AMERICA'S BEST KEPT COLLEGE SECRETS

AN AFFECTIONATE PROFILE OF EXTRAORDINARY COLLEGES AND UNIVERSITIES

Third Edition
Featuring Thirty Two New College Profiles

PETER L. ARANGO

TABLE OF CONTENTS

[handwritten annotations: "– also PRK-3 or g rules 2-6"]

Introduction

What do you do if you are a pretty good student, in the top half of your class, scoring above 500 on each of the SAT sub-tests and eager to find a group of colleges that match your interests and gifts? You want to find a college that challenges you, that promises preparation for success in the years after your college experience? And, you'd like to find a place that seems to attract the kinds of students with whom you would like to spend the next four years. The "name brand" schools seem to be out of reach and the regional options seem too familiar.

I was sitting in a dormitory at Western Washington University as I began the introduction to the second edition of this guide. The view from my window was spectacular – pine trees surrounding lovely homes, sloping down to Bellingham Bay. Bellingham is lush in its green beauty, and the university is one of the most elegantly designed and altogether handsome universities I have ever seen. Each building – from stately Old Main to the angular King Recreation Center – is perfectly set against a wooded backdrop. Distinguished programs at the university include nationally renowned departments of Vehicle Research, Watershed Studies, Native American Studies, and an experimental interdisciplinary college.

And, unless you live in the Pacific Northwest, chances are you have never heard of the place. That's why I updated the first edition and why I've added thirty colleges in presenting a third edition.

The response to the first two editions of America's Best Kept College Secrets was rewarding; families found colleges they would otherwise not have known, applied, and enrolled. Now, they act as ambassadors themselves, trying to communicate all that is exceptional at a college about which most of their friends or family may have known little or nothing.

My hope in presenting a third and updated edition is that in adding more distinctive post-secondary options, students and families will continue to find and appreciate excellent colleges and universities that will soon become more widely appreciated.

This book profiles some of the most highly regarded and effective colleges and universities across the country and yet, with the exception of those playing Division I sports, they remain largely unheralded outside of their region.

How can that be possible?

Every magazine and website delivers up-to-the-minute digestion of the latest trends in college admissions. The array of publications in the checkout line at the supermarket shifts from tabloids to college guides each fall. Experts from every corner weigh in with more and more advice about the hottest colleges in the country.

But it's always about the SAME colleges.

Even a quick examination of this book reveals profiles of a different order – colleges of character and quality that offer exceptional opportunities to well prepared students from around the country.

If you have picked up this book, chances are that you're the parent of a high school junior or senior, and you've already been around the block with a college counselor, or, you're an ambitious high school student trying to grab as much information as you can before the process gets away from you.

In either case, you probably already know that the competition for spots at the "Most Competitive Colleges" is insane. Harvard, Yale and Stanford admitted less than seven <u>percent</u> of the seventy thousand applications the three received in the most recent application season. As one counselor observed, "Pretty soon, they'll be taking zero percent."

Obviously, a great many able and ambitious students will have to consider other options. And where will they look? For the most part, those other options are by default the nearest public and private institutions. Most college applicants apply within their own region, and often within a hundred miles of their home. There's nothing wrong with going to college close to home, but for many students, part of the allure of the college experience is the promise of finding fresh new experiences in a setting that is different from what they have known throughout their high school years.

So, what do you do if you are a pretty good student, in the top half of your class, scoring above 500 on each of the SAT sub-tests and eager to find a group of colleges that match your interests and gifts? You want to find a college that challenges you, that promises preparation for success in the years after your college experience? And, you'd like to find a place that seems to attract the kinds of students with whom you would like to spend the next four years. The "name brand" schools seem to be out of reach and the regional options seem too familiar.

This book presents good options for ambitious, well-prepared students who may not fall within the tiny percentage of ridiculously well qualified superstars who land a spot at the colleges enjoying the greatest celebrity.

My hope is to bring other excellent options to your attention, recognizing that the single greatest challenge is in convincing the reader that these as yet unfamiliar colleges and universities demand further investigation.

The bottom line is that these are best kept secrets for reasons that have nothing to do with quality; graduates of these colleges are loud in their praise of their alma mater, and many of those graduates have gone on to distinguished careers in a variety of fields.

I know – it is daunting to take an unfamiliar path. Who knows where it might lead? Perhaps this generally conversational and "affectionate" guide can provide a sense of what the journey might look like.

There have been many good college guides written over the years, most of which fall into one of two categories: either they profile the most sought out and popular options, or they give statistical information about several thousand. The exception was the groundbreaking book by Loren Pope, entitled, *Colleges That Change Lives: 40 Schools that will Change the Way You Think About Colleges*, originally published in 1996. Pope, a college counselor and writer, did a great deal to draw attention to options beyond the Ivy League, and the 40 colleges identified in his book are among the most interesting of college options. Some of them will appear in these pages, although many have moved into the more competitive categories.

The criteria that I have used, however, in selecting the institutions profiled in this book are both objective and highly subjective.

I have been to each of the colleges over the course of almost forty years as a college counselor and have been impressed by the work that they do. In every case, from my first visit, I felt that a student from any part of the country and from any background would be welcome and well served.

In addition, and more objectively, I have limited this group to those colleges enrolling more than 50% of applicants, and colleges retaining more than 80% of enrolled students. In addition, the colleges selected are eager to enroll students from outside their region, are financially sound, and all are non-discriminatory in the selection of a first year class.

All statistics taken from the National Center for Educational Statistics http://nces.ed.gov/collegenavigator/

Some are small liberal arts colleges, some are technological institutes, there's one college of art and design, and some are comprehensive universities. Most are private, but some are public universities that deserve greater attention outside of their region. All of the selected colleges have programs that compete favorably with the more highly rated institutions.

This book is simply my best attempt to bring some excellent schools into the mix. If you want quality and are willing to look beyond the familiar, you will find exceptional opportunities in the pages ahead.

Two final notes:

1. **Region:**

The colleges are presented by region, simply as a means of balancing the array of best-kept secrets in some fashion. I could have presented the best-kept secret technological schools, or liberal arts colleges, or small universities, or comprehensive universities, or arts schools, or athletic programs, but, since these institutions actually are unfortunately little known outside of their region, I need to make sure the reader has some idea of where in the world the investigation might lead.

You'll find a short, and highly subjective, description of each of the regions as we move from one to the next. It isn't always easy to "read" a region from a distance, and my opinions are but my own, but at the very least you'll have a set of observations to question or debate.

2. **Type:**

I have included all sorts of colleges, including those with religious affiliation, single-sex colleges, rural colleges, technical colleges, fine arts colleges, small colleges, urban colleges, and large universities.

One of the sub-groups that ought to be identified is the very diverse group of colleges with religious affiliation (one of my students asked for a college with a religious *affliction* - not the same thing!)

You don't have to be Catholic to attend a Catholic college, or Lutheran to attend a Lutheran college, and for many students, the college experience at a school with a religious affiliation or heritage will have a notably non-religious character.

These colleges, like the rest, are characterized by strong academic programs and healthy residential life.

So, please, please don't eliminate a college because it has a "Saint" in its name; there are huge differences between colleges with religious affiliations, and I have included those that work well for students of any faith or any degree of faith, including the absolutely faithless. You don't have to be a saint, or even want to spend time with saints; rumor has it that there is plenty of good old-fashioned college hijinx at Georgetown, Notre Dame, Boston College and Villanova – and not only are these Catholic schools, three of them are Jesuit colleges.

By the same token, investigating a single-sex option does not indicate that your only interest is in that sex. The colleges for women suggested in this book and the colleges for men are spectacular places and worthy of your attention.

Come on. Give them a chance.

It is a challenging to consider colleges outside of the ordinary college conversation, but I also know many good students will find immediate reassurance if they take the time to do a little footwork.

Should you find the descriptions interesting, follow up by contacting current students through social media to make sure that the social and extracurricular life is as active and rewarding as I have indicated. The good news is that social networking allows immediate feedback on the most remote or regional of institutions. You can get the lowdown on any college simply by tracking down blogs written by current students (It's NOT stalking). Obviously, the wider the range of opinions, the more likely you are to get a sense of what the college is actually going to be like for you.

Happy hunting and be sure to spread the word when you find the ideal college match; it's time some of these secrets became well known!

The College Search

As a college counselor for more than forty years, I have watched thousands of students go through the process of identifying the colleges to which they want to apply. The search can be affected by any number of considerations from strong parental expectations to the availability of professional programs, from the opportunity to play a particular sport at a particular level of competition, to the organization of the curriculum. The whole enterprise is tricky because it comes upon a student too quickly and with incredibly high stakes, it involves people and institutions over which the applicant has no authority, and it demands the impossible ability to predict the future.

Every college has a campus, professors with degrees, a library, and dormitories. Some are in cities, some in the country; some are large, some small. For the most part, colleges and universities all offer a fairly standard set of courses, frequently called the Liberal Arts. Unless otherwise noted, most colleges teach languages, literature, history, math, science, and a rich variety of more specific disciplines attached to the arts, the humanities, or the sciences. Most colleges and universities prepare students for med school, law school, business school, and graduate school. Most colleges and universities offer counsel and advice given by faculty advisors. Most colleges and universities sponsor healthy residential life.

I can't describe the entire process in this book, but I can describe several types of colleges and universities, recognizing that broad generalizations are only the start of an investigation. Some aspect of the search may make all the difference for one student and not matter to another. So, as a starting point, here are some very general categories of post-secondary options:

Small Independent Liberal Arts Colleges

The small liberal arts colleges have traditionally offered an introduction to courses in language, literature, social science, life sciences, physical sciences, the humanities, mathematics, and the arts. In recent years, the small liberal arts colleges frequently also offer study in Computer Science, Neuroscience, and Ethnic or Cultural Studies. Classes are small and taught by professors; they have no teaching assistants. An emphasis is placed on strength of community and activities often include the entire student body. Athletics, extracurricular, and recreational opportunities abound, and considerable emphasis is placed on creating a strong sense of engagement in the life of the college. The size of a small liberal arts college can range from very small (200) to relatively large (2500). Two of these colleges enroll only men. Several enroll only women.

The excellent small liberal arts colleges described in this guide are:

Marlboro College, Bennington College, Endicott College, Simmons College (Women), Hartwick College, Eugene Lang/ New School, Drew University, Juniata College, Muhlenberg College, Allegheny College, Goucher College, Washington College, McDaniel University, Davis and Elkins College, Hampden-Sydney College (Men), Sweet Briar College (Women), Emory & Henry College, Hollins University, Lynchburg College, Randolph College, Guilford College, Presbyterian College, Wofford College, Furman University, Berry College, Agnes Scott College (Women), Eckerd College, Rollins College, University of the South (Sewanee), Rhodes College, Centre College, Millsaps College, Hendrix College, Southwestern University

Public Universities/ State Universities

Public universities are generally large, complicated institutions, offering instruction in the liberal arts as well as a wide range of specialized preparation for undergraduates seeking professional training (Nursing, Engineering, Music, Theater, Art, Architecture, etc) and even more specialized training in their graduate and professional schools. The number of opportunities available is huge, including big-time sports programs, specialized facilities, and a large number of students from a variety of socio-economic backgrounds. Not all classes are enormous, but many may be. In most instances, a student will work with Teaching Assistants (TAs) rather than professors until the junior or senior year.

The advantages of the public university include lower cost for in-state students, access to specialized professional programs as an undergraduate and the exciting jumbles of living with thousands of students of the same age. For some, the larger university may appear to offer more opportunities to become independent, and for some, the university allows a degree of anonymity; a student may not want to see the same people every day.

The excellent large public universities described in this guide are:

The University of Maine, The University of Vermont, The University of New Hampshire, The University of Connecticut, Alfred University, Christopher Newport University, Virginia Polytechnic Institute, Appalachian State University, University of North Carolina Wilmington, The University of North Carolina at Asheville, The University of Georgia, The University of Alabama Tuscaloosa, The University of Alabama Birmingham, The

University of Alabama Huntsville, The University of Mississippi, The University of Arkansas, Miami University , Indiana University, Ferris State University, The University of Iowa, The University of Missouri, Montana State University, The University of Montana, The University of Northern Colorado, Northern Arizona University, Cal State Stanislaus, San Francisco State University, Western Washington University

State Liberal Arts Universities and Specialized Public Universities

A small number of states have made a commitment to support relatively small colleges or universities dedicated to the liberal arts. These institutions do not have the words "Liberal Arts" in their title, but their mission is to provide the equivalent of the small liberal arts experience in a public setting. Some of these can be considered "Non-Traditional" in their method of instruction and character while others are similar to their larger cousins in pursuing big-time sports and in distinguishing pre-professional preparation. Most enroll fewer than 5000 students.

The excellent state liberal arts colleges and universities described in this guide are:

Saint Mary's College of Maryland, University of North Carolina Asheville, University of Montevallo, Sonoma State University, Southern Oregon University, The Evergreen State College

The Comprehensive Private University

Called "comprehensive" these universities offer all of the liberal arts, specialized professional programs such as Nursing, Engineering, Architecture, and Business. They also operate significant graduate and professional programs such a School of Law or Veterinarian School. In this guide, the comprehensive universities are not gigantic. For the most part, they are in or near cities and operate external enterprises that can offer internship. The comprehensive private university offers many of the benefits of the larger public universities at a smaller scale. For the most part, they will offer a highly competitive athletic program and specialized study. Examples of the private comprehensive university would include Johns Hopkins, Duke, Georgetown, Stanford, University of Pennsylvania, Vanderbilt, and Northwestern. Those famous universities accept a tiny proportion of applicants; this guide presents great options that accept more than 50% of applicants.

The excellent private comprehensive universities described in this book are:

Quinnipiac University, Fairfield University, College of Charleston, Stetson University
Belmont University, Samford University, University of San Diego, University of the Pacific, University of San Francisco, Dominican University, Pacific Lutheran University

Specialized or Technical Colleges or Institutes

This guide identifies a very few exceptional programs that are not for every applicant. In some cases the institutions are technical institutes; in some instances they are dedicated to a singular undertaking.

The excellent specialized or technical schools described in this guide are:

College of the Atlantic – Ecology/ Marine Ecology
Green Mountain College – Environmental Liberal Arts
Lesley University – Education
Curry College – Learning Difference Liberal Arts
Worcester Polytechnic Institute – Technology
Bard College at Simon's Rock – Early College/Liberal Arts
Johnson and Wales University – Culinary Arts/ Hospitality Management
Clarkson University – Technology
Paul Smith's College – Forestry / Hospitality Management
Alfred University – Ceramics
Rochester Institute of Technology – Information Science
The Culinary Institute of America – Culinary Arts
Virginia Polytechnic Institute – Engineering
Rose-Hulman Institute of Technology – Technology
Ferris State College – Materials Engineering/ Automobile
Colorado School of Mines – Petroleum Engineering
New Mexico Institute of Mining and Technology – Technology
Santa Fe University of Art and Design – Film

Colleges with a Strong Religious Affiliation or Conviction

Applicants may be familiar with Notre Dame, Georgetown, Boston College, or Villanova, all Catholic universities. Many of universities of a particular size (between 5,000 and 10,000 students) happen to be operated with a sense of purpose attached to faith. Almost all present their convictions in their statement of mission; all of the institutions in this guide do not demand or expect students to practice the convictions of their founders, but they do hold to principles consistent with their faith.

The excellent colleges and universities with strong religious affiliation described in this guide are:

St. Michael's College – Catholic
St. Anselm College – Catholic
Fairfield University – Catholic
Guilford College – Quaker
Berry College – Christian Non Denominational
Belmont University – Christian Non Denominational
Samford University – Alabama Baptist Convention
John Carroll University – Catholic
Earlham College – Quaker
St. Olaf College – Lutheran
Saint John's University/ College of Saint Benedict – Catholic
University of San Diego – Catholic
Thomas Aquinas – Catholic
Saint Mary's College – Catholic
University of San Francisco – Catholic
Dominican University – Catholic
Pacific Lutheran University – Lutheran
Whitworth University – Christian Non Denominational

Nontraditional Colleges

There are several ways to differentiate these colleges from the rest of the colleges and universities described in this guide. Some are intimate and student directed. Some concentrate so emphatically on a particular issue. A few have maintained a quality of character or identity that separates them from standard sensibilities. A few can be described as "quirky"; I suspect each of them would be delighted to be in this company.

The excellent nontraditional colleges described in this book are:

College of the Atlantic, Green Mountain College, Marlboro College, Bennington College, Bard College at Simon's Rock, Paul Smith's College, The Culinary Institute of America, Eugene Lang College/ New School, Warren Wilson College, Berry College, Coe College, Santa Fe University of Art and Design, Prescott College, California Maritime Academy, Thomas Aquinas College, The Evergreen State University.

The Northeast

As a region, the Northeast is rich in history, tradition, and colleges. When popular mythology turns to college, the archetypal image is of a gothic campus, autumnal foliage ablaze, set in a charming New England college town. Rolling hills surround leafy glades, and wood smoke climbs from ivied halls.

My friends in New England will forgive me, I know, if I suggest that New England is also subject to extremes of weather - often steamy in the summer and early fall and bitterly cold in the winter. A reference to Hamilton College in Thornton Wilder's *Our Town* describes a winter so cold, "students' ears are falling off."

I've learned that the great advantage of the New England climate is that it allows a full range of wardrobe choices, from flip flops and t shirts to parkas and scarves, any of which can be reasonably worn in any season.

Travel to the region is made easier by the development of several excellent small airports: Westchester, (New York), Hartford (Connecticut), Manchester (New Hampshire), Portland (Maine), Providence (Rhode Island), and Albany (New York), but most visits begin in New York or Boston.

The Connecticut River bisects southern New England, and its valley provides one of the few highways running north and south. Along that route lie many of the famous colleges (Yale, Wesleyan, Trinity, Amherst, Smith, Mount Holyoke, Dartmouth). More adventurous trekking carries the visitor to the Maine colleges and to the northern colleges - Williams, Bennington, Middlebury, UNH, and UVM. An area of about thirty square miles centered in Boston contains Harvard, MIT, Wellesley, Tufts, Simmons, Boston College, Boston University, Brandeis, Babson, Emerson, and Bentley. Brown, Johnson and Wales, Providence, Holy Cross, Worcester Polytechnic, Clark University, and Wheaton are only slightly outside of the Boston circle.

Columbia, Barnard, NYU, Cooper Union, Julliard, Fordham, Parsons, Pratt and the city colleges of New York are all within the five boroughs of New York City. Within easy reach are Sarah Lawrence, Bard, and Vassar to the north and Princeton, Drew, and Rutgers to the south.

I should probably say a little bit about universities in New England, because the model there differs from that in other regions of the country.

Each of the New England states has a university system - most with a flagship campus established in the 19th Century. The exception is the

University of Vermont, which was founded in the 18th Century and which was established as a private university. In the 19th Century, Vermont joined with the state's agricultural college and became a public university. Thus, the state universities in New England were largely established as agricultural and "mechanical" (engineering) colleges in the period following the Civil War.

All six state universities are now categorized as "research" universities with comprehensive academic programs, each, however, has at least one program that distinguishes it from its neighbors. The University of Maine is known for the Rubenstein School of Environment and Natural Resources. The University of Vermont has a highly reputed College of Natural Sciences, Forestry, and Agriculture.

Both the University of Rhode Island and the University of Connecticut offer programs in marine science. URI is a land grant/sea grant college with the Graduate School of Oceanography. Undergraduates at the University of Connecticut can enter Project Oceanology at Avery Point, Connecticut near Groton and New London.

The University of Massachusetts's flagship campus in Amherst, MA is a member of the Five College Consortium with Amherst, Smith, Mount Holyoke, and Hampshire. The University of New Hampshire is a mid-sized campus offering specialized programs in a setting similar to many independent small universities.

The outlying stretches are beautiful but not always easy to reach. A major east/west highway runs from Chicago to Boston; it's known as the New York State Thruway from Rochester to the Massachusetts state line, where it becomes the Massachusetts Turnpike, or the Mass Pike. Route 91 runs north and south from New Haven, Connecticut to Derby Line, Vermont on the Canadian border.

Some of the colleges in this book are north or south of the turnpike and east or west of Interstate Route 91. A good map will help an adventurous navigator successfully negotiate the smaller byways that lead to college treasure.

Maine

When most people think of Maine, they think of rocky coastline, they think of charming lighthouses standing in lonely contemplation of that coastline, and they think of lobsters.

All of which is true of the easternmost reaches of the state, but Maine is a big state, as New England states go, the largest of the New England states, with a coastline of almost two hundred and fifty miles. West Quoddy Head (go figure) is the easternmost piece of land in the contiguous United States, although various islands and spits of rocky islet are just a nudge more eastern.

The rest of Maine is equally impressive, if less frequently visited. Bordered by New Hampshire to the south, Maine is the only state in the United States to be bordered by only one other state. To the north, Maine bumps up against New Brunswick and Quebec. The interior of the state is paradise for those who love to spend time in the outdoors. Thickly forested, occasionally mountainous, Maine is known for its trails (the Appalachian Trail begins at Mount Katahdin) and numerous lakes and rivers. Moosehead Lake is the largest lake in the state, second only to Lake Champlain in New England, which is shared by Vermont, New York, and Quebec. The list of rivers in Maine is overwhelming and organized by the various unofficial divisions of the state.

Starting at the northern tributaries, the river regions are: The Saint John – including the Saint John River, the Allagash and the Aroostooc; Down East – the St. Croix and Machias rivers; Penobscot Bay – the Penobscot and Goose rivers; Mid Coast – St. George and Johns rivers; Kennebec – Kennebec and Androscoggin; Southern Maine – Saco and Scarborough.

Maine is known as The Pine Tree State, and it is a forested state. Logging and paper production were important industries in the state, and many of the smaller inland cities were attached to those industries. The largest cities in the state are Portland (about 90,000, including South Portland), Bangor (about 38,000), Lewiston, (about 36,000), and Auburn (about 23,000). The capital is Augusta (about 20,000). The two International Airports, Portland and Bangor, are served by major airlines and offer connection to most cities.

The University of Maine system extends throughout the state. The flagship campus, The University of Maine, is in Orono, a city of about 11,000 located north of Bangor, in the Penobscot Valley. The University of Maine at Augusta offers professional program on campus and online and is profiled in this book. The University of Maine at Farmington is actually older than the University of Maine and is one of the Council of Public Liberal Arts

College. The University of Maine at Fort Kent is small (about 1,500 students) in a region close to New Brunswick; many in the region are bi-lingual, speaking French and English. The University of Maine at Machias is truly "Downeast" Maine. The town is small (about 2,200) and campus brings about 1,200 students to a strong program in Marine Biology. The University of Maine at Presque Isle brings about 1,700 students to the largest city in Aroostook County. Presque Isle has a population of about 10,000.

Maine is home to several highly regarded colleges as well. Bates, Bowdoin, and Colby form a trio of frequently mentioned liberal arts college of quality. Bates is located in Lewiston, enrolling about 1,750 students in the oldest co-educational college in New England. Bowdoin is in Brunswick, a small city with lively celebration of the arts, near the shopping madness brought by the original L.L. Bean store and the other high-end stores that have adjoining outlets. Bowdoin enrolls about 1,800 students and is highly selective in admissions. The third popular college in the state is Colby, located in Waterville, enrolls about 1,800 and, with Bowdoin and Bates, is highly selective in admission.

The less commonly known independent college, profiled in this book is College of the Atlantic in Bar Harbor.

The University of Maine - Orono, Maine

Maybe it's the beauty of the campus, or the quality of food provided by the dining service, or the relatively small size of classes and the variety of excellent programs of study, or the excitement of big-time sports, or the quiet comfort of the town, or well maintained dormitories, or distance from the rattle of big cities - for whatever reason or reasons, students at the University of Maine are HAPPY.

And the stats... 2015

Number of Applicants: 11,500 / 83% Accepted
Undergrad Enrollment: 9,340 48% female/ 52% male
Avg. SAT Reading Comp 490- 590 / Math 480 - 600 Avg. ACT : 21 - 27
Total Cost: $23,100.00 (in-state) / $40,980 (out of state)
Received some form of financial assistance: 66%

I'm going to go out a limb here. The University of Maine may be the only public university I know in which students are openly grateful for the opportunity their state has afforded them. They are also open in recognizing that U. Maine is not an Ivy League ticket to Wall Street, but they appreciate the care with which their professors teach them, a campus they consider lovely, and the variety of programs that entirely meet their needs. One real measure of a university's ability to deliver on its promises is in the attrition rate; good schools keep their kids and few leave the University of Main. Dollar for dollar, Maine may be among the best "buys" in the Northeast. The university is a bargain for in-state residents and not a bad deal for out-of-staters as well. Facilities are considered excellent; a remarkable number of students describe their dormitories as very comfortable, and a truly remarkable number rave about the food, although many advise shopping carefully for the meal plan that suits a student best.

Located about sixty miles inland and about a hundred miles from the Canadian border, Maine is the northernmost of the universities and colleges reviewed in this edition. The University is set in Orono, a city of about ten thousand, and is the largest in Maine's system of universities (about 8,600 undergraduate students/11,500 undergraduate and graduate) and the state's flagship university. Maine was founded in 1862 by the same act of Congress that established most of what were called "land-grant" colleges (only Cornell and MIT are non-public land-grant institutions). Maine's campus is actually on an island between the Penobscot and Stillwater rivers. The campus was designed by Frederick Law Olmsted, the architect who framed Central Park in New York, the grounds of the White

House, and the elegantly crafted landscapes in which the nation's grandest estates have been placed. The most striking aspect of the campus, other than its lovely setting, is the University of Maine Mall (not a shopping center!), which extends from the library to the field house.

Although the temperature in Orono at mid-winter is only about three degrees lower than that in Worcester or Springfield, Massachusetts, Maine has a "north country" feel that has something to do with its extensive programs in forestry and sustainability, and an awful lot to do with the success of Maine's "Black Bear" championship ice hockey team. The Black Bears are strong in a number of sports and are the state's only Division I athletic program, but the fever pitch in the Alfond Arena when Maine takes the ice against archrival New Hampshire warms even the coldest of Maine winters. The Bears have twice won the national championship in hockey and regularly send players on to the NHL.

Maybe it's the beauty of the campus, or the quality of food provided by the dining service, or the relatively small size of classes and the variety of excellent programs of study, or the excitement of big-time sports, or the quiet comfort of the town, or well maintained dormitories, or distance from the rattle of big cities – for whatever reason or reasons, students at the University of Maine are HAPPY.

Students use words such as "welcoming", "friendly", "accepting", "generous" in describing their community, and it's clear that there is a strong sense of community in this not-very-large state university. Athletes, actors, dancers, scientists, environmentalist, fraternity/sorority, physically disabled, people of color – all seem to have a place on a campus that students call, "open to diversity". An uncommon number of student-written accounts describe their university as responsive, supportive, and working hard to meet the needs of its students. Most instruction is provided by professors who are well liked by students who find them informative and helpful. The curriculum is wide and deep; specialized programs in the College of Natural Sciences, Forestry, and Agriculture are distinctive, as are the several strong programs in psychology and neuroscience, but highly regarded programs are also offered throughout the five academic divisions (College of Business, Public Policy, and Health, the College of Education and Human Development, the College of Engineering, the College of Liberal Arts and Sciences, and the aforementioned College of Natural Sciences, Forestry, and Agriculture),

How does the experience at the University of Maine begin? First year students are welcomed into a program known as FYRE (First Year Residential Experience) dedicated to building a sense of community among incoming students. That kind of formal program is always an indication that the training of Residence Advisors has been taken seriously and that quality of residential life is a priority. Aside from that warm welcome, most new students are surprised to find that they have free admission to all of Maine's Division One athletic events (Go, Bears!) and are given two free tickets each semester to concerts and performances on campus.

Engineering and the Natural Sciences/Forestry/Agriculture get a lot of attention, but there are several other programs that are noteworthy and highly regarded. Among them is a program called New Media, which, as its title suggests, offers extensive exposure to the quickly changing media landscape. Courses in digital narrative and documentary are accompanied by courses in what is called, "Time-based sequence" in digital arts. The program is interdisciplinary and at the cutting edge of digital arts and journalism. I hear equally good things about the Music program, which includes performance majors and is under the umbrella of a growing School of Performing Arts, part of the College of Liberal Arts and Sciences. Other programs of note include an Athletic Training program in the College of Education and Human Development, Civil and Chemical Engineering, (actually ALL of the Engineering programs), and a rigorous Honors College, which depends upon core programs in the College of Liberal Arts and Sciences and the College of Natural Sciences. Honors students meet the General Education requirements in courses that are offered in small groups made up of Honors students. One of the requirements of the Honors College is the completion of an Honors thesis.

Outside of the classroom, Maine offers significant opportunities for recreation and activity, the most notable of which, given the university's location is the program known as Maine Bound. Women Rock – rock climbing for women, Biking and Bouldering, Katahdin Knife Edge Traverse, Surf Southern Maine, Sea Kayaking – all bring students into the wilderness, but a lot of activity can be found on campus in the Indoor Rock Climbing facility and the Ropes Challenge Course. Fitness programs are offered in the New Balance Student Recreation Center and Intramural sports abound, including indoor softball, floor hockey, and the Black Bear Attack Adventure race, which almost certainly does not involve fleeing from a black bear.

Student clubs and organizations are equally well subscribed and include all of the expected options in music, drama, journalism, political activity, and celebration of culture. At last count, Maine hosted more than two hundred different clubs, so I am forced to highlight only a small portion of the array.

Sports? Fencing, crew, cricket, rugby, triathlon, Alpine skiing, wrestling, ultimate frisbee.], capoeira, equestrian, figure skating, trap and skeet, yoga.

Cultural and Service? Best Buddies, South Asian Association of Maine, Helping Honduras, Iranian Social Hub, Hillel, Muslim Students Association, Deaf Culture Club, Autism Training Student Organization.

Other? Gamers, Black Bear Robotics, Home Brewing Club, Hip Hop and Swing Dance clubs,.

My favorites, however, are found in Animal and Veterinary Sciences division: UMADCOWS - caring for the dairy herd, the Maine Animal Club, several equestrian clubs and competitive teams, and the Standardbred Drill Team.

Fraternities and sororities have their place at Maine, and the Greek life seems healthy and positive. A strong Residential Life staff organizes a variety of living options, including theme based housing for new student, should they feel more comfortable in one of eight residential communities organized around Great Books, Technology, or Global Crossroads among others. The seventeen residential halls on campus are described by students as comfortable and welcoming.

There are two distinctive traditions at Maine that deserve at least a cursory description. In the first place, the crowd at any athletic event might cheer, "Go, Blue" in order to root the team to victory, but the true mascot is a black bear. Originally, Maine's mascot was an elephant (Go Figure!), but the arrival of a black bear cub on the sidelines of a football game apparently made the crowd go "bananas", so today, "Bananas the Bear" is the university's totemic animal. Once a famous song across the country, the "Maine Stein Song" is now sung at most events and often when the Bears score.

Varsity teams at Maine play in Division I in three separate conferences. The football team is a member of the Colonial Athletic Association, which includes William and Mary, Villanova, and Richmond, among others. The very successful hockey team plays in the Hockey East Association. The association currently includes the universities of Notre Dame, Vermont, New Hampshire, Boston College, and Boston University. All other sports play in the America East Conference, which brings competition with U Vermont and U New Hampshire.

College of the Atlantic - Bar Harbor, Maine

Imagine a college that takes ecology seriously – I mean REALLY seriously.

And the stats... 2015

Number of Applicants: 429 / 71% Accepted
Undergrad Enrollment: 378 70% female / 30% male
Avg. SAT Reading Comp 580– 690 / Math 530 – 640 Avg. ACT : 25 – 33 (scores not required)
Total Cost: $51,400.00
Received some form of financial assistance: 94%

Maine is celebrated for its rocky coastline, fisheries and lobster traps, and ruggedly stunning islands, one of which, Mount Desert Island, has famously welcomed families of enormous wealth and power. Much of Acadia National Park on the island was donated by John D. Rockefeller whose elaborate summer home is among those built by J.P. Morgan, Cornelius Vanderbilt, and the Astors. The town of Bar Harbor and communities of Northeast Harbor and Seal Harbor, located on Mount Desert, have long been a refuge for the most prominent families from the steamy confines of Boston, New York, and Philadelphia. In what might have seemed a curious impulse, Mount Desert is also the home of College of the Atlantic, a remarkable educational innovation, unique in its mission and uncommon in its ambition.

COA was founded in 1969, one of the last of the wave of experimental colleges that swept the end of the decade and one that has remained true to the vision of its founders. Today, almost four hundred students live and study on a thirty-seven acre campus overlooking Frenchman's Bay; they are all engaged in the study of human ecology, the college's only major. Well, that's not entirely true, or at least not completely true. COA describes itself as a liberal arts college in which all students design their own major... but every student majors in human ecology.

Confused? This is one instance in which you might actually get the best of both worlds.

Imagine a college that takes ecology seriously – I mean REALLY seriously. The extraordinary setting and natural resources make the place a living laboratory and a superior learning environment for those who think it is great to work in Acadia or take an hour-and-a-half boat ride to Duck

Island, one of the college's research stations, a twelve acre preserve protecting the largest breeding ground of Leach's Storm Petrels and Black Guillemots. If marine mammals are your preference, you can scoot twenty-five miles to Mount Desert Rock which offers a window into the world of whales, dolphins, and porpoises. If you don't know the difference between dolphins and porpoises, you probably need to enroll right away. Any description of resources available to students at COA has to include the world-class biological research facility, the Jackson Laboratory, one of the leading areas of research in Geonomics, Mammalian Genetics, Cancer Research, and Neurological and Sensory Research.

So, to make the picture a bit more complex, COA is a small (375 students) college located in a fabled Maine holiday destination next to one of the nation's most powerful research facilities. My own impression of the COA experience leads me to describe the college as an intensive professional school with considerable interest in the liberal arts.

All students take the core course in human ecology and must also take at least one course in history, a writing course, a quantitative reasoning course, and at least two courses from environmental science, human studies, and art and design. The requirements for a degree from COA also include community service, a writing portfolio, an internship, a final human ecology essay, and a final project.

Without majors, the courses in the college are separated into three areas of inquiry: Art and Design, Environmental Science, and Human Studies. Thus, even in this environmentally super-charged college, a student can develop concentration in Arts and Design, Field Ecology and Conservation Biology, Ecological Policy and Planning, International Studies, Literature and Writing, Sustainable Business, and Sustainable Food Systems.

The courses generally included in the Environmental Sciences are as one might expect, both comprehensive and marine sensitive: Organic Chemistry raises its formidable head, but so does Edible Botany; Introduction to Statistics and Research Design is offered in the same quadrant as the Art and Science of Fermented Foods.

Concentration in Arts and Design might introduce a student to a Visual Seminar in Photographic Syntax as well as a course in The History of Rock. Some courses are clearly conceptually based (The Reality Effect: Art and Truth in the 19th century) while others have a hands-on approach (Four Dimensional Studio Art).

Human Studies is concerned with the social sciences, of course, but the range of courses proceeds from Gender, Politics, and Science in Fairy Tales from the World to Philosophy at the Movies.

Chances are that students interested in the College of the Atlantic have self-identified as ecologically active; few arrive without having sustained interested in marine environments. The school is small and somewhat remote; Mount Desert is stunningly beautiful but about an hour from Bangor and about four hours from Boston ... if you have a car. As a result, the description of student life is probably more significant than it might be in examining other, more conventional, opportunities.

It goes without saying that environmental activism is an important part of the experience at COA. The regular trips to field stations like the frequent monitoring of projects begun as part of the curriculum or as part of internships takes planning and considerable time.
The payoff? Night skies at the Duck Island station are spectacular, and apparently, the view of the sunrise from the station's lighthouse is pretty remarkable as well. A Lunch break at Mount Desert Island includes a parade of whales breaching nearby. Yes, the environmental stuff is a huge part of life at COA, but so is recreation in the outdoors. The college's outdoor program offers a fleet of canoes and kayaks as well as Rhodes 19 and Sonic 23 sailboats. Camping equipment is checked out daily, with lots of COA trips into the mountains and rivers of Maine. Wintertime? Still time for exploration and camping.

The college maintains several distinctive programs and facilities that are animated and directed by students throughout the year. In addition to classrooms, labs, and library, COA operates The Osprey, a research vessel and floating classroom. The George B. Dorr Museum of Natural History, once the headquarters of the Acadia National Park is now curated by students who design and prepare every exhibit. Beech Hill Farm is a working, sustainable, organic farm, also operated students, faculty, and farm managers. The college also operates the Peggy Rockefeller Farm, more than one hundred acres of pasture on Mount Desert Island. All electricity used on the farm is generated by solar panels, and the entire property is in the Northeast Creek watershed. On campus, the college maintains a garden, a greenhouse, a herbarium, and an arboretum.

Regular college fun? OK, slightly modified but definitely present. The residences (NOT dorms) are wonderfully diverse and rich in character. Collaborative living is at the heart of the COA residential experience, and, while there are Residential Advisors in each facility, the expectation is that all residents will be mindful of the needs of others. The closest thing to conventional dormitory is Blair/Tyson, essentially a group of connected townhouses with group kitchens and cedar sided ski-lodge exterior. About twenty students live in Seafox, an authentic and authentically quirky New England seaside farmhouse. This is the largest of the residences with a porch that looks out on the sea; Seafox is also designated as a substance-free dorm. Six students live in Cottage, a converted gatehouse, which, in addition to comfy intimacy offers the residence closest to the Bus Stop. The first building constructed as part of the college, Peach House, holds eight students and is also designated as a substance-free residence. Also substance-free is David House, a small carriage house welcoming five students. The newest housing on campus is the Davis "Village", a complex of biomass pellet heated, solar powered, toilet composting small houses, separate from but adjacent to Seafox and the Deering Commons. The village is also designated as substance-free.

Students edit two publications throughout the year – Off the Wall, a student newspaper, and Edge of Eden, a literary journal. Open Mic nights take place in the great hall of the Turrets mansion, and a major cultural/social/musical/theatrical event of the year is "Fandango", a talent show that raises money for charity while allowing students to perform a surprising variety of talents, from the choral presentation of Finnish folk songs to an authentic Maori dance. Fandango also allows international students to carry some aspect of their culture into the program. Roughly twenty percent of the student body comes from outside the United States.

Unconventional in its focus, serious in its commitment to changing the world as well as its students, the College of the Atlantic is unique. It is not for everyone, but if a star-spangled night sky, breaching whales, organic food, and cozy collaboration appeal to you, there is nothing more invigorating than the experience COA promises and delivers.

Vermont

Vermont is known as the Green Mountain State for obvious reasons. It does have a plethora of "mountains", although to those accustomed to the grand panorama of the Rockies or the Sierras, the Vermont version of towering peaks may be a bit understated. What Vermont does not have is population. Alaska, both North and South Dakota, and Delaware beat Vermont in the population tally. Fortunately, Wyoming is still about one hundred thousand behind, although it would only take one oil strike to leave Vermont in its wake. As a point of comparison, the entire state of Vermont has fewer people than Oklahoma City or Las Vegas.

Lots of colonial history is attached to the state. The Green Mountain Boys, lead by Ethan Allen, were largely responsible for the successful recovery of Fort Ticonderoga in 1775. Following the Revolutionary War, the Republic of Vermont was tempted to join British Quebec, bordering Canada to the north. Having been excluded from the Continental Congress. Vermont eventually became the fourteenth state after the thirteen colonies; in claiming independence as a republic, Vermont joins Texas, California, and Hawaii as the only sovereign states.

Crisp winter skies, fresh maple syrup, rustic ski lodges (the Trapp Family singers migrated from Salzburg to bring the "sound of music" to Vermont), Vermont is also vacation paradise for those who love rivers and lakes. Lake Champlain separates Vermont from New York State and offers every imaginable water activity, including the hunt for "Champy", America's lake monster, apparently a separated relative of Loch Ness' "Nessie".

Burlington, Vermont's largest city and home to the University of Vermont, is at the northern end of Lake Champlain. A small city (forty five thousand), Burlington offers air service from the Burlington airport to major cities via Jet Blue, US Air, United, and Delta. The capital city of Montpelier has a population of about eight thousand, roughly the size of Middlebury. Visitors frequently seek out the particular commercial pleasures of Manchester, an unspoiled colonial village containing Orvis, the family owned fly-fishing entrepot, and outlet stores including Brooks Brothers and Ralph Lauren, as well as the impressively stocked Northshire Bookstore. The Connecticut River provides a border with the state of New Hampshire, and Route 91 provides speedy north/south connection with Massachusetts and Connecticut.

The University of Vermont is the state's flagship university. The Vermont state college system includes Lyndon State, Castleton State, Johnson State, and the Vermont Technical College. Private colleges include highly regarded Middlebury College, Bennington College, Saint Michael's College, Marlboro College, Norwich University, and Burlington College.

University of Vermont - Burlington, Vermont

For many who apply to UVM, however, the appeal of the place is in its location (already described as spectacular), its size (under ten thousand), its diversity of majors (seven undergraduate divisions as well as graduate programs), and its lively, active, generally happy student body. It isn't easy to compile a ranking of the happiness of student experiences, but were such a ranking available, UVM would be in the top ranks.

And the stats... 2015

Number of Applicants: 24,300 / 73% Accepted
Undergrad Enrollment: 10,992 56% female / 44% male
Avg. SAT Reading Comp 540- 640 / Math 540 - 650 Avg. ACT : 25 - 33
Total Cost: $29,700.00 (in state) $51,300.00 (out-of-state)
Received some form of financial assistance: 81%

Location. Location. Location.

The University of Vermont could not be more handsomely located. Lake Champlain, the sixth largest lake in the United States, abuts the small (very small) city of Burlington. Burlington is a picture-perfect college town, packed with great eateries, cafes, and clubs. A quick glance over the shoulder reveals the Green Mountains, the great outdoors, winter sports, and the best skiing in the East.

Is Vermont a crunchy, environmentally aware state? Yes. Is Vermont attractive to the jet set, prepsters and skiers? Yes. Students at the university are mostly white and mostly Christian, but the diversity of white is kind of impressive in this relatively small university. The work is tough enough and the reputation sound enough that the general tone of the place is both industrious and cheerful. Hippies and hipsters, jocks, skaters, boarders and skiers, aggies pre-meds, pre-vets all seem to enjoy each others' company and their privileged location.

The University of Vermont itself has a few quirky characteristics. It is popularly known as UVM rather than UVT because its Latin title is *Universitas Viridis Montis* or University of Green Mountains (that makes sense). Then UVM is a public/private or private/public university. UVM was founded as a private college in 1791, just as the foundling state abandoned it status as an independent republic to join the newly established United States of America. In the Nineteenth Century, the Morrill Acts established the Land Grant universities, of which UVM was one, thus taking on the role of the state's public university. Today, the university operates with funds from the state and with tuition paid by students, a good number of whom are from other states.

The university is an excellent small research university, generally included in the small group of public (ish) universities that offer highly regarded academic instruction. Known as the Public Ivies, the original group includes Michigan, Virginia, North Carolina, Miami University (Ohio), UC Berkeley, UCLA, Texas, William and Mary, and Vermont. UVM continues to enjoy a solid reputation, due in part to its success in placing its graduates in competitive graduate programs and in part to its many innovations in developing a sustainable campus.

For many who apply to UVM, however, the appeal of the place is in its location (already described as spectacular), its size (under ten thousand), its diversity of majors (seven undergraduate divisions as well as graduate programs), and its lively, active, generally happy student body. It isn't easy to compile a ranking of the happiness of student experiences, but were such a ranking available, UVM would be in the top ranks.

The totemic creature once prowling the northern tier of New England, the Catamount (also known as mountain lion or puma), is the school's mascot and a reasonable gesture toward the environmental concerns the Green Mountain State has championed and a gesture toward the elegant power of the university's Division One teams. Lots of schools have adopted cats of one kind or another (Tigers, Lions, Bobcats, Wildcats), but Vermont's Catamount prowls alone as a purely regional beast. Well, Maine suggests that their Black Bears are Maine Black Bears, but they look exactly like anyone else's Black Bears. In any case, while UVM is not generally seen as a sports-mad campus, two winters sports, basketball and ice hockey, draw crowds to some spectacular play.

Residential life is healthy, as is indicated by the high percentage that chose to live on campus throughout the four years. It is rare to see more than 50% remaining in dormitories at a university of this size, but the advantages of living on-campus are many. In describing the social scene at UVM, students quickly disclose that there are three thriving sorts of social activities, outside of clubs, organizations, team and intramural sports, etc. The Catamounts can prowl the Burlington nightlife, which gets high marks – the number of recommended clubs is overwhelming. Many will take to the outdoors; all the usual wilderness activities are within a short drive. Hiking, rock climbing, camping, rafting, sailing – all in a glorious setting. The skiing is excellent and there are a number of types of venues. There are some pretty stylish resorts, such as Stowe, Stratton Mountain, and the aforementioned Trapp Family Lodge, and lots of MUCH less expensive skiing as well. Some offer Nordic and some Downhill and some both. After a healthy snowfall, numbers of students slap on a pair of skis and cross-country wherever they want. Lots happens on campus, including an active calendar of student organized coffee houses at which budding singers/songwriters/stand-up comedians take the stage. The university brings in the usual array of big-name entertainment twice a year and provides a number of entertainment choices throughout the year. There are fraternities and sororities at UVM, but they hold no more sway in the social life of students than do a number of other organizations and associations.

OK, the setting is fabulous and social goodies abound. What about academics?

UVM is a relatively small university, and students report exceptional access to professors; many describe themselves as having found a mentor during their undergraduate careers. A fair number choose to stay to complete graduate work and reports on their preparation indicate that they have had a solid undergraduate training.

The university presents seven colleges (Divisions), an Honors College, a medical school, and a variety of graduate programs. They are: The College of Agriculture and Life Sciences, the College of Arts and Sciences, the college of Education and Social Services, the college of Engineering and Mathematical Sciences, the College of Nursing and Health Sciences, the Rubenstein School of Environmental and Natural Resources, and the School of Business Administration.

All of the divisions have distinctive programs or majors; perhaps among the most uncommon are the Green Forest Initiative sponsored by the Forestry Program of the Rubenstin School (and the internship at the Alaska Field Station), the programs in Rehabilitation and Movement Science in the College of Nursing (including Athletic Training and Movement and Exercise Science), and the program in Early Childhood Special Education, sponsored by the College of Education and Social Services.

Most applicants from outside the region will probably apply to the College of Arts and Sciences. One of the distinctive differences between UVM and many other public universities is that a significant number apply without a major. More than 30% arrive without having stated a major choice, and that does not include those in the Honors College. UVM offers the usual comprehensive smorgasbord from anthropology to zoology with some pretty interesting options. There are some good inter-disciplinary programs (Neuroscience and Eastern European/Russian Studies), thirty-seven majors including Film and Television and Classical Civilization.

The Honors College gets very high marks from students who, in many cases, chose it over some hefty "name-brand" liberal arts options.

Separate housing is provided in a stunning residence hall, replete with conference rooms, libraries, study centers, and handsome suite and single rooms. In addition, a residential faculty is available for discussion and formal lecture opportunities. About two hundred students join the Honors College each year, and in addition to getting first choice in registering for classes (a major advantage!), they also meet in council to advise the university on the development of new courses and new programs.

Students from outside the region may have the misconception that UVM is a snow-bound school for crunchy New Englanders, and in an attempt to correct that opinion, here are a few relatively current initiatives straight from Burlington.

The first comes from the Business School and the Engineering College, where enterprising students decided to invent a better golf club. "The Bomb", a high-end driver, was created at UVM and marketed by BombTech, a UVM start-up. From all accounts, it is one heck of a driver.

Dance students from Vermont take their salsa and meringue from alpine New England to … Mongolia? Yes, UVM has an exchange program with Mongolia University Arts College, promoting cultural exchange through dance.

If you have ever asked the question, "Are we happy?" you'll be pleased to find that the UVM Business School students are at work on the "hedonometer", a device that graphs the emotional state of people by measuring activity on Twitter. Imagine a ticker such as used on the Stock Exchange, graphing emotional booms and busts as Twitterscapes provide immediate data.

When UVM invites students to "Walk on the Wild Side", the invitation comes from horticulturalists teaching herbivores to find edible plants.

UVM has sent numbers of graduates into volunteer and service programs following graduation; alumni have flocked to the Peace Corps, and one recent graduate founded a program called Connecting Cultures, a service provided to Refugees from more than twenty countries who find themselves in Vermont. One outgrowth of that initiative was the establishment of New England Survivors of Torture and Trauma (NEST).

So, what else do Catamounts think about?

Her Campus based at the University of Vermont is the largest online global community for college women, identifying such issues as *The 8 Things You Do That Make You Not Seem Like Girlfriend Material,* and *11 Swimsuits We're Obsessed with for Summer 2014.* As a fairly neutral visitor to the blog, I was most impressed with a really sensible and helpful article on how to spend a happy and healthy spring break on campus, directed toward the many students who can't afford or manage to make the traditional "College Gone Wild" Spring Break.

Or, you might contact Adrian Ivakhiv, Professor of Environmental Studies, who maintains a blog entitled, *Immanence*, directed toward creating a space for environmental cultural theory. How many people follow Ivakhiv? A recent survey of the "top humanities theorists of the last century" was flooded with nominations. The winners, should you wish to pass them on in casual conversation, were: Michel Foucault, Pierre Bordieu, Max Weber, Sigmund Freud, and John Dewey. Umberto Eco finished a disappointing twenty-eighth.

As might be expected, there are blogs dedicated to Pasture Management and Orchard Maintenance; for example, the UVM Fruit Blog characterizes the thinning and codling moth population in the state. But there are also rabidly followed blogs attending to issues surrounding UVM's nationally regarded hockey and basketball teams.

Speaking of sports, UVM fields eighteen Division One teams, including a national championship teams in Skiing and basketball teams (both men's and women's) that have played a part in the NCAA tournament. Vermont's ice hockey team is a perpetual powerhouse, often appearing in the Frozen Four. Catamount teams are fairly well supported, but it is the hockey team that gets the most love. Gutterson Field House ROCKS during the hockey season, especially when playing traditional rival Dartmouth. Anyone watching the NHL will recognize the names of goalie, Tim Thomas, and sharpshooter Martin St. Louis, winner of the Hart Trophy, both former Catamounts.

Outdoor Magazine rates UVM among the Top Ten Collegiate Outdoor Programs, and the call of the wild is heard and obeyed. Club sports also abound, including all of the usual options plus Equestrian, Fencing, Brazilian Jiu Jitsu, Figure Skating, Bollywood Dance, and Olympic Weightlifting.

Saint Michael's College - Winooski, Vermont

How friendly is this college? Every Friday and Saturday night, Resident Advisors are out in the college quad, grilling up a midnight meal for the student body. Every night! Even when a Vermont winter brings feet of snow, those RAs are still serving burgers and dogs.

And the stats... 2015

Number of Applicants: 4,290 / 80% Accepted
Undergrad Enrollment: 2,123   54% female / 46% male
Avg. SAT Reading Comp 530– 630 / Math 530 – 610 Avg. ACT : 23 – 27
Total Cost: $52,155.00.
Received some form of financial assistance: 96%

It won't take much to convince a visitor that the northern reaches of Vermont are exceptionally beautiful, especially the region adjacent to Lake Champlain. Colchester is a bedroom community of Burlington, Vermont's largest and most exciting city. Let's be clear, Vermont is not really about cities; Burlington has a population of about 43,000 and is easily four times as large as the other celebrated Vermont "cities" – Bennington, Barre, Brattleboro, and Montpelier – and it is an active college town. The University of Vermont is a happening place, Lake Champlain is nearby, and Burlington offers a good small airport and a number of excellent restaurants, as well as virtually immediate access to some of the best skiing in New England.

Vermont is totally about mountains and lakes, and in that attractive environment, St. Michael's describes itself as a place that will change the way you see and care for the world. That's a rare opportunity to the 2200 undergraduate students who find their way to Winooski. Founded by a relatively low-key order dedicated to social conscience, the Society of Saint Edmund, conceived of Saint Michael's as a college providing the intellectual tools to live a purposeful life.

It is, in addition, the first college in the United States to offer a complete all-access pass to a major ski area, –Smuggler's Notch –as part of the tuition package. Obviously, the college is not all about, or even primarily about, skiing; it is a first rate academic enterprise and there is an active program of community service at Saint Michael's; more than 70% of the student body are involved in MOVE – Mobilization of Volunteer Efforts.

Saint Mike's has a Catholic tradition but is inclusive, adventurous, and occasionally pretty far out on the liberal college spectrum. For example, two areas of academic inquiry - Men and Masculinity and Gender Studies - recently put on Saint Michael's first

Drag Show, in which performers from the college and from Burlington performed in drag before an appreciative audience. Similarly, a recent appearance by YouTube blogger, Laci Green, "The F____ Word", animated weeks of conversation about feminism and the challenges facing feminists.

That's not all. Like some of the other small universities profiled in this book, Saint Michael's combines an engaging introduction to the liberal arts in a freshman seminar, a widely diverse curriculum, and a number of majors outside of the traditional liberal arts. The most notable, from my point of view, are found in the Department of Media Studies, Journalism, and Digital Arts - offering an unusual opportunity in a college of this size. Other pre-professional programs are offered in Education and Engineering, and some students will jump into the pre-Pharmacy program as well.

Now, in an attempt to overcome the resistance a number of high school applicants to a college founded by a Roman Catholic order, let's turn to student life and fun on campus.

First of all, Saint Michael's is residential; almost all of its students actually live on campus. That's a good thing. The campus is handsome and well maintained, and there are a number of interesting housing options in addition to the traditional dormitories. Special interest houses, apartments, and suites - all are available after the freshman year.

Sports are big at Saint Michael's and some of the programs are exceptionally successful. For the most part, Saint Mike's competes in NCAA Division II. The college belongs to the Northeast 10 Conference, made up of colleges of similar size and athletic aspiration. Basketball has been a hallmark sport for some time. Back when Saint Mike's was a college for men, the teams were known as the "Iron Knights"; now the college competes as the Purple Knights. The "Ice Knights", Saint Mike's ice hockey team has won the Division II national championship, and the women's lacrosse program has captured the NE 10 championship.

One of the hallmarks of the experience at Saint Michael's is that student-athletes feel very strongly that they have the best of both worlds - they very much appreciate the quality of instruction they receive, and they feel that athletic programs are well supported. One athlete noted that when travel for sports made it difficult for him to complete a project, his professor went out of his way to reschedule a tutoring sessions to make sure the did as well as possible.

The two extra-curricular programs that have most impressed me are the Wilderness Program and the Volunteer Fire Department.

Vermont is a snow state, and skiers and snowboarders rave about the opportunities available to them from late October until April. Smuggler's Notch and Stowe are both within range The Wilderness Program is huge at Saint Michael's and most students will be involved in at least one of the activities offered throughout the year. Rock climbing, skiing, snowboarding, might be expected in the Green Mountains, but Lake Champlain is also close at hand and sea kayaking is both a popular and extremely well developed program. Students also have the opportunity to become certified in wilderness medicine, and many do.
The very impressive Fire and Rescue Squad responds to almost three thousand calls a year and is entirely made up of student volunteers. Operating every day of the year, and every hour in the day, the Fire and Rescue Squad has become the model of college emergency teams and prepares hundreds of students in emergency medicine.

Nice kids, a four hundred acre campus in the Green Mountains with easy access to Burlington, unique academic and service opportunities, a successful athletic program - how can this gem remain a secret for long?

Green Mountain College - Poultney, Vermont

Green Mountain College directs its seven hundred or so students toward a greater emphasis on environmental literacy and active citizenship than its cohorts, and its location between the Green Mountains and the Adirondacks offers great opportunities in farming and the use of the wilderness. On the far side of the more traditionally designed campus are the Solar Garage, the Cerridwen Farm, and the Killington School of Resort Management.

And the stats... 2015

Number of Applicants: 973/ 68% Accepted
Undergrad Enrollment: 853   51% female / 49% male
SAT scores Recommended but not required
Total Cost: $47,758.00.
Received some form of financial assistance: 98%

Wow! Talk about a transformation! A few decades ago, Green Mountain was a comfy two-year college for women, handsomely set in prototypically quaint Vermont village. Today, same village, still quaint, but GMC has become a vibrant, ambitious, well equipped, and distinctive opportunity for men and women who have an abiding interest in the environment AND the liberal arts. An emphasis on environmental issues and environmental studies is at the heart of the curriculum, but Green Mountain offers an uncommon range of academic and social options not found in most charming New England settings.

Poultney is a small town (in a state with pretty much only small towns) about twenty miles south of Rutland, Vermont's third largest city (after Burlington and South Burlington) with a population approaching sixteen thousand. The town is charming, and one of the notable differences between GMC and the few equally dedicated to environmental education is a campus that looks more like Colonial Williamsburg than Vermont farm buildings. Handsome buildings, almost all of which are made of red brick and adorned with white columns are set on a well maintained and beautifully designed campus. Well-equipped classroom buildings, laboratories, and dormitories sit behind a formal entrance gate, and are arranged in quadrangles and open grassy space. At the edge of the campus, a stately white building houses the college's guest house, the Two Editors Inn. Two of the most notable residents in the Nineteenth Century were George Jones, first editor of The New York Times, and Horace Greeley, editor of the New York Tribune. Both were active abolitionists and both were/are considered among the most influential men of their age. The college owns and maintains the Two Editors Inn on the edge of the campus, a facility used by the college to welcome college visitors (including applicant families) for a one-night stay for free.

How big is Poultney, Vermont? Not counting the six hundred students at Green Mountain, the abiding population is about three thousand. Size of town and college does not seem to be much of an issue for students headed to Green Mountain College; they have more than enough to occupy their time and ambition and could care less about rollicking city life. Green Mountain is one of very few colleges that combine a focus on environmental education and John Dewey's "Progressive Education", a philosophy which guarantees that each student has authority in organizing and focusing the education to be gathered in this grounded and experimental college. Vermont has more than its share of interesting and uncommon colleges, but Green Mountain truly has no peers. A close comparison might be made to The College of the Atlantic, an enclave of fewer than four hundred students studying human ecology on Mt. Desert Island in Maine, or perhaps with Warren Wilson College a working farm and college next to Asheville, North Carolina, also known for its pioneering work in combining environmental studies and a liberal arts education. Green Mountain is a member of the Eco League, an association of colleges that dedicates themselves to environmental studies, allowing students at each to study at the other in order to experience sustainability in a variety of biomes. But Green Mountain College directs its seven hundred or so students toward a greater emphasis on environmental literacy and active citizenship than its cohorts, and its location between the Green Mountains and the Adirondacks offers great opportunities in farming and the use of the wilderness. On the far side of the more traditionally designed campus are the Solar Garage, the Cerridwen Farm, and the Killington School of Resort Management.

The college offers more than twenty-five majors, many of them in what might be considered the liberal arts - History and English- and some in what might be considered "professional" programs - Resort and Hospitality Management and Elementary Education with a Special Education Endorsement. These and the rest of the college's offerings, however, are all presented by the small (fewer than fifty) faculty members who endorse the tenets of Dewey's progressive educational theory.

In principle, the theory, as first explored by Locke and Rousseau, begins with the notion that truth and knowledge are gained through experience and observation rather than from the transmission of generally accepted ideas. OK, that explains the emphasis on experiential education at Green Mountain- learning by doing. Dewey was determined to integrate education and the society in which its citizens would live and work. His work had much to do with the development of the public school program in the United States, and his conviction that an important element in citizenship was pragmatic understanding of what a society needs. That is why Green Mountain endorses entrepreneurship as an important element in the preparation of its students to carry their environmental expertise into the marketplace and to the service of the community.

In case this college is starting to sound entirely too philosophical, remember that it is made up of college-aged students, most of whom are similar to their peers elsewhere in college land. Kids play rugby (and Quidditch) and they sing (frequently in Welsh). Maybe the roster of activities is a bit different from that at a more conventional college. Clubs include the Pre-Law and Pre-Vet clubs, and the Agora (philosophy), the Forestry Club, the Herbal Tribe, an Equestrian Club, Black Culture Club, Dream Mentoring Club, a fencing club, and one of the coolest activities I have ever seen.

The website dedicated to this book includes photos of the Green Mountain Solar Garage and the Green Mountain Tiny House, two extraordinary accomplishments designed and built by GMC students. The Solar Garage generates enough voltage to power electric vehicles even on the bitterest of Vermont mornings. In addition, it serves as a kind of hothouse in which crops sprouts can be developing before spring arrives. It also looks fantastic. Equally inventive and just as beautifully designed is the GMC "Tiny House". The Tiny House movement has delighted designers across the country, and the GMC version is not only great looking, but also a seventy square foot mobile home, easily pulled by a small car.

Before I go any farther, I should emphasize that Green Mountain has an honest-to-goodness very "collegiate" campus with residential halls, dining facilities, athletic facilities, and edifices that look entirely welcoming. The campus map looks very much like that of most New England College, except that it is also attached to a working farm. GMC athletes compete in six varsity sports in Division III. Their mascot, Larry the Eagle, inspires them to compete in golf, lacrosse, soccer, tennis, track, and volleyball. GMC also offers club teams in frisbee, and rugby.

So, having established that GMC is more than a constellation of ideas, I'll turn to the final two examples of traditions and sensibilities that set Green Mountain apart from other post-secondary destinations. The first of these is attached to the college's location in a particular stretch of New England countryside settled by Welsh immigrants attracted by the slate industry in Vermont and adjacent New York State. The region was among the most concentrated centers of Welsh population in the United States, and GMC has worked hard to maintain its Welsh heritage. The library has a large collection devoted to Wales and Welsh culture, and the school sponsors an annual Welsh Festival each fall. The college's anthem is performed in

Welsh as are the many numbers performed by the college's choir, and Cantorion, an a cappella group.

My guess is that only readers actively interested in Green Mountain's mission are still following this discussion, so I feel comfortable in addressing what was known as "The Great Oxen Slaughter Debate". It's a tricky case, in that the college's tradition of pragmatism and sustainability came into conflict with the gentle sensibilities of students, friends, and neighbors. One of the college's oxen was dramatically injured (no details here) and had to be put down. Its companion, heartbroken, would not accept another companion. Thus, the college reasoned, why not slaughter both and stock up some tasty meat for the use of the college's food service? The oxen had worked the fields instead of tractors and had become virtual college mascots. Lu and Bill were beloved. The battle raged, and the college finally capitulated, burying one and keeping the other. This would merely be an odd and sad story were it not for the clarity with which it demonstrates the sorts of principles by which this small college works.

Marlboro College - Marlboro, Vermont

Here's the thing – the entire process of education at Marlboro is based upon the student's interest in building and pursuing a course of study... independently. There are professors, of course, and courses, and regular class meetings, and grades, but the intent in the undertaking is to sharpen thinking and writing skills so that the student can undertake a two-year adventure known as "Plan of Concentration," or simply, "Plan." Having determined what he or she wants to study, a Marlboro student works in tutorials for two years in the development of a significant piece of work reflecting that concentration.

And the stats... 2015

Number of Applicants: 212/ 82% Accepted
Undergrad Enrollment: 230   52% female / 48% male
SAT and ACT scores are not required as part of the application,
Total Cost: $51,600.00.
Received some form of financial assistance: 80%

"We, its resident and affiliate members, shall foster among ourselves a sense of stewardship for the natural resources on which we depend and educate ourselves and other about the opportunities and obligations we share as citizens of a sustainable world"
Marlboro College Environmental Mission Statement

Vermont is a beautiful state from top to bottom.

However, one of the most terrifying stretches of roads in America is on Route 9, the New England Interstate Byway, and a two-lane ribbon stretching from Wells, Maine to Bennington, Vermont. It is, essentially, the only east/west route through the southern reaches of Vermont and New Hampshire. It's a fairly tame road until it crosses Route 91, the great highway running north and south; at that point is starts to get, well, twisty.

It is at its twistiest near the western end, from Bennington to Brattleboro, as the road climbs around Hogback Mountain. Fortunately, the route becomes more than civilized as it falls near the town of Marlboro, home of the Marlboro Music Festival, Vermont's largest Civil War reenactment, and Marlboro College.

Marlboro is a strikingly beautiful town, and the college looks like the most perfectly planned New England farmstead, tucked in the Green Mountains of Vermont.

If you've done any reading about colleges, you have probably encountered a short paragraph about Marlboro; it is an anomaly – a tiny college community made up of about 350 men and women and an active experiment in self-directed study and communal governance. Marlboro (the college) is absolutely NOT interested in frat parties, the big game, and mindless acquisition of college credits.

I don't often include a college's statement of mission –because most sound exactly the same – but Marlboro's is worth considering:

> *The goal of Marlboro College is to teach students to think clearly and to learn independently through engagement in a structured program of liberal studies. Students are expected to develop a command of concise and correct English and to strive for academic excellence informed by intellectual and artistic creativity; they are encouraged to acquire a passion for learning, discerning judgment and a global perspective. The college promotes independence by requiring students to participate in the planning of their own programs of study and to act responsibly within a self-governing community.*

So, the three elements that can't be ignored in this proposition are: that students are expected to become independent as students; that students had better figure out how to write exceptionally well; and that students, to some degree, actually run the show.

Here's the thing – the entire process of education at Marlboro is based upon the student's interest in building and pursuing a course of study... independently. There are professors, of course, and courses, and regular class meetings, and grades, but the intent in the undertaking is to sharpen thinking and writing skills so that the student can undertake a two-year adventure known as "Plan of Concentration," or simply, "Plan." Having determined what he or she wants to study, a Marlboro student works in tutorials for two years in the development of a significant piece of work reflecting that concentration.

I know, it sounds a bit fuzzy, so here are examples of three recent Plan descriptions:

Bachelor of Arts
THEATER

PLAN SUMMARY: An examination of the history and use of race as a thematic device on the American stage, culminating in a production of Rebecca Gilman's play, *Spinning into Butter.*
PROJECT: A performance of Rebecca Gilman's play, *Spinning into Butter.*

Bachelor of Science
BIOLOGY & MATHEMATICS
PLAN SUMMARY: A study of the anatomy and physiology of the human kidney, with the goal of using mathematical tools to predict the severity of kidney disease.
PROJECT: A paper detailing work on mathematical models of kidney functions.

Bachelor of Arts
ECONOMICS & PHILOSOPHY
PLAN SUMMARY: An interdisciplinary study of environmental management with a focus on collaborative, place-based and adaptive planning, drawing on economics, environmental philosophy and policy studies.
PROJECT: A case study of the Northern Forest planning initiative, examining history, process and outcomes.

None of this happens, by the way, without the student's first managing to get past the Clear Writing requirement. Marlboro seems to think that thinking and writing are connected, and so demands a series of experiences in which students write critically. Clear writing is expository, not creative, writing. Each student is expected to produce a 20-page portfolio in the first year demonstrating competency as a clear writer. A number of workshops and tutorials assist in the production of that portfolio.

Yup, not the usual "show up - sit in the back - buy the Cliff Notes" kind of education.

Clearly, the Marlboro College experience is not for everyone; in fact it is for less than a four hundred students. The college began in 1946, in part in response to the need for a substantial educational experience for men returning from World War II. From the start, it was assumed that these students were fully capable of governing themselves and should be involved in the administration of the learning community.

Here's where Marlboro gets even more distinctive: The college and the community are one, and the community is governed by a Community Constitution and directed by monthly Town Meetings, based on the tradition of New England town meetings. Students, teachers, and administrators, all have one vote. The meeting is run by Town Selectpeople who might be students or faculty. The Meeting determines EVERYTHING that happens in the community.

But, independent thinkers who write with sharp critical acumen must spend at least a few hours a week away from portfolio and Plan, don't they?

Actually, they do.

Skiing, both downhill and cross-country are, literally, at the student's doorstep. The Outdoor Program is ambitious, planning adventures virtually every weekend. Marlboro competes against other colleges in two sports – soccer and fencing, and play is a significant aspect of life at Marlboro. If a student wants to take a break from hiking, mountain biking, rock climbing or kayaking, there are opportunities to play basketball, softball, ultimate frisbee, or to take a class in yoga or martial arts. Vermont provides snow, lot of it, and a pond on campus freezes early, allowing pickup games of hockey and broomball.

I've cheated a little bit in bringing Marlboro to these pages. Most students come from within the region, but its distinctive reputation does bring it a fair number from far-flung states. Obviously, with fewer than three hundred students, in the total student population, and an entering class of fewer than seventy, all statistics are a bit tricky.

There are a few other equally distinctive colleges profiled in this book, but Marlboro is a rarity and not to be overlooked by the independent thinker seeking active participation in a community of learners.

Bennington College - Bennington, Vermont

Bennington offers the sort of almost in-bred literary hothouse that encourages a collaborative and occasionally competitive writing community. Aspiring writers seek out Bennington and practicing writers continue to practice in the company of other writers. In the same fashion that lab-intensive science communities turn out legions of innovative experimental scientists, Bennington creates a climate that suits writers, particularly those who aren't afraid to go slightly over the edge.

And the stats... 2015

Number of Applicants: 1,101/ 67% Accepted
Undergrad Enrollment: 775   64% female / 36% male
Avg. SAT Reading Comp 620- 720 / Math 550 - 650 Avg. ACT : 26 - 30
Total Cost: $64,090.00
Received some form of financial assistance: 91%

Bennington is small (fewer than seven hundred students) and notably unconventional college with an international reputation in literature and the arts. Its program is distinctive and notably "experimental" (students adopt "The Plan" rather than take on a major/ each year includes a Field Term); its student body independent and creative. The town of Bennington is colonial quaint, the mountains are gorgeous, the campus is distinctive in the flavor of its architecture, and the dorms are FABULOUS. By any measure, Bennington is one of the most comfortable places to spend four years. The food is good, and the intensity of student relationships makes Bennington a one-of-a-kind opportunity for the student who seeks a true intellectual and artistic milieu.

If you have heard of Bennington, you may have heard of the number of highly regarded literary figures who have studied at Bennington and have used that experience as grist for their literary mill, or perhaps, have heard of the extraordinary place that Bennington holds in the history of dance and dance education, or of the purposefully experimental character of the college in several decades, or of the whole scale release of members of the faculty who have sued the college. Actually, every one of those stories has something significant to add to an understanding of Bennington today.

The legacy of literary accomplishment attached to the college is remarkable. The college wasn't established until the early nineteen-thirties, and yet the number of successful authors outpaces much older institutions. Relatively recently published authors include:

Elizabeth Frank, Pulitzer Prize winner for her biography of Louise Bogan and Kathleen Norris, author of *Dakota, The Cloister Walk,* and *A Vocabulary of Faith*. Susan Wheeler, finalist for a National Book Award and the Director of Creative Writing at Princeton and Jonathan Lethem, author of *Motherless Brooklyn* and Disney Professor of Literature at Pomona. Michael Pollan, Professor of Journalism at Berkeley and the author of *The Omnivore's Dilemma* and Kiran Desai, Booker Prize winner of *The Inheritance of Loss*.

The two contemporary authors who have used the college as the setting for their provocative novels are Bret Easton Ellis, author of *Less than Zero, The Rules of Attraction, American Psycho* and Donna Tartt, Pulitzer Prize winner and author of *The Goldfinch* and *The Secret History. The Secret History* is an inverted mystery set at a very small unorthodox liberal arts college in rural New England and *The Rules of Attraction* is also set at an intimate and unconventional liberal arts college in rural New England. Both authors plumb the depths of human behavior (approaching depravity, especially in Ellis' *American Psycho*), and their account of college days travels far from jolly romances once set against the college backdrop.

Bennington offers the sort of almost in-bred literary hothouse that encourages a collaborative and occasionally competitive writing community. Aspiring writers seek out Bennington and practicing writers continue to practice in the company of other writers. In the same fashion that lab-intensive science communities turn out legions of innovative experimental scientists, Bennington creates a climate that suits writers, particularly those who aren't afraid to go slightly over the edge.

The history of dance in a formal academic setting began with Bennington's School of Dance, a celebration of the arts, directed by Martha Hill and illuminated by Martha Graham. Bennington became known as a college that took dance seriously and produced original choreography as a central point of focus. Today, the dance program is still highly regarded and remains reflective of several of the tenants that have become hallmarks of a Bennington education. In the first place, it is expected that from the start of the first year that students of dance will create new work. Bennington has long endorsed an active and self-initiated education; there aren't any sit-back-take-notes-ask-the-teacher kinds of majors at Bennington, and Dance is certainly determined to turn out professionals who know how to create. Part of that training comes in the Field Work term that will be described after I have had a chance to talk about the faculty.

There are two significant issues at work in any discussion of those who teach at Bennington.

The first is that they are expected to be practitioners of their craft. Bennington was the first institution to include the Fine and Performing Arts as part of a liberal arts curriculum and has long demonstrated the collaborative advantage of students working toward mastery in the company of established professionals. Working dancers, sculptors, writers, musicians teach at Bennington but remain active in the production of their own work.

The second is that Bennington, like other "experimental" colleges faces economic challenges that conventional schools might not. Established as a college for women in 1932, long identified as a college particularly championing the arts, operating without athletic teams to engage alumni, welcoming an unconventional student body, and a very small student body at that, Bennington simply lacks the sort of invested endowment that allows other institutions to weather hard times with composure. Figures vary, but Bennington probably has an endowment of fourteen million to sixteen million dollars, which may sound like a lot of money until you compare Bennington with comparable semi-quirky institutions. The endowment at Sarah Lawrence, for example, is more than one hundred and four million. The endowment at Warren Wilson College is more than fifty eight million. The endowment at the even tinier College of the Atlantic approaches thirty million dollars.

For many years, Bennington was the most expensive college in the nation. A concerted effort at righting the financial ship brought the college back into line with other competing colleges, although the current projected total cost including room, board, tuition, and fees is over sixty thousand dollars a year. It was in the effort to cut expenses while improving the quality of the student body that a number of professors were let go. Some were asked to leave and others were not offered tenure; a third group left in protest. That chapter has ended, and the college is on firm financial footing and served by professors of rare talent, all of which are practicing poets, artists, musicians, writers, filmmakers, dancers, or scientists.

At the heart of the Bennington academic experience is The Plan. From the start, Bennington has operated with the conviction that a worthwhile education proceeds from a student's taking charge of the process. Initiative, responsibility, and agency are at the heart of the Bennington experience. Working with advisors, students spend the first year working with an Assistant Director for Academic Services, beginning the process of identifying what they want to study and how they want to study it. That, in essence is The Plan, although it is expected that the plan will change during the course of a Bennington career as course work, tutorials, and Field Term inform a student's ambition and focus.

The Field Term is a seven-week off-campus opportunity to pursue an area of interest by gaining hands-on experience. Some Field Terms will be internships; others may be volunteer experiences. Students must take one Field Term each year, but as many would argue, what could be better than taking a new job every year, bulking up a resume, and perhaps, not being in Vermont in the darkest, coldest months?

What else matters in the realm academic? The clearly articulated expectation that each student will map out a plan and prepare the stages necessary to its completion creates strong bonds between students and faculty advisors. This is a close and uncommonly collaborative academic community. There are "areas" rather than departments, but the emphasis is on the work rather than territorial posturing; students know they are the heart of the college and enjoy the privilege of being taken seriously.

They may ask to be graded on a standard A, B, C, D scale, but grades are not required. Narrative evaluations provide the real assessment of a student's efforts.

And, the rest of the story?

Lots of outdoor activities at the doorstep and an endless parade of performances, recitals, cafes, coffee houses, recitations, installations, happenings, readings, lectures, and meetings. Here are a typical week's activities as a snapshot of Bennington life:

- Basketball
- Meditation in Motion | Yoga
- Interfaith Meeting
- Karaoke
- Senior Series | Questions about Grad School
- Environmental Change and Infectious Disease Speaker Series | Amphibian Population
- Declines: Complex Causes and Consequences for Global Amphibian Biodiversity Loss
- 40 Years Later: Rightsizing the United States Criminal Justice System | Glenn Martin
- Cities Art Forum | Lukas Ligeti
- Kickstarting Capitalism: Finding A Calling In A Clean Energy Future
- Poetry at Bennington | Spencer Reece
- Film Showing | "The Hungry Heart"
- Deane Carriage Barn Series Concert | Lukas Ligeti
- Room Tone Festival

Meditation in motions, yes, but also basketball. There's a weekly series of pick-up games, and some groups go off campus to play other colleges. In the fall Bennington also plays against other colleges in soccer. No mascot for Bennington, no membership in an athletic conference, but lots of great club sports, including frisbee, fencing, and a killer dodgeball program that attracts fourteen teams into violent dodgeball competition.

No fraternities or sororities (please!), but lots of activities, including environmental action groups, Bollywood flash mobs, a classic film series, swing and social dancing, lots of outdoor opportunities including skiing and sledding, tennis, and swimming.

If Donna Tartt and Bret Easton Ellis are to be believed, there may be some fairly enthusiastic and quasi-orgiastic, collegiately hedonistic activities after hours, but those are better left to the imagination, or, I suppose, to the many Bennington authors. Bennington is one of the colleges that can be described as self-selective; smart, artsy kids seek it out and find what they are looking for at this idyllic and active small enclave at the corner of Vermont, Massachusetts, and New York.

New Hampshire

New Hampshire has all the rich variety of the New England states. The New Hampshire coast feels very much like the adjacent coast of Maine, the mountains look a lot like Vermont's, the trees burst into autumnal color in the fall as do those in Massachusetts, and small towns boast a general store and the occasional covered bridge. Like Vermonters and Mainers, New Hampshire's natives are Yankees or French Canadian, proud of their heritage and inclined to view tourists and newcomers with some skepticism until they've proven themselves capable of understanding and appreciation the New England way of life.

New Hampshire is a bit different in one notable aspect, however. Proximity to Boston and particularly to the booming high-tech boom located in the western exurbs, the "Magic Circle", Route 128, brought a large influx of commuting families to New Hampshire, tripled the size of towns near the highways, and changed the character of the southern half of the state. Nashua, for example, once a textile city, then an empty textile city, now only 50 minutes from Boston even at rush hour, is the second city of New Hampshire.

"Live Free or Die." Apparently. There is no sales tax in New Hampshire, so a number of "border malls" attract Bay Staters from Massachusetts who come to New Hampshire to shop. There is also no income tax in New Hampshire, the state has the most relaxed gun laws in the nation, and there is no mandatory seatbelt law in New Hampshire.

For the visitor, however, the beaches on the coast, Franconia Notch, Mount Washington, and Santa's Village Christmas Time Theme Park in Jefferson will draw the greatest attention, although those in the know recommend a trip up to the northern border, near Pittsburg, where congregations of moose have given the area the name, "Moose Alley".

The college campuses in New Hampshire are worthy of a visit as well. Dartmouth College in Hanover is pretty much the poster-child of New England colleges, impressive white Georgian buildings surrounded by brilliant green lawns. Very Ivy! The University of New Hampshire is in Durham, a small city in the seacoast region of New Hampshire, about fifteen minutes south of Dover. Saint Anselm's College is in Goffstown, an extension of the city of Manchester. Franklin Pierce College is in Rindge, in the southwestern portion of the state, close by Mount Monadnock. New England College is in the far western county along the Contoocook River, along Route 202. Colby-Sawyer College located in New London, NH, near Lake Sunapee, about ninety minutes north of Boston.

University of New Hampshire - Durham, New Hampshire

This strong university is distinctive for five notable attributes: Location, Size, Student Body, Academic Profile, and Athletics. In fact, the university is pretty darned good, for a variety of reasons. Oh, and I should mention the UNH Dairy Bar, a sustainable food restaurant that serves a delicious breakfast and ice cream that surpasses description.

And the stats... 2015

Number of Applicants: 18,420/ 80% Accepted
Undergrad Enrollment: 12,831 54% female / 46% male
Avg. SAT Reading Comp 490‐ 590 / Math 5100 ‐ 610 Avg. ACT : Very few submitted
Total Cost: $30,750.00 (in-state) $43,730.00 (out-of-state)
Received some form of financial assistance: 56%

Durham, home to the University of New Hampshire is north of the population explosion, in a town of about 12,000, within easy reach of the New Hampshire coast and the Maine beaches. Boston's airport, Logan Airport, is about an hour and fifteen minutes from Durham. In many ways, Durham is the ideal location - near enough to Boston, Cape Cod, and the Massachusetts colleges, and the virtual gateway to northern New England.

This strong university is distinctive for five notable attributes: Location, Size, Student Body, Academic profile, and Athletics. Oh, and I should mention the UNH Dairy Bar, a sustainable food restaurant that serves a delicious breakfast and ice cream that surpasses description. Durham is not the college town that time forgot, but it does feel very much like the traditional movie-set college setting. All the usual amenities and big box stores are within easy reach, and two good airports bring students from outside New England. It is, dare I say it, a happy town. And, it is a town that revolves around the university. I can't think of an outdoor activity not immediately available; both beaches and good skiing are within an hour's drive. I'm not going to make a huge deal out of this, but UNH is safe.

UNH enrolls about 3,000 new students each year; the total population is around 12,000. There are relatively few universities that are large enough to be truly comprehensive and small enough to maintain a sense of community. One of the most significant experiences at UNH is that virtually all of its graduates complete course work on schedule; they can get into the courses they need to take. Again, without trashing other universities, UNH is unusual in offering a range of majors and programs and accessibility to those programs. There is an active fraternity and sorority scene at UNH, but again, the size of the university is manageable so that frat life does not dictate social activity. In addition, the amenities in a university of this size are simply easier to maintain. The food at UNH is excellent, often remarkably so. The dining halls feature meals-prepared-to-order (stir fry, etc), and there are a number of smaller convenient coffee shops around the campus, one of which is open until 4:00 am during the week.

The student body is less diverse than the university might wish; let's guess that about 20% might be considered students of color. On the other hand, minority students at UNH report that they feel welcome and that they have a place in the university. The majority of students are more polished (J Crew/ North Face/ Uggs?) than are the students at the other New England state schools, and they are athletic, ambitious, and kind. This is a happy campus attracting happy kids. In walking across campus, you'll see a range, of course, but the "feel" is very much like Boston College, Villanova, or Colgate. It may of interest to know that UNH often appears at the top of the unofficial polls for "hottest girls" and "smartest girls." Apparently the guys are ok too.

Academically, UNH has some distinctive programs, including a School of Engineering, a School of Business, the College of Health and Human Services, Forest Science, Resource Management, and Hospitality Management. Until recently, the university managed the New England Center, a top-flight hotel and conference center, at which Hospitality majors could intern. UNH regularly sends graduates to top graduate programs and is among the few of the state schools to win numbers of Fulbright Fellowships each year. The programs in marine biology and oceanography are conducted at the Shoals Marine Laboratory, jointly operated with Cornell University.

One unique program has recently received considerable attention. The UNH Innovation Center has as its mission the transfer of innovative ideas formulated at UNH into the wider world. Over the years UNHI has recognized a number of innovative programs, but with the reality of school violence, the obvious recent recipient of the UNHI award is the Prevention Innovation Research Center (PIRC). The curriculum developed by PIRC is now used by more than six hundred campuses to reduce relationship violence. The university not only sponsors innovative research and development but also is dedicated to promoting the results of that research for the improvement across the nation.

Finally, as fair warning to warm weather candidates, it has to be noted that UNH is a hockey school. Ice hockey is huge and hugely successful. Field hockey is also a signature sport, and the rest of the varsity programs compete happily in the conference called the America East Conference, a group of ten universities in Division IAA. The mascot of the university is the Wildcat, and Wildcat hockey fever is relentless; the ice arena is packed for every home game. The Cat Cup, however, is given to the winning team in intramural competition, and the intramural program at UNH is among the most active in the nation. Dorms, frats, and special interest groups compete for the Cat Cup throughout the year.

Saint Anselm College - Manchester, New Hampshire

It has become an unwritten understanding that no one runs for president without speaking at Saint Anselm College. The Washington Post referred to Saint Anselm as "the Benedictine college with a box seat on America's most riveting political theater."

And the stats... 2015

Number of Applicants: 3570/ 76% Accepted
Undergrad Enrollment: 1968 60% female / 40% male
Avg. SAT Reading Comp 490– 590 / Math 490 – 590 Avg. ACT : 21 – 26
Total Cost: $52,000.00
Received some form of financial assistance: 85%

There is quite a lot of press about Saint Anselm's as I write this profile, largely due to the excitement surrounding the New Hampshire Primary and the role the college as taken as the site of the New Hampshire Institute of Politics. It has become an unwritten understanding that no one runs for president without speaking at Saint Anselm College. The Washington Post referred to Saint Anselm as "the Benedictine college with a box seat on America's most riveting political theater." The institute has been in place for more than forty years, welcoming hundreds of presidential aspirants. Who knows what secrets its halls could tell?

The significant political identity of the college has long distinguished the college, and there is more to say about this remarkable program, but Saint Anselm has a number of other very attractive attributes, including a notable humanities program the college calls, "Portraits of Greatness", a rigorous curriculum in the liberal arts, a cooperative program in engineering which partners with Notre Dame, a program in archeological excavation in Italy, and the Meelia Center for Community Service. Despite its relatively small size (just under 2000), Saint Anselm competes in Division II athletics, sponsoring 20 varsity teams for men and women, including a men's ice hockey program that regularly lands at the top of the Northeast 10. In addition to its many fine qualities as an academic institution, the college is also noted for an exceptionally tasty menu on a daily basis. A recent lunch? Chicken pot pie. Buttered asparagus with breadcrumbs, broccoli stir fry, and Caprese panini. Wow!

Goffstown is virtually the eastern end of Manchester, New Hampshire's largest city. Concord, the state capital, is sixteen miles to the north. Boston is about an hour to the south, and Portland, Maine is about two hours to the north. Manchester is the largest city north of Boston with an airport that serves most of New England. The city also boasts several good museums and two major venues for sports and concerts. The New Hampshire Fisher Cats, are the Double A affiliate of the Toronto Blue Jays, and the Manchester Monarchs of the AHL are affiliated with the Los Angeles Kings of the NHL.

All of which is to reassure the college prospector worried about the connection between this friendly college and the Order of Saint Benedict. How Catholic is Saint Anselm? Well, there is a Benedictine abbey attached to the college, and the President of the college lives in the monastery, as does the Dean of the College and the college is still operated by the Order of Saint Benedict. On the other hand, an ordinary day at Saint Anselm feels very much like an ordinary day at any secular college - preppy kids on their way to class or sports laugh and scurry as they would anywhere else. Perhaps the only notable difference is that the dormitories are still single-sex for the most part. The campus is handsome and well maintained, athletics and social life are vital, and the range of courses is surprisingly diverse for a college of about 2000.

One of the qualities often present in the small Catholic colleges is a commitment to service, a commitment actively pursued at Saint Anselm. One obvious element is the development of an active branch of the college, the Meelia Center, with one purpose - the organization and facilitation of service learning and community service. More than nine hundred students volunteer at nursing homes, public schools, juvenile correctional facilities, and a number of organizations in Manchester. In addition to the work done in the Meelia Center, the college's Center for Experiential Learning arranges internships, career engagement, and study abroad. This clear sense of responsibility for educating men and women who will take a place in the world as civic leaders is also reflected in the courses of study offered at Saint Anselm.

Portraits of Greatness, the core humanities program required of all students, asks the fundamental question - can this individual be called 'great'? Investigation challenges the student to consider: The Warrior (The Iliad, the Homeric Warrior, and Alexander the Great), The Philosopher (Reading from The Bible, The Koran, Socrates, Plato, and Aristotle), The Citizen (Roman Republic, Cicero, Augustus), Ancient Artist (Greek art, Roman art, and the Classic tradition), The Convert (Saint Paul, Saint Mark, Saint Augustine), The Ruler (Charlemagne, Pope Gregory VII, Louis IX), The Townsman (Carolingian manors, Gothic Art, Saint Francis), The Poet (Marie de France, Chaucer), and The Teacher (Abelard, Thomas Aquinas). In the second year, the investigation continues with Michelangelo, John

Calvin, Queen Elizabeth I, Adam Smith, Thomas Jefferson, Ludwig van Beethoven, Darwin, Freud, Picasso, Camus, and Martin Luther King, Jr. In addition to the expected majors and courses of study, Saint Anselm's departments include: Nursing, Criminal Justice, Business, Education, and Classics. The Modern Languages include Chinese and Russian in addition to French, German, and Spanish.

Students characterize Saint Anselm as unfailingly friendly. Residential Halls organize a variety of social events and more than eighty clubs and associations keep the campus hopping. Some of that activity is in the athletic arena, as the college supports an extensive program of varsity sports and a number of club sports for those who want to get active but not at the top level of competition. Most notable among the club sports is rugby. Teams for men and women play regularly and compete against other club teams in New England. Similarly, softball, lacrosse, and field hockey club teams are active and well supported. My favorite of the club sports is the Synchronized Skating Club. Choral and instrumental music remain important to the college, and, in recent years, SAGA (Saint Anselm Gaming Association) has emerged as the arbiter of all things gaming – from video games to role-playing games.

Healthy, happy, earnest, generous – Saint Anselm's students are predictably appreciative of the opportunities they find on this well-appointed campus. Their appreciation grows beyond all containment, however, in two notable arenas.

The New Hampshire Institute on Politics is unique; not only does it act as a focus for political debate within the state of New Hampshire during the campaign years (and every year is a campaign year!), it also provides an academic program of unusual breadth. A visitor to the campus will appreciate the facility itself – a 20,000 square foot building built in 2001. The television studio is impressive, but the heart of the academic program is in the six classrooms and four seminar rooms. The classrooms are "smart classrooms" equipped with full audio and video capability, and the studio is the only live production facility in the Manchester area. As a result, television journalists from across the country make use of the college's facility. Then they, like any visitor, can adjourn to the quiet coffee shop within the Institute –The Common Ground Cafe – for a beverage and continued political discussion. I've seen a lot of coffee puns as the caffeination of America has boomed, but this one strikes just the right note of political and brewing savvy.

It is not surprising that the college has also established the Kevin B. Harrington Student Ambassador Program (named for late Massachusetts Senator Kevin B. Harrington – member of the Board of Trustees at Saint Anselm and a driving force in the establishment of the Institute). Student ambassadors essentially run the events that fill the campaign season, welcome speakers, and introducing candidates who headline special programs. Student bloggers rave about having met the most influential political figures face-to-face.

Less academic is the enthusiasm Saint Anselm brings to its support of its excellent Division II ice hockey teams. A quick look at the roster of the most recent men's teams reveals the powerful hockey network that brings outstanding players to this championship team. Players arrive from the best prep school programs and from the strongest New England traveling teams. By the way, the roster of the Women's ECAC championship team may actually be even more impressive, as it features prep school and New England stars and a fair sprinkling of hockey players from Wisconsin and Minnesota. In case the ice is not your thing, most of the rest of the varsity programs are exceptionally strong as well. Men's lacrosse has emerged as a perpetual power and is currently ranked in the top three in Division II.

Massachusetts

It's understandable that visitors tend to think that Massachusetts is Boston in the same way that New Englanders think that California is Los Angeles. OK, the sophisticates may know about Nantucket, Martha's Vineyard, Hyannis Port, Provincetown and Wellfleet, but the general impression is that the entire commonwealth revolves around the colonial hotspots in Boston and the Harvard/MIT nexus in Cambridge. The hundred or so colleges and universities in the state, however, are spread somewhat more widely and direct the visitor's attention to the other, equally fascinating areas outside of Beantown, The Athens of America, The Hub.

The earliest settlements were in Plymouth on what is known as the South Shore and Salem, on the North Shore. Hawthorne's House of Seven Gables and the history of the clipper ships still draw visitors to Salem; charming fishing villages such as Gloucester (*Gloss-ter*) still send fishing fleets out, even in the face of The Perfect Storm. On the North Shore, Endicott College, formerly a college for women, now enrolls 2200 students in a program emphasizing internship and coop experience. Gordon College in Wenham is a nondenominational Christian college of national reputation. Merrimack College in North Andover is a small Augustinian liberal arts college.

Closer to Boston, a constellation of colleges ring the city. Bentley University in Waltham enrolls more than 4000 undergrads in programs of business, management, and finance. Brandeis University, also in Waltham, is the premier nonsectarian Jewish sponsored research university in the nation, long regarded as one of the most successful research universities in the country. Medford is adjacent to Cambridge and is the home of nationally known Tufts University. In addition to Harvard and MIT, Cambridge is home to Lesley College, profiled in this book.

Within the city of Boston, the college visitor will meet Boston University, following Commonwealth Avenue from Kenmore Square to Alston along the Charles River. Northeastern University, known for outstanding cooperative education and for its School of Architecture, enrolls more than 20,000 resident and commuting students in its programs in the Fenway District. Simmons College, profiled in this book, is also located nearby in the area known as the Fenway. Among the other colleges associated in a group known as The Colleges of the Fenway, are Wentworth Institute of Technology (known for programs in computer engineering) and Wheelock College (known for programs in social work and education). The most comprehensive program in contemporary music, composition and performance is offered at the Berklee School of Music in Boston's Back Bay. The New England Conservatory of Music is located near Symphony Hall on Huntington Avenue. Emerson College, located near the Theater

District on the edge of the Boston Commons offers an outstanding program in communications within a liberal arts curriculum. Also near the Fenway in the Longwood district is Massachusetts College of Art and Design (MassArt). Just to the west of the Museum of Fine Arts is the School of the Museum of Fine Arts, associated with Tufts and Northwestern. Near the State House on Beacon Hill, Suffolk University has grown from an evening Law School to a comprehensive university enrolling almost 10,000 students in undergraduate and graduate programs. The School of Law is still its most prominently known program, although the Sawyer Business School is also growing quickly. The University of Massachusetts Boston enrolls more than 15,000 students on its campus at Columbia Point. Curry College, also profiled in this book, is located in Milton, adjacent to Dorchester and the Blue Hills Reservation.

Boston College is famously not in Boston (it's in Chestnut Hill) and not a college (It's a university). Equally celebrated, Wellesley College is within minutes of the city and part of the massive college cohort that frequents pubs and clubs in the hub. This posh suburb is also home to Babson College, perhaps the preeminent business program in a college setting. Also in Wellesley, but approached through Needham, is Franklin W. Olin School of Engineering, also known as "Olin," one of the most remarkable institutions founded in the last twenty years. Free at the start and intensely competitive, the Olin experiment is project based. There are no separate departments and no tenured faculty. Today, the brilliant applicants admitted to Olin pay half tuition. Slightly south of the city, Wheaton College in Norton offers an excellent liberal arts education in a beautiful setting halfway between Boston and Providence.

To the west (and there is actually an entire state left to describe) the first major settlement is Worcester, home of Clark University (in this book) and Worcester Polytechnic Institute (WPI). WPI is an outstanding engineering school, best known for the financial success of its graduates (7th highest salaries of any institution upon graduation) and its Gaming Weekend, during which hundreds of gamers descend upon the Institute for games of all kinds.

The Massachusetts Turnpike runs from Boston to Stockbridge, connecting east and west. Route 91 divides Vermont and New Hampshire and slits Massachusetts east and west from the Vermont line to New Haven. In the center of state, the Five Colleges establish one of the most ambitious collaborative educational opportunities anywhere. The University of Massachusetts, Hampshire College, and Amherst College are located in Amherst. Smith College is in Northampton, Mount Holyoke in South Hadley, just south of Amherst. Students enrolled at any one of the five may take course work on one of the other campuses during their undergraduate career.

South of Amherst (on Route 91) is Springfield, home of the NBA Hall of Fame and Springfield College, long prominent in teaching physical education. American International College is also located in Springfield.

Finally, the weary college visitor will take the Stockbridge exit and turn north on route 7, driving through the extraordinarily beautiful Berkshire Mountains to Williamstown, home of Williams College and the westernmost of the Massachusetts colleges and universities.

Endicott College - Beverly, Massachusetts

Is the campus reflective of the stately charm of the region? Absolutely! Do some of the dorms actually overlook the Atlantic Ocean? Again, absolutely! Visiting Endicott feels like visiting a beautifully maintained estate.

And the stats... 2015

Number of Applicants: 3,848/ 73% Accepted
Undergrad Enrollment: 2,877 62% female / 38% male
Avg. SAT Reading Comp 480– 570 / Math 500 – 590 Avg. ACT : 21 – 25
Total Cost: $45,500.00
Received some form of financial assistance: 94%

Endicott was founded as a college for women in the 1930's and has grown exponentially since its founding, now enrolling approximately two thousand, five-hundred undergrads (male and female) and another two thousand graduate students on its expansive campus. The college is impressively equipped in comparison with many of New England's liberal arts counterparts, but the most distinguishing feature in assessing Endicott's value as an option for those exploring colleges in the Northeast is its demonstrated commitment to experiential education and a vibrant program of internship placements.

I know. I tend to rave about these "hidden gems," waxing rhapsodic about colleges that most readers do not know well. Fair warning! Rave review about Endicott is coming your way.

In the first place, Endicott has beaches.

Notice, I did not say *access* to beaches; I said beaches. Beverly, Massachusetts is a seaside resort and residential community, and Endicott sits adjacent to three of Beverly's sandiest and most pleasant beaches. These are bayside beaches, great for sunning and splashing, but not roaring with surf. The college has a number of excellent qualities and would be highly touted even if it happened not to enjoy this privileged setting.

Endicott has an historic, extremely handsome campus on what is known as Boston's North Shore. Actually, in the circles of folks who know, Beverly and several of the beautifully situated towns that abut it sit on Boston's "Gold Coast." Rockport, Newbury Port, Gloucester, and Marblehead get most of the tourist traffic, offering picture postcard views of the rugged shoreline and of the fishing nets and lobster traps that are still in use in this seacoast economy. Beverly is more domestic; you won't be able to see many of the grand houses, although the Cabot House and the Hale farmstead give some sense of the history of the town. You'll notice the word "Hannah" on the emblem of city officials, signifying Beverly's claim as the homeport of the US Navy's first ship, the schooner Hannah, donated by the Glover family of Marblehead. Marblehead begs to differ. North Shore squabbling aside, Beverly has long attracted wealthy summer visitors, such as the fabulous philanthropist and artist, Isabella Gardiner, and the nation's most substantial president, William Howard Taft. California's Beverly Hills takes its name from settlers who longed to return to this seaside haven.

So, is the campus reflective of the stately charm of the region? Absolutely! Do some of the dorms actually overlook the Atlantic Ocean? Again, absolutely! Visiting Endicott feels like visiting a beautifully maintained estate.

Of course, all of the conventional and functional facilities are in place. Callahan Hall, the dining center, was recently renovated so as to seat more students and to provide separate stations at which food can be prepared. The Business School operates out of a high tech and flexible center, providing space for the development of projects and for the hands-on counseling that accompanies the internship program. The same large complex houses the Life and Sciences facility and the Judge Science Center. Athletic facilities include a number of playing fields, a stadium for football, soccer, lacrosse, and rugby, a spacious gymnasium, and the Post Center, dedicated to physical fitness and the teaching of Sport Science, Fitness, and Athletic Training. Fitness takes some effort, but the center provides some unusual amenities in the support of that effort. Not only does the Post Center include the most up-to-date equipment, it also provides thirteen high definition television screens to offer distraction/encouragement to those who sweat and strain. And, having raised the issue of sweat, I should note that Endicott is one of the few colleges in the Northeast that provides dormitories with air conditioning. Some of the most popular dorms have a view of the Bay and easy access to the beach, while others offer apartment-style living.

Much of the infrastructure has been recently updated, and the modern facilities are impressive. What sets Endicott apart as a campus, however, are the remarkable older buildings, many of which have stories to tell. The oldest building on campus, Alhambra Hall, was originally a tavern. Built in 1750, the tavern served the weary and thirsty travelers on the route from Salem to Gloucester. Absorbed into the Gardner estate, this summer home is now a residence offering its female residents an extremely comfortable dormitory with full kitchen. Several of the older buildings have been converted into residential halls, among them Hamilton Hall and Wenham Hall. Reynolds Hall was once an estate employing thirty gardeners, and several other buildings were carriage houses or stables. Tupper Manor has been converted into the college's Inn and Conference Center. Finally, Winthrop Hall is reputed to house a ghost who walks the hall each night. On Halloween, students hope to catch sight of the "Pink Lady"; almost all of them describe encountering her at some point in their adventure.

At the heart of the Endicott experience, however, is its distinctive academic program. In fact, Endicott is alone in the New England college scene in requiring internship experience of all undergraduates, regardless of major. Learning by doing has been at the heart of Endicott's mission as the college is determined to bridge the gap between classroom instruction and professional experience; In addition, Endicott believes that the two semester long (120 hour) immersions into a professional setting do more to help a student explore career than any counseling session. Endicott was way out in front in developing, not only providing an active mentoring of all students as they take on their internships, but working with those students to use those internships in charting their future course of study and professional planning. Several of the academic divisions offer even more extensive hands-on learning; the Early Childhood, Elementary, and Physical Education programs include student teaching, and the Nursing and Athletic Training programs send students into clinical settings.

The opportunities for some disciplines seem obvious, but Endicott has worked hard to open many doors. For example, the college established a relationship with the Ibbetson Street Press in Somerville that allows aspiring writers the opportunity to immerse themselves in Boston's literary world. Students meet the most highly regarded literary figures in the region as well as becoming intimately involved with the Visiting Authors series sponsored by Ibbetson Street Press. They help to write and produce a widely admired magazine and maintain a literary blog. In addition, they make the sorts of connections that allow them to seek further internship opportunities with other publishing houses, literary festivals, and bookstores.

Academic programs at Endicott are organized into eight distinctive areas. The School of Arts and Sciences offers the usual majors in the Humanities, social sciences, languages, and science. In addition, particular programs include: Bioengineering, Computer Science, Criminal Justice, and International Studies. The Business School offers degrees in Accounting, Business Management, Entrepreneurship, Finance, International Business, and Marketing. The School of Communication offers programs in Communication, Digital Journalism, and Marketing Communication. The School of Education is specialized; majors include: Autism and Applied Behavior Analysis, Early Childhood, Elementary, and Secondary certification. The School of Hospitality Management presents majors in

Hospitality Management, and Hotel Management. The School of Sport Science and Fitness Studies includes Athletic Training, Coaching Certification, Exercise Science, and Sport Management. The School of Visual and Performing Arts presents majors in Art Therapy, Graphic Design, Photography, Interior Design, and Studio Art. The School of Nursing carries students to the RN degree.

Campus life at Endicott is not entirely conventional, primarily because Boston is a short hop away by public transportation. There are a number of activities on campus throughout the week and on weekends, but Boston is a powerful draw and the other two hundred thousand students make the city a very attractive option. No fraternities or sororities operate at Endicott; the dormitories take on an identity of their own and plan social activities that welcome the entire community. A quick glance at the range of students' interests gives some sense of the variety of activities currently flourishing. Club sports include crew, rugby, ice hockey, sailing, dance, and cheerleading. Intramural sports include powder puff football, flag football, basketball, kickball, arena football, floor hockey, dodgeball, and indoor soccer. Clubs include the Endicott Musician collective, the Endicott Political Debate Society, the Endicott College Television Network, and the college Oratory Society.

On the varsity level, Endicott's Gulls compete in NCAA Division III in a number of appropriate conferences. The football program plays in the New England Football Conference against such rivals as MIT, the Coast Guard Academy, and Curry College. Most sports play in the Eastern College Athletic Conference, a constellation of colleges across the East Coast; those sports would include: Field hockey, basketball, women's volleyball, softball, tennis, cross-country, and soccer. The crew team rows in the New England Collegiate Rowing Association, and the men's volleyball team in the New England Collegiate Conference. Rugby plays in the Colonial Coast Rugby Conference, the ice hockey team in the Northeast Collegiate Hockey Association, and the equestrian team in the Intercollegiate Horse Show Association. Endicott's teams appear in conference championships with regularity.

Simmons College - Boston, Massachusetts

Although the total undergraduate population is around 2000, many classes will enroll fewer than 20 students; the average class size is 18. As a result, Simmons students feel attended to by the college and secure in the mentorship they receive from their professors, and the quality of teaching at Simmons is impressive.

And the stats... 2015

Number of Applicants: 4,000 / 52% Accepted
Undergrad Enrollment: 1,662   100% female
Avg. SAT Reading Comp 540– 640 / Math 530 – 620 Avg. ACT : 24 – 28
Total Cost: $53,800.00.
Received some form of financial assistance: 90%

Boston was once known as "the Athens of America" and the city, like San Francisco, seems somehow more cultivated than other urban areas. Those of us who know Boston with some degree of familiarity will quickly acknowledge that much of it is a mess and occasionally unlovely. But, for the most part, tourists and college students find the city appealing.

After all, there are approximately 250,000 college students in the greater Boston area.

Think about it. How can any city be more exciting than Boston with a quarter of a million fun-seeking, moderately intelligent, tuition paying kids standing ready to hit the clubs and pubs on any night of the week?

I start with the collective mass of studentdom because Simmons is a college for women (at the undergraduate level), and there is still a lingering antipathy towards the single-sex option in some applicants. In anticipation of that antipathy, I need to stress several advantages of the Simmons education. In the first place, although the college is clearly dedicated to an undergraduate liberal arts education, its graduate programs are exceptional and accessible to undergrads as well. Programs in Health Studies, Library Information Science Management, Social Work, Education and Business set it apart from other colleges of its size. In the second place, Simmons is not a regional insular residential experience; more than twenty-five percent of enrolled students self-report as students of color, and the college enrolls women from more than forty states and many international students. Simmons is serious about its students, and its students are serious about preparing for their lives ahead, but, in addition to adventures to be found in Boston, Simmons keeps an active profile on campus throughout the year. My favorite of the Simmons traditions is the celebration of Simmtober. Lots going on in every arena, but particular energy around Simmons Fund Monday, Trivia Tuesday, and Leadership Wednesday.

So, Simmons is a fairly large liberal arts college for women located in what many people would consider Boston's prime real estate.

The Fenway is the section of the city, attached to one of Boston's most attractive neighborhoods – the Back Bay Fens. Most tourists know the area through visiting Kenmore Square on the way to Fenway Park, home of the Boston Red Sox. Cultivated visitors also know that this corner of the city also includes the Isabella Stewart Gardner Museum and the Museum of Fine Arts. The Boston Symphony plays at Symphony Hall on Massachusetts Avenue, and the spectacular Emerald Necklace Conservancy is a system of contiguous parks designed by Frederick Law Olmsted.

Among Simmons' near neighbors are Boston University, Northeastern University, and the Berklee School of Music. Access to all areas of the city is easy through via subway or bus.

After having invoked the specter of 250,000 college students on the loose, I had better quickly state that Simmons is NOT a party school. Far from it – Simmons may have the most goal-oriented and serious students in the city.

Some of the seriousness of purpose may come from the cohort of "older" students on camp (over the age of 24!). Simmons recognized one of America's great social reformers, Dorothea Dix in encouraging returning students to find their place in this strong liberal arts college. The Dix scholars are entirely comfortable in mixing with the conventional college students, and a high proportion of transfer students also connect quickly with the institution.

I may be overly generous in stating this, but I think Simmons may have the smallest classes of any college of its type. Although the total undergraduate population is around 2000, many classes will enroll fewer than 20 students; the average class size is 18. As a result, Simmons students feel attended to by the college and secure in the mentorship they receive from their professors, and the quality of teaching at Simmons is impressive, some would say, "Wicked Good!"

I indulge in that curious Bostonian turn of phrase in order to mention that Gregory Maguire, author of the enormously popular, *Wicked: The Life and Times of the Wicked Witch of the West*, is a professor at Simmons and past chair of the excellent Simmons College Center for the Study of Children's Literature.

Boston is distraction enough, but student activities flourish on campus as well. A Campus Life program keeps things hopping, and more than 50 student clubs and organizations are active, including an a cappella group (The Sirens), dramatic productions, music in conjunction with the Fenway colleges, and an investment club.

A reasonable percentage of students at Simmons play sports, and the Simmons Sharks compete in soccer, basketball, field hockey, lacrosse, crew, volleyball, and swimming. Among intramural options are: Wiffle Ball, Ultimate Frisbee, Bowling, Dodgeball, and Turkey Trot (don't ask – you have to run!)

Facilities at Simmons are attractive and well maintained; much new construction has taken place in the past five years.

Lesley University, Cambridge, Massachusetts

"Those who can ... do; those who can't ... teach." And that unfortunate sentiment is at the heart of an educational disaster we call contemporary American education. Real teachers are a rarity, and from the start, Lesley has been about real teachers.

And the stats... 2015

Number of Applicants: 2,800/ 71% Accepted
Undergrad Enrollment: 1,929   75% female / 25% male
Avg. SAT Reading Comp 510– 610 / Math 470 – 580 Avg. ACT : 21 – 26
Total Cost: $42,000.00
Received some form of financial assistance: 80%

Lesley is unlike any other institution in this book and a resource many excellent candidates will not have discovered. In the first place, Lesley is made up of Lesley College, set in Cambridge (just north of Harvard Square), the Art Institute of Boston (Kenmore Square/Fenway), a graduate school that operates from a campus near Porter Square, and residential buildings located on Brattle Street. First impressions might be that Lesley is primarily a graduate institution (it sponsors thousands of learners earning the M.Ed. at sites across the country through an advanced program of distance learning) but more than two thousand undergrads find a remarkable experience in Cambridge and Boston as they encounter programs uniquely designed to prepare students for work in the fields of education, the arts, art education, or counseling.

"Those who can ... do; those who can't ... teach." And that unfortunate sentiment is at the heart of an educational disaster we call contemporary American education.

Real teachers are a rarity, and from the start, Lesley has been about real teachers. Edith Lesley began this school in 1909, convinced that the most important work to be done was work with young children. "Kindergarten education in America will soon become established as a permanent unit in our national educational philosophy. I plan not merely to set up just another training school; I plan for us to be different; to consider the individual of basic importance; to inculcate the ideal of gracious living; and to foster the traditions of American democracy."

Lesley has moved far beyond the training of excellent kindergarten teachers to a broadly based liberal arts curriculum on the Cambridge campus and to an exceptional program in fine arts on Kendall Square campus. The Art Institute of Boston offers major programs in Animation, Illustration, Fine Arts, Art History, Design, and Photography, all at the highest level of instruction in small workshop classes. The great advantage of the program, however, is that a student at the Art Institute can minor in any of the programs offered at Lesley College. So, for example, a Design major can minor in Art Therapy, Environmental Studies or a foreign language. Another great advantage of the association between programs for the student in fine arts is that Lesley College is a residential college (in a fabulous location!) with an undergraduate population of almost two thousand and all the social, residential, and athletic advantages of a conventional four-year college. For the artist, the city, instruction, and workspace feed the craft, while the college allows interaction with other humans rather than relegating the artist to isolation in a seedy garret or loft.

Lesley College does not feel quite like other residential colleges, however, because those who choose it are people who have a sense of mission in mind as they arrive. They may not want to be teachers or therapists, but they do want to make a difference in the world. The college has developed a strong sense of purpose and is clear in its mission. The experience at Lesley College is one animated by four core values: Democracy, Inquiry, Equity, and Community. Classes are small and taught by professors, not teaching assistants. The most notable aspect of the curriculum however, other than its grounding in fields of social service, is in the college's commitment to experiential education.

All students, starting in the first year, will take on an internship. By the time a student graduates from Lesley, it is expected that he or she will have spent hundreds of hours in practical application of courses taken. The list of internship opportunities is impressive and includes: The Children's Room, Operation Peace, Phoenix Media, JFK Library and Museum, Cambridge Health Alliance, New England Aquarium, Project HOPE, Mass. Adoption Resource Center, and the Cambridge Center for Families. The Internship office is active and works to place each student in an environment that will enhance major or minor programs.

The program in Early Childhood Education is probably Lesley's best known major program, but others of national reputation include: Art Therapy, Child Studies, Counseling, Special Education, Holistic Psychology, and Social Work. The Education Department includes majors in Early Childhood Education, Elementary Education, Middle School Education, Secondary Education, and Special Education. The Counseling program offers a dual BA/MA in Counseling Psychology and a BS/MA in Clinical Mental Health Counseling.

An immediate difference between the undergraduate experience at Lesley and that at almost any other college of its type is that the core faculty at each of the divisions is devoted to the instruction of undergraduates and teach as professionals in their field. Students speak with warmth and gratitude in discussing their instructors and hold the conviction that they could not have found a more gratifying experience in any other setting. Classes are VERY small; students report taking courses with fewer than twelve students in a classroom. Most classes will enroll fewer than thirty students.

OK, so the professional/educational opportunities are excellent; what about LIFE at Lesley? "Vacations were great, but I counted the minutes until I could get back to Lesley. It actually felt more like home than home." This is a small college in an advantaged location, near the heart of a student population of almost four hundred thousand. That perspective is important, because Lesley is still overwhelmingly female in its enrollment, currently stuck at about four women for every one man. The sense of community is intense and residential life is rich. One student describes life at Lesley as, "...exactly the right blend of on-campus activity and access to a big city. There's always something happening in the dorm, but the nearest T stop is outside my door and the whole city is at my feet. I love the games like humans vs. zombies and having comedians and concerts on campus, but I also love meeting students from everywhere when I go into Boston." Another student felt slightly overwhelmed in the first year, but quickly came to appreciate the opportunities the college offered. "It's hard coming to a city if you're not a city person, but everyone here is so friendly and the internships make so many connections that you're zipping all over in just a few months." One real advantage to life at Lesley is that this is not the kind of college that people end up in by default; they want to be teachers or counselors, or artists, or therapists. Classes bring bonding, as does placement off-campus. Friendships are the norm; few students report feeling overlooked or isolated. "Look, we're busy," reports one student, "but I can take classes at the Art Institute and Lesley and still have a great time on the weekends and veg out with friends in the dorm."

One major opportunity for an exceptional experience at this unconventional college is in athletic competition. The Lesley Lynxes play a varsity schedule in NCAA Division III men's and women's soccer, tennis, cross country, track, volleyball, and basketball, and in women's softball and men's baseball. It may be surprising to learn that the baseball team plays approximately thirty games a year, traveling to Florida for spring training. The Green and Gold Lynx teams often train and play in facilities operated by a local independent school, a cooperative practice that makes excellent use of limited court and field space in Cambridge. The Fitness Center is located on the Lesley campus, on the first floor of Doble Hall.

When it comes to best-kept secrets, Lesley has to be near the top. I can't imagine a better opportunity for those who want to consider a career in teaching, counseling, or the arts, and I can't imagine a more exciting and manageable location than Cambridge/Boston.

Curry College - Milton, Massachusetts

The history of the college and its legacy of respecting individual uniqueness has created a program of study in the liberal and communicative arts that serves students of great promise, many of whom are identified as having learning differences, particularly language based disabilities and attention deficit disorders. The PAL Program, (Program for Advancement in Learning) is a model of an ambitious and supportive college level program leading to the BA and BS degree, graduate school, and career.

And the stats... 2015

Number of Applicants: 5,450/ 87% Accepted
Undergrad Enrollment: 2,900 63% female / 37% male
Avg. SAT Reading Comp 430– 520 / Math 430 – 550 Avg. ACT: 18 – 22
Total Cost: $52,500.00.
Received some form of financial assistance: 71%

Curry is an attractive and ambitious college located just outside of Boston, adjacent to a leafy forest preserve. A visitor will quickly note the well-manicured lawns, the stately brick buildings, the happy crowds of students milling with the usual mix of Abercrombie polos, Nantucket red shorts, and tattered tee shirts. What the visitor may not note in a casual drive-through is the pride Curry students take in themselves and in their college. Most institutions boast of the care they give their students and the conviction they have that each student is a valuable individual; at Curry they mean it.

The first principle of Curry's mission is RESPECTING INDIVIDUAL UNIQUENESS, followed by BUILDING SUCCESS. The history of the college and its legacy of respecting individual uniqueness has created a program of study in the liberal and communicative arts that serves students of great promise, many of whom are identified as having learning differences, particularly language based disabilities and attention deficit disorders. The PAL Program, (Program for Advancement in Learning) is a model of an ambitious and supportive college level program leading to the BA and BS degree, graduate school, and career.

Curry began as The School of Elocution and Expression in Boston, a school that believed that, "expression is the outward manifestation of that which is already in the consciousness." An early professor and significant influence on the school was Alexander Graham Bell's father, and Bell delivered some of the college's most significant lectures in the "science of voice," and became chancellor of the college himself until his death in 1922. Curry became the first college in the nation to develop a program (PAL) for students with language based disabilities and quickly established itself as a pioneer in the field, now offering undergraduate degrees in twenty majors and graduate degrees in Criminal Justice, Business Administration, Education, and Nursing.

Currently enrolling about nineteen hundred students in a variety of undergraduate programs, Curry is, in every way, a strong residential college community with an active and diverse student body. Competing in Division III athletics and offering a wide range of co-curricular and extracurricular activities, Curry is unique in the ranks of New England Colleges and distinctively different from the colleges with which it competes.

Curry is NOT an LD college; it is an ambitious college with the most carefully conceived support for students with learning differences. That support is most obvious in the PAL program, but the respect with which the institution treats its students and the determination with which the college prepares all of its graduates for success clearly sets curry apart. In addition to the PAL program, for instance, Curry offers an interdisciplinary first year seminar, an Honors program open to scholarship winners, extensive opportunities for study abroad, and internships.

Major fields of concentration include the usual arts and sciences and more professionally based programs. It is not surprising that Communication is among the most popular majors at Curry; what may be surprising is that Curry has developed extensive programs in screenwriting. tele-journalism (Curry has its own student-staffed television station), broadcasting, public relations, and film studies. Other uncommon majors include: Community Health and Wellness, Nursing, Information Technology, Criminal Justice, and Graphic Design.

So, what's it like to live at Curry? Imagine enjoying a wooded campus only moments from Boston's largest green space – a safe, healthy, active college community – only minutes from the hub of central Boston and, obviously, close to the beaches of Cape Cod and the mountains of New Hampshire and Vermont. Students live in eighteen residential halls, in a configuration of options that is uncommon for a school of Curry's size. There are several large red brick, white columned residential halls (one of which is a replica of the Massachusetts State House), primarily occupied by first-year students. Other housing options include at least ten handsome homes, ranging in scale from the cottages to a Tudor mansion. One house is gingerbread Victorian; another is a white colonial. Although most of the dorms are coed by floor, a small house in the center of campus houses ten men; another houses nineteen women. There are residences with singles, doubles, suites, and each promotes a strong sense of community.

A new Student Center in the heart of the campus provides a state-of-the-art dining marketplace and a plethora of entertainments. Curry's students describe the new center as a "dream living room" with an outstanding dining room. Favorites in the marketplace are the made-to-order deli sandwiches, a lavish salad bar, and the made-to-order pizzas. The adjoining fitness center features every training machine and device imaginable, most of which have been adapted to allow exercisers to plug in an mp3 player or watch television as the sweat glistens. One nice feature of this fitness facility is the space given to group fitness: Pilates, cardio-kickboxing, Zumba, and hip hop aerobics.
Those who want competition can jump into a solid intramural program, offering the usual blend of sports for men and women. A particular favorite on this campus is floor hockey - not quite as brutal in terms of contact as ice hockey, but more than physical enough for an intramural tilt.

There is one surprising mystery on this campus: For reasons that have vanished in the haze of time, Curry's purple teams are known as the Colonels, and their mascot looks suspiciously like the Confederate officer only recently removed from the sidelines of the University of Mississippi. Despite their oddly southern mascot, however, Curry Interscholastic sports are played at the Division III level in the ECAC (Eastern College Athletic Conference) against rivals such as MIT, Fitchburg State, the Coast Guard Academy, and Endicott. Sports for men include football, soccer, ice hockey, basketball, baseball, and tennis. Women's sports include soccer, volleyball, cross-country, tennis, softball, and lacrosse. In addition, an active schedule brings club sports into excellent competition. Currently, Curry offers an equestrian team, rugby for men, rock climbing, skiing, and snowboarding.

Every college has its own "vibe", and Curry is distinctly less hedonistic and self-absorbed than most undergraduate student populations. A sense of community is important to the college and to its students; residential life is well organized and directed toward creating small communities within the college population of about two thousand. In addition, the most visible activity on this campus is ONE CURRY, a subset of the International One campaign to bring equality, justice, and opportunity to all. A major event on a recent weekend raised eleven thousand dollars to be donated to bring clean water to refugees in the Sudan, and it is that sort of generosity of spirit that animates residential life at Curry.

I cannot endorse this college and the PAL Program strongly enough. In counseling students with any sort of learning difference, I recommend Curry above all others.

Clark University - Worcester, Massachusetts

The answer is: Vienna, Zurich, and Clark University. The question: Where might one have heard Sigmund Freud and Karl Jung debate the basic principles of psychology?

And the stats... 2015

Number of Applicants: 7,304/ 54% Accepted
Undergrad Enrollment: 2,301   58% female / 42% male
Avg. SAT Reading Comp 560– 670 / Math 550 – 660 Avg. ACT: 25 – 30
Total Cost: $50,280.00.
Received some form of financial assistance: 80%

Worcester, Massachusetts is the self-styled, "Gateway to New England", and if that motto seems a bit disingenuous, please understand that this small industrial city less that sixty miles east of Boston suffers from the same set of inadequacies that all New England cities other than Boston suffer – it's hard not being Boston. Also known as "The Heart of the Commonwealth," "The City of Seven Hills," and "The Woo", Worcester is the second-largest city in New England, slightly larger than Springfield, Providence, Portland, or Hartford. Worcester is the home of the Polar Beverage Company and thus of the giant green shirted polar bear overlooking interstate highway 290. The city is also home to College of the Holy Cross, Worcester Polytechnic Institute, the University of Massachusetts Medical School, and the Higgins Armory Museum.

Clark University is located in the Main South neighborhood, on Main Street, about two miles from the center of the city. The use of the term "university" is slightly confusing for some applicants because we tend to think of universities as much larger than colleges, and Clark is about the same size as Smith, St. Olaf, and Lewis and Clark. Clark University was founded as a graduate university, the first institutions of graduate study in the U.S. Today slightly more than two thousand students are enrolled in the undergraduate programs at Clark; another nine hundred are on campus pursuing a graduate degree. Clark is a college of the liberal arts, but from the start, the school's character has been influenced by the most prominent researchers and practitioners in the field of Psychology.

The answer is: Vienna, Zurich, and Worcester. The question: Where might one have heard Freud and Jung debate?

The "Father of American Psychology", G. Stanley Hall was Clark's first president, and it was through his efforts that Carl Jung and Sigmund Freud came to the university; Freud's set of lectures introduced America to the nascent field of psychoanalysis. A statue of Freud remains on campus, allowing current generations of Clark student to sit on Sigmund's lap. Clark was home to many other iconic academics, most notably Franz Boas, the founder of cultural anthropology in the United States and Robert Goddard, former chairman of the University's Physics Department and pioneer in space and missile technology. Today, Clark is noted for an outstanding undergraduate program in psychology and a nationally ranked program in geology. That program has graduated more Ph.D.s in geology than any other in the country.

In his recent book, *Creative Schools*, author Ken Robinson referred to Clark as one of the colleges doing the most to bring about. He credits the leadership of Clark's president, David Angel for connecting the academic work undertaken at Clark with specific challenges facing cities such as Worcester and the wider world. He quotes President Angel:

> "We asked ourselves the question, 'If we want to be intentional at Clark at graduating students who are both strong on the traditional liberal arts criteria and can carry their education out into the world and be impactful, how do you cultivate the resilience of a young person when they hit a road bump?' How do they develop three-way creative solutions to problems? If you want to build those skills intentionally, you're much more effective if you do it in an authentic context. If a student is put on a project team and has a real problem to overcome, you see far more development."

Given the distinguished history of the place, one has to wonder why Clark is not included in the ordinary conversations about New England colleges. Perhaps it is the "grad-school-first" history of the institution, or Worcester, or the proximity of more celebrated neighboring colleges – for whatever reason, Clark remains poorly understood and little known outside of the region. Psych majors and geographers know and revere Clark; others need to catch up.

The campus is compact – primarily tucked into about two square blocks – easy to navigate and comfortable. Clark Hall, the oldest building and the iconic landmark is an odd brick confection, slightly clunky but certainly central. Many of the other buildings on campus are strikingly effective in their design. The Bioscience Center is a remarkably attractive place to study stickleback fish and the life cycle of fungi. Dining facilities and the Bistro are located in the well-appointed UC (University Center). The

Fitness Center is modern, well equipped, and well used; almost seventy percent of Clark's students are involved with athletics at some level.

From my point of view, however, the greatest advantage the campus offers its students is a variety of well-maintained dormitories. I'm not saying that dorms at other New England colleges are less than pristine, but I am frequently stunned at the condition of carpets, windows, doors, and walls in ivied halls at other institutions. Clark takes excellent care of its residential students and spruces up each dormitory every year.

It makes sense to turn to residential life at Clark first, in part because it is slightly different from that at some neighboring institutions. The First Year Experience (FYE) Program is a residential curriculum, resident advisors in the three first year dormitories run programs throughout the year which include the usual bonding and morale building initiatives and on-going instruction in such areas as personal finance and adjusting to diversity. Attention to study is emphasized more intentionally at Clark than in most first year residential systems; study spaces are designed to allow individual and group study. Several of the dormitories feature "smart" rooms as well. Although there are off-campus residential opportunities for upper class students, good housing options are available in an ingenious constellation of choices.

The single most notable difference between Clark and its cohorts may be in its decision to adopt Gender Blind/ Neutral Housing after the first year. That means students can live together in double rooms or suites without regard to gender; boys can live with girls. Gay, transgender, and bisexual students can live with whomever they wish. The policy is a housing policy, of course, but also a clear indication of the university's determination to be sensitive to the needs of a highly diverse student body.

The social scene at Clark indicates that a balanced and happy student body enjoys collegiate life without the direction of fraternities and sororities. Most weekend are filled with activity; a few students will leave campus on weekends as Boston and the rest of New England is within easy reach, but for the most part, small-scale and generally successful activities occupy a contented student body. It is not surprising, perhaps, that one of the most widely enjoyed options available to students at Clark is Cinema 320, an independent film series located in the Jefferson Academic Building. Ambitious and eclectic, Cinema 320 is a remarkable enterprise organized and run by undergraduates and it stands as an example of the kinds of enterprises Clark's students are likely to pursue. The film series is intellectually challenging and not at all the usual "chick flick" and blood-spattered action fare shown on most campuses on most weekends.

Clark's kids are smart, funny, and active; they join a cappella groups (The Clark Bars and Counterpoints), enjoy musical theater, support slam poetry, run a hip hop collaborative, run the CUBS (Clark University Brothers and Sisters - mentoring children in the neighborhood), engage in a variety of service projects, enjoy the celebration of the university's very diverse student body (The Muslim Cultural Society, Black Student Union, Latin American Students Organization, and OPEN - which welcomes the lesbian, gay, bisexual, transgender, and queer communities and their allies), and play a ton of sports - including intramural flag football, ultimate frisbee, soccer, volleyball, basketball, indoor soccer, and softball.

The interscholastic athletic program is an interesting mix of competitive options. Most of Clark's teams (the Cougars!) play in the NEWMAC - the New England Women's and Men's Athletic Conference. Other members of the conference include: Babson, the Coast Guard Academy, MIT, Mount Holyoke, Smith, Springfield, Wellesley, Wheaton, and WPI. The women's field hockey team is a perennial powerhouse and frequent conference champion. The Cougars can train in the Dolan Field House which houses a training center, an all-purpose gym floor, and a batting cage, or in the Kneller Athletic Center, which seats two thousand spectators, basketball courts, squash courts, racquetball courts, and a six lane competition swimming pool. Swimming and diving are among the most successful sports at Clark, as are field hockey, basketball, and baseball. Men and women row, play tennis, run track and cross-country. Women compete in softball and volleyball. Two programs, however, operate outside of the NEWMAC - Men's Lacrosse and Men's Ice Hockey. The Men's lacrosse team plays in the Pilgrim League against opponents such as Bowdoin, Skidmore, Plymouth State, and Babson. The Ice Hockey Program is true rarity - a club sport that plays a Division II schedule. Ice Cougars compete against Brown, Dartmouth, Wheaton, Wesleyan, Babson, and Coast Guard.

For all the success which Clark teams enjoy, the campus is not entirely aware of student athletes. Intramurals seem to capture most of the attention, and the general opinion is that Clarkies get a much bigger kick out of their intramural activities than they do in hanging around at the Holy Cross Rink watching the Cougars play Dartmouth.

Finally, the academic life at Clark is highly regarded by Clarkies and by those who know its programs. As noted earlier, psychology has long been the benchmark of Clark's academic reputation. An undergraduate may choose from the following concentrations: Developmental Psych, Social Psych, or Clinical Psych, and the reputation of the department remains first rate, producing a number of well qualified graduate students and clinicians. Geography is also highly regarded, offering a breadth of courses in four core areas: Nature-Society and Global Environmental Change; Globalization, Cities, and Development; Geographic Information Systems; and Earth Systems Science. The usual variety of courses in the sciences, humanities, and the arts are offered, as well as majors in Asian Studies, Communication and Culture, Ethics and Public Policy, Holocaust and

Genocide Studies, Innovation and Entrepreneurship, Jewish Studies, and Gender Studies.

Classes at Clark are taught by professors and more than half of the classes offered have fewer than twenty students in the classroom. And, in a remarkable fit of generosity, Clark offers an accelerated degree program, by which qualified students can earn a BA and MA in five years – the fifth year is tuition free! A tuition-free fifth year and two degrees! More than enough reason to investigate this remarkable small university at New England's gateway.

Worcester Polytechnic Institute - Worcester, Massachusetts

The range of activities at WPI is impressive and reflects the institute's technological bent and the advantages of attending a university of its size. Students new to WPI can be overwhelmed by the challenge of investigating the more than two hundred clubs and organizations available. Among the most unusual are a graphic design club, a Brazilian Students Association, a molecular gastronomy club, a Russian speaking association which welcomes Ukrainian, Turkmen, Kazakh, Armenian, Azerbaijani, Byelorussian, Georgian, Kyrgyz, Moldavian, Tajikistan, Uzbek, Estonian, Latvian, and Lithuanian enthusiasts, a Cyber Security Club, the Science Fiction Society, and the Society for Medieval Arts and Sciences.

And the stats... 2015

Number of Applicants: 10,230/ 50% Accepted
Undergrad Enrollment: 4,235   32% female / 68% male
Avg. SAT Reading Comp 600– 670 / Math 650 – 720 Avg. ACT: 28 – 32
Total Cost: $59,500.00.
Received some form of financial assistance: 92%

Interactive Media and Game Development! Hottest major in the tech world! And WPI does it right! Not only that, but this is one of the very rare colleges or universities in the four thousand undergrad range with a quiet and pretty campus near a small city and reasonably close to a great city – Boston. In addition, WPI has a healthy social life (lots of frats and sororities), Division III sports, and a dining plan that students actually like! Almost forty percent of the undergrad population is female, and they are a happy forty percent.

If you've begun to read this description, there is a pretty good chance that your interest is in the applied sciences, technology, or engineering. In addition to its highly publicized program in Interactive Media and Game Development, WPI offers the following: Biology and Biotechnology, Biomedical Engineering, Chemical Engineering, Civil and Environmental Engineering, Computer Science, Electrical and Computer Engineering, Mathematical Sciences, Mechanical Engineering, a School of Business, Social Science and Policy Studies, and a strong program in Humanities and the Arts. All of these offered in a small technological university enrolling about four thousand undergraduates. Two significant pieces of data should distinguish WPI from a number of other engineering or technological programs. More than one third of the undergraduates at WPI are female; commonly tech programs attract a predominance of men. The greater distinguishing characteristic is that an uncommon number of instructors who teach at WPI are female.

Worcester, Massachusetts is the self-styled, "Gateway to New England", and if that motto seems a bit disingenuous, please understand that this small industrial city less that sixty miles east of Boston suffers from the same set of inadequacies that all New England cities other than Boston suffer – it's hard not being Boston. Also known as "The Heart of the Commonwealth," "The City of Seven Hills," and "The Woo", Worcester is the second-largest city in New England, slightly larger than Springfield, Providence, Portland, or Hartford. Worcester is the home of the Polar Beverage Company and thus of the giant green shirted polar bear overlooking interstate highway 290. The city is also home to College of the Holy Cross, Clark University, the University of Massachusetts Medical School, and the Higgins Armory Museum.

Worcester Polytechnic Institute, widely known as WPI, is an equally overlooked college of quality, among the earliest of the engineering schools to have been founded in the United States, and long associated with groundbreaking technological discover. The term "polytechnical" refers to an institution's determination to offer a wide range of engineering, scientific, and technical studies. At WPI, for example, an undergraduate can enter into any one of fourteen areas of study and five combinations of programs, including pre-men, pre-law, pre-dental, and pre-vet programs. All of which are presented in the institute's motto – Theory and Practice.

Although, the curriculum at WPI is essentially an open curriculum with few required courses, at the heart of a WPI education, and one of the distinctive differences between WPI and similar technological institutes is a three-part series of requirements. The first two have to do with a real-world practicum. All students will undertake an Interactive Qualifying Project and a Major Qualifying Project. In addition, all students will demonstrate a Sufficiency in the Liberal Arts.

To Techies who shudder at the thought of more course work in the humanities, and languages, please be advised that the Liberal Arts program at WPI is attached to the institute's determination to prepare engineers and technological entrepreneurs with up-to-date and practical experience. The first course is one in Global Perspective and is a problem-based case study course. Other courses in the Liberal Arts include Actuarial Mathematics, Bioinformatics and Computational Biology, Economics, and Biotechnology.

The Interactive Qualifying Project is a hands-on problem solving project that connects problem solving and human or societal needs. An example of a recent Interactive Qualifying Project, for example, led to finding solutions to annual flooding and erosion in Namibia. Global Perspectives call about half of the projects and are arranged through WPI Centers in Thailand, China, South Africa, Hungary, Morocco, England, France, and Japan. Domestic Centers are found in Boston, Bar Harbor, and Santa Fe. An exciting new project allows students to work in New York and London in the Wall Street economic project.

The Major Qualifying Project is the senior year capstone project in the student's major field. Examples of recently completed Major Qualifying Projects in the Interactive Media and Game Development majors include: *Gone* - a first-person 3-D survival game in which the player is thrown in the mind of a mentally ill person and *Prota-Evolution*, a game in which the player controls evolution. Those interested in this field might also want to check out: *Captain Eagle vs. Doctor Catastrophe, Chronopigger, Blood Tide,* or *Grail to the Thief.*

More conventional fields yield equally interesting projects. A recent project in Mathematical Science looked at *Combinatorial Structures in Cryptography.* The Robotics Engineering program generated *Intelligent Vision-Driven Robot for Sample Detection and Return, Personal Assistive Robot,* and a *Calligraphy Bot.* The Biotechnology department generated *A Public Health Project in Methods of Schistosomiasis haematobium Control in Adasawase, Ghana.* A Workforce Expansion Proposal, for Putnam Investments came out of the School of Business, while a student from Kazakhstan developed a project examining *Salt Intrusion in Gatun Lake.*

The final appreciation of the academic program at WPI is in the area of original research. Not only is research alive and well at WPI, it is encouraged and made easily available for undergraduates. Biologists are looking at stem-cell research on ailing pets; environmental engineers are investigating ways in which metals can be recycled. Some of that work is done at the Institute's Surface Metrology Laboratory that uses a Laser Confocal Microscope.

After classes have ended, the WPI campus is a lively and healthy (and very safe) place. Weekday nights are usually filled with activities and study; weekends offer the entertainments planned by the fraternities and sororities, a very active activities committee, and a variety of college planned events. Most students stay on campus on weekends, and they report great satisfaction with the options presented in each term. Lots of activities are carried out by the dormitories and a sense of dorm identity does seem to have an important place at WPI. In addition, some uncommon amenities make life at WPI even more pleasant. The Food Service at WPI is actually provided in Morgan Commons, but was once delivered by a service known as DAKA. For reasons unknown, students still refer to their dining plan as DAKA and they like it. Particular enthusiasm is generated by the desserts, which include a highly regarded banana cream pie and chocolate chip cookies that are described as "legendary". For a special treat, they take a trip to one of New England's best seafood restaurants, The Sole Proprietor, for a tasty six-dollar sushi.

The range of activities at WPI is impressive and reflect the institute's technological bent and the advantages of attending a university of its size. Students new to WPI can be overwhelmed by the challenge of investigating the more than two hundred clubs and organizations available. Among the most unusual are a graphic design club, a Brazilian Students Association, a molecular gastronomy club, a Russian speaking association which welcomes Ukrainian, Turkmen, Kazakh, Armenian, Azerbaijani, Byelorussian, Georgian, Kyrgyz, Moldavian, Tajikistan, Uzbek, Estonian, Latvian, and Lithuanian enthusiasts, a Cyber Security Club, the Science Fiction Society, and the Society for Medieval Arts and Sciences.

Cub and recreational sports and activities include the usual sorts of recreational activities, but particular mention should be made of the dance team and the cheerleading team, both of which are excellent. WPI offers a highly competitive wrestling program among its athletic offerings, but also sponsors a freestyle wrestling club for those who would like to grapple at the club level. Good soccer, lacrosse, and hockey programs flourish, as do rugby, martial arts, and the pep band.

On the varsity level, the WPI Engineers compete in NCAA Division III in football, soccer, cross-country, field hockey, basketball, swimming, softball, and track and field. Two uncommon sports are rowing, (both men's and women's) and men's wrestling.

Bard College at Simon's Rock/The Early College - Great Barrington, Massachusetts

The college was born of the notion that the last two years of high school are a wasteland for the truly accomplished student.

And the stats... 2015

Number of Applicants: 200/ 89% Accepted
Undergrad Enrollment: 329   59% female / 41% male
SAT and ACT scores are not reported as most applicants will have just finished the first semester of the tenth grade year. The application is challenging, however, including prompts that seek close reading and personal reflection. It is only at Simon's Rock, for example, that the following prompt might be included in the assessment of a potential student:

> *"A young student has twenty-four 6" x 6" beautifully decorated, ceramic squares, which were given to her by her grandfather who made them when he himself was a young student. The young woman wishes to arrange the tiles on her floor in such a way as to cover as large a circular area as possible. How should she arrange the tiles to accomplish this? (Note that the tiles will not form a circle themselves, but must completely cover the circular area.) Write a two to four page essay explaining in detail the reasoning by which you arrived at your proposed arrangement and why it is a good one. You may include a description of some of your "first guesses," as well as diagrams showing your arrangements and the equations used to justify your claims. (Diagrams and equations may be hand drawn.) We are interested in your reasoning and your ability to communicate that reasoning rather than a "correct" answer."*

Detail the reasoning, write an essay, and prepare to take on the challenge and adventure of the nation's only fully accredited Early College.

Total Cost: $63,749.00.
Received some form of financial assistance: 91%

The Early College idea is not easy to describe; the opportunities are rich and unusual. The college itself puts it this way, "This is the general idea. It's like living in a picturesque rural village with four hundred people your own age, who want to talk about what you want to talk about."

That's certainly correct as far as it goes, but the four hundred are also exposed to gifted teachers and an array of concerts, lectures, exhibitions, and speakers. Students at Simon's Rock educate themselves in the company of other active, bright, engaged learners.

There are educational experiments and then there is Simon's Rock. Born of an idealistic impulse that brought Warren Wilson, Prescott, and Hampshire into existence, Simon's Rock is one of the few truly experimental enterprises which has managed to stay vital and relevant beyond the fervor of innovative reform that swept through the late nineteen sixties and the early nineteen seventies. Founded in 1964 on almost three hundred acres of Massachusetts's farmland, this is the only accredited four year early college. Just how early is enrollment in Simon's Rock? Most applicants have completed the tenth grade, but Woody Allen and Mia Farrow's son, Ronan, enrolled at the age of eleven. More conventional applicants, Joel and Ethan Coen, took their early education at Simon's Rock to one of the most successful long-term collaborations in film.

The college was born of the notion that the last two years of high school are a wasteland for the truly accomplished student. That idea had been championed earlier by Robert Hutchins, for example, at the University of Chicago and adopted by Shimer and Goucher, but no college had been established entirely for the purpose of bringing younger students to a full-fledged college experience. Early admission from the tenth grade was not unknown before Simon's Rock took hold, but it was distinctive in having been designed, from the start, with the early student in mind, and, as a result, Simon's Rock has a character notably different from that of any other college, including those in the experimental range.

The college has been located on the outskirts of Great Barrington from the start. Great Barrington is one of two towns of any size in what is truly Western Massachusetts; the other is Pittsfield, just south of Williamstown. Both are animated, winter and summer, by the streams of tourists who flock to the Berkshire Mountains – some in search of autumn leaves or rustic barns, some looking for a bit of culture at Tanglewood, Jacob's Pillow, or the Williamstown Theater. Great Barrington is just north of the Connecticut state line, just east of the New York state line, and just south of Stockbridge, the Normal Rockwell town. It's a small "city" of about seven thousand, formerly the summer retreat of wealthy New Yorkers. Restaurants are good and the local theater is beautifully restored.

There actually is a rock after which the college is named (a child named Simon was quite fond of it), and the rural campus retains a sense of agrarian, pastoral charm rare even in the far reaches of New England farmland. The college has shifted in scope and purpose a bit in the half-century since its conception, hence the shift in name: Simon's Rock to Simon's Rock Early College, to Simon's Rock College of Bard College (necessitated by the union of Simon's Rock and Bard), finally, Simon's Rock College of Bard. The alliance with Bard College makes sense from a number of points of view. In the first place, of course, the life span of experimental colleges is tenuous and connection with a more established institution lends some stability. In addition, the president of Bard College, then and now, Leon Botstein was himself a prodigy. Botstein entered the University of Chicago at sixteen, picked up a Ph.D. from Harvard, and became the youngest college president in the country at the age of twenty-three. An educational reformer, Botstein is also an accomplished musician and director of the American Symphony Orchestra. The connection with Bard was significant in safeguarding the program at Simon's Rock, but also significant in bringing two of Bard's signature programs to the early college.

The first of these, the Writing and Thinking Workshop, has been a hallmark of Bard's liberal arts curriculum and is a widely imitated method of developing effective writing. At Bard, and at Simon's Rock, the workshops are small and dedicated to active writing, response, and revision. For the most part, exercises are also attached to critical reading, creating a method by which writing is derived from the act of thinking critically, with intention.

The second of these, the Senior Thesis, is required of all graduates, and is intended to act as the capstone of a four-year adventure in thought and creativity. The Thesis may be a written work, a performance, an exhibition, an impact study; the format is chosen by the senior in initiating the Thesis project.

Happily, the marriage has also brought exchange between the two campuses, allowing Bard's best to teach at The Rock and allowing Rockers to join in Bard's exceptional programs of study abroad, including Bard's liberal arts college in St. Petersburg, Russia (Smolny College), Al-Quds University in Jerusalem, and the American University of Central Asia.

Let's put a few things on the table that ought to concern any parent about to spend approximately fifty eight thousand dollars at the end of a child's tenth grade year or any student about to leave the comfortable, if predictable, halls of a good high school.

In the first place, the college is small (about four hundred students), and the location, while beautiful, is rural and more than two hours from New

York or Boston. The social setting is that of a conventional college, allowing far more independence in some ways than a high school student might find. No fraternities or sororities, and no interscholastic sports.

On the other hand, the students have the strongest of positive feelings about the quality of instruction, the engagement of their professors, and the range of opportunities brought to them on a daily basis. One current student put it this way in a recent blog:

> *"Honestly I'm having a hard time understanding some of the negative review on this website, and I'm very sorry for those who feel like they've had a bad experience. As the school itself stress, SR is not for everyone. Students coming because they are excited about being challenged academically will thrive here. Student coming just to escape high school will not. Student coming here cause to have wild parties will not. No, the social life is not incredibly great. Yes, town sucks. But I have never felt like I have been more challenged, that I have fit in more, that I have been more excited about my prospects."*

Residential life in the first year is more closely supervised in dormitories set aside for first year students. Residence Directors and Residence Assistants are very much involved in the transitional year.

As this blogger suggests, Simon's Rock is an energizing experience for those who have genuinely outgrown their secondary school and absolutely thirst for a genuine college-level experience. Some do transfer to a larger school after two years, and the placement record of those students is impressive. An equal number remain, continuing to explore his or her own intellectual interests in the company of a diverse and challenging peer cohort.

The physical side of life at the Rock is organized around a program called Active Community Engagement. Some measure of that engagement takes place in small group work in Health and Wellness, attending to the identification of responsible social choices. Another area of engagement is in Participation and Service; students are required to join in the organizing of several community service projects. Finally, first year students are required to take part in one of the options offered by the Athletic Center in yoga, rock climbing, squash, ultimate frisbee, or any number of other recreational activities. Simon's Rock offers three team sports: swimming, soccer, and basketball. These teams play a reasonable schedule against small college and local high school teams.

A residential early college is, by definition, not the norm; its students, unsurprisingly, are independent, intellectually aggressive, liberal, and widely diverse in any meaning of the word. OK, so diversity is the norm at

Simon's Rock. Not for everyone, this exceptional experiment continues to offer a select few the opportunity of a lifetime, and the strong support of its graduates speaks to the success of the experiment.

Rhode Island

First of all, Rhode Island is not actually an island; it's an easy drive from the Connecticut and Massachusetts colleges for the searching families. Providence is one of the "second" cities in New England, with Worcester and Portland, and a gateway to all the attractions of the coastline. Visitors from the west will be stunned to find that a driver can cross the state at its widest span in under an hour. Boston is within an easy drive as are the beaches of Cape Cod. The city of Providence is home to Brown University located in the historic College Hill District of the city, filled with restored colonial buildings and flanked by lively commercial streets. Providence College, private and Catholic, is located about two miles to the west of central Providence. Providence is a liberal arts university; administered by Dominican friars, well know for a very strong intercollegiate athletic program. Bryant College, profiled in this book is in Smithfield. Roger Williams University, one of the few to offer an undergraduate degree in Marine Biology, is in Bristol, Rhode Island on Mount Hope Bay. RWO also has a strong program in architecture. Any trip to Rhode Island should include a visit to Newport, long celebrated for the remarkable mansions built in this ocean resort. The setting is the lovelier for the presence of immaculately maintained colonial buildings; Newport may have the most concentrated collection of colonial buildings in the nation. Newport is also home to the Naval War College and Salve Regina University, long Catholic and now coed.

One best kept secret that may attract only a few is the International Yacht Restoration School in Newport and Bristol. On the other hand, fans of Boston's sports will delight in visiting the Boston Bruins' affiliate in the American Hockey League, The Providence Bruins. Rhode Island's Bruins play in the Dunkin Donuts Center in Providence. The Red Sox Triple A affiliate, the Pawtucket Red Sox (PawSox) play in Pawtucket, just outside of Providence.

Johnson and Wales University - Providence, Rhode Island

Johnson and Wales is an unusual institution in that it has transformed itself almost completely in the last two decades and remains in motion if not in transition. - it developed an outstanding program in Culinary Arts, it developed a major program in Hospitality, and it developed a string of satellite campuses, each of which offered particular advantages to students interested in business, culinary arts, or the hospitality industry.

And the stats... 2015

Number of Applicants: 11,899/ 81% Accepted
Undergrad Enrollment: 9,173   55% female / 45% male
Avg. SAT and ACT: Not Reported
Total Cost: $43,000.00.
Received some form of financial assistance: 90%

Bam!

Where can I find a college that prepares me for a career and puts me to work...now?

Well, that would be Johnson and Wales, on any of its four campuses.

Bam!

Emeril Lagasse asked the same question, and turned down a scholarship to the New England Conservatory of Music in order to follow his dream of becoming a master chef. Lagasse choose Johnson and Wales University in Providence Rhode Island, and today supports the university through a variety of charity events. He's not the only culinary superstar to have found his or her way to Providence. A short list might include: Chef Rahman "Rock" Harper, winner of *Hell's Kitchen,* Chef Adrianne Calvo, author of *Maximum Flavor,* Chef Tyler Florence, host of *Tyler's Ultimate,* Chef Michelle Bernstein, James Beard Award winner and co-host of Food Network's *Melting Pot,* Chef Anna Olson, host of *Fresh With Anna Olson,* and Chef Jeremy Fox, partner of Ubuntu in Napa, California.

Of course, an equally motivated student might have found Johnson and Wales in order to study Criminal Justice, or Fashion Design, or Advertising, or Robotics, or Software Engineering.

What kind of place IS this Johnson and Wales?

Johnson and Wales is an unusual institution in that it has transformed itself almost completely in the last two decades and remains in motion if not in transition. Begun as a business school in nineteen-fourteen, Johnson and Wales was a regional business university until it took three significant steps - it developed an outstanding program in Culinary Arts, it developed a major program in Hospitality, and it developed a string of satellite campuses, each of which offered particular advantages to students interested in business, culinary arts, or the hospitality industry.

I'll spend most of this article describing what a student might find at the Providence campus, but the thought that has gone into the creation of the ancillary programs and locations reflects the forward thinking administration of the new Johnson and Wales.

In the course of a century Johnson and Wales (founded by Gertrude Johnson and Mary Wales) has evolved from a privately owned school of business education to university enrolling more than seventeen thousand students, about ten thousand of which study as undergrads on the Providence campus. As the university grew to maturity, it added undergraduate and graduate programs, now offering undergraduate degrees in the College of Culinary Arts, the School of Engineering and Design, the College of Management (includes the School of Business and School of Hospitality), and the School of Arts and Sciences.

Currently Johnson and Wales also offers comparable programs in Charlotte, North Carolina, North Miami, Florida, and Denver Colorado. Can a student start at one and work at another? Or at all four? Sure, why not?

It's interesting to see what else they've been up to. The first satellite campus was in Charleston, SC, where J and W offered food service, hospitality, and travel-tourism. The next campus was in Norfolk, VA, where food service programs were available. Graduate programs (criminal justice and education) were begun in Providence as the Business School was established. The campus in North Miami offered business and food service, and the Providence campus expanded to include the Hospitality College, the College of Culinary Arts and the School of Technology, as well as the School of Arts and Sciences. Next came a campus in Vail, CO, followed by the establishment of marketing and business in Goteborg, Sweden. Consolidation of programs ended the campuses in Charleston, Norfolk, Vail, and Goteborg, but new facilities were set up in Denver and Charlotte.

I take the time to walk through the various initiatives because I admire the university's willingness to adapt to changing needs and conditions and because every initiative has grown from an understanding of the changing demands of the work environment into which its graduates will enter.

From the start, Johnson and Wales has been practical. The association with real-world enterprises has been an important part of the J and W experience for decades; equally important is the university's development of what they call "learning labs". The labs may be kitchens or design centers or research facilities, or hotel lobbies. The fashion lab provides the opportunity to design and market and to follow market trends as they are occurring. The hospitality lab may be the Bistro 61 Restaurant, or the pop-up Taqueria. A foodservice major may run an entire establishment by the senior year; a design major may be putting together a window display for Crate and Barrel. Some of the labs are on=campus workspaces; others are on the job. In any case, study is more than enhanced by practical experience.

And here is where I think Johnson and Wales may have an edge on a number of other programs: In addition to the extensive program of sponsored internships (Disney, Facebook, Major League Baseball, Marriott, NASCAR, and thousands more), J and W actually owns and operates the Radisson Hotel Providence Airport Hotel and the restaurants it contains. It also owns and operates the Doubletree hotel in Charlotte. Oh, and the culinary students act as the food service operation for the seventeen thousand students enrolled at J and W.

I am emphasizing the culinary program, so I ought to identify the possibilities available for those who want to study the arts, beginning with the observation that the university has worked to create a balance between the operational skills (business and management) as well as the culinary skills; graduates know "how to" and "how to manage others". Programs include: Baking and Pastry Arts, a B.S. in Baking and Pastry Management, a B.S. in Culinary Nutrition, a B.S. in Food Service Entrepreneurship, A B.S. in Food Marketing, a B.S. in Hotel and Lodging Management, a B.S. in International Hotel and Tourism Management, a B.S. Restaurant, Food and Beverage Management, a B.S. in Sports, Entertainment, and Event Management, a B.S. in Travel, Tourism, and Hospitality Management,
And, should you not see yourself as a person inclined toward the culinary arts but still wish to get a hands-on education in a field that might actually provide employment, perhaps you might consider any one of the rest of the Johnson and Wales "menu":

Counseling Psychology, Criminal Justice, Equine Business Management, Equine Business Management/Riding, Liberal Studies, Media and Communications, Accounting, Creative Advertising, Entrepreneurship, Fashion Merchandising and Retail Marketing, Finance, Information Systems Analysis, Computer Programming, Electronics Engineering,

Graphic Design and Digital Media, Network Engineering, Robotic Engineering, and Software Engineering.

OK, it's clear that Johnson and Wales means business when it sets out to prepare its students, but what is life like on the Providence campus? In the first place, the calendar is set up so that internships and international experiences are easy to schedule. In addition, there is a very limited summer term because it is expected that students will get out and get into whatever field they want to explore. Sixteen thousand kids do live on that campus, however, and the usual sorts of collegiate things are on hand. There are a number of fraternities and sororities on campus, although the great majority of students are not actively involved in the Greek scene. Part of the advantage to be had in attending Johnson and Wales is in making use of the resources of Providence, one of America's oldest cities and increasingly a city given to cultural activity. The presence of Brown University, the Rhode Island School of Design, and easy access to Boston makes Providence a great city for college aged social life.

The Wildcats of Johnson and Wales play in NCAA Division III in the Great Northeast Athletic Conference. Varsity teams participate in soccer, basketball, cross-country, track, and golf. There are numerous recreational activities offered on and off campus, but, as indicated earlier, much of the emphasis at J and W is on the experiential preparation for career, leaving less time for full-scale commitment to an athletic team. No matter how the Wildcats fare in the Great Northeast, or in Denver, or in Miami, or in Charlotte, the proof is (heh) in the pudding.

Connecticut

There are so many misconceptions about Connecticut that it is probably not worth trying to explain the incongruous collision of industrial river towns, manicured horse farms, backwoods shacks and yurts, ordinary suburban sprawl, urban blight, and the truly overwhelming affluence of the Gold Coast towns – Greenwich, New Canaan, Darien, Westport, Southport, Weston, and Wilton. These mega-snappy towns (and their component villages, such as Old Greenwich, Riverside, Cos Cob) are all located in Fairfield County, the county closest to New York City and the county from which executive commuters have maintained their status as masters of the universe while retreating in the evening to the winding roads, expansive lawns, and cool breezes wafting from Long Island Sound. Fairfield University, profiled in this book, is located in Fairfield, a pretty town at the western end of Fairfield County, bordering Redding, Easton and Westport –small Gold Coast gems – and Bridgeport, which is a small industrial city.

Connecticut is a small state, and the college seeker can traverse the entire college realm in an easy day's drive in most cases. Yale University is in New Haven, just to the east of Fairfield and Bridgeport. Wesleyan University is in Middletown, an industrial town on the Connecticut River, north of New Haven and south of Hartford. Trinity College, one of the well-established small liberal arts colleges competing in the conference known as NESCAC (New England Small College Athletic Conference), is located in the south end of Hartford. The Coast Guard Academy and Connecticut College are both found in New London, a coastal town on Long Island Sound, equidistant to Boston and New York.

The only college visit outside of the Hartford/New Haven nexus would be to the University of Connecticut, the state's flagship university, located in Storrs, a small town in Connecticut's northeast corner, north and east of Hartford and Providence, and just south of Worcester. UConn's "Huskies" (Get it? UConn? Yukon?) are among the nation's most successful athletic teams, providing Division I national championships in men's and women's basketball and soccer.

University of Connecticut - Storrs, Connecticut

Quite aside from athletic arena, the University of Connecticut is a big deal in New England. It is the most competitive of the public universities in the region, by far the most successful in terms of national athletic prominence, and generally conceded to be the regional public research university with the fastest trajectory into the front ranks of nationally recognized universities.

And the stats... 2015

Number of Applicants: 31,280/ 50% Accepted
Undergrad Enrollment: 18,395 49% female / 51% male
Avg. SAT Reading Comp 550-650 / Math 590-690 Avg. ACT: 26-30
Total Cost: $28,274.00 (in-state) $48,454.00 (out-of-state)
Received some form of financial assistance: 62%

Husky mania has swept New England and may have infected the rest of the nation as well. Unexpectedly, Husky gear is now more commonly spotted that Georgetown's Bulldogs or Syracuse Orange; national championships for both men and women raised their visibility, and the streak of undefeated women's teams in basketball has made them a true powerhouse in Division I athletics.

Quite aside from athletic arena, the University of Connecticut is a big deal in New England. It is the most competitive of the public universities in the region, by far the most successful in terms of national athletic prominence, and generally conceded to be the regional public research university with the fastest trajectory into the front ranks of nationally recognized universities. As the newest university of national prominence in the region, UConn may not be as highly regarded as it ought to be.

When I say newest, please remember that the Northeast popped out colleges and universities at a ridiculous rate between the founding of Harvard in Cambridge (1636) and the establishment of Middlebury in Vermont (1800)

The Northeastern college map included: Yale (1701), Princeton (1746), Columbia (1754), U. Penn (1755), Brown (1764), Dartmouth (1769), Williams (1793), Hamilton (1793), Bowdoin (1794), and Union (1795). In the subsequent decades, West Point, Amherst, Colgate, Wesleyan, Mount

Holyoke took their place in the region. By the start of the Civil War, there were one hundred and eighty-two colleges in the United States.

None of these was the University of Connecticut.

UConn began as the Storrs Agricultural College in 1881. The Storrs brothers donated the land, and by the turn of the Twentieth Century, the institution had become a land-grant public university known as the Connecticut Agricultural College, by 1939, the University of Connecticut.

From these relatively humble beginnings, however, the university has recently taken on considerable momentum. Today UConn enrolls more than thirty thousand students, about half of whom are undergrads. The operating budget of the place is in excess of two billion dollars, and the number of projects and grants attached to the university push that figure even higher into the stratosphere. Storrs is a sleepy town actually a village with a population of about ten thousand) almost completely dedicated to the support and operation of a truly impressive national university.

For those not familiar with the scale of things in New England, it is probably necessary to say that nothing is very far from anything else. OK, the Maine schools have a bit of a trek, but the rest are all actually in fairly close quarters. Storrs is about twenty-five miles from Hartford, forty miles from Providence and Worcester, and eighty miles from Boston. Given that in any other setting, Storrs could be considered a bedroom for Hartford commuters, it is the more remarkable that the village remains, essentially, a farm town with a university on the side. The northeastern corner of Connecticut is dairy country, and the number of small towns between Storrs and those big-city destinations makes any drive quite diverting. It was to this quiet corner that Paul Newman brought his idea of a camp for chronic and terminally ill children. If you wonder where all the profits from Newman's Own products go, it is to The Hole In The Wall Gang Camp in Ashford, a stone's throw from Storrs.

So, to return to the description of the university, UConn is a somewhat unexpected institution of considerable size and complexity in a fairly under-explored part of the state. I have made reference in other sections of this guide to the Public Ivies, a group of state supported institutions of exceptional academic strength. The original group included the commonly esteemed universities such as Berkeley, Michigan, Virginia, North Carolina, Texas and a few smaller campuses such as Vermont and Miami University in Ohio.

The obvious advantage in attending one of the Public Ivies is in receiving an excellent education at a much lower cost than at one of the celebrated private institutions, and comparative shopping is an excellent idea in evaluating the colleges to which a student applies. In addition, an advantage frequently overlooked is in encountering a rich variety of curricular options, many of which allow study in considerable depth. UConn is the only university in New England with a Med School, Law School, Dental School, Pharmacy School, and School of Social Work.

The University of Connecticut is a highly regarded research university, particularly in preparation for professional careers, and increasingly for its innovation in Bioscience and Bioengineering. Undergraduates can choose from among more than one hundred majors and areas of concentration. The University offers instruction through a School of Fine Arts, the School of Agriculture, health, and Natural resources, the School of Business, the School of Engineering, the School of Education, the School of Liberal Arts and Sciences, the School of Nursing, the School of Pharmacy, the School of Social Work, and an experiential two year program in Agriculture through the Ratcliff Hicks School.

A random romp through the online course catalog will provide an overwhelming array of courses and programs. As in an examination of any large and complicated university, the more helpful description is in how the university presents itself to its students and how the complexity of university life is managed.

Here's a pretty impressive statistic indicating that UConn is exceptional in its ability to provide service and support to its undergraduate students – ninety-five percent of them return after their first year. That rate of retention puts UConn in the company of some fairly spiffy institutions. An excellent rate of retention, in my opinion, reflects the students' estimation of the value of their experience, some degree of comfort with the institution's practices, and a healthy social life.

UConn's students talk about their coursework and majors with real satisfaction. Yes, they understand that some general education requirements will involve classes in a large lecture setting; there are fifteen thousand undergraduates at work here, but none feel themselves at risk of not being able to get to the courses they need in order to complete their program of study. It is worth emphasizing that taking on a course of study at UConn is easily managed; advisors and professors are helpful and the institution has anticipated the needs of students at the introductory levels of study. As might be expected, courses in the sciences and engineering are uniformly excellent, but most other programs are equally well regarded. Students in Fine Arts describe their experience as remarkable. The School of Fine Arts has traditional strength in Art and Art History, but other areas, such as Dramatic Arts, Media Design, and Music are equally powerful. The Connecticut Repertory Theater is the production arm of the Acting and Theater Arts program at UConn, active throughout the year. I have heard rave reviews of Resource Economics, Public Policy, Information

Technology, Computer Science, and Nanotechnology and Ethics, Creative Writing, and all of the pre-professional programs.

In addition to finding their course work satisfyingly challenging and rewarding, students report excellent support from their instructors. Even in a large lecture class, professors are quick to respond to email and set up appointments that meet the student's needs.

I should quickly identify two of the elements that are at work in creating an uncommonly high degree of student satisfaction with the university. The first of these is the clear sense that UConn has become increasingly selective in admission, now admitting about fifty percent of applicants, a far lower percentage than that at other regional state universities. The other is that this lovely campus is beautifully maintained and updated. The quality of facilities is obvious and very much appreciated. As it is in other areas, UConn is on the move, and students feel they are part of the emergence of a great university.

Quinnipiac University - Hamden, Connecticut

It isn't unusual for a college to immerse itself in political issues; almost any college newspaper will poll its students and write about national issues. The Quinnipiac Institute, on the other hand, is a regular contributor to the New York Times, The Washington Post, CNN and other major news outlets. Its polling of New England and New York is considered to be the gold standard of analytical statistical modeling.

And the stats… 2015

Number of Applicants: 23,400/ 62% Accepted
Undergrad Enrollment: 6,553   60% female / 40% male
Avg. SAT Reading Comp 490-580 / Math 490-610 Avg. ACT: 23-27
Total Cost: $57,360.00.
Received some form of financial assistance: 82%

"Quinnipiac-Piac-Piac, Quinnipiac, Piac!" Not a cheer you've heard frequently? Well, that is about to change. Not only is Quinnipiac an increasingly popular destination for students in the region, it is also now a frequent contender for Division I national championships in men's ice hockey and coming on very quickly in men's and women's lacrosse, men's and women's soccer, and men's and women's basketball. The Bobcats have prospects in virtually every professional sport with current all-stars playing notably in the NHL; the prominence of Quinnipiac athletes reflects the university's rapid rise in the ranks of New England's colleges and universities. In the same fashion that Elon moved up from an almost purely regional college to a national institution, Quinnipiac is destined to find itself welcoming applicants, particularly those who have heard about the Quinnipiac Polling Institute, Quinnipiac's outstanding program in Business, Pre Law, Nursing and the associated professions in Health Sciences. This is probably the time to note that while Quinnipiac offers a full range of courses in sciences and the liberal arts, interest in professional preparation is evident in the number of internships and cooperative course work made available, and it is in that context that I would like to introduce the Quinnipiac Polling Institute.

It isn't unusual for a college to immerse itself in political issues; almost any college newspaper will poll its students and write about national issues. The Quinnipiac Institute, on the other hand, is a regular contributor to the New York Times, The Washington Post, CNN and other major news outlets. Its polling of New England and New York is considered to be the gold standard of analytical statistical modeling, Most recent studies, including an assessment by FiveThirtyEight.Com, have numbered the Quinnipiac poll among the four or five most accurate polls in the nation, competing with Gallup and the Pew Research Center. The university houses this institute, but it operates independent of the rest of the university. The researchers on staff are almost two hundred Quinnipiac students; they may be majoring in statistics, or sociology, or political science, or history. They do the brunt of the polling work as part of a work-study program administered by the university. Without leaving their undergraduate career, they enter into the world of professional pollsters and gain remarkable experience in a sophisticated field of political prediction.

The Quinnipiac story is an unusual one in the traditionally ivy covered tales of New England's institutions of higher education, and, curiously, has much to do with the migration of programs from two other universities. Northeastern University, now a powerful presence in Boston, began in New Haven; its departure to Beantown left a gap in the state's ability to offer commercial education. Quinnipiac was named after the tribe that had first occupied the region and quickly set out to provide quality education in business management. The college grew quickly and quickly outgrew the original campus in New Haven; the move to suburban Hamden gave the rapidly expanding institution an opportunity to welcome yet another migration; the University of Bridgeport's highly regarded Law School came to Quinnipiac in 1995 and Quinnipiac University came to also include a strong medical college with an undergraduate Nursing School as well, currently offering one of the most successful programs in the nation for those seeking a degree in any of the Health Science related fields such as Nursing and Physical Therapy.

Now enrolling more than nine thousand students, almost seven thousand of which are undergraduates, Quinnipiac is the rare "mid-sized" comprehensive university in the Northeast. Graduate programs are world-class, but the undergraduate programs are equally intriguing. Because Quinnipiac is so distinctive in terms of its "niche" programs in polling and medical science, I'm going to start with a description of the general Quinnipiac experience and then settle in on some academic programs in particular.

Look, Quinnipiac is a relative newcomer in the crowded array of well-established institutions in New England. Outsiders visiting the smaller, more tradition-laden campus at Middlebury or Bowdoin may consider Quinnipiac's Hamden campus less "collegiate", but students here L O V E it; the most common word used to describe the campus in any conversation is "beautiful", and it has considerable charm for those of us who appreciate the clean lines of relatively modern buildings, air conditioning, sensible spaces ordered in sensible ways, and a setting directly adjoining a lovely green space, Connecticut's Sleeping Giant State

Park. Hamden is a suburb of New Haven and close to major transportation hubs, easy access to New York and Boston and close to the Connecticut shoreline. Although Quinnipiac has three campuses, the newest in North Haven is strictly an academic setting and the York Hill campus holds the university's athletic facility, the TD Bank Sports Center, including one of the most impressive basketball/hockey arena in the region. Actually, Quinnipiac has TWO arenas– the Kahn Basketball Pavilion and the Northford Ice Pavilion; each seats just under four thousand spectators, although when hockey fever hits. Bobcat fans pack every inch of the ice arena.

There are fraternities and sororities at Quinnipiac, dormitory associations are strong, and the relatively unusual size of the residential cohort (about five thousand) allows Quinnipiac to feel small and cozy while offering a wide diversity of people and living options. The dining hall gets reasonably good reviews; as in any institution, some appreciate what can be done when feeding thousands of students daily. "Make sure you get the food when it first comes out," is the advice given by one canny sophomore – good advice in sampling any institutional cuisine. A first year program (FYRE – First Year Residential Experience), which introduces them to Bobcat lore, the traditions of the university, and residential expectations; they also take a course in which they look at and discuss the relationship between the individual and the community. The program includes an extensive orientation under the direction of their Resident Advisor, a student living with them in their dormitory.

Sports are important at Quinnipiac, and, as a Division I university, the Bobcats recruit talented athletes to compete against other universities in the Metro Atlantic Conference; Bobcat hockey is a cat of a different stripe, however, pitting Quinnipiac's women and men against the entire cast of characters in ECAC hockey. The ECAC includes all of the Ivy colleges and the remarkable smaller schools that have contended for and won national championships. Quinnipiac joins Colgate, St. Lawrence, Union, and RPI as a non-Ivy member of the ECAC. Union College won the NCAA Division I championship in 2014, defeating Minnesota, and Quinnipiac made it to the Championship game in 2013, losing in the final to Yale.

Opportunities for recreation outside of the varsity athletic world include a ton of fitness options, including classes and workshops scheduled throughout the day. Intramural sports are widely enjoyed, especially the heartless competition for top honors in co-ed kickball. Tennis, golf, swimming, skating, running, hiking, camping, horseback riding are all available as are tap dancing, salsa, weightlifting competitions, and indoor rock climbing. Clubs and organizations galore, including most of the usual spread (interest groups, ethnic support, publications, music, dance, and bands. Spirit groups abound, including rabid Bobcat hockey fans linked together as Ice Cat Cheerbladers; they manage to provide dance and cheer support while figure skating. Lots of publications and musical groups are available, including a cappella fans and theater rats. The unusual groups are the Quinnipiac Ballroom Society, Quinn PR, which is a public relations group offering free guidance to any who want to be relating publicly, and the Asian Novelty in Media Entertainment society (ANIME). The Ed McMahon Mass Communication Center operates an all-digital TV production studio, and increasing numbers of students are preparing for a career in the media.

Quinnipiac won't be a best-kept secret much longer; there are few universities of this size in New England with the kinds of professional programs that Quinnipiac offers. It is not a "rich kid" school, as its emphasis on work-study and professional preparation indicates, and it has the kind of grounded school spirit that a student wanting big-time college sports might enjoy.

Fairfield University - Fairfield, Connecticut

The academic profile is extensive, and the athletic mission is equally compelling, but I want to start with what may be a slightly provocative observation: Fairfield is preppier than Villanova and Boston College, less rabid than Notre Dame, less metro than Georgetown, and boasts a handsome campus in one of the most wonderfully well located small city in New England.

And the stats... 2015

Number of Applicants: 9,978 72% Accepted
Undergrad Enrollment: 3,982   59% female / 41% male
Avg. SAT Reading Comp 540-620 / Math 550-650 Avg. ACT: 26-30
Total Cost: $59,840.00.
Received some form of financial assistance: 89%

Although Fairfield is not mentioned as frequently as Georgetown or Villanova, it has many of the qualities that make those institutions nationally regarded. As is the case in almost every other conversation about national reputation, it probably has something to do with championship seasons and impact sports at the Division I level. Fairfield is one of the nation's twenty-eight Jesuit universities (like Georgetown and Villanova) and does play at the Division I level. It is also an emerging pre-professional power in the Northeast, a wonderfully balanced and spirited college, and a great option for the student who wants all the advantages of a university in a relatively small (3500 students) setting. In fact, Fairfield is actually much closer in size and "vibe" to Bucknell, Richmond, and Lehigh than it is to Villanova.

The academic profile is extensive, and the athletic mission is equally compelling, but I want to start with what may be a slightly provocative observation: Fairfield is preppier than Villanova and Boston College, less rabid than Notre Dame, less metro than Georgetown, and boasts a handsome campus in a wonderfully well located small city in New England. If there is a downside to the Fairfield experience – and I believe there are many spectacular opportunities here – it is in the homogeneity of the student body. It's a good-looking student body and a well-dressed student body (pink polo shirt with the collar turned up/ Uggs/ Northface/ J Crew), but also a kind student body and one that is ready to embrace the college's mission of education for an inspired life. The Jesuit influence is clear in the university's publications and public pronouncements; many of the academic offerings are influenced by the notion of an inter-disciplinary competency that is at the core of a life dedicated to faith and justice.

But let's be clear, here. The students at Fairfield are NOT monks; a quick look at the banners in the gymnasium reveals that they are STAGS. The statue of the stag (named Lucas) is at the center of the campus, and, while the mythological and theological import of the stag may have something to do with a prescient messenger from another world, these stags are very much of this world. They seek a professional life and have ambitions of success in this world. And, you can hang the tag of "party animal" on the antlers of some of these stags. In fact, the closest comparison, in terms of student body, is probably with Gonzaga, another smallish Jesuit university with an active and avid undergraduate population. Fairfield calls students from New England, and Gonzaga from the Northwest, so the uniform dress code is slightly different, but both institutions are simultaneously true to their Jesuit heritage and jam-packed with athletic fervor and fondness for hi-jinks of a Saturday night.

The casual visitor will quickly note that Fairfield is a less jumbled campus than some of its New England cohorts. It has the advantage of having been set in something like several city blocks on a two hundred acre campus in a quiet neighborhood only a few miles from Long Island Sound.

And, about Long Island Sound... roughly four hundred lucky upper class students win the lottery and jam into rental units located off the main campus and on the beach rather than living in on-campus dormitories. Local residents wish there were a few more units available for ordinary folk, but the stags love the water! In fact, most of the notable traditions celebrated by Fairfield's students have something to do with "The Beach", by which they mean Fairfield Beach. Beach residents host weekly parties, called the Floating Naut, rotating the hosting duties among the more than eighty student houses on the beach. Although things have calmed down considerably, the annual "Clam Jam" brought virtually the entire student population (and crowds of other young fun-in-the-sun seekers) to Lantern Point for a blow out before exam week in the spring. Some Fairfield residents took umbrage at the annual fete and apparently attempted to tame the event. Current students may refer to the weekend as "Spam Jam" at this point, recognizing its heritage and its distance from the excesses of years gone by. "Clam" or "Spam", the beat goes on. During the year, the beach is also the site of "Mock Wedding" – exactly what it sounds like – and "Powder Puff", another senior event, usually held in November.

If this description seems to have sunk to the level of "Beach Blanket Binge", remember that Fairfield has no fraternities or sororities; these beachy celebrations are loud and raucous, but absolutely typical of undergraduate frolic. Less typical is the high degree of engagement in community service and international justice. In addition to the hundred forms of ordinary service carried out in and near Fairfield (including the Annual Hunger Clean Up, a day in which students work with more than forty agencies to raise money for the homeless and hungry), Fairfield's students are active in the Relay for Life and the Adrienne Kirby Family Literacy Project; almost one hundred and fifty students volunteer in Early Learning and Head Start programs. If anyone doubts the investment of Fairfield's students in social action, all that is necessary to set the record straight is a quick look at the work undertaken by the Ignatian Solidarity Network, a national organization of students and graduates of Jesuit universities. Founded in memory of Jesuit missionaries killed in El Salvador, the network promotes missions across the country and around the globe. Fairfield's students are among the most heavily involved, leaving the pleasant campus in Connecticut to work for social justice and Word Fair Trade or to teach at the Red Cloud Indian School on the Pine Ridge Indian Reservation in South Dakota.

Social life and service aside, the most distinctive aspect of a student's experience at Fairfield is in the classroom, where a dedicated faculty teaches a core curriculum and courses across more than forty major programs. It is in this arena that the Fairfield advantage is most obvious. The requirements established by a core curriculum speaks to commitment to the liberal arts and to the process by which a general education both supports major fields of study and informs the values with which a graduate enters the world. The skills the core promotes are entirely worthwhile: Objectivity, critical acumen, effective communication, dexterity with symbols and symbol-systems, aesthetic appreciation, and familiarity with developing methodologies. Before graduation, then, each student will meet courses in Math and Natural Science, History and Social Science, Philosophy, English, Arts, Language, and U.S. and World Diversity.

That's a familiar enough academic landscape. The huge difference between Fairfield and some other institutions of comparable size is in the diversity of professional programs offered in addition to the usual constellation of academic majors. English students and philosophers, pre-meds and pre-law will find everything they need, but so will those who seek a degree in Engineering (computer, electrical, mechanical, software, and automated manufacturing), Nursing, Business (Accounting, Finance, International Business, Information Systems, Marketing) and Education.

A number of programs are highly regarded, but it probably makes sense to recognize the impact that the Charles F. Dolan School of Business has had in the region. Not only is the comprehensive slate coursework impressive, the facility includes what is known as the BEST classroom, a space that simulates the floor of the American Stock Exchange. Thirty-four workstations offer Bloomberg terminals and real time tickers. Graduates of the Dolan School have taken their place in the world of business and finance around the world and have animated much market research in this quiet corner of Fairfield County.

Quiet is not the word to describe the action in the Webster Bank Arena in Bridgeport, formerly known as the Arena at Harbor Yard, the Stags home court in basketball. There are great athletic facilities on campus - Alumni Hall, the old gym in which the 1979 Stags stunned the nationally ranked Holy Cross Crusaders, a spiffy baseball stadium, Lessing Field on which the soccer team plays. The issue is that Fairfield basketball is the signature sport, at the heart of the university's competition in the Division I Metro Conference. Ten thousand spectators flock to the arena to watch the Stags battle Iona, Niagara, Marist, Canisius, and Manhattan, and St. Peter's for a bid to the NCAA field of sixty-four. With the addition of women's rowing, Fairfield now offers more than twenty Division I varsity sports. That's impressive for a school of this size, but perhaps equally notable is the participation of almost eighteen hundred in intramural and club sports. A quick tally indicates that almost eighty percent of Fairfield's students are actively involved in some form of athletic competition each year.

The Jesuit colleges seek to balance academic challenge, social justice, and healthy competition, and Fairfield is certainly among the most successful in maintaining that balance. The handsome Connecticut campus sets it apart from some of its more urban counterparts, and the relative homogeneity of its student body makes the social scene a bit more predictably "collegiate", but the strength of feeling the university elicits from its graduates places Fairfield among the New England colleges most worthy of investigation.

New York

There are five separate mind-sets in terms of New York's college setting: The first, obviously, is the city – four of the five boroughs offer a truly urban college experience; the second is "Upstate" – Albany, the capital district, Syracuse, the Finger Lakes, and the St. Lawrence; the third is alternatively Western New York State or The Snow Belt, and includes Binghamton, Rochester and Buffalo, the fourth is Long Island, and the fifth "the other suburbs," Westchester, Rockland, Orange, Putnam, Sullivan, Ulster, and Dutchess Counties.

Most of the New York City schools are widely celebrated and enjoy an acceptance rate lower than attended to in this guide, and the city also offers some of the most highly reputed specialized programs in the nation. For example, the following represent the range in the fine and performing arts: the Julliard School, the Joffrey Ballet School, Parsons The New School for Design, Pratt Institute, the American Academy of Dramatic Arts, Manhattan School of Music, Cooper Union, and the School of American Ballet.

The near suburbs to the north of New York City are located in Westchester and Rockland Counties; the next nearest colleges are found in Putnam, Dutchess, Sullivan, and Ulster Counties. A major airport in Westchester allows easy access to towns and villages from Bronxville to Poughkeepsie.

Driving in the city is alternately nerve shattering and easy. The grid of streets and avenues is actually a snap to navigate (unlike Boston's city streets). The problem is that Manhattan is an island and entering involves crossing bridges, fighting traffic, and negotiating some slightly terrifying highways. Parking, on the other hand, is impossible.

The good news is that excellent routes are available in every direction from the city. The Long Island Expressway can be crowded, but its exits are appropriately labeled, and directions are clear. Several highways run from the city to the west and to the north. Visitors from other regions are often surprised to learn that what would be an ordinary afternoon's drive connects New York with most of the major cities in New England.

Philadelphia is less than two hours from New York, and Boston is about three and a half hours from the city. The drive to Portland, Maine takes less than five hours.

Upstate New York, on the other hand can seem more distant, in part because rough weather can make the drive from New York or Westchester to Syracuse or Potsdam more of an adventure.

Generally, life in New York City is exciting, expensive, and often exhausting. Students who need a big city setting can thrive in New York, but it is not for everyone.

The near suburbs – Long Island, Putnam, and Westchester – are convenient in that a trip to the city is always possible, but the pace (and cost) of living is more reasonable.

Upstate New York offers fabulous opportunities in the outdoors. The Adirondack Mountain chain stretches from the Mohawk Valley (near Colgate University and Hamilton College) to the Saint Lawrence River (Clarkson and Saint Lawrence). Separated from the Green Mountains by Lake Champlain and Lake George, the Adirondacks are part of the Laurentian mountains of Canada. Spectacular hiking, camping, fishing, rock climbing, skiing, skating, bobsledding, and almost any other outdoor activity is available in the Adirondacks. Lake Placid is probably the most famous of the Adirondack resort towns, but the entire region is rightly considered one of America's great natural treasures.

Western New York is more difficult to describe, in that it contains a southern tier touching the Pennsylvania border, the Niagara region which includes Niagara Falls, and, on its eastern edge, Rochester and the Finger Lakes.

All of the northeastern states deal with vagaries of weather, of course, but it should be noted that much of upstate and western New York can be considered likely to have the heaviest snowfall in the East and often the coldest temperatures.

Clarkson University - Potsdam, New York

Clarkson's grads were recently ranked in the top 20 best-paid starting salaries in the country (average starting salary $57,900.00)

And the stats... 2015

Number of Applicants: 7,400 62% Accepted
Undergrad Enrollment: 3,247   55% female / 45% male
Avg. SAT Reading Comp 520-620 / Math 570-670 Avg. ACT: 24-29
Total Cost: $59,920.00.
Received some form of financial assistance: 100%

In the northern tier of New York State, the town of Potsdam is a pretty Victorian town in Saint Lawrence County, equidistant from Syracuse and Montreal. Near the Canadian border, Potsdam is located on the Raquette River, and also close to Lake Champlain; Burlington, Vermont is about three hours to the east. This northern town is home to Clarkson University and one of New York's state universities, Potsdam State University. A student population of about 7000 brings the total population in the town to about 18,000. Saint Lawrence University, another excellent North Country school is only a few miles away in Canton, New York.

Any student serious about a technical education, global economy, or a degree in engineering should consider Clarkson. Recently, the US Association for Small Businesses and Entrepreneurship named Clarkson the National Model Undergraduate Program in Entrepreneurship. The university has developed programs outside of the traditional fields of technology, including a very strong business school, and an extensive and well regarded Arts and Sciences division. It is a tech school, however, that Clarkson first found its national reputation, and it is as an outstanding school of technology that it continues to attract some students from beyond the region. Oh, and Clarkson's grads were recently ranked in the top 20 best paid starting salaries in the country (average starting salary $57,900.00).

Here's the thing about Clarkson: The programs in applied engineering are remarkable; the Center for Advanced Materials Processing (CAMP), for example, promotes cutting edge research on the application of high-technology materials and is one of the most influential centers of applied technology in the country...and at the same time ... Clarkson is a hockey mad male enclave (2000 men/ 850 women) at the northern fringe of New York, sitting on the border with Canada.

I first realized that dichotomy after joining a professor in his laboratory devoted to research on the physicochemical properties of polypeptide and polysaccharide multilayer films. These were not Hollywood releases, mind you, but an extension of the work Clarkson has been doing for decades in the application of polymers. Only moments earlier, I had been at the hockey rink, watching some of the best skaters in Division I hockey prepare for another season competing for a national title.

So, who goes to Clarkson? For the most part, Clarkson's students are practical, bottom-line, grounded, sensible, ambitious kids; they want to find a career in science or business, and 98% of them are employed in a field of their choice upon graduation. Some of those graduates have been specifically trained in areas rarely considered by other schools, even colleges of technology. Among the areas of study most highly reputed at the college are: Advanced Materials Science, Biotechnology, Environment & Energy, Entrepreneurship and Global Supply Chain Management.

Ordinary, goofy kids go to Clarkson as well. They may not be deeply enmeshed in physico-chemical properties, but they do get a well organized and thorough education in science, Business Administration, Entrepreneurship, or Biotechnology, One of the areas that has long been of special interest at Clarkson is the application of physical therapy and the development of Assistive Science, creating technology and methods that make a difference in the lives of the disabled and injured. This is a real-world, real-life kind of school that proudly asserts that at least one of every eight graduates is a corporate CEO or partner in a business.

Northern New York is an outdoor kind of setting, and the possibilities for wilderness activities are limitless. A Social committee organizes on campus activities and the university sponsors clubs and organizations ranging from the gaming club to the women's rugby club, from the gay-straight alliance to the autonomous robot club. The fraternities tend to host the most raucous of parties, but they do not have a stranglehold on social life on campus.

Finally, most of Clarkson's teams compete in Division III; nineteen varsity sports are offered, many of them highly successful in their conference. However, hockey rules at Clarkson.

The men's and women's hockey teams are very strong Division I programs, frequently in contention for a national championship. From the first practices in the fall to the last games in the spring, the ice arena is the place to be for Clarkson students; most do not miss a single home game. Hockey fever is rampant and great fun. So, for the technologically minded student, or for the determined entrepreneur, this North Country university of about 3000 may be a great admissions bargain.

Paul Smith's College / The College of the Adirondacks - Paul Smith's, New York

Paul Smith's College is located INSIDE the Adirondack State Park. What's so cool about that? Well, Adirondack State Park is the largest park in the contiguous fifty states, protecting over SIX MILLION ACRES of forest and lakes. That makes it slightly larger than the state of Vermont. Adirondack is bigger than Yosemite, Yellowstone, Glacier, the Grand Canyon, and the Great Smoky Mountains National Parks. COMBINED.

And the stats... 2015

Number of Applicants: 828 98% Accepted
Undergrad Enrollment: 892 35% female / 65% male
Avg. SAT Reading Comp 410-530 / Math 420-540 Avg. ACT: 18-24
Total Cost: $41,200.00.
Received some form of financial assistance: 100%

I know. It seems as if EVERY college I describe is a hidden gem and remarkably more worthy of investigation than the next. In the case of Paul Smith's, however, I think I can be reasonably secure in guessing that nobody you know knows much of anything about this exceptional school. Even people who think they know a lot about colleges don't know about Paul Smith's. Why would I recommend a college that most people don't recognize? It's not for everyone, but for the student genuinely interested in working in forestry, fisheries, wildlife science, hotel management, culinary arts, or land management, Paul Smith's may one of the best programs in the country.

In the first place, the college is located INSIDE the Adirondack State Park. What's so cool about that? Well, Adirondack State Park is the largest park in the contiguous fifty states, protecting over SIX MILLION ACRES of forest and lakes. That makes it slightly larger than the state of Vermont. Adirondack is bigger than Yosemite, Yellowstone, Glacier, the Grand Canyon, and the Great Smoky Mountains National Parks. COMBINED.

So, there's that.

And, *Outdoor Magazine* rates Paul Smith's College as one of the top ten colleges for those who love the outdoors.

Did I mention the location?

106

Not only is the college located within one of the most striking and pristine of forested parks, not only is it literally on the waterfront of a crystal clear lake, not only is it less than twenty miles from Lake Placid, site of two Winter Olympic Games... it is also as close as a college can get to the experience of living in one of the great examples of arts and crafts stone and wood architecture.

The Adirondacks are strikingly beautiful and have attracted people who love the outdoors for generations. About half of the land within the park is privately owned, and there are more than thirty golf courses within the park. So, although the natural landscape has been well protected, this is also a vacation destination. The elaborate lodges (mansions made of logs) built at the end of the nineteenth century are known as the Great Camps and are among the most striking examples of the arts and crafts movement in American architecture. An early and very popular destination at the edge of Lake Saranac was Paul Smith's Hotel. Teddy Roosevelt and P.T. Barnum were among the many celebrated guests, and the popularity of the hotel was such that after the death of Paul Smith, the town took on his name.

The association of hotel and restaurant management and the understanding of natural resources came together when the college was founded in 1946. Within a few years, the college had developed a number of programs that can only be called unusual.

There is a liberal arts program with most of the usual majors in the humanities and the sciences. The backdrop is, of course, an added inspiration for the liberal arts student, as is a beautifully crafted and completely modern library with smart classrooms and wireless. In fact, a student can sit on a deck overlooking the lake, download the Odyssey, and read on an autumn afternoon. There is also a wonderful outdoor classroom, built by students and used by classes in the liberal arts as well as in the programs having to do with the outdoors.

Similarly, a well-established program in Business Management and Marketing offers a four-year program which features cooperative experience in collaboration with a network of Adirondack enterprises. In the senior year, Management and Marketing majors will essentially become consultants for the business they advise. A small program in Engineering Technology allows graduates to become certified in surveying and in Geographic Information Systems, using GPS technology to create cartographic surveys.

The signature programs at Paul Smith are three: Natural Resources and Conservation, Parks, Recreation, Fitness, and Leisure Studies, and Personal and Culinary Services.

The program in Natural Resources and Conservation includes Environmental Science, of course, but the real richness of program comes in the rest of the majors: Fishing and Fisheries Science and Management, Forest Management/Forest Resource Management, Forest Resources Production and Management, Forest Sciences and Biology, Forest Technology, Forestry, Urban Forestry, Land Use Planning and Development, Wildlife Fish and Wildlife Science and Management, Natural resource Management and Policy.

Obviously, a program of this scope does not take place in an ivory tower. Paul Smith's is a highly experiential college, and the hands-on approach may be most clearly felt in the area of Resource and Conservation. Students work in what is essentially a fourteen thousand acre classroom. Forest technicians have the opportunity to learn in a working sawmill. In the spring, they may be involved in the tapping of maples and in the production of maple syrup.

In addition to the courses offered in Natural Resources and Conservation, students working in the Parks, recreation, and Leisure Studies major actually work in several of the college's facilities, including the exceptional Visitors Interpretive Center. The Center is a working classroom as well as a resource for those traveling in the Adirondacks. In addition to offering miles of trails for hiking, opportunities to ski and snowshoe, the Center maintains a native species butterfly house. Of the many extraordinary facilities maintained by the college, none is more impressive than Dillon Park, a facility designed to meet the needs of disabled people who want to hike, canoe, fish, and camp. Students are actively involved in programs that make those experience accessible to people who would otherwise not have the opportunities in the outdoors to which Paul Smith's is dedicated.

I'm not going to suggest that any applicant is swayed by the smell of freshly baked croissants, but no visitor to Paul Smith's should miss an opportunity to stop by the A.P. Smith Bakery. Students in the Personal and Culinary Services program produce bread, cakes, cookies, and pies each day in the college's ovens. Majors include Baking and Pastry Arts and Culinary Arts/Chef Training. The culinary program is accredited by the American Culinary federation, and the work done in the college's Statler Hospitality center is outstanding. Training continues in the Ganzi Restaurant, named in honor of Wally Ganzi, CEO of the Palm Restaurants. The Ganzi kitchen contains eight full service food laboratories dedicated to advanced food preparation. All students in the Culinary program will do paid internships in kitchen from Aspen to Zurich.

The outdoors calls Paul Smith's students to all the activities this privileged location has to offer. Hiking, camping, skiing, rock climbing, fishing, sailing, swimming! In addition a program of interscholastic and recreational sports pits the Bobcats of Paul Smith's against teams in the

Yankee Small College Conference of the NAIA. Competitive teams play soccer, rugby, basketball, skiing, volleyball, and cross-country. More interesting occupations include what the college calls "Timbersports" - pole climbing, log birling, logrolling, chopping (Horizontal Chop/Vertical Chop/Hard Chop), bow saw, chainsaw, splitting, sawing, pulp toss, ax-throw, and pack-board relay.

There's a radio station on campus and all the usual clubs and activities. An open Mic night and seasonal "flings" liven the campus. No fraternities or sororities exist on campus, which is almost entirely residential.

Ithaca College - Ithaca, New York

It isn't celebrity sighting that brings students to Ithaca; they come because they find a small college experience in what is essentially an undergraduate university setting. The professional schools and the liberal arts programs all live under the same roof, allowing prospective captains of industry, broadcast journalists, and hockey playing physical therapists to share this handsome campus.

And the stats... 2015

Number of Applicants: 118,207/ 59% Accepted
Undergrad Enrollment: 6124   57% female / 43% male
Avg. SAT Reading Comp 510-610 / Math 520-630 Avg. ACT: 23-28
Total Cost: $57,200.00.
Received some form of financial assistance: 95%

Ithaca College is an exceptional and relatively large college, nationally famed for its program in communications, highly regarded in the fields of physical therapy, and business, set in the middle of a great college town!

Most people who have heard of Ithaca, New York associate the town with Cornell, the large quasi-State/quasi-Ivy prominent research university and occasional athletic powerhouse. That's probably a good thing since, despite its current identity as one of the liveliest of college towns (Cornell and Ithaca College bring almost twenty-six thousand students to town every fall), in frontier times, Ithaca was known as "The Flats" and less charitably as "Sodom", due to the profusion of gaming, horse racing, and Sabbath breaking in the small community. Today Ithaca is a small city with little industry and the many diversions that suit a college town. Located not-so-far above Cayuga's waters, Ithaca is on the south end of Lake Cayuga, the longest (forty miles) of New York's Finger Lakes. The Ithaca Gun Factory was the prominent local industry, dumping shot from its shotgun testing into the local water supply. Today, things have changed, for Ithaca is the North American home of Tenzin Gyatso, the fourteenth Dalai Lama.

Ithaca College is not small; more than six thousand five hundred undergraduates find their way to this relatively under-appreciated large college. Actually, Ithaca is one of those "if-you-know-about-colleges-you-know-about-Ithaca" phenomena because it has a universally appreciated school of communications and has graduated the current President of the Walt Disney Company and David Boreanaz, Buffy's forbidden vampire love and Dr. Temperance Brennan's boy toy on *Bones,* among many other notables in the field of communications. It isn't celebrity sighting that brings students to Ithaca; they come because they find a small college experience in what is essentially an undergraduate university setting. The professional schools and the liberal arts programs all live under the same roof, allowing prospective captains of industry, broadcast journalists, and hockey playing physical therapists to share this handsome campus.

In fact, Ithaca enrolls undergraduates in five separate schools: The School of Business, the School of Health and Human Performance, the School of Humanities and Science, the School of Music, and the Roy H. Park School of Communications. While the most sensational information in this profile may describe opportunities in the Park School of Communications, there are many reasons to consider Ithaca for students interested in a liberal arts, business, health science, or music. In addition to more than a thousand courses offered in more than a hundred degree programs, Ithaca is a genuinely friendly and unusually spirited large college. Classes are small for the most part, and a great mixture of students from many backgrounds, undivided by fraternity or sorority affiliation, enjoy the quality of life in this active college and in this active college town.

Ithaca began as a school of music in 1892 and quickly expanded, adding a School of Expression and Dramatic Arts. By the end of World War II, Ithaca had become known for its work in theater, music, music education, physical therapy, and radio. The addition of a liberal arts curriculum and a strong business school brought the university to its current size. About eleven hundred students graduate each year – about a third are in the School of Humanities and Science, the School of Business, and the Roy H. Park School of Communications. These days, the fewest graduates are in the School of Music.

The School of Business offers majors in Accounting, Business Administration (with concentrations in Corporate Accounting, Finance, International Business, Management, and Marketing) and Legal Studies. The two most notable aspects of the program offered by the School of Business are the ambitious placement of students in internships and the well-developed curriculum in Legal Studies. Internships carry students to Wall Street, London, and beyond. The major in Legal Studies prepares undergraduates for Law School, but also introduces interdisciplinary study in the liberal arts and business. An internship is required of all majors, and internships in London or Washington allow undergraduates to observe the reality of law in practice.

The stars of the Ithaca curriculum, however, are found in the Roy H. Park School of Communications and the School of Health Science and Human performance.

The Park School of Communications offers a major in Cinema and Photography allowing undergraduates to study still photography, cinema production, and screenwriting. The major in Communication Management and Design is more clearly aimed at the corporate market, providing instruction in Instructional Technology and Corporate Communication. Similarly, the major in Integrated Marketing Communication prepares graduates for work in a corporate setting. Documentary Studies and Production, Film, Emerging Media, Journalism, and Television-Radio prepare graduates to work in the field of communications. All of these programs are enhanced by remarkable facilities, and all of these facilities are in place for an undergraduate population.

The student newspaper, The Ithacan is published weekly and on-line and is considered one of the most ambitious and successful weeklies in the college journalism world. The radio station, 92 WCIB broadcasts widely, essentially as a commercial modern rock station. IC TV (Ithaca College Television) is far from what the casual reader might imagine as a college television station. The station is part of the cable package offered in that part of New York State, providing original programming to more than thirty thousand households. Its news programming is superior, garnering the College Emmy, and its flagship program, Newswatch 16, has been in production for more than four decades. What really has people excited about IVTV, however, are the original program and series that the station has developed. More than three hundred students volunteer in order to maintain the daily operation of the station, creating regular programming of such shows as: *Food Fight Face Off* - a cooking show; *A Book By Its Cover* - a dark mystery show; *Game Over* - a review of video games; *The Big Red Faceoff* - devoted to Cornell ice hockey. Two recently developed programs grabbed considerable attention. *IVY* is a reality show following student at Cornell and Harvard; *The Race* was a reality series based on The Amazing Race.

Ithaca welcomes some of the most prominent individuals in every aspect of the field of communications to the campus each year in symposia and colloquia, but the most significant extra opportunity offered to a student at Ithaca is the possibility of doing work at the Pendleton Center in Los Angeles. Industry professionals work with students at the center as they take on internships in the fields of cinema, television, radio, new media, music, communication management, advertising, public relations, and journalism.

Those in the know are also well aware of Ithaca's exceptional program offered through the School of Health Science and Human performance. It is the area of Physical Therapy that the school is most widely known, and there are obvious reasons for its celebrity. One of the most established programs, Ithaca now offers a six-year doctorate degree, combining a strong background in the liberal arts and science with exceptional preparation for practice as a physical therapist. This program is highly competitive; applicants are admitted in the freshman year. All students in the Physical Therapy program have access to internships in the college's Occupational and Physical Therapy Clinic, located in the Center for Health Sciences. Ithaca's program has turned out the highest percentage of graduates successfully receiving accreditation through the CAPTE.

OK, what have I not told you about Ithaca?

Yes, snow happens.

You can either think of Ithaca as a winter wonderland set in a bountiful landscape of astounding natural beauty, or you can think of it as an isolated experience locked in winter's cold embrace. Students who come to Ithaca actually talk about the weather fairly infrequently. They are ready for snow and enjoy it. The bus to town runs year-round, so there's no inconvenience in getting to the very active social scene in the town of Ithaca. Beyond that, activities on campus abound and are well supported. This is not a suitcase school; once the bond is formed, Ithaca's students find a community of like-minded friends and enjoy their time on campus very much. In addition to the usual constellation of social events, the college offers special opportunities, such as "Urban Cowboy Night" - think mechanical bull riding.

Even a casual visitor to Ithaca will quickly catch the positive attitude that its students have about the place. To a degree that is uncommon anywhere, and perhaps unexpected in the occasionally chilly North, students LOVE Ithaca. They love the campus; they love their professors; they love the outdoors; they love the town. No fraternities, no sororities - just a great group of college kids who adore their school.

Somehow (and the origin is lost in the fog of history) the athletic teams at Ithaca are known as The Bombers. As far as I am aware, Ithaca is the only college in Division III with weapon delivery as its totem. There are numerous recreational activities available throughout the year, including a challenging and much used climbing wall, and interscholastic sports do claim the attention of the student body as well. The Bombers compete in what is called "The Empire Eight", a conference that from its name ought to be made up of colleges found in the Empire State, and for the most part it is. Typical rivals include Union College, Elmira College, and Hartwick College. Stevens Institute of Technology is the lone member from the Garden State of New Jersey. Ithaca's women compete inter scholastically in field hockey, gymnastics, swimming, crew, track, tennis, softball, soccer, and lacrosse. Men compete in football, soccer, crew, cross-country, basketball, swimming, track, tennis, and lacrosse.

Men can compete in baseball, football, and wrestling, while women can compete in field hockey, gymnastics, softball, volleyball, and golf. Both men and women can gear up for basketball, wrestling, crew, cross-country, soccer, lacrosse, swimming and diving, tennis, and indoor and outdoor track and field.

Ithaca offers a beautiful setting, a great collegiate experience, serious pre-professional training, and a great college town. It is as expensive as its peer private colleges, but generous in awarding scholarships on merit as well as on financial need.

Rochester Institute of Technology - Henrietta, New York

The Golisano College of Computing and Information Science enrolls about 2500 of RIT's undergrads because it offers programs rarely found at the undergraduate level. For example, in addition to Applied Networking and System Administration (I.T. jobs, anyone?), Software Engineering, and Computer Science, the engineering college offers a major in Medical Informatics, New Media Interactive Development, and Game Design and Development.

And the stats... 2015

Number of Applicants: 17,936 57% Accepted
Undergrad Enrollment: 13,460 32% female / 68% male
Avg. SAT Reading Comp 540-640 / Math 570-680 Avg. ACT: 26-31
Total Cost: $49,360.00.
Received some form of financial assistance: 95%

Let's start with the basics: RIT enrolls almost 14,000 undergraduate students in a variety of technological programs, and the quality of instruction is exceptional.

Forty years ago, when I first started talking with students about college choices, I had a heck of a time convincing families from outside the region to consider the two remarkable options outside of New England - Carnegie Mellon University and Washington University. Try getting into either one of those today!

Now I'm touting two compelling universities that are about to get extremely competitive, and two outstanding institutes of technology - Rose-Hulman in Indiana and RIT in Rochester.

Henrietta, NY, is a suburb of Rochester, located within metropolitan Rochester, a town of about 39,000 attached to a metro area of about 219,000, the third largest in the state of New York. Rochester is generally considered to be among the nation's most "livable cities," in part due to its general quality of life. It's considered a great place to raise a family, thus indicating that, while it may not be the most exotic or hypnotic of urban experiences, it is relentlessly safe, comfortable, and predictable.

The weather, as you already guessed, is also predictable; Rochester is in what is known as the humid continental climate zone - read that as hot summer/cold winter with the promise of about 60 snowy days a year. However, it should be noted that autumn in Rochester is magnificent, offering a truly spectacular show of fall colors.

There are three celebrated products of the Rochester region – the "white dog", a variation on the hot dog, popular in the area and sold at Rochester Red Wings games; Genesee Beer; and optical products, especially those developed by Eastman Kodak and Bausch and Lomb.

Rochester is the center of research in the field of optics, and RIT may be the world's capital of optical imaging. Don't let the high percentage of applicants admitted fool you; students come to RIT because they want a particular program and the opportunity to get to work. Oh, and almost everyone on this campus is working like a dog. RIT is tough.

Like many tech campuses, RIT offers state-of-the-art technical facilities; unlike most tech campuses, the place is actually attractive, spacious, and easy to negotiate. RIT looks like a very well endowed, tech-savvy, small university. Red brick dominates, but the interior spaces are widely varied.

Ok, very large campus, lots of brick buildings, great facilities, beautifully maintained – what besides setting makes RIT a great find?

The first principle in looking at RIT is that this is an institute that intends to train its students for a professional career. There is a general education requirement, and a student could major in Biology, or Chemistry, Economics, or Mathematics, but most course work will be done in a specific technological area, and RIT offers majors that are not offered anywhere else.

The institute includes a graduate program, and eight "colleges," dedicated to various areas of study.

The College of Liberal Arts and the College of Science are very much like similar programs in any tech school.

The College of Applied Science and Technology is directed toward providing training in fields in the marketplace – improving products and the systems by which production takes place. Some of the majors seem like ordinary engineering majors (Civil, Computer, Electrical) directed toward commerce, but others are distinctive. The most notable may be the major in Manufacturing and Mechanical Engineering combined with Packaging Science. RIT is widely known as the center for packaging research.

The Saunders College of Business offers the standard degrees in Accounting, Finance, International Business, and Management, as well as a major in New Media Marketing. These majors are very effectively combined with an extensive co-op program that I'll describe in a moment.

The Golisano College of Computing and Information Science enrolls about 2500 of RIT's undergrads because it offers programs rarely found at the undergraduate level. For example, in addition to Applied Networking and System Administration (I.T. jobs, anyone?), Software Engineering, and Computer Science, the engineering college offers a major in Medical Informatics, New Media Interactive Development, and Game Design and Development.

The Game Design program at the Bachelor and Master's levels is one of the few recognized by Microsoft's innovation award.

Great stuff so far, but the next two colleges truly set RIT apart from the rest of the tech field.

The College of Imaging Arts and Sciences attracts more than 2000 of the hardest working students in America. They love what they do, and they do it virtually around the clock. The divisions within the College of Imaging Arts and Sciences include: The School of Art (a professional school of painting, printmaking, sculpture, illustration, and medical illustration), the School of Design (a studio intensive school of graphic design, interior design, industrial design, and new media design), the School for American Crafts (departments of clay, glass, metal, and wood), the School of Film and Animation (film/video production, screenwriting, stagecraft, traditional and computer animation, and digital cinema), the School of Photographic Arts and Sciences (advertising photography, fine arts photography, photojournalism, imaging and photographic technology, biomedical photographic communications, and visual media), and the School of Print Media (electronic technology merges printing and publishing, graphic design, art, and photography).

These programs are the most selective at RIT.

The last of the colleges, The National Technical Institute for the Deaf, is the first technological institute for deaf students to be established in the world. 1200 deaf and hard-of-hearing students live and work with hearing students on the campus of RIT, earning a career focused degree or an associate degree.

Obviously, the specialized academic programs at RIT assume the application of skills learned at RIT in the workplace, marketplace, or studio. Central to an RIT education is a comprehensive program of cooperative education (co-op). Placement in a co-op program means full-time, paid employment in the field; most programs require a co-op experience and many encourage it. The office of Cooperative Education places students in work setting at such enterprises as Adobe Systems, NASA, Hewlett-Packard, Honda, Goggle, and Walt Disney World. RIT reports that each year more than 3600 students complete more than 5400 work assignments with more than 1900 employers, generating more than 30 million dollars in earnings. Real world/ real money!

But what's life like outside the classroom/studio/job site at RIT?

It's college life, tech style, which is to say that the work is hard and occupies a lot of time, and the male/female ration is tilted roughly 2 to 1.

On the other hand, RIT offers a zillion clubs and activities, a full slate of varsity and intramural sports, and a very active social scene. Club level sports are widely supported; the school's roller hockey club, for example, went all the way to a national championship. Of the many extra-curricular activities, two of the most highly reputed are the active theater program and the excellent weekly magazine.

There's no football at RIT, but the Division I hockey team is powerful and its fans are zealous in their support. The ice arena is famous/infamous for the Corner Crew, a loud and determinedly obnoxious cadre of Tiger hockey fans. School spirit is at its highest during the hockey season, and the place rocks when the Tigers are skating.

RIT has a fairly active fraternity life; the college hosts 18 fraternities and 13 sororities, and a ton of special interest houses. The institute's dorms are in good shape, but lots of sophomores, juniors, and seniors opt to live in college owned apartments; there are five apartment complexes owned by the Institute adjacent to the campus.

Alfred University - Alfred, New York

Ok, Alfred attracts artists, scientists, and ordinary college kids to a lovely campus in a lovely town. The admissions office at Alfred puts it best: "At Alfred University, we know our students are our greatest asset. They are talented, active, involved and just a little bit quirky. And we like that!" They surely do, because the mix of students is as interesting as the mix of academic offerings and equally impressive.

And the stats... 2015

Number of Applicants: 3,482 / 69% Accepted
Undergrad Enrollment: 1,920 55% female / 45% male
Avg. SAT Reading Comp 470-570 / Math 450-550 Avg. ACT: 21-26
Total Cost: $40,866.00.
Received some form of financial assistance: 100%

Ready to take on winter in Western New York? Fly into Rochester, rent a car, drive about an hour south to the village of Alfred, New York, and prepare to be astounded!

Alfred University is unique in the college universe.

In the first place, there are two colleges in Alfred, a village with a population of about 3500 permanent residents. Alfred University is the institution we are interested in at this point; Alfred State College of Technology is a branch of the State University System in New York. The village of Alfred is in what locals call the "Southern Tier," which indicates that it experiences significant variations of weather. The area is hilly and beautiful; the college is located on a hill above the village. Visitors from other regions are most likely to arrive in Alfred for the annual Hot Dog Festival, a festival celebrated each spring. Some celestially minded visitors may drive to Alfred in order to visit the largest telescope in the state, located on the Alfred University campus.

Both Alfreds were established by Seventh Day Baptists in 1836 as a non-sectarian teaching college called Alfred Select School. One of the 30 earliest colleges established in the United States, Alfred was the second coeducational college and the second college in the nation to enroll an African American student.

The two Alfreds split as the State of New York established its Agricultural College at Alfred. Alfred University is on one side of the street; Alfred State College is on the other.

Here's where things get a bit odd, and it has to do with the ways in which the State of New York runs its huge system of universities and colleges. The State University of New York (SUNY) operates four fully comprehensive universities in Buffalo, Binghamton, Albany, and Stony Brook. It also operates a State College system and a large Community College System. In addition, SUNY operates five statutory degree programs through the auspices of otherwise independent universities. The New York State Colleges of Agriculture and Life Sciences, Human Ecology, Industrial and Labor Relations, and the College of Veterinary Medicine are located on the campus of Cornell University. The New York State College of Ceramics is located on the campus of Alfred University.

Finally, Alfred may be the one of the smallest truly comprehensive universities in the nation, certainly feeling much more like a residential college than a university. Similarly, the 2000 students at Alfred have the opportunity to study in the College of Liberal Arts, the College of Art and Design, the College of Ceramics, the College of Business, and the Inamori College of Engineering. There is also a very small graduate program on campus as well.

The Ceramics program put Alfred on the map for some students, and it has brought a remarkable legacy to the university. Established in 1900, Alfred's programs in ceramic art and ceramic engineering set the standard for ceramic education in the U.S. By 1948, the college had established a graduate program, offering the MFA in ceramic arts.

So, there is a rich tradition of ceramic art at Alfred, well represented in one of the nation's most highly reputed collection, the Schein-Joseph International Museum of Ceramic Art. As a result, Alfred attracts some fairly accomplished artsy types.

However, there is an entirely different strain of ceramic adventure also well established at Alfred – the New York State Center for Advanced Ceramic Technology (CACT), a world-renowned center for research into ceramic and glass science. For example, Alfred is the only university in the country offering a Ph.D. in glass science.

As the Center puts it, "*The focus at Alfred University's CACT is advanced ceramic materials and processing, which include electronic ceramics... high-temperature structural ceramics... photonic ceramics and glasses... bioceramics and glasses... whitewares... advanced manufacturing processes, including nanostructured processing capabilities... computer modeling and simulation... and electromagnetic processing.*"

When NASA needs help in figuring out how to build a nosecone that doesn't flame out on reentry, whom do they call? Alfred!

Obviously, then, the single most popular major at Alfred is in the Fine Arts, with Engineering second, followed by Therapy and Counseling, Business, and Education.

Ok, Alfred attracts artists, scientists, and ordinary college kids to a lovely campus in a lovely town. The admissions office at Alfred puts it best: *"At Alfred University, we know our students are our greatest asset. They are talented, active, involved and just a little bit quirky. And we like that!"* They surely do, because the mix of students is as interesting as the mix of academic offerings and equally impressive. Would it surprise you to know that the university offers tours of campus on a seven-person bicycle?

Alfred has recently popped up in several publications as one of the "best buys" in college education. The total cost including tuition, room and board for the past year was about $31,000.00 for everyone except the NY State residents in the State College of Art and Design. That's at least $10,000.00 lower than most comparable institutions, especially those offering an average class size of about 18 students.

Finally, Alfred is named after King Alfred the Great, British king of legend. You may not be familiar with Alfred, but to those in the know, Alfred is perhaps the king most closely connected with issues of intellect. The statue of Alfred reminds students and visitors of the king's attainments, best described in the inscription of his statue in England:

> *"Alfred found learning dead, and he restored it. Education neglected, and he revived it. The laws powerless, and he gave them force. The Church debased, and he raised it. The land ravaged by a fearful enemy, from which he delivered it. Alfred's name will live as long as mankind shall respect the past."*

Thus, Alfred's teams are the Saxons, and most of those teams are what you would expect to find at a small university – baseball, football, basketball, soccer, lacrosse, swimming, cross country. The Saxons often emerge as one of the contenders for a national title in Division III football, playing against colleges that are larger than this university. Recently, the duties of Alfred's mascots have been divided between a thoroughly regal mounted Alfred The Great and his steed, Alden, and L'il Alf, a pudgy quasi-Saxon with cheerful bravado.

The quirk in this athletic program is in the competitive equestrian teams. Not only are they coeducational, they also compete in both English and

Western equestrian events. Horse lovers should also note that the university's excellent equestrian center provides instructional space for the academic classes in Equine Science. An Equine Science minor is available and includes courses in riding, equitation theory, and draft horse driving.

Finally, the university offers a major in Athletic Training with a minor in Exercise Science.

Hartwick College - Oneonta, New York

Hartwick is a happy college of about 1500 men and women, grounded in the liberal arts, but also providing very strong programs in nursing, biological sciences, and environmental sciences. The ways in which colleges describe themselves is often more smoke than substance, but in Hartwick's case, its intentions are borne out by its many fine programs and by its consistent support of its essential principles.

And the stats... 2015

Number of Applicants: 5,036/ 90% Accepted
Undergrad Enrollment: 1540   61% female / 39% male
Avg. SAT: not reported Avg. ACT: not reported
Total Cost: $52,270.00.
Received some form of financial assistance: 100%

If you haven't heard much about Oneonta, New York, you haven't made the pilgrimage to the National Baseball Hall of Fame in Cooperstown, or to the International Boxing Hall of Fame in Canastota, or the Herkimer Diamond Mines in Herkimer. If you have explored the area, you've been in what is known as the "Leatherstocking Region," of New York State, just north of the Catskill Mountains, and near Oneonta, a village of about 13,000 roughly 250 miles north of New York City. The term, "Leatherstocking Region," comes from the stories of James Fenimore Cooper, whose home was, oddly enough, in Cooperstown, and whose focus was often on the region described in his "Leatherstocking Tales."

The region is beautiful; Oneonta means, "city of hills," and the setting for a college town could hardly be more pleasant. The campus is literally built into the side of one of the hills and enjoys a panoramic view of the Susquehanna River Valley. Should the exceptional campus not provide scenic richness enough, an extraordinary resource is found at their Pine Lake Environmental campus, about eight miles out of town.

Hartwick is a happy college of about 1500 men and women, grounded in the liberal arts, but also providing very strong programs in nursing, biological sciences, and environmental sciences. The ways in which colleges describe themselves is often more smoke than substance, but in Hartwick's case, its intentions are borne out by its many fine programs and by its consistent support of its essential principles.

The first of these is independent learning. While Hartwick is by no means experimental or quirky in its academic program, it does emphasize at least three significant programs that make a difference in the way in which a student experiences his or her education. The most innovative of Hartwick's new programs is the Three Year Bachelor's Degree. The idea of completing an undergraduate career in three years may be attractive in terms of cost, but the greater advantage may be in the ways in which the program is structured. Attending to what the college calls, "The Liberal Arts in Practice Curriculum", the program combines traditional study in the liberal arts with experiential learning, including study abroad, internships, and service learning.

Hartwick students are encouraged to travel widely, and almost 60% will take the opportunity to study abroad in a program supported by the college. That's a high percentage and testimony to the competence its students feel in moving outside of the comfort zone established in cozy Oneonta. The emphasis on study abroad is directly related to Hartwick's commitment to promoting an awareness of "interdependence," of nations, of cultures, of individuals. Hartwick is rated among the top ten colleges in the nation in the percentage of students who study abroad.

More particular to Hartwick is the notion of collaborative research at the undergraduate level. The college supports a number of centers and programs that allow unusual collaboration between students and faculty from the start of the Hartwick experience.

The Pine Lake Environmental Center is both a woodlands classroom and a residential option.

Students can undertake original hands-on research in such areas as: Conservation Biology/Ornithology, Microbial Communities, Steam Ecology Research, and Entomological Taxonomy…. whew!

About 30 students a year elect to live at Pine Lake as well, in a rustic cabin or farmhouse. The research done at Pine Lake is done independently under the tutelage of a professor expert in one of the fields identified above.

Ok, there's actually one more center that will be of interest to all who cherish amphibians. Hartwick maintains the Amphibian Research Laboratory (ARL) allowing collaborative research in a number of areas of amphibian biology.

The environmental and natural sciences do rock at Hartwick, but equally active collaboration exists across the board. Recent examples of work done in preparation for the senior thesis, for example, include research on digital photography, an investigation into Caroline theater, archeological research on the steppes of Russia, and an examination of the role of women in political leadership positions.

Another significant aspect of academic and social life at Hartwick is the 4 - 1 - 4 plan. A student takes four courses in the fall, four in the spring, and in January select an intensive course or internship in a specialized program of their choice. This "Jan Plan" allows a great deal of flexibility in curriculum and further supports the interdependence of academic and real world education. Some recent off-campus January Plan options have included: "Doing Business in China", "Sacred Space in America - Washington, DC, Gettysburg, New York City," "People and Plants of Thailand." Options on campus have included: "Theater Production Workshop," "Life's Choices: Ethical Dilemmas," and LEGO Robotics Production."

I am going out of my way to describe the rich academic opportunities at Hartwick because the college is too often overlooked when considering liberal arts alternatives in the East, but please do not think Hartwick is a "grind" or an ivory tower intellectual hothouse. Hartwick's students are outgoing, athletic, socially active, and happy. The college's roots go back to 1797, and this small college continues to attract very nice kids who like the outdoors, sports, and their college.

The Hartwick "Hawks" play a Division III schedule, with particular success in swimming and diving, lacrosse, and volleyball. The casual (or serious) visitor to the Hartwick athletic website, however, might well miss the remarkable history of men's soccer at Hartwick College.

Most soccer fans are aware of the Division I soccer powerhouses; for the most part they are large universities - Indiana, UCLA, UC Santa Barbara, North Carolina, Connecticut. A few mid sized teams have snuck in - Stanford and Santa Clara. But the smallest college to win a national championship in the modern era is tiny Hartwick. The Hawks continue to play an ambitious Division I schedule; they open on the road at Penn State.

Soccer has only recently crept into the public eye; for years it was primarily found in the East and in a few cities - St. Louis, for example, and San Francisco. It is a tribute to the long legacy of superior soccer at Hartwick that the National Soccer Hall of Fame is located in Oneonta.

It is a tribute to the balance of academics, social life, and athletics at Hartwick that soccer is not the tail wagging the dog.

The "Leatherstocking" thing may be a bit peculiar for a high school senior starting the college search, but Oneonta is a lovely college town, and Hartwick a very good option for the student of ambition who has not yet broken into the top ranks of academic competition.

The Culinary Institute - Hyde Park, New York

A central part of the CIA experience is the extended placement in a recognized restaurant or winery, with a semester's work at one of the satellite campuses and the selection of a concentration (major) in American Food Studies: Farm-to-Table Cooking; Advanced Wine, Beverage, and Hospitality; or Latin Cuisines.

And the stats... 2015

Number of Applicants: 2.778/ 64% Accepted
Undergrad Enrollment: 537   48% female / 52%% male
The admissions process is notably different at CIA. A high school diploma or GED is required; as are letters of recommendation, and certain standardized tests may be used in placing students in classes. The major difference is that an applicant must complete at least six months working in a professional kitchen (not a fast-food restaurant!) unless the applicant has already completed culinary classes elsewhere.

Total Cost: $42,947.00
Received some form of financial assistance: 98%

"Food is Life" - motto of the Culinary Institute of America

"Almost every profession has an outstanding training ground. The military has West Point, music has Juilliard, and the culinary arts has The Institute." —Craig Claiborne, Celebrated Author and Food Critic, The New York

Many of us have become "Foodies"; we scan the food channels to watch the greatest chefs in the world prepare meals most of us will never taste. As culinary skill has become more widely appreciated, one institution has emerged as the oldest and most celebrated of the culinary colleges. Familiarly known as the CIA, this remarkable institution continues to attract aspiring chefs from across the country and around the world. For those who want something like a collegiate experience in the midst of world-renowned preparation for careers in culinary arts, the Hyde Park campus – the original campus – will offer more than imagination can summon. The CIA has satellite facilities in St. Helena (Napa Valley), California, San Antonio, Texas, and Singapore, and each of these locations offers a particular sort of culinary training, but the mother ship is in Hyde Park, in New York's Hudson Valley, although it was in New Haven,

Connecticut, in 1946, that education in the culinary arts took a new direction.

Established as the New Haven Restaurant Institute, the first mission of the Institute was "the elevation of the profession", a goal born of the recognition that professional chefs in the United States lacked the opportunities for apprenticeship that existed in Europe. From humble beginnings in New Haven to the relocation of the growing institute to the campus in Hyde Park (a former Jesuit retreat), the emphasis at the start was to bring the profession to the highest level of quality, and the start, that meant learning the secrets of the best chefs in Europe, and that meant chefs from France. It is no surprise that the CIA's Leadership awards, given to chefs who have truly elevated the profession, are called the "Auggies", named for celebrated French chef, Auguste Escoffier. The first courses set out to bring the tradition of fine European dining to an American palette. Today, of course, the Institute recognizes the quality of cuisine from around the world.

There are other strong programs in the culinary arts in the United States (Paul Smith's College in New York and Rhode Island's Johnson and Wales University are profiled in this book), but the CIA is unique in its emphasis on Culinary Arts rather than extending degrees in the wide range of courses associated with the management of restaurants, hotels, resorts, and food services in what is known as the "hospitality industry". At the Hyde Park campus, a student can earn the BPS, Bachelor of Professional Studies, in Culinary Arts Management, Baking and Pastry Management, or Culinary Science. Although the emphasis is clearly on things culinary, starting in the junior year, after earning the Associate degree in Culinary Arts, the bachelor's degree also requires course work in a central curriculum, including courses such as: Financial Accounting, Literature and Composition, Math or Science, Foreign Language, Economics, Marketing and Promoting Food, Human Resource Management, and Social Science.

Hyde Park's facilities include several restaurants, each presenting a particular culinary tradition or emphasis. I confess myself most fond of the Apple Pie Bakery, where the savory dishes include soups and salads, the breakfast pastries include Pain au Chocolate (Yum!), Cinnamon Raisin Danishes, and the Salted Caramel and Coconut Doughnut, a Brioche doughnut with caramel glaze and shredded coconut. The dessert menu includes Chocolate Mousse, Strawberry Religieuse (Strawberry and pistachio pastry cream with dragee chips, and the Chocolate Rum Cannele Bordelaise. Named for famous French Chef, Paul Bocuse, Hyde Park's Bocuse is an elegant French restaurant, famed for a number of dishes, starting with the Black Truffle Soup VGE (with vegetables). Locovores will seek out the American Bounty Restaurant, featuring locally grown and harvested food. The dinner menu includes Hudson Valley Moulard Duck

Breast, English Pea, Fava Bean, Spring Onion Risotto, and Beer Braised Beef.

A central part of the CIA experience is the extended placement in a recognized restaurant or winery, with a semester's work at one of the satellite campuses and the selection of a concentration (major) in American Food Studies: Farm-to-Table Cooking; Advanced Wine, Beverage, and Hospitality; or Latin Cuisines.

The Advanced Wine, Beverage, and Hospitality concentration calls the student from Hyde Park to "Greystone", in St. Helena, in the heart of the Napa Valley wine world. Formerly Greystone Cellars, operated by Christian Brothers, the main building, included in the National register of Historic Places, contains teaching kitchens, The Wine Spectator Restaurant, The Bakery Cafe by illy, The Conservatory Restaurant, the De Baun Theater, and the Spice Island Marketplace. Outbuildings include the Rudd Center for Professional Wine Studies, The Williams Center for Flavor Discovery, and the Ventura Center for Menu Research and Development. Visitors might enjoy stopping in at the Spice Island Marketplace; the shopping is extraordinary, and the Flavor Bar allows civilians to try the tasting exercises thrown at aspiring chefs.

Latin Cuisines will take the student to San Antonio, Texas. Located in the Pearl Brewery (an up-scale development adjacent to San Antonio's River Walk), the Center for Foods of the Americas explores the cuisine of Mexico, Brazil, Peru, Central America, and the Caribbean. Visitors to the Center are particularly taken with the CIA Bakery Cafe, which features pastry dishes from Latin America, Central America, and Mexico.

OK, so the culinary part seems pretty nearly irresistible… and campus life?

The Hyde Park campus does a good job of replicating the college experience, complete with Student Government, intramural and recreational sports, fitness, clubs, and very healthy residential life. Students can choose from a number of housing options – one of four residential halls housing from 230 to 280 students, six Adirondack style lodges (generally given to about 400 upper class students) grouped around a village green, and townhouses, accommodating eight students in single rooms. Each of the residence halls has a full time residential director living in the hall and organizing activities for its students. No surprise – each residence has a fully operational kitchen. All utilities, wireless, laundry, are provided, and a number of meal plans make dining on campus relatively delicious.

The SGA sponsors and funds student activities and entertainment, while SPICE (Student Programming Igniting Campus Events) plans most activities. The student newspaper, La Papillote (the method of cooking in parchment), is published every three weeks, and keeps track of issues that affect the profession and the campus. Clubs include: The Bacchus Wine Society, Baking and Pastry Arts Society, Black Culinary Society, Culinary Christian Fellowship, Gay Straight Alliance, the Gourmet Society, Women Chefs and Restaurateurs. The Student Recreation center includes a gymnasium with two basketball courts, a six-lane swimming pool, a sauna, racquetball courts, a fitness center, and various exercise and weight rooms. Natural turf fields and the tennis courts are used for outdoor sports. CIA competes in the Hudson Valley Athletic Conference in soccer, cross-country, basketball, tennis, and volleyball. Fitness classes include Pilates, Zumba, and yoga; intramural sports run throughout the year. Special competitions include billiards and floor hockey.

The New School - New York, New York

Eugene Lang College for Liberal Arts - New York, New York

The history of The New School is the history of progressive education in the United States.

And the stats... 2015

Number of Applicants: 5,662/ 66% Accepted
Undergrad Enrollment: 6,940 72% female / 28% male
Avg. SAT Reading Comp 500-620 / Math 490-620 Avg. ACT: 22-27
Total Cost: $62,315.00.
Received some form of financial assistance: 96%

What legendary institution not only claims Woody Allen, Reinhold Niebuhr, Marlon Brando Margaret Mead, and Tim Gunn among its luminary number, but also offers quality instruction in the liberal arts, a seminar experience, and residential options in a metropolitan setting?

Yup, The New School.

The New School is a university, enrolling more than six thousand undergraduates in seven prominent divisions: Eugene Lang College - The New School for Liberal Arts, The New School for Social Research, Parsons-The New School for Design, The New School for Public Engagement, Mannes College - The New School for Music, The New School for Drama, and The New School for Jazz and Contemporary Music.

A quick look at the programs and majors would entice the truly adventurous student in search of a stimulating curriculum; the further advantage of meeting that curriculum in the heart of Greenwich Village might be almost impossibly attractive. In fact, although The New School has been a significant force in American education since its founding in 1919, it is only since the creation of a distinct undergraduate program in the liberal arts - with a full-scale residential program - that The New School has emerged as a reasonable option for students from any state or region.

The history of The New School is the history of progressive education. The idea at the start was to offer affordable and accessible interesting coursework to working adults. A band of extraordinary professors from Columbia University, in response to the "Red Scare" that swept the U.S. after World War I, established a university in which they could teach without fear of prosecution for their convictions. From the start, The New School has attracted lively and challenging voices, often the most distinctive intellectual minds of their time: Hannah Arendt -the political theorist who posited the notion of the banality of evil and the author of The Origins of Totalitarianism, Franz Boas – considered to have pioneered the study of anthropology in the United States, Frank Lloyd Wright, William F. Buckley, Jr., Thorsten Veblen, Reinhold Niebuhr, Margaret Mead, Betty Friedan, John Cage, Woody Allen, and John Cage, to name a few. Its non-degree programs were adapted in 1933 as a graduate division, The University in Exile, was established in order to offer sanctuary to professors fleeing fascist Italy and Germany. Today, The New School for Public Engagement offers undergraduate and graduate coursework for those who seek continuing education. In the 1940s, the Dramatic Workshop, brought Stella Adler and Elia Kazan to The New School and provided the impetus for the creation of The New School for Drama. Students in its infancy included Brando, Tennessee Williams, and Rod Steiger. Parsons School of Design had a distinguished history as the first institution to offer a degree program in Fashion Design, Interior Design, Advertising, and Graphic Design. Its association with The New School began in 1970. The New School for Social Research carries on the tradition of graduate education in the social sciences. Similarly, The Mannes College of Music was an esteemed conservatory before joining with The New School in 1989. The New School for Jazz and Contemporary Music had already been established in 1986, allowing an uncommon range of study for a student interested in a performance or composition based degree in Music.

Whew! That's a ton of hyper-intellectual, slightly radicalized, Euro-Manhattan legacy to have to live up to! On the other hand, Lower Manhattan, and Greenwich Village in particular, is exactly the right setting for the rich swirl of ideas and sensibilities a place like the New School can offer. Yes, there are programs of considerable reputation, and yes, there are teachers with professional clout, but the remarkable opportunity The New School offers an undergraduate is total immersion in a culture of intense and ardent commitment to the life of the mind.

The various component programs are world-class, and I think I can assume that anyone interested in fashion or interior design already has Parsons at the top of the list. Similarly, Mannes and the Jazz and Contemporary Music schools self-select. The most under-regarded and most commonly misunderstood program is that offered by Eugene Lang College The New School For Liberal Arts, and it is with that college that the profile begins.

There are several particular characteristics of the program at Lang that any prospective freshperson ought to consider. The first, of course, is that Lang is a college dedicated to discussion in a seminar setting. The seminars begin with the first classes and continue through the course of the entire four years. Happily, the seminars are facilitated by professors who find the prospect of sitting at a table with eager undergraduates the most alluring of professional options. Look, a seminar is only as good as the participants who make it up, and any seminar has good days and less good days, but Lang's professors are smart, smart, smart and eager to get into it with the students in their care. Recently, Lang has required all students to take at least two lecture courses in their four-year career. Some purists are appalled, but, really? Two lecture courses? This is a seminar college.

Although comparison might be made between NYU and Lang (Greenwich Village), the truth is that Lang is actually a far less constraining college than NYU and most other colleges. Perhaps a better comparison, in terms of requirement, might be Brown. There are only a few required courses and no strictures that prevent a student from following his or her interests. There are requirements, of course, in earning a degree, but they are reasonable. Students are required to take Five required foundation courses: Writing the Essay 1, Writing the Essay 2, First Year Workshop, First-Year Advising Seminar, and Reading NYC, and, as noted earlier, two University Lecture (ULEC) courses. Yes, they are required. No, they are not onerous.

Lang seeks independent learners, and their widely varied curriculum and the number of degree options, while attractive to the independent learner, are also indicative of Lang's somewhat under-organized administrative structure. Big Brother is not hounding students to get registration done on time, and some of the facilities that are at the heart of instructional programs elsewhere (libraries) are hardly visible; it takes a bit of resilience to manage the Lang experience.

Lang began as an experimental college and has really only operated as a fully residential undergraduate institution since 1985. NYU is the big dog around the corner, and there are those who still feel that Parsons is the division of The New School that gets all the press; Tim Gunn, Heidi Klum, and Project Runway took Parsons to the masses and brought celebrity to its students. The truth, however, is that while all the divisions are hopping, Lang is emerging as one of the two or three most powerful undergraduate writing programs in the country. The Literature and Writing major is an impressive and demanding major at Lang, and one that is attracting students who seek the college for that opportunity rather than looking for the New York Experience. Those who choose the writing track will begin in the first year, ordinarily identifying the genre (Fiction, Poetry, Non-Fiction, Journalism) they intend to take on. Fiction in particular has gained considerable reputation, but all the genres offer the best students a seminar in writing for publication. The student interested in writing for the stage can find that opportunity in the Arts major, which includes Dance, Music, and Visual Arts, as well as Theater.

I don't know another college that offers students the opportunity to major in Liberal Arts (OK, maybe Evergreen State - take a look at that profile). This is the major that most completely reflects the experimental impulse that brought Eugene Lang College into being. Self-reflective, self-initiated, self-designed, the major in the Liberal Arts is all about enlightenment and broad self-education. The only downside that I can see is that majors in Liberal Arts can't double major, as a number of Lang students choose to do.

Outside of the classroom, the residential and social realities are probably not unexpected:

Hipsters abound, most smoke, and there are those who posture in and outside of the seminar rooms.

The dorms are more than adequate, but residential prices in NYC are bound to be higher than those in Iowa. My guess is that almost all freshmen live in student housing and about a quarter of the rest of the undergraduates stay within the college's residential system. There is something like a freshman residence - Stuyvesant Park Residence, a twelve-story suite-style building on East 15th Street. The 650 residents may attend any of the divisions, so a Lang freshperson might well live in a suite next to a group of Parsons freshpersons. The other residential building house somewhat smaller numbers, and each has its own attractive characteristics. 20th Street residence Hall, for example, is in the Chelsea district, cheek by jowl with galleries, lofts, cafes, and bistros.

No frats, no big-time sports, a complicated and spread-out constellation of divisions - social life requires just as much independent initiative as participation in the seminars. The college is aware of its limitations in terms of student-services, but chooses to remain true to its founding mission; there won't be a lot of institutional money thrown at lavish student recreational facilities or spas. The city is a playground, from the college's point of view, and it is hard to argue that virtually any kind of interest or enterprise is further than a twenty-minute subway ride away. In describing the social scene at Lang, the admissions office is delicate:

> "Nothing constrains what you do, where you go, who you are. There are so many groups to support your interests, so many places to find culture, art, politics, even sports. Contrary to reports that your classmates are the country's leading dodgeball targets, last year many of them played fierce games of volleyball and basketball. Not exactly wimpy activity."

Not exactly fierce either, but the point is that lots of colleges have sports and very few have Manhattan.

Smart and independent, on their own in New York City – some young people are going to find the challenge more than they want to take on. Lang is not for everyone, but if you are one who thinks it might be fun to battle in a seminar then walk to a magical used magazine shop on the corner of Sixth Avenue and 11th Street, wander through the floor-to-ceiling stacks of obscure magazines, and retreat to a street-side cafe with a brioche and a cup of real espresso... The New School and Eugene Lang might be just right for you.

The Middle Atlantic States

The Middle Atlantic states are defined by three notable cities, Philadelphia, Baltimore, and Washington, D.C., although the region attaches itself to several other cultural regions of note.

To the west, Pennsylvania borders on the Ohio Valley, and is midwestern and Appalachian in its sensibilities. Maryland abuts Virginia and West Virginia and is simultaneously kin to Southern, Northeastern, and Appalachian mind-sets.

Virginia is often included in the Middle Atlantic region, and suburban Washington, D.C. is clearly Middle Atlantic in its attitudes, but regions south of the "Beltway" quickly reflect a different past and sensibility. Charlottesville, for example, is 150 miles south of Washington and 70 miles north of Richmond; it is more Richmond than Washington and has all the charm and history of a southern city.

Metropolitan New York has its own distinctive character, but it is also a coastal entrepot, a trading city on the Atlantic, and as such, participates in the Atlantic metroplex, an urban span reaching from the Potomac to the Hudson. There are suburban interruptions and a few odd patches of open land, but the character of work and play remains fairly constant within the range.

The first of the Middle Atlantic states is New Jersey, currently "celebrated" in a series of "reality" television shows that emphasize the outrageous excesses of hedonistic, lightly educated, apparently soulless, well-tanned, childish oafs.

In the real world, New Jersey may be among the most complicated of states. New Jersey has the highest percentage of millionaire residents per capita and the second highest median income of any state in the nation. On the other hand, several New Jersey cities are notably below the poverty line and among the most desperately devastated by unemployment, drug addiction, and crime. Alpine, New Jersey in Bergen County is tied with Greenwich, Connecticut as the most expensive zip code in the United States; Camden, near Philadelphia is the most dangerous city in the United States.

New Jersey's Ivy, Princeton is located in Princeton, a movie-set town about halfway between New York and Philadelphia. Rutgers, the State University of New Jersey is in New Brunswick, about thirty minutes south of Manhattan. Rutgers and Princeton played in the first intercollegiate football game. Played in eighteen sixty-nine, the game see-sawed back and forth until Rutgers took the victory, six to four.

Rider University, enrolling about five thousand students, offers a strong program in Business and is located in Lawrenceville, a charming town adjacent to Princeton.

Seton Hall (Go, Pirates!) is a private Catholic university with outstanding programs in Business, Education, and Nursing. The university is located in South Orange, New Jersey, a suburb of New York and one of the few remaining municipalities to still use gas lit street lamps. Seton Hall is a basketball powerhouse.

Stevens Institute of Technology is an outstanding engineering school, site of three national Centers of Excellence and widely regarded for its programs in Technology Management. Stevens is located in Hoboken, part of New Jersey's Gold Coast, just across the Hudson from Manhattan.

Pennsylvania, too, is a complicated entity. Perhaps the best way to identify the personalities of this large state is to present its four largest cities: Philadelphia, Pittsburgh, Allentown, and Erie. Its capital is Harrisburg, located about a hundred miles northwest of Philadelphia. This part of Pennsylvania is also known as the Pennsylvania Dutch region, and with Lancaster, Harrisburg is at the center. In this region, the visitor will find a number of notable colleges and universities, including: Franklin and Marshall College, Gettysburg College, Dickinson College, and York College. Also in Central Pennsylvania (not far from Hershey Park!) is Bucknell University, home of the Bucky the Bison and Juniata College, profiled in this book.

Philadelphia is completely Middle Atlantic. The Philadelphia area is rich with post-secondary options, including: The University of Pennsylvania, Temple University, Swarthmore College, Haverford College, Bryn Mawr University, Villanova University, and Drexel University.

Pittsburgh is the largest city in Appalachia, about 45 miles from Wheeling, West Virginia. It is an Ohio Valley city, part of Virginia until the Mason Dixon Line was drawn. Three colleges are located in Pittsburgh - Carnegie-Mellon, the University of Pittsburgh, and Chatham University. Carnegie-Mellon is one of the most celebrated comprehensive universities in the country with strengths in many fields, including Architecture, Computer Engineering and Musical Theater. The University of Pittsburgh is a state-related university of about twenty-eight thousand in the university district of Pittsburgh. Chatham is a women's college at the undergraduate level and co-ed at the graduate level. Washington and Jefferson College is located in Washington, just west of Pittsburgh.

Allentown with a population of about 100,000 is the largest of the cities that mark the Lehigh Valley; the others are Bethlehem and Easton; this is steel country. The city is about 60 miles north of Philadelphia, 80 miles east of Harrisburg, and 90 miles west of New York. Its claim to fame? The Mack Truck. Allentown is a blue collar working class small city with a German heritage. Muhlenberg College, a private liberal arts college in Allentown with an excellent reputation in the sciences; Muhlenberg enrolls about twenty-two hundred students. Neighboring Bethlehem is the location of Lehigh University, noted for programs in Engineering and Business as well as the Liberal Arts. Easton, about mid-way between New York and Philadelphia, is the site of Lafayette College, one of the smallest (twenty-three hundred) in NCAA's Division I.

Erie currently has a population of about 100,000 and is part of the "Rust Belt", a string of cities from Detroit to Buffalo. A casino has helped bring tourists to Erie, as has the Presque Isle National Park. Erie is also known for the "lake snow effect" that dumps snow on the city. Allegheny College (Go, Alligators!), profiled in this book, is located in Meadville, about forty miles south of Erie.

So, that's Pennsylvania, except for the legacy of Amish and Quaker history, the first oil wells in the country, steel production, and extensive coal mining. Oh, and the nation's top production of mushrooms.

Maryland has the nickname, "America in miniature," because its landscape is so completely varied. Colleges and universities within the state are equally varied. The U.S. Naval Academy is in Annapolis, on the Severn River and Chesapeake Bay. St. John's College, a Great Books college, is also in Annapolis. The public institutions include the University of Maryland in College Park, Salisbury University in Salisbury, and the state's public Liberal Arts college, Saint Mary's, in Saint Mary's.
The Chesapeake Bay almost cuts the state in half; the "Eastern Shore" has attempted to secede from the state on several occasions and remains resolutely its own culture, born of wetlands and the largest estuary in the United States.

Baltimore is an "independent city," governmentally separate from Baltimore County, a seaport, and a city of neighborhoods. Johns Hopkins University is in Baltimore; Goucher College, profiled in this book, is in suburban Towson, and McDaniel is in Westminster. . Washington College, also profiled in this book, is in Chestertown, on Maryland's Eastern Shore. Hood College is in Frederick, in north-central Maryland.

The Washington-Baltimore Metropolitan area, including counties in Central Maryland and Northern Virginia, is the most educated and highest income statistical area in the United States.

Western Maryland, just south of the Mason-Dixon Line, is rural, agricultural, and attached to Appalachia. The only ski area in the state is found in Western Maryland, and the winter is harsher in the western portion of the state.

Drew University - Madison, New Jersey

Drew's academic program is uniformly sound, but there are three areas in which it is notable: Political Science, Theater, and off-campus programs, such as the Wall Street Program and the United Nations Program.

And the stats... 2015

Number of Applicants: 3,417/ 70% Accepted
Undergrad Enrollment: 537 62% female / 38% male
Avg. SAT Reading Comp 500-620 / Math 500-6000 Avg. ACT: 22-28
Total Cost: $61,106.00.
Received some form of financial assistance: 98%

Lots of college counselors all over the country know and love Drew.

What's not to love? Drew is a strong small liberal arts college of about 1700 undergraduates (the university includes a graduate program and a theological school) located on a wooded campus, about 15 miles from New York City. There simply are not very many good small liberal arts colleges located in a handsome setting virtually minutes from a major urban area. Drew is good enough in its own right, but its location is certainly enticing.

Madison, New Jersey is an historic and picturesque town of about 16,000, frequently featured as backdrop or setting on television programs or in films, as is the university. The Sopranos visited Drew on their college trip, and Alicia Keyes used the university in her video, "Teenage Love Affair." When The Daily Show did a "back-to-school" special, it filmed at Drew, and Friday Night Lights featured several of Drew's dormitories in an episode about New York. The Pocono Mountains and Jersey Shore are both within reach, and the college has long been recognized for its excellence in theater and the liberal arts.

And, for my money, students at Drew have the best nickname by far - "The Drewids." Their actual mascot name is "The Rangers," but who could ignore a pack of rabid Drewids? The Rangers (cough) play in Division III. the Landmark Conference, and I'll be turning to two other Landmark colleges as we move through the Middle Atlantic States - Juniata and Goucher.

Academically, there's a lot to like about Drew. Equally impressive are the many events and activities that enliven this campus; this is a college that hums on weekends as well as the academic week. Although almost any specific interest is represented by a club or group, two well-established activities are worthy of particular note. The Abuntu-Pan African Choir brings the diverse music of the African continent to the campus throughout the year. The Drew Rugby Football Club has been getting down and dirty since 1962, recently celebrating their fiftieth anniversary.

Drew was founded as a Methodist college. Most institutions founded before the Civil War were attached to one denomination or another. It is important to recognize that Drew's continued association with the United Methodist Church is largely limited to the governance of the Drew Theological School and the Graduate Division of Religion. A separate graduate school, The Casperson School of Graduate Studies offers humanities based graduate degrees and the M.A.T. There is no liturgical baggage in the undergraduate college, and the benefit of world-class scholars has notably advanced the fields of philosophy and history at the undergraduate level.

Drew's academic program is uniformly sound, but there are three areas in which it is notable: Political Science, Theater, and off-campus programs, such as the Wall Street Program and the United Nations Program.

Political Science is always among the most popular majors, along with Economics and Psychology. Classes at Drew are small and professors close at hand. Even though Drew is a university, there are no teaching assistants in the College of Liberal Arts.

Tom Kean, former Governor of New Jersey, was President of the university for fifteen years, during which time Drew became increasingly connected with political initiatives at the national level. Close relationships with the Clinton and Bush presidencies and Kean's continued involvement with the National Endowment for Democracy brought considerable attention to Drew, as did Kean's appointment as the head of the September 11 Commission, investigating the terrorist attacks of 9/11.

Enormously popular on campus, Kean built exceptional programs in Political Science and Government and began the process of organizing a program in Business. The Athletic Center and the Young Center for the Arts were completed during his presidency.

Drew's later president, Bob Wesibuch, has brought a number of other initiatives to the college, including a program in Business Studies, a program in Environmental Studies and Sustainability, and an Honors Program. Merit Scholarship support of applicants who have shown a capacity for leadership and who have been active in community service is also an indication of Drew's continuing commitment to sustaining a college of character. Current president, Dr. MaryAnn Baenninger has invigorated Drew's commitment to social justice and civic engagement.

The two signature off-campus programs at Drew – the Wall Street Program and the United Nations Program are exceptional opportunities for an undergraduate to spend an entire semester immersed in the heart of the financial district or in close contact with the Secretariat and NGOs at the UN. An additional program – the Semester in New York on Contemporary Art – includes an internship at the Guggenheim, Whitney, or Museum for Contemporary Art.

The Dorothy Young Center for the Arts boasts excellent facilities for the college's theater program, and was identified by the Princeton Review as the number one college theater. The program in Theater Arts is highly reputed and attracts excellent actors for several obvious reasons, at least two of which have to do with proximity to New York City –the availability of theater professionals who can teach and remain active in the city and the availability of internships and auditions on and off Broadway. A third incentive is the very attractive scholarships given to prospective theater majors. The Dance minor is also active and well regarded.

I'll take leave of the academic picture in a moment, but I do want to recognize the unusual programs available at Drew, truly unusual in a liberal arts setting of this size.

Major programs include the usual arts and sciences and: Biological Anthropology, Neurosciences, Pan-African Studies, and Women's and Gender Studies.

Minor programs include: Archeology, Arts Administration and Museology, Holocaust Studies, Jewish Studies, Linguistic Studies, Public Health, and Russian.

In addition to some uncommon and very good academic opportunities, Drew is a handsome campus, wooded and verdant. There are a number of truly pleasing vistas and really pretty common space. For the aesthetically minded, Drew will look exactly like what a liberal arts college is supposed to look like, and its students will come pretty close to fitting that bill as well.

There are no fraternities or sororities at Drew, but there are the usual sub strata of personalities and types. It should come as no surprise that a college with the emphasis that Drew places on theater would have a fair number of "theatrical" kids, in whatever meaning you care to take of that term. They will join the other sub groups – jocks, princesses, preps, intellectuals, entrepreneurs, world peaceniks – in a remarkably happy mix.

One hallmark of a strong college community is the regard with which students hold each other's accomplishments. Students at Drew support actors, the a cappella singers, dancers, athletes, writers, and politicos. When Drew offers the opportunity to study Sudanese exiles in Egypt, through a course entitled Faith and Exile, enrollment is packed.

Equally telling is the strength of feeling that "Drewids" have about their campus. They appreciate having a cute village such as Madison at their doorstep, and New York is always nifty, but they especially treasure their Spirituality Garden, the Magnolia trees by stately Tilghman House, regal Bowne Hall, the Black Box Theater, the Chapel, and the courtyard in front of Brothers College.

Drew's radio station is excellent, music is hopping, and Drew's great coffee shop, "The Other End," looks like a set for a 1950's beatnik cafe.

Ok, if Drew is so great, you ask, and so close to New York, and so pretty, why isn't it one of the "hot" colleges?

I'm not sure, but I think part of the issue has to do with its location. Unlike some of the New England colleges that are all tucked together in a cozy collegiate leaf pile, or the ruggedly isolated outliers on the fringe of northern territories, Drew is the only school of its type in what can appear to be a commuting suburb.

Also, it doesn't help to be close to Princeton.

One of the important changes of the Keane years was that the university began to shed its inferiority complex. The good news for you is that admission is not a brutal gauntlet; the bad news for Drew is that while some students seek out its exciting opportunities, others land there by default. It wasn't long ago that the same might have been said about students at Tufts or NYU, both institutions that have more than enough clout these days. Astounding as it is that Drew has remained under-appreciated, this is one college bound to be "discovered" soon.

Juniata College - Huntingdon, Pennsylvania

Juniata is a real college with real college kids who laugh and frolic as college kids are meant to do. It's not a frat house kind of school, and there is a seriousness of purpose about the place and its students, but the community is warm, inviting, and particularly rich in the traditions it celebrates.

And the stats... 2015

Number of Applicants: 2,207/ 74% Accepted
Undergrad Enrollment: 1,632 54% female / 46% male
Avg. SAT Reading Comp 510-630 / Math 510-620 Avg. ACT: not reported
Total Cost: $51,190.00.
Received some form of financial assistance: 91%

Juniata is another of the colleges that counselors adore and another college that is still under the radar on many college searches. Juniata's lack of flash, or, rather, its genuine modesty comes from a set of principles that are all about substance and conviction.

Don't worry. Juniata is a real college with real college kids who laugh and frolic as college kids are meant to do. It's not a frat house kind of school, and there is a seriousness of purpose about the place and its students, but the community is warm, inviting, and particularly rich in the traditions it celebrates.

Two recent decisions made by the college give some notion of how principles affect the campus and student life:

Juniata invited Maya Lin to design the college's Peace Chapel in 1989. Lin had just completed work on her extraordinary Vietnam Memorial, and there had been considerable furor over her design and her selection as the architect of that memorial. Lin was only 21 years old when she submitted her design – a simple and evocative wall that seems to rise out of its setting. Lin wanted the names of fallen soldiers to be predominating, and she wanted to keep the landscape of the park in which the wall was placed. Further, she wanted the wall to remind its viewers of a long scar. The monument was not in the tradition of great hulking spires and its design was controversial.

The Peace Chapel at Juniata was Lin's next commission. Visitors to Juniata are often surprised to find that the Chapel is not a building, but essentially a sculpture, a ring of rough-cut granite squares, set on a promontory above a stunning Pennsylvania landscape. The approach to the chapel is across fields and before lovely woods in the college's Baker-Henry Nature Preserve. The ring is held in a grassy approach and contains a smooth floor of grass within the circle. Understated, unassuming, this chapel is entirely of its landscape and yet a bold statement of its purpose. Not a bad analog to Juniata College's character.

The second decision was to build the Baker Institute for Peace and Conflict Studies. Other colleges may offer Peace Studies, but I don't know of another that has dedicated an entire building to the subject. It is an important and perhaps defining major at Juniata. Internships take Peace students to the West Bank, Northern Ireland, and to conflict-torn inner cities in the United States.

While Juniata is a college independent from any religious affiliation, it was founded by the Church of the Brethren in 1886. Without getting into all the complications of religious movements in the United States, it is at least worth noting that the Church of the Brethren, like their spiritual cousins – the Quakers – were people of strong convictions about pacifism. The college was not founded in order to promote the denomination's mission, but to provide the world with useful and active leaders.

One of the ways in which the college continues to present those values is in the Program of (POE), Juniata's version of major academic divisions. There are a number of conventional Programs of Emphasis – Art, English, Biology, Mathematics, and so on – and a few unexpected POEs – Accounting, Business and Finance, Communication and Theater Arts, Education, Information Technology, Anthropology, Social Work and Justice Studies, and Peace and Conflict Studies. More than 40% of Juniata's graduates, however, determine their own POE.

Usefulness remains an abiding concern, and the college does a great deal to support internships and off-campus programs that teach "real-world" skills. One of its recent initiatives is the JCEL, the Juniata Center for Entrepreneurial Leadership, which not only teaches students to negotiate the hazards of starting a business, but also provides loans for students interested in actually setting up a small business in Huntingdon.

But Juniata is not just about values, principles, and real-world readiness. It is also one of the few colleges left that truly enjoys a calendar of happy traditions. In defending the college's traditions, a student observed, "At Juniata, we believe that change is good... except for this stuff!"

Other colleges have Homecoming, Juniata does too, but in addition students are VERY attached to a few rare traditions, some of which are as old as the college, some of which are fairly new.

The newest may be EID Dinner, a celebration of Muslim culture and food at the end of Ramadan. The Muslim Student Association hosts the event, but the entire community participates. Students prepare the food, organize the entertainment, and perform; an especially popular student group performs the folk dance, Debk, popular in Lebanon, Syria, Palestine, and Jordan.

All Class Night was established in the 1930s and pits each class against the others in an all-out competition of song, skits, and spoofs of college personalities. The All Class Night Cup is awarded to the most successful class, and recent competitions have brought sheep on stage and a performance of the college president's joining the Juniata Blues Brothers.

Lobsterfest welcomes students to Juniata in the fall. At the end of the first week of classes, lobsters are flown in from Maine and eagerly consumed. This is an opportunity for college bands to rock out, and the dinner is followed by a Student Organization Fair, giving students new to Juniata a chance to sign up with any of the fifty or more organizations on campus.

Mountain Day is one of the two most eagerly anticipated traditions as all classes are suspended and the entire college heads out for a day of hiking, picnicking, and student-faculty tug-of-war. The announcement of Mountain Day comes as a welcome surprise in the first semester. Madrigal is the college's holiday celebration in December. Students at Duke may camp out all night for basketball tickets; Juniata's students (800 or more) wait in line, in tents for almost a week in order to get a coveted spot in the Madrigal Hall. Apparently the tenting is as much fun as the Madrigal itself, broken up with spirited exercise such as the Underwear Run, in which female tenters can race to the track in underwear or in Supergirl costume.

The year's final two traditions are the Mr. Juniata auction, in which campus hunks raise money for charity by agreeing to become "personal assistants" to the highest bidder, and Springfest, a muddy carnival.

Juniata competes in Division III's Landmark Conference. The male Eagles play baseball, basketball, cross country, football, soccer, tennis, track, and volleyball; women's teams play basketball, cross country, field hockey, soccer, softball, swimming, tennis, track, and volleyball. Football is not terribly successful; women's field hockey and volleyball do pretty well.

Here's the thing about Juniata: Its students love it. They know the location isn't sexy; they wish a more diverse group would find the college; football isn't great... but morale is through the roof and this is one happy campus.

Maybe there are more significant criteria in taking on the college search, but finding a college with exceptional values, a strong sense of tradition, and real character is rare. Juniata is truly an exceptional college.

Muhlenberg College - Allentown, Pennsylvania

It isn't easy to capture the sense of a college in a short description, but my observation is that Muhlenberg's students are ambitious, bright, active, and happy, and perhaps a bit more aware of and appreciative of what they see as a first-rate education.

And the stats... 2015

Number of Applicants: 4,714 / 53% Accepted
Undergrad Enrollment: 2,440 60% female / 40% male
Avg. SAT Reading Comp 560-660 / Math 560-670 Avg. ACT: 28
Total Cost: $57,300.00.
Received some form of financial assistance: 94%

Muhlenberg is one of the highly regarded colleges that offer admission to roughly fifty percent of applicants - slightly more in some years and slightly fewer in others. That level of selectivity puts Muhlenberg near the highly selective colleges that are not profiled in this book. I include Muhlenberg because it remains a distinctly superior college choice and is still somewhat more regional than other colleges of its quality.

Muhlenberg is one of the colleges nestled in Pennsylvania's Lehigh Valley, a quickly growing region that includes other notable institutions, such as Lehigh University and Lafayette University. Muhlenberg is about fifty miles from Philadelphia and about ninety miles from New York City. The city of Allentown is the fastest growing community in the state and is actually considered part of the New York Metropolitan Area. The Liberty Bell was hidden in Allentown during the Revolutionary War; a museum recognizes that distinction. In addition, a long legacy of brewing beer (from Schaeffer, Pabst, Guinness, and Sam Adams) also offers the visitor opportunity for diversion during a visit to Allentown.

It isn't easy to capture the sense of a college in a short description, but my observation is that Muhlenberg's students are ambitious, bright, active, and happy, and perhaps a bit more aware of and appreciative of what they see as a first-rate education. Unlike other colleges experiencing roughly the same degree of selectivity, Muhlenberg does not feel like anyone's second-choice; its students are confident and proud of their collegiate experience. In fact, there is an engaging assurance about Muhlenberg's students that signifies a rare confidence in the quality of the education and support given them in their time at the college.

Muhlenberg is located on an eighty-acre campus in a residential area east of Allentown's center. Established in 1848, the college reflects the variety of institutional architecture over more than a century-and-a-half of expansion. Muhlenberg is a liberal arts college of about twenty-two hundred students all of whom are undergraduates. Although Muhlenberg is still affiliated with the Evangelical Lutheran Church of America, its faculty and student body is made up of people of every faith and belief, and its mission is clearly inclusive, encouraging diversity. In fact, Muhlenberg enrolls a high percentage of Jewish students and is known for the quality of kosher meals served daily in the dining halls; the college actively seeks diversity. In my opinion, Muhlenberg is been a bit more dedicated to pre-professional education than some liberal arts colleges; the college does present well-organized mentoring of those seeking admission to medical school, law school, and other professions, and it has a very strong program in accounting, a major not offered by many liberal arts colleges of this size.

A quick look at Muhlenberg's mission and curriculum reveals the strength of program available in this happy college. In addition to a rich variety of courses within the traditional arts and sciences, the college presents three major pre-professional tracks and nine other coordinated tracks. Students are prepared for graduate programs in Medicine, Law, and Theology with the help of academic advisors experienced in those professional areas. Muhlenberg also works with other institutions and agencies to prepare students for careers in engineering, dentistry, occupational therapy, optometry, physical therapy, and music certification. A student seeking commission as an officer in one of the military services can join others in the Lehigh valley in a cooperative ROTC program.

In addition to the standard liberal arts courses in science, math, language, literature, the social sciences, fine arts, and economics, Muhlenberg offers majors in some unusual areas - for example:

Business Administration, Finance, Accounting, Economics

Dance, Film Studies, Media and Communication, Music, and Theater (VERY strong program in theater, among the most highly regarded)

French, German, German Studies, Jewish Studies, Russian Studies, Spanish, with Minor programs in Africana Studies, Asian Traditions, International Studies, Latin American and Caribbean Studies

Biochemistry, Computer Science, Environmental Studies, Neuroscience, Public Health, and Sustainability Studies

The college is committed to Global Education and more than half of Muhlenberg's students will participate in one of the college's programs outside the United States. Of particular interest are opportunities at The London Theater Program at Goldsmith's College of London University, Accounting, Business, and Economics at the University of Maastricht in the Netherlands, Media and Communication and Film at the University of Dublin, and Dance in Arezzo, Italy. Tuition costs and financial aid remain the same as those offered on-campus students; there is no extra tuition cost or loss of aid in traveling to an international campus.

It is worth noting that student opinion is enthusiastic in recognizing the incredible generosity of spirit and professional competence of their professors. Over and over again, Muhlenberg's kids express their gratitude for the interest that their teachers take in them and in their work. Advisors and mentors abound, but the real advantage in choosing a solid academic program such as this is in finding actively responsive professors in every course.

Carrying the enthusiastic good news into life outside of the college, many students begin their appreciative comments with a rousing shout-out to the food service for providing food of unusual quality and variety. I've already mentioned the kosher menu as remarkable for a college of this size, and, in an era in which the "food court" has replaced the dining hall, the cheerful ambience of Muhlenberg's dining hall and a variety of uniformly well-prepared meals do stand out. I can guarantee that most colleges do not earn the kind of enthusiastic approval that Muhlenberg has. There are other on-campus sources of snacks and specialized food, such as the popular "knoshery", but one of the most appreciated aspect about the dining hall is that it remains open throughout the day for drop-in snacking.

Dormitories are comfortable, and in a rare impulse of humanity, most are air-conditioned or about to be air-conditioned, an initiative most other colleges should imitate. I won't go full-rant at this point, but most colleges spend a lot of money on "splash", striking and elaborate facilities, but old dorms are hellacious in September, October, and May as heat rises to rooms on the third of fourth floor. There are lots of options with regard to configuration of rooms and suites and well-maintained living spaces. At this time, only two of the fraternities own their residence; others live in college owned houses. Greek life is moderately impactful during the rush weeks, but generally muted throughout the rest of the year. About twenty percent of students join one of three fraternities or one of five sororities, and those organizations do organize social events enjoyed by the college as a whole. The Greek system is not the stereotypical "frat boy" agent of excess. Muhenberg's kids work hard and are ambitious; this is NOT a party school.

It is an active school, however, with more than a hundred clubs and organizations at full membership. I would say that Muhlenberg has a slightly greater emphasis upon service than some colleges; I'm impressed with the number of students involved with Muhlenberg College Emergency Medical Services (MCEMS) which provides first responder service at no cost and confidentially. Members are certified EMTs or in the process of earning certification. There are a number of other service organizations, including the Peer Health Advocates, the Sexual Assault Support Services, and the Cardinal Key Society, extending welcome to visitors and promoting school spirit. Two of my favorite organizations are Best Buddies, the nationally affiliated organization linking students with people in the community with intellectual and developmental disabilities, and Dress Upon a Star empowering disadvantaged young women in the Allentown area by making sure that they are given lovely clothes for a magical prom experience.

As mentioned earlier, the theater program is excellent, and the performing arts have a prominent place at Muhlenberg. The Theater Association is very large and supports both man stage productions and the more than twenty student productions that take place each year. A cappella music is so popular that the college has founded an A Cappella Council to coordinate the activities of the six a cappella groups on campus. There are co-ed groups, male groups, female groups, and one group called the Chaimonics that performs in Hebrew at the Hillel center. Fusion is, quite appropriately, the group that combines vocal music and dance, particularly hip-hop. There are a number of other groups, including the Soul Sound Steppers, performing African dance.

The publications at Muhlenberg include an excellent yearbook, the Muhlenberg Weekly is the college's newspaper, and MBC, the Muhlenberg Broadcasting Community brings student work on campus television station, MCTV. Special interest clubs are many, from the Russian Club to the John Marshall Pre-Law Society. Active involvement in activities indicates a student population that is both ambitious and committed; seriously, Muhlenberg is an uncommonly active place! And then, there is the exciting and distinctive athletic tradition that is also part of Muhlenberg's obvious sense of pride and spirit. Students are involved in tons of intramural and recreational sports. To begin with, the college's Life Sport Center includes a tournament sized basketball court, a field house, a six-lane swimming pool, and courts for racquetball and squash. The new addition to the center (fabulous!) includes training facilities, cardio-fitness facilities, and a weight room, The college offers a full menu of intramural sports in every season and facilitates three club sports that operate at close to varsity status - men's ice hockey, women's rugby, and co-ed fencing.

The Muhlenberg Mules have a distinguished athletic legacy. Football was the first varsity sport, organized at the start of the Twentieth Century and made prominent with the arrival of a coach who would later go on to lead Syracuse University to national championships, but in his time at Muhlenberg take the Mules to its own championship, winning the Tobacco Bowl in the late 1940's. Today, Muhlenberg competes at the NCAA Division III level, as a member of the Centennial Conference (Johns Hopkins, Dickinson, Franklin and Marshall, Gettysburg, Haverford, Swarthmore, etc.) and the Eastern College Athletic Conference. Varsity teams for men include football, soccer, cross-country, golf, lacrosse, wrestling, track and field. Women's sports include volleyball, soccer, cross-country, field hockey, golf, lacrosse, softball, track and field. Many teams have won regional championships and both the men's and women's soccer teams are highly regarded.

Muhlenberg's facilities are first-rate, its academic reputation excellent, and its students proud and happy. The closest comparison I can think of outside the confines of this book is Bates College in Maine, similarly grounded and ambitious.

Allegheny College - Meadville, Pennsylvania

There are more central locations than Meadville, Pennsylvania, and larger, better-known colleges than Allegheny, but this college is confident in its own purposes in ways that many other colleges are not.

And the stats... 2015

Number of Applicants: 3,857/ 72% Accepted
Undergrad Enrollment: 2,203 55% female / 45% male
Avg. SAT Reading Comp 530-640 / Math 520-630 Avg. ACT: 23-29
Total Cost: $53.980.00.
Received some form of financial assistance: 100%

I'm not sure why a landlocked college south of Lake Erie would have adopted the alligator as its mascot, but perhaps the feisty critter represents something of the tenacity and spirit of this excellent small college.

It's been a while, but Allegheny won the Division III national championship in football back in 1990 (I said, it had been a while!). Championships are terrific, of course, but an article written in Sports Illustrated at the time, helps bring the college into perspective:

> *I cannot think of a single thing that has eroded public confidence in America's colleges and universities and undermined key educational values more than intercollegiate athletics as it is practiced by a large fraction of the universities in the NCAA's Divisions I and II. It is hard to teach integrity in the pursuit of knowledge, or how to live a life of purpose and service, when an institution 's own integrity is compromised in the unconstrained pursuit of victory on the playing fields.*

> DANIEL SULLIVAN President, Allegheny College

Allegheny beat Lycoming 21-14 in overtime last Saturday in the Amos Alonzo Stagg Bowl in Bradenton, Fla. The win gave the Gators from Meadville, Pa., their first Division III national football championship. Daniel Sullivan's reaction to the triumph was consistent with his words above, which came from a recent article. He said, "It's nice."

Indeed, the win was very nice for Allegheny, a small institution (enrollment 1,950) in western Pennsylvania that heretofore has bragged mostly that one of its graduates was President William McKinley and that it is the 32nd oldest college in the nation. Now, Allegheny's run-and-shoot offense has given it another reason to pound its chest.

Sort of.

That's because Allegheny—like most of the 208 colleges and universities that play Division III football—defines a clear, if restricted, space for sports inside its academic walls. Sullivan professes that the way Allegheny handles football, with quiet understatement, no athletic scholarships (which are not allowed in Division III) and an emphasis on balance among all endeavors, works because "football is seamlessly connected to everything else we do. Athletics are for the students. What we're about is teaching."

In the wake of the Gator victory, it was apparent that everyone, including the Allegheny players and coaches, wanted to keep the championship game in perspective. Rookie coach Ken O'Keefe, the 37-year-old architect of the Gators' 13-0-1 season, said, "Success is not measured in terms of wins and losses. We are developing students, players, people." So sure is O'Keefe that W's and L's aren't the essence of athletic success that he never mentions winning. Moments before the Gators took on previously undefeated Lycoming (12-0), he told them, "Play like champions. Four quarters total team effort. Relax and have fun. The results will take care of themselves."

I'm not touting Allegheny as a football powerhouse, or even as a paragon of athletic virtues. What the article suggests is that Allegheny has a strong sense of purpose and a strong sense of its own mission. There are more central locations than Meadville, Pennsylvania, and larger, better-known colleges than Allegheny, but this college is confident in its own purposes in ways that many other colleges are not.

One manifestations of that confidence is a very clear set of academic challenges.

The first difference between Allegheny and its peers is that the college requires that every student declare a major (ordinary) and a minor (not ordinary). In addition, each student participates in three seminars in the first two years. And, there are some particular course requirements that support the college's contention that education ought to be broad as well as focused - non-science majors (or non-science minors) will take a science in order to graduate. The college expects its graduates to be literate in science. Finally, and distinctively, in order to graduate from Allegheny, a senior must complete a Senior Project.

Starting at the end, the Senior Project is a huge deal and one that Allegheny's graduates value enormously. In some cases, a student will face comprehensive examinations; in all cases, a final presentation, performance, or project will reflect two years' preparation. A seminar in the junior year begins the process of defining and developing the project; faculty advisors work closely with students in this stage of the project. Earlier, in those seminars required in the freshman and sophomore years, the skills necessary to the completion of the project have been clarified.

If it sounds as if Allegheny is hard, it is. Students consider themselves to be loaded up with work, and they are ok with it, in part because they have such strong feelings about the professors with whom they work. Small colleges all advertise close relationships between students and teachers; at Allegheny they actually happen. Accounts of the Allegheny experience may quibble about snow and parking, but it is clear that students feel themselves both challenged and supported by their teachers. They like their professors, respect their professors, and feel their professors are truly collaborative in much of the work done at Allegheny.

Seriously, the strength of feeling expressed about professors is very unusual.

Meadville is a small town, and Allegheny a small college, so it is not uncommon for students to spend some part of their undergraduate career traveling. The college offers direct enrollment in a number of foreign universities, and helps students plan their off-campus experience. In addition, other innovative educational opportunities are also supported by the college through its office known as ACEL (Allegheny College Experiential Learning).

Outside of the classroom, Allegheny is also unique. Although the college draws heavily from its region (Western Pennsylvania, Ohio, and Western New York), it is the college of quality in its region and attracts ambitious, interesting, focused students. One student characterized his classmates as "Rust Belt Intellectuals," and while that contention cannot be tested, there is something to the notion of gathering bright kids from small towns and allowing them to blossom in a challenging environment. The strength of feeling Allegheny's students have for their college indicates that the experience is very good indeed. Unlike many other small college student bodies, this one is eminently appreciative of the opportunities the college provides.

This might be a good place to talk about diversity at Allegheny, and while there are not huge numbers representing other populations, the student body is inclusive and eager to support ethnicities, nationalities, and identities other than their own. One way in which the college endorses the impulse to think beyond the boundaries of small college and small town is in the sponsorship of colloquia and panels on controversial subjects.

A fraternity (and sorority) system is alive and well at Allegheny, and about 30% of the student body will affiliate. Other social groups are also active, and residences sponsor House Parties and other activities that rival the frolic of the frats. It is not surprising that Greeks and independents both support worthy charities and that some of the biggest college-wide events of the year are associated with raising money for charities. The college calendar includes several large-scale undertakings – Make a Difference Day, Second Harvest Holiday Food Drive, Senior Citizens Recognition Day, and Saturday Service Days. Many students are involved with Community Service and Service Learning through ACCEL, and the number of service hours provided by the Allegheny student community is reputed to be in excess of 2500 hours a year.

This generation of Gators seems to be able to balance workload and serious academic enterprise with worthy social consciousness, cheerful community life, a vigorous intramural athletic program, and lots of activities.

All of the usual clubs and organizations have grown up at Allegheny, but there are a few other obvious differences in the activity arena. For example, there's quite a lot going on in the performing arts, with various jazz bands, swing dance groups, dance teams, and various choirs all competing with the formal theater program and the experimental theater. There's a Legion of Allegheny Gamers (LAG), Animal Welfare advocates, Model UN, Neuroscience Club, a Meditation Club, Islamic Awareness Society, and, literally a hundred more activities.

I mentioned intramural sports because they involve almost all students at Allegheny and are widely followed. Varsity sports compete in Division III, and in addition to the major sports, Allegheny offers club teams in rowing, ice hockey, rugby, skiing and snowboarding, ultimate frisbee, water polo, equestrian, fencing, and triathlon. Intramural sports include: bowling, floor hockey, indoor soccer, tennis, walleyball, basketball (single sex and coed), dodgeball, golf, volleyball, flag football, racquetball, and softball.

Gators love their school, stay loyal to the college after they leave, and universally consider themselves fortunate to have had an Allegheny education. They come to love Meadville and many end up doing considerable public service in that community. Yes, it snows... a lot... but morale is high and as one student noted, "we're usually home on break during the worst of the winter."

Let me end this description of Allegheny with a word about humor. It's a rare college that has a sense of humor about itself; it's a mark of confidence and self-assurance. One clear indication of the abiding sense of humor at Allegheny is found in the naming of the library's coffee shop, "The Wrecking Ball." The library had been in the process of being renovated earlier when a 1500-pound wrecking ball broke loose and crushed a number of cars parked across the street. In colorful homage to the event, students tagged the new coffee shop with the uncommon name.

Equally charming, is the tradition that no female student is truly an Allegheny co-ed until she has been kissed on the thirteenth plank of a wooden bridge across a campus stream. It will not surprise most readers to learn that the thirteenth plank is stolen on a regular basis; the buildings and grounds crew keeps extra planks on hand to replace the trophies.

Goucher College - Baltimore, Maryland

Other colleges have libraries, with stacks of books, study areas, a few couches, and maybe an A-V room; Goucher has the Athenaeum

And the stats... 2015

Number of Applicants: 3,340/ 76% Accepted
Undergrad Enrollment: 1,477 67% female / 33% male
Avg. SAT Reading Comp 530-660 / Math 510-630 Avg. ACT: 23-29
Total Cost: $55,338.00.
Received some form of financial assistance: 98%

Newsweek Magazine tagged Goucher's students as the happiest in America a few years ago, and while that title may belong to several happy colleges in other regions as well, it is very much worth noting that Goucher is one of the few colleges that has managed a relatively recent shift in mission (from single-sex to coed in 1985) without getting tangled up in back-peddling rhetoric.

This is not your mother's Goucher.

Chances are pretty good that your mother didn't actually go to Goucher, so let's clarify the issue.

Not only has Goucher been admitting men for more than 25 years, it has shifted from the conventional and somewhat imitative curriculum of its first 100 years to a vibrant program charting new territory as it celebrates its 125th birthday.

By new territory, I mean Goucher was the first college to REQUIRE all students to take at least one semester in another country. New Territory also describes the remarkable new building called the Atheneum.

Goucher's campus is pretty - always has been - in a same-stone-building-on a-leafy-campus kind of way. Unlike many of the women's colleges approaching the same birthday milestones, Goucher actually had a plan, implemented in the 1950's. The idea was to use local stone, beige Butler Stone, in modern buildings that actually considered the natural contours of the landscape. As a result, Goucher looks both thoughtfully planned and pleasantly uncomplicated; there is no hodge-podge of older crumbling former mansions and unfortunate odd corners with failed cement experiments from the '60s.

Not only was the campus recognized by the National Registry of Historic Places for its sensible design, it remains unbelievably fortunate in its natural setting. Walking and riding trails take students into hilly woods, and the deer population is so healthy that drivers are warned to keep an eye out for bounding Bambis.

The idea was always to create a campus flexible enough to accommodate new buildings without seeming squished, and that plan has allowed the spectacular new facility, the Athenaeum, to take its place easily.

Other colleges have libraries, with stacks of books, study areas, a few couches, and maybe an A-V room; Goucher has the Athenaeum.

Located in the heart of the campus, the Athenaeum is a high-tech library, but it is also an art gallery and a conference center. The building houses a center for community service, classrooms, and the college's radio station. Oh, and exercise space and a cafe. 100,000 square feet of academic/community space built to the highest level of environmental standards, the Athenaeum is open 24 hours a day and is the only building of its kind on the campus of a liberal arts college.

So, if the campus is so cool, why does Goucher make everyone leave?

That would be in order to bring every student to the understanding of a global community. Other colleges allow or endorse study abroad; Goucher requires it.

In order to help meet the cost of taking time in another country, Goucher gives a stipend of at least $1200.00 to each student. The International office is active in helping students plan and arrange study internationally and also maintains a website devoted to accounts of students' experiences and insights; a monthly contest recognizes the best essays. In addition, the international study requirement can be met by taking one of the three week intensive courses actually offered by Goucher – and there are many.

ICAs (Intensive Courses Abroad) have been offered in such widely varying fields as: Dance in Brazil, Film in Berlin, Tropical Marine Biology in Honduras, Solving the Puzzle (?) in India, Religion, Nation and the State in Israel, Alternative Media and Culture in Slovenia and Bosnia.

And, should the short-term or semester academic options not meet the needs of a student, or, if a student wishes to pursue further hands-on experience in another country, Goucher gives academic credit for international internships.

Back on campus, there are three significant elements to the Goucher experience that ought to be emphasized.

The first is that, although the ratio of women to men is still an issue (but changing!), this is a balanced, open-minded, and happy campus. There is no one type that chooses Goucher; you'll see the full range from jocks to punks. One significant contribution made by Goucher's students is the game, "Humans vs. Zombies", now available on campuses around the country. The Goucher mascot is the gopher, and the school exudes a cheerful "gopher spirit" without being an athletic powerhouse.

The second is that this is a true liberal arts education with an emphasis on quality teaching. The prevailing opinion is that Goucher's professors could not be more supportive, available, and interested. Some of those professors are celebrated writers or performers who seem to find great pleasure in bringing their craft to the college. All the liberal arts are well represented, but creative writing and dance are particularly appreciated.

Towson is a very attractive community, offering a variety of restaurants and stores, but Baltimore is close at hand, and the college makes good use of its location. Students can do the city thing or seek internships that can only be found in Baltimore, such as working for the Baltimore Orioles or Baltimore Ravens.

The Goucher Gophers play in Division III in the Landmark Conference, often competing against Drew, the Merchant Marine Academy, and Juniata. Games against Johns Hopkins inspire Gopher Madness.

Saint Mary's College of Maryland - St. Mary's City, Maryland

The history of the college certainly sets it apart from other state supported institutions. Although the college was established as part of Maryland's system of higher education, it is NOT a part of the University of Maryland. It is called "Maryland's Public Honors College" and provides an exceptional and challenging education for about two thousand student in the liberal arts and sciences.

And the stats... 2015

Number of Applicants: 1,874/ 79% Accepted
Undergrad Enrollment: 1688 57% female / 43% male
Avg. SAT Reading Comp 570-650 / Math 530-630
Avg. ACT: 23-28
Total Cost: $28,500.00 (in-state) $43,350.00 (out-of-state)
Received some form of financial assistance: 75%

First things first.

Saint Mary's is NOT a Catholic college. It IS a public college offering an outstanding education to students as part of Maryland's public education system. The college is located on the banks of the Saint Mary's River, a tributary of the Potomac on the western shore of Chesapeake Bay. The town of Saint Mary's is the fourth oldest town in the United States and the site of the passing of the Maryland Toleration Act in 1649, establishing religious freedom in the colony. Once the capital of Maryland, the town is a valuable source of archeological and historical information and maintains an active interpretive center for many visitors.

Take a moment to consider this: A student from the State of Maryland will pay about twenty-eight thousand dollars for a year at Saint Mary's. That's TOTAL cost - tuition, room, board, fees...everything. The comparable cost at one of the private colleges in Saint Mary's peer cohort would be at least fifty thousand dollars.

In keeping with its mission as an honors college, all students are required to study within a Core Curriculum. At Saint Mary's, that means reading a book in common during the summer, choosing one of the First year Seminars, an International Language, and one course in Art, Cultural Perspectives, Humanistic Foundations, Mathematics, Natural Science, and

Social Science. The First Year Seminars investigate a number of unusual subjects, such as: Jane Austen and the Dating Game, Culture and Madness, From Jupiter to Jesus, Everything You Always Wanted to know About Death but Were Afraid to Ask, Math, Music and the Mind, and The Evolution of Altruism. One aspect of this experience that is unique to Saint Mary's is the "Fifth Hour." In addition to class time, each member of the seminar is required to be involved with an extra curricular activity that in some way reinforces and informs the conversation in the seminar.

Once the core requirements have been met, students may select from twenty-four major concentrations, ranging from Anthropology to Film, Theater, and Media Studies. The most popular major is Economics, but professors in every discipline get rave reviews from students who are well aware of the quality of instruction. The proof is clearly in the pudding, as it were, in that Saint Mary's has the highest rate of graduates going on to graduate study and an exceptionally high retention and graduation rate.

It is in the remarkable energy of student life that Saint Mary's most vividly separates itself from the pack of public institutions. In the first place, Saint Mary's supports more than a hundred clubs and activities, a remarkable number for a school of this size. I don't have enough space to highlight every organization, but several deserve mention. The Amnesty International and Invisible Children chapters are exceptionally active and may have something to do with the uncommon number of graduates who end up volunteering for the Peace Corps. A different kind of energy emerges in the Appreciation of Capoeira Club. A Gospel Choir, an Improv Company, and a Step Dance team bring performance to the stage. Recreational sports and activities are well represented with: Billiards, Board Games, Community Garden Club, Crew, Cross Country, Dance, Fencing, the Jane Austen Society, lacrosse, rugby, Model UN, Outdoor Adventure, Puzzle Club, Rock Climbing, Rubik's Cube Club, SCUBA, Skiing, soccer, softball, tennis, radio station, a cappella music, water polo, windsurfing, and SMUT(Saint Mary's Ultimate Team).

The Seahawks of Saint Mary's play Division III sports in the Capital Athletic Conference, but traditional rivals pop up in several of the signature sports, several of which merit particular notice. Saint Mary's men play soccer, cross-country, basketball, baseball, lacrosse, tennis, and sailing. The women play soccer, field hockey, cross-country, volleyball, basketball, swimming, lacrosse, tennis, and sailing. The men's soccer team plays Johns Hopkins, the men's basketball team recently arrived at the final eight in the NCAA Division III tournament. Men's baseball plays an ambitious schedule against such teams as Randolph Macon, Gettysburg, and Salisbury State. The lacrosse team takes on Drew, Denison, and Mary Washington.

It is the sailing team, however, that is Saint Mary's greatest pride. The Seahawks are among the top ten sailing teams in the nation, competing against such tradition powers as Navy and winning second place in the Inter-Collegiate Sailing Association finals last year. As I write, a current student and a recent graduate are preparing to compete in the London Olympic Games.

The college is literally on the banks of the Saint Mary's River, and sailing is available as a recreational activity for all students - Olympic aspirants and novice sailors.

Finally, students characterize their experience at the college as entirely enjoyable. They mention warm relationships with teaching faculty and enjoy the wide diversity of people from different backgrounds approaching their work with seriousness of purpose and their classmates with friendship and acceptance. It is also worth mentioning that the food at Saint Mary's is excellent and widely praised. The Great Room offer sushi and stir fry, a bountiful salad bar, and choice of entrees. In addition, several snack shops and coffee houses allow late night grazing. Drowsy Seahawks like stopping in at The Daily Grind for a cup of java, while locovores particularly appreciate the Food Co Op.

For a school of this size, the number of active traditions is impressive; the embracing of traditions indicates investment in and abiding fondness for the college. The most commonly occurring tradition is called "ponding", the tossing of a friend into St. John's Pond on his or her birthday. The Great Bamboo Boat Race has replaced the Great Cardboard Boat Race as a community event during Homecoming Weekend. Regardless of material, the race generates intense rivalry and good-natured competition. No better way to identify Global Warming that to indulge in the annual Polar Bear Splash in mid-winter, an act of courage/folly that involves more than a hundred students. Midnight Breakfast during exam weeks and the May Day streaking through campus are fun, but the event known as Christmas in April raises money for charity by auctioning off the services of teachers and students with gentle good humor.

Aside from its prominence as an obvious bargain, Saint Mary's is a healthy, challenging, interesting college that should be of interest to anyone seeking a quality small college in the liberal arts tradition.

Washington College - Chestertown, Maryland

Students do work hard and do enjoy the opportunities to work independently, but they also enjoy life on the Eastern Shore and look very much like Polo/J Crew college kids anywhere. There are fraternities at Washington, and they do provide much of the focus of social activity. However, parties are open to all students, and Greek life appears to be available to those who like it and not a big deal for those who don't.

And the stats... 2015

Number of Applicants: 5,318/ 56% Accepted
Undergrad Enrollment: 1,467 57% female / 43% male
Avg. SAT not reported Avg. ACT: not reported
Total Cost: $56,352.00.
Received some form of financial assistance: 95%

"It's hard to separate what we are from where we are."

That's a message the college hopes visitors will appreciate. This is a college with a distinguished history and an advantaged location.

The first thing to know about Washington College is not that it was virtually founded by George Washington –although that is fairly impressive – or that Washington College is the tenth oldest college in the country – also impressive – but that Washington College is located in a town that makes Williamsburg, Virginia look positively shabby.

Chestertown is the county seat of Kent County, Maryland, and the jumping off point for any exploration of Maryland's exquisite Eastern Shore. It is also an entire town on the National Registry of Historic Places, a perfectly preserved harbor town with incredible brick mansions facing the river.

The good news is that the town is beautiful; the less good news is that it's a bit precious, although there are college hangouts and plenty of pizza is available.

The college itself is distinguished in a number of areas aside from location and age.

Creative writers know all about Washington because the college offers an astounding prize to its best writer each year. The Sophie Kerr Prize for Creative Writing carries an award that has grown to at least $60,000.00.

Yes, a graduating senior trots off the stage with a check for sixty grand to start a lifetime of writing.

And, lest historical writing go unrewarded, the college added the George Washington Book Prize for the best writing about the Founding Era. That little baby carries a mere $50,000.00 award.

This is one college that puts its money where its tradition is. A strong liberal arts program has been the hallmark of Washington College academics for generations. Recent innovations have included one of the most impressive programs of visiting lectures in the nation.

The Harwood Series brings some of America's most eminent speakers and pundits to the college where they continue in the tradition of open dialogue established by Washington College professor, Dick Harwood, a journalist, media maven, and close friend of Robert Kennedy. Harwood brought lively political debate to Washington, and following his death, his son, John Harwood, has continued in his father's footsteps, bringing Karl Rove, John McCain, Robert Novak, Howard Dean, James Carville, Eugene McCarthy, Cokie Roberts, and others to the campus.

Washington is not just for literary or political types; great opportunities abound in the sciences as well, where independent and collaborative research is especially supported. The college is ranked in the top 50 undergraduate programs producing Ph.D.s in science.

There are no teaching fellows or teaching assistants at Washington, and the ratio of student to teacher remains slightly under 12:1. Reports from happy students at Washington indicate that their professors are uncommonly eager to offer assistance and support.

Students do work hard and do enjoy the opportunities to work independently, but they also enjoy life on the Eastern Shore and look very much like Polo/J Crew college kids anywhere. There are fraternities at Washington, and they do provide much of the focus of social activity. However, parties are open to all students, and Greek life appears to be available to those who like it and not a big deal for those who don't.

One of the most distinctive elements of life at Washington College is the paramount importance of one varsity sport – lacrosse. Although Washington has been competing in baseball since 1870 –Yes, 1870 – and although Washington's sailing and rowing teams are nationally known, its lacrosse team has captured the imagination of campus fans. The rivalry game (known locally as "The War on the Shore") with Salisbury State, another lacrosse power, is a huge event. More than two hundred lacrosse players from Washington have been named All-Americans, and the team won the Division III championship in 1998 and has been in the Division III championship game eight times. Recently, the men's tennis team has also emerged as a national power, competing annually for one of the top spots in Division III.

The Shoremen and Shorewomen compete in Division III as members of the Centennial Conference for all sports except rowing and sailing. The Centennial Conference is, as its name would indicate, a conference made up of institutions of similar academic ambition, all of which are more than one hundred years old. members include: Johns Hopkins, McDaniel, Swarthmore, Haverford, Ursinus, Muhlenberg, Gettysburg, Bryn Mawr, Dickinson, and Franklin & Marshall. In sailing, Washington is a member of the Middle Atlantic Intercollegiate Sailing Association (MAISA), which is a conference within the Intercollegiate Sailing Association (ICSA). The Washington College rowing teams are members of the Mid-Atlantic Rowing Conference (MARC).

I get a huge kick out of looking at Club Sports at colleges, because these are activities that have come directly from and are supported directly by, current student interest. At W.C., current club sports include: Equestrian Club, Trap and Skeet Club, Wilderness Adventure Club, Men's and Women's Rugby Clubs, and a Wakeboard and Waterski Club.

The college offers all of the usual activities (Baking Club and Mixed Martial Arts) and journalistic opportunities, and holds a few distinctive traditions in place as well.

The Goose Bump Jump is a November version of a Polar Bear dip, held in order to raise money for charity. The freezing plunge is followed by a MeltDown/Pig Roast as a thawing gesture.

The rest of us may celebrate President's Day, but at WC, students enjoy the George Washington Birthday Ball, a formal affair attended by students, alumni, and faculty.

The college's Early Music Consort and the Vocal Consort perform at the annual Renaissance Christmas Dinner, a time-hallowed tradition which has all the trappings of a beautifully choreographed collegiate celebration.

May Day does not. It is a blowout that involves much rowdy adventuring and the occasional discarding of clothing.

That mix of tradition and high spirits describes the lively tension at Washington between the carefully preserved and the innovative. Washington College is a great find for any student who seeks the balance of academic challenge and healthy residential life.

McDaniel College - Westminster, Maryland

One of the aspects of work at McDaniel that remains unusual and impressive is in the collaboration between teachers and students. Undergrads have a chance to take on original research under the direction of teachers, and some recent opportunities to participate in research and publication have come in such areas as: "Eating Disorders in Athletes," and "The Biochemistry of Color Pigmentation in Chameleons." Generally, the profs at McDaniel receive high praise for their attention to individuals and their mentorship of students.

And the stats... 2015

Number of Applicants: 2,966/ 76% Accepted
Undergrad Enrollment: 1,740 54% female / 46% male
Avg. SAT Reading Comp 490-600 / Math 490-600 Avg. ACT: 21-27
Total Cost: $50,150.00.
Received some form of financial assistance: 99%

From 1867 until July of 2002, McDaniel was known as Western Maryland College, which was confusing for several reasons.

In the first place, the college was named for the Western Maryland Railroad, not for its position geographically in the state. So, it was not easy to find Western Maryland in Western Maryland, if you see what I mean.

And then, Western Maryland sounded like a state college, which it was not.

Finally, the Western Maryland Railroad was merged with another railroad, and no longer really existed, so what the heck?

So, in 2002, the college was renamed as McDaniel, after a graduate and benefactor who had been of distinctive service to the college. By the way, the name change thing is not at all unusual: Duke was Trinity College; Rhodes was Southwestern at Memphis; Claremont McKenna College (CMC) was Claremont Men's College (CMC); James Madison was State Normal School for Women at Harrisonburg.

The problem is that not very many people outside of the Middle Atlantic region have heard of McDaniel, which is unfortunate because it is a very good small (1600) liberal arts college. The colleges that face McDaniel in the Division III athletic conference, the Centennial Conference, know McDaniel (and its mascot known as The Green Terror) well. This is one of the great small college conferences in the nation (Bryn Mawr, Dickinson,

Franklin and Marshall, Gettysburg, Haverford, Johns Hopkins, Muhlenberg, Swarthmore, Ursinus, and Washington College.

Several distinctive qualities separate McDaniel from its peers, the most notable of which is its campus in Budapest. McDaniel College Budapest is, in fact, the only American university in Hungary and a fully affiliated branch of McDaniel. Obviously, the opportunity to work with McDaniel teachers while in a program abroad is very attractive. Also, the long association with Budapest allows those who work in the program to offer great insight into the history and politics of Central Europe, and great information about travel in Europe as well.

But back home in the USA, McDaniel offers several reasons to attend the college – some of which may be compelling in your consideration of this option:

The first reason is The McDaniel Plan – an academic program that includes freshman seminar, Sophomore Interdisciplinary Studies (SIS), a writing course in the junior year. and the capstone in the senior year.

I know, the idea of a seminar for freshman is not that unusual, but the McDaniel versions do sound sort of spiffy: "Born to Buy: America's Consumer Society" and "Baseball: America's Favorite Game."

Similarly, the Sophomore Interdisciplinary Studies has included interdisciplinary investigation into "South Park and Contemporary Issues."

In addition to the requirements of the McDaniel Plan, student can take advantage of the 4-1-4 calendar which includes a January Plan. In January, students can travel, as students have done in exploring orphanages in Vietnam, or looking into Tropical Marine Biology in the Bahamas.

McDaniel does encourage community service, and the college has been recognized for the impact students have made in their community. Westminster Boys and Girls Clubs have benefited from countless hours of volunteer service, and one of the most popular activities is the raising and fostering of puppies to become service dogs for the disabled.

I mentioned Loren Pope's groundbreaking book, *Colleges That Change Lives,* in my introduction to this guide; it remains one of the very few books that identifies colleges that make a difference. McDaniel was recognized as one of those colleges and remains active in the consortium of colleges Pope identified as colleges of quality.

One of the aspects of work at McDaniel that remains unusual and impressive is in the collaboration between teachers and students. Undergrads have a chance to take on original research under the direction of teachers, and some recent opportunities to participate in research and publication have come in such areas as: "Eating Disorders in Athletes," and "The Biochemistry of Color Pigmentation in Chameleons." Generally, the profs at McDaniel receive high praise for their attention to individuals and their mentorship of students.

Outside the classroom, McDaniel is a comfy, happy campus, with an active but not monolithic Greek system. Social activities seem to be as easily managed through residence halls and special interest groups as through the frats, and the number of clubs and organizations on campus certainly speaks to the initiative of numbers of students. Music, for example, seems to be hopping, with a number of singer-songwriters performing, a folk-rock band (Turtle Buddy) that plays widely in the area, and an exceptional Gospel Choir that has traveled around the world.

Other groups include the canine companion trainers, a dance team, snowboarding and skiing clubs, a belly-dancing club, and a politically active group known as "Sophisticated Ladies." - who knows! One recent event that captured my imagination was a fashion show for charity in which all creations were made from trash. The "Re-Fashion" show linked environmentalists and designers in an on-campus gala.

McDaniel also participates in "Baltimore Collegetown," an association of the 100,000 students in the Baltimore area who join together for a variety of events and cultural opportunities. One of the best deals for McDaniel students is the discounted ticket rates available through "Collegetown" for all area concerts and shows. Orioles and Ravens tickets are also discounted for students.

In an attempt to intimidate their opponents in a tough Division III conference, McDaniel's athletes are known as "The Green Terror". The "Terror" play in the Centennial Conference with the Gettysburg Bullets, The Diplomats of Franklin and Marshall, the Blue Jays of Johns Hopkins, the Muhlenberg Mules, The Swarthmore Garnet, the Bears of Ursinus, and the Shoremen and Shorewomen of Washington College. The Lady Terror also play against the Owls of Bryn Mawr. Varsity sports include: football, baseball, basketball, wrestling, soccer, swimming, tennis, golf, lacrosse, track, field hockey, and volleyball. Almost everyone is involved with a varsity sport or an intramural team.

A great location, handsome campus, happy students, good teachers, excellent reputation - what's not to like about McDaniel? Newly re-named but providing a solid liberal arts education for over a century, McDaniel is one of the most interesting "undiscovered" colleges awaiting your investigation.

The South

The South is large and complex, ranging from Virginia and West Virginia in the north to Mississippi, to Arkansas and Texas in the west, and to Georgia and Florida in the south.

Those from other parts of the country tend to see "The South" as a monolithic region, virtually a separate nation, with attitudes and customs completely different from those in other regions.

Even the most cursory of visits, however, establishes the difference between the financial and commercial capitals of the "New South" – Charlotte and Atlanta – and the bastions of an older South – Savannah and Charleston.

Richmond and Charlottesville are within the sway of Washington, D.C., Nashville is the center of a national music industry, and Memphis, the home of southern blues and barbecued ribs, is also the home of the FedEx empire, the largest privately owned airline in the world. Raleigh, Durham, and Chapel Hill make up the "Research Triangle" – a high tech hotbed of science and technology.

Horse country in Kentucky and Tennessee has a different style of life from that on the Gulf coast; Appalachian mountain towns are only distantly related to towns on the mighty Mississippi.

You'd recognize the Hoover Mall outside of Birmingham, Alabama or the Citrus Park Mall in Tampa, Florida, or any of the hundreds of shopping areas that look exactly like their counterparts in California or Minnesota.

There are some notable differences that will strike those who arrive from the Northeast or the West Coast:

You'll see a lot of churches and meet a lot of people who take their religion fairly seriously.

Young people use "Ma'am" and "Sir" more frequently than their counterparts in other regions.

Football really matters, except in those states where basketball really matters.

Fraternities and sororities are far more common and significant in Southern colleges and universities.

A "casual" date in the South looks like a formal date in the Northeast and like graduation in the West. Girls wear makeup. I mean it; girls don't go to a football game in t-shirt and shorts, although boys may.

The term "Southern Hospitality" is not misplaced; you will be warmly welcomed to the college you attend in the Southland. The graceful traditions of the Old South have survived and its troubled past is evident as well.

A visit to Maya Lin's memorial to the Civil Rights Movement in Montgomery reflects the region's willingness to look at its history; you might think about the public recognition of issues of race in Boston, New York, Chicago, or Los Angeles.

Colleges and universities with national reputation in the region include: The University of Virginia, The College of William and Mary, Washington and Lee University, Duke, Davidson, the University of North Carolina, Wake Forest University, Furman, Clemson, Emory, the University of Georgia, Georgia Tech, the University of Florida, Auburn, the University of Alabama, Vanderbilt, Tulane, and the University of Tennessee.

Former students of mine have attended every college and university in that list and have become devoted to their school. Public universities in the South are excellent and very much worth investigating. Virginia and North Carolina will be beyond the aspiration of all but the most superior students in the first year; William and Mary, Georgia Tech, and the University of Georgia are also highly competitive.

Those looking for the large university experience might consider Tennessee, Florida, Florida State, North Carolina State, and the University of Alabama. Clemson and Auburn, in part due to their location in a small college town, have the feel of a mid-sized university and are both excellent choices for the student coming from outside of the region.

The stretch of southern states from Virginia to Florida may seem more familiar than the interior of the South, and there are some truly unfortunate misconceptions about the southern states, but it would be a shame to overlook the outstanding liberal arts options and the compelling specialized programs in the region.

It doesn't take long to see the charm of the Bluegrass region of Kentucky or the ante-bellum homes in Natchez. Lots of visitors stop in Nashville and Memphis; the troubled history of the Civil Rights Movement brings visitors to Birmingham and Montgomery. Literary types stop to see William Faulkner's Oxford or Eudora Welty's Jackson.

The universal response of those who trouble to make those visits is that they had no idea the South was so lovely or so vibrant.

Obviously, one way to consider the region is too look at the waterways, most notably the Mississippi River. The cities that grew up along the Mississippi run from Bemidji, Minnesota to New Orleans, and the regional attractions have to include Natchez and Vicksburg. The last of the Piedmont chain of mountains runs through Georgia to end near Huntsville, Alabama. The Great Smoky Mountain range rises along the border of Tennessee and North Carolina. The southernmost extension of the Appalachian Mountains, the Smokies takes its name from the fog that often shrouds its peaks. Knoxville, home to the University of Tennessee, lies about twenty miles north of the Great Smoky Mountains National Park. Chattanooga, Tennessee's fourth largest city, sits under Lookout Mountain and along the Tennessee River. No visitor to the region should miss the astounding Tennessee Aquarium, the largest freshwater aquarium in the world.

Civil War battlegrounds? Mostly in the South. Hmmmmm.

College trippers are probably familiar with Vanderbilt and Tulane. Auburn, Alabama's second state university, gets attention on the sports pages, and Kentucky basketball is legendary.

Rhodes College in Memphis, Tennessee. Rhodes has a stunning campus in a lovely neighborhood in Memphis, and has become a nationally regarded liberal arts college of quality. Imagine a campus that most closely resembles Princeton's filled with the most earnest, kind, ambitious students you can imagine, toss in a commitment to diversity and a generous program of financial aid, and add the savory tang of Memphis barbeque. Why is Rhodes not on every list of best colleges? We'll also consider the University of the South in Sewanee, Tennessee, Belmont University in Nashville, Samford University and the University of Montevallo in Alabama, Centre College in Kentucky, the University of Mississippi, and Millsaps College in Mississippi.

Virginia to Georgia is the span known as the Southeast; Kentucky, Tennessee, Alabama, and Mississippi make up the Central South. From the panhandle of Texas to the shores of Lake Pontchartrain, however, the region becomes less distinctly one sort of culture.

The Mississippi River defines most of the eastern border of Arkansas, separating West Memphis, Arkansas, from Memphis, Tennessee, but the state itself touches on Missouri, Louisiana, Tennessee, Texas, Oklahoma, and Mississippi. Some of Arkansas is lowland river country; the Arkansas Delta has rich dark soil. Some of Arkansas is prairie. Much of the northern section is mountainous; the Ozark Mountain region has been transformed by the creation of a number of lakes and has become a significant recreational destination. Little Rock, Pine Bluff, and Conway, home of Hendrix College, are located in the center of the state.

Louisiana has been in the news entirely too frequently recently. Hurricane Katrina devastated the southeastern United States, but left most enduring scars on New Orleans. The recent oil spill in the Gulf of Mexico will have environmental and economic consequences we have yet to imagine. For all of its unfortunate press, however, Louisiana is unique in its cultural history; each of its parishes reflects the tides of immigration over the centuries. The state was held by both the French and the Spanish, and the mixture of African, Indian, Spanish, and French language and culture has made its cities and towns distinctively more diverse than those in any other region.

Louisiana State University is located in Baton Rouge, the state's capital. The campus of Tulane University is in the "uptown" section of New Orleans, adjacent to the campus of Loyola University

West Virginia

I don't know what image you hold in mind when you think of West Virginia, but, until I visited the state, I thought primarily of Wheeling, the steel city on the Ohio River, a "smokestack", blue collar city attached by trade with sooty Pittsburgh.

Well, Pittsburgh has cleaned up quite nicely, and there's a lot more to West Virginia than I had originally understood.

The state came into being during the Civil War, when West Virginia split from Virginia. Following the war, as industry came of age in America, West Virginia's deposits of oil and coal made it an important resource for the Industrial Revolution. Mining and logging might have destroyed the state's remarkable topography, but West Virginia remains a beautiful state, especially in its forests, rivers, and hills. The Shenandoah River runs through Harper's Ferry, a historic site, and a great spot for rafting, fishing, and all water sports. The Greenbrier, a five star resort in White Sulphur Springs has welcomed twenty-six presidents and was the site of the first Ryder Cup golf match played in the United States. Sam Snead and Tom Watson have been club pros at the Greenbrier's course.

The Greenbrier is also famous for housing an enormous bomb shelter known as "The Bunker." Commissioned by the Federal Government as a refuge for national leaders in case of nuclear attack, the bunker was never used. It has since been decommissioned and is now open to the public.

The state's two preeminent universities, West Virginia University ("The Mountaineers") and Marshall University ("The Thundering Herd") are each excellent options for those students searching for a quality undergraduate experience in a larger educational setting.

West Virginia University has produced 25 Rhodes Scholars and is among the top 30 colleges in the nation in graduating Rhodes Scholars.

Marshall is a small research university of approximately 10,000 undergraduates. A recent movie, *We Are Marshall,* documented the aftermath of the plane crash in 1970, in which seventy-five members of the Marshall football team died. The crash, on November 14, 1970 drew the university more closely together, and the efforts to re-build the university's viability as a contending football team demonstrated the small university's resilience. The fountain commemorating the lost members of that team does not flow from November 14th until the start of spring football practice each year.

Budding CSI enthusiasts should also know that Marshall's graduate program in Forensic Science is generally regarded as the best in the nation.

Davis and Elkins College - Elkins, West Virginia

I can't think of another college of this size that begins to offer what D&E is able to offer. And, several of the programs, particularly those in Theater Arts, Marketing, Biology, Environmental Science, Sustainability Studies, and Hospitality and Tourism Management are highly regarded outside of the region.

And the stats... 2015

Number of Applicants: 1,812/ 58% Accepted
Undergrad Enrollment: 846   53% female / 47% male
Avg. SAT Reading Comp 440-530 / Math 430-550 Avg. ACT: 18-24
Total Cost: $40,112.00.
Received some form of financial assistance: 94%

I'm going to spend much more time on Davis and Elkins' location than I have with some other colleges because understanding the location is essential in understanding the college. This is a small college perched in the Potomac Highland surrounded by God's own forest; there is no lovelier setting, and no college that is more attuned to its environment.

Davis and Elkins College is a small college in Elkins, West Virginia, an artsy town in the Highlands adjacent to the Monongahela National Forest. In fact, Elkins is one of those "hidden gems" all by itself. Described as "vibrant", it is said that the town is, "where the mountains reach higher, the air is fresher, the streams run clearer, and the snows are deeper than any place you've probably visited before."

Elkins is home to a number of festivals and concerts, many of which are connected with the heritage of Appalachian arts, crafts, and music. Other traditions are explored in the town's Augusta Heritage Arts workshops – such as Cajun, jazz, blues, and "old time" music. Randolph County, of which Elkins is the seat, is chock full of artists, craftspeople, jewelry makers, quilters, weavers, and woodworkers.

Families visiting Davis and Elkins (D&E) often return with a car stuffed with newly acquired and eminently beautiful purchases.

The town and the campus are about a half-day drive from Washington, D.C., or Pittsburgh. An airport in Clarksburg provides the nearest air travel, although many book through Pittsburgh.

174

D&E is adjacent to the Monongahela National Forest and some of the eastern United States' premiere outdoor recreation sites. Within an easy lope, students can find skiing, climbing, hiking, biking, fly fishing, rafting. The challenging New River Gorge is only a few hours to the south, and many of the local rapids are more than challenging enough for the ordinary rafter.

As for the college itself, the most noteworthy indication of the conviction with which those who love D&E see the school is in the decision made by the college's president, G.T. "Buck" Smith who turned down the annual salary of $130,000.00 a year to work for free during the post-recession slump. Each week a message from Smith is posted on the college's web site, usually an encouraging or welcoming note.

The college is named for two of West Virginia's senators, Henry B. Davis and his son-in-law, Stephen G. Elkins, each of whom owned considerable tracts of property in the area. Today, the mansions of the senators are part of a hundred and seventy acre campus that houses the six to seven hundred students and the college's uncommon programs. The former Halliehurst mansion ice room is now a student club, and the Graceland Inn is a learning laboratory for students in the hospitality program; both mansions are on the National Registry of Historic Buildings, but many contemporary and well equipped buildings also sit handsomely in a setting that defies description; the forest and mountains are literally in view no matter where one walks on campus.

D&E is a Presbyterian College, affiliated with the Presbyterian Church and the Presbyterian heritage is still important to the college's mission. A handsome chapel is widely used, but students of many backgrounds attend Davis and Elkins. The student body is small and the teaching faculty lives in Elkins, so it is not surprising that the relationship between teachers and students is close. What is surprising is that the college's curriculum is as broad as it is.

All of the usual liberal arts are represented; uncommon programs include: a Bachelor of Science degree in Sustainability Studies. The Bachelor of Science degree is also offered in Environmental Science, Accounting, Business, International Marketing, International Management, Forestry, Finance, and Exercise Science, among others. The Bachelor of Arts is offered in the usual subjects as well as in Criminology, Theater Arts, Recreation and Fitness, and Hospitality and Tourism Management.

I can't think of another college of this size that begins to offer what D&E is able to offer. And, several of the programs, particularly those in Theater Arts, Marketing, Biology, Environmental Science, Sustainability Studies, and Hospitality and Tourism Management are highly regarded outside of the region.

Another surprising aspect of D&E's program is its conspicuous success in athletics. I'm not sure that there is a smaller college in Division II, the division that permits the awarding of some athletic scholarships. As a result, D&E's athletes emerge in national scouting in several sports. The baseball, basketball, swimming, cross country, and golf teams offer scholarships for men and women; softball and volleyball offer scholarships for women. School spirit is huge and the Senators are always well supported at every home event.

Perhaps the Presbyterian Church has been unusually generous; perhaps its graduates have been generous. In any case, D&E ends up giving financial aid to more than 80% of enrolled students ... and ... the total cost at Davis and Elkins is just over $30,000.00, putting it considerably under the total cost of comparable institutions.

Virginia

No state has a richer history than Virginia, and no state is more complicated.

The northern counties are essentially suburbs of Washington, D.C. and rife with governmental connections and affiliation with various high level offices of agencies essential to national security and well-being.

The Hampton Roads metropolitan area is home to the largest concentration of military facilities in the world, and Virginia Beach, the commonwealth's largest city, is also registered in the Guinness Book of World Records as the world's longest pleasure beach.

Fairfax County contains almost 14% of the population of the commonwealth and was the first county in the United States to hit the six-figure mark in median annual income. Vietnamese Americans have settled in northern Virginia, and Filipino Americans in Hampton Roads. Western Virginia was settled by Scotch-Irish immigrants, and that legacy remains important to the current day.

The land itself defies easy description. Much of historic Virginia is in what is known as the Tidewater region, along the eastern shore of the commonwealth. The land above the tidewater was better for agriculture, and it is in the Piedmont plateau that the large tobacco plantations emerged. The western border of the Piedmont is the Blue Ridge Mountain chain.

Two great national parks fall within the Blue Ridge Mountains – Shenandoah National Park and the Great Smoky Mountains National Park. The Blue Ridge Highway runs from Shenandoah National Park to the Cherokee Indian Reservation in North Carolina and the Great Smoky Mountains National Park.

Finally, the southern portion of the Appalachian Valley is the Cumberland Plateau. This hilly and densely forested region extends into Kentucky, Tennessee, and Alabama. Of the regions, this is the area most commonly referred to as "Appalachia", a region dedicated to logging and coal mining, and a region that has known significant poverty.

Appalachia has also provided some of the most enduring cultural legacies in the southern United States. Folktales, country music, clogging, bluegrass music, fiddle tunes, and folk music all owe a debt to the traditions of Appalachia. One of the region's hallmark celebrations is the annual Storytelling Festival, held each October in Jonesboro, Tennessee, just across the border from Bristol, Virginia.

From Jamestown and Williamsburg to the establishment of the C.I.A. in Langley, Virginia has been a commonwealth of uncommon influence in American history.

Visitors intent on college tripping will find themselves driving through a window into the past.

The college terrain is similarly varied.

"Mr. Jefferson's university," The University of Virginia, is consistently mentioned among the top public universities in the nation (along with Berkeley, UCLA, the University of North Carolina, and the University of Michigan). The other, and earlier, university of national prospect in Virginia is the College of William and Mary, founded in 1693, the second oldest college in the country after Harvard,

The two most selective independent colleges in the commonwealth, the University of Richmond and Washington and Lee, both draw from a national base, although both have a lingering aura of Southern gentility about them.

In Virginia, several state universities have received growing numbers of applicants from outside the commonwealth. For the most part, that growth has taken place in the Middle Atlantic region, with many new students arriving from New Jersey, New York, and Pennsylvania.

George Mason is in Fairfax County, about 15 miles outside of Washington, D.C., and, in addition to a number of the usual majors, offers an extremely strong program in creative writing, computer science, and economics. George Mason, often referred to as GMU, is the largest university in the Commonwealth of Virginia, enrolling almost 36,000 students. The Patriots of GMU shocked the national sports community by arriving in the NCAA basketball tournament Final Four in 2006.

James Madison University in Harrisonburg, Virginia is located in the northwestern corner of the state, at the head of the Shenandoah Valley. Formerly the state's Normal College for Women, JMU is now a very attractive coeducational university of increasing reputation. Recently, the JMU "Dukes" also had a notable upset in 2010 when their football team beat the 12th ranked Hokies of Virginia Tech.

Old Dominion University, once the Norfolk division of the College of William and Mary, now enrolls more than 25,000 students in a comprehensive university curriculum. As the university closest to the military complex at Hampton Roads, Old Dominion has developed a close relationship with many governmental agencies, including NASA.

Radford University was once Virginia's Teachers College, and now enrolls about 7500 undergraduates, many of whom will study in the excellent program in education.

The University of Mary Washington was once the women's college of the University of Virginia, but is now a strong liberal arts university with a comprehensive academic profile, a competitive Division III athletic program, and one of the oddest traditions in college-land: Devil-Goat Day. Fredericksburg, Virginia is lovely, and the University of Mary Washington is a spectacular campus. This is one of the public universities I most enthusiastically recommend.

Now, on to the profiles of Emory&Henry, Hampden-Sydney, Hollins, Lynchburg, Mary Baldwin, Roanoke, and Sweet Briar.

Fair Warning!

Some of the best college options in the South will have been founded by religious organizations and may remain affiliated with one Church or another. The colleges in this guide welcome students from anywhere and any system of belief; they do not demand attendance at religious services and they do not require courses in any particular religious tradition.

Similarly, the South has retained the tradition of single-sex education, and several of the best kept secrets in this region will be colleges for women, and in one case, a college for men. Obviously, the success of the colleges and the strong feelings of their students have earned them a place in this guide and, I hope, in your college search.

Be Open Minded!

Hampden-Sydney College - Hampden-Sydney, Virginia

Hampden-Sydney is not all about honor code issues, but it is about a manner of living that has largely disappeared in American culture. In addition to a fine education, the men of Hampden-Sydney are expected to develop the skills and attitudes of responsible and cultured men.

And the stats... 2015

Number of Applicants: 3,639/ 47% Accepted
Undergrad Enrollment: 1,105   100% male
Avg. SAT Reading Comp 490-600 / Math 500-610 Avg. ACT: 21-26
Total Cost: $54,266.00.
Received some form of financial assistance: 98%

This excellent college is a remarkable setting was founded in 1775 and is one of the ten oldest colleges in the United States. For a young man who hopes to find a school rich in tradition, Hampden-Sydney is an excellent choice.

Hampden-Sydney is one of three colleges for men in the United States. Located on an impossibly handsome campus of more than 1300 acres in rural Virginia, Hampden-Sydney is all about tradition. Men wear coat and tie to football games, and each entering student is presented with *To Manner Born, To Manners Bred: A Hip-pocket Guide to Etiquette for the Hampden-Sydney Man*, a guide to proper behavior. As at the University of Virginia, Davidson, Washington and Lee, and some other southern colleges, the honor code is taken very seriously.

In fact, the honor code is one of the most distinguishing aspects of community life at this old and widely respected college. It is easy to overlook the essential qualities of Hampden-Sydney while fixing entirely too much attention on the whole "preppy-southern gentleman- blue blazer frat house-boys' school" thing.

Established as the first private college in the South, just months before the outbreak of the Revolutionary War, Hampden -Sydney has played a significant role in Virginia and in the South. The Medical College of Virginia (now part of Virginia Commonwealth University) was founded at Hampden-Sydney in 1838. Similarly, one of the nation's most respected schools of Theology, the Union Theological Seminary, began at Hampden-Sydney before splitting off and moving to Richmond.

Today, Hampden-Sydney is a liberal arts college enrolling about eleven hundred men. Its curriculum is fairly broad, but the college places unusual emphasis on preparing its students to think and write effectively. Each student must pass a three-hour examination in Rhetoric, including a test of proper grammar and usage, and a fully developed argumentative essay. No matter what major a Hampden-Sydney man takes on, it is expected that he will be capable of writing correctly and at length.

The honor code has developed in a particularly effective fashion at Hampden-Sydney. Whereas there can be some gray areas in the question of reporting student offenses at the military academies, Washington and Lee, or Davidson, the honor system at Hampden-Sydney operates on two levels. There is no question that the principles endorsed in the honor code are taken seriously; the commitment to follow the honor code is taken for life, and asserts that no Hampden-Sydney student will lie, cheat, or steal, or tolerate those who do. A second system, covering the kinds of hi-jinx college boys get into - underage drinking, drinking, drinking to excess, drinking in the wrong place, etc... - are addressed by the Dean of Students, while honor violations are handled by a student court.

Hampden-Sydney is not all about honor code issues, but it is about a manner of living that has largely disappeared in American culture. In addition to a fine education, the men of Hampden-Sydney are expected to develop the skills and attitudes of responsible and cultured men. The much discussed handbook, "To manner born, to manners bred..." is not a snooty treatise on how to plan a cotillion, but a sensible handbook on the ordinary (maybe not so ordinary anymore?) practices that allow a man to move comfortably and responsibly in polite society. Yes, there is information about which fork to use, and how to shake hands properly, but the guide is essentially a short course in becoming a good man.

The college is virtually a movie-set campus, set against a backdrop of more than a thousand acres of Virginia rolling farmland. The central campus resembles a village green, with handsome buildings in the federal style creating the impression of an academic village. Facilities are modern, of course, and extensive. In fact, one of the charming elements of H-SC is the combination of savvy high-tech instructional practices plunked inside one of these impressive federal buildings on the green.

The single sex issue at H-SC is probably much more of an issue for applicants than it is for students at the college. It won't come as a surprise that the school week is given to study and the weekends to a vigorous social life. . It doesn't hurt that Hollins University and Sweet Briar College are both close by and both replete with young women eager to travel to H-SC

The three elements that create the very positive experience for the thousand young men who choose Hampden-Sydney are a challenging academic program with uncommonly accessible and engaged professors, active social opportunities that include volunteerism as well as fraternity sponsored events, and rabid interest in the fortunes of the H-SC Tigers in competition through the Division III Old Dominion Conference

Academic life is serious and directed toward the maximizing of career opportunities for H-SC's graduates. Not only have they developed effective writing and thinking skills, they have been grounded in course work offered in small classes taught by professors who live in or near the college. H-SC offers the usual liberal arts as well as Computational Physics, Economics and Commerce, Government and Foreign Affairs, Greek, Latin, Mathematical Economics, and Pre-Law and Pre-Medical programs. H-SC's students report a consistent and demanding workload, but also note the quality of teaching as well. Study abroad is easy and popular; many of Hampden-Sydney's second and third year students will avail themselves of the many programs the college sponsors.

It is probably worth mentioning at this point that the "Old Boy" thing is alive and well at Hampden-Sydney. Alumni cherish their own experience and consider new graduates to be part of a Tiger brotherhood that extends beyond Farmville. Graduates are actively involved in career mentoring and have been especially helpful in connecting recent grads with good first jobs.

Socially, the conventions of the collegiate South still obtain. Parties, dances, football games – all are carried out with deliberate attention to style. The prevailing opinion is that the men of Hampden-Sydney are sons of privilege, happily sporting pink polo shirts, madras shorts, or Brooks Brothers blazers and tweeds. In fact, there is some truth to the gloss of the Hampden-Sydney student body, generally a better dressed group than most their age. Is Hampden-Sydney self-consciously protecting an age gone by? There is a distinct tinge of satisfaction with maintaining traditions that other institutions have let go. On the other hand, there is some diversity among the 94% of students who are white, non-Hispanic; some are on financial aid and have not been to the manner born.

The twelve national fraternities on campus absorb roughly 40% of the student body and are significant in arranging social events on campus. H-SC will feel more notably fraternity heavy than schools in the north or west, but the fraternities, and other associations are relatively open to all comers at party time, and also active in a number of volunteer efforts.

The college supports a "Mentor" program that pairs veteran successful students with students who need support of various sorts. The program offers academic tutoring, and personal support as well. Mentors go through extensive training and become a significant resource on campus. The effectiveness of the mentors can be seen in the relatively low rate of academic distress in the first two years.

Community Service takes many forms at the college. For example, a recent initiative by a student at H-SC brought into being a program known as RAMPS (Ramp Access Made Possible by Students) which provides and installs modular steel ramps for seniors and people with disabilities. A long-standing tradition at the college is the Hampden-Sydney Volunteer Fire Department, founded in 1970, and now incorporated as a Prince Edward County fire department, although almost all of the volunteers are students at H-SC. The department also maintains an emergency first responder program, allowing students to receive training in emergency medical procedures.

The football rivalry between Hampden-Sydney and Randolph Macon College is one of the oldest in the South, The Tigers (Don't call them the Hamsters!) have faced the Yellow Jackets more than 115 times since 1893. Football has the cachet that only a century of tradition can bring, but basketball at H-SC is also successful, frequently capturing the conference crown. Lacrosse is huge, of course, at H-SC as it is throughout much of Virginia. The Tigers play a tough schedule outside of their conference, often facing top ten Division III teams.

Hampden-Sydney is an athletic school. In addition to the varsity athletes, about 70% of students are involved in intramural and club sports. Among the club options are rugby, fencing, bicycling, and swimming.

Sweet Briar College - Sweet Briar, Virginia

I remain impressed with Sweet Briar's ability to attend each student with care. It is a beautiful school with lovely traditions. For any young woman seeking a strong sense of community, and especially for any devoted to things equestrian, Sweet Briar should be in the mix during the college search.

And the stats... 2015

Number of Applicants: 789 / 94% Accepted
Undergrad Enrollment: 691   100% female
Avg. SAT Reading Comp 440-600 / Math 440-560 Avg. ACT: 21-28
Total Cost: $50,937.00.
Received some form of financial assistance: 100%

Finally, we arrive at one of the most beautiful colleges in the nation – Sweet Briar College.

Sweet Briar is a college for about 750 women built on a 3250-acre estate and designed by the architect who had much to do with creating the campus at Princeton and West Point; twenty-one of Sweet Briar's buildings have been placed on the National Registry of Historic Buildings. It would be easy to say that Sweet Briar is the Disneyland of colleges, almost TOO pretty and almost TOO beautifully set against an almost TOO perfect Virginia landscape, but the truth is that Sweet Briar is what college should look like.

Perfect? Awfully close.

I love writing about Sweet Briar, an unincorporated village (?) of about 820, almost all of whom are students at the college. Fortunately, the gorgeous campus is only about twelve miles from Lynchburg, which is a pleasant small city in the middle of Virginia.

And there is the food issue – it is almost certainly TOO good. Nobody can evade the freshman fifteen or twenty when facing fresh baked croissants each morning. I'm not going to talk about the ice cream desserts, because the rest of the college world doesn't need to know what they are missing. Suffice it to say, that dining at Sweet Briar is at a level culinary institutes would envy.

Horses? Stables? Equestrian paradise? Any young woman with serious ambitions as a rider should certainly consider Sweet Briar one of the most advantaged riding programs in the world.

Then, there's the abiding and almost overwhelming sense of tradition and spirit that makes the Sweet Briar experience uniquely compelling.
And, it's a pretty good college on top of all of that.

Sweet Briar does suffer, I think, as contemporary cynicism about southern gentility forces students to seek a gritty "real world" experience before entering the real world. There is also a sticky reality in that the exquisite setting was crafted from a working plantation that once held eighty or more slaves. Emancipation changed everything, of course, and the founding of the college was based on thoroughly modern ideas about the liberal arts and preparation for leadership and service in the contemporary world. Sweet Briar was never intended to be a finishing school or convent; active scholarship has long been central to the Sweet Briar experience.

It is no accident that Sweet Briar first became prominent in the academic world with the establishment of its programs abroad. The connection with St. Andrew's University in Scotland was established in 1932, well before other colleges and universities were looking beyond their own elm shaded pathways. The Sweet Briar junior year program in France is the oldest sponsored program in Paris; the Munster program is operated by Sweet Briar, William and Mary, and Vassar. The college is also invested in programs in Spain, Japan, Urbino, Rome, Beijing, Florence, Athens, and London. Study abroad remains an important element in the education of most Sweet Briar students, and the college has established scholarship funds to assist students in traveling abroad.

The on-campus curriculum supports the study of the liberal arts with two notable points of difference from other colleges of comparable ambition.

In the first place, Sweet Briar operates with an honor code that is central to the college's mission. "Sweet Briar women do not lie, cheat, steal, or violate the rights of others..." This pledge is memorized by all first year students and attached to every aspect of life in the college.

In the second place, Sweet Briar includes a "Physical Activity Requirement" that can be met through any number of athletic options, including riding, but can also be met by taking an Outward Bound course, a course from the National Outdoor Leadership School (NOLS), classes in dance or yoga.

A clear indication of the college's commitment to educating women for a place in the real world is the major in Engineering; Sweet Briar is one of only two women's colleges offering an undergraduate program in

Engineering. In addition, acceptance of Sweet Briar graduates at medical and veterinary schools remains impressive. A rigorous Honors program challenges students to engage in critical reasoning across disciplines.

Sweet Briar's graduates are more than ready to take claim their place in the world of work or study; fully 96% move on to graduate school or significant employment immediately following graduation. These ambitious young women have gathered considerable strength in their time in this strong academic program.

There are two ways to look at the plethora of traditions and institutions peculiar to Sweet Briar: One could consider them insular and precious; one could see them as remarkable opportunities for leadership. To an outsider, they may seem odd, but to the women who have lived with them, they represent all that is best about the Sweet Briar experience.

Let's start with the traditions, most of which are roughly comparable to the cherished practices of other women's colleges: Opening Convocation, Founders' Day, Step Singing, Freshman Caroling, Secret Sophomores, Big Sister/Little Sister, Senior Robes, Junior Week, Junior Banquet, Senior Toast, Faculty Show, Lantern Bearing, Hanging of the Banners, Rock and Hitching Post Fight... ok, we just stepped off the conventional conveyer belt into SBC legend.

Rock and Hitching Post – this is a paint fight in which first year students defend the hitching post and second year students defend their rock. Mayhem ensues.

Scream Night – At 10:00 on the night before first exams, students gather in the quad to scream. Snacks appear and mayhem ensues.

Halla Halla, Halla – sung when anyone has done anything of note, this song is meant as a tribute to good work:

> "Here's to (insert name)
> Halla, halla, halla
> Nothing you cannot do..."

Ring Game – when an SBC student becomes engaged, the class president calls the class together to form a ring. The engaged person identifies herself during the game.

The Scroll Game – when an SBC student is accepted into graduate school, the ring forms.

The Game – sophomores wishing to be tapped by Bum Chums... Oh, we're off the map again.

Sweet Briar has no sororities, but the place is crawling with "secret" societies. Some of these "clubs" are associated with particular enthusiasms (theater, singing, etc..), some are dedicated to service, and some are interested in spreading mayhem. Most have traditional rival clubs.

Paint N' Patches – serious about theater/ rivalry with Aint's N' Asses
Aints N' Asses – sketch comedy and spirit/ rivalry with Paint N' Patches

Bam – recognizes hard work and accomplishment/ no rivals

Bum Chums – try to uncover identity of new QVs/ rivalry with QV
QV – secret society elected as freshmen by class/ rivalry with Bum Chums

Chung Mungs – nicest on campus, exactly 13 members/ rivalry with Tau Phi
Tau Phi – most academic on campus/ rivalry with Chung Mungs

Earphones – enthusiastic singers/ rivalry with Sweet Tones
Sweet Tones – a cappella group by audition/ rivalry with Earphones

Fall On Nose – enthusiastic dancers/ rivalry with Tap N' Toes
Tap N' Toes – dance majors

SBC also has its share of conventional clubs and activities, including a very ambitious and effective outdoor program. SBC athletic teams are known as the "Vixens", and a program known as "Late Night Vixens," promotes a variety of community activities. In addition, it has to be said that road trips to Hampden-Sydney and various other colleges supplement the social scene at the college.

The Vixens play a Division III schedule in soccer, field hockey, lacrosse, softball, tennis, swimming, and volleyball. The equestrian program has won a number of national championships and has produced riders who have competed at the Olympic and international level of equitation. The facilities are extensive and impressive; the riding center occupies its own hundred-acres and features a huge indoor ring and three outdoor rings. A hunter trials course and seven schooling fields are adjacent to the center, and the facilities are available to competitive and recreational riders throughout the year.

Emory & Henry College - Emory, Virginia

So, an excellent academic institution with a laughably intimate student/faculty ratio, a long-standing commitment to community service, active and healthy campus life, strong school spirit, and a setting in one of the country's most lovely regions ... how has this gem of a school remained a secret to the rest of the nation?

And the stats... 2015

Number of Applicants: 1,471/ 72% Accepted
Undergrad Enrollment: 1,012   49% female / 51% male
Avg. SAT Reading Comp 430-560 / Math 430-550 Avg. ACT: 18-25
Total Cost: $44,784.00.
Received some form of financial assistance: 100%

I would have included Emory and Henry if only because it is the only college that insists on using the ampersand in its title ("&") rather than the word, "and," but Emory & Henry is so much more, one of the colleges profiled by Loren Pope in his *Colleges That Change Lives,* and one that continues to occupy a distinguished and unique place in the history of the commonwealth and in the ranks of liberal arts colleges.

E&H is small, currently enrolling about eight hundred students. The ratio of students to faculty? About ten to one. That's an incredible statistic and part of the reason for the uncommon success of E&H's graduates and part of the reason the campus is so relentlessly happy.

The college is located in the village of Emory in the Virginia Highlands in the region known as Central Appalachia. This is the southernmost and westernmost region in the commonwealth and one of the richest in terms of Appalachian culture. The Tri-Cities of Johnson, Kingsport, and Bristol provide a mid-sized airport, and adjoining towns include the home of the Barter Theater and the Lincoln Theater. The college is rooted in the history of the region; J.E.B. Stuart was a graduate and during the Civil War the college was used as a hospital for troops of the Confederate states. Equally strong is the college's commitment to service in the region.

In addition to nationally known performance groups in the region, this corner of Virginia is close to some of the most spectacular wilderness opportunities in the eastern United States. The entire campus of Emory and Henry has been designated a National Historic Landmark and lies virtually within a stone's throw of the Appalachian Trail.

Emory and Henry are not first names, but last. Bishop John Emory and Revolutionary patriot, Patrick Henry, gave their names to this college, founded in 1838. Today this small college is noted for the excellence of its teachers, many of whom have been identified as among the most effective professors by the Carnegie Foundation, and for the passion with which its students attend to study, community service, and football.

The academic profile is sound. Forbes Magazine ranks E&H among the top thirty liberal arts colleges, and most outside observers name it as one of the colleges of quality in the South. The college offers the usual array of liberal arts majors, and a few interdisciplinary programs that are uncommon. Among the interdisciplinary programs are: Athletic Training, Environmental Studies, International Studies, Public Policy and Community Service. Probably the most celebrated academic department is the Theater Department, in part because the college is affiliated with two equity companies of actors and offers undergraduate actors the opportunity to work in theater year-round.

My interest in E&H grew from its strength in three areas: Community Service, Campus Life, and Athletics.

The college has been among the most widely recognized in the country for its work in service learning. The Public Policy and Community Service major allows students to do course work in such fields as: Appalachian Studies, Political Economy, and Human Services. Every core course is attached to a community service commitment. Students give something like twenty-five hours of one-on-one community service for each course in the major.

Outside of the major field, students are also widely involved in community affairs. A distinctive program is in the Appalachian Center for Community Service. The Center describes its work with an emphasis on place - there is a commitment to a place-based model of service. "In all of its work, the Appalachian Center for Community Service seeks to take seriously the life of each place, and to provide student, faculty, staff, and community partners with opportunities to acquire and sharpen the intellectual skills, civic tools, and values necessary to be effective participants in the life of their place." The underlying conviction is that every place has the potential to be safe, healthy, and good for the people who live there. The college's location in Appalachia allows students to make a real difference in the lives of people of the region.

Real work with real people to make a real difference is grounded in the college's abiding sense of mission, which endorses humanitarian values, honesty, and responsibility. Affiliated with the United Methodist Episcopal Church, the college is based on transforming lives, but it is not a churchy school pressing religious values on its students.

In fact, E&H welcomes students from every background and from all walks of life. Its aim is to make the individual the best person he or she can be in order to make the world a better place for their engagement in it.

Ok, that's kind of daunting, I know. But the odd thing about E&H is that the campus is an exceedingly cheerful, happy, spirited place despite holding some very serious attitudes about education.

One of the elements that signify healthy campus life, from my point of view, are flourishing traditions. E&H has eight local fraternities and six local sororities, and the Greek system is alive and well; one of the traditions in the fall, for example, is the "Running of the Bulls," at which time, girls intending to pledge scatter at once toward the sorority they intend to join.

Many of the most cherished activities during the school year, however, are campus -wide. Service Plunge is a day at the start of the school year on which all new students go out to perform community service.

Another point of pride for the students of Emory & Henry is the sure knowledge that classes will NEVER be cancelled, no matter how vile or inclement the weather might become. According to campus legend, the college has only closed three times since its founding in 1836.

As any college must, E&H has its share of ghosts, some of which haunt Wiley Hall, the building used as a hospital during the Civil War. Apparently (apparitionally?) the ghost of a nurse named Freda walks the halls at night carrying a lamp. I have not seen this phenomenon, but it remains the stuff of legend.

Every athletic team touches "The Rock" before a game, in recognition of the contribution to E&H athletics by Coach Fred Self, whose motto, " Trust in your teammates; trust in yourself," has been important to the tradition of the "Wasps," the blue and gold teams of Emory & Henry.

E&H plays in NCAA Division III, and has been dominant in conference play in football, at one point putting together an unbeaten streak of 39 games. The Wasps earned their nickname in 1921, losing to Tennessee but with such ferocity that a reporter described them as a bunch of stinging wasps.

Passion and pageantry are the words most commonly used to describe the tradition of college-wide support for the football, basketball, and other athletic programs.

So, an excellent academic institution with a laughably intimate student/faculty ratio, a long-standing commitment to community service, active and healthy campus life, strong school spirit, and a setting in one of the country's most lovely regions ... how has this gem of a school remained a secret to the rest of the nation?

It is worth noting that Emory & Henry automatically considers all applicants for financial aid, and awards a number of merit scholarships without regard to need.

Hollins University - Roanoke, Virginia

The literary legacy and active interest in creative writing is truly distinctive and one of the reasons the university has gained considerable momentum in the last decade. Hollins has long been well known as one of the most successful of Virginia's colleges for women and as a campus of exceptional beauty; it stands ready to become a college of national distinction

And the stats... 2015

Number of Applicants: 1,785 / 56% Accepted
Undergrad Enrollment: 596   100% female
Avg. SAT Reading Comp 500-630 / Math 450-570 Avg. ACT: 20-27
Total Cost: $49,435.00.
Received some form of financial assistance: 99%

Hollins is a small university of about 1000 women, formerly Hollins College for Women, and it is a hotbed of literary activity. Annie Dillard and Natasha Trethewey are recent graduates and winners of the Pulitzer Prize. Winner of the Man Booker Prize in 2006, Keran Desai is also a graduate of Hollins. In addition, two of Hollins' professors have been nominated for National Book Awards this year. The literary legacy and active interest in creative writing is truly distinctive and one of the reasons the university has gained considerable momentum in the last decade. It is a great credit to the university that it is consistently recognized as having a superior teaching faculty, again among the top twenty-five colleges with best professors. Hollins has long been well known as one of the most successful of Virginia's colleges for women and as a campus of exceptional beauty; it stands ready to become a college of national distinction.

Here's the challenge for a university such as Hollins: The legacy of the genteel college for well-bred southern women is hard to shake, especially when the university's location is in a small and generally undistinguished city in the southwestern tip of the Commonwealth. Roanoke is a pleasant small city of about 90,000, but it is not a hip urban metropolis. Among the highlights of the cultural calendar in Roanoke are the Chili Cook-Off and the Big Lick Blues Festival; one of the points of interest in the city is the Roanoke Weiner Stand.

Fortunately, Virginia abounds with other colleges in the region, most notably Virginia Tech, Hampden-Sydney, Washington and Lee, and the University of Virginia. Commonly held notions about Hollins have included the road-tripping Southern Belles scooting off at the drop of a pearl necklace to H-SC, Washington and Lee, VMI, and UVA, and the hardened equestriennes caring more for their horses than their studies.

All of which was/is/may be true in part.
Equally true is the notion that, against all expectations, Hollins has attracted a wonderfully weird and attractive mix of bohemians, beatniks, hippies, preppies, belles, horse-crazy barn rats, political junkies, artists, and astounding writers.

I can't think of another campus on which the "stereotypical" student is so tough to define. There probably was a time in which the Hollins girl saw the college as the finishing school on the way to a "good" marriage. One short visit to the campus will quickly demonstrate that those days are mostly gone. The buzz around campus is as likely to be fiercely political or intensely aesthetic, and many students are decidedly NOT interested in road tripping to find a man.

I am always struck by colleges that have been able to sustain traditions that allow students of one generation to experience what students of another found meaningful. Bryn Mawr College in Pennsylvania, for example, is an academic powerhouse that still carries on well-established traditions. Like Bryn Mawr, Hollins has a fair share of traditions, and, like Bryn Mawr, they remain alive and important. The odd thing is that they are important to the eclectic mix of current Hollins students.

A few colleges do the Surprise Free Day Thing in the fall, and it is always an appreciated release from the first weeks of classes. At Hollins, the event is called "Tinker Day," as the day involves a romp up Tinker Mountain where a fried chicken picnic accompanies skits and songs. The real punch to the day, however, is in its anticipation. In the weeks before the "real" Tinker Day, seniors run through the freshman dorms banging pots in the wee hours, terrifying newbies and suggesting that the holiday is at hand. On the actual Tinker Day, seniors festoon graduation garb with decorations, bang the pots at dawn, hand out doughnuts, and help the new students dress up in fabulous costumes for the ascent of Tinker Mountain.

One of the newer traditions allows seniors to pass on their decorated robe to underclass women. Other, older, traditions recognize other rites of passage. The Front Quadrangle is off-limits to underclass students, so the ceremony of the First Step allows new seniors to claim their space for the first time. Apparently, those first footsteps may also be enhanced by goblets of bubbling Champagne. Similarly, Ring Night celebrates the transition from the junior to the senior year. Seniors select secret sisters, to whom the Hollins ring will be passed. That ring will, in all likelihood, be worn for a lifetime. On Hundredth Night, one hundred days before graduation, seniors are feted by sophomores and juniors.

There are no sororities at Hollins, but there are secret societies, which are both secret and social, and also dedicated to particular purposes.

The first, established in 1903 is called "Freya." Those in the know are aware of the pantheon of Norse deities and recognize that Freya was the goddess of love, beauty and fertility. Most of us invoke her weekly, as the word, "Friday" honors her – it comes right after "Wotan's Day" and "Thor's Day." At Hollins, "Freya," is dedicated to ideals of generosity. Anonymous members contribute various services to the community and oversee endowed funds that provide scholarships and loans for students in need.

One of the most moving of traditions at Hollins is one in which "Freya Walks." At moments of significance in the college or in the country, "Freya Walks" – hooded anonymous members walk the campus from ten until midnight, carrying a candle to signify their support of an issue. In the past, Freya has walked in support of desegregation, in support of women's rights, against violence. The college has shown its support of Freya's efforts by turning off lights, so that its members might walk in complete darkness.

The discussion of traditions underscores the enduring experience of an education apart from the ordinary institutional educational experience; a discussion of academic initiatives will give some sense of the ways in which Hollins women are very much prepared for the world into which they will emerge.

The first observation has to be that Hollins virtually started study–abroad, ramping up programs in the mid 1950's when most colleges were insular and entirely self–satisfied. Today, more than half of Hollins' students will spend an appreciable stretch of their college years in another country. Hollins maintains its own programs in Paris and London, and supports other opportunities in virtually every spot on the globe. Hollins programs operate in the usual destination cities – Florence, Rome, Athens, and in such unlikely spots as Legon, Ghana. In addition, a community service program brings a number of students to Jamaica each January to engage in an on–going series of projects on the island. A January short term as part of a 4-1-4 calendar allows Hollins to send almost 70% of its students into internships off campus as well.

On campus, the big dogs of the Hollins academic landscape are in the Creative Writing Program and the Batten Leadership Institute, although, the arts are flourishing as well. The visual arts remain strong, design in particular is highly reputed, and the theater program, already excellent, will be enhanced by renovation of the university's theater. A booming program in film has also recently captured a great deal of undergraduate interest.

The general education requirement at Hollins has been established in a program knows as ESP (Education Through Skills and Perspective). All students at Hollins build skills in thinking, writing, expression, quantitative reasoning, research methods and acquire perspective through the examination of cultures, social systems, aesthetic observation, language, and scientific inquiry.

The creative writing program is one of three options offered to the English major. The other two concentrations are Literature and Performance and Multicultural U.S. Literature. Creative writing has been a particular strength and interest of the college for more than fifty years, and the *Hollins Critic* is a well-established literary magazine of national reputation. Writers-in-residence have long helped promote good student writing, and the establishment of a residential creative writing center has further enhanced the climate in which writing is celebrated.

The number of successful writers with connection to Hollins is more than impressive; Hollins is one of the most successful writing programs in the country and a superb opportunity for the young woman who considers creative writing her future.

The Batten Leadership Institute was established at Hollins in 2002 in order to formalize the education of women seeking leadership skills. The Institute offers a Certificate in Leadership Studies following an intensive course of study and the successful completion of a student leadership project. Recent projects have included such initiatives as: A Student Coalition Against Viruses, Adware, and Spyware, free tutorial programs for public school students with reading difficulties, HIV, and AIDS awareness Projects, including a trip to Africa working in AIDS education.

The arts flourish at Hollins and weekly performances, readings, viewings, and demonstrations keep the campus hopping. An active outdoor program (HOP) takes students into the extraordinarily beautiful and easily accessible wilderness, where rafting, rock climbing, hiking, and skiing are available.
The athletic scene at Hollins revolves around two sports that have long been traditional at colleges for women: tennis and equestrian events. The Hollins tennis team competes in the Old Dominion Conference (without a nickname or mascot) and often emerges as Conference champ.

The riding program is one of the three or four most successful programs in the nation, often winning national championships. The Hollins Riding Center is located close to the campus and offers paddocks, pastures, more than forty well maintained stalls and a huge indoor riding facility. Riding rules at Hollins and Hollins rules in the world of equitation.

A college for women faces some challenge in this age, but the opportunities offered by this extraordinary small university are not to be found in many other institutions. Hollins is a rarity.

Christopher Newport University - Newport News, Virginia

Christopher Newport is an absolute bargain, both for in-state students (and they are the majority at present) and for out-of-state students. It is hard to imagine a more attractive opportunity than that of attending a university rising quickly in the ranks of academia, in the company of happy students, on a campus that is incredibly beautiful, for the price that CNU costs. Without much help from this guide, there is little doubt that this remarkable find will remain a secret for much longer.

And the stats... 2015

Number of Applicants: 7,366/ 56% Accepted
Undergrad Enrollment: 5,096 57% female / 43% male
Avg. SAT Reading Comp 530-630 / Math 530-620 Avg. ACT: 23-27
Total Cost: $26,232.00 (in-state) $36,690.00(out-of-state)
Received some form of financial assistance: 75%

Christopher Newport University is impossibly gorgeous!

Oh, and it's a fantastic bargain!

Oh, and students love it!

Christopher Newport looks like a movie set; the individual buildings are truly impressive, the design of the entire campus is elegant and purposeful. Many of the largest buildings are red brick and neo-Georgian, as might be expected at a university patterned at the outset after the College of William and Mary, but the newly constructed (well, it's all fairly newly constructed) Ferguson Center for the Arts was designed by Pei Cobb Freed and Partners, the firm directed by I.M. Pei, architects of the Kennedy Library, the Hancock Building, and, oh yeah, the expansion of the Louvre.

Imagine a university of about five thousand, dedicated to the teaching of undergraduates, offering modern and comfortable suite-style dormitory accommodations, remarkable facilities in every area of academic, residential, and athletic life, and one of the most strikingly handsome campuses in the nation. Christopher Newport may be a best kept secret today, but it is rising so quickly that this university will soon be among the most highly respected.

I'll be describing many of the exceptional physical qualities of the university, but first, I hope to communicate something of the exceptional character of the student body and the warmth with which any visitor to this campus will be met. The phrase students use to describe their habitual and cheerful greeting of each other is "door-holding", and they do hold doors and greet each other with pleasure as they cross this expansive campus. Some of the courtesy and good cheer arrives with the students, but some portion derives from the pride students take in their university and the gratitude they feel in attending CNU. The sense of appreciation and pride is palpable and extremely unusual in a public institution.

I had been working as a college counselor for about ten years when Richard Moll wrote *Public Ivies: a Guide to America's best public undergraduate colleges and universities.* The book recognized some of the obvious choices (UVA, William and Mary, UNC, Michigan, and Berkeley) and a few underappreciated (Miami University, U. Vermont). In subsequent years, others have been added to the list (U. Wisconsin, U. Washington, Georgia Tech), By every measure applied to the evaluation of public universities of high quality, Christopher Newport is the obvious next choice.

CNU began as an extension of William and Mary in the 1960's, offering course work to those in the Newport News/Hampton Roads area. By 1997, however, it was clear that the university had taken on a life of its own, and the split from W&M propelled Christopher Newport into its own impressive arc. The great advantage of the relatively late start is that the university grew up virtually in one piece. Almost a billion dollars has been spent in the last decade, creating a campus that rivals the most impressive in the land. Spacious, beautifully maintained, the CNU campus has the sort of aesthetic integrity that older colleges cannot hope to create.

Among the brick and mortar gems on this campus is the stunning Arts Center, which includes several performance spaces, dance studios, galleries, classrooms, and a theater acoustically designed so that a performer can be heard from any seat without use of microphone. CNU performances claim much of the stage, but visiting performers (Blue Man Group, Amy Grant, The Saint Petersburg Symphony, Patti Lupone, Straight No Chaser, Michael Crawford) regularly appear; students can attend for as little as $5.00. Equally impressive is the David Student Union (conference rooms, a post office, a dining court, and Chick-fil-A). As classically designed as the rest of the buildings, the Union also offers the post office, game rooms, and a second-story ballroom. The academic buildings are superior. The newest (well, they're ALL new) have gorgeous lecture halls and state-of-the-art classrooms. My favorite of the academic facilities is the Mariner's Museum, located within the equally impressive library. The museum houses the largest collection of maritime history in the hemisphere. That is entirely appropriate to an institution named for

Christopher Newport, a buccaneer who captained one of the three ships bringing the earliest settlers to Jamestown in 1607.

Social life at CNU, I am delighted to report, is also residential life. The university has added to its holdings in the neighborhood and has built extremely comfortable dorms, almost all of which are suite style, four students to a suite. In yet another uncommon observation, CNU has a sizeable Greek population (seventeen fraternities and sororities), but little angst about pros and cons of fraternal life on the campus. Many of the fraternities and sororities are housed in dormitories and all of them have a significant service component. In addition, there are another eight or ten other fraternal organizations that are particularly geared toward service and are non-residential. There is, in addition to lavish a residential apartment complex known as CNU landing available to upper class students, adjacent to Panera Bread and a Southwest Grill. The university sponsors more than two hundred and fifty clubs and activities in addition to recreational, intramural, and club sports. There is not room or time enough in this article to do justice to the extensive menu of available activities, but they run the alphabetical gamut from A to W, as suggested by these attached to the letter "A" A la mode – dedicated to fashion, fashion design, interior design, and personal styling, Agents with a purpose – agents of positive change, the Alexander Hamilton Society – debate on foreign, economic, and political issues, Altered Xpressionz –a break dancing club, American Sign Language Club, Anthropology Club, Arabic Club, the Association for Computing Machinery, and Astronomers Anonymous.

One residential certainty is that first-year students will be placed in a Learning Community, a residential assignment attached to a core of at least three academic courses in their fields of interest, taken in common with others in the community. Close attention to the experience of students in the first year has resulted in very little attrition from the first year to the second; students report great satisfaction with the program and with the courses. It should be noted that among the many (and I mean MANY) commendations that current students give their university is the clear appreciation of a teaching faculty that is accessible and devoted to the instruction of undergrads. Opportunities for original and shared research abound, and the faculty offers mentorship as a matter of course. The university is organized so that coursework is offered by a College of Arts and Humanities, the College of Natural and Behavioral Sciences, and the College of Social Sciences, which includes the Luter School of Business.

In honor of the free booting mariner, the university's team mascot is Captain Chris, and their teams are the Captains. Sports at CNU are also distinctive in that the university competes in Division III, as do other academically minded universities of about the same size (Chicago, Emory, Case Western, Carnegie Mellon, Washington University). As a result, athletes have exceptional facilities with which to train and compete. How successful is the program? CNU currently ranks among the top five Division III programs and has produced an extraordinary number of All-American athletes. Seeking more appropriate challenge, the university has moved from the USA South to the Capital Athletic Conference, joining institutions such as Mary Washington, Salisbury State, and Saint Mary's of Maryland. Among the most successful of programs are the women's softball and basketball teams. both of which have reached the highest ranks of post-season play. Men's baseball and basketball are also effective and well supported. It should be mentioned that the Captains have a notable home court/field advantage in that the university's cheer squad is exceptionally good. Club sports are also popular and well equipped. A surprising favorite is the ice hockey club; also popular are the rugby and soccer clubs.

Finally, Christopher Newport is an absolute bargain, both for in-state students (and they are the majority at present) and for out-of-state students. It is hard to imagine a more attractive opportunity than that of attending a university rising quickly in the ranks of academia, in the company of happy students, on a campus that is incredibly beautiful, for the price that CNU costs. Without much help from this guide, there is little doubt that this remarkable find will remain a secret for much longer.

Lynchburg College - Lynchburg, Virginia

Lynchburg attracts athletes and sports play a large part in campus morale and spirit. The Hornets play in the Old Dominion Conference and have established themselves as a power in a number of sports, most notably baseball until recent years, as soccer, both men's and women's, has taken center stage.

And the stats... 2015

Number of Applicants: 5,515/67% Accepted
Undergrad Enrollment: 2,161   60% female /40% male
Avg. SAT Reading Comp 460-550 / Math 440-540 Avg. ACT: 19-24
Total Cost: $45,925.00.
Received some form of financial assistance: 100%

Lynchburg is a small city of about 80,000 in the foothills of the Blue Ridge Mountains, about an hour east of Roanoke. It's a pleasant enough city, fairly quiet, once a tobacco capital and industrial city, now modestly active. It is a city of colleges, hosting Lynchburg and Randolph College, two liberal arts institutions and Liberty University, the largest evangelical Christian College in the world.

The focus point of an applicant's visit to Lynchburg may well be an introduction to the newly constructed Drysdale Center, a multi-purpose building of more than seventy thousand square feet, housing a student center, fitness center, multicultural center, space for dance and aerobics, a game room, and a food court. It's a pretty impressive building and gives testimony to Lynchburg's vitality.

Lynchburg College has an affiliation with the Disciples of Christ, an enrollment of about 2500, and a place in *Colleges That Change Lives*. Its location in Virginia, its affiliation with the Disciples of Christ, and the proximity to Liberty University may give the impression that Lynchburg is a "churchy" kind of school. The college is proud of its religious affiliation, but the core values the college promotes are values that might be at the heart of the most secular of liberal arts institutions: Academic Rigor, Active Learning, Commitment to Success, Integrity, Diversity, Community, Wellness, and Sustainability. Students at Lynchburg enjoy the full range of collegiate activities during their time in the college - including a healthy social and athletic life.

The values Lynchburg stresses have much to do with the qualities that earned the college a place in the list of *Colleges That Change Lives* – active preparation for success and earnest interest in the development of character.

A visitor to Lynchburg quickly notices three significant differences between Lynchburg and some of the other colleges with which it competes:

1. Lynchburg is big for a liberal arts college; of the 2600 students on campus, 2200 are undergraduates. The good news in maintaining a student population of that size is that the curriculum is wide and many of the activities offered on campus are on a large scale.

2. Lynchburg's campus is attractive and impressive in its scale. Dormitories and classrooms are handsome enough, but the newest academic and athletic spaces are truly impressive. One notable facility, for example, is the ambitious television broadcast center.

3. Athletes find Lynchburg and make a notable contribution to the morale and spirit of the place. For years, baseball was king at Lynchburg, but recently, a number of sports have edged into national prominence, appearing at the highest level of Division III championship play.

What difference does size make in framing the curriculum? Lots.

Lynchburg's students can major in the usual arts and sciences, but also have the opportunity to explore such major programs as: Accounting, Athletic Training, Communication Studies, Journalism, Criminology, Economic Crime Prevention, Exercise Physiology, Teacher Education, Marketing, Nursing, and Sport Management.

The graduate program is small, but one of the doctoral programs offers the Ph.D. in Physical Therapy. The presence of an active graduate program in an applied field like physical therapy allows undergraduates in allied fields, such as athletic training and exercise physiology, invaluable resources not commonly found in a small school setting.

Equally impressive is the on-going association with the Bonner Foundation, identifying Lynchburg as one of twenty-seven colleges in the country committed to the development of leadership and service. Lynchburg students annually contribute in excess of 40,000 hours of service to the community.

Distinct centers of academic and community interest have been established on campus; many students will be attached to one of the centers during their career at Lynchburg. The current centers are: The Clayton Nature Center – a nature preserve of almost 500 acres offering environmental education and recreation; The Center for Family Studies and Educational Advancement, The Beard Center on Aging; The Walter G. Mason Center for Business Development and Economic Education; The Center for Economic Education; The Donovan Media Development Center.

The facilities at Lynchburg are impressive, particularly the newest academic building, Schewel Hall, home to the Business Development and Education Center and the Donovan Media Development Center. The building is snappy in a number of ways, but the most eye-catching are the television studio and multiple editing rooms. Media projects can be completed at virtually a professional level, including the presentation of broadcast, video, or film in high definition. The building also contains a small and exceptionally attractive, auditorium.

Social life at Lynchburg is less influenced by fraternities and sororities than many southern colleges, in part because there are only five fraternities and six sororities on campus, in part because the emphasis on service and leadership takes a great many students out into other sorts of activities. Of course weekends also include the festive frolic that is college life, but the general tone of the campus during the week is purposeful. In addition to the usual assortment of publications, performances, artistic, and musical organizations, current clubs include an anime club, a Playstation college football tournament, scuba diving, wilderness medicine, and an odd association of students mobilizing for the right to carry concealed handguns.

Go figure.

Lynchburg attracts athletes and sports play a large part in campus morale and spirit. The Hornets play in the Old Dominion Conference and have established themselves as a power in a number of sports, most notably baseball until recent years, as soccer, both men's and women's, has taken center stage. The men's soccer team went to the NCAA Division III finals and has appeared in championship series frequently. The women's team has won the ODAC championship ten times in recent years and has also appeared in the championship rounds of the Division III tournament. The field hockey team may be equally dominant, having won the conference championship fourteen times in the last twenty years. In fact, all sports at Lynchburg are well above average, and participation at the varsity level is impressive. Club and intramural sports are also extremely popular, with options such as lacrosse, fishing, water skiing, equestrian, and scuba.

Randolph College - Lynchburg, Virginia

Throughout the twentieth century, the college was known for four abiding strengths: The academic rigor of its program and the excellence of its teaching faculty; remarkable loyalty to the college, inspired in part by well established traditions; an honor code that animated every aspect of college life; an equestrian program equal to the best in the country.

All indications are that nothing has changed.

And the stats… 2015

Number of Applicants: 1,353/ 81% Accepted
Undergrad Enrollment: 675   64% female / 36% male
Avg. SAT Reading Comp 480-600 / Math 470-600 Avg. ACT: 20-29
Total Cost: $47,860.00.
Received some form of financial assistance: 99%

Lynchburg, Virginia is a city of about seventy-five thousand, and to the visitor, it will quickly establish itself as a quiet, elegant small city with more than its share of handsome homes. It's a city Thomas Jefferson used as a country retreat, and it's only about twenty miles from the Appomattox Courthouse in which Robert E. Lee surrendered to Ulysses S. Grant to end the Civil War. The charm of a well-appointed Southern city is palpable; Lynchburg is a city with rich history, but not a museum piece or theme park city as are some other Southern destinations. There are several colleges in or near Lynchburg, including Randolph, Lynchburg College, Liberty Baptist, and Sweet Briar College. In fact, the student population during term time adds another sixteen thousand students to the mix. The Blue Ridge Mountains are visible from the campus, and the Blue Ridge Parkway offers a sensational drive north or south.

Randolph College is located on one hundred acres in the heart of one of Lynchburg's most beautiful and historic areas. Several Virginia colleges vie for the title of "most stunning campus", and Randolph is certainly a contender, especially among those in a city setting. The buildings are red brick and graceful; several are included in the National Register of Historic Places. The Maier Museum of Art is the college's nationally celebrated museum, holding one of the foremost collections of American art in the South. Most impressive, from this author's point of view, is the degree to which beautifully maintained classic buildings are completely functional and impressively responsive to the needs of a college continually growing and changing. Main Hall is a showpiece and an active, bustling, happy and effective home to classrooms, offices, the Student Activity Center, and a dormitory for several hundred students.

Like many colleges that were single sex (female) until fairly recently, Randolph's campus feels a bit more carefully tended to, its interiors a bit more thoughtfully decorated, than its more careless peers. Randolph starting enrolling men in 2006, and is now almost forty percent male. The success with which the college has attracted an ambitious student body of both sexes is due in large part to the extraordinary reputation the college enjoyed in its many years as Randolph-Macon Woman's College, established in Lynchburg in 1893, at a time in which the education of women was seen as "dangerous". The college was highly regarded nationally and seen as one of the prominent institutions of its type; its chapter of Phi Beta Kappa was the first granted to a women's college in the South. Throughout the twentieth century, the college was known for four abiding strengths: The academic rigor of its program and the excellence of its teaching faculty; remarkable loyalty to the college, inspired in part by well established traditions; an honor code that animated every aspect of college life; an equestrian program equal to the best in the country.

All indications are that nothing has changed.

Many colleges claim that they offer small classes and close association with a caring teaching faculty. At Randolph, it would be difficult to find a class enrolling more than twenty students; the average class size is twelve. Beyond the classroom, Randolph's profs are not just accessible; they are virtually inescapable. Teachers eat with students, go on trips with students, and sit in the bleachers rooting for Randolph's Wildcats. They are as actively involved in the life of the college as they could possibly be. Reports from students about their experience at Randolph invariably begin with a rave review of a class and of a professor. The college offers twenty-five major and fifty minor concentrations in fields ranging from Art History and Museum Studies (an exceptional program conducted in a world class museum owned by the college) to the experimental Design Your Own Major, an increasingly popular interdisciplinary option for the ambitious and self-directed student.

Two majors not commonly found in a college of this size are Education, leading to licensure, and Sports and Exercise Studies. No matter what major a student decides to take, the chances are good that the course of study will involve at least one semester abroad. The National Association of International Education honored Randolph as one of sixteen colleges and universities recognized for its commitment to global education. The Davenport Global leadership Program offers an exceptional opportunity for women who hope to be of service in an international setting.

Traditions continue to hold an important place in the life of the college. There are several that have stood the test of time, most notably the competition known as the Even-Odd Rivalry. Juniors and first-years team up against sophomores and seniors in a yearlong series of events, ranging from pie eating to pie tossing. A pumpkin parade challenges sophomores in the decoration of jack-o-lanterns, and an annual performance of a Greek play is both an academic and artistic highlight of the year. My favorite tradition at Randolph for many years was the annual "Tacky Dance", in which students ransacked local thrift shops (and parents' closets) to assemble the most obviously tacky attire.

Many of the Virginia colleges subscribe to an honor code. At Randolph, the code is an important part of every aspect of student life, so securely established that exams are not supervised; a student picks up a copy of the examination, completes it in any one of a number of quiet spaces, and returns it when done. To a degree uncommon even in those colleges that have long held an honor code, the trust among students is exceptional. One difference in the application of the code is that while there is an Honor Council made up of students that deals with breaches of the honor code, it is not expected that any student will report on any other student; part of the climate of trust on campus derives from the conviction that each student is responsible for himself or herself.

Finally, the equestrian program remains the signature athletic program at Randolph and one of the best in the country. How does a college in a lovely suburban area manage to maintain an ambitious equestrian program? Well, Randolph owns and operate a hundred acre riding facility in the foothills of the Blue Ridge Mountains, about eight miles from campus. The facility includes two rings and an amphitheater, a schooling ring, and a forty-stall barn. Randolph competes in the Intercollegiate Horse Show Association, traveling widely, and has been ranked in the top three collegiate riding programs in the nation.

Other activities and clubs enliven student life, including an active Model United Nations program, the aforementioned Greek Play, a radio station, a cappella groups, and the ubiquitous Humans Vs. Zombies.

The Randolph Wildcats compete in NCAA Division III in the Old Dominion Athletic Conference. Men ride and compete in soccer, cross-country, basketball, tennis, and lacrosse. Sports for women include riding, cross-country, basketball, soccer, volleyball, softball, tennis, and lacrosse. One of the unusual aspects of intramural sports at Randolph is that in some cases, members of the faculty compete as well. Ping-pong is likely to pit a student against his or her physics teacher in a battle to the finish.

Finally, and not unimportantly, Randolph is a bargain. The total cost for a year at Randolph is about forty-seven thousand dollars, considerably less expensive than comparable colleges of its reputation. In addition, the college very generously supports students with financial need and offers merit scholarships as well.

Virginia Polytechnic Institute and State University - Blacksburg, Virginia

Virginia Tech has come of age in the last twenty years, growing exponentially as a center of scientific and technical innovation. Its great strength at the moment, aside from the powerful appeal of nationally ranked athletic teams, is in the array of courses and majors available in this lovely setting.

And the stats... 2015

Number of Applicants: 20,744/ 73% Accepted
Undergrad Enrollment: 24,247 72% female / 58% male
Avg. SAT Reading Comp 540-640 / Math 570-680 Avg. ACT: Not Reported
Total Cost: $25,837.00.(in-state) $41,868 (out-of-state)
Received some form of financial assistance: 68%

Virginia Tech is officially the Virginia Polytechnic Institute and State University, also known in earlier times as VPI. Now firmly established in the public's mind as Virginia Tech, this eminently interesting university has developed into an exciting opportunity for a student wishing to enjoy the bustle and spirit of a large, comprehensive university with a powerful presence in Division I athletics, nestled in a lovely and historic town in the mountains of Virginia. Small town charm, beautiful mountain vistas and major league comprehensive university - a very rare combination.

Blacksburg is a mountain town in southern Virginia just south of Salem and Roanoke on US Highway 81, an incredibly beautiful drive through the Blue Mountains of Virginia. The town has been identified as "The Best Place to Raise Kids", probably not that enticing to prospective college students but reassuring to prospective families. The university is challenging, thriving, active, exciting, spirited, and fun, but I do have to note two particulars that often arise as families from other regions consider the university.

The first is just interesting: When Virginia Agricultural and Mining changed its name to Virginia Polytechnic Institute (VPI) in the late 1800's, it was obvious that with the change came the need for a new school cheer. The winner of the cheer competition produced the following rousing strain-

Hokie, Hokie, Hokie, Hy!
Tech, Tech, VPI
Sol-a-rex, Sol-a-rah
Poly Tech Vir-gin-ia
Ray rah VPI
Team! Team! Team!
What's a "Hokie"? A fan of Virginia Tech. At some point, this curious identity was attached to the sound made by the Virginia wild turkey. In that moment, the Hokies began to use "Gobbler" as their mascot. Go figure.

The second point often raised is more serious and has to do with the shooting that took place on campus in April of 2007. A mentally ill student killed thirty-two students and wounded twenty-seven others. It was a devastating event and one that is still in the minds of those who remember the accounts of the shooting. Could it have happened anywhere? Of course, and there is nothing to indicate that Virginia Tech is any more vulnerable or unsafe than any other location. I

The University has come of age in the last twenty years, growing exponentially as a center of scientific and technical innovation. Its great strength at the moment, aside from the powerful appeal of nationally ranked athletic teams, is in the array of courses and majors available in this lovely setting.

Its technical side remains strong; the College of Engineering is highly regarded; the Engineering College is ranked in the top ten of public universities. At least eight of its programs are regularly included in the top twenty in the nation – civil engineering, electrical and computer engineering, engineering science and mechanics, environmental engineering, industrial and systems engineering, mechanical engineering, biological systems engineering, and chemical engineering. The College of Agriculture and Life Sciences is equally distinguished.

The great advantage of VA Tech is that, in addition to the technical strength one expects in a polytechnic institute, the university is also well respected for its programs in business, architecture, natural resources, landscape architecture, growth management, and education. But wait! That's not all. VA Tech offers instruction through seven separate undergraduate academic colleges: College of Agriculture and Life Sciences, College of Architecture and Urban Studies, College of Liberal Arts and Human Sciences, Pamplin College of Business, College of Engineering, College of Natural Resources and Environment, and the College of Science. Students interested in becoming a veterinarian can also take course through the graduate College of Veterinary Medicine.

It's worth noting that admission to vet schools is exquisitely difficult and made MUCH more accessible to those who took an undergraduate degree in the university offering the graduate program. In addition to the standard curriculum, the university sponsors cooperative educational opportunities, study abroad, and a remarkable number of on-campus research facilities. Among those most admired are the Virginia Bioinformatics Institute and the Institute for Creativity, Arts, and Technology. Two other programs of interest are the universities programs offering study outside the United States. VA Tech operates the Caribbean Center for Education and Research and the Center for European Studies and Architecture.

The university's history and the traditions of the region contribute to the strength of another uncommon opportunity – membership in the university's Corps of Cadets. Unlike ROTC/AFROTC/NROTC programs the Corps is a separate student body, living and working in cadet barracks rather than in the other residential halls. About a thousand students a year enter the Corps of Cadets, march at public functions (and GAMES!) and carry on a tradition in place since the 1800's. Described as a twenty-four hour, seven days a week, four year, residential program developing practical, ethical leadership, the Corps requires its cadets to wear the Corps' uniform at all times in order to demonstrate each student's commitment to the life and code of the Corps. One obvious responsibility of the cadets is the firing of the school's cannon when the football team scores.

All of the usual high-jinx and community activities take place at VA Tech; the range of clubs and organizations is enormous; performing arts, music, dance, publications, service, virtually any interest is met with an organization eager to offer opportunity. Some of the activities are not found on other campuses, the Kendo/Kumdo club, for example offers instruction in that martial art.

Hang gliding and parasailing? Helping Animals Learn to Trust (HALT)? Hokie Ambassadors? Azwaz, the Indian a cappella group?

Yup. VA Tech has 'em all and another several hundred more, and two state-of-the art athletic centers allow another impressive array of activities, from bowling and darts, to home run derby and Wallyball. Indoors, Outdoors, the opportunities for active participation are available around the clock.

Greek life is significant as it is at most public universities, attracting about twenty percent of the student population. Twenty of the fraternities and sororities have houses on campus, and another eleven maintain houses off-campus. Roughly forty percent of students live on campus in dormitories that are modern, well maintained, and comfortable. Most offer suite apartments to all but freshmen.

At last, we come to athletics, the focus of much public attention to the university. Virginia Tech is an athletic powerhouse, playing nineteen Division One sports in the Atlantic Coast Conference. Fans of most sports know that conference as the ACC, a conference that pits Hokies against teams from Duke, Clemson, Virginia, Florida State, North Carolina, and Notre Dame. The flagship sports have brought the university much acclaim, and graduates have gone on to prominence in Major League baseball, the NFL and the NBA. There is a particular kind of school spirit that grows up around nationally ranked, successful athletic programs. Traditional rivalries, heated competition, truly gifted athletes bring the school together and provide an exciting experience available to every student. The Hokies take their Hokie pride seriously; it's worth remembering that school spirit is a great comfort as students go away from home for the first time.

North and South Carolina

The Research Triangle of Raleigh, Durham, and Chapel Hill has certainly accelerated investment in research in North Carolina, and the growth of Charlotte as a financial nexus of the "New South" has added to Carolina's infrastructure. As a result, North Carolina offers a number of exceptional and interesting options to students from outside the region.

UNC Chapel Hill is considered one of the "Public Ivies," an outstanding research university with a national reputation. In addition to the University of North Carolina's flagship campus in Chapel Hill, the state system includes Raleigh's North Carolina State and several strong branches of the University of North Carolina, two of which (UNC Wilmington and UNC Asheville) are profiled in this book.

Davidson College, located in a small college town just north of Charlotte, was known as, "The Princeton of the South," until its recent emergence as one of the top five liberal arts college in the country. Princeton may now have become, "The Davidson of New Jersey."

Duke would be a premier university even if it were not a perennial contender for the NCAA basketball championship. One visit is ordinarily enough to convince the most ambitious of applicants to include Duke as a long-shot application.

Wake Forest University in Winston-Salem is a strong small university with outstanding undergraduate and graduate programs. Know as, "The Fighting Baptists," in early days of athletic competition, they are now, "The Demon Deacons," and a power in the ACC.

Shaw University founded in Raleigh by the American Baptist Home Mission Society was the first college for African-Americans established in the South. Recently re-animated by sound fiscal management, Shaw enrolls approximately 2500 undergraduates. A major highlight of recent years was the restitution of Shaw's marching band ("Platinum Sound") with 130 members in the annual Honda Battle of the Bands in the Georgia Dome. The band was featured in the recent movie, *Drumline*.

Once a "best-kept secret", Elon University, located outside of Greensboro, is now widely sought, especially by those who value study abroad, a strong major in communications, and a campus that has been declared a national botanical garden. Elon enrolls about 5000 undergraduates, more than half of whom arrive from out of state.

South Carolina is less well known to applicants from other regions and, like North Carolina, offers the full range of recreational activity, from beautiful beaches on their outer banks, to wild rivers and forests along the Appalachian Mountains.

The two flagship state universities, USC (University of South Carolina) and Clemson are known to those who follow Division I sports. Both offer excellent programs.

Increasingly popular, the College of Charleston, also a public university, is actually in Charleston, but no longer a college. A university with almost 10,000 students, the College of Charleston is especially known for its programs in marine science.

Readers of Pat Conroy's work will be familiar with The Citadel, a state-supported residential military college in Charleston. The Citadel is no longer entirely a military college, but military tradition remains strong at The Citadel, The Military College of South Carolina. Its undergraduates make up the Corps of Cadets; an evening program enrolls civilians. The Citadel accepts almost 70% of applicants, but the requirements for acceptance into the Corps of Cadets include stringent physical requirements, similar to those attached to enrollment in the armed forces.

A strong contender for the most impressive campus in the United States is Furman University in Greenville, South Carolina. Furman is the largest and the most academically esteemed of South Carolina's independent liberal arts colleges and is also an uncommonly active and happy campus. One of the smallest colleges participating in athletics at the Division I level, Furman has graduated a number of professional athletes, perhaps most notably in golf. Beautiful, balanced, happy, Furman is one of the colleges most appreciated by students from outside the region and is profiled in this book.

Our investigations will bring us to Guilford College, in Greensboro, Appalachian State University in Boone, the University of North Carolina at Wilmington, Warren Wilson College in Swannanoa, University of North Carolina at Asheville, Furman in Greenville, Presbyterian in Clinton, and Wofford College in Spartanburg, South Carolina.

Guilford College - Greensboro, North Carolina

Guilford is probably a bit more politically active than liberal arts colleges of similar size and location. The tradition of civil disobedience remains alive, and the college supports a number of social initiatives that are distinctive. For example, a Native American program has been in place at Guilford since 1982, offering support to Native American students enrolled at the college and establishing awareness of issues of importance to that community. Other long-established programs include the Africana program, the Latino program, and the LGBTQA program.

And the stats... 2015

Number of Applicants: 3.001/ 62% Accepted
Undergrad Enrollment: 2,137   53% female / 47% male
Avg. SAT Reading Comp not reported Avg. ACT: not reported
Total Cost: $47,175.00.
Received some form of financial assistance: 100%

There are three distinctive features that might make Guilford an excellent option: It is a college in the liberal tradition of the Quaker colleges; it is a small college located within a small city; it is exceptionally successful in athletics. For those not familiar with North Carolina, Greensboro is the third largest city in the state, roughly in the center of the state, part of the Piedmont Triad with High Point and Winston-Salem. Greensboro has a population of about 250,000, and the Guilford campus is a lovely forested campus on the city's northwest side. Third oldest coeducational college in the country, Guilford is primarily Georgian in appearance' red brick buildings and a leafy quadrangle give the college an entirely collegiate appearance. This is a college within the city – a distinct campus of more than 350 acres separates the college from its quarter of Greensboro.

The Quaker heritage is an important part of Guilford's story, although the college's enrollment is less than 10% Quaker. The Society of Friends (Quakers) has been involved in education from the start; William Penn's establishment of a community in the colonies that supported freedom of religion may have been the start of Quaker influence on American education. The principles that have been of greatest importance in the establishment of the Quaker colleges are these: Peace, Equality, Integrity, and Simplicity. The contemporary implementation of these principles in contemporary Quaker colleges has been found in a curricular emphasis on social justice and peace studies.

At Guilford, still associated with a Friends' Meeting, the values central to its mission include student-centered instruction, a values-rich education, and a global perspective. All of which sounds pretty darned serious until one sets foot on campus – where good natured, happy, healthy, active, spirited, absolutely normal college kids romp as college kids are wont to do when taking a break from a demanding academic program.

So, what does the Quaker thing mean to a non-Quaker?

In the first place it means calling professors by their first name. Disrespectful? Not so much. Actually, the convention promotes the notion that there is equality in the work that each person does in the community.

Guilford is probably a bit more politically active than liberal arts colleges of similar size and location. The tradition of civil disobedience remains alive, and the college supports a number of social initiatives that are distinctive. For example, a Native American program has been in place at Guilford since 1982, offering support to Native American students enrolled at the college and establishing awareness of issues of importance to that community. Other long-established programs include the Africana program, the Latino program, and the LGBTQA program.

The college's mission is to engage its students with an emphasis on ethics, not solely out of conviction or principle, but also to prepare students to live and work in a smaller and more transparent world. The core values of the college and an emphasis on honesty are significant in its continuing affiliation with the Colleges That Change Lives; Guilford is determined to change many lives.

The student population at Guilford may seem slightly older than that at comparable liberal arts institutions, as Guilford has worked hard to bring educational opportunities to returning students. Of the 2600 full time students at Guilford, roughly 28% are between the ages of twenty-five and thirty-nine. The Bonner Foundation has taken special interest in Guilford's mission in educating principled leaders from an older cohort.

Finally, the athletic teams are known as The Quakers, a slightly less provocative title than the "Fighting Quakers," a sobriquet claimed by Sidwell Friends School in Washington, D.C. and occasionally by the University of Pennsylvania. Guilford's Quakers are pretty good in most sports, but have had some national success in basketball. It will come as no surprise that its most famous/notorious athlete alumnus is Lloyd Free, known to generations of NBA basketball fans as "World B. Free", the Prince of Mid-Air, and the current director of player development for the Philadelphia 76ers. Lloyd helped Guilford win the NAIA championship, then changed his name to "World B." It is hard to imagine how this NBA scoring champ with a 44 inch vertical leap dominated the Old Dominion Athletic Conference.

I'm a sucker for traditions, as careful readers of this book have now surmised, and one of Guilford's traditions particularly tickles me in that it reveals the college's warm sense of community and the whimsical nature of its students.

Guilford has its share of urban legends and campus myths, but one that lives beyond the campus is the haunting of Hobbs House. "Carolina By Moonlight" and other ghostly sources consider Hobbs one of the most celebrated of Carolina's haunted houses; tradition has it that Mary Hobbs was trapped in the attic when pranksters set fire to her home; apparently she still walks the halls of her former home, kind of spooky for the current residents, but not a major issue for most of the year.

Mary Hobbs hall is the oldest residential building on Guilford's campus and a prime residential choice for several reasons beyond its rich historical legacy. In the first place, it is air conditioned, and in Carolina, that's a good thing. In the second place, the campus Coffee Collective is located in the basement of Hobbs, and that's a good thing too. Finally, the residents of Hobbs are known as, "Hobbits," so how cool is that?

Lots of colleges do the trick and treating thing, but for decades, Guilford has gone out of its way to offer a safe Halloween experience for children of Greensboro, particularly for children of families not otherwise able to enjoy the holiday. Students prepare costumes for several hundred children, load them with treat bags, and take them through the campus, ending up at Hobbs, where well-mannered ghosts entertain them in a "haunted house."

The academic picture at Guilford is most clearly defined by the great respect and fondness Guilford's students have for their teachers; most students report a strong relationship with one or more mentor. A First Year Experience provides the transition from high school to college and is fairly well respected by freshmen who find their footing quickly at Guilford. The curriculum is a bit more expansive than at most liberal arts colleges, offering degrees in Forensic Accounting, Peace and Conflict Studies, and Sports Management in addition to the expected majors.

An extensive array of programs abroad supported by the college encourages study off campus, with centers in Ghana, China, England, France, Germany, Japan, Scotland, Ireland, the Netherlands, Wales, Mexico, Washington, D.C. and the American West.

Those who study college enrollment know that most liberal arts campuses are disproportionately female; relative few are actually 50/50 male/female.

Guilford is close - 47% of students are male; 53% are female. One final incentive to include Guilford in a college search is the college's generosity in awarding merit or need-free scholarships. A recent publication indicated that Guilford grants some form of financial assistance to more than 90% of current students, a considerable portion of that through merit scholarship.

There are no fraternities or sororities at Guilford, and the many social activities on campus are organized by individuals and groups. Among the notable extracurricular offerings are a highly regarded campus radio station and both the men's and women's rugby teams.

Some students feel that Guilford's intercollegiate athletes form a sub group within the college, but the relatively low-key athletic profile (with the exception of basketball) keeps the student body relatively cohesive. The golf team is also very successful and plays on a championship course designed by Pete Dye about ten minutes from the campus. Intramural sports are extremely popular and involve almost 60% of all students.

University of North Carolina Wilmington - Wilmington, North Carolina

Oh, and did I mention the beach?

Seriously!

Wrightsville beach is about twenty minutes from campus; it is a four-mile beach island on the same bank of beaches that stretch from North Carolina to Cape Cod, broad, sandy, and great for any beach activity. Fishing is good; surfing is as good as it gets on the East Coast.

And the stats... 2015

Number of Applicants: 11,523/ 59% Accepted
Undergrad Enrollment: 1,2964 61% female / 39% male
Avg. SAT Reading Comp 550-630 / Math 560-640 Avg. ACT: 22-26
Total Cost: $21,391.00 (in-state) $35,419.00 (out-of-state) Received some form of financial assistance: 68%

The University of North Carolina has long been among the premier public universities in the nation. Located in Chapel Hill, UNC is among the most competitive of state universities for out-of-state applicants; for more than a decade, UNC has been as tough as the most selective of private colleges. The university has more than one campus, however, and recently, the rest of the country has come to realize that the UNC campus in Wilmington, North Carolina might actually have some advantages over its better-known older brother on Tobacco Road.

In the first place, Wilmington, North Carolina is a spectacular location for a campus. The city is virtually a postcard for the National registry of Historic Buildings; although the city of Wilmington was not officially founded until 1797, the area is mentioned in the reports brought back to Europe by explorer Giovanni da Verrazzano in 1524. Known as the Port City, Wilmington is in the southeastern corner of North Carolina, between the Cape Fear River and the Atlantic beaches. Nearby Wrightsville Beach is among the most sought out beaches for surfing and windsurfing, and there are too many excellent golf courses in the area to mention. Wilmington is a port city, a shipbuilding city, and a major film center on the East Coast. Screen Gems has a large studio in Wilmington, and many, many movies and television shows have been filmed there. Soapy *A Walk to Remember,*

One Tree Hill, Dawson's Creek, and adventures such as the *Teenage Mutant Ninja Turtle* epic have been filmed in Wilmington.

The university occupies 650 acres in Wilmington, almost one third of which has been set aside as green space. A wildflower preserve, wetlands, and many oaks and pines are set aside the university's modern and excellent facilities. Only the Alumni House, a perfectly preserved southern mansion, speaks of an older architectural tradition. In recent years, the university has grown to almost 13,000 students, 12,000 of whom are undergraduates.

UNCW was founded relatively recently, and brought into the UNC system recently, and sat for some time in the shadow of its bigger brother in Chapel Hill; to be honest, there was a time in which UNCW was seen as the less academic, "party" option in the state system.

That has changed.

In the first place competition for spots in the state university system has grown as Carolina has emerged as a financial and research center on the New South. In the second place, UNCW has programs and facilities that are not found elsewhere.

One significant innovation has been in the establishment of a multi-disciplinary experiential learning model. The program known as ETEAL (Experiencing Transformative Education through Applied Learning), allows students to combine internships, study abroad, research, independent projects, and service projects in a highly individualized program of critical thinking and applied learning.

Marine biologists have long been attracted to the region, but the university scored a notable triumph when it became the center of research and education in a massive variety of subjects, from Aquaculture to Business of Biotechnology, from Coral Reef Ecology to Estuarine and River Ecology. An enormous Center for Marine Science, opened in 2000, allows laboratory research and docking facilities. In addition, UNCW has the only fully operational teaching aquarium on a college campus.

Marine studies and Marine Science are attached to many of the undergraduate divisions, so that some may be studying as biology majors and others as business majors. Programs also allow students to study the harvesting of oysters or the economics of fish hatcheries.

The university is organized into five divisions – Arts and Science, Health and Applied Human Sciences, Business, Education, and the Graduate School. In addition to bachelor's degrees in the liberal arts, the university offers the following undergraduate degrees: Bachelor of Music, Bachelor of

Fine arts in Creative Writing, Bachelor of Science, and Bachelor of Social Work. Pre-professional interdepartmental programs prepare graduates for the Allied Health Professions, Medicine, Law, Dentistry, Veterinary Medicine, Optometry, Pharmacy, Physical Therapy, and Engineering.

One notable recent development has brought the university's strong film department into closer connection with the booming film industry in Wilmington.

UNCW is a residential campus; about 4500 students live on campus in one of the dormitories, residence houses, or apartments. The remainder live within fifteen minutes of the campus in a variety of housing options, most of which have been coordinated by an off-campus housing office, The Seahawk Perch, one division of the Dean of Student's Office. In my experience, UNCW does a better job of coordinating and maintaining a close relationship between off-campus housing and the university's residential life system than any university I have visited. And, as testimony to the quality of on-campus housing, the occupancy rate has been at 100% for the past three years.

One distinctive program for first year students combines academic and residential opportunities. Called "Learning Communities," this option allows students with particular interests to meet basic requirements while living with and studying with others who share their interest. Among recent Learning Communities UNCW has offered: Dance is Life, Cultural Anthropology and World Citizenship, A Community of Caregivers, Physics, History and the West from 1650, German Music and Literature, Vital Signs – Navigating the Journey from Freshman year to medical School.

UNCW offers the full range of university level activities and organizations. About 10% of the students are actively engaged in fraternities or sororities. The campus recreation center is hopping and recently re-modeled to bring an even higher level of service to the all students. It offers the usual social amenities, an indoor track, a climbing wall, weight and exercise facilities as well as space for various clubs and activities

A short list of clubs and organizations on campus might include: an Anime Club, many publications, a Screenwriting Club, the Dance Company, Flicker Film Society, The High Seas (men's a cappella singing), the Irish Dance Club, the Pep Band, Physical Graffeeti (alternative dance), Sea Belles (women's a cappella singing) MainStage, a theater company, Teal TV (television production), a ton of service organizations, and the odd assortment of professional societies (American Fisheries Society).

Oh, and did I mention the beach?

Seriously!

Wrightsville beach is about twenty minutes from campus; it is a four-mile beach island on the same bank of beaches that stretch from North Carolina to Cape Cod, broad, sandy, and great for any beach activity. Fishing is good; surfing is as good as it gets on the East Coast.

Intercollegiate athletics at UNCW are in Division I, and the UNCW Seahawks play in the Colonial Conference against opponents such as James Madison and George Washington. The men's basketball team in particular plays some powerful teams each year, including Ohio State and Wake Forest.

UNCW's color is teal with red and gold as accent colors - slogans read, "Feel the Teal!" and students flaunt rainbow flip flops in testimony to Teal Power. The Teal Men compete in baseball, basketball, cross-country, swimming, tennis, golf, soccer, and track; women's sports include basketball, cross-country, golf, soccer, softball, swimming, tennis, track, and volleyball. The list of club and intramural sports is staggering; in addition to the usual (Ultimate Frisbee), UNCW offers, field hockey, ice hockey, rugby, crew, lacrosse, sailing, surfing, windsurfing, wakeboarding, water polo, horseshoes, and kickball.

Appalachian State University - Boone, North Carolina

The first thing to recognize about Appalachian State is that it is a state school - about 88% of enrolled students are from North Carolina. And, like any state school, it is notably less expensive than its private counterparts. So, at this small university of about 16,000 students the total cost for a year - including tuition, room, and board - is about $32,554.00 for an out-of-state student; that's about one semester at a comparable private college. By comparison, the annual total cost at Davidson in North Carolina is about 60,921.00.

And, despite its affordability, App State is not a factory!

And the stats... 2015

Number of Applicants: 1,496/ 72% Accepted
Undergrad Enrollment: 16,255 51% female / 49% male
Avg. SAT Reading Comp 530-620 / Math 530-620 Avg. ACT: 23-27
Total Cost: $19,387.00 (in-state) 32.554.00 (out-of-state)
Received some form of financial assistance: 68%

Those who follow college football are well aware of Appalachian State. The Mountaineers traveled from Boone, North Carolina to Ann Arbor, Michigan to hand the Wolverines of Michigan a stunning loss in 2007, becoming the first Division IAA school to defeat a ranked Division I football power. For reasons other than football, Time Magazine identified Appalachian State as its College of the Year in 2001. I'd like to say that the Michigan game has not been the deciding factor as students from other regions have begun to explore App State, but the truth is that national exposure revealed what Carolinians have known for years - Appalachian State is one beautiful, cost-effective, and ambitious small university in a fabulous setting.

Boone is located in the Blue Ridge Mountains of northwestern North Carolina and sits at an altitude of more than 3000 feet, making it one of the most elevated of institutions west of the Mississippi. Obviously, the town is named for Daniel Boone, and a statue of the explorer was crafted using the likeness of an App State professor. The charm of this small town in the mountains is evident from the first visit. Ablaze with color in the fall, likely to see snow in the winter, fresh and mild in the spring - Boone is like the prettiest New England hamlet. Appalachian State sits in the middle of the town with increasingly impressive facilities.

The first thing to recognize about Appalachian State is that it is a state school – about 88% of enrolled students are from North Carolina. And, like any state school, it is notably less expensive than its private counterparts. So, at this small university of about 16,000 students the total cost for a year – including tuition, room, and board – is about $32,554.00 for an out-of-state student; that's about one semester at a comparable private college. By comparison, the annual total cost at Davidson in North Carolina is about 60,921.00.

And, despite its affordability, App State is not a factory!

Most classes enroll fewer than thirty students and many fewer than twenty; the average class size is 27 and the ratio of students to faculty is about 16 to 1 – better than many private options. The statistic that best reflects the quality of education and life at Appalachian State is its retention rate of almost 90%; students are happy and happy to stay.

Appalachian State began as a teacher's college and it has remained a leader in the field of education. The greatest number of majors is in Education, with concentrations in specialized fields of Education, such as Communication Disorders, Educational Administration, Adapted Curriculum in Special Education. Of the almost three thousand undergraduate degrees issued in recent years, more than nine hundred were in Education. It is worth noting, however, that the University's recent emphasis on Entrepreneurial Studies, and the creation of the Center for Entrepreneurship has attracted increasing numbers of students to programs in that center. Recently two App State design students took top honors in an international competition in industrial design, demonstrating the opportunities for innovative work outside of the classroom.

App State is organized around separate undergraduate academic colleges: The College of Arts and Sciences, the College of Fine and Applied Arts, the Walker Business College, the Reich College of Education, the Hayes School of Music, the College of Health Sciences, and the University College.

Accounting, Finance, and Management degrees are offered through the Walker Business College, and the College of Health Science contains the highly regarded program in Nursing. The University College allows interdisciplinary study and offers the distinctive courses in Sustainable Development and Appalachian Studies.

Appalachian State is a large state university, enrolling almost seventeen thousand students. Unlike any similar institutions, however, App State has the feel of a responsive private university, particularly in the development of its orientation program for students new to the university. Called, First Ascent, the four-day wilderness program pulls first year students into small groups for an experience at Wilson Creek area in Pisgah National Forest, a spectacular setting in which to make first friends. Like most of the programs at App State, First Ascent is a crazy bargain. The total cost of taking the trip is under $250.00 and includes all equipment and specialized climbing gear.

On campus life is equally active, with sports and outdoor activities occupying a somewhat greater portion of student attention than at some institutions. The Student Rec. Center includes a 50-foot climbing wall, and the Outdoor Club is huge. Varsity sports are well supported, and it is with considerable pride that the Mountaineers point to their success in the twenty Division One programs offered by the university.

The victory over Michigan in football will long live in legend, but Appalachian State has long been a small university powerhouse in football, winning the NCAA Division One (Football Championship) national title for the last three years in a row, the first team to win three championships in a row. In addition to the other ordinary varsity sports, the Mountaineers have won national titles in mountain biking and cyclo-cross. The basketball team faces strong regional competition from Davidson and Wake Forest. App State competes in the Southern
Conference and is the only university to have won the competitive cup for both men's and women's sports in the same year...eight times!

Fraternities and sororities have their place at Appalachian State, but an active social calendar is planned for campus-wide events. Club sports such as rugby, lacrosse, climbing, equestrian, ice hockey, skiing, and fencing keep the active student body fit as well.

Finally, the Sousaphone section of the Mountaineer Marching Band has rightly captured the attention of all true lovers of marching music. The band is excellent and absolutely rocks "The Rock", the Kidd Brewer football stadium. What sets the band apart from the many excellent southern marching bands is a self-proclaimed "Wall of Sousa-Sound", tuba music at its finest.

Warren Wilson College - Swannanoa, North Carolina

The motto of Warren Wilson has long been:

"We're not for everyone…but then, maybe you're not everyone."

And the stats… 2015

Number of Applicants: 1,176/ 72% Accepted
Undergrad Enrollment: 822   55% female / 45% male
Avg. SAT Reading Comp 530-640 / Math 480-480 Avg. ACT: 23-28
Total Cost: $44,282.00.
Received some form of financial assistance: 94%

I know - Swannanoa, North Carolina doesn't sound all that glamorous, which is a shame because this small town is effectively the eastern edge of Asheville, one of America's most beautiful small cities in what some think is one of the most spectacular settings for any city.

Asheville, North Carolina is the largest city in western Carolina with a modest population under eighty thousand. At about 2400 feet, set against the Blue Ridge Mountains, Asheville has the charm and sophistication of a genteel country retreat. Tourists flock to the Biltmore Estate, commissioned by the Vanderbilts in the 1880's as a companion to the estate in Newport, and outdoor enthusiasts find their way to this comfortable city on their way to adventure. Cool, fresh summer breezes have made Asheville and Brevard the preferred refuges of those who can afford to "summer" outside of the humidity and heat of a Southern summer. So, shops are quaint, and artisans abound. Asheville is one of the rare destinations that always exceed expectations in any season.

Parents love Asheville and are fortunate to have the city as a jumping off point when exploring the distinctive program at Warren Wilson.

Warren Wilson is a truly unique experimental college, known for what it calls the "Triad" of work, service and academics. Students enrolled at Warren Wilson are required to work in an on-campus job and to perform at least 100 hours of community service before graduating.

The motto of Warren Wilson has long been:

"We're not for everyone...but then, maybe you're not everyone."

Self-aware, unique, Warren Wilson escapes being precious by remaining utterly and entirely "grounded" in real work.

Warren Wilson began as a farm school, and the farmland is still part of the campus. The sounds and smells of farm life remain attached to the campus, and Warren Wilson works hard to maintain a balance between academic and experiential education. The outdoors plays a large part in the life of Warren Wilson students; the North Carolina Outward Bound Program has a chapter on the Warren Wilson campus. The view of the mountains animates and soothes WW students, but it is the intensity and purpose of life at Warren Wilson that truly sets the college apart from its peers, even from those also consciously dedicated to establishing a community as well as an academic venture.

There are other colleges that believe in the value of work as part of the undergraduate experience. Several are Appalachian; three (Alice Lloyd, Berea, and College of the Ozarks) remain dedicated to educating students from the region who would otherwise not have the opportunity to receive a college education. Sterling College in Vermont offers few course options outside of environmental studies. Ecclesia College in Arkansas is a missionary college. Blackburn in Illinois is private but closely connected with the Presbyterian Church.

Work is a significant part of what the Warren Wilson experience is all about. Students maintain the college and the farm, working in teams. Some of the work is in the dormitories or dining hall, some in the barns and fields. More than one hundred "crews" keep the college running - fixing broken plumbing, baking bread for the next meal, repairing computers.

A student I know at Warren Wilson worked for several years coordinating "service learning" opportunities for other students; she arranged trips and home-stays, all of which were connected with the Bonner Leadership initiative in community building. She loved the work and felt that it was important and meaningful; on the other hand, as one who often traveled with projects, she put in many more hours than the fifteen required per week. She didn't begrudge the time, but she has other interests she felt she could not pursue. One of those interest is ornithology, so, she approached her professor of ornithology and suggested that there might be a place for an "ornithology crew." She will be working as a campus ornithologist in her next semester, training others to preserve and build habitats for native birds.

It may seem odd to begin the description of the Warren Wilson experience with work, but many of the most attractive elements of the college's identity are wrapped up in the intensity and commitment that the work crews generate. And, of course, students depend on peers to keep the plumbing working, the library functioning, and the highly reputed "Cow Pie Cafe" turning out organic goodies.

Oh, the students are paid for the work they do – about $3500.00 – reducing the total cost of a year at Warren Wilson to about $30,000.00. Even without any financial aid, WWC is among the bargains among colleges with a national reputation. Special scholarships are given to incoming students who bring special skills or talents to the work program. A number of merit, academic, and leadership scholarships are also available.

The academic portion of the Triad is designed with particular attention to the college's mission. Thus, every student will engage in studies that attend to issues of awareness, responsibility, and sustainability, no matter which of the many major fields they choose..

The First Year Seminars, for example, are broadly interdisciplinary investigations into a range of topics that engage even the most jaded of first year students. Recent seminars have included: Ecosystems in Time, Space, and Mind; Power, Privilege, and Community; Animals and Society; and Wanderlust.

In addition to the seminar, Warren Wilson's first year students must also take on a demanding course in College Composition – an equally esoteric mix of topical issues. Last year, the College Composition courses included Write What You Eat: Food, Culture, and Social Responsibility and Gothic America.

The environmental sciences remain popular, of course, and the campus farm allows hands-on experience in Sustainable Agriculture; other majors include Sustainable Forestry and Conservation Biology. In recent years, however, there has been a notable surge in interest in creative writing and the arts. The college's decision to support an ambitious master's level program in Creative Writing has brought many teaching writers to the campus and animated the writing program at the undergraduate level. The Theater program is also on the rise and increasingly popular.

Warren Wilson was the first desegregated college in the South and remains an active and liberal community. Don't look for fraternities or sororities or much in the way of athletic fervor, but there is a healthy social life on campus, and Warren Wilson is a very residential campus. Frequent coffee houses showcase excellent student performers, many of whom step up at the open mic nights. "Who ARE these people?" a recent transfer student asked. "Do they actually go here?" They do, and they go on to careers as songwriters and performers.

The college does support a few intercollegiate varsity teams which compete in soccer, basketball, cross country, and swimming. At the moment, the most successful team is probably the Mountain Bike Team, a co-ed team that competes throughout the region.

Recreation is often centered on the extraordinary outdoor opportunities available within minutes of the campus. In addition to caving, climbing, cycling, and hiking, WWC is closely associated with the North Carolina Outward Bound Program and with the most challenging whitewater course in the South, the Nantahala Outdoor Center in the Great Smoky National Park.

I am fond of Warren Wilson and would love to bring it to life in the pages of this book, but, obviously, this is one of the colleges that demand a close examination by those who would consider this innovative, challenging, and unusual collegiate experience, WWC is truly about the Triad, and unless a student is animated by the prospect of spending as much time in work and community service as in the library, WWC is the wrong choice. But for those who do, there is no better, happier, college in the nation.

University of North Carolina at Asheville - Asheville, North Carolina

UNC Asheville is a powerful public liberal arts college enrolling about 3800 students on a campus in one of the country's most beautiful settings. Oh, it also offers a spirited Division I athletic program.

And the stats... 2015

Number of Applicants: 3,090/ 73% Accepted
Undergrad Enrollment: 3,804 56% female / 44% male
Avg. SAT Reading Comp 560-660 / Math 530-620 Avg. ACT: 23-29
Total Cost: $19,928.00 (in-state) $34,799.00 (out-of-state)
Received some form of financial assistance: 75%

I am continually impressed with what UNC Asheville has to offer students each year. This is a small public university that is determined to bring the equivalent on an Ivy education to the mountains of North Carolina. A quick glance at the weekly calendar might include the Men's tennis regional tournament at Duke, an address by Henry Louis Gates, Jr. on Genealogy, Genetics, and African-American History, a reading by Rick Bragg, the production of a play written by an emerging Cuban playwright, and the annual "Boo Fest", a Halloween experience for local children sponsored by the UNCA's athletes.

In writing about Warren Wilson College in Swannanoa, adjacent to Asheville, I raved about the city of Asheville, one of the most pleasant small cities in the country. At the risk of boring the careful reader, I'm going to incorporate that description in presenting the equally impressive UNC Asheville. Asheville, North Carolina is the largest city in western Carolina with a modest population under eighty thousand. At about 2400 feet, set against the Blue Ridge Mountains, Asheville has the charm and sophistication of a genteel country retreat. Tourists flock to the Biltmore Estate, commissioned by the Vanderbilts in the 1880's as a companion to the estate in Newport, and outdoor enthusiasts find their way to this comfortable city on their way to adventure. Cool, fresh summer breezes have made Asheville and Brevard the preferred refuges of those who can afford to "summer" outside of the humidity and heat of a Southern summer. So, shops are quaint, and artisans abound. Asheville is one of the rare destinations that always exceed expectations in any season.

The more commonly recognized campus of the University of North Carolina is in Chapel Hill, while the increasingly popular UNC Wilmington continues to attract large numbers of applicants. UNC Asheville is distinctive for several reasons – an incredible location, one of the lowest price tags of any college in this book, access to the wilderness, and an NCAA basketball team that almost took Syracuse out of the national championship hunt – but the primary distinction is that the State of North Carolina established UNC Asheville as the state's liberal arts college. It is one of seventeen colleges in a state college system designated as a liberal arts college. The prominence of UNC Asheville within that peer cohort is made clear in the decision to place the headquarters of the Council of Public Liberal Arts Colleges on the Asheville campus. Noteworthy among the members are Evergreen State University in Washington, Sonoma State University in California, Saint Mary's College in Maryland, and the University of Montevallo in Alabama – each profiled in this edition.

What does a liberal arts college of quality look like when administered by a state system? It looks almost exactly like any one of a number of excellent private colleges with a discount of almost twenty percent for out-of-state students and a ridiculously low cost for in-state students. UNC Asheville offers a comprehensive array of majors in the arts and sciences and a few programs that would be unusual in any setting. For example, a student can major in Atmospheric Science, studying climatology and weather forecasting. A major in Ethics and Social Institutions is under the Department in Interdisciplinary Studies and examines the process and outcome of social change. The first comment Asheville students make is that this is one serious, ambitious, demanding college. There is fun to be had, particularly in exploring the outdoors, but the coursework is demanding, the professors attentive, and expectations high. Allowing for the necessary bias that comes with loyalty to one's institution, several students contend that Asheville is closer to Duke or Davidson in its aspirations than to most public universities. UNCA is slightly bigger than Colgate, and slightly smaller than Bucknell, enrolling about 3000 students in the undergraduate programs. The key to the UNCA experience in the words of many students is enjoying the facilities available in a state supported university with the access and responsive attention given in a small college.

The slogan presented at UNCA is UNC Asheville – Seriously Creative! Both of those elements are clearly present and much appreciated. Several students begin a conversation about their experience by trying to balance the pleasure they take in studying in the company of eager students like themselves with the pleasure they take in meeting professor with active interest in their subject and in the wider world. A purely liberal arts curriculum will necessarily mean meeting a variety of subjects and subject areas in navigating all the possibilities available. One much appreciated phenomenon is the enriching of the upper level Humanities classes as students contribute their experience gathered in pursuing their major.

In much the same fashion, residential life, extra-curricular life, and athletics all profit from the odd mix of state university facilities and small college atmosphere. Perhaps it is the seriousness of purpose that permeates the college, or the immediacy of a truly extraordinary experience in the outdoors, the rich creative character of the exceptionally intellectual small city, or the absence of football and a large fraternity scene – for whatever reason, UNCA is somewhat arty, liberal, and palpably welcoming. This is a happy college filled with happy students. They find ways to amuse and entertain themselves; social life is relative low-key, informal, and active. A variety of options in residence and dining are available, and some students do choose to live off-campus after the first year (Asheville is awesome!), but the dining service and the dorms get high marks as well.

Finally, I can't think of another university of any size that engages so many students in the intellectual and creative life, an almost overwhelming number of options in the outdoors while supporting a genuine NCAA powerhouse program in basketball, and pretty darned good Division I programs in soccer (men and women) and baseball. The Bulldogs moved up from the NAIA and have joined the Big South Conference, in which they have become a dominant force. It is great to see a relatively laid-back student body pour into Kimmel Arena to root the Bulldogs to victory. NCAA tournament appearances have pitted UNCA against Arkansas, Syracuse, and Pittsburgh.

Presbyterian College - Clinton, South Carolina

Presbyterian is annually among the top colleges providing professors recognized for outstanding teaching; it houses a vibrant Confucius Institute and maintains close connections with sister schools in China and Germany; it is a college devoted to public service; it has recently established its own School of Pharmacy on campus; it is the site of the world's largest bronze statue of a Scotsman in the world.

And the stats... 2015

Number of Applicants: 1,506/ 54% Accepted
Undergrad Enrollment: 1,146   55% female / 45% male
Avg. SAT Reading Comp 480-600 / Math 480-610 Avg. ACT: 21-26
Total Cost: $47,832.00.
Received some form of financial assistance: 100%

Presbyterian is the smallest college (1200) in NCAA Division I sports, one of the very few colleges to have an article of clothing as a mascot (the Blue Hose, represented by a Scotsman in a kilt - with blue stockings), and one of the few to have a reasonably completely authenticated haunted building within a district of buildings listed in the National Register of Historic Places.

OK, if those attributes don't compel the college applicant to pause, consider these: Presbyterian is annually among the top colleges providing professors recognized for outstanding teaching; it houses a vibrant Confucius Institute and maintains close connections with sister schools in China and Germany; it is a college devoted to public service; it has recently established its own School of Pharmacy on campus; it is the site of the world's largest bronze statue of a Scotsman in the world.

The Presbyterian colleges are among the most generous in terms of scholarship and financial support and are equally distinguished in extending their mission to traditionally underrepresented minorities and international students. Presbyterian is a church related college and holds principles that have animated the college from its founding.

Today Presbyterian welcomes students regardless of religious background or conviction, but includes several precepts as central to the life of the community. Among those that set the college apart is the conviction to "help students develop moral and ethical commitments including service to others, to help students attain a sense of dignity, self-worth, and appreciation of other persons of diverse backgrounds, and to encourage in students an appreciation for teamwork and for physical fitness and athletic skills that will contribute to lifelong health." The college's motto, "While we live, we serve," describes this college's mission in brief.

Presbyterian is an outstanding liberal arts college with coursework in all areas of the humanities, arts, and sciences. Unusual opportunities abound for the students interested in pursuing a career in education; major programs in Education and Early Childhood education, and Elementary Education are offered, as is a major in Physical Education. Accounting and Business Administration are undergraduate programs, and pre-professional programs are offered in every field. The college has recently brought a College of Pharmacy to the campus and considers strong preparation in the undergraduate program in giving preference to graduates of Presbyterian. The Confucius Institute was established by Presbyterian College and Guizhou University in order to promote the teaching of Chinese at Presbyterian and its partner colleges and by the Office of Chinese Language Council International of China to promote the mutual understanding between the two nations.

Presbyterian is one of the liberal arts colleges that include freshmen seminars, capstone experiences in all majors, internship opportunities for all students, and a broad-based program of studies directed toward international issues. I'll be turning to life in Clinton, S.C. in a moment, but one obvious advantage of attending a small college in a small town is that professors live within minutes of the campus, are actively involved in every aspect of college life, and are accessible in the extreme. Almost every student review includes glowing appreciation of teachers' efforts to help students.

So, life in Clinton, South Carolina. Clinton is not far from Greenville or Columbia and is within a few hours of beaches and mountains, but its primary attraction is in its comfortable, safe, homey small town atmosphere. Part of the easy acceptance of small town life has to do with the many opportunities Presbyterian's students find to engage in community service - and the by the extraordinary energy and excitement brought to campus by an ambitious athletic program. In addition, for a small college, this place is rich with extra-curricular activities and happy residential life. In addition, there are fraternities and sororities there are six national fraternities on campus and three national sororities; about 45% of men enter into Greek life and about 40% of women. Each fraternity has a house on campus; the fraternity houses together comprise fraternity court. Residential life outside of the fraternities is well directed and varied. The college offers eleven residential halls, eleven townhouses, and fifteen apartments. Of those, one residence is set aside for men only, and five are for women only.

Extra-curricular activities include a number of service opportunities, of course, including Habitat for Humanity, Big Brother/Big Sister, Special Olympics, and many more. Other popular activities several vocal groups, chamber ensembles, several bands (including a Pep Band), a bagpipe ensemble, a handbell ensemble, a brass ensemble, a strong theater program, ultimate frisbee, foam warriors, and a ton of intramural sports.

The prominence of Division I sports on this campus is a striking and important part of the life of the college and of its mission. This is an active student body; almost everyone is involved with some form of physical activity, from dance to football. Crowds at athletic events are huge, and excitement about teams is felt throughout the college. The giant eight foot bronze statue of Cyrus, the Scotsman, will remind the visitor of Braveheart; it's a terrifying Scots warrior, poised to do some serious bashing. The decision to move up to Division I was not taken lightly; the college in no way intended to dilute its academic program or its mission of service. Athletes who find their way to Clinton enjoy all the benefits of close association on a small campus; everyone knows who they are. They also climb on a bus and drive eleven hours to Columbus to play Ohio State. As ESPN put it, "The schedule is from hell, but Presbyterian is loving life in D-I."

Furman University - Greenville, South Carolina

This manicured and handsome campus is uniformly impressive, from the stately Duke Library to the cabin built by students on the shore of Furman's lovely lake, an exact replica of the cabin in which Thoreau wrote Walden. The Asian garden sits near a crystal pond, the Eco-Cottage is next to the lake, and the Florentine Bell Tower stands at the edge of a peninsula, allowing the sixty bells in the carillon to sound over the water on a South Carolina evening. In fact, there is no corner of the campus that is not among the most spectacular in terms of vistas and views.

And the stats... 2015

Number of Applicants: 4,583/ 69% Accepted
Undergrad Enrollment: 2,810   57% female / 43% male
Avg. SAT Reading Comp not reported Avg. ACT: not reported
Total Cost: $59,051.00.
Received some form of financial assistance: 96%

It hardly seems possible that Furman is included in a collection of best-kept college secrets; Furman is one of the most beautiful colleges in any region and quite possibly the most beautifully appointed college in the South. The American Society of Landscape Architects places the Furman campus among the most beautiful places in America! The casual visitor, struck by the lavish landscaping and stunning vistas might well understand why the college is often called, "The Country Club of the South," but may not be familiar with the recent study revealing that Furman has sent more students on to earn a Ph.D. than any other private liberal arts college in the South – that includes Davidson and Sewanee – and has produced six Rhodes Scholars and seventeen Truman Scholars.

Furman is located in Greenville, South Carolina, the state's third largest city, located in the northwest corner of the state, almost exactly halfway between Atlanta and Charlotte. Greater Greenville has a population of about four hundred thousand and offers all the amenities and opportunities found in a major city. Of particular interest to the college student are the several arena available as concert venues and a raft of sports teams located in the city, including: The Greenville Drive, a Single A farm club of the Boston Red Sox, The Greenville Force, an indoor football team, the Greenville Road Warriors, an ECHL hockey team, the Greenville

Groove, a minor league basketball team, the Greenville Derby Dames, professional roller derby team, and the Greenville Griffins, a professional rugby team. Some of the most exciting sporting events in town, however, take place on the Furman's campus, where this small university (twenty-seven hundred students) plays traditional rivals in Division I athletics.

Furman for many years was associated with the Southern Baptist Convention, during which time its teams were known occasionally as "The Christian Hurricanes". Since the split from the Baptists, Furman has become more diverse and more ambitious, welcoming students from every background and belief. Today, Furman's teams are known as "The Paladins," a far more interesting and evocative moniker.

Recent financial good fortune has solidified Furman's status as one of the most financially successful of Southern colleges. A twenty million dollar bequest twenty years ago was followed by several even more significant gifts. The bequest of more than a hundred million dollars from the estate of John D. Hollingsworth was certainly an important addition to the Furman endowment. In addition, just as North Carolina's Duke University receives the largest share of the billion-dollar investments administered by the Duke Endowment, Furman is also a beneficiary, receiving annual allotments that help to bring the Furman financial picture into a very strong position, and thus allowing considerable financial assistance to students in financial need.

This manicured and handsome campus is uniformly impressive, from the stately Duke Library to the cabin built by students on the shore of Furman's lovely lake, an exact replica of the cabin in which Thoreau wrote *Walden.* The Asian garden sits near a crystal pond, the Eco-Cottage is next to the lake, and the Florentine Bell Tower stands at the edge of a peninsula, allowing the sixty bells in the carillon to sound over the water on a South Carolina evening. In fact, there is no corner of the campus that is not among the most spectacular in terms of vistas and views. Some of us who are hostage to the game of golf find the eighteen hole golf course on campus mildly irresistible, realizing that it is among the best courses in the state and the course on which several future PGA and LPGA players played to the championship level in their college years.

Landscape and spectacular buildings aside, Furman is one heck of a school. The Furman academic journey begins with the First year Seminar, conducted in small sessions with a professor on a number of topics. Recent seminar subjects have included: American Gothic: Innocent Vision to Nightmares; Clothing as Self-Expression; Greece and Japan- Connections and Comparisons; Global and Green Computing; Exclusion and Damnation: Go to Hell; Rogue States; and Introducing Quantum Mechanics.

Once grounded, Furman's students can choose from more than forty major programs of study, formally grouped in eight separate areas: Humanities, Science and Mathematics, Fine Arts, Business Disciplines, Multidisciplinary Majors, Education, and Interdisciplinary Majors. Students can also pursue pre-professional programs in Engineering, Law, and Medicine, as well as Military Science.

The two distinctive opportunities made available within Furman's curriculum are the Study Away program and the May Experience. The May Experience allows students to take an optional three-week course after Commencement. The courses present a wide range of interests and many travel off-campus. For example, a recent May Experience took students from Furman to New Zealand to study Communication, Culture, and Identity. All the ordinary opportunities for international study and exchange are available to Furman's students, but the Study Away program is designed and directed by members of the Furman faculty who travel with students (recently to Spain, Italy, and India), advise students in their course work, and accompany them as they explore the nations they visit. One key aspect of both the May Experience and Study Away is that costs are covered in the Furman tuition.

Meanwhile, back in Greenville, life at Furman is pretty close to idyllic. Reports from students rave about the many opportunities to be involved on campus. Furman is a Southern school and a relatively conservative school. Kids tend to be identified as "Southern Preppy", by which they mean wearing light blue or yellow and true southern brands such as Southern Tide, Vineyard Vines, Southern Proper, Ralph Lauren, and Brooks Brothers, lots of pastels, seersucker, poplin, madras, polo shirts, topsiders, an occasional bow tie, and fresh, fresh, fresh good looks. Yes, Furman's students are a great looking group. They work very hard and consider their work to be worthwhile, then join the dance company, or the players, or the orchestra, or the FUtones (a cappella), or run triathlons, or play club lacrosse, or rugby, or frisbee, or do Aikido, or work on the newspaper, or the radio station, or the television station, or student government, or the Creative Collaborative.

Residential life is exceptionally well administered, and the reports from students are strongly appreciative of every living option, including freshman dorms and the fourth year option, apartment life in The Vinings at Duncan Chapel, a luxury apartment complex on the edge of the campus. Fraternities and sororities live in sections of the dormitories, not in separate housing.

Finally, Furman is an ambitious and successful athletic competitor at the Division I level in the Southern Conference, playing against such traditional rivals as Davidson, The Citadel, Wofford, Elon, Samford, and Appalachian State. The university sponsors eighteen intercollegiate sports for men and women as well as offering sixteen club sports. While all of Furman's teams are excellent, those gaining the greatest celebrity in the last decade have been championship teams in football, tennis, golf, soccer, and rugby. Furman has sent a number of graduates on to professional sports, including NFL football players, several who have gone on to play Premier League Soccer, Ryder Cup golfer Brad Faxon, and two World Golf Hall of fame players from the LPGA – Commentator Dottie Pepper and Betsy King.

It has been great fun to write about Furman and to remember just how delightful this college has been on every visit, but the proof is in the pudding. Take a trip to Greenville, walk through the Furman gates, stroll around the lake, and see if you can ignore the charm of this remarkable university.

Wofford College - Spartanburg, South Carolina

Like Furman and Wake Forest, Wofford attracts a healthy, happy, preppy, active, sporty student body that intends to take up a career as a doctor, lawyer, or corporate chief. The students are good looking and friendly, and the campus has the feel of a college in which poise and good looks prevail. Wofford is a small college playing big-time sports, and that commitment brings energy and focus to social life on campus.

And the stats... 2015

Number of Applicants: 2,565/ 77% Accepted
Undergrad Enrollment: 1,658   51% female / 49% male
Avg. SAT Reading Comp 530-630 / Math 530-640 Avg. ACT: 24-30
Total Cost: $51,504.00.
Received some form of financial assistance: 91%

Most of us from outside the region know relatively little about South Carolina and its cities. We may have seen photos of historic Charleston, and that is likely to be about it. Spartanburg, however, has at least two notable distinctions that may bring it to mind more often. In the first place, BMWs are built in the western end of Spartanburg County. In the second place, the Carolina Panthers train at Wofford in Spartanburg each summer. The city is about two hundred miles north of Atlanta and about eighty miles west of Charlotte, North Carolina. It's a thriving small city with both industry and corporate headquarters (Denny's Restaurants and Extended Stay America).

The Wofford campus is probably the most handsome section of the city, beautifully groomed and entirely designated as a National Arboretum – stunning when the magnolias blossom. More than five thousand Trees have been planted since 1992.

The college is located on about one hundred and seventy acres on the edge of the city and has managed to create something like distinct "neighborhoods" without losing the integrity and beauty of a well-established and eminently traditional southern college. The athletic facilities are impressive and grouped at one corner of the campus, while the academic buildings cluster together in another. The fraternities and sororities have their own distinctive section, and common areas tie the entire campus together.

Like Furman and Wake Forest, Wofford attracts a healthy, happy, preppy, active, sporty student body that intends to take up a career as a doctor, lawyer, or corporate chief. The students are good looking and friendly, and the campus has the feel of a college in which poise and good looks prevail. Wofford is a small college playing big-time sports, and that commitment brings energy and focus to social life on campus.

What difference do big-time sports make in the composition of the student body? Unlike virtually all of its peers, Wofford enrolls slightly more males than females – 51% to 49%. By comparison, the next best ratios, at Wake Forest or Davidson, are 48% male and 52% female. At happy Warren Wilson, 39% of the student body is male.

Long recognized as one of the strongest private options in the South, Wofford is increasingly well regarded outside of the region. Some of its current momentum derives from the energy brought by an ambitious president – Benjamin Dunlap.

All colleges tend to tout the academic and personal clout of a sitting president, but in Wofford's case, they actually do have a real live wire. Dunlap is a Rhodes Scholar and Harvard Ph.D. who has been a Fulbright Fellow in Thailand, a principal ballet dancer in the Columbia, S.C. ballet, the host of numerous programs on public television, and one of "Fifty Remarkable People" invited to participate in the Technology, Entertainment, and Design Conference.

Wofford has been a thoroughly reputable college since its founding in 1845, but Dunlap's presidency has enhanced the curriculum and program by establishing four initiatives that distinguish Wofford from its peers.

The first of these is its support of opportunities for students to study abroad; Wofford has been among the most successful in promoting foreign study, with more than eighty percent of graduating students having had the experience of studying or working abroad. More than half of those students have earned academic credit in countries in the developing or underdeveloped world. Open Doors has rated Wofford among the top ten colleges on an annual basis.

In the second place, Wofford has attracted Michael Curtis, fiction editor of the Atlantic Magazine to Wofford as an endowed professor and writer-in-residence. As a result, creative writing at Wofford is highly evolved. An annual competition brings publication to the most successful of authors.

The Community of Scholars Program invites ambitious students to invent projects worthy of ten week's attention during the summer and to find mentors on the faculty to assist in the carrying out of those projects. Rather than expecting students to scurry for spots assisting a professor in

240

research the professor thinks valuable, the Community of Scholars Program challenges students to come up with cross-disciplinary projects of their own.

SENCER (Science Education for New Civic Engagement and Responsibility) was developed by Wofford's Biology Department as a way of teaching science and math in a context of real world problems and initiatives. Course work is intended to empower students to feel themselves in partnership for change.

Finally, Wofford is cited by the Bonner Leadership Foundation as one of the colleges most actively involved in service for learning and community outreach. In addition to the ordinary compliment of service opportunities available through the college, Wofford's students have taken it upon themselves to engage actively with the city of Spartanburg in the Twin Towers Program, bringing student leadership to many city initiatives.

All the conventional benchmarks cite Wofford as a college of uncommon attainment and note particularly the engagement that Wofford's students feel in their own education. High marks given professors in student surveys and the objective research carried out by the various agencies that look at student engagement place Wofford in the top ranks of effective colleges.

Residentially, Wofford is unique in that it offers the entire senior class the opportunity to live in the Wofford Village, the extremely attractive apartment style complex including residential and academic facilities. And how do students relax?

The Greek system provides significant social activity, attracting about forty percent of men and about fifty percent of women, but the W.A.C. (Wofford Activities Council) is also highly active. The big news, however, almost every weekend is on the field or on the court.

Wofford is the second smallest college in Division I. Only Centenary College in Louisiana is smaller, and Centenary is moving down to Division III this year, leaving Wofford the distinction of being simultaneously the smallest and the most effective per capita in the country. How good are sports at Wofford?

Only sixty-four teams are selected to play in the NCAA basketball tournament known as "March Madness;" Wofford arrived in that select company in 2010 and almost knocked off Big-Ten powerhouse, the University of Wisconsin. Basketball is huge at Wofford, and beyond its opponents in the Southern Conference, Wofford's Terriers play against the giants of the NCAA - Georgetown, Minnesota, Xavier, Cornell. In most recent competition, Wofford emerges as the champions of the Southern

Conference, losing to BYU in a hard-fought battle in the NCAA March Madness. The football team is highly successful in the Southern Conference, champions in 2010, and made it to the quarterfinals of the Division I (smaller colleges) championship. Like the basketball team, the football team enjoys the modern and impressive athletic facilities recently completed in order to support the ambitions of a Division I school. Both baseball and soccer teams have also emerged as conference champions.

College of Charleston - Charleston, South Carolina

The life of the city is inevitably part of the life of the university, but the strength of programs here, and the variety of opportunities available should make COC an interesting option for anyone seeking a university in a manageable urban setting.

And the stats... 2015

Number of Applicants: 11,179/ 78% Accepted
Undergrad Enrollment: 10,440 63% female / 37% male
Avg. SAT Reading Comp 452-620 / Math 510-610 Avg. ACT: 203-27
Total Cost: $44,342.00.
Received some form of financial assistance: 74%

The word "college", evokes images of a small liberal arts institution, but the College of Charleston is a public university enrolling more than ten thousand undergraduates on a campus included in the Registry of Historic Buildings in the heart of Charleston, South Carolina. COC combines an elegant architectural past and contemporary design, presenting stately buildings of historic note and up-to-date facilities with every modern amenity. An exceptionally successful athletic program and a strong set of fraternities and sororities have made COC a happy choice for students from every region.

A recent graduate of the Honors College, a Creative Writing major, blogged about her first impression of the College of Charleston; her voice is more particular and comprehensive than mine, so please enjoy this account by Leah Knapp:

> *"I visited College of Charleston for the first time in April of 2010. On a Friday morning, my mother, sister and I set out for the Admissions Office to find our tour guide. We walked through Cougar Mall, past the clock in front of the Sottile House, and finally through Cistern Yard. Spanish moss draped across tree branches like Christmas tinsel and hot-pink azaleas burst from each side of the herringbone walkway. I tripped on a disrupted cobblestone and looked up, mortified, only to realize that none of the students walking around me had noticed—or if they did, they didn't care. Randolph Hall stood regally above the Cistern, where I'd read that students*

graduated in white sundresses and dinner jackets. Tan, smiling students passed by, many of them with swimwear under their clothes. I was smitten.

"I'm going to college here," I said decisively, before the tour even began."

Are all visitors to COC smitten? Probably not, but many do trust a strong first impression followed by good information to settle into this lively university in the midst of a lively and historic city.

The College of Charleston's setting has much to do with its evolution as a prominent university. Charleston is not just one of several distinctive cities in the Southeast; it may be (with Savannah) the city that most completely reflects the traditions, culture, and aspirations of the South. Evidence of Charleston's prominence in the Antebellum South is evidenced in its plantation era homes and public buildings. Charleston was at the heart of the cotton trade and the slave trade, and both have left historic buildings and ports. Charleston also had a sizeable number of free people of color, and those African-Americans who came to the city from the Sea Islands and the Low Country speaking the Creole language known as Gullah. Rich in cultural history, Charleston is equally impressive in its support of art and music. The annual Spoleto Festival is one of the most vibrant art festivals in the nation, bringing performers of every type to Charleston during the seventeen-day festival in the spring. For students, however, the charm of the city includes great places to eat and relax. One of the most helpful publications written by current students identifies the many local establishments that give discounts to COC students.

The life of the city is inevitably part of the life of the university, but the strength of programs here, and the variety of opportunities available should make COC an interesting option for anyone seeking a university in a manageable urban setting.

COC is a public university, part of the state university system in South Carolina. Although the university is one of the country's oldest, founded in 1770, its emergence as a national institution really began with its incorporation in the State College System in 1970. Growth was rapid, and in short order, the university established itself with more than sixty-six programs granting an undergraduate degree. In addition, COC is one of the few land-grant universities participating in both Sea Grant research and outer space research through the National Space Grant and Fellowship program.

The academic program consists of more than fifty possible major areas of study offered in seven academic divisions: The School of the Arts, School of

Business, School of Education, Health and Human Performance, School of Humanities and Social Science, School of Science and Mathematics, and the Honors College. In addition to the separate schools, facilities pertinent to academic interests have also been established. For example, COC operates centers dedicated to work in particular majors. These are five of the more uncommon centers:

The Halsey Institute of Contemporary Art includes a significant collection and exhibition space but is also in the service of one of the signature programs offered at COC. The university is the only one in the nation that offers a major in Arts Management and specialization in the combining of historic preservation and urban planning.

The Carter Real Estate Center housing the full-time professors in Real Estate, offered by the Department of Economics and Finance.

The N.E. Miles Early Childhood Development Center operates an accredited school for children from the ages of two to five as part of the school of Education.

The Avery Research Center for African-American History and Culture houses a collection describing slavery, the Gullah culture and the civil rights movement as well as acting as a research facility.

The Dixie Plantation is an eight hundred acre ecosystem allowing study of longleaf pine forests, wetlands, savannahs, tidal marshes, and saltwater ponds. Both historic Preservation and Forest Management make use of the plantation.

Undergraduate education is sound, professors admired, and classes kept reasonably small (the average size is about twenty-six per class). The Honors College is a particularly good option for students who want challenge, inter-disciplinary study, and independent study, under the supervision of a Peer Facilitator. Students in the Honors College can major in any area.

Residential life at COC includes an active and healthy Greek system. The university has had a number of fraternities and sororities on campus since the mid-Eighteen Hundreds; currently fourteen national fraternities and eleven sororities carry out recruitment of new member during the school year. Five of the fraternities live in a fraternity house; nine sororities have a house of their own. Most students live in one of the eleven modern residence halls, or in one of the nineteen historic homes owned by the university.

Rollicking spirit can be found throughout the university, particularly in support of the COC Cougars, a perennial powerhouse in several Division I athletic programs. Basketball and baseball are probably the best-known programs, and they are very successful. The university often sends its basketball teams to the National Invitational Tournament or the NCAA's March Madness. COC baseball is high-powered, sending graduates into the major leagues. Two of the most successful program, however, are less widely known. COC's equestrian program regularly competes in the highest level of national competition and often lands at the top of intercollegiate equestrian teams.

I've saved the most impressive program for last. COC has an extraordinarily successful sailing team, almost always one of the top two or three in the nation. The team consists of a coed squad and women's squad, both of which compete at major regattas. The team currently sails eighteen 420's, eighteen FJ's, eight lasers, and two J22 sloops. The depth of the program is impressive, but I have been most struck by the remarkable work the sailing team does in educating and recruiting students new to sailing. The sport of sailing is not available to many people in the real world; at COC, experienced sailors will be delighted to welcome a new student aboard.

Georgia

There is more to Georgia than Atlanta, although the more than five million people living in greater Atlanta certainly give the city real preeminence in the Southeast. The commercial and media capital of the "New South", and the home of Coca Cola, Atlanta is a "happening" place (CNN, Ted Turner, and the fourth highest concentration of Fortune 500 companies in the US) and rich in culture and tradition.

Emory University is a national and powerful university. Located in the Druid Hills area of the city, Emory is home to the Carter Center and closely associated with the Center for Disease Control and Prevention. The Yerkes National Primate Research Center, one of the eight research center of the National Institutes for Health, is located on the Emory Campus.

Georgia Institute of Technology (Georgia Tech) is located in midtown Atlanta and remains one of the nation's most influential technological universities and is often included in "The Public Ivies," public institutions that compete with the most celebrated private universities.. A Division I athletic power, Tech athletes are known as the Yellow Jackets, but immortalized in song as, "The Ramblin' Wrecks from Georgia Tech." Georgia Tech has graduated Nobel laureates and astronauts, as well as a number of corporate chiefs.

The Atlanta University Center includes three of the most influential of the historically black colleges.

Clark Atlanta University enrolls 3400 students on 126 acres in the heart of Atlanta. Among its graduates, Clark can number Ralph Abernathy and Marva Collins. Through faculty member, W.E.B. Du Bois, the university has long been associated with the National Association for the Advancement of Colored People (NAACP).

America's oldest historically black college for women, Spelman College is well endowed and highly regarded. Graduates include Alice Walker, Marian Wright Edelman, and Alberta Williams King, Martin Luther King, Jr.'s mother. Among the notable faculty in recent years attracting almost 60% of students from outside the region, are Toni Cade Bambara and Howard Zinn.

Morehouse College, one of three all male colleges in the U.S., was founded after the Civil War, currently enrolls almost 3000 undergraduates, and is the home of the collection of Martin Luther King Jr.'s documents. Notable alumni include: Martin Luther King, Jr., Julian Bond, Maynard Jackson, Edwin Moses, Samuel L. Jackson, and Spike Lee. The Morehouse marching band, widely known as, "The House of Funk," has appeared on the Today Show and at the Super Bowl.

Agnes Scott College, one of the nation's premier colleges for women, is located in Decatur, a large suburb of Atlanta. Currently accepting fewer than 60% of applicants, Agnes Scott is more selective than the colleges profiled in this book, but its extraordinary generosity in offering financial assistance to first year students (99% receive some form of financial aid) makes it a truly worthwhile option for female applicants. Agnes Scott is also a national college, enrolling the great predominance of its students from outside Georgia. You have probably seen Agnes Scott, as it is often used as the backdrop for films or television shows about "college." Its appearance, for example, in *Road Trip: Beer Pong* probably did little to enhance the college's academic reputation, but an impartial viewing does certainly endorse the college's beauty.

Also worth investigation is the nation's oldest state chartered public university, the University of Georgia in Athens, Georgia. Established in 1785, Georgia is an uncommonly handsome state university and especially well located in one of the South's most active cultural centers. Athens is the home of R.E.M., the Indigo Girls, and the B-52s and remains a thriving center for music and clubbing.

Our profiled institutions in Georgia are Berry College in Mount Berry, adjacent to Rome, Georgia, Agnes Scott College in Decatur, a near neighbor of Atlanta, and the University of Georgia in Athens.

Berry College - Mount Berry, Georgia

Founded in 1902, Berry stands for values that once animated Main Street America – principles that may not be commonly embraced in every quarter these days, but which the college has continued to hold with pride. The college is not large (about 2100 students) but offers a rich array of courses and programs.

And the stats... 2015

Number of Applicants: 3,801/ 61% Accepted
Undergrad Enrollment: 2,085 61% female / 39% male
Avg. SAT Reading Comp 530-630 / Math 530-630 Avg. ACT: 24-29
Total Cost: $44,388.00
Received some form of financial assistance: 98%

Mount Berry is essentially a rural attachment to the city of Rome, Georgia, almost equidistant from Chattanooga to the north, Birmingham to the west, and Atlanta to the east. Rome is a handsome city in its own right, but the gem in this region of Georgia is Berry College.

You may think you have seen an expansive campus, Cornell, say, Stanford, or Duke, but Berry College has the largest contiguous campus **in the world** – twenty-seven THOUSAND acres. The military academies are big, but Berry is gigantic!

To be fair, much of the campus is landscaped garden and pruned forest and even a few mountains, but the effect of stepping into this lavish landscape is stunning. The central buildings look like a movie set, and the campus has been the backdrop of a number of films, including *Remember the Titans,* and *Sweet Home Alabama.* The combination of handsome collegiate architecture and rolling countryside makes this campus among the most impressive anywhere. No matter what else the visitor plans to see in exploring this extraordinary setting, a visit to the oldest structures, The House of Dreams (Miss Berry's mountain retreat), The Possum Trot Church, and the Roosevelt Cabin.

Founded in 1902, Berry stands for values that once animated Main Street America – principles that may not be commonly embraced in every quarter these days, but which the college has continued to hold with pride. The college is not large (about 2100 students) but offers a rich array of courses and programs. Degrees are offered in The Campbell school of Business, the Charter School of Education and Human Sciences, the Evans School of

Humanities, Arts, and Social Sciences, the School of Mathematical and Natural Sciences, and the Division of Nursing.

Not strictly a Christian college, Berry describes itself as, "a comprehensive liberal arts college with Christian values." The general application of those values is in emphasizing the importance preparing its graduates to work hard and to make a contribution to their community. Some of the words that appear in Berry's descriptions of itself have to do with "practical work experience," "community service," and " work done well."

Christians of all denominations are invited to explore their religious faith and to consider themselves responsible for making principled use of the courses they take. Don't mistake this emphasis on values as having abdicated academic challenge; Berry combines a strong academic commitment with an eye on life after college.

The practicality of Berry's mission, and the straightforward expression of Christian values have attracted philanthropists who see Berry as an outpost of the American Dream. Its first incarnation was as a school dedicated to providing an education to local impoverished children. Martha Berry felt that the best education was one that combined classes with hard work; the first boys at Berry worked for two days and attended classes for four. Sunday, obviously, was a day of rest. Martha Berry's influence was widespread, and the institution grew from a school for boys and girls to a comprehensive liberal arts college, still endorsing the "regenerative power of work." "The head, the heart, and the hands," reflects Martha Berry's vision for a well and usefully educated person.

An early supporter of Martha Berry's efforts was Henry Ford, whose contributions helped to "seed" an endowment that is now in excess of six hundred and fifty million dollars. Already the college with the most acreage per student, Berry is among the colleges with the highest endowment per student. That endowment is actively used to support the education of students who might otherwise not be able to afford the liberal arts education. The total cost of a year at Berry is relatively low (about $32,000.00), and the college extends financial assistance to more than 80% of incoming students. The average financial aid package is about $20,000.00.

So, this remarkable college, steeped in Christian values, attracts a very interesting and unusual student population.

In the first place, Berry students expect to work.

Lots of colleges offer on-campus employment, but Berry's work experience is notable in two important areas. The principal operating at Berry is that students profit from "meaningful" work, and, as a result, the work programs actually make a difference in the quality of life on campus. And, unlike most programs, Berry's students are not only allowed to find advancement (and increased pay!), but also actively encouraged to develop student generated enterprises, which include a business plan and marketing strategies.

Now, about Berry's students: They are uniformly positive, energetic, and generous. The operative word, I think, is *healthy.*

They like to roam the trails, watching the deer that cavort just beyond the central quadrangle. Sixteen thousand acres of the campus is a Wildlife Management area, supervised by the Georgia Department of Natural Resources. A three mile paved trail allows runners, cyclists, and rollerbladers connects the main campus and the mountain campus. Other trails have been identified for mountain bikers and horseback riders.

Berry's tradition of observing Martha Berry's birthday with Mountain Day allows a quick snapshot of the culture of this college. Held on the first Saturday in October, the celebration includes a "Mountain Day Olympic" competition involving the entire student body, organized by residential hall. The egg toss and tug-o-war occupy much of the afternoon, but the real energy is in the preparation of the t-shirts proclaiming the superiority of one dorm over the rest. A talent show on Friday evening has prepared the college for the two other major events of the weekend.

The first of these-the Grand March – gathers as many as five thousand people at the foot of Lavender Mountain. Traditionally, Berry's undergraduate women wear pastel pink and the men blue to represent the uniforms of Martha Berry's day. The participants drop a contribution (the number of pennies representing their age) into a basket supporting a scholarship.

Martha Palooza – is an all-night carnival held in the college's Clara Bowl. This is a real carnival – Ferris wheel and rumbling rides – and entertainment throughout the night. A bonfire, bands, outdoor movie all compete with the carnival rides and attractions until sleepy students set up sleeping bags and camp out at the end of a long night.

At this point it is worth noting that Berry's academic offerings are equally distinctive. In addition to the usual constellation of majors in the liberal arts, Berry offers major concentrations in Exercise Science, Early Childhood Education, and Animal Science. The college has divided instruction into programs offered by the Campbell School of Business, the Charter School of Education and Human Services, the Evans School of Humanities, and the School of Mathematics and Natural Science. In recent years, the Liberal Arts, Education, and Business have graduated about the same number, reflecting real balance in the curriculum.

The athletic profile at Berry is slightly unusual, in that the college has recently moved from the NAIA to NCAA Division III. Varsity athletes compete in soccer, basketball, equestrian, golf, tennis, cross-country and track. Men also compete in baseball and women in volleyball and swimming and diving. Newly added is lacrosse for both men and women. Berry's mascot, the Viking, appears at most athletic events, and is a frequent performer at other campus events. Students support their teams and enjoy a wide variety of recreational sports including: golf, kickball, inner tube water polo, frisbee, dodgeball, racquetball, soccer, softball, disc golf, horseback riding, snow tubing, river rafting, and camping.

Agnes Scott College - Decatur, Georgia

Once one of the "Seven Sisters of the South", the elite group of the most admired colleges for women in the South, Agnes Scott has happily moved into the Twenty-First Century, taking its place among the best colleges in the region while remaining a staunch advocate of education for women.

And the stats... 2015

Number of Applicants: 1,394/ 68% Accepted
Undergrad Enrollment: 837   100% female
Avg. SAT Reading Comp & Math 1090 - 1300
ACT: 23-29
Total Cost: $48,832.00.
Received some form of financial assistance: 100%

Agnes Scott is one of the most distinguished colleges in the South, rich in tradition, ambitious, generous, lively, and exciting. Once one of the "Seven Sisters of the South", the elite group of the most admired colleges for women in the South, Agnes Scott has happily moved into the Twenty-First Century, taking its place among the best colleges in the region while remaining a staunch advocate of education for women.

Imagine a college so impressive that it has been the site of more than thirty films, running the gamut from *Driving Miss Daisy* and *The Blind Side* to *Scream 2*. The campus looks totally like "college" with manicured gardens, sweeping lawns, gothic buildings, and elegant interiors. Agnes Scott is a picture book college located in the picture book town of Decatur, a charming village lined with coffee shops, bakeries, restaurants, and boutiques. The, put these two impressive settings in the suburb of Atlanta, a city of more than five million people and thirty colleges and universities. This no convent!

Women's colleges have remained popular for several reasons; in addition to long-standing tradition and loyalty, every student leader, every team captain, every head of every activity, every academic star is a woman. There is a lot of evidence to suggest that a college for women with the academic clout of Agnes Scott empowers graduates to move into the highest levels of enterprise, government, and education. It is equally true that there is something about the sense of community in a women's college that is sustaining and strong; women at Agnes Scott report feeling independent, valued, and mentored. They also love their campus, their professors, their dormitories, the food service, and their traditions. I'll describe "Black Cat" in some detail later, but it is clear that those who come to Agnes Scott take great pride and pleasure in becoming "Scotties" forever. While tradition is important, Agnes Scott has been the most emphatically academic of the "sisters", less attached to horses, barns, and an ever-present strings of pearls. In its founding and in its mission, Agnes Scott may be best compared to Mount Holyoke. Georgia's colleges are well supported by the state, and the generous Woodruff Scholarships add to the competitive financial advantage of attending Agnes Scott.

I am such a fan of tradition that I had best get to the particular academic opportunities available to Scotties of the current generation. Atlanta is not to be overlooked as an educational resource; not only can the women of Agnes Scott cross-register with Emory (School of Public Health), Georgia Tech (Joint MBA program) , and a number of other institutions, the city itself is rich in terms of cultural activities and opportunity for internships. The college itself sets out to excite and develop the intellectual curiosity of first year students by assigning each to a seminar program attached to their dormitory section. Conversations begun in seminar carry over into evening and weekends, not only broadening the impact of the seminar, but also creating strong ties of shared inquiry with a small group of classmates, Recent offering in the Foundation Skills seminars have included: Making American Girls - cultural history of American girlhood, The Coca-Colonization of Europe - Debating American Culture, The Search for Other Worlds - exploring the idea of the search for life in the universe, Travelers as Learners/ Learners as Travelers - exploring the idea of the "journey", 21st Century History, The Bible and Human Rights in Atlanta, The Secret City - the Manhattan Project, "How Do I Look?" - Visual Politics, Personal History, Feminist Practices, Gender and Music, Media, Communication and the Shape of Our World, Dramatic Leadership - leadership as expressed in Drama, What to Do About Disagreement, and Choices: A Study of Economics and Leaders from Film and Television Narratives.

Pretty nice array of options. And that is just the start of the Agnes Scott experience.

The general scope of the student's academic progress is described as "Summit" - a four year sequence of programs and courses designed to enhance leadership, global awareness, and a broad set of skills in a particular discipline. Starting with the orientation program, students take courses directed toward these aims with the mentoring of a Summit Advisor who contacts incoming students before they arrive at Agnes Scott and who continues to offer direction and advice throughout the four years.

The college is small and relationships with the teaching faculty are strong. One innovation at Agnes Scott is an Academic Fair at the very start of the year, during which new students and their parents can meet with the teaching faculty in every department, talk about the particular demands and requirements for study in the departments, and explore the possibilities of combining study across several departments. The fair also allows time for questions about study abroad and internships as well. During the course of a career at the college, both professors and advisors are actively supportive in preparing graduates for fellowships, graduate school, and professional training.

Agnes Scott is uniformly excellent in every academic arena, but there are some distinctive programs not commonly found in a college of this size. The number of excellent universities in the city allows Scott to offer dual degree programs in Computer Science, Nursing, Engineering, and Public Health.. Several options are available for those who want to start graduate work while still an undergrad. The MBA program with Tech is one of the opportunities, as is the concurrent enrollment with the Rollins School of Public Health at Emory. Agnes Scott has also developed an interesting option for those who have completed, or are about to complete the undergraduate degree but who have not taken course work necessary to preparation for medical school, veterinary school, or dental school. The Post-Baccalaureate Pre-Medical Program is a thirteen-month program accelerating preparation for professional schools.

There are several significant aspects of the Agnes Scott experience that set the college apart from comparable liberal arts colleges. The first is an exceptionally vibrant Honor Code and Honor Court. Participation in the Honor Court is among the more important leadership positions given students. The impact for most students is in the strong sense of trust that is felt throughout the community. Shared responsibility for the establishment of authentic trust allows professors to give unsupervised, take-home examinations and exams that are self-scheduled, a great advantage in a busy semester. The second is an on-going commitment to public service, a commitment that begins with a day of service during the first week of the school year. The third is in the wealth of opportunities of every sort available in Decatur and Atlanta. Decatur's pleasant shops and cafes are a five-minute walk from the heart of campus, and the city of Atlanta is within a five-minute ride. One of the generous gifts of the student activity council is the discounting of ticket costs for virtually any activity in the city. Concerts, plays, sports – all are offered at half-price. Residential life is centered around the comfortable (and spacious) rooms in the traditional residences, each of which contains kitchen, social, and laundry facilities.

Finally, Scotties love their traditions, two of which are particularly lovely. Each of the classes has its own identity (and it own color and song); early in the fall, competition between the classes moves into hyper-drive, bringing excesses of decorative display and even more frequent performances of class songs. The week is called "Black Cat" and culminates on campus in a vigorous exchange of satiric performances in music and dance expressing superiority in every quality. With the end of the week, the freshman class is formally recognized and allowed to fully feel themselves Scotties for life. A gala dance at a splendid venue in Atlanta is a semi-formal recognition of the unity of Scotties in a social setting. Exams are stressful at any college. Scotties feel appropriately challenged during exam week and are grateful for "Pajama Jam", late night pancake extravaganzas that feed the hard-working scholar and allow a pajama break when most needed.

Agnes Scott competes in athletics in NCAA Division III as members of the Great South Athletic Conference. Scotties play at the varsity level in soccer, cross-country, volleyball, basketball, softball, and tennis. The Scottie Dog mascot is prominently featured on uniforms to the great advantage of the teams. Over the years, tennis has been the most successful team, frequently capturing the conference championship and sending an occasional player into the NCAA national championships.

Highly regarded in the Southeast, Agnes Scott should be among the options considered by any young woman eager to find academic challenge and a warm sense of community.

University of Georgia - Athens, Georgia

College counselors use the term, "Public Ivy" to refer to the relatively few public universities that rank at the top of America's academic institutions. Although it has changed over the years, the list generally includes Berkeley, Michigan, Virginia, UCLA, Wisconsin, Miami University, UNC, and Texas. It would be crazy not to include the University of Georgia on that list.

And the stats... 2015

Number of Applicants: 20,918/ 56% Accepted
Undergrad Enrollment: 26,882 57% female / 43% male
Avg. SAT Reading Comp 470-660 / Math 570-660 Avg. ACT: 26-32
Total Cost: $22,680.00 (in-state) $40.890.00 (out-of-state)
Received some form of financial assistance: 95%

College counselors use the term, "Public Ivy" to refer to the relatively few public universities that rank at the top of America's academic institutions. Although it has changed over the years, the list generally includes Berkeley, Michigan, Virginia, UCLA, Wisconsin, Miami University, UNC, and Texas. It would be crazy not to include the University of Georgia on that list.

Georgia, also known as UGA, is a big, complicated, public university with all the red tape and logistical challenge that any institution of more than twenty-seven thousand students is bound to have. That said, it is also truly distinctive, not only in the range of academic opportunities it offers, and it is a wide range indeed, or in the remarkable facilities it has built, but also in the texture of tradition and daily life.

"How 'bout them Dawgs!" This question/endorsement refers to Georgia's exceptionally talented football team. All of UGA's teams (Georgia Bulldogs) have the same mascot, "Uga", an English bulldog of distinguished lineage; Uga makes an appearance at every football game, dressed in a Georgia red jersey with a varsity "G" emblazoned on his chest. He's worn a tuxedo to the Heisman Trophy awards dinner and often wears green on Saint Patrick's Day, but Georgia's dog has come to symbolize the gritty toughness of Georgia's teams and the down-to-earth, self-deprecating humor of a first-rate university in a first-rate college town only about an hour away from Atlanta, a first-rate city.

The great Big-Ten college towns, Ann Arbor or Madison, are loaded with colorful tradition and celebration of college life. The University of Georgia is important, of course, and the city's largest employer, but it is a remarkable music scene that has made Athens a celebrated destination. There are festivals devoted to country music, bluegrass, and rock music, all of which pay tribute to what the music industry has called, "The Liverpool of the South". Contemporary groups in the 80's such as R.E.M., the B-52s sprang from a well-established music scene in the city, followed by other popular groups, such as Widespread Panic and Danger Mouse.

I include a colorful description of Athens because Georgia is a bit different from the other southern universities with which it might be associated. Yes, sports matter here as they do at the rest of the colleges belonging to the Southeastern Conference (SEC), generally considered the most uniformly talented football conference in the nation. The annual tilt against the University of Florida, known to Georgians as "The World's Largest Outdoor Cocktail Party:, and the equally significant rivalry game versus Georgia Tech, "Clean, Old Fashioned Hate" are both important moments in the collegiate year. There are a number of other activities and qualities, however, that set Georgia apart from the rest; it isn't easy to describe the "attitude" of a campus, but even the casual visitor will get the Georgia Vibe within minutes of walking through its celebrated arches.

In the first place, the University of Georgia is old. Most people are surprised to find that the historic North Campus looks and feels like the campus of an Ivy League college. UGA was established in 1785, before Georgetown or UNC and was patterned after the campus at Yale. Stately buildings in the Federal and Antebellum classical styles flank a beautifully landscaped central green, and the entire North Campus has been designated an arboretum by the State of Georgia. The venerated Arch at the edge of the Old Campus welcomes walkers coming from downtown Athens. Since the university occupies almost eight hundred acres, the Old Campus is but a small part of this complex university. Most people speak of the North and the South campus, but the area between the two, the Central Campus, is the home of the college's Student Center and bookstore, as well as the football stadium, Sanford Stadium. There is also an East Campus that has developed as the university had need of more academic and instructional space, and most students will be housed in high-rise housing on West Campus.

I can't begin to identify all of the programs available to an undergraduate at UGA; after all, the university offers more than a hundred and seventy majors and programs through its seventeen separate schools and colleges. Suffice it to say that Georgia has anything you might want to study and more than adequate resources for its instruction. I do want to highlight some of the extraordinary academic opportunities, however, but please understand that these are but a fraction of what is to be found in exciting Athens, Georgia.

One of the reasons Georgia has become one of the preeminent southern universities is that the state established Hope (Helping Outstanding Pupils Educationally) Scholarships funded by the state's lotteries. The scholarships are merit based and assist about nine hundred thousand students a year to the tune of about three billion dollars per year. The impact of the scholarships was felt primarily by UGA and Georgia Tech, two ambitious programs that compete with other excellent colleges and universities across the nation. The merit bump given to outstanding students meant that some of the best who might have gone elsewhere remained in Georgia.

Merit scholarships aside, UGA has some pretty nifty options for undergraduates. The Honors College is an exceptionally challenging and rigorous program, open to the most highly qualified entering students. The Franklin Residential College is patterned after the colleges of Oxford University in England, bringing students and resident faculty together for study and conversation. Should that seem pleasant, UGA's students may also apply to the university's program in Oxford, England. There, students live in the city and attend classes for the semester or for the year.

Other study abroad programs are also impressive. The university actually owns two other centers abroad. One, in Cortona, Italy, offers immersion into Italian language, culture, and history; the other, a campus of more than one hundred acres in the San Luis de Monteverde Mountains of Costa Rica offers a series of courses by season, making use of the natural environment as a classroom. For example, in the fall, students learn about the biology and economy of coffee, Tropical Biology, and as part of the school of Environmental Design and Landscape Architecture study farm and hotel management in Costa Rica. Later in the year, courses are offered in Avian Biology, Nutrition Education in Latin America, and Outdoor Recreation and Geology.

Back home in Athens, other notable programs distinguish this university from many others. The university maintains the State Botanical Garden of Georgia, thirteen separate libraries including one that is entirely electronic, an institute of Oceanography, a magnificent observatory, an institute in Artificial Intelligence, the UGA Institute of Bioinformatics, the Coastal Plain Arboretum, the UGA Bioenergy Research Systems Institute, and the Georgia Museum of Natural History.

As might be expected, facilities are modern and extensive in every area of student life, including one of the largest recreation centers in the world. The Ramsey Center includes two gymnasiums, three swimming pools, an indoor track, a climbing wall, eight full-sized basketball courts, and numerous courts of every other sort. The Tate Student Center is a virtual student service city, replete with restaurants, cafes, lounges, gaming centers, and theaters. Many of the university's lingering traditions have to do with sports and football in particular. One, "The Dawg Walk", assembles students outside the Tate Center to form a human tunnel that runs to Sanford Stadium, home of the Georgia Dawgs, allowing the football team to march to the accompaniment of the Redcoat Marching Band.

UGA is a southern school with many of the enthusiasms that the other southern universities experience. Football is king, and sports in general are widely enjoyed and supported. Intramural sports and club sports are equally popular, and the university is known for its active and fit student body. About twenty-five percent of UGA's undergrads will pledge the fraternity or sorority system and the university is proud of its long-standing history of fraternal life. There are also honorary societies and Georgia and a few secret societies as well. The seven hundred clubs and activities on campus seem to absorb the attention of most students, and for those not given to on-campus activities, the city of Athens and its music scene beckons.

A university of this size contains all sorts of people, so identifying a "typical" student is unlikely. Lots of kids travel abroad, play sports, are active in student leadership, work in the college's radio or tv station, sing, dance, act, paint, study. One recent graduate, however, embodies the kinds of diversity of experience an active student might find at UGA. Colton Fowlkes majored in Biology and Psychology with a minor in Religion. His claim to fame came in his portrayal of the Bulldogs' sideline ascot, "Hairy Dawg", a more rambunctious canine than the well-behaved Uga. His work in the mascot suit was both strenuous and gratifying; it is "Hairy Dawg" who tumbles wildly when the Georgia team scores or wins. Colton also found time to work with UGA Miracle, a charity that raises funds for Children's Healthcare of Atlanta. Colton's story is not unique; many undergraduates at Georgia are given the opportunity to take on significant positions of leadership.

Like its counterparts at Berkeley or Michigan, the University of Georgia is an exceptional educational opportunity and one of the "best buys" in terms of total cost. Perhaps the most impressive statistic of all is that more than ninety percent of students entering as freshmen return for the subsequent years. That rate of retention is ridiculously high for a large public university. This is one happy campus!

Florida

There is sunshine in Florida, and this long peninsula – the longest coastline in the United States – offers seaside communities on the Atlantic and the Gulf of Mexico. Despite the wild beach party image of Florida portrayed in films and television however, the state is actually made up of at least five distinguishable sections, each of which has its own character.

South Florida, from Miami to Pompano Beach, including Coral Gables, Fort Lauderdale, Palm Beach, Boca Raton, and Deerfield Beach is considered one metropolitan area and has the characteristic mix of cultures – Latin American, Caribbean, and European. Many "snowbirds" and retired people live in the South Florida Metropolitan region, and the predominant political affiliation is more liberal than in other regions of the state. The University of Miami. Florida International University, and Florida Atlantic University are found in this section of the state.

Atlantic coastal Florida, extends from Pompano to Jacksonville. Jacksonville is the largest city in the state, and, as a city in northern Florida, experiences the varieties of weather similar to those experienced in coastal Georgia or South Carolina. The northern section of the Atlantic region is known as the "First Coast," in part due to the founding of Saint Augustine –the first settlement in North America – in 1565. A long stretch of white beach runs south from Saint Augustine to Titusville and Cape Canaveral, including the race-car and tourist destination of Daytona. Colleges and universities found in this region include Stetson University in Deland, Jacksonville University, Embry–Riddle, and Flagler College in Saint Augustine.

Stetson, profiled in this book, is located between Daytona and Orlando. The center of the state, from Lake Okeechobee to Deland, includes the heart of Florida's agricultural economy and the happiest place on earth. Citrus and minerals have brought great wealth to the central region of the state; the bluegrass region of Kentucky has nothing on the horse farms of Ocala. Orlando, established by the citrus industry, is Florida's largest inland city, and, since the establishment of destination tourism with Disney World, Seaworld, and Universal Orlando Resort, the most visited city in the United States.

Not strictly part of the central region, Gainesville is the home of the University of Florida. Rollins College is located in Winter Park, one of Florida's oldest resort towns, adjacent to Orlando. The University of central Florida is located in Orlando.

Florida's "Panhandle" – also known as "West Florida" or the "Emerald Coast" stretches from the Alabama border to the west and the Georgia border to the north to the Gulf of Mexico to the south. The state capital, Tallahassee, and Pensacola are Panhandle cities, and the region is home to Florida State University.

Finally, the cities of St. Petersburg, Tampa, and Clearwater make up a distinct region. St. Petersburg may be the "sunniest" city in the U.S., located on the Gulf of Mexico and Tampa Bay and, until recently, known for the number of retired people who made the city, "God's Waiting Room." Now an eminently modern city with a younger demographic, St. Petersburg is a popular vacation destination. Tampa is an older city, distinguished by a remarkable mix of cultures and architecture. The University of South Florida is located in Tampa, as is the University of Tampa and St. Leo's University.

Eckerd College is located in St. Petersburg.

Eckerd College - Saint Petersburg, Florida

Obvious advantages to students of Marine Science and Environmental Studies appear in the most cursory investigation of Eckerd's programs. What is harder to appreciate is the degree to which this small college has taken leadership in American educational innovation. Eckerd was selected as one of Loren Pope's Colleges That Change Lives after only having been in existence for thirty-five years. In its short history, however, the college had already contributed several significant ideas to the college community.

And the stats... 2015

Number of Applicants: 3,459/ 73% Accepted
Undergrad Enrollment: 2,083 62% female / 38% male
Avg. SAT Reading Comp 510-630 / Math 510-610 Avg. ACT: 23-29
Total Cost: $53,508.00.
Received some form of financial assistance: 95%

Let me begin by asserting that Eckerd is an astoundingly good college deserving wide celebration from coast to coast. Eckerd certainly belongs in any conversation about liberal arts colleges located in a city setting, or any conversation about liberal arts colleges consistently bringing innovation to a sound academic curriculum, or any conversation about liberal arts colleges with sensitivity to contemporary social issues.

How remarkable is this campus?

Well, for a start, it has one hundred and eighty-eight acres of waterfront!

The Eckerd campus is literally <u>ON</u> the Gulf of Mexico, more inspiringly located in a city setting than any place I can think of, including the spectacularly designed campuses of UC San Diego, UC Santa Barbara, and UC Santa Cruz. This campus is ridiculously pretty, and the buildings have been designed so that almost every one offers breath-catching views of the coastline.

Obvious advantages to students of Marine Science and Environmental Studies appear in the most cursory investigation of Eckerd's programs. What is harder to appreciate is the degree to which this small college has taken leadership in American educational innovation. Eckerd was selected as one of Loren Pope's *Colleges That Change Lives* after only having been in existence for thirty-five years. In its short history, however, the college had already contributed several significant ideas to the college community.

One of the most copied of Eckerd's innovations is the 4-1-4 academic calendar, also known as the "Jan Plan," allowing students to concentrate on one particular endeavor during the month of January. Northern colleges leapt at the chance to cut down heating bills by farming kids out in January (OK, they probably had some academic goals as well), but Eckerd's notion was that education was enhanced by variety of types of engagement and that particular interests demanded greater intensity of concentration. The significance of this introduction of flexibility in the academic year is hard to overemphasize.

I am most moved and impressed, however, by two of Eckerd's more recent innovations.

The first of these may appear inconsequential unless it is compared to policies elsewhere. Lots of colleges are famous for having "Animal Houses" – crazy, drunken, irresponsible, social units, usually fraternities; Eckerd, on the other hand, has "Pet Dormitories" – residential halls allowing students to bring a pet to college. It doesn't take a genius to know that there's something about a dog or cat that's often good for a college kid far from home. And, really, can a schnauzer do more damage than five frat boys with a fire extinguisher?

The decision to allow pets in the dormitory may seem like a small accommodation, but it is not only unique; it is revealing. Eckerd values compassion, connection, and commitment. The sort of person who is attracted to a college that allows pets is exactly the sort of person who can make the most of an Eckerd education.

How many pets arrive at Eckerd? About three hundred... counting guinea pigs and fish.

The second policy is among the most brilliant of insights.

St. Petersburg has long been a city attracting an older population. Other colleges might have considered this situation a deficit; Eckerd assumed that with age came wisdom. The college has implemented a number of programs that allow younger learners and older learners to work collaboratively. In addition, Eckerd has brought mentors and tutors from the St. Petersburg community into the life of the college.

Please don't make the mistake of thinking that these are geezers playing checkers. Elie Wiesel, a Nobel Laureate, has been a visiting professor of Humanities at Eckerd since 1993. Recently Wiesel and John Prendergast, former head of African Affairs at the National Security Council, and a visiting professor at Eckerd, presented a program entitled, "From the Holocaust to Darfur: If We Had Only Learned Our Lesson." It is no surprise, then, that Eckerd would dedicate an entire year to a college-wide examination of the plight of Africa.

An annual colloquium brings Nobel Prize winners to campus, and notable literary and political luminaries have given their talents to the college over the past two decades. The college supports a "Diplomat in Residence" program, currently hosting a career officer with the U.S. Information Agency, a former resident at Tufts' Fletcher School of Law and Diplomacy. The Leadership Development Program and the Center for Creative Leadership are highly regarded, and The Academy of Senior Professionals brings journalists, authors, lawyers, executives, and a variety of other professionals to the campus as visitors and mentors.

This infusion of real world, experienced expertise brings the level of inquiry in the humanities to an exceptional level.

Classes at Eckerd are small and the professors get rave reviews, particularly for their active engagement in the progress of their students. The difference between Eckerd and most other small liberal arts colleges is that profs jump into sustained mentorship from the start.

The obvious curricular strength at Eckerd is in Marine Science. Like Maine's College of the Atlantic, Eckerd is perched on the edge of a living laboratory; the Gulf of Mexico is a classroom. And, should the Gulf not provide enough excitement, the department supports a wide variety of courses abroad, including a field study of marine mammals in New Zealand during the winter term.

Another great idea from the fertile minds at Eckerd?

Hundreds of yellow bicycles are strewn about the campus, available for students who want to peddle to or from.

Frats and Sororities? Not so much. Social life at Eckerd is characterized by a tidal pull between academics and the laid-back life of a college on the beach. The residences have been given Greek names, and the dorms make up the primary social focus. The newest residence halls are extraordinary handsome, and students come to feel affiliation with their dormitory.

Almost every description of Eckerd makes note of the mix of types who find their way to the college. It may be that the combination of location, reputation, and programs brings preppies, beachies, grinds, jocks, political junkies, writers, and mariners together in an odd jumble of undergraduates. The mix suits the college well, and students appreciate the opportunity to meet a variety of people on this astounding campus.

It will come as no surprise that Eckerd's athletic teams are called the Tritons. Lest you think this is a Little Mermaid – Under The Sea – reference, this Gulf Coast college plays tough competition in the Sunshine Conference, taking on a Division II schedule. Soccer and Basketball are hot, drawing crowds and considerable attention. Men's and women's volleyball have recently had considerable success, and intramural and recreational sports are well supported.

Kickball and dodgeball are especially active in the intramural world, whereas the co-ed sailing program and club lacrosse program have the greatest current interest.

The Eckerd Search and Rescue Team responds to more than five hundred distress calls a year. Trained by the Coast Guard, Eckerd students provide emergency medicine, firefighting, and open water rescue. Eckerd is the only college in the country to offer an opportunity in marine emergency rescue.

Despite its distinctive programs, I find Eckerd among the most difficult of colleges to profile.

Some of that difficulty comes in the uncommon mission the college has taken on. In addition to its liberal arts undergraduate program, Eckerd welcomes lots of returning and nontraditional students. Classes in the liberal arts college are uniformly good and do not mix, for the most part, with classes offered to less traditional populations.

Study abroad pulls many of Eckerd's liberal arts students off campus, and since the city of St. Petersburg is essentially attached to Eckerd's campus, the character of the city affects the college's social scene in significant ways.

Put simply, there is no such thing as a typical Eckerd student. It makes sense that this remarkably creative college has attracted a remarkably diverse student body.

Rollins College - Winter Park, Florida

When independent school counselors think of Florida, they think of Rollins; when they think South, they think Rollins. When they think gorgeous, without fail, they think of Rollins. Today almost 40% of undergraduates are graduates of independent schools and almost 40% are from New England or the Middle Atlantic states.

And the stats... 2015

Number of Applicants: 4,858/ 57% Accepted
Undergrad Enrollment: 2,670 59% female / 41% male
Avg. SAT Reading Comp 550-640 / Math 550-640 Avg. ACT: 25-29
Total Cost: $62,433.00.
Received some form of financial assistance: 87%

Winter Park is a spiffy small city in central Florida, the earliest planned city in the state and long a haven for New Englanders escaping from rough winter weather. Today a suburb of Orlando, Winter Park is minutes from the Disney World and Universal Studios. The city itself sponsors a number of festivals and celebrations, museums, and activities; beautiful, up-scale, and temperate, Winter Park alone is a draw for Rollins College.

Consider then the particular setting of an elegantly landscaped campus built by the shores of a sparkling lake, and Rollins, like Furman and Sweet Briar, moves into the company of colleges that are almost too good-looking. Even the most well prepared visiting applicant will think "Country Club" on first glance. It has been said that one can't be too rich, too thin, or too fit. For a variety of reasons, the tanned and fit Rollins student body is almost uniformly impressive. Famous alumnus, Fred Rogers, wasn't all that tan or rich, and there is room on campus for the ordinarily presentable human being.

When independent school counselors think of Florida, they think of Rollins; when they think "South," they think Rollins. When they think gorgeous, without fail, they think of Rollins. Today almost 40% of undergraduates are graduates of independent schools and almost 40% are from New England or the Middle Atlantic states. As a result, there is a climate of broader ambition and a far more sophisticated student body than that felt at near neighbor, the University of Central Florida.

The college recognizes its advantaged setting in describing college as, "location, location, location." The weather is often perfect, and the

Spanish-Mediterranean architecture is stunning. Lake Virginia is lovely – home to Rollins' water skiing and sailing programs. The crew rows at Lake Maitland nearby. Just to make the scene a bit more paradisical, the college has constructed a number of gazebos along the shore, complete with wi-fi access!

What does Rollins have to offer besides a beautiful setting and beautiful people?

There are three aspects to life at Rollins that are notable:

In the first placed, life at Rollins is balanced. Perhaps a better way of putting it is to say that students at Rollins are remarkably happy. Students consider the academic burden reasonable and find themselves well prepared for career and life. This is not a dreary, "college-is-hell," kind of campus; to a degree not found at comparable schools, Rollins kids love their college and are delighted to be there.

In the second place, the professors are universally admired and respected. The quality of interaction between students and their teachers at Rollins is exceptionally positive. Lots of colleges advertise small classes and responsive faculty; the overwhelming regard with which Rollins teachers are held is uncommon.

Finally, a strong program in the liberal arts is enhanced by the presence of an esteemed graduate school of business and by majors in International Business, International Relations, and Latin American and Caribbean Studies. The Theater Arts and Dance major is also highly regarded. In addition, Rollins does a great job of assisting its students in finding excellent opportunities for study abroad.

Rollins has established programs in a number of locations, bringing Rollins faculty and students to: Sydney, Shanghai, Hong Kong, Tokyo, London, Lancaster, Trier, Rabat, and Salvador. A recent survey identified Rollins as one of the top ten liberal arts colleges in terms of percentage taking advantage of the opportunity to study abroad.

Long-standing traditions indicate healthy school spirit, and, Rollins enjoys one of the great college traditions, "Fox Day", on which the appearance of the statue of a fox on the horseshoe lawn signals a college holiday. Al's Pancake Flip eases the pressure surrounding exams by offering a late night, pancake laden study break.

Fraternities and sororities play a very large part in the social life of the college; estimates of the degree of affiliation vary, but it's reasonable to guess that at least half the student body has been involved with Greek Life. Greek Week is a celebration of all things Greek, and a chance for the Greeks host a number of carnival activities. Open to the entire campus, Greek Week is an entertainment bonanza.

The annual Lip Sync brings out the rock star in entirely too many Rollins students who perform throughout the night in an all-out competition. In a more disturbing aside, faculty and staff also compete. Equally diverting, and even more arduous is the Rollins Dance Marathon. Couples are sponsored and attempt to dance throughout a twelve-hour marathon to raise money for the Miracle Children's Network.

Too much sun in Florida? Wait for the annual snow-day! A snow machine arrives at the campus center, and before you can say, "Jack Frost," snowmen appear on formerly sunny lawns.

Several cultural events associate the college with the city of Winter Park. Three are particularly important to the college: Winter With the Writers, which brings notable contemporary authors to the campus; Campus Movie Fest, celebrating student films, and the Bach Festival, a nationally renowned choral festival begun in Winter Park in 1935.

The athletic program at Rollins is outstanding. Once primarily known for water skiing and baseball, Rollins has become a power in the Sunshine Conference in many sports and a strong contender for national honors in Division II. The first recorded contest was a baseball game played in 1885 between Rollins and Stetson; both have remained exceptionally strong baseball schools, sending players on to the professional ranks. Rollins remains the smallest college ever to play in the College Baseball World Series in Omaha.

In addition to baseball and waterskiing, still a significant sport at Rollins, the college offers excellent programs in golf, lacrosse, soccer, swimming, rowing, basketball, and volleyball.

Finally, the teams at Rollins are known as the "Tars," one of the most curious of all college sports tags. What is a Tar? From most accounts, the name refers to the once-popular figure of "Jolly Jack Tar," representing the British sailor. During World War I only a few men were left on campus, training in sad rowboats, and apparently, they were called, "Tars," in fun.

You won't be surprised to learn that the name is not universally popular, especially among varsity athletes, who might prefer to be known as "pumas" or "tigers." In addressing the controversy, a recent issue of the Rollins Magazine put it this way:

> *"For the purposes of athletics, "Tar" conveys the requisite qualities of aggressiveness, indomitable spirit, and power, with a certain jauntiness thrown in that seems to fit Rollins.*

No reptilian Moccasins or mythological Tritons for us; Rollins alumni sail our lives with the wind at our back and a boundless horizon before us, and we know how to survive the occasional hidden reef or violent storm. We're Tars on the Seas of Fate."

In 2005 cheerleaders welcomed "Tommy Tar," a mascot who has been described as a cross between Popeye and the Pillsbury Dough Boy.

Stetson University - Deland, Florida

The first private educational institution to be founded in Florida, Stetson has a number of other firsts - first baseball game in the state, first basketball game, first school of music. This relatively small university (about twenty-four hundred undergraduates) not only competes in Division I, but also offers more than sixty majors and exceptional programs in Business and Music.

And the stats... 2015

Number of Applicants: 10,986/ 61% Accepted
Undergrad Enrollment: 2,841   61% female / 42% male
Avg. SAT Reading Comp 540-650 / Math 430-630 Avg. ACT: 24-28
Total Cost: $55,176.00.
Received some form of financial assistance: 100%

Wait, Stetson... like the HAT?

Yup. Although the university was founded in the last decade of the nineteenth century by Henry Addison DeLand, it was John B. Stetson's hat fortune that got the new institution off to a great start. In recognizing Mr. Stetson's generosity, the university has taken on his name and profession as the mascot and moniker of its Division I athletic teams; the Hatters play in the Atlantic Sun Conference, and mascot, "John B." appears at all games.

Today, Stetson is a highly regarded university offering undergraduate degrees through the College of Arts and Sciences, the School of Business Administration, and the School of Music. Several other graduate programs, including the College of Law, are on satellite campuses.

It was DeLand who developed this part of central Florida and for whom the city of about thirty thousand is named. Almost equidistant from Daytona and Orlando, (Seaworld and Disney) DeLand boasts an historic downtown area with a number of nineteenth century buildings. Relations with the university have always been important to the city, and residents remain actively involved in events on campus.

The first private educational institution to be founded in Florida, Stetson has a number of other firsts - first baseball game in the state, first basketball game, first school of music. This relatively small university (about twenty-four hundred undergraduates) not only competes in

Division I, but also offers more than sixty majors and exceptional programs in Business and Music.

I don't often quote a university's mission statement – most sound identical – but Stetson's is remarkable, not only for the range of its commitments, but for the tone of the piece itself. Most sound a bit ... well ... ponderous. Well-meaning and sincere, but slightly self-important. The Stetson mission is written in language clearly directed to the students they hope to serve:

> *At Stetson University, we dare students ....*
> *to push beyond their comfort zone*
> *to go far beyond success*
> *to be significant*
> *A Stetson University education helps students do all three, and more, through inspired learning, attention to values, and valuable life experiences.*
>
> *There's a big difference in the way Stetson approaches education, compared to schools with student populations the size of cities.*
>
> *Stetson University: Our students engage in small-group learning, in classes led by Ph.D. professors who share expert knowledge, serve as mentors, and teach students how to apply what they've learned. Students practice skills in real-world settings. Professors conduct research with undergraduates. Students learn how to think critically and creatively, surmount challenges and solve problems. These important skills are needed no matter what 21st century profession or career a student moves into after graduation.*
>
> *Others: Students are unable to receive individual attention because they are in giant lecture halls with 300 of their BFFs, and are often taught by grad students. Professors teach hundreds, not handfuls, which leaves scant time for mentorship or one-on-one discussions. Information is imparted, but facts alone don't provide a well-rounded education.*
>
> *At Stetson, life begins the day students walk on campus, not four years later at graduation. Residential campus life grants students the space and opportunity to develop their social and leadership potential.*
>
> *The Stetson combination of academic excellence, lively campus life and attention to civic and social responsibility*

positions students to reach their full potential as informed citizens of local and global communities. Students graduate with a professional skill-set, independent judgment, a global perspective, a grounding in ethics and a strong sense of leadership.

Yes, we cost more than some other schools. But you get what you pay for.

Stetson students do more than succeed. They become significant.

In fact, the tagline on much of Stetson's publications offers the challenge: "Dare to be Significant!" That is an interesting point of emphasis and one that makes sense in what is a close and exceedingly friendly community.

The two most commonly reported observations about Stetson, in fact, are that the faculty is amazingly accessible and supportive and that the student body is inclusive, friendly, and uncommonly happy. One obvious indicator of the university's sincerity in promoting the success of its students is in the staffing of the Academic Success Center. The Center provides tutoring and disabilities resources as many such offices might, but beyond that actually offers mentoring in areas such as Success Coaching and Academic Improvement – one-on-one mentorship designed to bring enhanced academic performance in a student's field of study.

The range of majors is impressive, including some that are rarely offered at universities of this size. For example, a Stetson student can elect to major in Africana Studies, Business Law, Music Combined with Business, or Sports Management, as well as in more commonly found majors in the humanities, arts, and sciences. Faculty are highly regarded in all fields, but in the College of Arts and Sciences, Psychology and Biology are particularly popular. The School of Business Administration and the School of Music enjoy national celebrity and considerable prestige.

The School of Business Administration intends to provide practical experience as well as comprehensive information. The programs within the school are: Accounting, Business Administration, Business Law, Economics, Family Enterprise, Finance, International Business, Management, Management Information Systems, Marketing, and Sport Management. There are several distinctive opportunities made available to Business majors. The Roland George Investments Program allows students to manage a real investment portfolio of more than three million dollars. The Joseph C. Prince Entrepreneurship Program gives Stetson's students the chance to see how a new business venture is conceived and managed. A very pleasant extra for Business majors is the summer program in Innsbruck, Austria.

Stetson may well enjoy the greatest national reputation as a result of its exceptionally highly regarded School of Music. Make no mistake; this is a top-flight conservatory. A talented group of about sixty new musicians is admitted by audition in order to keep the total enrollment in conservatory at about two hundred. Perhaps the intimacy of instruction and mentorship has something to do with the quality of the teaching faculty, all of whom are exceptional professional musicians. Perhaps that mentorship is also enhanced by staffing the school with more than sixty of those professionals. Experts work with students in Brass, Percussion, Guitar, Jazz Composition, Music Education, Music History, Music Technology, Music Theory and Composition, Piano, Organ, and Harpsichord, Strings, Voice, and Woodwinds. Performances on campus showcase the Concert Choir, the University Orchestra, the University Symphonic Band, the Jazz Ensemble, the Choral Union, the Stetson Women's Chorale, Stetson Men, the Stetson Opera Company, the Chamber Ensemble, the Flute Orchestra, The Clarinet Choir, The Trombone Choir, the Percussion Ensemble, the Guitar Ensemble, the Chamber Orchestra, the Barron Quartet, the Hatter Brass, and the Horn Ensemble.

So, there is quite a lot going on at any time, in addition to the many programs organized by the student activities committee, the fraternities, and the sororities. Service groups are well supported, and there are more than one hundred activities sponsored on campus. One that has a national draw is the Mock Student Senate, the oldest collegiate Senate, and one that welcomes delegations from many other colleges in its annual conference.

Finally, Stetson is mad about the Hatters. Over the past decade, baseball has been the premiere sport at Stetson; Hatters routinely win their conference championship. The excitement about Stetson football is building as the university prepares to restore its football program. Other programs of note include Women's soccer, rowing, basketball, and golf. Stetson has an outstanding cheer squad and increasingly successful teams in cross-country, men's soccer, tennis, women's sand volleyball, softball, tennis, and lacrosse. Men's lacrosse has recently been added as a varsity sport. Club sports include Aikido, equestrian, croquet, fishing, mixed martial arts, and shooting.

Sewanee - The University of the South - Sewanee, Tennessee

One special manifestation of the British tradition is in the Order of the Gownsmen. Gownsmen (and women) are inducted into the order upon reaching a notable level of academic excellence. The Gownsmen are permitted to wear the traditional black academic gown and are delighted to do so. The verb, "to gown," indicates the ceremony by which the gown is first presented to an inductee. "O.G." is the abbreviation of the order, as used in conversation. One of the many "ghosts" featured in Sewanee legend is, "The Headless Gownsman," reputed to walk the halls of academic buildings at night.

And the stats... 2015

Number of Applicants: 2,997/ 65% Accepted
Undergrad Enrollment: 1,631   52% female / 48% male
Avg. SAT Reading 650-670 / Math 570-690 Avg. ACT: 26-30
Total Cost: $49,700.00.
Received some form of financial assistance: 75%

Well, which is it?

"The University of the South" or "Sewanee"?

And where is Sewanee, anyway?

The University of the South, more commonly known as Sewanee, has produced twenty-five Rhodes Scholars - an impressive statistic. In fact, I should pause long enough to note that production of Rhodes Scholars is about as accurate indicator of excellence as anything I can think of; it is certainly more indicative than ranking in a news magazine. In having produced twenty-five, Sewanee ranks fourth among all liberal arts colleges.

Located in a mountain campus of 13,000 acres and enrolling about 1400 undergraduates, Sewanee is splendidly rural, a quiet and lovely, magical campus about halfway between Nashville and Chattanooga. Associated from the start with the Episcopal (Anglican) Church, Sewanee often seems more British than southern. "The Order of the Gownsmen" (upperclassmen with outstanding academic records) often wear the academic gown during the class day, and teachers usually do. Traditions of this sort abound and are sustained by the strong sense of historical connection with the universities of Oxford and Cambridge. A strong literary tradition also persists at Sewanee. The Sewanee Review, like the Kenyon Review, is a literary magazine of international importance. The collection of papers belonging to Tennessee Williams is housed at Sewanee, and English remains the most popular major.

Sewanee looks like a British college and the improbable combination of classical education and a remote mountain location in the Cumberland Plateau adds a quality of character to Sewanee and to the Sewanee education that can only be described as one-of-a-kind. One indication of the range of opportunities available in this setting is the menu of activities sponsored by the Sewanee Outing Club. Got some time on your hands? Within easy reach – cycling, caving, climbing, and fifty miles of trail on campus. Then, with a bit more time to spend, join the club backpacking in the Smokey Mountains, or canoeing on the Rio Grande, or tackle some winter camping in Colorado. The Club maintains gear that can be checked out at any time.

Sewanee's students have picked Sewanee because they found something rare and good in a college that has remained true to its mission and character despite the shock waves in American culture.

Is this a "magic mountain," a "bubble," outside the ordinary sway of life in Twenty First Century America?

You bet!

The first indicator of the distance that Sewanee establishes in the invention of itself is in the naming of its campus. The entire thirteen thousand acres, rising from the town of Winchester, Tennessee to the spires of All Saint's Chapel is known as "The Domain." Although only the central thousand acres have been developed and form the visible campus, the entire "Domain" belongs to the college.

The second will be in the remaining traditions cherished by current students, the most visible of which is that of wearing "formal" clothing to class.

Once men wore coat and ties, ladies wore dresses. Things have relaxed a bit in that guys now may wear a collared shirt and jacket, gals slacks and a blouse, or in a spirit of compromise, the academic gown and a pair of shorts. True college life prevails here as well in that everyone wears flip-flops rather than oxfords or pumps. The tradition of dressing indicates respect for the classroom experience and a sense of participation in an enterprise of real importance.

One special manifestation of the British tradition is in the Order of the Gownsmen. Gownsmen (and women) are inducted into the order upon reaching a notable level of academic excellence. The Gownsmen are permitted to wear the traditional black academic gown and are delighted to do so. The verb, "to gown," indicates the ceremony by which the gown is first presented to an inductee. "O.G." is the abbreviation of the order, as used in conversation. One of the many "ghosts" featured in Sewanee legend is, "The Headless Gownsman," reputed to walk the halls of academic buildings at night.

Two social groups, the Highlanders (Scots) and the Wellingtons (Brits) wear distinctive regalia and often appear on the sidelines of football games and other athletic events.

Other notable traditions include "Passing Hello," by which every resident of the Domain is encouraged (compelled?) to greet every person met on any walkway. Thus, the campus is a far more visitor-friendly campus than any other.

Finally, The Honor Code is more than a tradition. As it is at some other Southern colleges, the Honor Code is taken seriously and is adhered to in every aspect of life in the college.

Finally, it has to be said, the University of the South is owned by the Episcopal Church.

As is true of the great universities of Europe, the influence of the Church is most visible in the college's architecture - Gothic and sandstone. In addition to the undergraduate college, the University maintains a School of Theology and a School of Letters, both graduate programs. The Episcopal Church is actively involved in the stewardship of the college, but, with the exception of "churchy" tourists arriving for the celebrated Festival of Lessons and Carols in December, the place is decidedly more collegiate than religious.

Sewanee is a bastion of the liberal arts, perhaps a bit more "literary" than some of its peers, but still preparing a healthy number of graduates for med school, law school, and business. The presence of the Sewanee Review and the Tennessee Williams letters does attract a fair number of literary pilgrims, and the annual series of lectures and convocations brings the contemporary literary scene to a happy cadre of English majors.

The academic program will look familiar - requirements in general education, the usual majors and electives. What will set the experience apart in the academic realm is the cumulative synthetic experience of a lifetime - the comprehensive examination, or "Comps." The comprehensive exams usually take place in the last months of the senior year and pull together the entire academic experience in one last, exhausting marathon.

So, Sewanee is traditional, and slightly Southern, and slightly Episcopalian, and completely rural, and outstandingly beautiful.

Spirit runs high here and the loyal student body is every bit as active and engaged as one might guess. In addition to the usual extra-curricular activities (newspaper, radio station, music, film, dance, etc), Sewanee has an active Emergency Medical Squad that responds to emergencies in the Domain and a volunteer fire company as well.

Wilderness and outdoor opportunities are everywhere. Not only are there rapids to run, rocks to climb, trails to bike, there are also a number of caves to spelunk, and the spelunkers love to initiate newbies into the thrill of caving.

An activity/sport that sets Sewanee apart is the nationally ranked equestrian program. The Co-ed program competes across the region and is both a varsity sport and an individual challenge.

The Sewanee Tigers compete in Division III in every other sport, offering successful programs in football, soccer, baseball, basketball, lacrosse, tennis, cross country, field hockey, softball, swimming, tennis, track, volleyball, and golf. The college operates a challenging nine-hole golf course on the Domain.

The athletic tradition at Sewanee is the stuff of legend; Sewanee was a pioneer in inter-collegiate athletics in the South.

In the 1880's Sewanee was among the most powerful football programs in the land, an original member of the SEC. One of football's most celebrated marathons took place near the end of the Nineteenth Century and featured the Sewanee Tigers.

In 1899, Sewanee defeated five colleges in six days on the road, including: Georgia, Georgia Tech, Texas, Texas A&M, Tulane, LSU, and North Carolina. The college was undefeated that year, finishing with a record of twelve wins and no losses – a national championship performance.

The college remains ardent in its support of its Tigers. A recent article in its magazine connects the frenzy that is football with the dignity of the Episcopal Church in the following description.

The surviving last line of an old football cheer:

> *"Rip 'em up! Tear 'em up! Leave 'em in the lurch.*
> *Down with the heathen. Up with the Church.*

Yea, Sewanee's Right!"

The heathen may have been the Methodists of Vanderbilt, which would date the cheer in the 1890s; the cheer was sometimes also used against Hampden-Sydney. Now used as an alternative motto and often shouted at the end of the alma mater. When used with the alma mater, it is preceded by an extended pause and the phrase "Hit it!"

Belmont University - Nashville, Tennessee

Located in "Music City," Belmont is the only institution in the world to offer an accredited degree in Music Business. The Mike Curb College of Entertainment and Music Business is a professional school entirely dedicated to every aspect of the music and entertainment industry.

And the stats... 2015

Number of Applicants: 5,665/ 83% Accepted
Undergrad Enrollment: 5,837   83% female / 39% male
Avg. SAT Reading Comp 530-630 / Math 530-630 Avg. ACT: 23-29
Total Cost: $45,340.00.
Received some form of financial assistance: 88%

Belmont is a comprehensive Christian University in an historic section of Nashville, only a few blocks from Vanderbilt and the city center. Like the other Christian colleges in this book, Belmont is both a community of faith and an exceptional academic enterprise. Belmont is the fastest growing Christian university in the country, now enrolling more than seventy-five hundred students from every state and more than twenty countries.

The university describes itself in the following fashion:

> *Belmont University is a student-centered Christian community providing an academically challenging education that empowers men and women of diverse backgrounds to engage and transform the world with disciplined intelligence, compassion, courage and faith.*

In recent years, Belmont has shifted that focus somewhat, severing ties with the Tennessee Baptist Convention and becoming governed by a Board of Trustees from all Christian denominations.

Located in a neighborhood setting, Belmont has grown quickly. Now a university with an enrollment of almost 6000 (4800 undergraduates), Belmont has become a highly regarded professional and pre-professional school with an exciting Division I basketball program.

My purpose in presenting this Christian university in the South is to draw attention to a program that is not only unique, but also remarkable.

Located in "Music City," Belmont is the only institution in the world to offer an accredited degree in Music Business. The Mike Curb College of Entertainment and Music Business is a professional school entirely dedicated to every aspect of the music and entertainment industry.

Mike Curb was a musician, record company executive, musical entrepreneur, and the former Lieutenant Governor of California. In addition to his many other enterprises, he founded Curb Records in Nashville, recording such artists as Wynonna Judd, Tim McGraw, LeAnn Rimes, and Hank Williams, Jr. Through his efforts, the Curb Events Center was constructed at Belmont, and the school of entertainment and music business, established in 1971, became internationally known.

The Curb School offers a Bachelor of Business Administration in Music Business, a Bachelor of Science or Bachelor of Arts in Entertainment Industry Studies, a Bachelor of Science or Bachelor of Arts in Songwriting, and a Bachelor of Science or Bachelor of Arts in Audio Engineering Technology.

An Audio Engineering student has to jump in with coursework in Physics and Math, but quickly moves into Electronics and Circuit Theory, recording Technology, Critical Listening for Audio Production, Auditory Perception and Hearing Science, and Physics for Audio Engineering.

Songwriters take a general education course of study at the start, but then meet the Survey of Music Business, Copyright Law, Studio Production, Lyric Writing, Fundamentals of Harmony, Ear Training, Music Theory, Commercial Music, Music Theory, Evolution of the Popular Song, and a series of showcases and seminars.

Those pursuing the business degrees hit Macroeconomics, Accounting Principles, Integrated Accounting Principles, Foundations of Entrepreneurship, Business Law, Managing Information Systems, Business Finance, Principles of Marketing, Principles of Management, Business Ethics, and Strategic Management. Then, the business student chooses an emphasis on Music Production or Music Business.

The Entertainment Industry student begins with Mass Media and Society, then moves into The Entertainment Industry, Entertainment Industry Economics, Creative Entertainment Technology, Intellectual Properties, Sociology of Music, Sociology of Film, Entertainment Distribution and Promotion, and course work in Literary Studies or Creative Arts.

All of which suggests that the professional degrees offered by Belmont are substantial and almost immediately applicable in the field of one's choice. The preparation might be considered more than adequate, but the university takes it one step further with a series of internships that place students in their field as early as the sophomore year. The university sponsors more than four hundred career-specific internships each year. In addition, the university's recording facility is used by such artists as Dave Matthews, Sheryl Crow, and Bob Seeger. The university also operates RCA Studio B (where Elvis, Roy Orbison, and Dolly Parton were recorded) in conjunction with the Country Music Hall of Fame.

Having identified the curriculum, let me quickly say that the campus is handsome, well organized and effective. The mansion from which the university sprang is an impressive building; most of the residential halls are new and well equipped. A quick visit to Belmont will attest to the university's recent growth into national prominence.

There are but two significant areas left to discuss - alumni and basketball.

Belmont's alumni include Trisha Yearwood , Lee Ann Womack and Brad Paisley. Hundreds more are active at the highest level of the recording industry, providing essential connections for Belmont graduates attempting to break into the field.

At the last CMA awards presentation, the entertainer of the year (Paisley) was an alumnus, and the writer of the best song of the year (Tom Douglas) is a member of the Songwriting faculty.

As for basketball, the Belmont Bruins shocked the sports world in 2007, almost bouncing Duke from the NCAA tournament in a thrilling 71-70 contest. Basketball remains Belmont's premiere sport, but the university competes fully in a Division I schedule in the Atlantic Sun Conference.

Rhodes College - Memphis, Tennessee

Every college enrolls some good kids with impressive ambitions and dreams; over the years, I have come to believe that Rhodes is unusual in that it has a concentration of truly impressive students. The Rhodes experience is a happy experience; life at Rhodes is active and meaningful. While there is no one type of person who picks Rhodes, I describe the average Lynx (their mascot) as bright, kind, loyal, engaged, eager to try new things, fond of tradition, and generally poised for success wherever they end up.

And the stats... 2015

Number of Applicants: 3,882/ 60% Accepted
Undergrad Enrollment: 2,031   58% female / 42% male
Avg. SAT Reading Comp 600-690 / Math 600-690 Avg. ACT: 27-34
Total Cost: $55,640.00.
Received some form of financial assistance: 91%

Rhodes College belongs in the company of Whitman, Macalester, Lawrence, Grinnell, and Sewanee, all superior small liberal arts colleges attracting strong students from outside their region and increasingly numbered among the nation's most respected colleges of their type. Just as Macalester offers the small college experience in the city of Saint Paul, Rhodes is one of the few eminent small colleges located in the heart of a major city.

Rhodes looks like an Ivy college in an earlier era, but its facilities are modern and more than adequate. For those of you approaching the South for the first time, Memphis is unique in several aspects. In the first place, Memphis operates the second-busiest commercial airport in the world, second only to Hong Kong. Memphis is the corporate and operational home of FedEx, but numbers of other cargo planes and major airlines fly from Memphis around the world. The city was at the heart of the cotton trade, located as it is on a bluff above the Mississippi River. Memphis is the largest city on the Mississippi, almost as rich in musical tradition as Nashville and certainly a contender when talk of barbeque begins to arise.

I'm not sure a casual observer could tell the difference between a campus photo of Princeton and a similar shot at Rhodes. I believe that with the possible exception of a small quadrant on Duke's campus, Rhodes has the most "Gothic Collegiate" architecture in the South. Applicants on tour immediately appreciate the elegant setting and beautifully maintained grounds on the one hundred acre wooded campus in the middle of Memphis, within yodeling distance of the city's excellent zoo and Overton Park. Recent visitors have been delighted to find that the college's original dining hall, the "Refectory", bears a stunning resemblance to the imagined Great Hall at Hogwarts School of Witchcraft and Wizardry. If you want to see a good representation of life on campus, take a trip to Rhodes via Instagram – fabulous!

Rhodes was included in the first edition of Loren Pope's *Colleges That Change Lives*, his groundbreaking book on the character of colleges outside the Ivy League and remains distinctive in its ambitions and its successes. Over the course of the subsequent years, Rhodes has continued to distinguish itself. Newsweek Magazine recently named Rhodes the number one service-oriented college in the nation, and the plethora of clubs, activities, service projects, internships, and opportunities to study abroad make Rhodes a remarkably responsive and active small college.

Every college enrolls good kids with impressive ambitions and dreams; over the years, I have come to believe that Rhodes is unusual in that it has a concentration of truly impressive students. The Rhodes experience is a happy experience; life at Rhodes is active and meaningful. While there is no one type of person who picks Rhodes, I describe the average Lynx (their mascot) as bright, kind, loyal, engaged, eager to try new things, fond of tradition, and generally poised for success wherever they end up. When students and recent graduates talk about the college, the three elements they mention most are strength of the community, extraordinary relationships with professors, and the Honor Code. It may seem odd to put the code in that light, but both community and relationships with professors are based on an abiding sense of trust, an enterprise this college takes seriously. Community doesn't just happen; kids have to step up to take leadership in a variety of ways to make the Rhodes experience as lively and rewarding as it is. The number of clubs, organizations, and service opportunities is impressive, but so is the engagement in student government, including participation in the Honor Council.

There are some distinctive programs at Rhodes, and I will describe them is greater detail, but be assured that the core of the humanities and science programs is solid and very much appreciated by the graduate schools that more than a third of Rhodes graduates attend upon leaving the college. The college challenges prospective students to become "essential", by which they mean taking responsibility for the success of each class and activity, but also taking responsibility for living a meaningful life in the years following college. Classes are small; about fourteen students make up an average class, although some advanced classes are even smaller.

English, Biology, Computer Science, History – all areas of study are highly regarded. There are some uncommon academic programs that reflect the college's commitment to diversity and global awareness. Among the interdisciplinary programs are: Africana Studies, Archeology, Asian Studies, Gender and Sexuality Studies, Latin American Studies, Neuroscience, and Urban Studies.

Recently, Rhodes established the Mike Curb Institute for Music at Rhodes. Mike Curb's career in production and recording is legendary, and his interest in music education led him to establish the excellent program in Nashville at Belmont University. Memphis has its own very rich musical legacy, and the students in the Curb Institute work to preserve that legacy while also bringing new music to the campus. The college works in concert with the Stax Museum, the Rock and Soul Museum, and the Blues Foundation. One unique opportunity at Rhodes allows students to work in the building in which Elvis Presley wrote many of his songs. Students can also join in the house concerts presented frequently, called "An Evening with Elvis."

Rhodes supports education abroad through a number of affiliations; the Buckman Center for International Education offers advice and counsel as students prepare to enter into study internationally. The center offers assistance on every issue from the completion of necessary studies while away from Rhodes to planning travel and residential opportunities.

Rhodes also sends students to some fascinating programs operated by specific centers. So, for example, a Rhodes' students can attend the International Business Case Studies, Business in the EU, and Religion in the Low Countries. A center in Wyoming sets students in Teton National Park and Yellowstone National Park, studying Rocky Mountain Ecology. The Sociology of Martin Luther King, Jr. in Practice, takes students to St. Augustine in a peace-based study of the Civil Rights Movement. There is one more international programs that is distinctive to Rhodes, Field Studies in Namibia, which not only presents students with several ecosystems, including the Naukluft Desert, but puts them in contact with indigenous people, NGOs, and Namibian officials.

Back on campus, life is pretty fantastic.

I would not ordinarily start with a description of a building, but the recent renovation of the college's dining facility, The Burrows Refectory was one of the most impressive spaces on any college campus, the sort of dining hall that demanded comparison with the great Gothic halls. The renovation added more space, a new serving center, and, in the process created a new quadrangle. It's pretty, and efficient, and sparkling, but it also fit perfectly with the classic building and makes this a true heart of the campus experience. Do not be misled; although Rhodes students call the Refectory, "The Rat", there is nothing rat-like about it.

Dining is simply one aspect of community life, and Rhodes is determined to create and maintain a strong communal character to this college. There are fraternities and sororities, and they are popular with about fifty percent of the student body. That's a higher percentage than at some colleges, but has far less impact than Greek life at most southern universities. For one thing, the fraternities and sororities are not residential, and each is organized around four "pillars" as well as social events and activities. The pillars are: Philanthropy (and there's a lot of service commitments), Leadership development, Academic Achievement, and Intramural Athletics. Generally, about eighty percent of students are involved with some form of service, and virtually all are engaged in one of the more than a hundred clubs and activities on campus. All of the usual opportunities (Music, Dance, Theater, Publications, Arts, Service, Sports, Student Government) are available. Three interesting opportunities might be found in Quidditch, Contents Under Pressure (an Improv Troupe), and the Swing Dance Club.

My contention is that colleges with strong traditions allow students of every generation to feel a strong sense of community and campus pride. The seriousness with which students take the Honor Code and the deliberations of the Honor Council demonstrate the importance of that code to the life of the community. Rhodes has a host of other traditions (Don't step on the College Seal!), but the activity that most gladdens students may be the pancake study breaks. Pancakes of all sorts are cooked up all evening during the exam weeks, and the cooks may be students, faculty, of even one of the deans!

There are plenty of Wildcats, Bobcats, Cougars and other feline mascots, but Rhodes may be among the few sports team named after the Lynx. Rhodes is an NCAA Division III athletic college, participating in the Southern Athletic Association. You'll know something about Rhodes in noting the athletic competition they seek. The football team, for example, plays Pomona-Pitzer (CA), Berry College (GA), Sewanee/University of the South(TN), Washington University (MO), University of Chicago (IL), Hendrix (ARK), Centre (KY) and Millsaps (MS). Both Men's and Women's sports play similarly ambitious schedules with good success. Athletic facilities are first-rate; the Bryan Campus Life Center impressive offering a gym, a fitness center, an indoor track, racquetball courts, squash courts, a training facility and an extra gym, available for intramural and pick-up sports.. Oh, and there's also a snack bar and a ballroom.

Rhodes College is an extraordinary college set in an extraordinary city. For the student who wants both campus-based community and access to a city, Rhodes can't be beat.

Centre College - Danville, Kentucky

In addition to enviable academic success on campus (70% of Kentucky's Rhodes Scholars have graduated from Centre), the college also maintains centers in China, England, France, Japan, and Latin America, and offers short-term courses in New Zealand, Vietnam, Greece, Australia, Cameroon, Russia, Turkey, and India.

Consumer Reports adds its own approval to the Centre College experience, naming it, "… the number one value in private liberal arts education."

And the stats… 2015

Number of Applicants: 2,494/ 72% Accepted
Undergrad Enrollment: 1,387   52% female / 48% male
Avg. SAT Reading Comp 550-650 / Math 560-680 Avg. ACT: 26-31
Total Cost: $49,440.00.
Received some form of financial assistance: 98%

Recent publication of the Forbes.Com America's Best Colleges list included three relatively surprising names in the top rank, two of which are featured in this book:

Whitman College in Washington, Wabash College in Indiana, one of the three remaining colleges for men, and Centre College in Danville, Kentucky.

Consumer Reports adds its own approval to the Centre College experience, naming it, "… the number one value in private liberal arts education."

High praise for a small (1600) liberal arts college located in Danville, Kentucky, south of Lexington. Danville is a quaint small city, the "Home of Bluegrass." boasting the Great American Main Street Award from the National Trust for Historic Preservation.

In addition to enviable academic success on campus (70% of Kentucky's Rhodes Scholars have graduated from Centre), the college also maintains centers in China, England, France, Japan, and Latin America, and offers short-term courses in New Zealand, Vietnam, Greece, Australia, Cameroon, Russia, Turkey, and India.

Those centers reflect one of three promises made in "The Centre Commitment." The first of these guarantees is that each student will have the option to study abroad. The second is that each student will have the opportunity to undertake an internship during his or her career at Centre. The third guarantees that each student will complete the course of study leading to graduation within four years, or the college will provide up to a year of additional study without charging tuition.

These guarantees speak to an uncommon determination on the part of the college to provide an exceptional experience for its students.

In its establishment of its study abroad program, for example, the college has created residential centers administered by the college. In almost every case, the cost of attending a Centre program abroad is the same as attending the college in Danville; all financial aid still applies. Should those programs not meet the needs of an individual, extensive opportunities for affiliated programs abound. Two notable sets of opportunities also exist during Centre Term and on Summer Trips.

Centre Term is the three-week intensive study period in January. Centre's professors travel with students in the examination of volcanoes in New Zealand or dance in Bali. Courses have been offered in Vienna, Prague, Costa Rica, Beijing, Greece, Spain, and Peru.

Summer trips also involve traveling with Centre faculty and allow students to earn credits while engaging in meaningful activity abroad. For example, recent trips have taken Centre's students on an archeological dig in Israel and to Strasbourg, where from college owned apartments, students received a "survival course" in French and preparation for trips throughout France, Germany, and Switzerland.

Centre is one of a small number of colleges that participate in the Shepherd Higher Education Consortium on Poverty, an immersive program that connects students studying the effects of poverty with firsthand experience as interns with service and advocacy agencies. Centre's students travel from Danville to New York City, for example, to work as Homeless Outreach interns with the Bowery Residents Committee. The college works hard to provide a distinctive collegiate experience on the Danville campus without losing sight of the greater world.

Life on campus is equally engaging, as Centre's students rave about their professors and consider them to be friends and mentors as well as highly competent teachers. The general tone of the campus is positive, healthy, balanced, and active. Centre is not as well known as its counterparts in other regions, but its students absolutely feel that they have enjoyed an exceptional academic and social experience.

The recent validation from Forbes and other ranking surveys have helped Centre's students to persuade others that the Centre experience is equal to the best of liberal arts colleges.

Socially, Centre is slightly "land-that-time-forgot" in the best sense of the phrase. For example, the campus is safe. I mean REALLY safe. Danville is a nice town and the relationship between college and town is strong.

The Greek system is important; fully sixty percent of men and women will pledge and join a fraternity or sorority. Even students who do not choose to enter into the Greek system appreciate the efforts that the Greeks make to bring the campus to life. The most significant social events during the year are often sponsored by a particular fraternity or sorority. For example, "Hawaii Phi O" and "Sigma Chi-Yote" are cited as examples of excellent parties, and most are open to the entire campus.

Rush takes place in the second semester, allowing students the chance to think carefully about whether they want to pledge or not. Most of those not in the Greek system remain friends with many who are.

To a degree unusual on campuses these days, drug use is uncommon; a first violation of the college's policy with regards to drugs will bring expulsion. There are few smokers on campus, and most students will end up involved in a varsity sport or an intramural sport.

Finally, Centre, although very much a Kentucky college, is not as "southern" as many other colleges in the region might appear to be. The student body is attractive and healthy, but concern for dress and makeup is notably less a pressure than it is at some neighboring schools. One reasonable comment about Centre's female students is that they take care of themselves, but don't turn into vapid, weight-obsessed, tanning divas.

Sound pretty good to me.

The traditions specific to Centre are slightly less archaic than those at some other equally hallowed institutions. There is a "mortal kombat" moment when new pledges "run the field" toward the house they've picked, mashing into each other as they tumble from end-to-end. Pretty tame.

An impulse toward "naturism" is revealed in the tradition known as "Running the Flame," a naked streak toward a sculpture, "The Flame," in the center of campus. Apparently the greatest disincentive for Running the Flame is that when naked runners are apprehended by campus security, they are questioned at length where they stand...in the raw.

"Dead Fred," refers to the image of former Chief Justice of the Supreme Court, Fred Vinson, a celebrated athlete at Centre and devoted son of Phi Delta Theta.

During his lifetime, Vinson shook off the weighty affairs of state to attend Centre's football games with his Phi Delt brothers. Today, they honor his memory by bringing his portrait to every game. Dead Fred also appears at odd moments in the school year, most notoriously in the front row of the televised Vice Presidential Debate between Dick Cheney and Joe Lieberman.

The most ardently held of all Centre's traditions, however, harks back to 1921.

The Praying Colonels of Centre first traveled to Cambridge, Massachusetts to play Harvard University in 1920. Harvard had won the national championship in 1919 after an undefeated season and a victory in the Rose Bowl. As Centre's team arrived at Harvard Stadium, they met a Crimson squad that was both undefeated and unscored upon.

Harvard's supporters were rocked by the play of Colonels, who managed to take a 14-7 lead at the end of the first half. Harvard bounced back and won by a score of 31 - 14. When the Harvard captain attempted to give the game ball to Centre's premier running back, Bo McMillan, McMillan shrugged it off, saying, "We'll be back."

In front of a crowd of 45,000 the next year, Centre shocked Harvard (who had not lost a game since 1918), winning by the score of 6-0.

ESPN and the Associated Press include the Centre victory as one of the greatest upsets in the history of sports in the Twentieth Century. The College adopted the "impossible formula," *C6H0* on every surface within range. The wall of Centre's post office still holds the original formula, and rumor has it that several local cows ended up with *C6H0* painted on their flanks.

That 1921 Centre team went on to prove their victory was anything but a fluke, defeating Virginia Tech, Auburn, Clemson, and Arizona before finally losing to Texas A&M in the Dixie Classic, now known as the Cotton Bowl.

Centre's teams are still known as the "Colonels." They compete in Division III's Southern Collegiate Athletic Conference in nineteen intercollegiate sports. Almost half of Centre's students will participate in intercollegiate sports, and virtually all will enjoy one of the college's intramural tournaments.

Like Whitman in Washington or Bates in Maine, there is something about Centre that attracts happy, earnest, good kids. There is simply no chance that this highly regarded and thoroughly excellent institution will not climb into the ranks of nationally esteemed liberal arts colleges.

Auburn University and the University of Alabama System

In terms of variety of distinguished public universities, Alabama may have the right to boast about the three universities in the University of Alabama System a well as the other notable public university, Auburn University. The University of Alabama System consists of three very different but equally interesting campuses, each with a distinctive character and history. Tuscaloosa is the site of the state's flagship university, the University of Alabama, enrolling more than thirty thousand students. Birmingham, Alabama's largest city, is the home of the University of Alabama at Birmingham (UAB) enrolling about twelve thousand undergraduates, and the University of Alabama in Huntsville (UAH) enrolls about eight thousand undergrads in a city in northern Alabama best known for the NASA Space Center. Auburn University, Alabama's great rival, enrolls about twenty-five thousand undergrads in the fastest growing city in the state, Auburn in eastern Alabama.

Auburn University - Auburn, Alabama

Auburn is the university to attend if you are interested in engineering, or architecture, or applied science and technology, and that does attract a significant portion of the undergraduate population. The aerospace program is well known, and that too attracts a certain sort of student. The Greek system is strong on both campuses, but Auburn's may be a bit less visible, slightly more diversified. Is Auburn a bit less self-consciously southern? I think so, but I'm sure feelings run strong on both campuses. Auburn feels a bit more rural because of the agricultural setting, and Auburn's kids may be more firmly attached to the campus grounds than Alabama's. Other than those observations, I can only suggest that Auburn seems slightly more determined to create a sense of "family" among its undergraduates.

And the stats... 2015

Number of Applicants: 16,958/ 83% Accepted
Undergrad Enrollment: 20,629   51% female / 49% male
Avg. SAT Reading Comp 520-630 / Math 540-645 Avg. ACT: 24 – 30
Total Cost: $29,164.00 (in-state), 46,438.00
Received some form of financial assistance: 78%

Most people know that the rivalry between Auburn and Alabama is fierce, and is played out in the annual battle for bragging rights, a football game known as the "Iron Bowl", takes place in Birmingham, neutral territory. To be honest, "fierce" doesn't even come close to describing the intensity of the rivalry. Partisans on both sides of the divide will no doubt contend that their university is truly superior, and allegiances run deep and across generations, but the two great public universities developed in different ways and to serve different purposes, so the visitor to either of the universities will find active, engaged, purposeful students who think the world of their alma mater.

What's the difference between the two from the student's point of view? Both have fun-loving, ordinary kids not yet certain of career or vocation, but Auburn is the university to attend if you are interested in engineering, or architecture, or applied science and technology, and that does attract a significant portion of the undergraduate population. The aerospace program is well known, and that too attracts a certain sort of student. The Greek system is strong on both campuses, but Auburn's may be a bit less visible, slightly more diversified. Is Auburn a bit less self-consciously southern? I think so, but I'm sure feelings run strong on both campuses.

Auburn feels a bit more rural because of the agricultural setting, and Auburn's kids may be more firmly attached to the campus grounds than Alabama's. Other than those observations, I can only suggest that Auburn seems slightly more determined to create a sense of "family" among its undergraduates. Sports are huge at both schools, and the balance of athletic power swings back and forth relatively evenly.

Auburn was established in 1856 as the East Alabama Male College, a private college sponsored by the Methodist Church, but became the Agricultural and Mechanical College of Alabama in 1872, and the Alabama Polytechnic Institute in 1899. Long known as "Auburn", the university took the name officially in 1960. From the start, the university provided the state and the region with men and women educated in practical fields, such as engineering and architecture; as the university matured, it developed considerable strength in other areas as well, now presenting a wide variety of programs and majors.

National reputation in the earliest programs remains impressive and demonstrates the evolution of new courses to meet contemporary challenges. The School of Agriculture, for example, now offers programs in Aquaculture, Horticulture, Biosystems Engineering, and Plant Pathology. The Pre-Vet program is widely admired, and the university is particularly well regarded for its remarkable work in the rehabilitation of injured raptors (hawks, eagles, owls, harriers, kites, ospreys) through the Southeastern Raptor Center; injured birds are rescued by volunteers throughout the region and transported to Auburn where they receive medical treatment sand are returned to the wild if viable.

The School of Engineering is highly regarded in every area of study and particularly proud of innovative work in Computer Science and Wireless Engineering, as well as in its well established program in Aerospace Engineering. Hundreds of Auburn graduates have worked for NASA; at least six have been astronauts. Currently, a graduate of the program in Aerospace Engineering heads the Kennedy Space Center. Other areas of enviable strength in what might be considered polytechnical fields are to be found in the outstanding School of Forestry and Wildlife Sciences, the College of Human Sciences, the College of Science and Mathematics, the School of Nursing, and the School of Pharmacy.

The Liberal Arts are equally well represented among undergraduates, offering the expected course work as well as excellent programs in Communications and Journalism, Communication Disorders, Social Work, and Theater. The Harbert College of Business offers an exceptional variety of professional courses, including Accounting, Marketing, Finance, and Aviation and Supply Chain Management. The School of Education offers supervised certification and coursework in Kinesiology and Special Education.

Respected as these programs are, the School of Architecture has claimed particular distinction over the course of the past decade, identified as one of the top programs in Architecture and Design in the nation. Auburn's programs in Industrial Design and Interior Design have recently won top honors, and the program in Landscape Architecture is equally highly regarded.

Auburn's central campus was designed by Frederick Law Olmsted, celebrated for his design of New York's Central Park, Stanford and Berkeley, and Vanderbilt's Biltmore Estate in Asheville. The red brick buildings are beautifully set in an expansive and verdant series of quadrangles; Auburn is lively and stately, one of the most attractive of southern universities, and its active social and extracurricular scene makes it among the most pleasant as well.

As is true of many southern schools, the Greek systems are important at Auburn; roughly twenty-five percent of men and about thirty-five percent of women are affiliated with a fraternity or sorority. Other sorts of social relationships abound as the university sponsors several hundred clubs and organizations. Dorm life is also good, as are the many dining options, and undergrads take particular pride in describing their years at Auburn as being part of a large and fun-loving family.

Some of that fun comes in the terrific pride Auburn's students take in their athletic teams. No fan of professional football is unaware of Cam Newton, currently Super Bowl quarterback for the Carolina Panthers, one of the most dominant athletes in America, and winner of the Heisman Trophy as Auburn's quarterback in 2010 . In addition to a football team that is often among the most successful in the nation, Auburn has won national championships in swimming and diving and track and field and is equally successful in both men's and women's basketball, baseball, and golf. Less well known but equally successful is Auburn's national championship equestrian team.

Auburn's mascot is the Tiger. "Aubie" the tiger appears at every game and also shows up in the dining halls, on Auburn's tv broadcasts, in the academic buildings. Often wearing glasses and a button-down shirt, Aubie roams the campus building spirit. The cry, War Eagle!" during athletic contests is often confusing to those outside the Auburn family. The tiger is the only mascot, but the appearance of an eagle at the pivotal moment in a football game against Georgia caused the fans to scream "war eagle" as the team marched down the field. Auburn has been playing football against the University of Georgia since 1892, establishing the oldest football rivalry in the South.

Tradition is strong at Auburn, and many of the most important traditions and characteristics of the university were brought to the Agricultural and

Mechanical College of Alabama in 1890 with arrival of George Petrie, the first Alabaman to earn the Ph.D (from Johns Hopkins), a historian who changed the university's name to the Alabama Polytechnic Institute, brought the school colors (burnt orange and navy blue) from his undergraduate days at the University of Virginia, administered the athletic program, coached the football team in the first game against Georgia in 1892, and composed the "Auburn Creed"

I believe that this is a practical world and that I can count only on what I earn. Therefore, I believe in work, hard work.

I believe in education, which gives me the knowledge to work wisely and trains my mind and my hands to work skillfully.

I believe in honesty and truthfulness, without which I cannot win the respect and confidence of my fellow men.

I believe in a sound mind, in a sound body and a spirit that is not afraid, and in clean sports that develop these qualities.

I believe in obedience to law because it protects the rights of all.

I believe in the human touch, which cultivates sympathy with my fellow men and mutual helpfulness and brings happiness for all.

I believe in my Country, because it is a land of freedom and because it is my own home, and that I can best serve that country by "doing justly, loving mercy, and walking humbly with my God".

And because Auburn men and women believe in these things, I believe in Auburn and love it.

–George Petrie

University of Alabama - Tuscaloosa, Alabama

Alabama isn't just about football; it's a large research university providing what it calls the capstone of public education in the state. Many of its programs are highly regarded and its preparation for the professions is impressive and widely admired.

And the stats... 2015

Number of Applicants: 33,786/ 51% Accepted
Undergrad Enrollment: 30,752 54% female / 46% male
Avg. SAT Reading Comp 490-620 / Math 500-630 Avg. ACT: 21-31
Total Cost: $27,205.00 (in-state) $42,339.00 (out-of-state)
Received some form of financial assistance: 76%

The crest of the University of Alabama includes the school's nickname, "Crimson Tide", a reference to the powerful sweep of an Alabama football team, which, in defeating Auburn in 1907, fought so resolutely that their uniforms stained red with Alabama clay, seemed a tide overwhelming the Auburn side. The rallying cry for Alabama's fans since then has been, "Roll Tide."

Alabama isn't just about football; it's a large research university providing what it calls the capstone of public education in the state. Many of its programs are highly regarded and its preparation for the professions is impressive and widely admired. The university has developed three distinctive academic programs that set it apart, and it is the description of those programs that will follow a brief account of the university's history.

Alabama's story is complicated and occasionally disturbing. The founding of the university occurred almost as the state came into being. Established in 1831, it was one of the first universities built on the frontier. The rough and ready habits of folks on the frontier was apparently part of the university's first years; although it had a fine library, one of the largest in the nation, the university was also the site of brawls and the occasional gunfight. Consequently, the trustees transformed the university into a military school just before the outbreak of the Civil War. Many cadets graduating from Alabama served as officers in the army of the Confederate States of America, demonstrating skills they had acquired in Tuscaloosa. The Union army burned most of what had been the university, leaving the state to start the construction of the campus virtually from charred remains. It was in Tuscaloosa in June of 1963 that Governor George Wallace barred the gates of the university to African-Americans attempting to register. The event, known as "Stand At The Schoolhouse Door", was Wallace's attempt to stop desegregation mandated by the Supreme Court. Troops from the National Guard were mobilized, and Wallace eventually had to stand aside. The last of the unfortunate legacies which the university has endured has to do with the uncommon strength with which the fraternity and sorority system ruled the university's Student Government Association.

Although more than twenty-five percent of men and more than thirty-five percent of women remain active in Greek life at Alabama, the campus is notably democratic, supportive of rights of all students, and increasingly diverse. The divisions of the university offer comprehensive education across a variety of disciplines, ranging from Culverhouse College of Commerce and Business Education to the College of Communication and Information Science. Alabama offers an extremely successful program in Nursing through the Capstone College of Nursing and equally regarded programs in most disciplines through the College of Arts and Sciences, the largest of Alabama's academic divisions, enrolling about six thousand five hundred students.

I do want to highlight three distinctive programs because they reflect the lengths to which the university has gone in the last decades to move to the forefront of higher education.

Alabama has crafted a particular niche in the literary world by developing a curriculum in Book Arts that links fine arts and literature, creative writing and the craft of printmaking and bookbinding. Alabama's Creative Writing program is excellent; students in the Book Arts program have created works that accompany every reading by the Creative Writers, designing broadsides and typeface appropriate to each work. And, in an exceptionally innovative burst of connection, the Book Arts has also partnered with Environmental Sciences to create textiles of particular strength and texture.

Coming from a more commercial point of view, the university has created a major in Management Information Systems, a complex fusion of information technology and business administration. Students invent ways to make firms more successful by harnessing existing information technology, emerging technology, and social media to create the design of projects and the scope of their presentation. Graduates of the Management Information System curriculum are prepared to step immediately into significant positions in Health Care Information and Management, Management Communications, International Sales and Business, Supply-Chain Management, and Computer Management.

Finally, one of the most original of ideas came with the creation of the Blount Undergraduate Initiative. Scholars selected for the initiative are students at the university, but the program is privately financed as an intensive introduction to the liberal arts in a residential, seminar based Minor in Liberal Arts. Scholars travel from the Blount experience into their prospective major with an uncommonly extensive preparation in critical analysis, critical writing, and effective speech.

All of that now said, it is time to move to the element of the university that gets the most attention in the greater world, an athletic program matched by very few universities in the nation. Alabama's football team has been preeminent since the end of the Nineteenth Century. The Crimson Tide have won fifteen national championships. Fifteen! Alabama's stadium, Bryant-Denny Stadium holds more than a hundred thousand fans screaming, Roll Tide! The university's sports programs in every area are well supported and contribute to the spirit and pride which students feel in their university.

University of Alabama at Birmingham - Birmingham, Alabama

All aspects of public health are represented in this teaching facility, making it one of the most advantaged of pre-medical, pre-veterinary, pre-dental programs in the region. The school of Nursing is, of course, outstanding, and the opportunities for research extensive.

And the stats... 2015

Number of Applicants: 5,710 86% Accepted
Undergrad Enrollment: 11,679 58% female / 42% male
Avg. SAT Reading Comp 500-640 / Math 490-640 Avg. ACT: 21-27
Total Cost: $524,405.00 (in-state) $33,957.00 (out-of-state)
Received some form of financial assistance: 89%

The University of Alabama at Birmingham is a distinctly different residential and academic experience. Begun as an extension of the University of Alabama, Birmingham quickly developed its own character and purpose. Located in the southwest quarter of Birmingham, the university is an urban campus with the advantage of sitting in the middle of one of the most active medical centers in the state. The UAB Health System is one of the largest in the United States, and the associated medical professions are a large part of the curriculum developed at the university. STEM courses (Science, Technology, Engineering, and Mathematics) are important at UAB and many programs allow undergraduates to take graduate work as they become advanced in their major course of study. All aspects of public health are represented in this teaching facility, making it one of the most advantaged of pre-medical, pre-veterinary, pre-dental programs in the region. The school of Nursing is, of course, outstanding, and the opportunities for research extensive.

It's not all about medical science, however. The liberal arts and humanities are well represented and the university's Business School is widely admired, as is the Law School. Undergraduates are slightly older on average than at some universities, as UAB caters to those returning to school or starting a collegiate career after having worked. There are residential dormitories and an active program of social activities including a lively Greek system. All the ordinary clubs and organizations flourish, but UAB is particularly well known for its success in Model UN and Mock Trial. The UAB Mock Trial team has won national championships, defeating traditional powers such as Harvard and Berkeley.

Athletically, the UAB Blazers have become a frequent participant at the highest level of competition in basketball, often contending in the NCAA tournament in March. March Madness grabs the attention of the entire nation, but at UAB, the fever runs high

University of Alabama Huntsville - Huntsville, Alabama

It is likely that no university in the country can match the program that UAH has developed in Atmospheric Science. Aspiring daredevil atmospheric scientists can join in the chase, hunting down tornados and mapping hurricanes.

And the stats... 2015

Number of Applicants: 2,104/ 82% Accepted
Undergrad Enrollment: 5,618   43% female / 57% male
Avg. SAT Reading Comp 520-670 / Math 530-650 Avg. ACT: 24-30
Total Cost: $23,532.00 (in-state) $35,606.00 (out-of-state)
Received some form of financial assistance: 87%
University of Alabama in Huntsville - Huntsville, Alabama

The third in the state's university system is the University of Alabama in Huntsville, the smallest of the three, but in some aspects the most intriguing. Huntsville is a small city, just south of the Smokey Mountains and the Tennessee Valley; outdoor opportunities are remarkable, and the regional experience something close to four real seasons. It is an oddity in the South in that it has vestiges of its place as a cotton marketing entrepot while operating at the most sophisticated level as the U.S. Space and Rocket Center at the George C. Marshall Space Flight Center and the site of the largest military arsenal in the United States. During World War II, Huntsville had become home to the Redstone Arsenal, and it was there that the Ordnance Guided Missile Center was developed. The most prominent rocket scientists in the world were brought to Huntsville, and it was there that Werner Von Braun and others brought the Redstone Rocket and the Apollo Lunar Landing Programs into being. Space and Rocket technology and military hardware are still important in the life of the city, and one of the great advantages enjoyed by UAH is the active support of technology industries. The recent development of a booming industry in biotechnology firms has created the Huntsville Biotech Initiative has brought yet another sophisticated set of skills to the Huntsville community.

UAH is among the most successful undergraduate preparation in the areas of astrophysics, atmospheric science, and aerospace engineering. Seriously, if an applicant is interested in any of these fields, there are very few collegiate options that can offer what UAH can. It should not come as a surprise that weather is of particular interest in much of the South and Southeast; the region has some dramatic weather and considerable variety of serious weather issues. It is likely that no university in the country can match the program that UAH has developed in Atmospheric Science. Aspiring daredevil atmospheric scientists can join in the chase, hunting down tornados and mapping hurricanes.

Samford University - Homewood, Alabama

The prevailing climate at Samford is one of cheerful hard work. Samford's students want to make something of themselves and want to carry valuable skills from their undergraduate experience into their professional lives.

And the stats... 2015

Number of Applicants: 4,557/ 60% Accepted
Undergrad Enrollment: 3,051   65% female / 35% male
Avg. SAT Reading Comp 510-620 / Math 500-610 Avg. ACT: 23-29
Total Cost: $42,270.00.
Received some form of financial assistance: 98%

Homewood is a suburb of Birmingham, Alabama's largest city. Metropolitan Birmingham has a population of more than a million and a quarter people, while the population of Homewood, a leafy residential suburb, is about twenty five thousand. Birmingham is an important financial center in the Southeast and a city with significant cultural and recreational attractions.

Few people outside of the South have heard much about Samford, which is a shame because it is a gorgeous, happy, productive small university in a city setting. It isn't easy to portray the tenor of a place; statistics don't give the real character of a university. Although I have no statistical basis for making the argument, I think Samford may be one of the two or three healthiest and happiest universities in the country.

It is southern, and anyone hailing from another region will quickly come to understand that southern colleges have their own distinctive flavor. You'll notice that your fellow students are careful about grooming, dress as if they are young professionals, and occasionally look as if they have spent an hour finding just the right shade of eyeshadow to match a skirt and sweater set.

And, a major issue has to be faced in looking at any institution in Birmingham. Memories of the Civil Rights struggle are still vivid, and Birmingham was at the heart of that struggle. It is no accident that the Civil Rights Institute was built in Birmingham and no surprise that the legacy of the movement may be stronger there than in any other city.

And all of that is a good thing.

Birmingham has confronted its past and has celebrated the heroes who marched for freedom. In Birmingham, the conversation about race is honest; it was in Birmingham that segregation ended. Birmingham today is all about diversity.

Samford was founded by Baptists (as a passel of Southern universities were, as were Brown and the University of Chicago) and today welcomes students of all faiths and backgrounds. The university retains a Christian mission, which in practice involves an emphasis on service and preparation for a life of purpose. The influence of the Baptist Church is no longer felt, and many students spend four years at Samford without attending chapel or church.

The campus is lush and beautifully maintained, and upbeat events are planned on a daily basis. The Samford Bulldogs play a tough Division I schedule and sports are definitely a hot topic in any conversation, but don't let the whole southern drawl and easy charm thing fool you; Samford kids work hard and take their work seriously. Academics matter, and the organization of the undergraduate program demonstrates the degree to which a very small university (4930 undergrads) operates in order to prepare its graduates for success in the world of work and service.

The prevailing climate at Samford is one of cheerful hard work. Samford's students want to make something of themselves and want to carry valuable skills from their undergraduate experience into their professional lives.

This tightly knit and eminently happy university is arranged into eight academic schools, reflecting the emphasis on professional preparation. By the time this edition is in print, the university will have opened two impressive new facilities - a comprehensive Health Sciences Center and a brand new facility for the Brock School of Business.

The Howard College of Arts and Sciences is named after James Howard, a social reformer who fought to improve the lot of prisoners in Eighteenth Century Britain. In addition to the usual core courses in the liberal arts (Classics, English, Philosophy, Mathematics, Physics, Biology, Chemistry, Political Science, and Psychology), Howard College offers degrees in Communication Studies, Geography, Journalism, Religion, and World Languages and Cultures.

The School of the Arts offers majors in Music, Theater & Dance, and Visual Arts. For a small university, Samford produces a number of excellently well-prepared graduates in each of the fields, with an especially long history of success in music. Graduates can claim a degree in Vocal Music, Piano, Piano Pedagogy, Organ Performance, Instrumental Performance, Church Music, Music Theory and Composition, Instrumental Music

Education, Vocal Performance, and Vocal/Choral Music Education. In addition, the university offers a BS degree for students fond of music who intend to go to medical school. Degrees are offered in Theater, Technical Theater, and Musical Theater. A BFA in Graphic Design and a BA in Visual Arts is also presented in this division.

The Brock School of Business is organized into three significant departments: The Department of Accounting and Management Information Systems, The Department of Economics, Finance, and Quantitative Analysis, and the Department of Entrepreneurship, Management, and Marketing. A quick look at the Brock School of Business reveals that this course of study is grounded in a set of well-defined values. Unlike many business programs, elements of service and ethical practice take a prominent place in the school's curriculum and methods.

The Beeson Divinity School is a graduate school of theology.

The Orlean Bullard Beeson School of Education and Professional Studies offers programs in Teacher Education leading to certification in Early Childhood and Secondary Education. The school also prepares professionals for careers in Exercise Science and Sports Medicine, Family Studies, Paralegal Studies, and Interior Design.

The Cumberland School of Law is a highly esteemed law school on the Samford campus.

The McWhorter School of Pharmacy and the Ida Moffett School of Nursing offer instruction at the undergraduate and graduate levels. Both are considered among the most highly reputed in the region.

The academic demands at Samford are notable and consistent; students expect and value hard work. That is not to say that the Samford experience is grim or glum. In fact, the overwhelming perception of the university is that its students know how to find balance in their college years.

Social life is active, often centered around the activities of fraternities and sororities, but equally open to students who have not entered into Greek life. The large events of the year energize the entire campus.

As one might expect, Homecoming is one of Samford's most important traditions. Not only does the campus rally to support the Bulldogs as they take the football field against Wofford, the entire week is filled with activity.

On Monday, one of the most celebrated of southern traditions is observed, as Chik-Fil-A provides chicken and biscuits in the Ben Brown Plaza in the heart of the campus. On Tuesday, "decorate your own cupcake" evening hits the plaza. On Wednesday, how 'bout some "wings" and a ride on a mechanical bull? Thursday brings a paint ball war on the rec fields. On Friday, there's a bonfire, coronation of the Homecoming Queen, and s'mores.

Oh, and just in case you think the coronation thing is a minor event, you should know that another of the cherished events during the year is the competition for Miss Samford, one of the official preliminary contests in the determination of Miss Alabama. In 2005, Miss Samford became Miss Alabama, and then was crowned Miss America.

One of the highlights of the winter is Step Sing, a performance in which almost one thousand students will participate. Originally, male students gathered on steps to serenade the sororities at twilight. For the past sixty years, a lavish production, entirely organized, choreographed, and produced by students has benefited local charities. The step sing is a competition in which fraternities, sororities, and independent organizations vie for bragging rights as singers, dancers, and actors. Thousands of visitors arrive on campus for the annual event.

Another tradition that speaks to the general wholesome good heartedness of Samford's students is Rascal Day, a celebration of the awarding of the degree of Canine Jurisprudence to a pooch selected for that year. The original Rascal, a mixed breed dog of rare intelligence, attended classes at the law school for years. The Cumberland Law School brings a jazz band on campus, holds a parade, and awards the degree to a dog that best represents the qualities that made Rascal a beloved part of campus life.

In Alabama, a dog may be family, but football is king. The annual battle between Auburn and Alabama consumes the state, but the fortunes of Samford's bulldogs are equally compelling in Homewood.

Samford is a small Division I school, only marginally larger than Wofford, Division I's smallest college. Competing in the Southern Conference against traditional rivals Davidson, Elon, Charleston, Wofford, and Georgia Southern, Samford is highly successful in its seventeen varsity sports.

It is in its recreational programs that Samford distinguishes itself most particularly. The intramural athletic program is active, with both Greek and independent teams caught up in competition in the usual sports, as well as bowling, Texas Hold 'Em, billiards, Super Smash Brothers, dodgeball, and Quidditch,

Club sports include an active outdoor program, swing dancing, ultimate frisbee, lacrosse, and soccer.

This happy, healthy, earnest student body is primarily made up of students from Alabama and surrounding states, but warmly welcomes students from beyond the south.

University of Montevallo - Montevallo, Alabama

So, the campus is fantastic, the location is excellent, and the student body is unique. There are a number of obvious post-secondary choices in this region; as most people know, the rivalry between the University of Alabama and Auburn University is intense and occupies a lot of public conversation. Big time sports and the fraternity/sorority whirl are a powerful attraction for most young people leaving high school. The students who choose to attend Montevallo have made the decision to seek the particular opportunity that a college of Montevallo's stature and mission afford. They enjoy an active life on campus and support the purple and gold Montevallo Falcons as they compete in Division II sports, but it is clear that this is a community that has a sense of purpose and a sense of service.

And the stats... 2015

Number of Applicants: 1,821/ 74% Accepted
Undergrad Enrollment: 2,664 68% female / 34% male
Avg. SAT Reading Comp 500-600 / Math 460-590 Avg. ACT: 20-26
Total Cost: $24,720.00 (in-state) $35,280.00 (out-of-state)
Received some form of financial assistance: 89%

I wish I could pick readers up and transport them to the stunning campus of the University of Montevallo, one of the most beautifully landscaped and designed colleges that I know of. Several of the buildings were built before the Civil War and are on the Registry of Historic Places. In fact, the entire center of the campus is a National Historic District. The paths are paved with red brick, and many of the buildings are also crafted of handsome brick. Much of the design of the campus was done by the firm that designed the Biltmore estate in Asheville and Central Park in New York City. Montevallo is a lovely campus, but it is included in this book because it is also an ambitious university with some distinctive programs and one of the very few public universities designated as a liberal arts college, a member of the Council of Public Liberal Arts Colleges.

Montevallo is a small town almost exactly in the center of the State of Alabama, just south of Birmingham and north of Montgomery. The county in which Montevallo is located, Shelby County, has a per capita income among the top hundred in the nation. The closest super exciting shopping is in Hoover, the upscale suburb of Birmingham about ten miles north of Montevallo.

So, the campus is fantastic, the location is excellent, and the student body is unique. There are a number of obvious post-secondary choices in this region; as most people know, the rivalry between the University of Alabama and Auburn University is intense and occupies a lot of public conversation. Big time sports and the fraternity/sorority whirl are a powerful attraction for most young people leaving high school. The students who choose to attend Montevallo have made the decision to seek the particular opportunity that a college of Montevallo's stature and mission afford. They enjoy an active life on campus and support the purple and gold Montevallo Falcons as they compete in Division II sports, but it is clear that this is a community that has a sense of purpose and a sense of service.

The university has a long tradition of providing some of the region's most talented teachers, and the major programs in Education are outstanding, including a major in the Education of the Deaf and Hearing Impaired. The legacy of those sorts of specialized programs has meant that this university committed to the liberal arts houses the College of Liberal Arts, the Michael E. Stephens College of Business, the College of Education, and an extraordinary College of Fine Arts.

Montevallo is a small town, and the university itself enrolls only slightly more than three thousand students, and yet, the productions in Musical Theater rank with the best of theater productions. The College of Fine Arts offers the Bachelor's degree in Fine Arts (BFA) in Acting, Directing, Design and Technical Theater, Musical Theater, Ceramics, Graphic Design, Drawing, Painting, Photography, Printmaking, Sculpture, and New Media. The Bachelor's of Arts degree is offered in Communications, Mass Communications, Composition, Instrumental Performance, Music Education-Choral, Music Education-Instrumental, Organ Performance, Piano Pedagogy, Piano Performance, and Vocal Performance.

Whew! And that's just a small part of what happens at Montevallo!

The School of Education not only offers the usual course work and certification, but also presents Child and Family Studies, Dietetics, Interior Design, and Kinesiology. The Stephens Business College offers Accounting, Finance, Business Management, Management Information Systems, and Marketing.

Graduate programs on campus allow students to pursue specialized programs in Speech - Language Pathology, Counseling, and the MBA.

Montevallo's campus is lovely, but in a far-sighted moment of inspiration, the university bought one hundred-and-fifty acres of unlovely land about three miles from the campus and began the process of restoring its natural beauty while building a powerful observatory, from which students can do major astronomical research. This observatory is one of the very few built to be fully accessible to people with disabilities. Thus in one stroke, Montevallo demonstrates its mission to build as wide a community as possible.

Equally innovative was the university's development of the Vallo-Cycle Bike Share program. On an environmental level, the program seeks to lessen the carbon footprint in Shelby County. On an educational level, the program was developed with the Department of Kinesiology. Finally on an aesthetic level, the program has inspired creative projects in bicycle-parking design.

Equally generous is the university's work in safeguarding the Ebenezer Swamp Environmental Preserve. While we, the uninformed, might think of a swamp as less than fascinating, the sixty acres of wooded wetlands just north of the university is a significant point of environmental impact. This area is the headwater for the Cahaba River Watershed. For those not yet familiar with the Cahaba River, it remains the longest free-flowing river in the country and the source of an incredibly rich biodiversity of fish. Obviously, the work done by Montevallo students at the Ebenezer Swamp Wetlands Research and Interpretive Center is an incredible opportunity for the study of environmental science.

Obviously, there's a lot going on at Montevallo, and much of student activity outside the classroom is focused on a wide variety of service opportunities and organizations, such as Habitat for Humanity, Amnesty International, and Best Buddies, a big brother/big sister program connecting with children with intellectual and developmental disabilities. Music is HUGE, of course, as is theater, but so are more physical pursuits, such as wrestling, the dance team, and bass fishing. There is a Montevallo Organization for Gaming, and a Yarn Club.

About fifteen percent of the enrolled student body becomes active in fraternities or sororities, all of which are housed in sections of the dormitories. Applicants from other regions will be delighted to earn that all eight of the residence halls are air conditioned, although it must be said that the general range of temperatures during the school year in central Alabama is not unpleasant.

I can't emphasize strongly enough the advantages of attending one of the public liberal arts colleges, like Montevallo, UNC Asheville, Saint Mary's in Maryland, or Mary Washington in Virginia. Consider the incredible array of opportunities I have just described and then consider the cost of attending Montevallo.

Millsaps College - Jackson, Mississippi

The student body is almost universally clean-cut, handsome, athletic, and goal oriented. Don't mistake the general level of ambition for homogeneity; Millsaps is among the most racially diverse of the southern colleges, and eminently diverse for a college in the Deep South. What draws students to Millsaps is the energy around the attainment of personal and professional skills. Millsaps students see themselves as having an obligation to make the best of the opportunities given to them.

And the stats... 2015

Number of Applicants: 2,851/ 57% Accepted
Undergrad Enrollment: 842   49% female / 51% male
Avg. SAT Reading Comp 510-640 / Math 520-630 Avg. ACT: 23-29
Total Cost: $48,654.00.
Received some form of financial assistance: 100%

Millsaps College in Jackson, Mississippi is another of the *Colleges That Change Lives*, a small liberal arts college located in the heart of Mississippi's capital, only blocks from the home of Eudora Welty. Millsaps is known for an outstanding program in business administration and offers a 5-year MBA. A strong connection with the Methodist Church animates Millsaps and is at the heart of the college's program known as "Faith & Work Initiative," connecting career and service.

Jackson is the capital of Mississippi and the state's most vibrant city. Jackson is pretty; Millsaps is gorgeous!

Millsaps was founded in 1890 by Major Ruben Millsaps as a liberal arts college affiliated with the United Methodist Church. Today, the affiliation with Methodism remains, but the curriculum is entirely secular. Major Millsaps' generosity is also honored by the enduring pride in the college mascot, Mr. Major. The college's athletic teams are known as the "Majors" and the "Lady Majors."

Among the distinctions accorded to Millsaps, is the title, " Best College in the Deep South." It was no accident that Loren Pope included Millsaps in his collection of *Colleges That Change Lives*, and the role of the college in educating well-prepared and effective leaders in the South remains clear.

There are three elements of the Millsaps experience that ought to be emphasized in describing this Methodist college in Jackson, Mississippi:

The first of these is that the student body is almost universally clean-cut, handsome, athletic, and goal oriented. Don't mistake the general level of ambition for homogeneity; Millsaps is among the most racially diverse of the southern colleges, and eminently diverse for a college in the Deep South. What draws students to Millsaps is the energy around the attainment of personal and professional skills. Millsaps students see themselves as having an obligation to make the best of the opportunities given to them.

The second of these is that the fraternities and sororities are really important, with unexpected depth of purpose. The Greek organizations are social and residential, but they are also committed to significant issues and social causes. Identification with a particular mission sets each of the organizations apart and identifies their first principles. Work in support of the "Make A Wish Foundation," or " The Children's Miracle Network," with "The March of Dimes," or "AIDS Awareness," animates much of the energy of the Greeks during the course of the year.

Finally, while many students at Millsaps are not Methodists, a great many find direction in their Christian faith. Students do less talking about their convictions than acting upon them; most will engage in some kind of service work during the course of their career at Millsaps. I found this statement by a Millsaps senior to be indicative of the general level of insightful reflection on the value of an education in an institution such as Millsaps:

> "In his book, Desiring God, John Piper asserts, "If we take our doctrines into our hearts where they belong, they can cause upheavals of emotion and sleepless nights. This is far better than toying with academic ideas that never touch real life. "

That senior, Chad Bowen, worked as a Lily Intern in a church in South Jackson; the Lily internship program places students in more than a hundred foundations, schools, and work sites in which active mentoring is offered by professionals in a field the student might want to enter.

Millsaps supports a variety of student initiatives, sending students abroad to study and do service work, and encouraging independent research as well. One sophomore recently established a non-profit program called, "Operation Re-Hydration," in sub-Saharan Africa, distributing a product similar to Pedialyte. Millsaps students raise funds and run the program entirely on their own.

So, active, principled, ambitious, decent kids come to Millsaps in order to begin a lifelong process of education and service. They study on campus, travel to the college's biocultural preserve in the Yucatan, seek a five year MBA, do original research in science, mount a major production in the excellent Theater Arts program, jump into the Ford Fellowship Teaching Program, or develop their skills in an ambitious writing program.

But, do they have any fun?

Yup.

One of the most surprising campus-wide events at Millsaps is Diwali, the Hindu Festival of Lights, sponsored by Millsaps Masala, the college's Indian Students Organization, the festival features spicy food, music, and dance. A recent performance of "Bolly-Fusion", dance and fashion, was the hit of the Diwali show.

More conventional collegiate antics take place during "Major Madness," an all-out celebration of spring. There are a number of "Major" moments and opportunities at Millsaps, including Majorly Dramatic (the theatrical organization), Major Melodies (the show choir - think GLEE), and Major Noise (the pep band). The SAPS Board
organizes weekly events that range from Scavenger Hunts to golf outings. And the Greeks open their social events to the entire campus.

Outside of work and service, the activity most Majors and Lady Majors have in common is the very ambitious and successful athletic program. Millsaps plays in the Southern Collegiate Athletic Conference of Division III, offering fourteen varsity sports for men and women. Definitely purple and white, the Majors and Lady Majors have won conference championships in football, basketball, and baseball. Lacrosse for men and women has recently been added to the athletic program as a club sport. Other very popular club sports include the dance team, cheerleading, and fencing. Recreational or intramural sports include rugby, inner tube water polo, dodgeball, volleyball, soccer, flag football, and softball.

Millsaps is a beautiful, happy, goal-oriented school in a lovely capital city in the deep South. For a student with a sense of purpose and adventure, Millsaps could be one of the great bargains available on the current admission scene.

University of Mississippi - Oxford, Mississippi

It should be noted that the undergraduate program at Ole Miss is relatively small. About twenty-two thousand students attend the university; slightly more than eighteen thousand are undergraduates. By comparison, the undergraduate population at Boston University is more than twenty-four thousand. The University of Mississippi offers class size and faculty mentoring equivalent to any private comprehensive university.

The stereotype of the Ole Miss student is of a southern preppy, well dressed, somewhat conservative, keen on sports, and loyal-for-life to his college. The actuality is that there is no single "type" at Ole Miss, but the quality of life does breed strong attachment and pride

And the stats... 2015

Number of Applicants: 16,101/ 81% Accepted
Undergrad Enrollment: 1,101   56% female / 44% male
Avg. SAT Reading Comp 480-590 / Math 490-590 Avg. ACT: 21-27
Total Cost: $22,704.00 (in-state) $34,752.00 (out-of-state)
Received some form of financial assistance: 85%

I know. The image of James Meredith meeting the hateful response of segregationists at the gates of the University of Mississippi does not fade easily. And it is true that Mississippi was at the heart of some of the most disturbing scenes of the Civil Rights battle in the South. It is surprising today, therefore, to discover the charm, beauty, and enlightened good will of the University of Mississippi and its home in Oxford, Mississippi.

The university itself is something of a surprise – an excellent academic institution, both affordable and open to students in the normal reaches of scores and grades.

We'll turn to the university itself in a moment, but the first observation has to be that Oxford, Mississippi is pretty much what a college town should look like, assuming that the college town is set amidst magnolias and historic antebellum mansions. *Travel and Leisure Magazine* recently named Oxford one of the ten "Coolest College Towns," an honor the town has long deserved; *USA Today* picks Oxford as one of the top six.

Not only is the town ripe with charm, in conjunction with the university, Oxford has become a true center of culture in the region. William

Faulkner's historic retreat, Rowan Oak, now maintained by the university, is a much-visited literary monument and a good example of antebellum Greek Revival architecture. Readers of Faulkner's work will also recognize the historic buildings around The Courthouse Square and will enjoy the attractive modern business that flourish there. Square Books, one of the most highly regarded independent bookstores in the nation holds collections of important signed works, and the variety of restaurants and eateries on The Square has included such favorites as: Ajax Diner, The Bottle Tree Bakery, The Blind Pig Pub, Bouré, City Grocery, the Downtown Grill, Irie, Parrish Baker Pub, Proud Larry's, The Rib Cage, Rooster's Blues House, Varsity Grille, and Waltz on the Square.

Oxford is strikingly handsome and eminently historic, but the town is also progressive and up-to-date. Bike trails wind through the town, and Oxford is at the heart of a "happening" music scene. Whereas the music scene was most firmly established in Athens, Georgia, Austin, Texas, or Chapel Hill, North Carolina, today that mantle has fallen on Oxford, home to Beanland, The Cooters, Kudzu Kings, Blue Mountain, George McConnell, Caroline Herring, and the Sweet Tea Recording Studio. Sweet Tea has recorded such contemporary icons as Modest Mouse, Elvis Costello, The Hives, Counting Crows, Jars of Clay, and Buddy Guy.

And, if that were not enough, the Gertrude C. Ford Center for the Performing Arts on the campus of the university hosts concerts, Broadway shows, and was the location of one of the televised debates between Barack Obama and John McCain.

The university and Oxford are home to a number of internationally celebrated programs, including the Yoknapatawpha Conference, the Faulkner Conference, the Oxford Conference for the Book, and the Southern Foodways conference, a celebration of southern cuisine. Summer also brings fireworks, outdoor concerts and a Shakespeare Festival.

And, author John Grisham has chosen to make his home in Oxford.

For all its sense of place and history, Oxford is primarily a college town, and the life of the university animates the life of the town. Some of that life is academic and cultural, and, inevitably, some of it derives from the place SEC sports plays in this region.

The university's athletic facilities are impressive. Vaught-Hemingway stadium holds more than seventy thousand rabid fans of Ole Miss football, and Oxford-University Stadium features one of the nation's finest collegiate baseball facilities. The Palmer-Salloum Tennis Center is home to the SEC championship tennis team; Tad Smith Coliseum is an SEC favorite, hosting basketball for men and women. Golfers love the newly reconfigured Ole Miss Golf Course, one of the top tips from Golf Inc. Magazine.

How important are sports at the University of Mississippi?

Well, current NFL icons, Peyton and Eli Manning, were raised by their dad, Archie Manning, the best quarterback Ole Miss has ever seen. Manning wore number eighteen in his glory days at Mississippi and ever since then, the speed limit on the campus has been eighteen miles per hour. An odd tribute, perhaps, but indicative of the respect the university holds for excellence.

That pursuit of excellence extends to the curriculum as well. Twenty-five graduates have won Rhodes Scholarships, almost all of them graduates in the College of Liberal Arts. A rising program in creative writing has claimed national attention, and the Master of Fine Arts in Creative Writing is distinctive and highly regarded. An initiative sponsored by the English Department is digitizing some of the world's most ancient manuscripts. The Forensic Chemistry program is one of only ten such programs in the country, regularly sending its graduates to agencies such as the FBI. A team of physicists from the university was instrumental in designing and creating the world's most powerful particle detector for the Large Hadron Collider, the world's most powerful atom smasher.

The university is made up of fourteen separate schools or colleges, four of which are professional schools. The Schools of Law, Pharmacy, Medicine, and Nursing provide professional training at the highest level. Undergraduates may study in the Schools of Engineering and Nursing, and graduate programs are found in the remaining schools.

The largest number of undergraduates is found in the School of Business Administration, The College of Liberal Arts, and the College of Education. Other undergraduate programs are found in the School of Accountancy, the School of Applied Sciences, and the School of Education. Business claims the greatest number of majors, followed by Education and the Liberal Arts.

One flagship program is found in the Media Department, where the journalism program produces a number of highly successful print and media journalists each year. Forensic Science and Criminal Justice are also very popular majors.

At this point, it should be noted that the undergraduate program at Ole Miss is relatively small. About twenty-two thousand students attend the university; slightly more than eighteen thousand are undergraduates. By comparison, the undergraduate population at Boston University is more than twenty-four thousand. The University of Mississippi offers class size and faculty mentoring equivalent to any private comprehensive university.

The stereotypical Ole Miss student is southern preppy, well dressed, somewhat conservative, keen on sports, and loyal-for-life to his college. The actuality is that there is no single "type" at Ole Miss, but the quality of life does breed strong attachment and pride.

The university recently decided to abandon the mascot known as "Colonel Reb," a goateed plantation owner with a broad hat in favor of a more politically correct totem. The current mascot is a black bear known as Rebel Bear, but the clear choice of the current student body was the adoption of Star Wars military legend, Admiral Ackbar. So, to please the alumni, Ole Miss still fields "Rebel" teams, but the climate on campus is notably more Robot Chicken.

It is heartening to hear the crowd chant "To Hell With LSU," instead of, "The South Will Rise Again." Times in Oxford are a-changing.
And yet...

This article can close with no better evocation of the Ole Miss that was, and in part, still is, than they revered Ole Miss cheer, known to generations of "Rebels" and "Ackbars" as "Hotty Toddy":

Are you ready?
Hell, yeah! Damn Right!
Hotty Toddy, Gosh almighty
Who the hell are we, Hey!
Flim Flam, Bim Bam
OLE MISS BY DAMN!

Hendrix College - Conway, Arkansas

Hendrix is in Arkansas, but the "feel" of the college is very similar to its true peers – Rhodes, Whitman, Grinnell, Macalester. Not only is Conway more like an enlightened Midwestern town than a small Southern city, the overwhelming impression one gets in visiting Hendrix is that this is an ambitious and tolerant liberal arts college.

And the stats... 2015

Number of Applicants: 1665 / 83% Accepted
Undergrad Enrollment: 1,358 55% female / 45% male
Avg. SAT Reading Comp 540-660 / Math 540-660 Avg. ACT: 25-31
Total Cost: $.54,302.00
Received some form of financial assistance: 100%

Hendrix is a "Best Buy" and a great option for an adventurous student eager to see a part of the country often left unexplored. Those fond of the outdoors will be stunned with the opportunities waiting in the Ozarks, just beyond the attractive city of Conway.

Conway is the second-fastest growing city in Arkansas and a thriving small city in the Little Rock metropolitan area. Charming, this city of about fifty thousand is known as the "City of Colleges," as three are located in town, of which, Hendrix is the most highly reputed. Conway High School is a sound and modern secondary school, one of the largest in the state. Its mascot is notable – the "Wampus Cat" is a six-legged cat, boasting "four to run with the speed of light and two to fight with all its might."

The Hendrix mascot is the Warrior, estimable enough, but hardly comparable to the Wampus Cat! In every other regard, however, Hendrix is among the most attractive of college options. Secondary school counselors have long admired Hendrix and have included it in the discussion of the most highly regarded small liberal arts colleges.

Another of the *Colleges That Change Lives*, Hendrix College is among the most progressive colleges in the South. Located in a suburban town outside of Little Rock, Hendrix enrolls students from across the country, including a significant number of students of color; Hendrix has no fraternities or sororities. The 1300 students at Hendrix are happy and active and grateful to have found themselves in the company of teachers who enjoy teaching.

I think it may be necessary at this point to emphasize three observations that have been made by most visitors to Hendrix.

1. Yes, Hendrix is in Arkansas, but the "feel" of the college is very similar to its true peers – Rhodes, Whitman, Grinnell, Macalester. Not only is Conway more like an enlightened Midwestern town than a small Southern city, the overwhelming impression one gets in visiting Hendrix is that this is an ambitious and tolerant liberal arts college.

A Hendrix friend passed on a scathing article about Hendrix posted online. I believe it accurately reflects the degree to which Hendrix is not a typical regional college.

> *"The school itself tries, like any liberal arts school, to brainwash its students into super acceptance and American/Christian hate through its required first year class, Journeys. Students are brainwashed to sympathize with Islamic terrorists, see Christianity as silly, and to reject any American ideals."*

I hadn't heard liberal education described as "brainwashing into super acceptance," but if that's what liberal arts colleges do, Hendrix is in the mix.

2. Accepted students who have visited Hendrix chose the college over a number of other excellent options. To be fair, Hendrix is more affordable than many other equally ambitious colleges, and its financial aid policy is generous. But what appears again and again in the testimony of those who have found Hendrix is that they were won over by the warmth of welcome they received in visiting the college and convinced that Hendrix is a "friendlier" campus than the others they had explored.

Not only is the campus friendly, it is also impressive and quite beautifully landscaped. The facilities at Hendrix are modern and first-rate; residences are universally well appointed.

3. Loyalty and strength of affiliation are common at many of the Southern colleges, but, for the most part, the depth of attachment at most of them has something to do with fraternity and sorority, big time sports, and "old boy" traditions.

Hendrix inspires an impressive degree of loyalty; its students and its graduates absolutely love the place! But, there are no fraternities and sororities, sports have a place equal to a number of other important activities (like Student Congress), and traditions are inclusive and welcoming to all. Without making too much of the issue at some other comparable institutions, Hendrix does not suffer from an inferiority complex; its students are genuinely glad to be there and are happy to return after the freshman year.

It's hard to measure happiness or to use it as an index of a college's viability, but Hendrix students are hardworking and happy to a degree not found at many other colleges.

Academic life at Hendrix is demanding; most students describe themselves as having more work to do than they can complete in the course of a week. The library isn't bursting on Saturday night, but fills quite nicely on Sunday afternoon and evening.

A program known as "Your Hendrix Odyssey" contends that "You learn more when you do more," and requires that all students choose three Odyssey experiences from the six available categories: Artistic Creativity, Global Awareness, Professional and Leadership development, Service to the World, and Undergraduate Research.

In case this requirement seems a bit "fluffy", consider that a project in Professional and Leadership Development, for example, has to involve more than one hundred hours of engagement in some sort of contracted endeavor. There's no phoning in any part of the Odyssey experience.

Hendrix is nationally known for the quality of its undergraduate research, and its reputation may largely depend on its strength in the natural and biological sciences; the college reports that its graduates have an acceptance rate at medical schools approaching 90%.

More than half of the college's graduates end up in graduate or professional programs within two years of graduation, a significantly higher proportion that found at most colleges. Acceptance at law school has been running at about 90% in recent years, and the college is ranked among the most successful in producing Ph.D.s in the sciences.

The science programs are strong and numbers of graduates do seek them out, but a number of other programs are equally compelling. Involvement in the Theater Program at Hendrix is common, and the number of students participating in productions is far higher than at comparable institutions. The quality of the Theater Arts major is well recognized, and numbers of its graduates have found success in the performing arts after having graduated from Hendrix.

The absence of the Greek hierarchy allows Hendrix to enjoy an active social scene that is both inclusive and imaginative. For example, the largest fundraiser of the year, and one of the most enjoyed celebrations, centers on the selection of Miss Hendrix. At most southern colleges, the competition would lead to pageants at the state and national levels, but at Hendrix, the winner is male and in drag. This, by the way, is more than a swimsuit competition; the talent component is extremely important.

The single most emphatically endorsed tradition at the college is known as "Shirttails," in which new students wearing a long white shirt and boxer shorts serenade the dormitories. Think Tom Cruise in *Risky Business* and you'll have some idea of what the choreography looks like. Each residential group tries to outdo the others in the performance of their debut in shirttails; there is little doubt that the evening does a great deal to break the ice at the start of the year.

The Hendrix Warriors play in the Southern Collegiate Athletic Conference in Division III against other colleges of similar size and ambition. Actually, this is one of the most interesting conferences in Division III, uniting colleges from Georgia (Oglethorpe) to Colorado (Colorado College). Traditional regional rivals in the SCAC include Rhodes, Millsaps, Sewanee, Centre, Austin, and Southwestern.

In a recent survey, Hendrix was named as one of the top twenty colleges in terms of its athletic facilities, and the 100,000 square foot Wellness and Athletic Center is a stunningly impressive facility. It houses all of the usual amenities and an indoor climbing wall.

Almost 40% of Hendrix students end up having played on at least one intercollegiate team, and many join in other active athletic endeavors. The Warriors offer the usual array of sports for men and women, including lacrosse, swimming, and a championship baseball team. Cheerleading and Dance Team are also varsity sports. Ultimate frisbee and a strong Outing Club are also highly visible.

Hendrix is a far more attractive option than many other colleges enjoying greater selectivity, and this secret won't stay undercover much longer!

University of Arkansas - Fayetteville, Arkansas

The university raised a BILLION dollars much of which went to the funding of the Honors College (Recently established and now among a very select group, including Harvard, Berkeley, Princeton, MIT, and Yale in having multiple Gates Cambridge Scholarship recipients). The Walton family trust donated three hundred million dollars to the university - the largest single gift ever given to an institution.

And the stats... 2015

Number of Applicants: 18,984 / 62% Accepted
Undergrad Enrollment: 121,836 52% female / 48% male
Avg. SAT Reading Comp 500-610 / Math 510-620 Avg. ACT: 23-28
Total Cost: $23,066.00 (in-state) $35,156.00 (out-of-state)
Received some form of financial assistance: 79%

Fair Warning! This is a RAVE review, a totally over-the-top genuinely enthusiastic description of what I think may be one of the most remarkable collegiate opportunities in the nation.

The University of Arkansas has six campuses within the state, but it is the flagship campus at Fayetteville that has captured the attention and admiration of those keeping track of major universities. In an attempt to remain mildly objective, permit me to highlight a baker's dozen of observations about Arkansas that might be of interest to the college-bound student:

- Among the speakers and performers recently appearing on campus - Tenzin Gyatso, 14th Dalai Lama, Snoop Dog, Anderson Cooper, Malcolm Gladwell, Benazir Bhutto, the Foo Fighters, Jane Goodall, James Earl Jones, President Bill Clinton, The Roots, Salmon Rushdie, The Flaming Lips, Elie Wiesel, Magic Johnson, John Legend, Condoleezza Rice, and Steve Wozniak.

- The university raised a BILLION dollars much of which went to the funding of the Honors College (Recently established and now among a very select group, including Harvard, Berkeley, Princeton, MIT, and Yale in having multiple Gates Cambridge Scholarship recipients). The Walton family trust donated three hundred million dollars to the university - the largest single gift ever given to an institution.

- Among many distinctive and nationally recognized academic programs, the University of Arkansas has a distinguished program in Middle Eastern Studies, including a generous program of Middle East Studies Abroad scholarships.

- The student to faculty ratio is approximately 19:1.

- The Stella Boyce Concert Hall offers more than 300 Hundred Concerts each year.

- Eleven buildings on campus have been added to National Registry of Historic Buildings.

- Tuition expenses have been offset by contributions by the athletic department of more than a million dollars to the general operating budget.

- Club sports at Arkansas include Bass Fishing, Shotgun Sports, Boxing, Quidditch, Paintball, Water Skiing, Triathlon, Men's Ice Hockey, Men's and Women's Rugby, men's and Women's Ultimate Frisbee, and Bowling.

- The University Recreation center offers instruction in African Dance and Bollywood Dance.

- The university has three miles of sidewalks inscribed with names of graduates. At this point, more than 170,000 names of graduates are inscribed in Senior Walk.

- The Music Department is designated an All-Steinway School.

- The most successful athletic program in the NCAA is Arkansas' program in track and field. Arkansas has won 41 National track and field championships. Football and basketball are showcased more frequently, but it is track and field that is the true Razorback dynasty.

- The university's Fine Arts Center was designed by Fayetteville native and graduate of the University of Arkansas, Edward Durell Stone, Stone is a major figure in the development of modern architecture in the United States, having designed the Radio City Music Hall, The Museum of Modern Art, The Kennedy Center, and the General Motors Building.

Arkansas is a big, complicated, lively university in one of the most attractive of college towns. Fayetteville is a happening town, in part because of the university, but also because the Walton family has been actively supporting the city's cultural life for several decades. The location is superb; Fayetteville is on the edge of the Boston Mountains in the Ozarks, a lovely mountain region.

The university was founded in 1871 on farmland that rose above the town. For that reason, the university is sometimes referred to as "the Hill". Old Main in the heart of the campus is an impressive brick building with two towers, one of which plays the college's alma mater every day at five o'clock. Today the building hosts a number of administrative offices, including those of the J. William Fulbright College of Arts and Sciences.

The setting is impressive and the more lovely for including two arboreta within the university's three hundred and forty five acre central campus.

The Fulbright College of Arts and Sciences is the center of academic affairs for most undergraduates enrolling at Arkansas. Departments included in this college include all the arts and humanities, math and science, and some other interesting programs, such as the School of Social Work, Communications, Journalism, Geosciences, Sociology and Criminal Justice, and the Department of World Languages, Literature, and Cultures. The highly esteemed MFA program in Creative Writing and Translation is one of the few English programs to offer literary translation as a professional degree.

Arkansas is a top-flight research university; the formal designation given by the Carnegie Foundation is "very high research university", placing Arkansas in the top two percent of research universities in the nation. Consequently, study as an undergraduate is animated by research carried out in every department and college. In addition to the Fulbright College of Arts and Sciences, Arkansas is made up of the Dale Bumpers (former Secretary of Agriculture) College of Agricultural, Food, and Life Sciences, the Fay Jones School of Architecture, the Sam Walton College of Business, the University of Arkansas College of Education, the University of Arkansas College of Engineering, the University of Arkansas Graduate School, and the University of Arkansas School of Law.

Bill and Hillary Clinton both taught in the university's school of law at the start of their careers; Hillary Clinton founded the university's legal clinic.

One highly regarded program allows about four hundred exceptional entering students to enroll in Arkansas' Honors College; almost three thousand undergraduates and seven hundred professors participate in honors courses or programs, but those attached to the Honors College in particular are an impressive group. Almost one hundred and fifty of them are National Merit Scholars, and a high percentage will go on to win the most prestigious of postgraduate awards. Honors College undergrads study abroad at about the same rate as other students in the university, and it is worth noting that it was Arkansas Congressman and Senator, William J. Fulbright, former Chairman of the Senate Foreign Relations Committee, and President of the university at the age of thirty-nine, who founded the Fulbright Program in 1946. The program, supporting the exchange of students and scholars around the world has allowed more than two hundred and ninety thousand American students and another one hundred and eighty thousand foreign students to travel and study.

Arkansas has all the elements of fun and diversion that make a college campus stimulating. Residential life is well supervised and healthy. Arkansas is like most southern universities in maintaining an extensive system of fraternities and sororities. One sorority, Chi Omega, was founded at Arkansas, and in recognition of the university's contribution to the sorority, Chi Omega donated an elegant Greek Theater to the university; the facility has since been included in the National Register of Historic Places.

The Greek Theater is one of the distinctive traditions that make the Arkansas experience memorable. I appreciate the generosity with which one group extended its efforts to serve the university as a whole. Today, the Greek Theater has joined the other facilities in the National Register of Historic Places and is often used for concerts, plays, and pep rallies. Similarly, the tradition of the Senior Walk is inclusive. Every graduate's name is placed on the walk which now extends for miles around the campus. It took a great deal of effort to carve names individually, so the invention of the "Sandhog", a machine that etches names, was significant in allowing the hundreds of thousands of names to find their place on the walk.

Having made reference to the "Sandhog", the time has come to wallow for a while in the naming of Arkansas' teams. Known as the Cardinals (the school's color) until the first decade of the Twentieth Century, Arkansas' football team went undefeated and played with fierce intensity. At a pep rally in 1909, the coach made reference to the team as having played, "like a wild band of razorback hogs". The razorback is thought to be related to the wild boar, and is considered dangerous. From that point on, Arkansans referred to the teams and themselves as Razorbacks, and eventually, as "Hogs".

Any sports fan knows the signature cry that arises whenever Arkansas meets a foe. It is interesting to hear a single fan give the cry; it is terrifying to hear the entire stadium erupt. The printer word can only mildly express the rallying power of the Razorback War Cry, but here goes:

Calling The Hogs (instructions)

Begin by screaming "WOOOOOOOO"

As the scream gets louder, raise arms, fingers wiggling up and down.

After about six seconds, close fists and bring arms down hard in a fist pump.

As the fist pumps, Scream the word, "PIG".

Call the pigs home by yelling, "SOOOOIE".

After the third call, add (at full volume) RAZORBACKS!

In 2014, the Razorback War Cry received a patent, thought to be the first patent given to a university's cheer and among the first given to a sound. It will not be surprising to learn that the mascots appearing at athletic contests are porcine. An actual Razorback is on hand, of course, but so too are "Sue E", a female mascot that dances with wild abandon, "Pork Chop", a child-sized mascot, and "Boss Hog", a nine foot inflatable mascot.

Arkansas loves its hogs, and the athletic tradition at the university is similar to that at any of the Southeastern Conference athletic powerhouse programs, such as Alabama or Mississippi, but the Arkansas version includes significant appreciation of sports other than football. The university sponsors nineteen varsity sports and more than two hundred contests on campus per year, giving many opportunities to call those hogs.

Track and field (men's and women's) enjoys the greatest consistent success, essentially dominating Division I for more than five decades. Both baseball and basketball have won national championships, and SEC competition in swimming, volleyball, cross-country, gymnastics, soccer, golf, and tennis are at the highest level. Although it is not a varsity sport, the men's Rugby team competes nationally.

Patented war cry, beautiful setting, highly respected research facilities, ambitious student body – there is a lot to like about Arkansas.

Texas

For all the bluster and regional patriotism Texans proclaim when out of the state ("Don't Mess With Texas!"), there really are many different experiences of Texas as one travels across the Lone Star expanse.

Rather than attempt to pinpoint the gradations of cultural difference from Amarillo to Waco, it's probably worthwhile to identify the three major urban areas (Houston, Dallas-Fort Worth, and San Antonio), and the most significant college towns.

Houston is the fourth largest city in the United States and the nation's busiest port. In addition to a widely varied industrial and commercial base, Houston is home to NASA's Mission Control Center ("Houston, We Have A Problem!") and to the first domed sports stadium. Those who visit will quickly learn that Houston's climate is classified as *humid, subtropical* - hot and goopy in the summer and wet in the winter. Houston enjoys more than ninety-nine days of temperature above ninety degrees each year. No wonder it is the most "air-conditioned" city in America. The University of Houston, Texas Southern University, and Rice University are located in Houston.

Dallas is landlocked and a center of banking and commercial enterprise. Considered more sophisticated and polished, Dallas grew from a cotton town to a major financial center with a wide variety of cultural and recreational opportunities. Like Houston, Dallas has a humid subtropical climate, but also picks up warm (!) winds from the north, often boasting some of the highest temperatures in the nation. In fact, Dallas is only bettered by the Mojave Desert and portions of Nevada in summer temperatures.

Major universities in Dallas include the University of Dallas and Southern Methodist University.

SMU is a remarkable and exceptionally interesting small comprehensive university located in a lovely section of the city. I would have devoted an entire chapter to the exceptional programs available at SMU had the university not attracted a significant number of students from outside of Texas and outside the region. I love SMU, but I have to acknowledge that it is probably not a very well kept secret at this point.

If you have not had a chance to consider this gem, take a look. Its six thousand undergraduates live in an exceptionally attractive and lively quarter of the city and have the opportunity to study in some of the country's most exciting programs. Of particular interest are the programs in journalism and media and the exceptional professional programs in dance, theater, and art offered by the Meadows School of the Arts of SMU.

Fort Worth has its origins as a stockade and stop along the Chisholm Trail. Growing into prominence as a center of the cattle trade, it won the nickname, "Cowtown." Today Fort Worth retains its western heritage alongside a growing technological industrial base. Fort Worth is home to Texas Christian University's Horned Frogs.

The third of the major cities in Texas is San Antonio, home of Trinity University, formerly profiled in this book, now admitting about 48% of applicants.

The Texas college appearing in this book is Southwestern University in Georgetown, just north of Austin.

Southwestern University - Georgetown, Texas

Southwestern's location is outstanding, and its campus is considered among the most impressive for the size of its student body. The campus is beautifully maintained and intelligently laid out, and the signature buildings are predominantly crafted of gray stone. I have always liked all varieties of Gothic, lots of Georgian red brick and white columns or Victorian gables, but I have to admit that I have been won over by Southwestern's buildings made of gray stone.

And the stats... 2015

Number of Applicants: 3,487 / 50% Accepted
Undergrad Enrollment: 1,538 58% female / 42% male
Avg. SAT Reading Comp 520-630 / Math 530-630 Avg. ACT: 23-28
Total Cost: $49,090.00
Received some form of financial assistance: 100%

There are a few matters to clear up right at the start, the first of which is to identify Southwestern as a small liberal arts college rather than a massive regional university. Made up of the Brown College of Arts and Sciences, and the Sarofim School of Fine Arts, Southwestern is the oldest institution of higher education in Texas, enrolling about thirteen hundred students in an outstanding undergraduate experience.

Georgetown, Texas is a charming small town in Texas Hill Country (Red Poppy Capital of Texas!), north of Austin. Today, Georgetown and Austin have grown closer together, but the Georgetown's Victorian Central Square is still a point of interest and worth the trip from Austin. Georgetown was the first city in America to be named a Great American Main Street, and the college's location in a town with character is a major attraction. Texas Hill Country is noted for its rugged beauty and, increasingly, for successful vineyards. The nearby Balcones Canyonlands Preserve is home to numerous songbirds and a profusion of wildflowers.

Austin, the capital city of Texas, Live Music Capital of the United States, is home to the University of Texas, and is a fascinating city and college town. Southwestern enjoys its cozy location in charming Georgetown and its close relationship with all that Austin has to offer; the Longhorns of Texas are no more than twenty-five miles from the Southwestern campus.

In addition to the liberal arts curriculum at Southwestern, the university is also home to two notable initiatives. The National Institute for Technology in Liberal Education is headquartered at Southwestern and promotes innovation in the use of technology in teaching; work done at the institute is shared with colleges and universities around the world. The National Hispanic Institute has created a Center for Hispanic Studies at Southwestern in addition to its Leadership Institute at Villanova in Pennsylvania. The presence of the institutes and the School of Fine Arts allows Southwestern to offer the Bachelor of Arts, Bachelor of Science, Bachelor of Music, and the Bachelor of Fine Arts degrees – a greater variety than most small colleges can offer.

Southwestern's location is outstanding, and its campus is considered among the most impressive for the size of its student body. The campus is beautifully maintained and intelligently laid out, and the signature buildings are predominantly crafted of gray stone. I have always liked all varieties of Gothic, lots of Georgian red brick and white columns or Victorian gables, but I have to admit that I have been won over by Southwestern's buildings made of gray.

Architecture aside, the plan of the campus is brilliant. The college owns more than seven hundred acres, about one hundred of which make up the central campus. The decision was made to order that campus in a series of arcs so that landscaping, flowing water, and campus roads are graceful in connecting and containing the buildings and facilities of this ambitious college. Of particular note is the ten-acre academic mall, a grassy expanse in the heart of the campus. Many students consider it to be the most attractive meeting place on campus, and almost every student will greet every other student on the mall during the course of the day.

The academic program at Southwestern is not entirely conventional, I am pleased to report, reflecting the influence of a prominent educational philosopher named Mortimer Adler, who published an educational manifesto in the 1980's entitled, The Paideia Proposal. Paideia at Southwestern refers to a three-year program (although some freshman will be permitted to start in the first year) of seminar, civic engagement, an intercultural or diversity experience, and collaborative guided research or creative project. Paideia professors stay with their Paideia seminar group throughout the three years.

A recent project allowed a senior to connect a course in 20th Century American Literature and a course in Native American Religion. As a junior, she was fascinated by the connections she began to see between the two areas of study and turned her attention in her senior year to writing about Native American trickster mythology and Alan Ginsberg's poem, Howl. Happily, that project landed her a book contract before graduation.

Other Paideia enterprises do include fieldwork and a service component; a seminar group may build a community garden or work with the homeless population in Georgetown. In every case, participation in the program does include a summative project or performance.

Other significant intellectual experiences at Southwestern come about as the university extends itself to bring a variety of thoughtful and provocative voices to the campus. Two significant programs are the Shilling Lecture Series, which has brought speakers such as Bill Moyers, Former President Jimmy Carter, and Archbishop Desmond Tutu, and the Writer's Voice series, which has welcomed authors including Tony Kushner, Michael Chabon, Robert Pinsky, and Margaret Atwood.

The quality of life outside the classroom is enhanced by the eminently sane organization of the campus, a good residential life program, an active but not overwhelming Greek system, easy access to Austin, and the proximity of extraordinary recreational opportunities in the Texas Hill Country.

There are some traditions at Southwestern that enliven the place and are distinctive.

SING is a program of musical performances and skits that take place during Homecoming Weekend. Preparation for SING is extensive, and, although the quality of individual acts may vary, the total impact is uniformly impressive.

"Barcus" is a not-so-secret-secret-society, named in honor of former president of the university. The character appears at various athletic and community events, elegantly haberdashered in an ancient suit, bowler hat, and mask, followed by other members of the society, wearing sunglasses and long robes. "Barcus" traditionally arrives in a Model T Ford, yellow and black – the school's colors.

"Mall Ball" is a festive explosion of good spirits, held in the spring and fall on the extensive lawn in the heart of the campus.

The Southwestern "Pirates" play in the Southern Collegiate Athletic Conference in Division III against rivals such as Hendrix, Austin, Millsaps, Oglethorpe, and Rhodes. Although Southwestern has not fielded a football team for some time, it has recently emerged as a contender in men's and women's lacrosse. In addition to the usual array of intercollegiate sports, Southwestern offers an extensive program of support for Outdoor and Wilderness activities, ultimate frisbee, inner tube water polo, and a bowling league.

The Midwest

The Midwest is more than a region, of course; it is a mind set and a tradition of down-to-earth-plain-speaking common sense and hard work. Even the great cities of the Midwest, Chicago, Milwaukee, Detroit and Minneapolis, are cities that do things. For the most part, the Midwest is not a tourist destination, and for the most part, the Midwest is under-appreciated.

Aside from values born on the prairie and established in working the soil, the Midwest offers striking landscapes, beautiful towns, and thousands of lakes. Unlike some other regions that were defined from the start by the course of rivers and boundaries of valleys, the Midwest is about railroads.

The early mountain men may have slogged their way west on foot, but the great shift in population came with the expansion of railroad lines. Without a great mountain range in the thick of things to make travel difficult, rail connections east and west, north and south allowed easy transport of grain and livestock. Today, the small cities and town in which Midwestern colleges and universities are located pretty much follow the path of railroad expansion.

There are two flavors of Midwestern to be experienced in this section – the Great Lakes and the Prairie.

Lines of demarcation are not always clear. Minnesota has a bit of both; despite its ten thousand lakes, the western edge of Minnesota is on the prairie. Both Indiana and Illinois drop to a southern border with Kentucky, but Illinois has a stretch from Chicago to Waukegan on the Wisconsin line following the shore of Lake Michigan. The upper reaches of Wisconsin, Minnesota, and Michigan are their own region – rich in natural resources and positively Canadian in climate and attitude.

The State of Missouri often pops up in trivia contests as it is bordered by eight other states – Iowa, Illinois, Kentucky, Tennessee, Arkansas, Oklahoma, Kansas and Nebraska. That is a lot of real estate, and the diversity of experiences to be had in the state is remarkable. The capitol, Jefferson City, is virtually the center of the state, in the region known as Mid-Missouri. Kansas City is on the western border, adjacent to Kansas, and Saint Louis is on the eastern border, across the Mississippi from Illinois. Washington University, the highly ranked comprehensive university is located in various areas of Saint Louis and suburban Clayton, although most residences are in Forest Park. Saint Louis University, the second oldest Jesuit college in the country is located on Lindell Boulevard in Saint Louis. The major artery running between Kansas City and Saint Louis is Interstate Route 70; about a third of the way across the state, almost due north of Jefferson City, is Columbia, Missouri, the home of Stephens College for Women and the flagship campus of the University of Missouri. The Missouri University of Science and Technology is in Rolla.

Ohio

Ohio has an unfortunate image when it comes to college searches, and I don't really know from what set of misconceptions it has been sprung.

The state has essentially the same climate as New York or Pennsylvania, maybe a bit warmer south of Columbus, easily as snowy on the banks of Lake Erie. The colors in autumn are spectacular; lots of settings are hilly or on riverbanks. Some of the snappiest suburbs with the snappiest boutiques and manicured lawns are to be found Ohio; charming and interesting small towns dot the landscape.

Yes, the river towns have the mark of the industrial age, and Cleveland is where the petroleum industry got its start, but the three flagship cities – Cleveland, Cincinnati, and Columbus – have extraordinary cultural, commercial, and recreational opportunities for the visitor and college student. No trip to the Buckeye State would be complete without a stop at the Rock and Roll Hall of Fame, for example.

And, the state is chock full of excellent colleges and universities.

The largest and most celebrated, of course, is the Ohio State University, located in Columbus, Ohio's capital city. One of the great Midwestern land grant universities, Ohio State is atop the Big Ten in athletics and increasingly successful in academic endeavors as well, in part due to the energetic leadership of President E. Gordon Gee, formerly President of Brown University and the Chancellor of Vanderbilt University. Columbus is also home to Capital University and Ohio Dominican University. Ohio Wesleyan University is located in Delaware, now a suburb of the city.

Kenyon College, currently the most selective college in the state and celebrated for its literary tradition and its strength in preparing students for professional schools, is a small liberal arts college located in the village of Gambier, about fifty miles north of Columbus.

Denison University, enrolling about 2200 students on a lovely campus in the handsome town of Granville, Ohio, is about 30 miles east of Columbus.

Cleveland is a city of neighborhoods, one of which, University Circle, a five hundred and fifty acre cultural and educational compound, includes Case Western Reserve University, a nationally known comprehensive private university enrolling about four thousand undergraduates. John Carroll University is located in University Heights, and Oberlin College, the first college to admit women and black students, and the oldest continuously operating music conservatory in America is in Oberlin, Ohio, a very small city southwest of Cleveland, known as, "the hotbed of abolitionism," during the years preceding the Civil War.

The College of Wooster sits in Wooster, Ohio, just south of Akron in lovely countryside near the Amish communities of northern Ohio. To the south is Hiram College, in Hiram, Ohio, about an hour from Cleveland, Akron, and Youngstown in the northwestern quadrant of the state.

Wittenberg College is located in Springfield, about forty miles west of Columbus, and north of Dayton. To the south and west, Cincinnati is home to the University of Cincinnati and Xavier universities. Miami University is located in Oxford, Ohio, north of Cincinnati and just east of the Indiana line.

John Carroll University - Cleveland, Ohio

One of the most successful of John Carroll's programs is the Muldoon Center for Entrepreneurship, which includes the Entrepreneurship House, a residential option for freshmen who may be interested in pursuing the course of study in the Business School. Graduates of John Carroll have taken positions of importance in a number of enterprises; more than five hundred companies in Northwest Ohio are owned or run by alumni of John Carroll, making internships and job placement all the easier to find.

And the stats... 2015

Number of Applicants: 3,873 / 83% Accepted
Undergrad Enrollment: 3,113 47% female / 52% male
Avg. SAT Reading Comp 500-590 / Math 500-610 Avg. ACT: 21-27
Total Cost: $50,090.00
Received some form of financial assistance: 100%

In a quiet neighborhood of Cleveland and highly regarded is John Carroll University, a Jesuit university, and one of several Jesuit universities of high quality in the Midwest. John Carroll occupies a handsome 60-acre campus in University Heights, adjacent to the Cleveland suburb of Shaker Heights. Nothing more completely identifies the distinctive character of the John Carroll experience than its two primary missions: The development of intellectual inquiry and critical reasoning, and the promotion of social justice and community service. It is no accident that almost one third of an entering class is made up of first generation college students. Generous financial aid and a number of merit scholarships have brought the John Carroll education to students who could not otherwise afford to attend.

John Carroll has been out in front in a number of ways for years, but several new initiatives deserve close attention. The first of these, The John Carroll Access Initiative has been successful in increasing financial assistance and has resulted in John Carroll's appearing frequently on the "Best Buy" lists published annually. The Wilson teaching Fellows program has allowed students strong in Science and math to explore a career in teaching. JC developed a program in Computer Science with Healthcare Information Technology that allows students to become adept in the development of software to be used in the healthcare system. The Mike Cleary Program is Sports Studies allows undergraduates to acquire skill useful in sports management or sports administration. John Carroll has also partnered with NBS in creating a "Meet The Press" fellowship in political journalism.

So, just how Catholic is John Carroll? Well, any Jesuit institution is going to be influenced by the example of Saint Ignatius Loyola and committed to the idea of Spiritual Exercises. There are Jesuits on campus, some of whom teach at the university. The mission of the university, however, translates perfectly well into any tradition. John Carroll hopes to inspire students to excel in learning, leadership, and service. In describing the role of religion in the curriculum and in the community, the university is quite clear:

> "John Carroll University welcomes students and faculty from different religious backgrounds and philosophies. Dedicated to the total development of the human, the University offers an environment in which every student, faculty, and staff person may feel welcomed. Within this environment there is concern for the human and spiritual developmental needs of the students and a deep respect for the freedom and dignity of the human person. A faculty not only professionally qualified, but also student oriented, considers excellence in interpersonal relationships as well as academic achievement among its primary goals."

That "student oriented" thing is at the heart of instruction at John Carroll, In the College of Arts and Sciences and in the Boler School of Business, participation in a core curriculum with close faculty mentoring is central to the John Carroll experience. One of the hallmarks of rigorous Jesuit education is the core curriculum. There are many active and distinguished departments at John Carroll and the university graduates a wide variety of majors, but all students will take a First Year Seminar, two semesters of a foreign language, three philosophy courses, and two religion courses. Several distinctive programs for foreign study are sponsored by John Carroll – the Belfast Institute in Peacebuilding and Conflict Transformation, the Boler School of Business Semester in London, and the Italian Studies program in the Vatican City. Also popular are the London Liberal Arts Semester and the Casa de la Solidaridad in El Salvador.

Global education is available to those who have chosen engineering as a course of study as well. Course work is available at the Dortmund University of Technology in Germany and at England's Hull University.

One of the most successful of Carroll's programs is the Muldoon Center for Entrepreneurship, which includes the Entrepreneurship House, a residential option for freshmen who may be interested in pursuing the course of study in the Business School. Graduates of John Carroll have taken positions of importance in a number of enterprises; more than five hundred companies in Northwest Ohio are owned or run by alumni of John Carroll, making internships and job placement all the easier to find.

John Carroll is one of two universities in the world that have developed a program in "Crisis Mapping," an interdisciplinary approach to the response of critical issues in real time. Tufts and John Carroll have developed an intriguing set of criteria that demonstrate the emergence of crisis and the immediacy of response. Recent projects have looked at Haiti and Egypt as examples of regions that have experienced crisis, and have examined the ways in which governments, NGOs, and business respond to incidents in the contemporary world.

The organization of residential life is somewhat more thoughtfully developed at John Carroll than at some other middle-sized universities; residential options include lifestyle and academic choices. The general tone of campus life is purposeful and earnest; students enjoy their time at JCU, but are slightly more restrained than the general unwashed mass of hedonistic pleasure seekers who see college as tanning, laundry, and gym. Intramural competition, strong friendships, and lots of community service give the John Carroll student experience a quality few other colleges can offer.

There are many on-campus residential options for those who opt into the fraternity and sorority system, but, rather than send the Greeks out into separate space, the university has set aside floors in the residential halls, with social lounge space designated for the fraternity or sorority.

The Simple Living option allows students who want to enhance their spiritual and service lives by gathering with like-minded students. Students electing this option carry their mission into service work with communities in Cleveland.

The Healthy Living option offers the guidance of a nutritionist and physical trainer, regular practice of yoga, and produce found at area organic food stores. This option is also free of drugs and alcohol.

The university offers more than ninety student organizations and clubs, including very active programs in music and theater. Those interested in recreational sports can find an ambitious rugby club for men and women, lacrosse, rowing, field hockey, ultimate frisbee, a sailing team, and an ice hockey club. Intramurals include the usual sports plus flag football, dodgeball, racquetball, a three-point shooting contest, euchre (a card game), floor hockey, and a home run derby.

The Blue Streaks of John Carroll play a Division III athletic schedule in the Ohio Athletic Conference. Conference play pits the Streaks against such teams as the Ohio Northern Polar Bears, the Marietta Pioneers, the

Wilmington Quakers, the Muskingum Fighting Muskies, and the Heidelberg Student Princes, and the dreaded Mount Union Purple Raiders (perennial football champions in Division III).

The College of Wooster - Wooster, Ohio

There is no way to truly communicate the warmth, loyalty, and good-hearted spirit on this campus; Wooster's students feel at home from the very start and spend their four years making others feel as if they too have a place at Wooster. A quick tour of campus will present the excellence of the college's facilities, and it won't take long to see and feel that uncommon "spirit" of the place that sets it apart from lots of other colleges of its size.

And the stats... 2015

Number of Applicants: 5,497 / 59% Accepted
Undergrad Enrollment: 2,049 55% female / 45% male
Avg. SAT Reading Comp 540–650 / Math 560–670 Avg. ACT: 25–31
Total Cost: $55,500.00
Received some form of financial assistance: 99%

For the right student, the College of Wooster may be the most remarkable opportunity presented in this book. Counselors have been raving about Wooster for years; it combines an active and challenging academic program with a distinctive quality of life. Those in the know have long understood that this small college, set in a small town south of Cleveland and east of Akron, is a rarity. Not only is Wooster one of Loren Pope's *Colleges That Change Lives*, a charter member of the Great Lakes College Association, and an active champion of international education, its traditional association with its Presbyterian founders allows it to proudly boast one of the few collegiate bagpipe bands, replete with highland dancers. Once known as "The Presbyterian Steamrollers," the unaffiliated Wooster teams are now, the "Fighting Scots," and they fight effectively in the North Coast Athletic Conference.

There is no way to truly communicate the warmth, loyalty, and good-hearted spirit on this campus; Wooster's students feel at home from the very start and spend their four years making others feel as if they too have a place at Wooster. A quick tour of campus will present the excellence of the college's facilities, and it won't take long to see and feel that uncommon "spirit" of the place that sets it apart from lots of other colleges of its size. The commitment to internationalism has long brought real diversity to the campus; there is a genuine climate of appreciation for difference. In addition, community service, activities, and sports keep this campus hopping. One third of all students are involved with one of the musical groups on campus, almost as many with other performing arts. A third play a varsity sport. One hundred percent fill the gymnasium when the Scots have a home game and fill the theater when students perform. The clarity of purpose is demonstrated in Wooster's having been cited as one of the most successful colleges in mentoring original research.

Like Davidson, Macalester, and Centre, Wooster was established by the Presbyterian Church, and like those colleges, that founding impetus had much to do with the direction and purpose of the college from the very start. In 1870, much had yet to be worked out in the aftermath of the Civil War. Wooster's founding president was clear in stating the mission of this college:

> "The sameness of our origin as men and women carries with it our original and essential equality. Had our national life been the true expression of our national creed, slavery would have been forever impossible. Caste, in whatever name, strikes at the soul of our humanity and liberty."

In the same fashion, Wooster was established as a coeducational college from the start, clear in its expectation that it would hold women to the same level of expectation that it did men.

Although the college is no longer a Presbyterian college, one legacy of that affiliation is very much a part of the Wooster experience today - an uncommon commitment to a strong international presence on campus. Wooster reaches out into the world with a number of service and educational programs and has long enrolled a higher proportion of international students than most colleges of its type.

Missionaries left Wooster and traveled the globe, establishing strong ties with institutions and individuals. The Wooster in India program, for example, was founded in 1930. At that time, Wooster became connected with a sister school, Ewing College in Allahabad, India. Today, Wooster enrolls students from more than thirty nations, having developed programs that have welcomed international students as few colleges have done. Babcock Hall is a residence in which international students live in a cross-cultural living environment with students native to the United States. Luce Residential Hall offers six separate foreign language living centers in Russian, Chinese, French, German, Spanish, and Classics

In addition, Wooster offers instruction in seven foreign languages and promotes study abroad in sixty countries. As a side note, those travelers sent artifacts as well as students; the college has owned an Egyptian mummy since 1885 when it was donated by an alumnus who had purchased four in Egypt for the price of eight dollars each.

In addition to nationally reputed programs in the sciences, especially Chemistry, Wooster is known for its Independent Study Program, through which all students work one-on-one with an advisor in completing an independent project. This notion of a capstone academic experience has been copied by other colleges, but few have as successfully sustained a college-wide independent study program as Wooster has. Upon the successful completion of the Independent Project, students are awarded the coveted Tootsie Roll – yes, the chocolate candy. Look for the Tootsie Roll on the college's web site; it stands for a job well done.

Other traditions help Wooster separate itself from the pack of Ohio colleges, none more stirring than the corps of bagpipers who appear at a number of the college's most significant events. Pipers lead the marching band onto the football field, and pipers lead the procession at graduation.

Few colleges have a solitary bagpiper; Wooster has a minimum of five who appear in kilts, as do the one hundred and seventy members of the Fighting Scot Marching Band. Pipers are attracted to Wooster, of course, but enticed as well by the Scottish Arts Scholarship that identifies and supports talented musicians.

These aren't the only musicians or performers at Wooster. The Ohio Light Opera Company is the resident professional company of the College of Wooster, for example, and in continuous rehearsal and performance throughout the year. In addition to the expected performances of Gilbert and Sullivan's light operas, the company also produces musical theater, such as Camelot or Guys and Dolls. Wooster has long offered a strong program in Theater and now enrolls students in a major in Theater and Dance.

Two of the most significant traditions at Wooster involve the archway of Kauke Hall, at the center of the handsome campus. Freshman march through the archway on their way to their first convocation and are led back through the arch by the aforementioned pipers on graduation day. The entire student body rises to the challenge when snow falls heavily as tradition has it that classes will be cancelled if the entire archway can be completely packed with snow. "Packing the Arch" is one of the moments that creates a bond of friendship in shared labor.

There are fraternities and sororities at Wooster, but they play a less prominent role than at many similar colleges, in part because they are not nationally affiliated. Most social activity revolves around the residences. And most Wooster students have friendships that extend beyond fraternity or residence hall. Wooster is simultaneously an active academic community, a workshop in international understanding, an impressive athletic power in the region, and a very comfortable social setting for varieties of students of every type. Some fraternities and sororities live in sections of dormitories; some students join the College of Wooster Pipe Band, some belong to the Light Opera Company, some begin life work in theater. This is a healthy and happy campus, filled with motivated and effective students.

One hallmark of school spirit at Wooster is the very high proportion of students who play intercollegiate varsity sports; almost half of the men at Wooster have played at least one sport. The Fighting Scots excel in a number of sports for men and women, but the tradition of victory in basketball is particularly compelling. Wooster has shared the North Coast Athletic Conference championship in basketball with only one other college during the course of the last decade. The Wooster/Wittenberg rivalry in basketball is heated, and the games between these two teams always fill the stands. These are the only two teams in the NCAC that have won more than fifteen hundred games, and they are the two teams that set the standard for the league. Baseball, lacrosse, track and field, swimming and diving– all are good and well supported.

The other fifty percent of Wooster's students jump into club and intramural sports, of which the cricket club, ice hockey club, equestrian club, cheerleaders, dance team, ultimate frisbee club, and WOODS (Wooster's Outdoors Club) are most active.

Who ends up at Wooster?

The admissions process here is eminently sensitive and humane. Counselors and consultants appreciate the care with which applications are considered and the degree to which the college extends itself to ambitious students whose academic journey is still in process. My own experience has been that Wooster does a better job with the kids I send than almost any other college in its current range of selectivity.

Ohio Wesleyan University - Delaware, Ohio

For all these highly commendable and progressive initiatives, Ohio Wesleyan is a down-to-earth and active campus, on which a strong Greek system and sports play a large part in campus life. Known athletically as the "Battling Bishops", Ohio Wesleyan is an athletic power in soccer and lacrosse, virtually always at the top of its conference year after year.

And the stats... 2015

Number of Applicants: 3,981/ 74% Accepted
Undergrad Enrollment: 1,734 53% female / 47% male
Avg. SAT Reading. Avg.565 / Math Avg.562 ACT: 22-28
Total Cost: $54,750.00
Received some form of financial assistance: 100%

Ohio Wesleyan University (also known as OWU - pronounced: "Oh - Woo") in Delaware, Ohio is noted for the percentage of international students enrolled each year; Wesleyan is among the most generous in aiding applicants from outside the United States and enrolls a large number of international students - among the top ten most international of colleges by percentage of enrollment. In addition, the celebrated programs in international study and travel learning set this small college apart from many. OWU is also determined to promote "theory-to-practice", developing internships that support courses offered in the curriculum. It is not surprising that Ohio Wesleyan is often cited as one of the most successful in bringing entrepreneurial studies to the liberal arts program. A new major in Business has certainly added to the university's breadth of interest. This small university, located in what has become a suburban neighborhood of Columbus, is impressive in the range of majors and programs offered (more than 90) and in its determination to combine service for learning with active recruitment of a diverse student body. OWU is also unusual in its sponsorship of students with financial need and its identification as a "gay-friendly" college, meeting the six criteria developed by the Campus-Pride organization. It will come as no surprise that Ohio Wesleyan joins the select number of colleges identified as *Colleges That Change Lives*.

For all these highly commendable and progressive initiatives, Ohio Wesleyan is a down-to-earth and active campus, on which a strong Greek system and sports play a large part in campus life. Known athletically as the "Battling Bishops", Ohio Wesleyan is an athletic power in soccer and lacrosse, virtually always at the top of its conference year after year. The college's mascot, a stylized and feisty "bishop", rivals Wake Forest's "Demon Deacon" as one of the most bizarre pieces of religious/athletic iconography.

Delaware was once a small town near Columbus; today, the pleasant and uncommonly clean city of Columbus extends to the shaded campus of Ohio Wesleyan. Students flying in to Columbus (a major hub) will find themselves only a short cab ride from the campus. They will also find themselves on a leafy, attractive, and well maintained campus that has all the security and sense of community of a small liberal arts college with the many amenities of a major city. Two major league professional sports teams play in Columbus– The Columbus Blue Jackets of the National Hockey League and the Columbus Crew of the MSL – and a number of significant commercial empires have their base in Columbus.

OWU, like all the colleges with "Wesleyan" in their title, began as a Methodist college, and those Methodist roots have a great deal to do with the international flavor of the current student body and the high degree of commitment to community service and social justice. The college remains affiliated with the Methodist Church, but it is not a "religious" school; in fact, despite the generous volunteerism of OWU's students, there are some who would characterize the college as having a highly developed social life.

Academically, OWU is somewhat more comprehensive that its near neighbor Kenyon, in that it offers majors in a variety of areas outside of the traditional liberal arts, such as Ancient, Medieval and Renaissance Studies, Accounting and Journalism and offers a Bachelor's degree in Music. In addition to a strong program in Music, OWU is known for its Department of Practical Politics and Government, named after a distinguished professor. The Arneson Institute on Politics and Public Affairs was founded on principles fostered by Ben Arneson, including the pledge he asked majors in his department to sign:

> *"With a view to serving the public interest and regardless of the nature of my future vocations I pledge that, upon leaving college, I will devote a portion of my time to active and definite participation in public affairs."*

Perhaps as a result of Dr. Arneson's influence, Ohio Wesleyan provided the highest number of Peace Corps volunteers per capita of any American college in the 1960's and 1970's.

The Woltemade Center for Economics, Business, and Entrepreneurship promotes programs in business management and entrepreneurship through the Department of Economics, Fellows are selected to work directly with faculty on research, and many apply for scholarships through Operation Enterprise.

The Sagan National Colloquium highlights an issue of pressing concern and brings speakers and panelists to Ohio Wesleyan to engage in a year long colloquy on the subject. A recent Colloquium examined global opportunities for global citizens and brought Gloria Steinem among others to the campus. As part of the colloquium, a team of Ohio Wesleyan students traveled to Mexico with a professor to explore the, "Mexican Migration Experience."

Outside of the classroom, life at OWU is balanced and active. The Greek system is alive and well; about a third to a quarter of students join a fraternity or sorority during their time on campus, and the Greeks are generous in opening their activities to the entire student body. In addition, a number of other activities claim the energy of OWU's students. A cappella music and improvisational comedy groups perform regularly, and a plethora of clubs and organizations compete for student engagement. The Cricket Club, Ice Hockey Club, SciFi Role Playing Club, Rugby, and Outdoor Club meet throughout the year, as does Pet Pals, a group that visits the local Humane Society.

Traditions abound, the most notable of which are Step Show and Songfest. The Step Show originated with the Student Union on Black Awareness and challenged the Greek system to Step It Up and Break It Down, "stepping" as historically black fraternities have done. The competition is lively and carefully choreographed. Songfest is also a spring tradition, bringing celebrated popular recording artists to the campus for a weekend of music and merriment.

Athletically, the Battling Bishops are widely feared. Both the men's and women's soccer teams have won numerous conference championships, as have the baseball, lacrosse, and golf teams. OWU has won the North Coast Athletic Conference all-sports trophy for seven of the last twelve years, and is consistently among the top twenty-five colleges in the country in the Sears Cup competition.

Wittenberg University - Springfield, Ohio

And, as a final point of persuasion, Wittenberg has recently announced that there will be ZERO percent increase in tuition for the coming year. That's impressive, enough, but Wittenberg has frozen tuition for FOUR years in a row. Students entering Wittenberg in the 2016 - 2017 school year will be paying what students paid in 2012!

And the stats... 2015

Number of Applicants: 4,840 / 91% Accepted
Undergrad Enrollment: 1,964 57% female / 43% male
Scores not required: Avg. SAT: 1140 Avg. ACT: 25
Total Cost: $50,562.00
Received some form of financial assistance: 99%

Ohio may have more college gems per square mile than any other state; Wittenberg University is certainly among them. Springfield is a city of about a hundred thousand west of Columbus and north of Dayton. To be ruthlessly honest, the greatest of Springfield's assets is probably the handsome campus of Wittenberg University. The university was founded by the English Evangelical Lutheran Synod of Ohio and remains affiliated with the Lutheran Church, although the current student population is certainly less Lutheran than the founding fathers might have hoped and even more certainly less evangelical.

There are three important elements to keep in mind in considering Wittenberg. The first is that it is a very small university, enrolling fewer than two thousand students. The second is that the campus is lovely. The third is that Wittenberg has long had a reputation for treating its students well. Its professors are revered and highly accessible. Students rave about their course work and have the highest regard for those who teach here. It comes as no surprise to learn that Wittenberg's teachers have won more Fulbright Awards than any other college in Ohio.

Oh, and I probably ought to mention that Wittenberg loves its athletic teams and supports them vociferously as they claim title after title in the North Coast Athletic Conference, the first conference to make the commitment to equal emphasis on men's and women's sports. To the chagrin of rivals such as Allegheny, Denison, Wabash, Wooster, and DePauw, Wittenberg's Tigers have won the most conference championships in football, women's basketball, field hockey, and volleyball. And, as a final point of persuasion, Wittenberg has recently announced that there will be ZERO percent increase in tuition for the coming year. That's impressive, enough, but Wittenberg has frozen tuition for FOUR years in a row. Students entering Wittenberg in the 2016 - 2017 school year will be paying what students paid in 2012!

Although Wittenberg is a university, it operates very much like a liberal arts college, offering the usual majors in the humanities, arts, and sciences. The college does have strong programs in Business Administration, Financial Economics, Geography, and Education, and all of its majors are well regarded by current students. One recent graduate raved, "Every one of my professors was brilliant, enthusiastic, and caring!" For many years, one of the commitments that set Wittenberg apart was a program designed to support entering students who might find academic difficulty. The success rate of the college is evident, not only in the retention of a high percentage of entering students, but also in the remarkably high number of graduates that go on to do graduate study in their field.

Of the many excellent majors, the Department of Theater and Dance has won particular celebrity. More than twenty-five courses in Dance are offered by the department, including: Ballet, Tap, Jazz, Modern, Folk, Chinese Folk, Dance Technique, and Theater Movement. Further study introduces Motif Description, Dance Notation, Dance Ethnology, Dance Composition, and Dance Kinesiology. Theater courses include Acting, Directing, Stage Design, Improvisation, the History of Theater, Theater for Children, Playwriting, Costume and Makeup Design, and Lighting and Sound Design.

In addition to the many performances on campus, students are encouraged to enter into internships and to take on independent study.

Outside of the classroom, this beautiful campus hums with activity. Service is particularly prized at Wittenberg and is pursued in a number of organized enterprises. Witt's students are involved with Circle K, a national service organization, Habitat for Humanity, and the March of Dimes. In addition, many other students contribute their talents through special events and sales. The Art Department, for example, makes ceramic "Bowls for Rice" which are sold in order to raise money for charity. *The Torch* is the campus newspaper, and WUSO, the campus radio station involves a large number of students. Two a cappella groups have emerged in the last few years, *Just Eve*, a women's a cappella group, and *WittMen Crew,* a men's group. Not surprisingly, Wittenberg also sponsors an Anime Club, a Comic Book Club, and several outdoors associations promoting fishing and camping. More unusual are *Pocket Lint*, an improvisational comedy troupe, an Irish Dance Club, a Swing Dance Club, and a Role Playing Guild. Fraternities and Sororities have their own chapter houses at Wittenberg, although not all members live in the chapter house. About 33%

of men join fraternities and about 44% of women join sororities. Considerably more women live in chapter houses. Most of the student body happily lives in one of the University's well-maintained residences, many of which are the most historic and attractive of the university's buildings.

Finally, Wittenberg loves its Tigers and has reason to show Tiger Pride. The university offers twenty-three varsity sports - eleven for men and twelve for women. Men play football, soccer, cross-country, basketball, swimming and diving, lacrosse, baseball, tennis, golf, and track. Women play soccer, field hockey, volleyball, cross-country, basketball, swimming and diving, lacrosse, tennis, golf, track, and softball. Wittenberg football has enjoyed decades of success, compiling a record of six hundred and ninety-seven wins, the most wins in Division III football history.

Miami University - Oxford, Ohio

After all, Oxford, Ohio is the picture postcard of the ideal college town. Seriously, a visitor will be charmed within minutes as the main street of this city of about twenty thousand people is clearly in existence to provide an idyllic experience for the sixteen thousand students who find their way to Miami. Oxford looks like the town that time forgot with elegant small movie theater, malt shops and provides every imaginable amenity for college students since the university settled in this southwest corner of Ohio.

And the stats... 2015

Number of Applicants: 25,301 / 66% Accepted
Undergrad Enrollment: 15,813 51% female / 49% male
Avg. SAT Reading 550-650 / Math 570-680 Avg. ACT: 25-30
Total Cost: $29,423.00 (in-state) $45,527.00 (out-of-state)
Received some form of financial assistance: 78%

I have made reference to *Colleges That Change Lives* throughout the course of this guide, recognizing the groundbreaking work Loren Pope did in identifying colleges that were worthy of close investigation. In the same fashion, Richard Moll's guide, *The Public Ivies*, had a great impact on college counseling, in that it highlighted the public universities of superior quality across the nation.

The original eight universities profiled were: The College of William & Mary, Miami University, the University of California, the University of Michigan, the University of North Carolina at Chapel Hill, University of Texas at Austin, University of Vermont, and the University of Virginia. For those outside the Midwest, it may come as a surprise to see Miami University in the company of Michigan and Virginia, but those who know the university have no doubt that it belongs in the ranks of the most attractive public options.

After all, Oxford, Ohio is the picture postcard -Hollywood backdrop -ideal college town. Seriously, a visitor will be charmed within minutes as the main street of this city of about twenty thousand people is clearly in existence to provide an idyllic experience for the sixteen thousand students who find their way to Miami. Oxford looks like the town that time forgot – elegant small movie theater, malt shops – and has provided every imaginable amenity for college students since the university settled in this southwest corner of Ohio.

If the town is simply charming, the university is jaw-dropping-honest-to-gosh spectacular.

I don't know why every college movie is not filmed at Miami; the buildings are uniformly "just right" – just the right blend of red brick and white column, just the right scale, set in just the right place, surrounded by just the right landscaping. Paths cross in just the right ways at just the right angles so that this small university seems even more closely connected as a community than one might expect. Miami cherishes the sorts of traditions that are more frequently found in the smaller, private colleges than in a public university. Don't walk on the school seal, make sure you all pass on the same side of the tree as you cover campus, pack the stadium when Miami's Red Hawks play Ohio University's Bobcats in what is known as "The Battle of the Bricks." Both universities are noted for spectacular red brick architecture, so this football competition may be singular in its appreciation of the universities' aesthetic character. Super sugary baked treats sold in the campus student center pay tribute to those sold at "Tuffy's Place" an Oxford institution until it closed in 1973. The two most widely known traditions at Miami have to do with the years after college. Miami is known as "The Cradle of Coaches", having provided some of the most successful college football coaches in the nation. The "Miami Merge" refers to the uncommonly high percentage of graduates who marry inside the Miami family. Almost twenty percent of Miami's graduates will marry another Miami graduate.

And, at the risk of waxing a bit too superficial, the students pretty much fit the bill as well. I'm sure there are those who quibble that Miami's students are entirely too good looking, or dressed too well, or too cheerful, or too optimistic; I can understand that visitors from other state universities might find it hard to believe that the general level of student approval of the place is distinctly palpable. The stereotypical view of Miami has labeled the place, "J. Crew U," and this is a well scrubbed and apple cheeked, eminently healthy student body on a beautiful and safe campus.

Miami's students love their school, and with good reason.

There's a reason Miami's students didn't end up in Columbus; they get what is essentially a private school experience for a public school price.

Miami's course of instruction is offered in six divisions: The College of Arts and Sciences, the Framer School of Business, the School of Engineering and Applied Sciences, the School of Education, Health, and Society, the School of Fine Arts, and the Graduate School.

No matter what their major, all Miami students complete what the university calls the Global Miami Plan Core, which includes 36 hours of foundation coursework in English Composition, Fine Arts, Humanities, Social Science, Global Perspectives, Natural Science, and Mathematics or Formal Reasoning. This core guarantees a liberal education even in a professional or pre-professional course of study. In addition, each student, regardless of major, will complete a capstone experience in the major field. For some, the capstone may involve a workshop or seminar; for others, the capstone may involve research or a creative project.

Two distinctive programs also set Miami apart from the run-of-the-mill state university experience.

The first of these is the Western Program, an interdisciplinary college-within-a-college, housed the adjacent campus of the former Western College for Women. The program offers two majors – Individualized Studies and Interdisciplinary Studies, both of which involve significant contact with interdisciplinary faculty.

Miami's Honors Program significantly reduces class size, offers opportunities for research and creative expression, and can include a strong residential option.

At the risk of touting one program over many others, this description of a year's activities in the Honors Program residence gives a sense of how the Honors Program can enhance the undergraduate experience.

Events that took place in the Honors and Scholars Hall last year included: A Rave Dance Party, Undergraduate Research Series—The What, How's and Why's of Research, Bowling for Columbine: Film-Viewing and Discussion, Pizza and Prof monthly meetings, Pre-Med Study Series, Finals Week Midnight Breakfast, Massage Therapy and Stress Relief Workshops, Formal Hall Dinner (in the style of Cambridge University), Service-Learning with the Developmentally Disabled, Sensual Foods and Aromatherapy Night, Casino Night, and a March Madness Finals Party.

Sensual Foods and Aromatherapy Night? How can you beat that?

Well, Miami is so very Midwestern in many ways, that it should not come as any surprise that among its distinctions, it is the founding home of several fraternities and sororities, and a campus with a significant Greek presence.

Among the fraternities which began at Miami are Alpha Delta Phi, Beta Theta Pi, Phi Delta Theta, Sigma Chi, Delta Zeta, and Phi Kappa Tau. Not surprisingly, Miami is known in some circles as the, "Mother of Fraternities."

Today, Miami hosts at least fifty fraternities and sororities; it's a big deal on this campus.

Athletics are also a big deal, although Miami manages to keep a sense of perspective even in this arena. Known as the, "Cradle of Coaches," Miami has produced some of the most celebrated football coaches in the history of the sport, (both Ohio State's Woody Hayes and Michigan's Bo Schembechler!) and, at one time, football reigned supreme.

Not so much these days.

The Miami Red Hawks play in the Mid-America Conference against traditional rivals such as Ohio University and the University of Cincinnati, and against nationally ranked teams from other regions, such as the University of Florida. Recently, Miami has returned to dominance in the conference, but its greatest days of glory came with the collegiate career of Ben Roethlisberger, quarterback of the Pittsburgh Steelers, whose exploits as a Red Hawk were legendary.

Currently, the preeminent team of campus is the Miami University ice hockey team, a top-ten team nationally, and the runner-up for the 2009 NCAA Division I hockey championship, having lost to Boston University in overtime. Fan frenzy for the hockey program provides a major outlet for pent up energy in a long Ohio winter.

A curious and delightful sport recently emerging at Miami is synchronized skating, in which endeavor Miami is dominant nationally. In fact, those who wish to do synchronized ice-skating have made Oxford the Mecca of the sport.

Should spectators and ordinary students wish to get down and dirty, Miami offer almost two hundred intramural sports and clubs, in which almost 80% of undergraduates participate.

In conclusion, Miami is one of the few public institutions profiled in this book because it is a remarkable and affordable overlooked opportunity.

Indiana

Let's take a look at Indiana, adjacent to Ohio and just below Chicago.

Indiana University is located in Bloomington, fifty miles south of Indianapolis, and one of the most attractive college towns in the country. IU is a large state university with several renowned professional schools, the School of Music being on a par with Julliard as one of the finest in the nation.

Ball State University (BSU) is a state run university on a thousand acres in Muncie, known for years as "Middletown," the exact center of population in the United States.

Purdue University is yet another public university, located in West Lafayette, about seventy miles northwest of Indianapolis. Purdue was established as an agricultural and technical college and offers highly celebrated technological programs, including extensive coursework in aviation and aviation technology; it is no accident that more than twenty astronauts have graduated from Purdue. Today, Purdue is mentioned with Michigan, Georgia Tech and Virginia Tech as outstanding public options in engineering and technology.

So, on to Rose-Hulman, DePauw, IU, Wabash, and Earlham – all profiled in this book.

DePauw University is located in Greencastle, Indiana, almost equidistant from Indianapolis and Terre Haute in the west central region of the state. Flights to Indianapolis will serve the visitor from other regions most easily.

Indiana University is in Bloomington, a city of about eighty thousand, located in south central Indiana and known as "Gateway to Scenic Southern Indiana.

Earlham College is in Richmond, Indiana, a small city on the border with Ohio. Three airports are within easy driving distance of Richmond; flights can land in Indianapolis, Cincinnati, or Dayton.

Wabash is located in Crawfordsville, 45 minutes northwest of Indianapolis and about 150 miles south of Chicago; Rose-Hulman is located in Terre Haute.

Earlham College - Richmond, Indiana

"Fully Present". Not a typical statement of aspiration, but Earlham is not a typical liberal arts college. Academically superior, widely recognized and admired, Earlham is about more than a classroom experience. The college sets out to create an environment and set of expectations that invites its students to become "fully present", both energized and mindful.

And the stats... 2015

Number of Applicants: 2001 / 65% Accepted
Undergrad Enrollment: 1,076 55% female / 45% male
Avg. SAT Reading and Math 1240 Avg. ACT: not reported
Total Cost: $53,510.00
Received some form of financial assistance: 97%

"Fully Present". Not a typical statement of aspiration, but Earlham is not a typical liberal arts college. Academically superior, widely recognized and admired, Earlham is about more than a classroom experience. The college sets out to create an environment and set of expectations that invites its students to become "fully present", both energized and mindful.

Richmond, Indiana is a cozy small city, and the Earlham campus is both lovely and extensive, occupying more than eight hundred acres on the edge of town. The center of the campus is known as the "Heart", and it is an elegantly landscaped and beautifully maintained campus. The back regions of the campus are essentially forest and lovely wilderness. The nationally regarded Biology Department and Earlham's students maintain a museum of natural history on campus, the Joseph Moore Museum, open to the public without charge. It is rare for a college to let students run a museum, some of whom will take a degree in Museum Studies, some of whom will act as tour guides or animal keepers. As is true with all of Earlham's programs, however, the primary focus is student engagement.

Earlham may be the college most attractive to students from outside the region, one of the few Quaker Colleges, and perhaps one of the most "Quakerly." Although Earlham has a graduate program for teachers (M.A.T. and M.Ed.), it is primarily an eminently well-respected liberal arts college, most notable for its historic mission. That mission is best expressed in the college's own statement:

The mission of Earlham College is to provide the highest quality undergraduate education in the liberal arts, including the sciences, shaped by the distinctive perspectives of the Religious Society of Friends (Quakers). Earlham emphasizes: pursuit of truth, wherever that pursuit leads; lack of coercion, letting the evidence lead that search; respect for the consciences of others; openness to new truth and therefore the willingness to search; veracity, rigorous integrity in dealing with the facts; application of what is known to improving our world.

Generally seen by its collegiate neighbors as somewhat "quirky," Earlham students might better be characterized as "authentic." Characterized by jealous students at a competing school as "dirty hippies," an Earlham student responded, "Hippies? Maybe. Dirty? No."

In fact, one of the first observations that many visitors make about Earlham is that the campus is spiffy, students look great, and the tone of the college is almost uniformly cheerfully productive.

A major difference between Earlham and the other colleges to which it might be compared is in the closeness of faculty to students. Every college touts the accessibility of its faculty to undergraduates; at Earlham, those relationships are best described as respectful friendships; the faculty, as authentic as Earlham's students, has joined in a partnership with these active and socially committed learners on this handsome campus. One hallmark of the relationships established at Earlham is that all in the community are called by first name; there are no honorifics – Doctor, Professor, etc. It will come as no surprise that Earlham is also one of the *Colleges That Change Lives*.

Fortunately, Earlham students do not take themselves too seriously. With an eye to the dilemma facing any athletic team competing as a Quaker team, Earlham has adopted this self-aware fight song as they cheer.

" Fight, Fight, Inner Light!
Kill, Quakers, Kill!
Beat 'em, Beat 'em, Knock 'em Senseless!
Do it 'til we reach Consensus!"

"Consensus" is one of the words that illustrate the college's Quaker tradition. As one Earlham wit put it, " We can't agree on anything but the idea of consensus." The impulse to reach decisions based on discussion and shared deliberation is a hallmark of the Earlham experience, and, while the effort put into process can occasionally seem exceedingly time consuming, the result is that every member of the community feels fully invested.

Is this a politically charged campus?
 Yes.

Does principle matter more than practicality at times?
 Yes.

Is all of that a great deal of fun?
 Absolutely!

Don't mistake the emphasis on process and connection for a retreat from academic excellence; the Earlham experience is broadening in the best sense of the liberal arts and truly challenging.

There are several curricular innovations that set Earlham apart from its peers, almost all of which are connected with the college's determination to educate in a context of global responsibility. Earlham emphasizes connections with programs that unite students of similar scholarly aspiration.

One of those connections, of course, is with the consortium of colleges included in the *Colleges That Change Lives*; the key to inclusion in that group is an emphasis on student engagement in lifelong learning.

Another highly significant connection is with the Bonner Foundation, which sponsors Bonner Scholars in a four-year program of study and service to the community. Earlham's center supporting service, internships, and careers has been renamed the Bonner Center in recognition of the impact that more than two hundred Bonner Scholars have had on the life of the college.

The Davis United World College Scholars Program supports graduates of United World Colleges entering Earlham. The UWC programs around the globe promote internationalism and participation in global citizenry. Recently, Earlham has won recognition as the American college enrolling the largest number of Davis Scholars; more than forty have joined the first year class in each of the past three years.

Earlham was a founding member of the Great Lakes College Association, a confederation of thirteen Midwestern liberal arts colleges. The Association has been of great service to many of the member colleges, but Earlham may be the college that has served the Association most profoundly.

For example, the foreign language program at Earlham is outstanding. Not only does Earlham offer languages that other colleges do not (Japanese), but it also supports an extensive program of study abroad, opening its centers to students from other colleges. The Earlham program in Japan is widely known, and the major in Japanese is one of Earlham's most highly regarded. More than sixty percent of Earlham's students will study abroad during, and the clear commitment to internationalism animates much of the conversation about the college's goals.

One of the programs found only at Earlham is an intensive immersion in foreign language. In addition to Japanese, the study of other modern languages is highly reputed. The English Department is both popular and eminent, and the Biology major is among the most respected.

In addition, Earlham offers a variety of majors not commonly found in a liberal arts program, such as Peace and Global Studies, Neuroscience, Outdoor Education, Business and Nonprofit Management, teaching English to Speakers of Other Languages, Medieval Studies, and Journalism – all of this in very small classes to an undergraduate population of about twelve hundred.

It should not come as a surprise that Earlham is completely free of fraternities and sororities; social life is organized around the residences and special interest groups. The college works hard to provide at least one major activity each weekend (dances, concerts, etc.), but students report that most on-campus parties are open to all. Richmond is a small city, so most social activity is located on campus. The strength of community is such, and the regard with which people hold each other is such, that spur-of-the-moment spontaneous celebrations often end up involving a significant portion of the student body. A performance by an improv group, for example, or a costume party springs up without much advance notice.

Sports are alive and well at Earlham, although many more students are involved with intramural and recreational sports than with interscholastic, varsity, teams. Teams representing Earlham are known as, "The Hustling Quakers," and the mascot, once the feisty, "Mr. Quaker" has been replaced with "The Quaker Army," a force of more than eight hundred students who have been inducted into the corps of Earlham supporters and who wear t-shirts modeled after the U.S. Army's and the Salvation Army's garb.

Earlham fields a football team, but the more popular sports seem to be soccer and lacrosse. Club sports include rugby and equestrian, and the Quakers also hustle in Ultimate Frisbee. Recreational sports include racquetball, frisbee golf, the climbing wall challenge, kickball, chess (?), wiffleball, and triathlon.

No discussion of recreational activities at Earlham would be complete without mentioning the Wilderness Programs and "The Hash."

Earlham pioneered the use of wilderness experiences to effect transition to college, offering the first program to incoming first year students as early as 1970. The extensive programs today include trips to Utah, and Big Bend National Park. Students new to Earlham can bond, for example, while canoeing through Western Ontario's Caribou Forest.

"The Hash," is a curious phenomenon. Hashing involves running, to a degree, and imbibing, at times, and generally coursing, as chasing hares with hounds once coursed. Earlham's "kennel" meets on Saturday mornings for hashing, and it is rumored that some of the Quaker hashers also compete in Interhash, the global hashing experience.

So, call it "quirky" or call it "authentic"; the Earlham experience is distinctive, challenging, and highly worthwhile.

Indiana University - Bloomington, Indiana

And, at the risk of raving, every one of those divisions is highly regarded and celebrated nationally. Two, the Jacobs School of Music and the School of Journalism, are among the top two or three of their kind in the U.S. The Jacobs School is the largest school of music in the world and ranked with Julliard and Eastman as the best in the country. The School of Journalism has produced more than thirty Pulitzer Prize winning journalists.

And the stats... 2015

Number of Applicants: 36,362 / 76% Accepted
Undergrad Enrollment: 36,419 51% female / 49% male
Avg. SAT Reading 520-630 / Math 540-660 Avg. ACT: 24-30
Total Cost: $24,417.00 (in-state) $47,270.00 (out-of-state)
Received some form of financial assistance: 78%

A great state university ought to be exciting, and challenging, and responsive, and beautiful, and fun. A really great state university ought to offer football on Saturday afternoons in the fall, basketball in a crowded arena, festive celebrations throughout the spring, and, perhaps, one of the best conservatories of music in the world. Indiana University is an exceptional institution; there simply are very few universities of this size and ambition that deliver as personal and as satisfactory experience as that found at IU. One small example of the university's uncommon responsiveness to individual concerns is the building of a twelve-foot sculpture on campus for the explicit purpose of providing shelter for the endangered species of bird, the chimney swifts. That's a remarkable sort of investment for a university of this complexity.

Indiana University is located in Bloomington, Indiana, a city of about seventy thousand that happily welcomes IU's forty thousand students each year. The extraordinarily beautiful campus of the university aside, the city of Bloomington has much to recommend it. This is a jumping college town with a very active music scene. Eradicator Records, Secretly Canadian Records, BlueSanct records, and Plan-It-X Records have grown up as local bands have emerged, among them The Fray. There is an equally active program in theater and opera in Bloomington; there is nothing like a world-class school of music and eager ethnomusicologists to bring an astounding variety of music to various venues in the city and on campus. The country's oldest winery and the Tibetan Cultural Center add to the mix of opportunities available in addition to the many excellent restaurants found in several neighborhoods near the university.

The first observation any visitor will make in visiting Bloomington or IU will be that the amount of limestone used in architecture is stunning. Indiana limestone comes from local quarries and brings stately gravity to virtually every building on the thousand-acre campus. The university is consistently mentioned as having one of the most impressive campuses in the nation.

This handsome and inspiring campus is home to a College of Arts and Sciences, the Maurer School of Law, a School of Library and Information Science, the Jacobs School of Music, the Kelly School of Business, the Division of Labor Studies, the School of Health, Physical Education, and Recreation, the School of Education, the School of Public and Environmental Affairs, the School of Journalism, and the School of Informatics and Computing.

Whew!

And, at the risk of raving, every one of those divisions is highly regarded and celebrated nationally. Two, the Jacobs School of Music and the School of Journalism, are among the top two or three of their kind in the U.S. The Jacobs School is the largest school of music in the world and ranked with Julliard and Eastman as the best in the country. The School of Journalism has produced more than thirty Pulitzer Prize winning journalists.

What kind of experience does the run-of-the-mill ordinary student have at IU? Fantastic! The reviews from students uniformly describe their delight in the beauty of the campus and with the rush of activities, including big time Division I sports. They also routinely report that class work is challenging, professors and instructors accessible, and facilities first rate. The mix of types of students is rich, and while some might be tempted to see a wide divide between the fraternity/sorority kids and the "arty" kids, the truth is that with forty thousand students to choose from, it isn't hard to find someone who matches your interests. Although the strength of the separate programs might intimidate those who are not yet sure of career path or academic interest, many students report finding excellent counsel at IU and the ability to switch in mid-stream. One student reports easily changing from a major in the Theater Department to a major in the School of Business.

As one might expect, the opportunities for engagement in the life of the university are seemingly endless. The university suggests that there are over seven HUNDRED clubs and organizations, many created by students during their time at IU. Want to study Baltic and Finnish, explore emerging financial markets, learn Ballroom dancing, organize a demonstration in support of a free Tibet, play hockey, learn judo, anchor the news on the student television station, join the robotics club?

Before looking at residential life and the Greek scene, it is essential to highlight several of the traditions that set IU apart. The rest of what was once the Big Ten (Michigan, Michigan State, Ohio State, Iowa, Minnesota, Purdue, Northwestern, Wisconsin, and Illinois) are great places and worthy of your investigation. Indiana has always had a slightly more personal character, despite its size, perhaps in part because of its strong traditions. The first of these is the Little 500, a bicycle race modeled after the Indianapolis 500, which raises money for student scholarships. An entire Hollywood movie was written about the race (Breaking Away), and spectators come from everywhere for the event – including spectators such as Barack Obama and Lance Armstrong. Equally productive in terms of income is the annual dance marathon, which has raised in excess of seven million dollars for charity. The largest of student events outside of athletics is the IU Sing, again a fundraiser, ordinarily involving as many as three thousand students. Speaking of things athletic, one of the loudest and most appreciated traditions at IU is the Marching Hundred, the university's marching band. One of the best marching bands in the country, the band now numbers more than two hundred-and-fifty musicians, most of whom are not enrolled in the School of Music.

Residential life is exceptionally well organized. The university's eleven residential halls are set in what might be called three separate neighborhoods, each of which has its own theme and style. Each also has its own dining facilities and academic support services. Student apartments are also available as are a variety of Learning Communities, welcoming like-minded students interested in the Outdoors, Media Studies, religion, Service, and a host of other interests.

Indiana University is home to one of the largest and oldest fraternity and sorority systems anywhere. The number of Greek organizations is staggering, but only about seventeen percent of students join and live in chapter housing.

Finally, IU is a proud member of what is still known as the Big Ten Conference, despite the addition of Pennsylvania State University and the University of Nebraska, which brought the number of competitors up to twelve. The Big Ten is the oldest of the NCAA's Division I conferences and is rich with history. Bloomington is considered one of the top ten collegiate sports towns, and the twenty-four varsity Hoosier teams are loudly supported by Indiana's boosters. The history and tradition of Indiana basketball is especially prized, and the Hoosiers have found most consistent success in that sport.

Charming, challenging, supportive, exciting – this great midwestern university is an exceptional bargain in every way.

Depauw University - Greencastle, Indiana

The balance between a strong academic program and a lively social scene makes DePauw a most attractive option. This is a college in which togas might be seen in a first-rate production of a Greek tragedy, in a splendidly staged musical comedy, or in one of the sixteen fraternity or fourteen sorority houses on campus. As a result, this relatively small school has the kind of school spirit more commonly found at Notre Dame or one of the Big Ten schools.

And the stats... 2015

Number of Applicants: 5,304 / 57% Accepted
Undergrad Enrollment: 2,215 54% female / 46% male
Avg. SAT Reading 530-640 / Math 560-660 Avg. ACT: 25-29
Total Cost: $55,896.00
Received some form of financial assistance: 97%

DePauw is a small university offering its 2200 undergraduates the opportunity to study in expansive programs without the distress of bumping up against graduate students and competing for facilities and attention.

Students have the opportunity to dive into an ambitious curriculum, including entrepreneurial studies as part of the Management Fellows Program and exceptional majors in the highly regarded School of Music. DePauw sends a high proportion of students abroad and into internships, and is among the most successful in preparing graduates for further study. I also include DePauw among the colleges doing the best job in all the fine arts, and the Prindle Institute for Ethics among exceptionally interesting undergraduate opportunities.

But what may be the most obvious appeal of DePauw from a distance is its VERY active social life; it has been nominated the college with the highest proportion of students pledging into the Greek system; approximately 80% of students enter into fraternities and sororities (that has to be a record!). At least two prominent national sororities were founded at DePauw - Kappa Alpha Theta and Alpha Chi Omega. The wonderful mix of traditions at DePauw allows the Greek system to flourish, the athletic program to flourish, and the arts to flourish as well. Big news at DePauw is the construction of the new dining facility and student center, a new athletics and recreation center, and the transformative engagement of the annual ArtsFest, a month long celebration of the arts.

Actually, however, the entire student body can be characterized as preppy, well dressed, and gorgeous. Ok, there are probably a few ordinary mortals strolling the campus, but a quick scan on an admissions visit will yield a remarkable number of outgoing, happy, enthusiastic, athletic, handsome people.

For those who worry about transitioning to Indiana, it should be noted that Greencastle, Indiana is the archetypical college town, cute and accommodating the University's needs.

In fact, anyone who is interested in a small college with strong arts, music, science, business management, or athletics will find that their experience at DePauw will feel like four years on any eastern campus, although their classmates may be a bit better dressed. And, any college that graduates Barbara Kingsolver AND Dan Quayle is obviously open to some variety of achievement.

The balance between a strong academic program and a lively social scene makes DePauw a most attractive option. This is a college in which togas might be seen in a first-rate production of a Greek tragedy, in a splendidly staged musical comedy, or in one of the sixteen fraternity or fourteen sorority houses on campus. As a result, this relatively small school has the kind of school spirit more commonly found at Notre Dame or one of the Big Ten schools.

Professors at DePauw get rave reviews, regardless of subject or discipline. In every published account, students wax grateful, particularly commenting on the degree to which their teachers take an interest in them and their work. Faculty are both respected and widely liked.

The academic offerings are solid, although the School of Music probably has a greater national reputation than other programs. The Prindle Institute has developed an on-going series of lectures, colloquia, symposia, and classes that examine issues surrounding ethical decision-making. Work done at the Institute is shared in other divisions in order to broaden the field on inquiry.

Other popular majors include Asian Studies, Black Studies, Film Studies, Conflict Studies, Women's Studies, European Studies, Jewish Studies, Russian Studies, Latin American and Caribbean Studies, Religious Studies, Environmental Studies, International Relations, Neuroscience, Geoscience, a degree in Communications and Theater, and Education Studies.

Traditions abound at DePauw, not a few connected with the Greeks and their "recruitment" - the word "rush" is not used at DePauw.

Boulder Runs happen intermittently throughout the year as naked students streak from their residence hall to and around a boulder outside East College. The Boulder Run is an integral part of "Recruitment Night," as pledges are attached to their society.

Many activities take place in Bowman Park, an amphitheater and open-air recreational space. The green in front of Bowman Gymnasium is a popular spot for picnics, meetings, and outdoor concerts.

Although it is not on campus, Marvin's Restaurant has loomed large in the memory of DePauw's students since 1978. Home of the Garlic Cheeseburger (GCB), Marvin's is exactly the sort of casual eatery a small college town should boast. Its greater service, however, is that the GCB is available by delivery through the wee hours of the morning.

Anyone familiar with Indiana knows that there one of the most significant events in the year is the Indianapolis 500. Students at Indiana University created their own version, the Little 500, a fifty-mile bicycle race.

In 1956, cyclists at DePauw created the Little Five Bike Race in order to raise money for the American Cancer Fund. The race once shot through the streets of Greencastle but now takes place in Blackstone Stadium. Students are serious about the race and train assiduously; alumni return from around the world to race yet again. Currently the race includes the signature DePauw student race and alumni races for age groups of under forty, under fifty, under sixty, and masters.

The Little Five still raises a considerable amount of money for charity and is the highlight of a week of celebration. It has also produced a number of prominent road cyclists who have gone on to professional careers in bicycle racing. Although DePauw has a strong tradition in sports, no sport has produced as many professional athletes as bicycle racing.

Of all the abiding traditions at DePauw, however, the annual football game against rival athletic power, Wabash College is the most highly anticipated.. The game, known as the Monon Bell Classic, is one of the oldest rivalries in football and occasion for much social activity on both campuses. The Monon Bell itself is a 300-pound trophy, protected with hyper-vigilance by the winning college. DePauw and Wabash have won almost equally, but the strength of lunacy around the competition probably falls to Wabash.

The week before the Monon Bell Classic is alive with other competitions between the two colleges, a few shared events such as concerts, and much carousing into those wee hours when the GCB becomes a necessity.

DePauw's athletic teams are the Tigers, and they play a tough schedule in the North Coast Athletic Conference against rivals such as Allegheny Denison University Hiram College Kenyon College Oberlin College, Ohio Wesleyan University, Wabash College, Wittenberg University, and the College of Wooster.

The one Division III national championship team in DePauw's history is the women's basketball team, a perennial conference standout. The women's softball and golf teams have won regional championships, coming close to the national title tilt. Exquisite indoor tennis and swimming facilities have made those activities available to students at the interscholastic and recreational levels.

Club sports are hugely active at DePauw; almost 90% of students will have been involved with interscholastic or club sports. Popular options include crew, equestrian, fencing, hapkido, rugby, dance, taekwondo, weightlifting, indoor cycling, pilates, water aerobics, yoga, zumba, and tai chi.

Tiger pride is rampant and loyalty to their college distinguishes DePauw alumni. Should the prospect of attending a vibrant, balanced, ambitious college sound appealing, please do consider this gem in Indiana.

Rose - Hulman Institute of Technology - Terre Haute, Indiana

The good news for applicants is that this highly regarded college, widely appreciated in the world of engineering and science, is a bit less bone-crushingly competitive in the admissions struggle and a great option for the serious student.

More good news is that the Institute's programs are solid from top to bottom and the teaching faculty, almost all of whom hold the Ph.D., are excellent and happy to be in the classroom.

And the stats... 2015

Number of Applicants: 4,404 / 59% Accepted
Undergrad Enrollment: 2,338 27% female / 73% male
Avg. SAT Reading 550-650 / Math 640-740 Avg. ACT: 27-32
Total Cost: $58,740.00
Received some form of financial assistance: 97%

Rose-Hulman declares itself, "the nation's top undergraduate engineering, science, and mathematics college."

That sets a pretty high standard, and yet from all accounts, it is entirely defensible. The Rose-Hulman Ventures program, so much more than a series of internships, has produced an astounding number of significant breakthroughs, all designed by undergraduate students. Interested in Biomedical Engineering? A current junior found a place at a manufacturer of medical equipment, as a freshman, literally in the first weeks of the school year. Asked to design an apparatus to be used in carrying out brain surgery, Katina Volitch came up with a design that allows the removal of brain tissue so that it can be preserved for further study. Now in production, that student's contribution is a significant part of the company's current marketing.

That is just flat-out incredible, but for Rose-Hulman, ho-hum, same old yearly miracles.

Rose-Hulman is an anomaly; the acceptance rate approaches sixty percent in most admissions seasons, and yet the quality of programs and native ability of its students is clearly superior. Enrolled students are uniformly excited by the education they receive, and loyal graduates cannot speak too highly of their experience at Rose-Hulman. Consider this: The middle fifty percent of enrolled students score between 640 and 740 on the Math subtest of the SAT.

What's the problem?

Well, it could be Terre Haute.

Terre Haute, nicknamed the "Dirty Haute," "Capital of the Wabash Valley," "Queen City of the Wabash," is the site of the federal death row at the Terre Haute Federal Correctional Facility. It was in Terre Haute that Timothy McVeigh, the Oklahoma City bomber was executed. Fortunately, Indiana State is also located in Terre Haute, bringing ten thousand students to the city each year.

Indiana is a tough sell outside of the region in any case, and Terre Haute has not stirred the imagination of applicants from across the country.

And, there's the name.

Originally founded as Rose Polytechnic Institute and then generously aided by the Hulman family, the Institute's name is a bit clunky, lacking the punch of acronyms such as M.I.T., R.P.I., R.I.T., or the abbreviated Cal Tech.

Of course Harvey Mudd, another exceptional undergraduate school of math and science faces the same challenge, but it is one of the Claremont Colleges and located in Southern California.

The good news for applicants is that this highly regarded college, widely appreciated in the world of engineering and science, is a bit less bone-crushingly competitive in the admissions struggle and a great option for the serious student.

More good news is that the Institute's programs are solid from top to bottom and the teaching faculty, almost all of whom hold the Ph.D., are excellent and happy to be in the classroom.

The academic departments include:

Applied Biology and Biomedical Engineering, Chemical Engineering, Chemistry and Biochemistry, Civil Engineering, Computer Science and Software Engineering, Electrical and Computer Engineering, Engineering Management, Environmental Engineering, Humanities and Social Science, Mathematics, Mechanical Engineering, and Physics and Optical Engineering.

Most accounts credit Rose-Hulman as the first school of engineering to develop and offer Chemical Engineering. Current students and graduates mention that program as among the strongest, and Chemical Engineering is still one of the Institute's prominent departments.

There are some noteworthy aspects of academic life at Rose-Hulman, including Rose-Hulman Ventures, an outstanding co-op and internship program, the Challenge X Competition, the Efficient Vehicle Team, and the Human Powered Vehicle Team.

Rose-Hulman Ventures is essentially an entrepreneurial company providing engineering solutions to real-world enterprises. Industry and Institute come together in a facility about five minutes from the campus. The project was supported by a fifty million dollar grant from the Lilly Endowment and allows students to work as engineers on real projects. Products are developed which become the property of the industry entering into the partnership, and student-engineers have the opportunity to develop applied engineering skills.

The vitality of Ventures serves as a model of partnership between industry and education and is distinctive in bringing student engineers into the workforce as problem-solvers at an early point in the engineering career.

The co-op and internship programs allow students in any discipline the opportunity to put their studies to the test in a work environment, and also provide income during the process.

Speaking of income, one statistic that will endear Rose to the hearts of many parents is that almost 100% of graduates have a job upon graduation; average salary of new graduates? $60,000.00 a year!

The Challenge X Team, Efficient Vehicle Team, and the Human Powered Vehicle Team are applied engineering competitions outside of the curriculum. Rose is among the most successful in engineering competitions of all sorts and encourages travel across the country to participate.

Current students and graduates share virtually the same opinion of their time at Rose:

Work is incredibly hard.

The Faculty is fantastic and accessible (no Teaching Assistants).

Social life is hard to sustain with the workload demanded.

They can't imagine a better education.

The warmth of feeling extends beyond the classroom, as Rose students describe each other as interesting and genuinely kind. School spirit is high, and loyalty very real.

The Institute offers almost ninety clubs and organizations outside of the classroom which allow Rose students to get together in a variety of enterprises. Most of the organizations are found at other colleges, but a few are distinctive.

The concrete canoe club, for example provides an opportunity to build and race –you guessed it – a concrete canoe.

Other options? The board game club, a model railroad club, a robotics team, Engineers Without Borders, and a paintball club reflect the range of interests in this most interesting student body.

An intramural program attracts about 70% of students and offers a wide variety of leagues and sports. Club sports at Rose include ballroom dance, fencing, bowling, martial arts, lacrosse, water polo, volleyball, yoga and scuba.

Twenty-one varsity teams compete in NCAA Division III. The Fighting Engineers field teams in the traditional sports, including football, basketball, baseball, softball, swimming, track, cross country, tennis and golf. They load up a varsity rifle team with eleven top ten NCAA finishes.

By the way, the rifle team is co-ed.

As is true of most engineering schools, Rose is predominantly male (73%), but social life for both genders is enhanced by the proximity of ten thousand students at Indiana State in town.

Wabash College - Crawfordsville, Indiana

The upside at Wabash is a sense of belonging and participation in a unique educational and social experience. It may go without saying that Wabash alumni are zealous in their support of their college. In many ways, four years at Wabash are four years at a college that time forgot. For a young man in search of a life-long affiliation, Wabash is unbeatable.

And the stats... 2015

Number of Applicants: 1,259 / 70% Accepted
Undergrad Enrollment: 926 100% male
Avg. SAT Reading 500-600 / Math 520-640 Avg. ACT: 22-27
Total Cost: $49,380.00
Received some form of financial assistance: 100%

Wabash, like Morehouse and Hampden-Sydney, is a college for men. It is no surprise, then, that Wabash enjoys a level of self-conscious spirited tradition that is rarely found in co-ed institutions. As at Hampden-Sydney, those traditions also include particular attention to the qualities that denote gentlemanly conduct. At Wabash, the code is known as, "The Gentleman's Rule," and its precepts are simple: "A Wabash Man is to conduct himself at all times, both on and off campus, as a gentleman and responsible citizen."

Wabash men speak with pride in describing the rule, and in endorsing the quality of education they have received in this small college in Crawfordsville, Indiana. They also note that Wabash may be distinctive in the degree to which tradition is attached to the life fraternal. For example, one of the highlights of the Homecoming Weekend is the Chapel Sing, during which each fraternity sings its own songs and then joins with the brothers (and few independents) in singing the school fight song... for forty-five minutes! The official mascot name of the college is the Little Giants, but jealous rivals like to call Wabash's teams, "The Cavemen," not a fair appraisal but indicative of the ferocity with which Wabash's teams play.

The upside at Wabash is a sense of belonging and participation in a unique educational and social experience. It may go without saying that Wabash alumni are zealous in their support of their college. In many ways, four years at Wabash are four years at a college that time forgot. For a young man in search of a life-long affiliation, Wabash is unbeatable.

There are three distinctive aspects to the Wabash experience:

1. As one of the last colleges still enrolling only men, Wabash has a culture that admires and encourages loyalty, spirit, friendship, and shared purpose. No college can promise that the undergraduate years will be distraction-free, but the absence of at least one distraction for some part of the week does allow room for other interests.

2. Let's assume that a relatively high level of testosterone breeds competition and an inclination toward things athletic. Although Wabash plays in the NCAA Division III, there are those who would call it a "jock" school, in the best meaning of the term. My guess is that more than half of the enrolled students play a varsity sport or one of the club sports (rugby, crew, volleyball) and something like ninety percent are involved in intramural sports. "Wabash Always Fights" is the self-proclaimed motto of the athletic program, and the degree to which Wabash spirit is visible at almost any contest is remarkable.

3. Many colleges are apologetic in describing the importance of the fraternity system in the shaping of the residential experience. Not Wabash. There are students at Wabash who don't join, and they are well served by a residential program that provides excellent housing options and a host of activities that are campus wide. More than half of men at Wabash, however, live in one of the fraternity houses that abut the campus. Because the fraternity system has grown up as it has, Wabash has as many fraternity houses as schools four times its size.

Close relationships with professors, a challenging liberal arts curriculum, and an abiding sense of tradition make the Wabash experience perhaps a bit more intensely collegiate than that found elsewhere. It is no wonder that they have an uncommonly active and engaged alumni body. One of the advantages of the loyalty Wabash men feel is the cultivation of major gifts, gifts which have brought the college's endowment to more than three hundred and fifty million dollars. Wabash enjoys one of the highest per capita endowments among liberal arts colleges.

Finally, the facilities at Wabash are first rate. The college has maintained architectural integrity, building stately buildings in red brick, adding columns and cupolas in white. The lawns are spacious and well groomed. Wide pathways connect the buildings and the campus as a whole is impressive. Athletic facilities are particularly impressive for a school of this size. The Allen Athletics and recreation Center houses fitness facilities, practice areas, training rooms, a wrestling room, a natatorium, an indoor track, and four multi-purpose courts. Little Giant Stadium can seat about five thousand, but a recent tilt against rival DePauw in the annual battle for the Monon Bell brought more than eleven thousand spectators to the stadium. As a point of comparison, Portland State University, a Division I (FSC) football team has no stadium; Montana State's stadium can seat only four thousand more than Little Giant Stadium. Wabash has a modern ballpark for baseball; Wabash basketball plays in Chadwick Court, a large facility enlivened by the "Chadwick Crazies", super-fans who bring additional fervor to the already volcanic sound in the arena. A separate facility offers competition for indoor track. Tennis players have a tennis center offering six outdoor and three indoor courts. Wabash offers a remarkable education and true school spirit.

Illinois

There is a great deal more to Illinois than Chicago, but, let's be honest – Chicago is a fabulous city and an amazing place to go to college.

There are a number of colleges and universities located in or near Chicago; college guides usually include the University of Chicago in Hyde Park and Northwestern University in Evanston as two of the most esteemed universities in the Midwest, and both are certainly worthy of much acclaim.

DePaul University is the largest Catholic University in the world, serving more than twenty-five thousand students on several campuses, the two most prominent being in Lincoln Park and in Chicago's Loop. DePaul is noted for the quality of teaching in a university of enormous size and scope. Several of the programs at DePaul have won national attention, and DePaul's location in the City of Chicago, its active service learning program, and its distinctive programs in communications, journalism, and theater ought to make it an interesting option for the student who is ready for big-city life.

The theater program at DePaul is among the best in the country and is a conservatory program at the undergraduate level. Admission is highly competitive and includes an audition or interview. Anyone interested in Costume Design, Costume Technology, Lighting Design, Scenic Design Sound Design, Stage Management, Theater Technology, Dramaturgy, Playwriting, or Acting should consider DePaul. For years, the university has produced its student shows in the Blackstone Theater in the heart of Chicago; recently the name of the theater has been changed, but the prime location places DePaul's production at the center of theater in the United States.

Lake Forest College, profiled in this book, is located in Lake Forest, about thirty miles north of Chicago in an elegant suburban setting on Lake Michigan.

There are a number of public universities in Illinois, including the University of Illinois in Urbana/Champagne, its branches, Northern Illinois in DeKalb, and Southern Illinois in Carbondale. Illinois State is located in Normal, Illinois.

Bloomington, Illinois is adjacent to Normal and is home to Illinois Wesleyan University. Illinois Wesleyan is one of the great undiscovered gems in the region, a college of rare quality, comparable to Whitman or Bates, but currently enrolling fewer students from outside the region than it should. I would have loved to offer a profile of Illinois Wesleyan, one of my favorite colleges in the Midwest, but it currently accepts about 50% of applicants and is more selective than the Best Kept Secrets.

Bradley University is in Peoria, southwest of Chicago, and is a small (6500) comprehensive university with one of the best basketball teams in the country. Like Gonzaga, Bradley has jumped onto the front page of the Sports Section and is a legitimate contender for an NCAA national championship in basketball.

Augustana College, a Lutheran college which still bears the imprint of its Swedish founders, is located in Moline, one of the "Quad Cities" on the northwestern border with Iowa. Augustana's Fighting Vikings won three NCAA football championships in a row.

Knox College is in Galesburg, south of Peoria, and Monmouth College is about thirty miles west of Peoria. Knox is profiled in this book.

Monmouth is an up and coming small college with a strong Scottish legacy. The Fighting Scots have emerged as a football powerhouse, and Monmouth is also recognized as the founding chapter the first sorority, Pi Beta Phi, and of Kappa Kappa Gamma.

Lake Forest College - Lake Forest, Illinois

Unlike most colleges of its size, Lake Forest offers an uncommonly wide range of course offerings. LFC has called itself, "Chicago's National Liberal Arts College," with good reason. An Ethics Center, a program in Urban Studies, an ambitious Theater department join Economics and Business and Education in broadening this solid liberal arts curriculum. The introduction of Islamic Studies, Asian Studies, and Communications has further broadened an already ambitious slate of offerings.

And the stats... 2015

Number of Applicants: 3,451 / 55% Accepted
Undergrad Enrollment: 1,607 57% female / 43% male
Avg. SAT Reading and Math: 1520 – 1790 ACT: 23–28
Total Cost: $53,545.00
Received some form of financial assistance: 98%

Lake Forest College is located in a charming town, the most northerly of Chicago's "Gold Coast" towns, celebrated in *The Great Gatsby* as the place in which Tom Buchanan's polo ponies were bred. Lake Forest is still a polo town, and the elegant homes in the most affluent of north shore suburbs are among the most sought by Chicago's financial elite. Lake Forest is quite literally on Lake Michigan and extremely leafy. The influence of English gardens remains in the landscaping of the quaint town center and on the grounds of Lake Forest's estates. The college itself occupies one hundred and seven acres literally on the shore of Lake Michigan.

The college, on the other hand, has worked hard to bring under-represented minorities to the campus for years. At the moment, for example, more than five hundred of the college's thirteen hundred students are ethnic minority students or international students. In addition to a large number of international and ethnic minority students Lake Forest supports an equally large number of very talented students on scholarship. Presidential, academic, leadership, music, science, social justice, theater, and writing scholarships of up to $20,000.00 have made this tree lined and extremely pretty college a lively campus and a sophisticated base from which to explore the city of Chicago.. The college helps in this regard by maintaining the Center for Chicago Programs. The Center arranges internships and academic opportunities, invites prominent speakers and performers from the city to the campus and facilitates the easy access to the city for fun and recreation. Recently, the college also instituted the "Lake Forest College in the Loop Program", allowing students to take classes in the heart of Chicago as well as investing up to three hundred hours of credit bearing internships.

The campus is divided into three areas on the edge of a town that Fitzgerald described as "...the most glamorous place in the world." Happily, the college offers an extraordinary range of building style - from the gray rock of the neo-Gothic music building to the cheerful neo-Victorian administrative building, to red brick dormitories, yellow post-sixties steel and glass, and one truly exceptional example of Midwestern gabled Gothic. Hotchkiss Hall now housing the Psychology, Sociology, and Anthropology departments was once the gymnasium, and is now known as the "Harry Potter" building, as to students it seems to resemble a corner of Hogwarts.

Unlike most colleges of its size, Lake Forest offers an uncommonly wide range of course offerings. LFC has called itself, " Chicago's National Liberal Arts College," with good reason. An Ethics Center, a program in Urban Studies, an ambitious Theater department join Economics and Business and Education in broadening this solid liberal arts curriculum. The introduction of Islamic Studies, Asian Studies, and Communications has further broadened an already ambitious slate of offerings.

LFC encourages research and is particularly successful in creating opportunities for the active collaboration of students and their teachers; numbers of Lake Forest students have been published as co-authors of original research. Internships and study abroad are also easily coordinated and encouraged, as are significant programs of independent study. LFC offers internship programs in Paris and Granada, Spain, an Ancient Civilizations program in Greece, and a Border Studies program on the U.S.- Mexico border. Other programs allow students to study in Prague, Costa Rica, England, India, Italy, Japan, Russia, and Tanzania.

Should a student chose to remain on campus, a visit to the Center for Chicago Programs building initiates internship programs and a wealth of other opportunities, including a semester-long residential program in "the Loop." Travel from LFC to Chicago is as simple as a fifteen-minute walk to the Metro station which carries students to the Ogilvie Transportation center in downtown Chicago. From there, the entire city is only one transfer away.

Chicago is an important part of the Lake Forest experience, but plenty happens on-campus as well. Both the theater and music departments sponsor performances that attract the entire student body. In addition, more than fifty activities offer opportunities for participation and leadership. The number of fraternities and sororities is small (two frats/five sororities) and their role on campus clearly involves community service. Some other interesting clubs include: Mr. Game (LFC gaming club), Voices of the World (Gospel music singers), F.L.A.S.H. (Forester Laughing

Association of Super Heroes – an improv comedy troupe), WMXM (88.9FM on your radio dial), Best Buddies (service organization working with disabled people), the "e" Team (plans campus entertainment/coffee houses, etc.), and LEAP (League for Environmental Awareness and Protection).

I always look to see what sorts of uncommon traditions or celebrations fill the year, and there are several at Lake Forest that strike me as particularly interesting. The first of these is the Iron Chef Competition, in which students compete in the preparation of odd and challenging dishes provided by the "commissioner." LFC is exceptionally committed to the Relay for Life as more than four hundred and fifty people ran in support of the American Cancer Society. The International Dance Club moves into the public eye with its annual display of belly dancing – always a crowd pleaser! Another four hundred volunteers turned out for the Gates Day of Service, providing more than a thousand hours of volunteer service to communities in the area. Finally, it probably has occurred to some readers that Illinois may experience an occasional flurry of snow? The response from students at LFC to an unusually heavy recent snowfall speaks volumes about the kinds of kids who find this college – the dorms bake. Gingerbread men, cupcakes, all pour into the lounge as the winds blow and the snows mount.

LFC has an unusual proportion of students involved in service organizations, including spring trips for Habitat for Humanity. An equally large number are involved in recreational and club sports. Among the club offering offered in recent years are: cheerleading, fencing, dance team, aikido, karate, riding, rock climbing, sailing, golf, baseball, lacrosse, rugby, ultimate frisbee, and water polo. Recreational sports are also numerous, including ice hockey, flag football, Give Grub, basketball, volleyball, and racquetball.

The athletic program at Lake Forest is equally adaptive, offering a full range of sports at the Division III level, including one of the most successful handball teams in the nation. LFC plays in the Midwest Conference in a number of sports, including basketball, baseball, soccer, cross-country, track, swimming, and golf. The Foresters are cheered on by "Boomer the Bear", the LFC mascot, especially in their ambitious schedule in ice hockey. The men's and women's hockey teams play in the Midwest Collegiate Hockey Association.

Illinois Wesleyan University - Bloomington, Illinois

If this book accomplished nothing other than bringing Illinois Wesleyan to the attention of the college bound, I would be delighted. Not only is Illinois Wesleyan the model of the effective, responsive, well designed, thoroughly successful small liberal arts college/university, it is also an institution that hums with positive energy and which engenders deep feelings of attachment and loyalty among its students and graduates. I won't say that this is a university that time forgot (many of its buildings are state-of-the-art), but there is a sense of mutual respect and affection that sets this solid college apart from many of its peers.

And the stats... 2015

Number of Applicants: 3,427/ 60% Accepted
Undergrad Enrollment: 1,893 56% female / 44% male
Avg. SAT Reading 490-620 / Math 660-760 Avg. ACT: 24-30
Total Cost: $52,690.00. Received some form of financial assistance: 100%

If this book accomplished nothing other than bringing Illinois Wesleyan to the attention of the college bound, I would be delighted. Not only is Illinois Wesleyan the model of the effective, responsive, well designed, thoroughly successful small liberal arts college/university, it is also an institution that hums with positive energy and which engenders deep feelings of attachment and loyalty among its students and graduates. I won't say that this is a university that time forgot (many of its buildings are state-of-the-art), but there is a sense of mutual respect and affection that sets this solid college apart from many of its peers.

Part of that climate is due to its setting and traditions. Bloomington-Normal are the twin cities about equidistant from Chicago and St. Louis. With a population of about one hundred and twenty-five thousand, the cities make up the fifth largest urban area in the state. Bloomington in particular is a city of considerable charm, prosperous and especially appreciated by golfers; Golf Digest picked the city as one of the top five metro golf cities in the nation. The cities offer numerous parks, a cultural district with an outstanding center for performing arts, and U.S. Cellular Coliseum. Comfortable, friendly, welcoming - Bloomington is exactly the sort of city from which a healthy, happy college such as Illinois Wesleyan ought to have emerged.

Healthy, happy, productive, engaged, responsive – Wesleyan students love their school and believe themselves to have landed in the best of all collegiate worlds. They think the campus is more beautiful than many of the more celebrated colleges, and they are absolutely right. One stunning feature of the campus is the variety of trees to be found on the main campus and in the college's arboretum. It is very cool that the college has more than twelve hundred trees and more than one hundred and fifty specific species, but the best part is that the college has not only identified every single tree by species, but made that identification available in a beautiful on-line map of trees (you can search for the map on the college's web site – http://www.iwu.edu/treemap/). The buildings on campus are equally impressive. As one student put it, "They're either really old – which is cool – or they're brand new – which is also cool." The older buildings are refurbished and eminently comfortable, and the new buildings are impressive. For the most part, the tree -shaded campus is built around a central green space, the Eckley Quadrangle. Residential buildings occupy one corner of the campus; classroom buildings, laboratories, and the student center are within an easy walk from every residence. The first impression the visitor will have is that this campus has been out together thoughtfully. The buildings are impressive, and it's clear the college is more than solvent, but the real difference is that all aspects of college life appear to have been placed with students in mind.

The campus is beautiful; the students are animated, ambitious and talented. Moreover, the teaching faculty appears to have an investment in the lives of their students that is truly rare. Teaching is uniformly admired; most students rave about the quality of instruction. Their more vocal admiration, however, is for the many ways in which their professors go out of their way to connect and support their students. The university is relatively small (two thousand students), and maintains a twelve to one student to teacher ratio in every department. The evolution of a strong liberal arts college into a small university allowed the development of three separate but entirely equal entities. The College of Liberal Arts is the oldest of the divisions; The School of Fine Arts was established in the nineteen-twenties, and the School of Nursing was established in the late nineteen-fifties. All three divisions have grown in strength and are well regarded for the preparation they provide, and each of the three has a particular area of strength that has won considerable.

The College of Liberal Arts offers the Bachelor of Arts and the Bachelor of Science degree in a wide range of majors, including the conventional humanities and sciences and a few uncommon departments, such as Business Administration, Cognitive Science, Women's Studies, and Greek and Roman Studies. Although Biology, Business, Psychology, Political Science, Chemistry, American Studies, and English enroll the greatest number of graduates, IWU is known for its remarkable program in Modern and Classical Languages and Literature, a major that allows the student to delve into Chinese, French and Francophone Studies, German, Italian, Japanese, Russian, Latin, and Ancient Greek.

The School of Nursing is an exceptional opportunity in that IWU offers admission directly to the Nursing Program; the course of studies begins in the freshman year, and the Bachelor's in Nursing is earned in four years at IWU. Clinical placement begins in the second year, and the university offers placement in almost fifty clinical sites. The program blends the excellent program in Nursing with a sound liberal arts education and adds a focus on global health care issues. The average class size in the Nursing program is about seventeen, roughly the same as other courses at Illinois Wesleyan.

The School of Fine Arts is comprised of three divisions: The School of Art, the School of Music, and the School of Theater Arts. The Ames School of Art offers studio courses in a full range of subjects, from Ceramics to the BA in Acting, with an excellent program in Graphic Design. The School of Theater Arts offers a BA in Theater, the BA in Musical Theater, and the BFA in Theater Design and Technology. A minor course of study of offered in Theater Dance. Currently, IWU has a number of recent graduates appearing in and behind the scenes of a number of Tony winning Broadway productions.

The School of Music offers admission by audition; a student must be admitted to the university and selected by the department of Music as well. The School of Music offers the Bachelor of Music, the Bachelor of Music Education, and the Bachelor of Arts in Music. Major areas include Composition, Instrumental Performance, Piano Performance, Vocal Performance, and course work in a wide range of options such as Conducting, Keyboard Theory, Opera, and Fundamentals of Harmony.

One of the most impressive elements of the quality of life at Illinois Wesleyan is that the general level of satisfaction with social life is high, and uniformly high even among the two-thirds of students who do not enter into fraternity and sorority life. This is a small community, appreciative of the excellence of instruction they receive and willing to take on the rigor their teachers demand. A plethora of student activities animate the campus, including an active chapter of Best Buddies - working with intellectual and developmental disabilities, Amnesty International, the Illinois Wesleyan Pride Alliance, and the supportive organization known as To Write Upon her Arms, dealing with issues of addiction, depression, and self-injury. More celebratory activities include the Cohesive Dance Company, an Improv Troupe, Lyrical Graffiti - a spoken word company, and the Phoenix Theater. The Capoiera Club, CineClub Francais, and Vegans and Vegetarians Victorious Association also draw numbers of members.

The Student Activity Committee provides campus wide entertainment on a weekly basis, and in comparison with the events appearing on most college campuses, IWU's array of shows is exceptionally varied and good. The Greeks do offer social events to the community as a whole and are generous in their sponsorship of fundraising and service activities. About thirty percent of men and women are active in fraternities or sororities, and the chapter houses are residential. Most of the houses are found on campus.

Finally, the Titans of Illinois Wesleyan fight fiercely in the College Conference of Illinois and Wisconsin (CCIW), in which they meet rivals Rose-Hulman, Augustana, Carthage, Millikin, North Central, and Wheaton. The Titans compete in nine varsity sports for men and eight for women. Currently, the men play football, soccer, cross-country, basketball, swimming, baseball, tennis, golf and track; the women compete in soccer, cross-country, volleyball, basketball, softball, tennis, golf, and track. It is in basketball that the Titans have won the greatest success. The men's team has reached the Division III Final Four several times in recent years, and the women's basketball team recently won the 2012 Division III National Championship.

Knox College - Galesburg, Illinois

This is not a college full of smooth operators and socially nimble party boys and girls; there is social activity on campus, and Knox students are certainly within normal limits in terms of college fun, but they see themselves as kind, smart, politically aware nerds, and they aren't ashamed to admit it.

And the stats... 2015

Number of Applicants: 3,221 / 68% Accepted
Undergrad Enrollment: 1,399 58% female / 42% male
Avg. SAT Reading and Math 1150 – 1380. Avg. ACT: 25 – 30
Total Cost: $53,510.00
Received some form of financial assistance: 97%

Knox College is a happening place these days. Although the college has long been highly regarded and successful, it has taken on some academic initiatives that ought to make it particularly interesting to certain kinds of learners. In the first place, Knox offers three academic terms, during which a student takes only three courses. That's more concentrated than the standard four or five course load and slightly less daunting for some than the "block" plans offered at Colorado College and Cornell College.

In addition, Knox offers what they call "immersive learning". These are term long opportunities, part classroom and part practice, and these do bring term-long intensive study of one area. The terms, however, are not standard academic classes. The Japan Term immerses students in history, economics, religion, culture, and includes a two-week trip to Japan. The Open Studio Term gives artists the chance to sink into a major project. The Repertory Theater Term concludes with a production. The Clinical Psychology Term allows students to investigate a career in social work, clinical psychology, counseling. This term includes a two-week internship. The Green Oaks Term is an interdisciplinary experience in community building at a biological field station.

Knox College, in Galesburg, Illinois, truly is a historical campus; Old Main, the college's oldest building is the only remaining site of a Lincoln-Douglas debate. That's Abraham Lincoln and Stephen Douglas... on the campus of Knox College. Galesburg is a town built to serve the railroads; it is a junction of several major lines. "Railroad Days" celebrate the importance of the railroad to Galesburg, and it is easy to hop a train going almost anywhere.

Also on the edge of the college campus is the prairie; this is heartland farm country.

Knox also appears in a popular series of "collegiate" stories, first appearing in *The Saturday Evening Post* and then in one volume as *At Good Old Siwash* by George Helesen Fitch, Knox Class of 1897. Fitch portrayed Knox as the model of hearty collegiate humor and hi jinx.

The college took the name "Siwash" as its mascot until it became sensitive to the derogatory nature of the term in its use in describing the Chinook tribe of the Pacific Northwest. Since 1993, the athletes of Knox College have been identified as, "The Prairie Fire." By the way, the "prairie fire" is not just a nickname; each spring students actually set fire to the prairie at the seven hundred acre biological research area called Green Oaks in order to renew growth and maintain biodiversity.

So, although Knox has not been in the public eye at that same level of notoriety since the early 1900's, surely some of the sentiments about quality education remain alive today:

Mind you, old head, I'm not saying that a little education isn't a good thing in a college course. I learned a lot of real knowledge in school myself that I wouldn't have missed for anything, though I have forgotten it now. But what irritate me are the people who think that the education you get in a modern American superheated, cross-compound college comes to you already canned in neat little textbooks sold by the trust at one hundred per cent profit, and that all you have to do is to go to your room with them, fill up a student lamp with essence of General Education and take the lid off.

At Good Old Siwash, by George Fitch

The very good news is that Knox is not at all coming at anyone already canned; in fact, the Knox way of offering a college education is a bit different from that presented anywhere else.

At Knox, a student takes three courses at a time for a period of ten weeks; the academic year is made up of three ten-week blocks. The 3-3-3 Plan allows in-depth study and concentration of a few subjects. It also allows a killer six-week vacation from the middle of November until the start of January.

The Knox plan is great for those who have a short attention span, but even more useful for those who want to take a very demanding course and hope to be able to spend concentrated time in study. Coursework is rigorous at Knox, but taking only three courses at a time seems to eliminate much of the stress a demanding curriculum might otherwise bring.

So, who ends up in Galesburg, Illinois studying hard in a 3-3-3 academic plan?

Oddly enough, the answer is a very distinctive and idiosyncratic group of students who most frequently describe themselves as, "quirky."

The exact parameters of quirkiness are unclear, but the general agreement seems to be that Knox students are ambitious, bright, and somewhat hyper-focused. Academics are important to a significant portion of the student body, and the college has produced some top-notch scholars. Community seems to be equally important; lots of Knox students report spent in building friendships around shared passions - community service, video games, politics, the arts.

It is no accident that the Creative Writing Program has emerged as one of Knox's most popular and most celebrated programs. The creative writers uniformly describe themselves as "liberated," set free by professors who care about their work but who do not proscribe what good writing should be. Creative, expressive, active - Knox breeds engaged and productive students.

Here's one hallmark of a school with a curiously broad sense of self: About a third of the students are involved in the Greek system, but the overwhelming sentiment of the campus is liberal - actively, vocally, occasionally confrontationally, liberal. Those who join the fraternities and sororities remain closely involved with those who don't, and the general feeling on campus is that Knox is a community, no matter which affiliations a student might choose to make.

One tour guide out it this way:

"Most of us weren't in the "in crowd" in high school, for reasons we are pretty proud of. We have personality and principles, and we probably seem a little bit "out there" compared to the frat boys at Illinois or Northwestern."

Galesburg is a small town and Knox is a small college, but the fourteen hundred students seem to like each other very much and find their professors absolutely spectacular. They use the word "nerd" to mean someone who devotes himself or herself completely to a passion. Knox students have the capacity to "sign on" to their academic life, their extra-curricular life, their political life, and their social life; they feel an attachment and a sense of gratitude to their college.

One student writing about Knox put it this way:

"Knox can be best described in one word: unique. The fact there are so many intelligent students from all over the country and globe in this little Midwest school is mind-boggling. Add to this the diversity and free spirited attitude of the student body, the high caliber of professors, the fantastic course offerings and all the activities/events on campus, and you have a very special place to, learn, grow and prepare yourself for your chosen field. I love my friends, the campus is pretty and the charm of an old-fashioned downtown packed with cool restaurants and stores is just steps away. I can't imagine being anywhere else!"

Traditions are strong at Knox and several are particularly valued. In addition to the annual setting fire to the prairie, Knox students start the year by gathering in front of Old Main to shake hands with everyone in the community. Known as "Pumphandle," the tradition has been alive at Knox since 1885. The most happily pursued tradition, however, is "Flunk Day." Flunk Day is planned in secret, sprung upon the college early in the morning with shouts and the ringing of the college bell. What follows is a carnival featuring inflatable sumo battles, various types of bouncing spaces, rides, concerts, a visit from Abraham Lincoln , and the usual sorts of collegiate mayhem following a day free of classes and obligations.

Knox students love their college, but agree that athletic prominence is not one of the attainments of the college's various interscholastic teams.

Knox plays in Division III's Midwest Conference and enjoys an active schedule of games in a variety of sports, including football and wrestling. A recent headline touting a victory by the basketball team tells the story – "Goodbye Losing Streak: Men's basketball wins at Monmouth College!" The Prairie Fire play with intensity and pride, but interscholastic athletics are in balance with every other activity at Knox. Club sports are well supported and allow Knox students to play water polo, rugby, lacrosse, frisbee, and to pick up fencing as an activity.

Finally, the tradition begun by Lincoln and Douglas remains alive at Knox. Debate, participation in the Model UN, strong advocacy in Common Ground (LGBTQA), and Students against Sexism in Society attract numbers of Knox students, as do an Amnesty International, Food for Thought, and Students Without Borders. Knox is an uncommon college attracting uncommonly decent and uncommonly interesting students. Take the time to investigate this gem of a college.

Michigan

Yes, there are two Michigans – The Lower Peninsula and the Upper Peninsula.

Residents of the Upper Peninsula are occasionally known as " Da Yoopers" because the shortened form of Upper Peninsula for those in the know is the U.P. The U.P is the sixteen thousand square miles of Michigan above the Mackinac Bridge, bounded on the north by Lake Superior and on the southeast by Lake Michigan and Lake Huron. Wisconsin is to the southwest of the U.P. The U.P. is about a quarter of Michigan, but only about three percent of the state's population is found there, as this is some kind of formidable climate; the Keweenaw averages about two hundred and thirty inches of snow a year.

There are three state universities in the Upper Peninsula – Lake Superior State in Sault Ste. Marie, Northern Michigan University in Marquette, and Michigan Tech. in Houghton.

Michigan Tech began in response to the intensive mining enterprises in the U.P. and is still a very strong technological institute. It's snow and ice country, so ice hockey, broomball, skiing (Tech operates its own ski area) and snowboarding are huge. There may not be many who seek the frozen north, but if you do, Superior, Northern Michigan and Michigan Tech are excellent options.

The Lower Peninsula is the mitten-shaped part of the state that most people think of as "Michigan."

The flagship university in the state is the University of Michigan in Ann Arbor, one of the "Public Ivies," and an outstanding academic university in virtually every field. In addition, Ann Arbor may be the ideal college town.

Lansing, home of Michigan State University, is north of Jackson in the south center of the state. MSU is also an outstanding public university and would be among the profiled in this book (the current rate of acceptance has ranged from 70% to 73% in recent years), but it is extremely well known and enrolls numbers of students from around the country and around the world. Michigan State is among the most welcoming and attractive universities in the region and an excellent choice for a student interested in any of its hundreds of programs of study.

Starting in the easternmost portion of the state, in and near Detroit, there are four universities that are largely regional, but worth investigating.

The first of these is Wayne State University, a city university, located in Detroit. Wayne State offers a strong program in the liberal arts and prepares numbers of Michiganders for excellent professional programs, most notably law and medicine.

The College for Creative Studies is also in the heart of Detroit and is among the most innovative in its professional curriculum. Obviously attached at the start to auto design and engineering, the college quickly expanded to offer degrees in graphic arts, product design, advertising, interior design, animation, transportation design, illustration, and photography.

Eastern Michigan University is a state university, not a branch of the University of Michigan, located in Ypsilanti, west of Detroit. Twenty-two thousand students attend Eastern Michigan, many of whom are attracted by exceptional programs in education.

Nineteen thousand students attend Oakland University, located in Rochester Hills and Auburn Hills, affluent northern suburbs of Detroit. Oakland offers more than a hundred major programs and a number of graduate professional programs.

Albion College is located in Albion, equidistant from Jackson and Battle Creek on Route 84, the highway that runs from Detroit to Chicago. "Albion" is the oldest known name for the Island of Great Britain, and the men and women of Albion College are known as "Britons." The British Eighth is the college's marching band, dressed in the bright red and very familiar uniforms of the guards at Buckingham Palace. Albion is a handsome and active small liberal arts college competing in the MIAA with Alma, Adrian, and Olivet.

Central Michigan University in Mount Pleasant (home of the Soaring Eagle Casino) is also a state university separate from the University of Michigan and Michigan State. Central enrolls almost thirty thousand students, most of whom are from Michigan, in a variety of programs, including the celebrated Center for Professional and Personal Ethics. Mount Pleasant is north of Lansing.

Alma College, an excellent small liberal arts college is located between Lansing and Mount Pleasant. Alma is one of the colleges identified as a "College With a Conscience", a college with outstanding community involvement. Alma was founded by Presbyterians and retains its Scottish heritage. Known for its excellence in the arts, Alma is uncommon in that more than a third of all students have been involved in drama production during their time in the college.

Ferris State University was founded as the Big Rapids Industrial School, and this strong local university prepares more than fourteen thousand students for business and professional careers, most notably in optometry and pharmacy. In a rare departure from established format, the Engineering Technology Program at Ferris, truly a distinctive program, will be reviewed in this edition.

Olivet College, south of Lansing, is affiliated with the United Church of Christ and was founded by the same missionaries who founded Oberlin College. Originally known as "New Oberlin," Olivet was one of the first colleges to join the Michigan Intercollegiate Athletic Association, the country's oldest athletic conference. Today, Olivet plays in Division III.

Some of the most interesting options emerge as the college visitor travels to the western portion of the state. Western Michigan University in Kalamazoo began as a teachers college and now enrolls more than twenty-five thousand students on an impressive campus in this city of about eighty thousand people. Western is a comprehensive university, still strong in education, but increasingly noted for its programs in engineering and applied technology. Western Michigan offers an outstanding program in aviation in its College of Aviation, and is equally well known for its work in Paper Engineering and Behavior Analysis. The annual Conference on Medieval Studies is held at Western Michigan as well.

Kalamazoo College, profiled in this book, is adjacent to the campus of Western Michigan University in a pleasant quarter of the city.

Calvin College is located in Grand Rapids, a city of almost two hundred thousand, about forty miles east of Lake Michigan. Calvin is an outstanding comprehensive liberal arts college, one of the strongest in the region, and would be profiled in this book, were it not that its affiliation with the Christian Reformed Church places it in a specialized subgroup of colleges. Calvin is one intelligent hotbed of thought and study, but the college does retain what it calls a "Discrimination Policy," exerting its right under the First Amendment to make decisions about hiring and admission based on religious criteria.

Hope College, in Holland Michigan, is also associated with the Reform Church in America and retains a conservative Christian environment. Known for its excellence in the sciences and the arts, Hope enrolls about three thousand students in a liberal arts course of study.

Whew!

Michigan has its share of colleges, but this book will fully examine only two of the best - Albion and Kalamazoo - and bring the remarkable program in Engineering Technology at Ferris State into the conversation.

Albion College - Albion, Michigan

The Held Equestrian Center is three hundred and forty acres dedicated to competitive riding, the care of horses, and the development of equine skills. Albion competes nationally in hunters, jumpers, western, and dressage. The center offers a barn capable of stabling seventy-nine horses, a welcome center and classroom, three arenas, and miles of trails. The center offers instruction, coaching, symposia, clinics, and a variety of boarding options. I don't know of a coeducational liberal arts college of this caliber offering a similar equestrian program.

And the stats... 2015

Number of Applicants: 4,866 / 61% Accepted
Undergrad Enrollment: 1,268 50% female / 50% male
Avg. SAT Reading 510-590 and Math 520 -640 Avg. ACT: 22-27
Total Cost: $49,685.00
Received some form of financial assistance: 100%

Albion - the oldest known name of the island of Great Britain, and the name of the first college in the state of Michigan to receive a chapter of Phi Beta Kappa. Today Albion College athletic teams remains the Fighting Britons, and the college trots out the British Eighth, a red-coated marching band reminiscent of the Guards at Buckingham Palace at each home football game. But for all the banners and pennants, red coats and brass, Albion College is a thoroughly midwestern small college community of about fifteen hundred students - close-knit, industrious, and kind.

Recognizing that liberal arts colleges often appear relatively similar let me introduce two remarkable and distinctive opportunities available at Albion.

The Whitehouse Nature Center is a one hundred and forty acre classroom, offering more than five miles of roads and trails, four hundred species of plants, and one hundred seventy species of birds. As Albion likes to put it, this is a classroom with a river running through it. Opportunities for environmental study, the study of environmental ethics, bee keeping, and bird keeping make this center truly unique.

The Held Equestrian Center is another three hundred and forty acres dedicated to competitive riding, the care of horses, and the development of equine skills. Albion competes nationally in hunters, jumpers, western, and dressage. The center offers a barn capable of stabling seventy-nine horses, a welcome center and classroom, three arenas, and miles of trails.

The center offers instruction, coaching, symposia, clinics, and a variety of boarding options. I don't know of a coeducational liberal arts college of this caliber offering a similar equestrian program.

The town of Albion is in the same county as Kellogg's Battle Creek and just off the interstate that links Chicago and Kalamazoo to Ann Arbor and Detroit. For many years, Albion was particularly well known for the strength of its pre-professional programs; the college sent numbers of graduates on to become lawyers, doctors, and dentists in southern Michigan. Today, the college continues to prepare its students exceptionally well for professional and graduate programs, but is also increasingly known for the strength of programs in the liberal arts, for innovative programs in student wellness and health, and for a distinctive group of Institutes and Centers designed to propel Albion's graduates into success after college.

The obligation to build a bridge to post-collegiate opportunities is often assumed but rarely made explicit; Albion puts that determination at the top of priorities with what they call The Albion Advantage Pledge:

Our pledge for your future.

Albion will help you realize your professional goals, offering thoughtful guidance and support from the moment you arrive on campus until you begin your life's work.

With that in mind, the college has designed a four-year sequence that includes specific preparatory guidance. A thoughtful introduction to the academic and social demands of college life begins with what Albion calls The First Year Experience. The academic component includes a first year seminar (How Women Changed the World, Through the Looking Glass-Film and Video as Art, "Hooking Up"- the Evolution of Sexuality and Dating) and a common read. A recent Common Reading Experience selection was: "A School for My Village: A Promise to the Orphans of Nyaka" by Twesigye Jackson Kaguri. In addition to on-going orientation throughout the first semester, the social component includes residential programs that reinforce good learning strategies and convocations that are connected with the year's common read.

In subsequent years, Albion's students enter into a broad liberal arts curriculum with the opportunity to enter into particular study in the commonly offered programs in the arts, sciences, and humanities as well as rather uncommon majors in Anthropology and Sociology, Athletic Training, Communications, Exercise Science, Trans American Studies, and several interdisciplinary concentrations such as Neuroscience, Professional Management, and Human Services.

The development of institutes directed toward preparation for specific fields has set Albion apart and generated a good deal of interest from other colleges. The institutes and centers currently in place are: The Gerstacker Institute for Business and Management, the Center for Sustainability and the Environment, the Schmur Center for Teacher Development, the Gerald R. Ford Institute for Leadership in Public Policy and Service. and the Institute for Premedical Professions and Health Sciences. The three critical elements at work in each of the centers and institutes are the mentoring of individuals throughout the course of their study at Albion, the presentation of exceptional lecturers and experts in residence, and the placement of students in meaningful internships or off-campus programs. This initiative is well beyond the standard career office protocol found at most colleges.

With their academic and professional careers well in hand, it is no wonder that the social scene at Albion is hopping. Fraternities and Sororities play some part in organizing campus activities (there are six fraternities and six sororities on campus), but the greater impact comes from the many energetic students following interests outside of the classroom. Any college publishes a list of clubs and organizations, and many seem predictably alike. At Albion, however, the warmth and ingenuity of the student body is clear in the range of opportunities they have created for themselves.

For example, the organizations that are simply recreational include: Albion Anime, Brit Knits (teaching knitting skills), the Albyonne Medievalist Society, the Snow Carvers League, and the Student Farm. For the creative and performing student, Albion offers: *Adrenaline* - a drumline that appears at basketball games, *Bella Voce* - an a cappella treble group, the Albion College Dance Team, the *Dead Pinocchio Theater* - an experimental performance theater, *Euphonics* - a cappella jazz and pop, and the Albion College Players. Service opportunities include Best Buddies, Circle K, and Habitat for Humanity, but also include the Bitone Project, linking Albion's students with the Bitone Children's Home in Uganda, the Ngwani Project in Cameroon, Service Project Appalachia, and Wayfarers International Group for Service (WINGS).

Now, that is an exceptional list of activities and testimony to the wit, compassion, and energy of this exceptional student body.

The Britons competes in the Michigan, Intercollegiate Athletic Conference of the NCAA's Division III, playing against such traditional rivals as Kalamazoo, Olivet, Hope, Calvin, and Saint Mary's in most sports and against competition in the Midwest Lacrosse Conference in that sport. Sports for women include soccer, cross-country, equestrian, volleyball, basketball, swimming, lacrosse, tennis, softball, golf and track. Men compete in football, soccer, cross-country, equestrian, basketball, swimming, baseball, tennis, lacrosse, golf, and track. Recreational sports include equestrian frisbee, canoe, hockey, karate, ski and snowboard, and water polo.

Kalamazoo College - Kalamazoo, Michigan

Kalamazoo prides itself on the part it has played in the promotion of study abroad; for more than sixty years, Kalamazoo has been one of the most ambitious colleges in its program of study outside the United States. Today that initiative takes K students to forty-two programs in twenty-six countries, on six continents.

And the stats... 2015

Number of Applicants: 2,366 / 70% Accepted
Undergrad Enrollment: 1,461 57% female / 43% male
Avg. SAT Reading 530-680 and Math 550-690 Avg. ACT: 25-30
Total Cost: $52,654.00
Received some form of financial assistance: 100%

Kalamazoo College, a college of such confirmed excellence that I have to believe its time on the "hot" college list is bound to arrive. Kalamazoo College is one of those *Colleges That Change Lives*, and its remarkable innovations in curriculum and methods have much to do with its academic success.

The college is set almost perfectly on its own hillside, tree-lined, classically "collegiate" campus - some Georgian red brick and white columns, some faux Victorian - literally across the street from Western Michigan University. This is literally the best of all three worlds, as Western Michigan is a venue bringing the most popular concerts to Kalamazoo, Kalamazoo is a clean and safe city with all the amenities, and the K College campus is a knockout.

 K College is famed for the "K Plan," by which the college has mandated a broad and effective education for each student, including faculty mentors, career and service internship, study abroad, and an ambitious senior project. The aspect of the "K Plan" that had the most impact was the college's determination that the cost of studying abroad would be no greater than the cost of studying at Kalamazoo. In its essence, the "K Plan" has four equally significant elements: A broad and deep exposure to the liberal arts, experiential learning, intercultural and international experience, and independent scholarship.

Some elements of the "K Plan" have been modified in recent years. About eighty-five percent of K College students will study abroad, and almost all will enjoy an internship experience; the college maintains relationships with more than fifty universities across the globe and with hundreds of internship opportunities. From the start, Kalamazoo has believed that there is practical value in carrying one's education into a real-world experience. It is not common to find an excellent liberal arts college with an eye on career development.

The contemporary "K Plan" also includes a rigorous capstone experience. In order to graduate, a K College student will complete an independent project, the Senior Individualized Project (SIP), AND pass a comprehensive examination in his or her major field of study.

If that sounds rigorous, it is, and Kalamazoo has taken a distinctive place in American education, currently standing among the top twenty colleges and universities in the nation in the number earning the Ph.D. in chemistry, life sciences, foreign language, economics, English and literature, and psychology.

Students new to Kalamazoo will find themselves very well cared for. The college runs what is called the "First Year Experience," which begins with a commonly read book during the summer and includes "Land Sea," an optional eighteen day hiking, canoeing, backpacking trip in southern Ontario. After an intensive orientation program, first year students are assigned to a seminar group that meets throughout the year for discussion-based critical thinking. First year students are assigned a faculty advisor and a peer mentor. The process is highly successful and is part of the reason that few leave K College during their career.

Another reason Kalamazoo has been so successful in retaining students, in addition to quality programs and extensive study abroad, is that almost ninety percent of all students have received some form of financial assistance.

Kalamazoo prides itself on the part it has played in the promotion of study abroad; for more than sixty years, Kalamazoo has been one of the most ambitious colleges in its program of study outside the United States. Today that initiative takes K students to forty-two programs in twenty-six countries, on six continents.

The first principle is that travel and study will takes place through the Integrative Cultural Research Project; CIRP takes students into engagement with local culture in college-supported programs in Australia, China, Costa Rica, Germany, Japan, Kenya, Mexico, Senegal, Spain, and Thailand. Fieldwork in the community is accompanied by a reflective essay describing the project the student has undertaken.

And, on campus?

Well, one distinctive element of the K College experience is the diversity of the student body; almost twenty percent are people of color, a significantly higher percentage than that found at many small colleges. Another significant difference between K College and its liberal arts peers is that it enjoys the advantages of a well-conceived campus and the activities of an engaging city.

Indicative of the college's enlightened student body is the regard with which the college's annual Crystal Ball is held. The Ball is hosted by Kalamazoo's Kaleidoscope (Gay, Lesbian, Bisexual, Transgender, and Ally Organization), usually involves dressing in drag or costume, and is a long-standing tradition at the college.

There are at least two distinctive social traditions at Kalamazoo that should be noted. In addition to the frolic and festivity that accompanies Homecoming and the Fall Fest, K College has sponsored a Day of Gracious Living since 1974. This is a surprise day off for the college and can include a trip to the beach on the shore of Lake Michigan. In the midst of winter, K College offers a Casino Night that brings out the gambler in each of its students. This is a huge casino blowout and much appreciated by students each year.

K College attracts bright kids, and bright kids can occasionally be a bit "quirky", as those who love Kalamazoo might agree.

Does a student walk across campus in a banana suit?
Well, yes.

And is there a circus club on campus?
Again, yes.

How do these bright kids like their college?
Very much!

The overwhelming opinion is that Kalamazoo has brought a responsive and helpful faculty to a demanding and rigorous curriculum; K College students work hard, but they feel rewarded in the work they do.

Sports at Kalamazoo are not uniformly well supported, but several of the teams have won national recognition, and those teams are a source of great pride. Kalamazoo's Hornets plays a Division III schedule in almost every sport, although its dominant men's tennis team (The National Junior Championships are played at Kalamazoo every year) plays against the strongest competition it can find in order to prepare for conference and NCAA championships. Kalamazoo's tennis team has won the conference every year from 1936 – 2010. Only the success of Kenyon's swimming team (31 NCAA championships in a row) is a more impressive string of victories.

In recent years, Kalamazoo's swimming and diving program has also been dominant, having won twenty-five MIAA championships. K College plays traditional rivals Albion, Alma, Rose-Hulman, Olivet, and Hope in the usual configuration of sports, including football, soccer, tennis, volleyball, swimming, track, and cross country. Ice hockey is the most popular club sport although the student body is actively involved in more than eighty activities, organizations, and intramural offerings.

Ferris State University - Big Rapids, Michigan

Finally, and unexpectedly, Ferris is one of three colleges in the nation that offers a degree in Welding Engineering Technology, allowing one to learn everything there is to know about what Ferris calls weldments. While I remain entirely ignorant of what a weldment is, I do know that the average salary of graduates from this program is just under sixty thousand dollars a year in the first year after graduation.

The total cost of attending Ferris State in 2015 was $22,265.00 for in-state students and $28,055.00 for out-of-state students.

And the stats... 2015

Number of Applicants: 10,426 / 78% Accepted
Undergrad Enrollment: 13,373 53% female / 47% male
Avg. Avg. ACT: 19-24
Total Cost: $22,295.00 (in-state) $28,205.00 (out-of-state)
Received some form of financial assistance: 94%

Big Rapids, Michigan is certainly a name to conjure with, evoking rugged terrain and hearty woodlands adventure. The City of Big Rapids, however, home to Ferris State, is an industrial city about fifty miles north of Grand Rapids, and equidistant from Chicago to the west and Detroit to the east. Big Rapids is a great location from which to explore Michigan; it's almost exactly the midpoint of Michigan's lower peninsula.

Ferris State University is part of Michigan's public university system, currently enrolling about fifteen thousand students on campus and a considerable number at the satellite campuses - Dowagiac, Grand Rapids, Flint, Lansing, Traverse City, and University Center. At the Big Rapids campus, the university is organized around eight colleges, one of which, the College of Engineering Technology, is the subject of this article. The other colleges are: Arts and Sciences, Business, Education and Human Services, Health Professions, the Kendall College of Art and Design, Michigan College of Optometry, and Pharmacy. Ferris State is an active and ambitious public university with all the amenities and organizations college students have come to expect. In addition, the Division I Ferris State Bulldogs are among the powerhouse ice hockey teams in the country, battling for the NCAA championship in the Frozen Four. Hockey is the premiere sport at Ferris and crowds are vociferous in their love of the Bulldogs.

The College of Engineering Technology, however, is distinctive enough and interesting enough on its own to claim some attention from any student eager to reach the most advanced programs in industrial technology in the largest school of engineering technology in the world.

A quick review of the departments contained in the College of Engineering Technology will present the obvious specialization of these cutting-edge programs: The School of Automotive and Heavy Equipment, the School of Built Environment, CEEMS (Computer Engineering/Electronics/Mechanical Engineering/Surveying), and the School of Design and Manufacturing.

Just in case these programs sound entirely vocational, the course of study in each department is definitely engineering at the highest level.

For example, in the School of Automotive and Heavy Equipment, the Bachelor of Science is offered in Automotive Engineering Technology, Automotive Management, and Heavy Equipment Service Technology. As a student of Automotive Technology, one would take coursework in Calculus, Physics, several liberal arts courses, Technical Writing, Manual Transmission Drivelines, Automotive Brake Systems, Auto Electricity, Electronic Fuel Management Systems, Engine Flow Analysis, Material Science, Kinematics of Mechanisms, Metrology, and Prototype Development.

The BS in Automotive Management is far more clearly directed toward a business model with greater concentration on accounting, marketing, distribution, and communication skills, but Calculus and Material Science also come into play as well. The B.S. in Heavy Equipment Service Engineering is every bit as math and science laden, with particular courses work in Advanced Hydraulic Control Systems, Software Systems, Material Science, and Fleet Management.

Let's say your interest is in learning how buildings, bridges, and highways are actually built; you'll be digging into the School of Built Environment, where the major programs include: Architecture and Facility Management, Construction Technology and Management, and Heating, Ventilation, Air Conditioning, and Refrigeration. The Architecture and Facility Management programs offer degrees in Architectural technology and Architectural Sustainability. The B.S. Programs offered in Construction Technology and Management include Building Construction Technology Management and Civil Engineering Construction Management.

The School of CEEMS is wicked challenging and right up the alley of anyone interested in robotics, security systems, network systems, or automation. The school offers six separate degree-granting programs.

The first of these, Computer Networks and Systems is far less theoretical than other CS majors, putting great emphasis on the applicability of hands-on skills to technical employment. The priorities in this department are: Network implementation and administration, Network Communication Theory, Test, Design, and Applications, Real-time Control Networks, Operating Systems, Computer Control Systems Design, Microprocessor, Digital and Electronic Theory and Application Micro-controller Applications, Designs, Programming and Integration Software Development and Applications Project Management.

Whew! And that's just the Computer Network and Systems program.
Energy Systems Engineering is a B.S. program with an emphasis on solving energy related problems. Students will have hands-on experience with Electronic Grid Control, Alternative Fuel Experimentation, Energy Efficiency, and Chemical Processing.

The degree in Mechanical Engineering Technology probably comes closest to a standard engineering program with required coursework in Calculus, Physics, Dynamics, Thermodynamics, Kinematics, and Material Science.

The program in Product Design Engineering Technology is essentially a design major with coursework in Statics-Strength of Materials, Advanced Tolerancing, Applied Thermodynamics, and Advanced Machine Design. As would be the case in any design program, much of the work is project-based, geared toward industrial application.

The degree in Surveying Engineering is an engineering degree with emphasis on Material Science, GIS and Cartography, and Photgrammetry.

OK, so let's assume you are the one person in fifty who is keen to get your hands on Plastic and Rubber Materials Manufacturing? This is the place, with a BS program that allows one to work in Plastics Engineering or Rubber Engineering, two fields that apparently have come into high demand in the development of medical technology.

Finally, and unexpectedly, Ferris is one of three colleges in the nation that offers a degree in Welding Engineering Technology, allowing one to learn everything there is to know about what Ferris calls *weldments*. While I remain entirely ignorant of what a *weldment* is, I do know that the average salary of graduates from this program is just under sixty thousand dollars a year in the first year after graduation.

I'm just saying.

And get a load of total cost for both in-state and out-of-state students!

Wisconsin and Iowa

Wisconsin and Iowa may not have the glitz and glitter of New York or California, but they do offer all that is best and most valuable of the midwestern experience. Both states are farm states and both states produce much of what ends up on America's tables. Wisconsin is known for dairy (Green Bay has its Cheese-Heads for a reason!), and Iowa is known for grain.

Both states are defined to a degree by water. The Mississippi flows on the eastern border of Iowa, and the Missouri is the western border. Wisconsin is bordered to the north by Lake Michigan and Lake Superior.

The capital of Wisconsin is Madison, which is also a booming college town. In fact, only Austin manages to share that lively balance between political hub and college Mecca.

Madison is a great college town; the University of Wisconsin is a huge campus, almost a thousand acres, located between two beautiful lakes – Monona and Mendota. One of the many amenities enjoyed by students at Wisconsin is the availability of sailboats for hire at the student union, perched right on the shore of Lake Mendota. Loyal Badgers follow their teams in the Big Ten and in national contests.

The University of Wisconsin has twelve campuses – the flagship at Madison and branches in Eau Claire, Green Bay, La Crosse, Kenosha, Platteville, River Falls, Stevens Point, Superior, and Whitewater.

Marquette University is a Jesuit university, located in Milwaukee. Marquette has particular strength in Communications/Journalism and Engineering, but is highly regarded in several academic areas as well. The university enrolls about eight thousand undergraduates and another four thousand graduate students.

Three more of Wisconsin's independent colleges have attracted attention outside the region – Lawrence University, Beloit College and Ripon College, profiled in this book.

Some are aware of Ripon because it recently became the first college to offer free bicycles to any students who promised not to bring a car on campus. Some are aware of Ripon because its forensics team is as successful as the Red Hawk Division III athletes. Forbes places Ripon in the 19th spot among the best private colleges in the Midwest, and many believe that the anthropology classroom in The Temple of Doom was based upon Ford's experience as an undergraduate at Ripon. (Actually, the classroom can be found on the campus of the University of the Pacific.)

An unusual resource is the Ceresco Prairie Conservancy, a living classroom – one hundred and thirty acres of native prairie. Off campus programs are well supported as well– internships and study abroad are common. Almost eighty percent of Ripon's students will work off campus.

The town of Ripon, Wisconsin is known as the birthplace of the Republican Party, an honor it shares with Jackson, Michigan. The town of Ripon has a population of about seven thousand and is about ninety minutes north of Madison and about thirty minutes west of Fond du Lac.

Beloit, profiled in this book, is in a small city (about thirty five thousand) virtually on the border with Illinois, about equidistant between Chicago and Madison. The city, home to a Hormel meat plant and a Frito Lay plant, is celebrated as the site of the world's largest can of chili. Beloit is also the home of Korn Kurls, the first popular snack food.

There are three public universities in Iowa – Iowa State, University of Northern Iowa, and the University of Iowa. Iowa State is located in Ames, a small city about thirty minutes north of Des Moines, smack in the middle of the state. Iowa State is a strong university with particular reputation in the sciences. Its teams, the Cyclones, play in the Big Twelve Conference, but enjoy a long-standing rivalry with the University of Iowa, a Big Ten school.

Northern Iowa is, not surprisingly, in a small city in northern Iowa – Cedar Falls. UNI is known for its extensive program of study abroad.

The University of Iowa, in Iowa City, is one of very few large state universities profiled in this book.

There are several outstanding independent colleges in Iowa, the most celebrated of which is Grinnell College. Grinnell is a very highly ranked liberal arts college located in a small city about an hour north of Des Moines. Until recently, Grinnell was both respected and envied, as it had long been a bastion of excellence and recently fortunate in riding the "dot com" boom to one of the highest endowments among all liberal arts colleges.

Cornell College (not to be confused with Cornell University) is an innovative liberal arts college in Mount Vernon, Iowa, about twenty minutes east of Cedar Rapids. Cornell is one of very few colleges offering the "Block Plan." Students studying in the Block Plan (also known as OCCAT – One Course At A Time), spend a block of three-and-a-half weeks studying one course intensively. The academic year is divided into nine blocks. Cornell has been operating under the Block Plan since 1978.

Cornell has a very handsome campus and is nationally regarded for the success of its Mock Trial team, perennial champions of national contests.

Beloit and Ripon in Wisconsin are profiled in this book as are Coe College in Cedar Rapids and the University of Iowa in Iowa City.

Beloit College - Beloit, Wisconsin

Back on campus, the prevailing word of choice is intimacy, in the very best meaning of the word. Beloit is small (about thirteen hundred students) and a self-identified "bubble". International students are clearly a significant part of the Beloit experience, and the college does have an open window on the world, but the shared experience of life on campus creates a sense of community that is palpable.

And the stats... 2015

Number of Applicants: 2,281 / 69% Accepted
Undergrad Enrollment: 1,303 58% female / 42% male
Avg. SAT Reading 540-710 and Math 540 -660 Avg. ACT: 24-30
Total Cost: $52,270.00
Received some form of financial assistance: 99%

Beloit is yet another of the excellent colleges recognized by Loren Pope in his *Colleges That Change Lives,* and the college continues to promote the values and practices that attracted Pope as he compiled his original list. Beloit is the oldest continuously operating university in the state of Wisconsin and its buildings are the oldest academic buildings north of Chicago.

Located halfway between Chicago and Madison, Beloit has the qualities that both those cities might present. The high proportion of students entering from the Chicago area brings a level of worldly-wise sophistication; the folks from Wisconsin are grounded in the plain speaking, grass-roots common sense of the Upper Midwest. If there is any concern about Beloit's student body it might be that it is actively and occasionally vehemently liberal; it has been hard for conservative students to find their voice on campus.

For many years, Beloit was known for the "Beloit Plan," essentially an attempt to meld the liberal arts experience with "real world" experience. The Plan called for one semester of off-campus internship or travel for every four spent on campus. As a result, Beloit's students were notably more willing to study abroad in the 60's and 70's than students at many other comparable small colleges.

Today, Beloit is known for several departments in particular. Its Geology department is popular, and students of Geology frequently travel on geological expeditions. The Anthropology department is also highly esteemed as a disproportionate number of its graduates have gone to earn the Ph.D. in that subject. A strong program in Literature and Writing has been enhanced by the visiting writers program, which has brought such writers as Billy Collins, Ursula le Guinn, Robert Stone, and Denise Levertov to campus for the year. The Beloit Fiction Journal is now published at the college, and students serve on the editorial board. Beloit also maintains two working museums on campus – a museum of anthropology and a museum of art. Students not only use the holdings of the museums in research, but are involved in curatorial work as well.

Beloit enrolls students from every state, but it remains predominantly Midwestern; 60% of enrolled students are from the Midwest. 8%, however, are international. The college maintains a close relationship with Fudan University in China, exchanging both students and faculty with that university. Other international programs are also attractive, and more than half of Beloit's students will study off-campus during their career. Almost eighty percent will also be involved in an internship or research project as well. Collaborative work is encouraged, and many Beloit students will end up co-authoring an article after having done original research with a professor.

Beloit connects with the real world in a number of ways; internships are supported by scholarships and grants, and the program knows as CELEB (Center for Entrepreneurial Leadership at Beloit) us allows business ideas to incubate. Research fellowships are also available. Finally, the college offers intensive summer programs in language, including coursework in Arabic, Chinese, and Russian. Beloit's Cities in Transition program brings Beloit's students into close examination of cities in China, Senegal, Ecuador, Nicaragua, and Russia.

Back on campus, the prevailing word of choice is *intimacy,* in the very best meaning of the word. Beloit is small (about thirteen hundred students) and a self-identified "bubble". International students are clearly a significant part of the Beloit experience, and the college does have an open window on the world, but the shared experience of life on campus creates a sense of community that is palpable.

Not only does Beloit generate strong feelings of attachment, it maintains real bonds of loyalty. Beloit's students love their college and are grateful for the opportunities they find here. They recognize that their professors are exceptional and exceptionally willing to engage with students. They recognize that they, themselves, are an unusual and talented, highly engaged student body.

Fun at Beloit is most often found in spontaneous adventures with classmates who share a sense of goofy humor. The fraternity thing is very limited at Beloit; not only do very few join, they are far from the conventional "frat boy" model, often a serious student or active volunteer. As is the case in virtually every college and university, there are more women than men at Beloit, so dating can be a bit tricky. In a community this close, friendships seem more common than pairs.

Every college has traditions, and Beloit has one that is truly unique. Beloit annually publishes the "Mindset List," a compendium of people, events, and ideas that comprise the frame of reference of the class entering college that year.

2019 LIST
Students heading into their first year of college this year are mostly 18 and were born in 1997.
Among those who have never been alive in their lifetimes are Princess Diana, Notorious B.I.G., Jacques Cousteau, and Mother Teresa.

Since they have been on the planet:

- *They have never licked a postage stamp.*

- *Hong Kong has always been under Chinese rule.*

- *The announcement of someone being the "first woman" to hold a position has only impressed their parents.*

- *They have avidly joined Harry Potter, Ron, and Hermione as they built their reading skills through all seven volumes.*

- *The therapeutic use of marijuana has always been legal in a growing number of American states.*

- *Surgeons have always used "super glue" in the operating room.*

- *The Lion King has always been on Broadway.*

- *TV has always been in such high definition that they could see the pores of actors and the grimaces of quarterbacks.*

Beloit is a Division III school, competing against other small colleges in the region. Its teams are popularly known as the "Buccaneers," but the distinctive activity on campus in ultimate frisbee and frisbee golf. The Beloit Ultimate Frisbee Family (BUFF) competes in national ultimate frisbee tournaments, and Beloit students set the world record for number of hours (72) in the longest frisbee game.

Ripon College - Ripon, Wisconsin

Long interested in leadership as a mindful enterprise, Ripon is the heart of the Collaborative Leadership Network, based in Ripon's Leadership Studies Program. Similarly, the National Forensics League, the honorary society dedicated to the promotion of forensic competition among high school students grew from the National Forensic League tournaments held at Ripon from the nineteen twenties. Today, Ripon College supports an ambitious forensics team, competing nationally in eleven forensic events in tournaments throughout the year. As an NCAA Division III athletic school, Ripon does not offer athletic scholarships, but as a Division I Forensics school, the college offers a number of forensic scholarships, available to the most talented students by audition.

And the stats... 2015

Number of Applicants: 1.493 / 67% Accepted
Undergrad Enrollment: 840 53% female / 47% male
Avg. SAT Reading 500-630 and Math 470 -680 Avg. ACT: 22-27
Total Cost: $44,917.00
Received some form of financial assistance: 98%

You'd drive right through Ripon if you were on your way from Green Bay to Eau Claire or Wausau. Well, you'd have to turn north again to get to Wausau, or, you could rumble southeast to Milwaukee, or slightly southwest to Madison. You're about one hundred and eighty miles northwest of Chicago and about eighty miles northwest of Milwaukee. Ripon is on the edge of the Fox River Valley and is a small city of about ten thousand people, charming in the way that historic small towns are charming, and especially notable in that it is one of four "birthplaces" of the Republican Party in the United States. If you've a mind to track down the others, you'll need to travel to Crawfordsville, Indiana, Jackson, Michigan, and Exeter, New Hampshire. Thus, the Little White Schoolhouse in Ripon is on the Registry of Historic Places. Main Street offers the usual snack, pizza, and sundry amenities necessary to college life.

Ripon College belongs to the cohort of excellent and ambitious small liberal arts colleges that sprang up in the Midwest in the eighteenth century. Like its peers, Ripon has graduated doctors, lawyers, scholars, corporate chiefs, and educators galore. In its current iteration, Ripon is noted for thoughtful mentoring of individual students, an array of uncommon major programs exceptional in a college of this size, remarkable achievement in forensics, and a rich extracurricular life.

Oh, and the total cost of a year at Ripon is about forty-five thousand dollars a year, and more than ninety percent of students receive some form of financial aid. That sounds notable to me!

The student body is small, talented, ambitious, active, and kind. The enrollment at Ripon is just under a thousand students, allowing a degree of intimacy and mentorship not found at most colleges. The universal acclaim with which the teaching faculty is described is due, in part, to the exceptional interest they show in the progress of each student. Ripon is a small community, and the commonly shared cultural and recreational activities put faculty in close contact with students at concerts, lectures, carnivals, and athletic events.

Long interested in leadership as a mindful enterprise, Ripon is the heart of the Collaborative Leadership Network, based in Ripon's Leadership Studies Program. Similarly, the National Forensics League, the honorary society dedicated to the promotion of forensic competition among high school students grew from the National Forensic League tournaments held at Ripon from the nineteen twenties. Today, Ripon College supports an ambitious forensics team, competing nationally in eleven forensic events in tournaments throughout the year. As an NCAA Division III athletic school, Ripon does not offer athletic scholarships, but as a Division I Forensics school, the college offers a number of forensic scholarships, available to the most talented students by audition.

The program of study at Ripon may seem fairly conventional at first glance – two semesters with an optional "Maymester". What sets Ripon apart, however is that, in addition to an array of majors that includes the usual arts, sciences, and humanities, the college offers programs in Anthropology, Leadership Studies, Psychobiology, National Security Studies, Business Management, Exercise Science, and minor concentration in Museum Studies, Dramatic Literature, Classical Studies, Entrepreneurship, Military Studies, and Theater Production. In that regard, it doesn't hurt that Harrison Ford is a graduate and friend of the college.

There are active fraternities and sororities, but they are housed in the residences so that the small community remains centrally residential and well connected. Ripon's academic program is rigorous, and athletic offerings are ambitious; it is somewhat surprising that the number of social and special interest activities seems to multiply year after year. This is a busy campus, even in the dead of winter, and the jolly engagement in activities and organizations keeps these students energized and active.

College Days, the student newspaper, the Forensics Team, and Ripon radio, WRPN, are highly visible activities, drawing the talents of dedicated students throughout the year. Ripon's students are involved with service and issues – Amnesty International, Circle K, EGOR (the Environmental Group of Ripon), Network (gay, lesbian, bisexual and transgender ally support and social change organization for Ripon students, faculty, and staff), St. Jude Up 'til Dawn. Equally active are the more entertaining or purely social organizations, such as: Cinemaniacs, and the Heavy Metal Society. Some quirky organization's unique to Ripon are the Armchair Association (a philosophy discussion club) and Parallax (a fine arts journal). Students looking to break a sweat might engage with the fencing club, the lacrosse club, the rugby club, the ultimate frisbee club, the equestrian club, the outdoor club, the rrRumba ballroom dance club, the Red Hawks Dance Team, the college cheer and stunt squad, the mixed martial arts club, or the paintball club. Of course, some will end up near BAR (Billiards and Recreation of Ripon – darts/cribbage/bowling/euchre/air hockey, etc...)

As the presence of a red Hawk cheer and stunt squad might suggest, Ripon's teams are, in fact, the Red Hawks, and they compete in NCAA Division III sports in the Midwest Conference against such traditional rivals as Beloit, Grinnell, Cornell College, Lake Forest, Knox, and Lawrence. Rally the Red Hawk appears at games and at civic and celebratory events in Ripon (book him for your next birthday!). Ripon offers football, soccer, cross-country, basketball, swimming, track, baseball, golf, and tennis for men, and soccer, volleyball, cross-country, basketball, swimming, softball, tennis, golf, and track. An interesting athletic twist is that the Ripon Red Hawks compete up a level in Division II in cycling in the Midwest Collegiate Cycling Conference.

Not only is Ripon a major bargain among ambitious liberal arts colleges, and not only is the college an uncommonly active place, it is also relentlessly innovative. One great idea that lost its funding was the "Velorution" initiative, by which each student who pledged not to bring a car to campus was given a new Trek 820 mountain bicycle, helmet, and lock. Perhaps the campus will be wheeling again by the time this book hits the stands.

Lawrence University - Appleton, Wisconsin

Lawrence is an academic powerhouse and a cultural Mecca. The range of coursework and complementary events offered by the university approach those of a much larger institution, and the students accepted into the Conservatory are among the most gifted in the nation. Lawrence promotes engagement in learning, and it succeeds beyond all expectations. Pride in the university is palpable, and strong relationships with mentoring professors are obvious.

And the stats... 2015

Number of Applicants: 2,774 / 73% Accepted
Undergrad Enrollment: 1,511 54% female / 46% male
Test Scores Optional / Not Reported
Total Cost: $53,790.00
Received some form of financial assistance: 97%

I sound like a broken record, I know... but how can Lawrence University not be among the most sought out colleges in the Midwest? The abiding strength of its program in the liberal arts is widely recognized, and the Conservatory of Music is among the best in the country. Happily, the admissions office is once again taking leadership in connecting with potential Lawrentians. Early on, Lawrence joined the ranks of colleges no longer requiring SAT and ACT scores; about a third of applicants choose not to present their scores. Now they have revised their policy with regard to Early Decision, making three application cycles. Finally (Hurrah!) Lawrence no longer asks for an application fee.

Lawrence is a small university, enrolling about fifteen hundred students on a handsome campus located in one of the more charming small cities in the state. Downtown Appleton is lively and only about a block from Lawrence's campus, offering good theater and music, restaurants, and coffee shops. That's a bonus because life on campus is incredibly rich. I'll get specific about course offerings later, but Lawrence is an academic powerhouse and a cultural Mecca. The range of coursework and complementary events offered by the university approach those of a much larger institution, and the students accepted into the Conservatory are among the most gifted in the nation. Lawrence promotes engagement in learning, and it succeeds beyond all expectations. Pride in the university is palpable, and strong relationships with mentoring professors are obvious.

In the interest of attracting those who have not yet explored the Upper Midwest, I'll have to take a moment for some undisguised appreciation of the area. Appleton and the Lawrence campus are literally on the Fox River; the Lawrence campus is divided by the river – academic and residential buildings on one side, athletic fields and facilities on the other. Appleton's postcard pretty neighborhoods abut the Lawrence campus, about an hour-and-a-half north of Milwaukee and about a half hour south of Green Bay. Even the relatively balanced football fan will find the trip to Green Bay and to the Green Bay Football Hall of Fame worth the short detour.

Those who know Wisconsin and who appreciate the beauty of the northernmost reaches of the state have long been attracted to Door County, a prominent vacation spot, with almost three hundred miles of shoreline. Lawrence owns and operates a retreat center called Bjorklunden, Swedish for "the birch grove by the lake" for the use of Lawrence students during the academic year and during the summer. The estate is on Lake Michigan just south of Baileys Harbor. Students love to take some time in visiting Bjorklunden and find an impressive range of seminars and symposia. A weekend might bring an extended discussion of gender studies, a meeting of the Viking Conservative Club, or training for the fencing squad.

Three quarters of the students at Lawrence major in one of the liberal arts and sciences, with English and the Natural Sciences claiming the largest numbers. About twenty-five percent of Lawrence's students are enrolled in the Conservatory of Music, and about half of those are pursuing the dual degree, a B.A. and the B.Mus.; the wealth of opportunity within both programs is exceptional.

All freshmen participate in the Freshman Studies seminar for the first two terms at Lawrence. In small classes, the freshmen consider some fairly important issues: *What are the best sorts of life for human beings? Are there limits to human knowledge? How should we respond to injustice and suffering?* The entire freshman class reads the same books throughout those terms, so discussion can follow students to the dining hall and dormitories. A sampler of current titles includes: Alison Bechdel's *Fun Home,* Brecht's *The Life of Galileo*, Plato's *The Republic, The Bhagavad-Gita,* and Miles Davis' *Kind of Blue.*

The B.A. program includes all of the arts and sciences you would expect to find in a college of this quality, and then ... other programs include: Anthropology, Art History, Biomedical Ethics, Chinese, East Asian Studies, Cognitive Science, Computer Science, Ethnic Studies, Film Studies, Gender Studies, Geology, Innovation and Entrepreneurship, Japanese, Latin American Studies, Linguistics, and Neuroscience.

Students in the Conservatory will take approximately a third of their course work in the college of liberal arts and the remaining two thirds in the Bachelor of Music Degree Program, which offers the Major in Performance, the Major in Music Education, and the Major in Theory and Composition. Concentrations include: Bass, Bassoon, Cello, Clarinet, Composition, Dance, Flute, Guitar, Horn, Jazz and Improvisational Music, Music Education, Musicology, Music Theory, Oboe, Organ, Percussion, Piano, Saxophone, Trombone, Trumpet, Tuba-Euphonium, Viola, Violin, and Voice.

And what do Conservatory students do outside the classroom? There are no differences between the Conservatory students and others on campus in terms of in terms of residential life, extra-curricular activities, and athletics They are college students doing what college students do, but they can also join: The Lawrence Symphony Orchestra, Wind, Ensemble, Symphonic Band, Concert Choir, Cantala, Viking Chorale, Jazz Ensemble, Jazz Band, Opera Theater, Gamelan, Percussion Ensemble, and the Improvisational Group know as IGLU (Improvisational Group Lawrence University).

Balance. Me than most student bodies, Lawrence's seem to know how to keep engaged in their studies, active in clubs, organizations, and sports, and maintain happy and healthy social relationships. The co-curricular life includes the usual opportunities to become involved in student government, community service, honor societies, environmental organizations, religious, and creative groups. Some of the uncommon opportunities are: the Great Midwest Trivia Contest, Lawrence Improv (Optimistic Feral Children), Shakthi (Bollywood Performing Arts), Students for Justice in Palestine, Swing Dance, and a Printmaking Club.

Residential life The traditions that have emerged over the years at Lawrence and the particular role played by fraternities and sororities give a reasonably good sense of the balanced, sensible, sane, intelligent, responsible and slightly quirky Lawrentians. Every school has a seal proclaiming the college's spiritual core. At Harvard it's *Veritas* (Truth), at Yale it's *Lux et Veritas* (Light and Truth). Lawrence's seal? *Light! More Light!* It's in English, but the phrase comes from the dying words of Johann Wolfgang von Goethe, arguably the smartest guy of his time. Makes sense, impressively literary, but it is a bit... quirky. Every college has a fight song; Lawrence's (*Go, Lawrence Go!*) was written by one of the most prominent choral director of the time (1940) and describes what was once an annual part of Homecoming festivities – sending a burning raft down the Fox River. Not happening these days, but the song lives on. The burning raft may be a connection to the practices of the Vikings, the team name. Lawrence teams were not always Vikings; they were known as Blue-Somethings. The swim team, for example, was the Bluefins. Finally, the campus icon, "The Rock", was stolen, returned, stolen, returned, stolen, etc. until one of the dorms buried it. It was raised after nineteen years, then stolen, and now is lost.

About twenty-five percent of men join fraternities and they live in fraternity houses. Sororities do not have separate houses. Both provide social events that are open to the entire community and both play a quiet role in the college's life. The variety of student activities and the number of co-curricular activities keep the place humming.

Viking sports offer fifteen varsity sports which compete in the NCAA's Division III in the Midwest Conference. Men play football, soccer, cross-country, basketball, hockey, swimming, indoor track, fencing, golf, tennis, track, and baseball. Women play soccer, volleyball, cross-country, basketball, indoor track, swimming, fencing, softball, and track. Club sports include crew for men and women and coed ultimate frisbee.

Coe College - Cedar Rapids, Iowa

Current students and graduates speak fondly of their professors, describing them as endlessly accessible, patient, and wise. The affection with which Coe students speak of their teachers is distinctive and reflects the strong sense of community this college has engendered. The excellent record of placement in professional and graduate programs indicates that Coe students are well prepared and well represented by their college.

And the stats... 2015

Number of Applicants: 3,403 / 55% Accepted
Undergrad Enrollment: 1,436 56% female / 44% male
Avg. SAT Reading 500-640 and Math 530 -640 Avg. ACT: 22-28
Total Cost: $49,220.00
Received some form of financial assistance: 98%

The Field of Dreams and corn often get the glory when conversation turns to Iowa, but the other excellent gift to a grateful nation is Coe College in Cedar Rapids, Iowa. Coe is more than active enough, but should you wonder about the region, Cedar Rapids is a thriving cultural center for Eastern Iowa, home to the Iowa Cultural Corridor, the Paramount Theater, and a good museum of fine arts. Concerts and performers regularly appear at the U.S. Cellular Center, and the Anaheim Angels farm club, the Cedar Rapids Kernels, play baseball in a brand new stadium.

Cedar Rapids also has an interesting history of accommodating ethnic groups outside of the Iowan mainstream. The first Muslim mosque in North America was built in Cedar Rapids, and the city is home to the only exclusively Muslim cemetery in the United States. Large numbers of Cambodian and Hispanic immigrants have found work in Cedar Rapids, and the city is home to an African-American museum and the National Czech and Slovak Museum. Coe has traditional ties with the Presbyterian Church and is still mostly white and mostly midwestern, but its excellent programs and uncommonly generous financial support of its students (92% receive financial aid) has brought interest from students of many ethnicities from many regions.

A great deal has been happening at Coe in the last few years. The campus is much enlarged, primarily due to new construction of apartments now part of the residential system. A lottery system makes the apartments available to upper class students. The dining facilities are also much improved in an expanded and renovated dining hall with many options at every meal. The library, the science building, and the fine arts center have also had very recent upgrades. It's clear that Coe is a college on the rise.

Coe offers the usual majors and opportunities for off-campus study abroad through the Associated Colleges of the Midwest, and, in addition, offers, a degree in business management, and majors in elementary education, public relations and communications, neuroscience, athletic training, and music performance; other majors include accounting, athletic training, and English as a second language. The most significant of curricular differences between Coe and its peer institutions is that in addition to the B.A. and B.S., Coe offers a degree in Nursing and a degree in Music.

The Music program at Coe is widely known and highly regarded, as is the English Department. It is rare for a college of this size, with very small class sections, to offer a curriculum as wide as Coe's.

Coe is an academic school and its students study hard; they also have plans for the future. A clear commitment to preparation for the world of work is reflected in the provisions of the Coe Plan. The "Coe Plan" obviously assumes that college graduates may want to be employable – a delicious hypothesis. The Coe Plan offers students have the opportunity to learn from industry and academic professionals at such work sites as Walt Disney World, the State Department, and the Seattle Zoo. Students have the opportunity to follow their research to institutions and agencies in the Unites States and to laboratories in China, Germany, and the United Kingdom. Coe is also affiliated with the Washington Term and the New York term, making well organized off-campus experiences available to students in virtually any major.

Current students and graduates speak fondly of their professors, describing them as endlessly accessible, patient, and wise. The affection with which Coe students speak of their teachers is distinctive and reflects the strong sense of community this college has engendered. The excellent record of placement in professional and graduate programs indicates that Coe students are well prepared and well represented by their college.

Coe is also unusual in having created an extensive and ambitious writing center, now employing more than sixty students, many of whom are asked to speak nationally on the process of assisting students in writing. Volunteerism is a part of the Coe tradition as is active engagement in extracurricular life. Virtually all students at Coe have played a part in making one or several activities come to life during their time at the college. Ranging from Artists Anonymous to the College Republicans, the ambitious activities program presents more than eighty options and promises the opportunity to start new clubs each year.

Although many of the clubs, musical groups, theatrical productions, service groups, and publications are highly successful, there are two sorts of particular organizations that represent the diversity of interests and energies at Coe. The first of these is to be found in the organization of *Coe V Day,* an activist movement to end violence against women and girls, *Children of Promise*, a group working with local children whose parent has been incarcerated, and *Coexist,* a group that takes on tough questions in discussion of conflicting religious and political convictions. The second sort of group might be described as whimsical. *Geekfest* encourages all Coe students to find their inner geek, the Horror Flicks club is dedicated to discussion of the genre, the *Walahroo Drumline,* an oddly constituted pep band that appears on the sidelines of Coe's games, and the *Kohawk Otaku Anime Club.*

There are fraternities and sororities at Coe, but they tend not to dominate the social scene and play a limited part in the college's residential life. The Activities Committee keeps things hopping on most weekends, and several friendly spots offer entertainment and relaxation. The college coffee shop (Charlie's) is the scene of a variety of performers, including singer-songwriters, solo artists, poets, and impromptu karaoke. Live concerts feature prominent bands and the annual Big Band concert.

Cedar Rapids offers many entertainment and dining options and is easily accessed from the campus. The college organizes events in the city, such as first-release films in local theaters, ice-skating, or bowling.

Of all Coe's tradition, Flunk Day is the most treasured. The day is a surprise holiday, announced by the slipping announcements known as "broadsides" under the doors of the residences. Flunk Day has been a rite of spring at Coe since 1911. In the early days secrecy was necessary as the skip day was against college rules. Today, merriment reigns and the campus is transformed into a carnival.

One graduate, a newspaperman, wrote that the four most significant words in the English language are: "Flunk Day is tomorrow."

If Flunk Day is a once-a-year celebration, support of the Coe College Kohawks takes place throughout the year. The name "Kohawk" has been at Coe since 1922, when the Athletic Council sponsored a competition for a college mascot; until that time, Coe's teams were known simply as the "Crimson and Gold." A deadlocked election could not decide between the "Rangers," the "Ramblers," and the "Trojans." The chairman of the German Department saved the day by explaining that "Hawks" represented "Hawkeye State" – Iowa's state nickname.

Coe Hawk was shortened to Kohawk, and the "Kohawks", Coe's ranked Division III football team plays a schedule that is at once ambitious and obscure. Those in the know understand that competition with Augustana, St. John's (Minnesota), and Gustavus Adolphus is competition of the highest order. One of these Division III powers is likely to emerge in contention for the national championship. Kohawk pride is rampant, and most Coe students are involved with athletics on the interscholastic or intramural level. Other sports involve a number of students, and the level of participation in interscholastic sports at Coe is high.

Cornell College - Mount Vernon, Iowa

Make no mistake, however, this Cornell has more than enough to offer on its own. In fact, this smaller Cornell offers a strong sense of community, tradition, an uncommonly effective teaching faculty, a great location, engaging students, and the One Course At A Time academic calendar.

And the stats... 2015

Number of Applicants: 1,915 / 74% Accepted
Undergrad Enrollment: 1,086 53% female / 47% male
Avg. SAT Reading 520-680 and Math 520 -650 Avg. ACT: 23-30
Total Cost: $50,625.00
Received some form of financial assistance: 98%

Cornell College is often confused with the larger Cornell University in Ithaca, New York. This very much smaller Cornell is one of very few colleges operating on the "One Course At A Time" educational model known more widely as the Block Plan, but when that plan is mentioned, attention usually goes to Colorado College. Make no mistake, however, this Cornell has more than enough to offer on its own. In fact, this smaller Cornell offers a strong sense of community, tradition, an uncommonly effective teaching faculty, a great location, engaging students, and the One Course At A Time academic calendar.

Since Cornell is the only college in this guide that presents course work in blocks, it makes sense to start by describing how a block plan works. The plan offers some great advantages, but I am sure any reader wants reassurance that the student does not miss out on course work that might be done in a conventional program. In fact, the number of course hours matches almost exactly the hours logged in a semester. Instead of juggling four or five courses, working on four or five sets of assignments, contending with four or five professors, a Cornell student works on one course, prepares one set of assignments, and works with one professor. In addition to the advantages concentration might bring, the students in the course share a common schedule, allowing friendships to develop. Each one is part of a small cohort working with a professor who gets to know the student very well. It's easy to identify concerns and to get extra consultation and help. Projects and class trips are easy to schedule. And, as a final enticement, the eighteen day block is followed by a four day "Block Break"; a student finishes a block on Wednesday and is free until the following Monday. In effect, the block plan allows the college to offer a "semester break" every month.

Each student takes a single course for a period of eighteen class days. The class usually runs from nine in the morning until eleven and from one to three in the afternoon. The schedule promotes close study of a subject and the opportunity to take on an internship during the block, and it also brings the mastery that can only come from total immersion. Some of the examples Cornell presents may be helpful illustrations of how the block can work. Courses in Political Science can monitor campaigns and elections in real time. A Microeconomics course of China's emerging economy can travel to China for the entire block. Imagine the luxury of preparing a performance for an entire block, uninterrupted by other duties and obligations. For example, Cornell has invited professional puppeteers from New York to work with theater students in writing, directing, designing, and performing a major production.

I've used the word "concentrated" to describe the One Course At A Time plan, but I am tempted to use the word to describe the entire Cornell experience. The entire campus is included in the National Register of Historic Places and is set squarely in the midst of Mount Vernon, Iowa, a charming small town, recently cited as one of America's Coolest Small Towns. That designation came as a writer for *Budget Magazine* wrote, "Every now and then you stumble on a town that's got everything right – great coffee, food with character, shop owners with a purpose." The town's population is small, about four thousand, and the college is a significant part of the town's culture. Cornell is located in wooded, hilly country within a half hour of Cedar Rapids and equally close to Iowa City and all the fun and frolic of the University of Iowa.

The campus itself could be described as "concentrated", not cramped or confined, but nicely proportioned so that no one facility is far from any other point on campus. Thomas Commons is at the heart of the daily experience of Cornell, not only because a particular strength of Cornell is its dining service. To be sure, Cornell's dining experience has been recognized as one of the top five in the US. The food service has determined to use local and fresh food prepared thoughtfully and offering a wide variety of choices. And, as might be expected, the folks who work in the dining hall are exceptionally friendly and responsive. The building itself has been newly renovated, which allowed the expansion of dining space and the creation of two other dining options, the Hilltop Cafe and Zamora's Market. At the heart of the building, however, is the central meeting point on campus, a space widely known as "The Orange Carpet." That space is in part performance space, meeting or lecture arena, gathering point for clubs and organizations, and a comfortable spot to lounge for a bit, expecting to see most of the student body pass by.

Residential life at Cornell is thoroughly residential; virtually all students live on campus. First year students live in one of four recently renovated dormitories, each of which has a themed common space. One offers a stage, another a game room, another a study center with individual study spaces, and the fourth an extravagantly equipped kitchen. Those areas are open to any student in any of the four dormitories. Upperclass students can live in suite-style residences or choose to live in one of the many Living and Learning Communities. Recent communities have been organized around Environmental Community Outreach, Gastronomics, Music, Artistic and Creative Expression, and Students United Against Poverty.

There are fraternities and sororities at Cornell, but they play a unique role appropriate to the college's clear sense of community. Seven fraternities and eight sororities have been around since the nineteen twenties, but none are nationally affiliated. They do not live in separate housing, and their activities are open to the entire campus. They are active in intramural sports, as is almost every student at some point in the college career. The range of recreational options runs the gamut from football, basketball, volleyball, disc golf, and softball to yoga and extreme fitness. More than one hundred clubs and organizations flourish at Cornell. Some of the less frequently found clubs include: The Archeological Society, Knot Just for Grannies, Sci Fi Club, Medieval and Renaissance Club, the Muslim Student Organization, and an active band of Cheerleaders. The campus radio station, newspaper, literary magazine, and theatrical productions join the A Cappella Vocalist Society, Slick Shoes (Dance), Wordsmiths, and the Lyrically Inclined (slam poetry and spoken word).

The co-curricular activity for which Cornell is best known, however, is the nationally ranked and widely feared Mock Trial team. Mock Trial combines the best of debate, improvisational theater, and legal strategy. Cornell's team is open to any student regardless of major, attracting a wide variety of talents necessary to competition. A single case is given each year; colleges prepare as lawyers during the pre-trial negotiations and in the presentation of the case. Other students act as witnesses or as individuals providing specialized testimony. Cornell's team has been widely successful, earning national ranking; several students have been named All-American Attorney or All -American Witness. The All-American designation is more commonly given to athletes, and Cornell can claim quite a few athletic stars. The college offers nineteen varsity teams, all of which compete in the NCAA's Division III Midwest Conference. Cornell's Rams frequently butt heads with traditional rivals, Grinnell, Lawrence, Ripon, Beloit, Knox, and Lake Forest, but the most heated may be with Coe College. The oldest football rivalry west of the Mississippi is the Cornell-Coe game, first played in 1891. The most dominant of Coe's sports currently are the wrestling and volleyball teams. Coe's wrestlers have won national championships and more than twenty All-American citations.

The women's volleyball team has captured conference championships and has advanced to national championship tournaments.

University of Iowa - Iowa City, Iowa

Iowa is a remarkable public university in that it is home to what many believe to be the strongest writing program in the United States. It is also home to one of the most highly ranked teaching hospitals and medical schools as well. In addition, the university is noted for its programs in speech pathology and nursing, and was the first university in the country to give academic credit for creative work. Iowa is an innovative, responsive, highly effective research university with a remarkable campus and extraordinary facilities.

And the stats... 2015

Number of Applicants: 24,097 / 81% Accepted
Undergrad Enrollment: 22,354 52% female / 48% male
Avg. SAT Reading 480-620 and Math 540 -7000 Avg. ACT: 23-28
Total Cost: $20,861.00 (in-state) $40,190.00 (out-of-state)
Received some form of financial assistance: 88%

The University of Iowa, also known as "Iowa" or "U of I," is hardly a well-kept secret in Iowa; twenty thousand undergraduates seem to have found out about the place. A quick trip to the Iowa admission office makes three stunning facts jump immediately into focus. Eighty percent of classes have fewer than thirty students, Fifty-six million dollars are available annually as scholarship for undergraduate students, and more than thirty Learning Living residential

In other regions, however, Iowa has missed out on the acclaim given to Michigan or Wisconsin, universities with which it should properly be compared. The rest of the Big Ten are certainly notable universities, and each has its own particular strength. Indiana University, for example, has world-class school of music, and Purdue's engineers have helped land man on the moon.

Iowa is a remarkable public university in that it is home to what many believe to be the strongest writing program in the United States. It is also home to one of the most highly ranked teaching hospitals and medical schools as well. In addition, the university is noted for its programs in speech pathology and nursing, and was the first university in the country to give academic credit for creative work. Iowa is an innovative, responsive, highly effective research university with a remarkable campus and extraordinary facilities.

The campus is enormous – 1900 acres of beautifully manicured lawns, elegant buildings, and the Iowa River, which splits the campus into an east campus and a west campus.

The center of the campus is a remarkable constellation of five historic buildings known as the Pentacrest. The heart of the city and of the campus, the Pentacrest is made up of the Old Capital Building, and four lecture halls, each of which is stately and impressive. The campus also contains two notable museums in addition to state-of-the-art classrooms, athletic facilities, residences, fraternities, sororities, and an athletic hall of fame.

All of the academic programs are excellent and are organized into eleven divisions – College of Liberal Arts and Sciences, Tippe College of Business, College of Engineering, College of Pharmacy, College of Education, College of Nursing, Graduate College, College of Law, Carver College of Medicine, College of Dentistry, College of Public Health, and University College.

One of the points of pride with the University's historians is that Iowa was the first university in the United States to admit men and women on an equal basis in 1855.

The Iowa Writer's Workshop was founded in 1936 and has produced thirteen Pulitzer Prize winners. Members of the writing faculty are Pulitzer winners as well, and have included such luminaries as Philip Roth and Kurt Vonnegut.

The Daily Iowan, an ambitious and highly regarded student newspaper is published every day from Monday through Friday, entirely staffed by student writers and editors. Opportunities abound in all branches of communication including film, video, and television. The university's television station provides coverage of local and national events and is a public television station.

Student life is active – perhaps notorious; Iowa was included in the annual survey of the top "party schools" in the Unites States. Iowa City is an active college town, and the university has supported a number of civic enterprises that bring entertainment to the city and to the university. There are a number of events that mark the progress of the year – Homecoming, Family Weekend, Riverfest, and the Cultural Diversity Festival.

One major form of recreation and entertainment is in following the Iowa Hawkeye athletic program, and most notably, Hawkeye football. "Herky the Hawk" Iowa's mascot, appears at football games and at other occasions as needed. Iowa competes in the Division I Big Ten Conference, and enjoys annual contests with in-state rival, Iowa State.

Football is king in the Big Ten, but the Hawkeyes have long been the dominant wrestling power in college athletics, sending many athletes into Olympic competition. Wrestling hasn't captured the following that some other sports enjoy in other regions, but here in Iowa, wrestling is a very big deal. *Sports Illustrated* named the Iowa wrestling program one of the "sports dynasties" of the Twentieth Century. Iowa is also noted for men's gymnastics and women's field hockey, baseball and softball. In all, Iowa competes at the Division I level in twenty-four varsity sports.

Iowa football attracts a crowd of eighty thousand to its stadium, and another twenty thousand to various celebratory tailgates nearby. The competition in the Big Ten is pronounced, but Iowa has played the spoiler in several seasons, and most recently won a major victory over undefeated Michigan State. Football weekends are impressively extreme, and school spirit at Iowa is equally evident.

Minnesota

The word, "Minnesota" is taken from the Dakota term for "sky tinted waters," and the state is properly known for its ten thousand lakes. Minnesota is a recreational wonderland, although its northern territories are among the coldest places reported each winter. And, the stories you have heard about the mosquito being the state bird are mostly true. But there are no warmer, more welcoming, people than Minnesotans – from International Falls to St. Cloud.

The state is Germanic and Scandinavian in its European heritage, and in the "Iron Range" probably a bit more Finnish and Swedish than the lower portions of the state. The Dakota and Ojibwe met the Sioux in Minnesota and reservation lands are found throughout the state.

For the purposes of this book, there are two Minnesotas – one centered on the Twin Cities of Minneapolis and Saint Paul and the outlying and more northerly sections of the state. Several of the state universities and colleges are found in the north, most notably Bemidji State University and Moorhead State University. St. Cloud State University and Mankato State University are located in the lower half of the state, closer to the Twin Cities.

The colleges and universities profiled in this book are positioned in relation to "The Cities."

The University of Minnesota (known as the "Golden Gophers") is the most highly esteemed of Minnesota's universities, offering a comprehensive university experience in the city of Minneapolis. Minnesota is a highly regarded member of the Big Ten and an outstanding research university.

Hamline University and Macalester College are both nicely set in Saint Paul. Macalester is one of the top liberal arts colleges in the region and well known across the nation. Hamline is an excellent small university, profiled in this book.

Northfield, Minnesota is south of The Cities and north of Rochester. The outlaw Jesse James pulled a bank robbery in Northfield, but today, the charming town is best known as the location of Carleton College, recently ranked the eighth best liberal arts college in the country, and St. Olaf College, one of the highly ranked colleges profiled in this book. Northfield is less than an hour's drive from Minneapolis.

Saint John's University and Saint Benedict's College are adjacent to each other in Collegeville, Minnesota northwest of The Cities and just west of St. Cloud. Collegeville is about an hour and twenty minutes from Minneapolis.

Gustavus Adolphus is located in St. Peter, a small city southwest of The Cities and north of Mankato. St. Peter is about an hour and a half from The Cities.

Hamline University - Saint Paul, Minnesota

Hamline is diverse, and as a result, many student activities are remarkably inclusive. For example, the Hmong Student Association supports Hmong students on campus but also works to bring the Hmong experience to the wider student body. The same could be said of the Asian Pacific Coalition or Fusion, the network for multiethnic and multiracial students.

And the stats... 2015

Number of Applicants: 3,417 / 70% Accepted
Undergrad Enrollment: 2,242 58% female / 42% male
Avg. SAT Reading 470-610 and Math 480 -570 Avg. ACT: 21-27
Total Cost: $47,862.00
Received some form of financial assistance: 100%

Hamline is in an advantaged neighborhood called Hamline-Midway, about halfway between the heart of Saint Paul and central Minneapolis. The area is a quiet, residential neighborhood, known as an active and safe community. There are also approximately seven hundred businesses located in the Hamline-Midway area and easy access to any point in the Twin Cities.

Hamline is a rare example of a small and extremely successful comprehensive university located in a residential area of a major city. As a result, Hamline's students have the opportunity to explore city life without having to be tossed into the hurly burly of city living. Ninety percent of first year students live on campus, and most continue in student housing - which includes residential halls, housing by special interest groups, and apartment style housing.

What would bring a student from another region to Hamline?

The students - Hamline's eighteen hundred undergraduates are ambitious, positive, friendly, and engaged; they are an unusual student cohort, and visitors from other regions are uniformly impressed with Hamline's students.

Internships - One hundred percent of undergraduates complete an internship, collaborative, field-based research or service-learning project. A recent grant added another $300,00.00 to pay students on internships.

Scholarship – Twenty-four students in the last thirteen years have won Fulbright Scholarships.

Diversity – Hamline currently enrolls a student body that is approximately twenty-eight percent people of color.

Service – Year in and year out, Hamline is recognized by the President's Higher Education Community Service Honor Roll for community service and civic engagement.

A Guarantee – Hamline guarantees that an enrolled student will earn a bachelor's degree in four years or they pay the difference.

A Plan – Although the Hamline School of Law and the Hamline School of Business are on campus, the undergraduate program includes the Hamline Plan, a general education program that teaches critical thinking, communication skills, and problem solving. The plan is intended to provide a broad background applicable to any major and to meet the expectations employers have of college graduates.

Hamline offers more than fifty areas of study, including all of the liberal arts and pre-professional majors as well as Accounting, Athletic Training, Chinese, Criminal Justice, Education, Exercise and Sports Science, Forensic Science, International Business, Latin American Studies, Italian, Linguistics, Marketing, Urban Studies and Social Justice.

Academically the university delivers, promising small classes (student-to-faculty ratio is 12:1) and consistent mentoring. This is a university that believes in preparing its graduates for the world of work and for a life of civic responsibility; career development and placement is outstanding.

In addition, Hamline maintains partnerships with several universities outside of the United States. Hamline students may take courses for credit at the Universitat Trier in Germany, the Universidad Catolica de Valparaiso in Chile, the Universite Gaston Berger in Senegal, and the Akita International University in Japan.

Outside of the classroom, a lot is in motion much of the time. Varsity teams are good and are well supported, and the variety of people and interests on campus is impressive.

Hamline is diverse, and as a result, many student activities are remarkably inclusive. For example, the Hmong Student Association supports Hmong students on campus but also works to bring the Hmong experience to the wider student body. The same could be said of the Asian Pacific Coalition or Fusion, the network for multiethnic and multiracial students.

Wonderfully creative groups have emerged, identifying themselves with a sly sense of humor:

Knitwits – the knitting club; Merely Players – a theater–going club; HUGS – the Hamline University Gaming Society; Mamadada – club sponsoring the all campus arts show; and the Broke Starving Writer's Club – evidently a writing group.

Many students are involved with service and community, and a number of organization and associations assist in organizing those efforts.

Debate and journalism thrive, and the Student Congress is an effective and well–respected governmental agency within the university. Students report that the Congress is effective and responsive to student voices. A capella singing, orchestral music, and theater are all alive and well, and students are pleased by the facilities in these areas.

While there is no stereotypical "Hamline Student," most work hard and care about their work. Social life and community life are balanced with rigorous study.

Athletic teams at Hamline are known as, "The Pipers," and compete most notably in basketball and ice hockey. Both men and women have won regional championships in hockey, and the basketball team is the stuff of legend, among the most successful over a very long period of competition.

In fact, Hamline considers itself the "birthplace of collegiate basketball," as the sport was brought to the college only a year after its invention. The men's team had its first game in 1895 and the women a year later. Baseball and swimming are also strong, as is women's volleyball and softball.

Both men and women can play lacrosse on Club Teams, as well as having the opportunity to become involved with ultimate frisbee, club ice hockey, and club soccer. Some of the recreational options include rock climbing, outdoor recreation, a cycling club, and the Quidditch Flying Pipers.

For the earnest student eager to live and learn in a safe and active city setting, Hamline may the best–kept secret of them all.

St. Olaf College - Northfield, Minnesota

"Oles" have fun and frolic, just like real college students, and the spirit on campus is good. Athletic events are well supported; many more attend football games than attend chapel. The rivalry with Carleton always provides some cheer, and local traditions like the Midnight Breakfast served at before the start of exams and the Lutefest spring concert give some notion of what this wholesome and healthy college experience is all about. It is a rare college that is able to create the strength of community Oles feel while challenging them with a powerful academic experience.

And the stats... 2015

Number of Applicants: 4,875 / 51% Accepted
Undergrad Enrollment: 3,034 58% female / 42% male
Avg. SAT Reading 560-700 and Math 570 -690 Avg. ACT: 27-34
Total Cost: $53,100.00
Received some form of financial assistance: 89%

St. Olaf College is a Lutheran College steeped in the tradition of the Lutheran colleges. Located in Northfield, Minnesota, across town from Carleton, St. Olaf is probably best known for its outstanding program in choral music. St. Olaf's choir is featured each Christmas Eve in broadcasts seen and heard around the world. Music is HUGE at St. Olaf's, but math is equally reputed, and the college's international initiatives send St. Olaf's students to 110 off-campus programs. In fact, students can pick from more than one hundred and ten off-campus programs, including international programs that draw about seven hundred students a year into study abroad. By the time they graduate, about two-thirds will have studied outside the United States.

St. Olaf is handsome, beautifully maintained, offering a giant variety of courses to about three thousand students from across the country and around the world.

There's no way around the Scandinavian and Lutheran character of this college; this is a college founded by Norwegians, and the current student body looks more Scandinavian than any outside of northern Minnesota, but St. Olaf welcomes students from all 50 states and 30 countries; about 15% of St. Olaf's students are people of color. Since 1996, St. Olaf's has produced more Rhodes Scholars than any liberal arts college in the country. The question, I know, for kids from outside the region, and outside the Lutheran faith, is whether there is room on this spectacular campus for other denominations, other religions, perhaps even (gasp) nonbelievers.

My observation is that those commendable and very attractive Midwestern virtues of kindness and hard work really do prevail. The Lutheran thing is important to the College, but only about 200 of the 2000 students make it to the daily chapel service. "Oles" have fun and frolic, just like real college students, and the spirit on campus is good. Athletic events are well supported; many more attend football games than attend chapel. The rivalry with Carleton always provides some cheer, and local traditions like the Midnight Breakfast served at before the start of exams and the Lutefest spring concert give some notion of what this wholesome and healthy college experience is all about. It is a rare college that is able to create the strength of community Oles feel while challenging them with a powerful academic experience.

Everyone has a slightly different sense of what makes a college handsome, and there are some who prefer Carleton's yellow hue, but I find the three hundred acre hillside campus of St. Olaf to have more perfectly blended the traditional and the modern. Many of St. Olaf's buildings are exceedingly good looking - as are its students.

But these are not just a bunch of apple-cheeked Lutherans dashing around a handsome campus; in stunning opposition to the choices made at other liberal arts colleges, Math is the second most popular major. In fact, St. Olaf is nationally recognized as a Math powerhouse. How this can be with an internationally celebrated program in Music, I do not know, but somehow, St. Olaf manages to attract a remarkable and remarkably talented group of students. One measure of the strength of the academic program at St. Olaf is in the number of graduating students who have been nominated for the most prestigious fellowships and scholarships available. It is remarkable that St. Olaf has had five Rhodes Scholars since 1995 and ninety-nine Fulbright Scholars. The level of academic rigor is impressive; students describe their experience in the classroom as incredible.

There are regulations about alcohol on campus, and although off-campus parties do exist, the general level of social life is fairly healthy and improbably happy. St. Olaf's students love their college, have a great time, and go on to become contributive members of their community. The college regularly hosts more than a hundred activities, clubs, and organizations. Much is made of music at St. Olaf, and that celebrity is well deserved; in addition to the ambitions of the Chorale, the college's Jazz ensemble, was recently honored by Downbeat Magazine as the best in the country. They will travel to Cuba over spring break to play with Cuban musicians. Theater is strong, and the dance program offers merit scholarships to exceptional dancers.

The "Oles" play in Division III in the Minnesota Interscholastic Athletic Conference, the MIAC, generally at their best in swimming and diving, although the men's cross-country team has recently emerged as dominant in the conference. Most anticipated perhaps is the traditional football rivalry with neighbor Carleton College, in place since 1919. The annual "Cereal Bowl," pits the Oles against the Carls for zip code dominance, and the event is always the highlight of a fairly chilly late fall. Football is not the only sport claiming enthusiastic support. as the "Oles" participate in all the traditional sports as well as Alpine and Nordic skiing for men and women and wrestling for men.

Saint John's University - Collegeville, Minnesota

The College of Saint Benedict - Collegeville, Minnesota

The relationship between Saint John's and Saint Benedict is best described as a collegiate partnership. These are two separate colleges, about three miles apart, on a shared expanse of land of about three thousand acres. The huge campus includes forests, prairie, and lakes – it is an incredible resource. The colleges share the legacy of the Benedictine Order and both are administered by the Benedictines. Roughly sixty percent of enrolled students are Catholic, but the university and the college actively welcome individuals of any background or faith. There are no required religion classes.

And the stats... 2015
Saint John's
Number of Applicants: 1,469 / 79% Accepted
Undergrad Enrollment: 1,789 100% male
Avg. SAT Reading 480-620 and Math 490-600 Avg. ACT: 23-29
Total Cost: $50,384.00
Received some form of financial assistance: 100%

College of Saint Benedict
 Number of Applicants: 1,768 / 82% Accepted
Undergrad Enrollment: 2,020 100% female
Avg. SAT Reading 520-620 and Math 480-620 Avg. ACT: 23-29
Total Cost: $51,759.00
Received some form of financial assistance: 100%

I see a number of families that want to apply to Notre Dame, primarily because they like the tradition and spirit that animates the university. Notre Dame is in that group of exceedingly competitive universities, however, and Notre Dame expects freshmen to be able to thrive in a core curriculum that includes calculus. In searching for a college option that offers much of the best of the Notre Dame experience, I have found that the college that comes closest is St. John's University in Minnesota.

There are a bunch of St. John's across the country; St. John's in New York City is a Catholic basketball powerhouse, and the St. John's in Santa Fe and Annapolis are "Great Books" colleges, ideal for the broadly intellectual true student of the liberal arts.

The Collegeville, Minnesota St. John's is a college for men and is attached at the hip to Saint Benedict's College for Women. Both offer exceptionally solid instruction and well regarded preparation for graduate and professional programs. What sets St. John's apart is a healthy tradition of athletic achievement and the active involvement of most of the student body in a sport of some kind. Between interscholastic and intramural teams, 97% of "Johnnies" are sweating every day. The football team is a perennial finalist in Division III championship play, and the coach, John Gagllardi, in his coaching career of more than sixty years has won the most victories of any coach in the NCAA. The excitement surrounding St. John's teams is part of the high level of spirit and morale on this campus.

In addition, the Benedictine Abbey Church on campus was designed by preeminent Bauhaus architect, Marcel Breuer; the Abbey Church is considered one of the signature buildings in collegiate architecture. The Church is one of eight Breuer buildings on campus, making Saint John's among the most consistently designed college campuses. St. John's is a Benedictine college, and the Benedictine order has generally been less directive in its management of education than the Jesuits. Most of the students at St. John's are Catholic, but there is no required religious observance and students of other faiths are welcome. The two thousand seven hundred acres of the St. John's campus are remarkably inviting, including the central campus, prairie, hiking trails, lakes, and wetlands.

There are two hallmarks that signify the health of this partnership.

The first is that more than ninety percent of first year students return for the second year. The rate of retention and the glowing description of the quality of instruction speak to the academic health of the institutions. The extraordinary expression of school spirit on both campuses defines this unusual partnership as highly successful.

The second is that admission to graduate programs and the high proportion of students studying abroad indicates that mentoring and advising work well on both campuses.

The relationship between Saint John's and Saint Benedict is best described as a collegiate partnership. These are two separate colleges, about three miles apart, on a shared expanse of land of about three thousand acres. The huge campus includes forests, prairie, and lakes – it is an incredible resource. The colleges share the legacy of the Benedictine Order and both are administered by the Benedictines. Roughly sixty percent of enrolled students are Catholic, but the university and the college actively welcome individuals of any background or faith. There are no required religion classes.

Each college has its own campus and its own traditions. Both colleges have access to the same resources and share instruction. Classes are co-ed; residences are single-sex.

The College of Saint Benedict is the only Benedictine college for women in the country, currently enrolling about two thousand women, many of whom have been attracted by the college's highly successful Institute for Women's Leadership and the spectacular Benedicta Arts Center.

The Benedict Blazers play in Division III and are very well supported by fans and spectators. Roughly forty percent of Saint Benedict's students play on one or more of the college's twelve varsity sports. Saint John's may get the press, but Saint Benedict's has won fifteen basketball championships and is often represented in post-season play in most sports.

The Johnnies of Saint John's are among the most successful athletic powers in collegiate sports. Long a preeminent football power, Saint John's made conference history by winning Minnesota Intercollegiate Athletic Conference championships in all four fall sports in the same season. Football, soccer, cross country and golf were all MIIC champs, and the golf team went on in the spring to win the Division III national title.

Both rugby and lacrosse are also strong. The rugby team has been established for more than forty years and competes against Division II colleges. Lacrosse competes in the Upper Midwest Lacrosse League.

438

University of Missouri - Columbia, Missouri

What sets the experience at the University of Missouri apart from other state universities?

An incredibly beautiful and thoughtfully designed campus, for a start.

A healthy (and I mean HUGE) Greek system balanced with hipsters, hippies, apple-cheeked farm kids, serious science nerds, enterprising proto-entrepreneurs, literary types, slam poets, superb musicians and actors, and world-class athletes.

An athletic program that attracts support across every sub-group, creating uncommonly high morale throughout the year and enormous pride in Tiger teams.

And the stats... 2015

Number of Applicants: 21,163 / 78% Accepted
Undergrad Enrollment: 27,642 52% female / 48% male
Avg. SAT Reading 520-650 and Math 530 -660 Avg. ACT: 23-29
Total Cost: $23,597.00 (in-state) $38,624.00
Received some form of financial assistance: 81%

The University of Missouri is a big (slightly fewer than twenty-eight thousand undergraduates), complicated (one of six universities in the nation that has a medical school, a vet school, and a law school), that somehow manages to make its students feel spirited, happy, competent, and hugely proud of their Mizzou Tigers. The range of academic strengths is exceptional as is the responsive mentoring given to incoming students. Public universities often lose a considerable number of students between the freshman and sophomore year; 87% of enrolled students return for the sophomore year at Missouri.

We'll be looking in depth at Missouri's incredible programs in Journalism and the Performing Arts, but the one quality of the collegiate experience that we have not spent much time in exploring is fun, and the University of Missouri is fun.

I don't mean to suggest that Mizzou is not an academic institution of national reputation or anything less than effective; it is a very good, highly regarded, and ambitious university - and it is fun to be a student at Mizzou.

What sets the experience at the University of Missouri apart from other state universities?

An incredibly beautiful and thoughtfully designed campus, for a start.
A healthy (and I mean HUGE) Greek system balanced with hipsters, hippies, apple-cheeked farm kids, serious science nerds, enterprising proto-entrepreneurs, literary types, slam poets, superb musicians and actors, and world-class athletes.

An athletic program that attracts support across every sub-group, creating uncommonly high morale throughout the year and enormous pride in Tiger teams.

Once again, I wish I could plunk every reader down right in the middle of this campus in order to begin to communicate the stunning quality of this university's setting. Columbia is a small city of about one hundred thousand, equidistant from Kansas City and Saint Louis. It is one of the cities most frequently mentioned as among the best cities in which to live. In addition to the activities available on campus, the city of Columbia has a thriving cultural and entertainment life easily accessed by students and visitors.

The entire campus is registered by the State of Missouri as a botanical garden. The oldest part of the campus (the Red Campus) is the center of the academic buildings and is largely made of red brick. The somewhat newer Gothic White campus is crafted of native Missouri limestone. The fabulous Memorial Union, which could have been picked up at Duke and dropped in Columbia, is a prime example of limestone architecture at its best.

The athletic facilities at Mizzou are stunningly extensive. An entire Sports Park has brought together the Arena, two stadiums, playing fields, practice fields, the gymnasium and field house. How extensive are the resources available to students? The Recreation Center is about three hundred thousand square feet. And, for balance, entire campuses are set aside for the medical facilities, the Research Center, including the University of Missouri Reactor Research Center. Oh, and then, residential real estate worth millions of dollars abuts the eastern and western edges of the university in order to accommodate the approximately seventy fraternities and sororities.

The University of Missouri has a law school, a med, school, a vet school, and the largest reactor of any university in the country. Obviously, it has numerous academic strengths. Rather than enumerate every possible major and minor concentration, this profile is going to concentrate on two programs that are widely recognized as simply preeminent.

The first of these is the "J School- the Missouri School of Journalism. The "J" School was the first school of journalism in the United States and still accounted one of the finest in the world. Any aspiring journalist should certainly consider Mizzou in the company of programs such as Northwestern, Syracuse and Columbia, which are excellent but predominantly graduate level programs. The program at Missouri is characterized by what is known as "the Missouri Method" - a mixture of classroom instruction and lots of hands-on experience. That method begins as early as the freshman year and offers aspiring journalists the opportunity to get involved with any of the media outlets the university sponsors. The classroom work is done on a separate journalism campus, adjacent to the central, Red Campus, academic cluster. The journalism quadrangle is equally impressive architecturally.

The hands-on approach takes journalism students to the highly regarded Columbia Missourian a web-first newspaper that operates twenty-four hours a day and is considered one of the best newspapers in the region. Or, the more internationally minded might gravitate to Global Journalist, directed to journalists, covering developments in global journalism. Some will enjoy broadcasting on KBIA, the NPR station that features programs from Public Radio International and which develops professional broadcasters from the university. Some will join the staff of KOMU, the only university owned commercial television station that allows students to operate a newsroom as a working journalism laboratory. Others may join MOJO Ad, the student-staffed professional advertising agency or Missouri Digital News.

Classroom instruction includes concentration in the following major areas: Arts and Culture Journalism, Business and Economic Journalism, Convergence Photojournalism, Convergence Radio Reporting and Producing, Convergence Television Reporting, Emerging Media, Entrepreneurial Journalism, International Strategic Communication, Magazine Design, Magazine Publishing and Management, Magazine Writing, Multimedia Producing, Multi Platform Design, News Design, News Editing, News Reporting, Photojournalism, Radio-Television producing, Radio-Television Reporting, Science and Health Journalism, Sports Journalism, Strategic Communication/ Account Management/ Art Direction/ Copywriting/ Interactive, Media Planning/ Research, Visual Editing and Management, and Watchdog Journalism.

Whew!

Now, to the Performing Arts, specifically Theater and Music.

The major concentrations in Theater are made available through the university's college of Arts and Sciences and include a liberal arts core curriculum. The Theater program offers the B.A., M.A., and the Ph.D. but has produced numbers of actors, writers, and stage technicians from the undergraduate program. In addition, the university sponsors special programs such as the World Theatre Workshop, Interactive Theatre, Troubling Violence Project and Missouri Playwrights Workshop, creating a diverse community of aspiring theatre artists and scholars

The School of Music offers the B.A., the B. Mus., the B.S. in Music Education, and the Jazz Certificate Minor. The B.A. is not a professional music degree and allows the undergrad to pursue a variety of other interests during the course of a four-year career at Mizzou. The Bachelor of Music degree is a professional degree allowing the student to pursue a major in Performance (brass, classical guitar, percussion, piano, strings, voice, or woodwinds), Music Theory, Music History, or Composition. The Bachelor of Science Degree in Music Education is a professional degree, preparing teachers of music. The Jazz Certificate program includes performance, composition, improvisation, harmony, and ensemble.

OK, so Mizzou is an exceptional academic and professional university. It is also an athletic powerhouse, sending Tiger teams to competition in the Southeast Conference (SEC) of the NCAA's Division I. Once part of the Big Twelve, and traditional rival of Kansas University (Rock, Chalk, Jayhawk!), Missouri shifted conferences to enter into the toughest football conference, now playing against LSU, Alabama, and Florida.

The West

It's presumption, I know, to lump an area from Iowa to California in one chunk, but the number of profiled colleges outside of California is slim. The concentration of colleges is lower, in the first place, and population in the western states is thin in some regions.

Nebraska, the Cornhusker State, is north of Missouri and Kansas on the Great Plains. The capital city of Lincoln is also the home of the University of Nebraska. Not far from Lincoln is Hastings, Nebraska, the city in which Kool-Aid was created in nineteen twenty seven. Kool-Aid Days are still celebrated in Hastings on the second weekend in August. The state's largest city is Omaha, location of Creighton University, an outstanding Jesuit university with an enrollment of about five thousand undergraduates.

Montana is both a mountain state and a plains state. The western third of the state is the most visited, gateway to Yellowstone and Glacier Parks. Both the University of Montana in Missoula and Montana State in Bozeman are in the western third of Montana. Only Billings has a population in excess of one hundred thousand; Missoula and Great Falls are the next largest with a population approaching fifty thousand.

Colorado is also a state with many borders, adjoining Nebraska, Kansas Wyoming, New Mexico, Utah, Oklahoma, and Arizona. Of course, Colorado also offers access to the Southern Rocky Mountains as well as the Great Plains. As a result, Colorado is considered one of the Western States, one of the Mountain States, and one of the Southwestern States. Denver is roughly in the center of the state. Boulder is northwest of Denver; Colorado Springs is due south. Golden, home of the Colorado School of Mines, is west of Denver.

New Mexico is truly the Land of Enchantment, offering stunning landscapes and a window into the past. The state flag is red and gold with the luminescent symbol of the sun significant to the Pueblo people of the Southwest. Keresan is one of the languages still spoken in the state, as well as Spanish and English. Native Americans play an important part in the history of the state and remain a vibrant culture. The capital of the state is Santa Fe, where the Santa Fe University of Art and Design and a campus of saint John's College (The Great Books College) are located. It will come as no surprise that the University of New Mexico at Albuquerque is found in Albuquerque, the state's largest city, as is the Art Center Design College. New Mexico State University's main campus is in Las Cruces, and the New Mexico Institute of Mining and Technology, profiled in this book, is found in Socorro.

Arizona, the Grand Canyon State, offers a wonderful variety of climate and landscape, from the pine forests of Flagstaff to Saguaro National Park on the eastern edge of Tucson. About one quarter of the state is federal land, home to the Navajo nation, the Hopi tribe, and many other tribes and nations. Arizona supports three large public universities – the University of Arizona in Tucson, Arizona State in Tempe, and Northern Arizona University in Flagstaff; NAU is profiled in this book. Prescott College, also profiled, is located in the charming and historic town of Prescott, former capital of the Arizona Territory, about halfway between Flagstaff to the northeast and Phoenix to the southeast.

Montana State University - Bozeman, Montana

Specific programs are just a few of the excellent opportunities available at a great price in one of the most heart-stopping settings. MSU is among the most productive in graduating Goldwater Scholars and is home to the Museum of the Rockies. The dorms are good, the skiing starts in October, Yellowstone is at your door, and Bozeman is a great college town.

And the stats... 2015

Number of Applicants: 13,799/ 84% Accepted
Undergrad Enrollment: 13,298 56% female / 44% male
Avg. SAT Reading 510-630 and Math 500 -630 Avg. ACT: 21-28
Total Cost: $19,760.00 in-state $34,351.00 out-of-state
Received some form of financial assistance: 87%

How on earth could a university have anything more to offer than Montana State? Beautiful Bozeman, an academic program of incredible breadth and depth, a Division I athletic program... OH... and with an annual total cost of about twenty-three thousand dollars for in-state students and thirty-eight thousand for out-of state students. No wonder almost half of MSU's students are from outside Montana.

The western third of Montana is breathtakingly beautiful. Both Missoula and Bozeman are heaven for skiers, campers, hikers, fishermen and rafters who swarm to the area to take full advantage of the vast outdoor experiences available.

Visitors to Bozeman can explore the surrounding mountains including Bridger, Gallatin and the Tobacco Root Range that provide some of the finest skiing in the West. Bozeman is also the gateway to the Gallatin National Forest, Custer National Forest, and Yellowstone National Park, and is a curious feel of a modernized western town and comfortable college town. Fly fisherman already know about Bozeman and appreciate the opportunity to shop at Simms Fishing Products.

Each of the cities has its own considerable charm and each of Montana's public universities is remarkable in its own way. MSU is Montana's Land Grant university now known as the Bobcats, but originally the Aggies. There was a time when Montana had the skiers and MSU had the cowboys;

those days are long gone. Montana State and Bozeman are pretty hip and slick these days, although the rodeo team does remain world class.

Like other Land Grant institutions, MSU is extremely strong in the natural sciences and in those sciences as applied to Agriculture, Engineering, Business, and Nursing. There are three other uncommonly successful programs at MSU, however, and they deserve mention in this short profile.

Paleontology. Who knew? Montana State is not only a hotbed of speculative and theoretical paleontology, offered as a major through the College of Arts and Sciences in the Earth Science Department, but also a major research institution, sending both undergraduate and graduate paleontologists out into the field. I confess that I had no idea what paleontologists did until I encountered the MSU initiative. From what I can gather, research has gone in three directions. The first has to do with theropods (the group of primarily carnivorous dinosaurs that includes birds) from the Cretaceous of Montana and abroad (China, Africa, Argentina). A recent project involves the documentation of reproductive features within the theropod–bird lineage.

OK.

The second area is study of fossil eggs, dinosaur reproductive biology and paleoecology, and the evolution of reproductive traits in birds.

Uh huh.

And the third?

Taphonomy of bone beds and nesting grounds, deciphering processes of fossil preservation, and paleoenvironmental reconstruction of fossil-bearing strata, including both vertebrate and invertebrate fossils in marine and terrestrial deposits.

All of which takes students out into every corner of Montana and the world. One of the most notable efforts to protect fossils on federal land was organized by professors and students at MSU.

The next extraordinary area of accomplishment has to do with biotechnological research. I first became aware of the incredible resources at Montana State when some of the brightest kids I knew spent an internship summer in Bozeman working on developing grass seed that would only grow to a predetermined height – no need to mow the lawn...ever!

The programs at MSU are not only innovative, but also directed toward commercial application. The university directs more than one hundred million dollars in research annually. In the academic areas, ground breaking research is done in: agricultural biotechnology; laser/optical engineering; infectious diseases; life in extreme environments; engineering and applied science, including environmental engineering; molecular and cellular biology.

The commercial applications are often developed at the Montana State University Innovation Campus, located on approximately 100 acres adjacent to the Montana State campus. Innovation Campus provides an environment that assists and supports start-up companies and state-of-the-art facilities for well-established companies. Faculty, researchers, and scientists work with private and government researchers and scientists to push forward cutting-edge science; students gain hands-on learning experiences and often author research papers, and in some case, file patents that turn out to be quite valuable.

What kinds of facilities and equipment are made available at the Innovation Campus? How about an Animal Resources Center, a CBE Microscopy Facility Imaging and Chemical Analysis Laboratory, a Magnetic Resonance Laboratory, a Plant Growth Center the Spatial Sciences Center, a Subzero Science and Engineering Research Facility, and a Transportation and ITS Laboratory. Biotech work done by undergrads has taken them into biofilm engineering with bacterial biofilms, bio-inspired nanomaterials, optical technology, and sub-zero science and technology.

Fantastic!

The third area in which Montana State is making a name for itself is in the School of Film and Photography. The school offers a wide range of courses in film and video production, but has established expertise in an arena not often considered - Science and Natural History Filmmaking.

This was the first program to take on the specific challenges of filming Natural History and in its success has become the most celebrated program of its kind in the world. Graduates are highly prized and are among the most prolific Natural Science documentations working today. MSU's grads have been broadcast on The Discovery Channel, National Geographic, The Science Channel, CNN, Sixty Minutes II, Larry King, CBS Evening News, and NBC Nightly News. In addition, MSU's filmmakers have provided major work for museums and conservatory agencies, for the National Park Service, the National Science Foundation, the Department of Agriculture, NOAA, NASA, the Wildlife Conservation Society, the Sierra Club, the Audubon Society, and the Nature Conservancy.

Where does the footage come from? Literally from around the world - the Pribilof Islands to Easter Island, the Galapagos, Australia, Japan, Mongolia, Africa, Chile, and under the seas.

These specific programs are just a few of the excellent opportunities available at a great price in one of the most heart-stopping settings. MSU is among the most productive in graduating Goldwater Scholars and is home to the Museum of the Rockies. The dorms are good, the skiing starts in October, Yellowstone is at your door, and Bozeman is a great college town.

For the fourteen thousand undergraduate students, Bozeman offers bison burgers, wood fired pizzas, monster burritos, and great music. While I have highlighted three specific and highly unique programs, it would a great mistake to miss some of the other exceptional programs – such as the major in Equine Science, a rigorous program in Architecture, an increasingly celebrated program in Music Technology, the Space Science Engineering Lab, and the great work done by the Ethicats – MSU's team competing at the Ethics Bowl.

Montana State's Bobcats compete in the Big Sky Conference against such traditional rivals as the Grizzlies of Montana, Northern Arizona's Lumberjacks, the Vikings of Portland State, and the Weber State Wildcats. There is no doubt that the most successful Bobcat team is the rodeo team, winner of eight national championships and host to thirty College National Finals Rodeos. The Bobcat Alpine and Nordic ski teams are also exceptionally successful, producing athletes who compete at the highest level in their sport.

University of Montana - Missoula, Montana

The Wildlife Biology Program allows students experiential opportunities to work with wildlife populations from bison, moose, and bears to sage grouse and eagles. Students use resources available at Glacier National Park and Yellowstone National Park and at the National Bison range, less than an hour from campus. Many are encouraged to study outside the ordinary curriculum, exploring watershed hydrology, fish biology, and fisheries. Or, looking beyond the US, students can spend nine weeks in Botswana working with Wildlife Africa Conservation Team.

And the stats... 2015

Number of Applicants: 5,345 / 93% Accepted
Undergrad Enrollment: 11,692 93% female / 47% male
Avg. SAT Reading 480-610 and Math 490 -590 Avg. ACT: 20-26
Total Cost: $17,909.00 (in-state) $34,102.00 (out-of-state)
Received some form of financial assistance: 100%

Missoula is the location of Norman Maclean's *A River Runs Through It* and so equally well known by fly fishermen everywhere. The famous line from the novel is often quoted by natives of Missoula, particularly when discussing the difference between their college town and Bozeman. "...the world outside, which my brother and I soon discovered was full of bastards, the number increasing rapidly the farther one gets from Missoula, Montana." Missoula is known as the Hub of Five Valleys, the Bitterroot feeds into the Clark Fork on the southwest side of town, and the Big Blackfoot River meets the Clark on the east side of town. Missoula is about three hours from Glacier and a bit farther from Yellowstone. Great skiing, however, is within a thirty-minute drive.

The two college towns may have a rivalry, but these two institutions have few rivals outside the state. The University of Montana enjoys all the benefits of easily accessible outdoor recreation and is often included in Outdoor Magazines list of top ten schools for students who love the outdoors. As the elder of the two prominent universities in the state, UM is the flagship university, divided into colleges, each of which serves a particular academic mission. Undergraduates on the Missoula campus may enroll in the College of Humanities and Sciences, the College of Forestry and Conservation, the Phyllis J. Washington College of Education and Human Sciences, the College of Visual and Performing Arts, Davidson

Honors College, the School of Business Administration, and the School of Journalism.

Each of the colleges has notable strengths, but certain programs are distinctive or unique. Within the Humanities and Sciences. A vibrant program in Ethics and Public Affairs is hosted by the Mureen and Mike Mansfield Ethics Center. The English Department hosts Montana's Creative Writing Program, one of the oldest and highly regarded writing programs. Regional poet Richard Hugo described his involvement with the Montana's Writing Program, "A creative writing class may be one of the last places you can go where your life still matters." Within the College of Education, an exceptional program in Communicative Science and Disorders prepares professionals working with acquired and developmental disorders of speech, language, and hearing. The School of Journalism considers Print/Photo Journalism and Radio/TV, but students at work as journalists during their undergraduate career explore the changing face of journalism as they are involved as writers and reporters in virtually every medium. The School of Business Administration offers majors in Accounting and Finance, Management and Marketing, International Business, and Management Information Systems.

It is in the College of Forestry and Conservation, however, that two truly distinctive programs reside.

Students in the Ecosystem and Conservation Science track are quickly absorbed into the university's Avian Science Center, looking at birds and their ecosystems, the research team looking at Bark Beetle Ecology and Evolution, Population and Disease Ecology, Quantitative Wildlife Ecology, Global Climate and Ecology, Ungulate Ecology (balance between predatory risk and foraging for ungulate herbivores such as caribou), and the Terrestrial Ecosystem Ecology Lab.

The Wildlife Biology Program allows students experiential opportunities to work with wildlife populations from bison, moose, and bears to sage grouse and eagles. Students use resources available at Glacier National Park and Yellowstone National Park and at the National Bison range, less than an hour from campus. Many are encouraged to study outside the ordinary curriculum, exploring watershed hydrology, fish biology, and fisheries. Or, looking beyond the US, students can spend nine weeks in Botswana working with Wildlife Africa Conservation Team.

Back on campus, life is pretty sweet. Obviously, outdoor recreation is fully supported with bike-ski workshops, equipment rental, skills classes (avalanche awareness!), a climbing wall, and an endless array of trips to mountains, rivers, whitewater, and wilderness. Fitness classes and facilities, swimming, hiking, running, all continue through the year as do intramural sports, such as inner tube water polo and dodgeball, spikeball and indoor soccer. Club sports abound, including lacrosse, equestrian, fencing, hurling, rugby, triathlon, and ultimate frisbee. The university's golf course, laid out in the shadow of Mount Sentinel is spectacular when the snow melts.

Greek life exists at Montana, but at a slightly less frenetic pace than at some other public institutions. Eight fraternities and four sororities have a place in campus social life, but the majority of students make and find their own fun in and outside of their residences.

The Grizzlies of Montana play in Division I of the NCAA, in the Big Sky Conference, a conference that pits Grizzly against the Bobcats of Montana State. The entirety of tilts against MSU is referred to as the Brawl of the Wild; at the end of the year, each team (men's and women's) get points for victories bringing domination to one of the two Montana teams. The football team and the basketball team both play significant games outside of the conference. A great afternoon in Missoula might bring the Grizzlies up against the Mustangs of Cal Poly or the Mustangs of UC Davis – the bear versus the horse. A stadium seating twenty-six thousand fans is almost always filled to capacity.

Colorado School of Mines - Golden, Colorado

Colorado School of Mines was tough to get into last year. It should be one of the most highly respected colleges of its kind, and I am pleased that its reputation has finally reached a number of applicants. The rate of acceptance has moved steadily lower in the last five years, but it remain less well known than other schools of comparable excellence, so, despite its increased selectivity, it remains in this book.

And the stats... 2015

Number of Applicants: 12,340 / 36% Accepted
Undergrad Enrollment: 4,456 28% female / 74% male
Avg. SAT Reading 590-680 and Math 640 -720 Avg. ACT: 28-32
Total Cost: $49,685.00
Received some form of financial assistance: 100%

Most folks have heard of Golden, Colorado because it is the home of the Coors Brewing Company, and the American Mountaineering Center, the National Renewable Energy Foundation, the National Earthquake Information Center, the Colorado Railroad Museum, the resting place of "Buffalo Bill" Cody and the home of Jolly Rancher candies.

People who know anything about colleges know it as the location of the Colorado School of Mines.

Colorado School of Mines is a small (3300 students) public university, dedicated to engineering and applied sciences, attached from the start to the exploration and extraction of natural resources, and the most celebrated institution carrying out "material engineering."

In many ways, the story of "Mines" is the story of the American West.

Founded in 1873 by the Episcopal Church, the small college of mining was attached to a divinity school. Quickly claimed by the Colorado Territory and by the newly minted State of Colorado when the territory achieved statehood in 1876, Colorado School of Mines began "groundbreaking" work in the study of mines and mining, developing the first experimental mine, owned by the school, located on Mt. Zion.

The first subjects taught were in the Applied Sciences and Mining Engineering - including Chemistry, Physics, Metallurgy, and Drafting. By the 1940's, Geology, Petroleum Engineering, Geophysics, and Petroleum

Refining had been added. As a result of research done from the start at "Mines", one of the most significant collections of minerals in the world is housed in the Colorado School of Mines Geology Museum.

Today, prospective "Orediggers" can elect a major field from a wide variety of fields, including Engineering (Civil, Electrical, Mechanical, Environmental), Engineering Systems, Bioengineering, Chemical Engineering, Metallurgical and Materials Engineering, Mathematical and Computer Science, Economics and Business, Chemistry, Physics, Engineering Physics, Geological Engineering, Geophysical Engineering, Geophysics, Mining Engineering, Petroleum Engineering, and International Political Economy.

If this sounds like a fairly practical course of study, please understand that one of the hallmarks of the Colorado School of Mines story is that its graduates are among the most highly paid of college graduates, ranking only behind those of Caltech and MIT. Competition for places in the first year class is the most competitive of any public institution in the state, and the school's national reputation in fields having to do with exploration, extraction, production, and utilization of natural resources is unmatched.

The curriculum is specifically directed toward the stewardship of natural resources, and it can be argued that no institution in the country is more perfectly placed to make a difference in the lives of the next generation. That mission is clearly in place as "Mines" enters the second decade of the current century. The school hosts the state's Science Olympiad and the Science Bowl and remains a resource for students throughout the region.

It has to be said that Colorado School of Mines has changed significantly since the early days in some ways.

For example, residential life has become prominent and well organized. Well designed residence halls and student apartments meet the needs of the entire student body and activities, more than a hundred of them, fill the hours outside of the classroom.

Athletics play a part at "Mines". There is a pretty good football team, and the "Orediggers" have a superb cycling team and a nationally known mountain biking program. Runners have emerged as a significant force as "Mines" has entered into competition at the Division II level. A number of athletes compete in soccer, volleyball, cross-country, basketball, swimming, wrestling, baseball, golf, and softball. Swimming, rock climbing, recreational sports, fishing, hiking, skiing, and ultimate frisbee are among the intramural and club sports.

The facilities at Colorado School of Mines are first-rate and impressive, but the single greatest indication of "Mines" identity is found in looking to the mountains.

Today, a giant monogram, the letter "M", stands atop Mt. Zion, built by boulders carried by generations of Mines students. The "M" is illuminated every night and decked out in colorful lights as holidays approach. The monogram was first constructed in 1908 by two hundred and fifty students and a train of burros. Before long, the impulse to light the giant "M" was irresistible, and Homecoming in 1932 saw the first illumination; by the 1940's automatic lighting was in place and is now computerized and made more energy efficient with the introduction of LED lights in place of incandescent bulbs.
Each fall, freshmen carry a ten-pound rock up to the "M" and apply a fresh coat of whitewash. Seniors have the opportunity to return to Mt. Zion to carry their rock back down the mountain.

No tradition worth its salt exists for long without attracting attention from rivals longing to spoil it. Legend has it that a crew from New Mexico Tech carried rocks to add the "N" on one side of the "M" and a "T" on the other. Apparently the prank was met with some show of disapproval, and the monogram has been safe ever since,

Other traditions also enliven the school year.

"E Days," or Engineering Days, bring a three-day spring fling in which an elaborate fireworks show is put on and students compete in a cardboard canoe race.

The Mines Band has performed in traditional costume of red and black plaid shirts, jeans, hiking boots, and hard hats for more than fifty years.

Finally, each graduate of Colorado School of Mines receives a silver diploma. The diploma is etched onto a sterling silver plate and presented at graduation.

University of Northern Colorado - Greeley, Colorado

No description of UNC would be reasonable without recognizing that extraordinary friendliness of this campus and the rich sense of community found here. Students here are happy, hard working, and relentlessly nice. Activities on campus are inclusive and positive. It makes a difference, for example, that the extensive programs run by the college's outdoor program, Outdoor Pursuits, loans all equipment at no cost, offers workshops and training at no cost, organizes trips at no cost. It makes a difference that they love Greeley and appreciate the character of their town. It makes a difference that students "get" that they enjoy the rare opportunity to study on a campus surrounded by natural beauty. It makes a difference that they feel enormous pride in their university and genuine fondness for the professors who know them in and outside the classroom

And the stats... 2015

Number of Applicants: 7,831 / 71% Accepted
Undergrad Enrollment: 9,469 63% female / 37% male
Avg. SAT Reading 480-570 and Math 470 -590 Avg. ACT: 19-25
Total Cost: $21,983.00 (in-state) $33,527.00 (out-of-state)
Received some form of financial assistance: 90

I'm a fan of relatively small public universities that manage to create a strong sense of identity and community, particularly those that have come of age in the shadow of the larger, more athletically dominant "flagship" state university.

UNC is certainly one of the most attractive, set in the lively small city of Greeley (Pop. about 100,000), one of America's great college towns, about an hour north of Denver. UNC is not quite a mile high (4,780 ft) in altitude, but it does have a remarkable window on the Rockies, and is within easy reach of Breckenridge, Copper Mountain, Keystone, Crested Butte, the Arapahoe National Forest, and the three and a half million acres of Colorado's wilderness. Greeley itself has the charm of a rodeo town brought happily into the circle of snappy college town with big city amenities. The town and university are incredibly well matched. Greeley is lively with great restaurants, shopping, forty miles of bike trails and a stunning number of cultural events, including a rodeo stampede, jazz festivals, and world -class concerts in spectacular venues. UNC adds the intellectual and creative mix of an ambitious university, sponsoring speakers, performances, and, of course, athletic events throughout the year. Folks from outside of Colorado tend to think of the state as snow-covered, and there are some magical winters, but the state also enjoys three hundred days of sunshine each year, even when the snow is on the ground.

I'll get to the academic and social profile shortly, but no description of UNC would be reasonable without recognizing that extraordinary friendliness of this campus and the rich sense of community found here. Students here are happy, hard working, and relentlessly nice. Activities on campus are inclusive and positive. It makes a difference, for example, that the extensive programs run by the college's outdoor program, Outdoor Pursuits, loans all equipment at no cost, offers workshops and training at no cost, organizes trips at no cost. It makes a difference that they love Greeley and appreciate the character of their town. It makes a difference that students "get" that they enjoy the rare opportunity to study on a campus surrounded by natural beauty. It makes a difference that they feel enormous pride in their university and genuine fondness for the professors who know them in and outside the classroom. Asked what makes UNC special, one student responded, "My teachers are invested in my success. Here and after I leave"" That's a pretty remarkable endorsement. Equally impressive are the comments from those who come to UNC from other states. Many say that the campus has felt like home to them from the time they arrived.

Just under ten thousand undergraduates are enrolled at UNC, attending classes which are uncommonly small for a public university; more than sixty percent of classes have fewer than thirty students. They are purposefully engaged in study in one of the six divisions known as colleges: The College of Education and Behavioral Sciences, the College of Humanities and Social Sciences, Monfort College of Business, the College of Natural and Health Sciences, the College of Visual and Performing Arts.

Although the university's undergraduate curriculum consists of more than one hundred and thirty programs and majors, UNC's beginnings were in teacher education, and the varieties of programs and connections made over the years are impressive. Majors offered in the College of Education and Behavioral Science include Psychological Sciences, Counseling Psychology, Applied Psychology, Special Education, Teacher Education, Applied Statistics, and Research Methods, Educational Leadership, and Educational Technology. The college also operates centers and institutes dedicated to particular issues, including: Urban Education, Gifted and Talented, Teaching Students with Disabilities, and Interpreter Training.

The College of Humanities and Social Sciences starts first year students in what it calls "Clusters", in which the cluster is organized around a theme.

Each freshman takes a composition class linked to three other liberal arts courses in the company of the same group of freshmen cohorts. The structure allows freshmen to build connections across courses, develop strong relationships at the start of their college career, and organize helpful study groups. Some recent themes have been: Global Interactions–Then and Now, Gender and American Culture, and Exploring Culture/ A Way of Seeing and Being. Entering students pick their first three options and are informed of their assignment before they arrive on campus.

Majors in the College of Humanities and Social Sciences include the usual core subjects (English, Philosophy, Modern Languages, and Political Science) but also include a few unexpected major fields – Africana Studies, Hispanic Studies, Geography and GIS.

It is clear that the College of Natural and Health Sciences see their mission as the preparation of students who will make a contribution to the world they inhabit. Study of the sciences and mathematics may be significant for those who enter any of the health professions, therapeutic fields, counseling, or any field of public service. The college is divided into eight schools or departments: Biological Sciences, Chemistry and Biochemistry, Earth and Atmospheric Sciences, Human Sciences, Nursing, Physics and Astronomy, and Sports and Exercise Science.and Rehabilitation.

The School of Human Sciences prepares students for work in specific service-related fields. Within the school, students may major in Audiology and Speech Language Sciences, Community Health, Gerontology, Nutrition and Dietetics, Recreation, Tourism and Hospitality, That is quite an array of offerings in a program intended to prepare students for work in the helping professions.

Three statistics jumped out at me when I looked into the College of Performing and Visual Arts. The first is that about thirteen hundred students are enrolled in programs in that division; that's thirteen hundred out of a student population of about nine thousand. The second is that the college employs ninety professionals who are active in their field; they do art, music, theater, and dance. The third is that the college makes more than three hundred performances available to the community each year. That is one full schedule.

An interesting development within the college is the establishment of a certificate program in arts entrepreneurship.

The Monfort College of Business is well regarded, often mentioned among the emerging business programs in the nation. Majors are offered in Finance, Management, Marketing, and General Business. The College also offers a major in Software Engineering in conjunction with Natural Science and Health Sciences.

The transition from academic programs to residential life is made all the easier by introducing the Residential Learning Communities. Students and choose to live in communities with others who share their hope of exploring a particular set of issues. One sort of community is Interest Based Communities, looking at The Global Village, Women's Community, or Leadership, Other cohorts in these communities might include those who choose Spectrum which offers a safe zone supported by the GBLTA Office in which to discuss identity. First Generation allows students to live in the company of others making a difficult adjustment to life away from home. One community is created for those who transfer into UNC, and one is set aside as a Pet-Friendly community. Academic communities welcome those interested in the Performing Arts, Biology, the Monfort School of Business, Pre Nursing, the Presidential Honors students, and Cumbre, which includes students working toward an ESL endorsement. The final set of communities include the mentoring of a residential professor, ranging from one who teaches Criminal Justice to one who teaches Dietetics.

And, having mentioned Dietetics, the time has come to talk about food at UNC. The subject deserves particular attention because the university. Students *rave* about the food at UNC. They love the care with which food is prepared, and are particularly proud of their chef who has won national honors. They love the variety of options available, including two dining halls that serve an "all-you-can-eat menu" featuring a gourmet salad bar. Much of the fruit and produce served is grown locally and the "food-to-table" movement is alive and well at UNC. Any specific considerations from allergies to dining hours during weeks of religious observance are happily attended to by the responsive dining staff.

Residential life is well organized with good support from Resident Advisors and counseling staff on the residential life committees. In addition to the Learning Communities, there are several very large residential halls, some of which are among the tallest buildings north of Denver. Almost all of the residences are built in suite format with full kitchens, laundry facilities, computer labs, practice rooms, and common areas. UNC has about twenty fraternities and sororities that play a part in the healthy social life at the university. This might be the time to suggest that Greeley is such an important part of the out-of class opportunities for UNC's kids, that the usual social structures are slightly less important than they might be at other universities. There are plenty of clubs and activities in full gear most of the time, but it is easy to find a great pizza or great music in Greeley as well.

The UNC Bears play in NCAA Division I in the Big Sky Conference against opponents such as Montana, Idaho, and Northern Arizona University, probably the closest in type and size to UNC. The university competes in two sports that the Big Sky does not offer - baseball, wrestling and women's swimming- so those sports participate in other conferences.

UNC wrestlers are very competitive in the Big Twelve, a major athletic conference. Students can be glad that the name of the UNC mascot was changed in the 1920's from "The Teachers" to "The Bears". The Butler-Hancock Sports Pavilion comes alive during basketball season when fans of the Bears create the cheering section they call, "Fear the Claw", a rowdy and rollicking gang of Bear fans, often encouraged by Klawz the Bear, the costumed mascot. The 2011 men's basketball team won the Big Sky Conference and took the team to the NCAA championship Tournament.

New Mexico Institute of Technology - Socorro, New Mexico

New Mexico Tech is another exceptionally impressive college that has seen a rapid increase in selectivity. So, although the rate of acceptance has moved steadily lower in the last five years, New Mexico Institute of Technology is unique in almost every aspect and belongs in this guide to extraordinary schools that might not be nationally recognized.

And the stats... 2015

Number of Applicants: 1,003 / 36% Accepted
Undergrad Enrollment: 1,633 30% female / 70% male
Avg. SAT Reading 550-640 and Math 570 -670 Avg. ACT: 23-29
Total Cost: $19,494.00 (in-state) $31,422.00
Received some form of financial assistance: 95%

"Where can I go to blow stuff up?"

OK, that's not actually a question most counselors hear, but the truth is that the New Mexico Institute of Mining and Technology is exactly where people go when they want to blow stuff up. Mythbusters goes to New Mexico Tech; Warner Brothers does research for the Roadrunner cartoons at New Mexico Tech. Oh, and Homeland Security has an ... "unusual" ... relationship with New Mexico Tech.

Established as the New Mexico School of Mines in the nineteenth century, New Mexico Tech has evolved into one of the premiere small technological universities in the world, especially interesting in its pursuit of certain fields outside the parameters of most tech school curricula. One commonly heard joke about Tech is that it is a research center that just happens to have a university, and that's not far from the truth. It also happens to be a place that offers air rifles, pellets, and targets for the weekly air rifle practice on Monday afternoons.

The basic facts about the place are these: New Mexico Institute of Mining and Technology is a very small university, enrolling about thirteen hundred students on a campus of about four hundred acres in Socorro, New Mexico, although Tech also OWNS another town that it uses as a research facility. Socorro is a small town - population is about nine thousand - located seventy-five miles south of Albuquerque at an elevation of more than four thousand feet. The town is on the Rio Grande and at the foot of the Magdalena Mountains. Outdoor recreation is nearby in the Cibola National Forest, the Bosque del Apache Wildlife Refuge and the Sevilleta Wildlife Refuge. The two most notable advantages of life in Socorro are that the sun shines three hundred days a year (!) and the town is the site of a well-documented UFO sighting.

It's the incredible activity on campus, however that sets New Mexico Tech apart from any other college in the world. A quick glance at the course catalog indicates that degrees are offered in Math, the Sciences, Chemical Engineering, Civil Engineering, Communication, Computer Science, Earth Science, Electrical Engineering, Environmental Engineering, Management, Materials Engineering, Mechanical Engineering, Mineral Engineering, and Petroleum Engineering.

A far more reflective indicator of Tech's ambition, however, is the range of its research centers.

The sexiest by far is the Energetic Materials Research and Testing Center (EMRTC). Energetic materials, by the way, is a scientific way of describing things that blow up, hence the assertion that if you want to see materials get energetic, you might want to visit Socorro. On the other hand, if you intend to operate a glass window showroom, you might want to move as far away from Socorro as possible. The early morning explosions apparently help Socorrans start the day. The seriousness of the work done at New Mexico Tech is made clear, however, by such experiments as recreating the car bomb left in Times Square and evaluating its impact and determining ways of avoiding or mitigating the blast.

Equally compelling and maybe just a bit more odd is the counter-terrorism and first responder research site at Playas, New Mexico. Playas was an actual town at one point with a real population doing real work at the copper smelting facility. When the smelter closed, residents were evicted, the bowling alley closed, the bar shut down. The State of New Mexico and New Mexico Tech approached the Bureau of Homeland Security and established this training and research site. Because the town is an actual real town, it offers a real life simulation as Homeland Security works with Tech to operate in times of crisis. Oh, and the guys get energetic with materials out here as well.

The Magdalena Ridge Observatory is primarily sponsored by the U.S. Naval Research Laboratory and is operated in conjunction with the Cavendish Laboratory at Cambridge University. Magdalena Ridge is near the summit of South Baldy Mountain at an altitude of about sixteen hundred feet. By the end of two thousand and thirteen, the observatory should be fully functional; the plan is to install a ten-element optical interferometer and a single-mirror 2.4-meter fast-tracking optical telescope.

Perhaps the stars are too far away to catch your attention. How about the Earth's interior? The IRIS (Incorporated Research Institutions for Seismology) Consortium has a lot to do with earthquakes and subsurface activity, but it also keeps track of violations of Test Ban Treaties. Central to that work is the Incorporated Research Institutions for Seismology (IRIS) Program for Array Seismic Studies of the Continental Lithosphere (PASSCAL) Instrument Center and EarthScope USArray Array Operations Facility which, as you might have guessed, is housed at New Mexico Tech.

Want to have your head in the clouds? The Langmuir Laboratory for Atmospheric Research is adjacent to the Magdalena Ridge Observatory. Apparently the site is particularly well located in that it is at some elevation and exactly where the greatest concentration of storms occurs.

The Petroleum Research and Recovery Center allows students to do extensive research in groundbreaking methods of gas and petroleum extraction. It goes without saying that this center is almost fully underwritten by state and federal agencies, and it probably needs saying that the work done is in the areas of Petrophysics and Surface Chemistry, Gas Flooding Processes and Flow Heterogeneities, Reservoir Sweep Improvement, Reservoir Evaluation/Advanced Computational Technologies, and Carbon Sequestration and Membrane Technology.

Finally, Tech operates the Institute for Complex Additive Systems Analysis (ICASA) in order to study large-scale infrastructure systems. In case that sound academic and fuzzy-wuzzy, the CIA finds the center absolutely essential in the training of analysts, scientists and engineers in the evaluating of critical information.

Yow!

All of this takes place on a campus with a distinctly Southwestern feel. The newest buildings, like the Student Center, are impressively modern; the library and dormitories are certainly attractive enough, but functional. Tech operates two all-male dorms, two all-female dorms, and two co-ed dorms. In addition, apartments are available to upper class students, and a good number live in what tech calls the Living/Learning Communities. Examples of the communities include one dedicated to sustainability, and one is all about computer science, one called "Spaceship Earth" is about the biosphere assessing.

Despite the obvious rigor of the program at New Mexico Tech, students do have the occasional odd moment for recreation, and the array of student organizations will also speak to the character of the exceptional students who find their way to Socorro. There is Student Government, newspaper, yearbook, and a radio station, as might be expected, but also a belly dancing club, a caving club, a ballroom dancing club, the Adventurer's

Guild (a gaming club), and a billiards club. The Society for Creative Anachronism has a chapter (College of St. Golias), and sports are represented with a great deal of cycling, running, rugby, soccer, skiing and snowboarding.

Santa Fe University of Arts and Design - Santa Fe, New Mexico

The curriculum at SFUAD is the more remarkable for its rapid implementation. Strength in the visual arts seemed likely, and the recent explosion of creative energy in the area of film and video had already pulled Santa Fe into the public eye. What came as a surprise was the power of the university's programs in contemporary music and music technology.

And the stats... 2015

Number of Applicants: 608/ 100% Accepted
Undergrad Enrollment: 950 54% female / 46% male

The admissions process is somewhat different at SFUAD in that a personal statement of goals and evidence of sustained attention to craft will carry significant weight in the process. Demonstration of talent will be considered carefully. An interview is required.

Total Cost: $44,685.00
Received some form of financial assistance: 100%

There is no other institution in this guide that is similar to Santa Fe University of Art and Design, in part because it has been a residential college from its earliest days in several iterations. Today it offers exceptional preparation for professional work in the arts and a residential community animated by the arts. Its professors are working artists of considerable reputation, and its lively celebration of film animates the college and the community. Finally, Santa Fe!

Full Disclosure: Santa Fe University of Art and Design is the reformed and reconstituted university built from the ashes of the College of Santa Fe, the exciting and innovative college forced into bankruptcy in 2008. Ordinarily, the financial disaster that played itself out at the College of Santa Fe would remove a college from consideration in a guide of this sort. There are at least three circumstances, however that make the University of Art and Design a compelling well kept secret.

In the first place, the financial mess was a very public mess. There was no cover-up and no fancy footwork. The lovely College of Santa Fe had been fighting against the tide for a very long time, trying to maintain what was essentially an experimental arts curriculum while providing continuing education through a weekend program and offering a degree in business administration. Originally founded as Saint Michael's College by the Christian Brothers, a Roman Catholic teaching order, the College of Santa Fe served too many masters, pleased none, and ran out of steam.

In the second place, when the crisis finally forced the college to shut its doors, the Governor of New Mexico, Bill Richardson, created a College of Santa Fe Task Force to figure out a way to preserve an arts university in the State of New Mexico. The end result of the initiative was that a new university was created through the partnership of the City of Santa Fe, the New Mexico State Governor's Office, and a private for-profit educational company, Laureate Education.

Finally, the infusion of resources from all three sources allowed the new university to open its doors on a campus that is a far more attractive and more effective than that of its predecessor college. Whereas the College of Santa Fe was exciting but shabby, SFUAD is exciting and spiffy.

Not only are the teaching and workspaces up to the standards of a first-rate arts school, but also the residences are handsome and comfortable. Perhaps the single most obvious difference on campus is the construction of an impressive tennis complex. The stadium is capable of seating a thousand spectators, and the facility includes six indoor courts as well as lighting for the seven outdoor courts.

Oh, and by the way, the university is in Santa Fe, a city whose name is virtually synonymous with patronage of the arts. It is hard to imagine a city more artistically minded, more endorsing of creativity, and more strikingly beautiful.

Santa Fe University of Art and Design would be fairly attractive even without its impressive curriculum.

The curriculum at SFUAD is the more remarkable for its rapid implementation. Strength in the visual arts seemed likely, and the recent explosion of creative energy in the area of film and video had already pulled Santa Fe into the public eye. What came as a surprise was the power of the university's programs in contemporary music and music technology.

Interestingly, SFUAD offers a Bachelor of Arts degree in Studio Art and a Bachelor of Fine Arts degree in Studio Arts. The BA program is a studio program with a complementary coursework in art history and other disciplines. The BFA program is a professional program in which skills and practices of a student's art are developed through coursework, internship, and thesis presentation.

A program in graphic design is intended to bring the aspiring designer to competence in design elements and to mastery of digital image making.

This is a professional program, preparing graduates to enter the field of graphic design immediately upon graduation.

The Moving Image Arts filmmakers work in a professional studio, the Greer Garson Studio, where films such as *No Country for Old Men* have been shot; the Garson Studio has been a Hollywood location for generations. Students can explore film, digital media, screenwriting, and production. One notable resource at SFUAD is The Screen, a remarkable cinematheque screening great works daily on a curved high definition screen.

The Photography programs include a BA in Photography, allowing the aspiring photographer to study the elements of photography in the context of broad education, and a BFA in Photography, essentially a professional preparation in the craft of photography in order to become a practicing photographer upon graduation.

Unlike many other arts schools or conservatories, Santa Fe offers three areas of professional training that stand outside of the traditional studio experience.

One legacy from the College of Santa Fe is the program in Creative Writing and Literature. The program offers coursework and practice in Creative Fiction, Nonfiction, Poetry, and Screenwriting. A capstone experience is the Senior Reading, in which the writer prepares a book-length manuscript.

A second unusual option is the large program in Performing Arts. Areas of concentration include Theater Performance, Theater Design, Theater Acting, Theater Music, and Technical Theater Design. Professional training as an actor, singer, dancer, designer, director – all are offered in this unusual and ambitious performing arts program.

Finally, the program in Contemporary Music combines Performance, Music Theory, Music Technology, and Recording Technology in a professional program preparing the graduate for a career in the music industry.

A significant difference between SFUAD and some other professional art or design schools is that Santa Fe has built four residence halls and several on-campus apartment houses for residential students; the program at SFUAD is entirely residential, which not only relieves the difficulty of finding housing in a precious city such as Santa Fe, but also creates a community of professional artists, living and working together.

The university has retained a strong sense of community by endorsing residential life, providing an excellent dining service, and many recreational activities. A gymnasium, rock climbing wall, tennis courts, squash and racquetball courts, and stunning opportunities in the Outdoors make SFUAD truly unique as a school of arts.

466

Of course, the most significant facilities and resources are the extraordinary work, rehearsal, digital, and studio spaces available in this fine arts Mecca. For the student who thinks a late night trip to the practice room or digital lab is the cat's meow, SFUAD is a wonderland.

Northern Arizona University - Flagstaff, Arizona

The university is located in Flagstaff, Arizona, one of the most attractive settings possible in which a small university might have been founded. The NAU campus is handsome, a mix of classic collegiate red brick and modern architecture, only moments from pizza, bars, and Target, but surrounded by the largest ponderosa pine forest in the contiguous United States. The university is at close to seven thousand feet in elevation, and the highest point in Arizona (a little over twelve thousand feet) is just to the north of Flagstaff in the Kachina Peaks Wilderness. Flagstaff was a lumber and Ranching town, and the center of "Old" Flagstaff still feels like a movie set from a good Western.

And the stats... 2015

Number of Applicants: 30,855 / 81% Accepted
Undergrad Enrollment: 23,238 58% female / 42% male
Avg. SAT Reading 470-590 and Math 480 -570 Avg. ACT: 22-27
Total Cost: $24,820.00 (in-state) $37,340.00
Received some form of financial assistance: 84%

NAU can appear somewhat anachronistic – a college that time forgot. I don't mean that it is outdated, or musty, but simply that it's hard not to think of wholesome good fun when Larry the Lumberjack bursts through a banner on the sidelines of a football game or bounces on to the court at an NAU basketball game. The oldest buildings on campus are hallowed and handsome (the center of the campus looks like a movie set) and the rest of the campus is a park with elegant modern residences and classrooms. NAU is essentially a wooded, green island in the middle of a bustling medium-sized city, and the happy hum of twenty thousand satisfied students make the place a pleasure to visit.

The university is located in Flagstaff, Arizona, one of the most attractive settings possible in which a small university might have been founded. The NAU campus is handsome, a mix of classic collegiate red brick and modern architecture, only moments from pizza, bars, and Target, but surrounded by the largest ponderosa pine forest in the contiguous United States. The university is at close to seven thousand feet in elevation, and the highest point in Arizona (a little over twelve thousand feet) is just to the north of Flagstaff in the Kachina Peaks Wilderness. Flagstaff was a lumber and Ranching town, and the center of Old Flagstaff still feels like a movie set from a good Western. Tourists flock to Flagstaff as it is an easy jumping off point for a visit to the Grand Canyon and literally a mile from great skiing at the Arizona Snowbowl. Flagstaff absolutely enjoys its four seasons, and the winter is often very snowy. Within an hour's drive, however, the visitor can stop in Sedona and Oak Creek Canyon, watch the sunset over red rocks, and drop almost two thousand feet in the process.

The State of Arizona supports two other significant universities - the University of Arizona in Tucson and Arizona State in Tempe. Northern Arizona, like many modern comprehensive universities, started as a teacher's college and emerged as a more complex university in the years following World War II. Today, NAU enrolls approximately twenty thousand students in one of six divisions. Most undergrads at NAU are enrolled in the College of Arts and Letters, the College of Social and Behavioral Sciences, or in the School of Business. I'll report on those divisions, The College of Education and the College of Health and Human Services and then turn to Engineering and Forestry.

The College of Social and Behavioral Sciences offers a really interesting array of major concentration, some of which might not be expected - Anthropology, Sociology, Political Science, Communications, Criminology and Criminal Justice, Geography, Ethnic Studies, Women's and Gender Studies. The college offers another distinctive program that appropriately brings opportunity to Native people who aspire to make a difference in an indigenous nation or tribe. Other universities offer Native American Literature and Native American Studies, but Northern Arizona has developed a program called Applied Indigenous Studies that promotes skills necessary to service and leadership within indigenous communities.

The College of Arts and Letters includes most of the humanities, a school of Music, a school of Art, and is especially celebrated for three distinctive programs: Cinema Studies, Asian Studies, and vocal and instrumental performance.

Cinema Studies is a minor field, but increasingly popular. Courses in Visual Culture, Hollywood and Crime, Race, Identity, and Film have become widely sought, and the series of excellent films shown each week is a long-standing tradition at the university.

The program in Asian Studies includes foundation courses such as: Gateways to Asia and the Asian-American Experience, and offers a wide range of other options including The Art of China, Islamic Art, Pre-Modern India, China since 1945, and Women in Asia.

The School of Music offers the B.A. in Music, the Bachelor of Music in Performance (voice or instrumental), and the bachelor of Music Education. Admission to all of these programs involves application to the university and application to the program. Admission to the Bachelor of Music in Performance also requires an audition.

The College of Education offers major concentration in Educational Leadership, Educational Psychology, Educational Specialties (including Bilingual Education and Special Education), and Teaching and Learning (Early Childhood, Elementary, and Secondary).

The W.A. Franke College of Business offers major concentration in Accounting, Business Economics, Computer Information Systems, Finance, Marketing, and Management.

The College of Health and Human Services maintains several very compelling programs and may be of great interest to students searching for professional education. Athletic Training, Communication Sciences and Disorders, Speech and Language Disorders, Public Health, Nursing, and Physician's Assistant.

OK, finally, the College of Engineering and Forestry. The Engineering divisions include Civil Engineering, Computer Science, Construction Management, Electrical and Computer Engineering, Environmental Engineering, and Mechanical Engineering.

The truly uncommon division, however, is the excellent School of Forestry. The university has done a great deal to develop the program, but two significant advantages to establishing a program such as this in Flagstaff are the heritage of extensive logging in the region and the presence of six climate zones within the State of Arizona.

After the second year in the core curriculum, candidates for the Bachelor of Science degree in Forestry take courses such as: forest ecology, watershed hydrology, silviculture, wildlife management, harvest planning, recreation planning, and wildland fire. Classroom instruction is impressive, but hands-on learning takes place at every level, supplements by internships and summer employment arranged by the university. One other notable opportunity is the five-year B.S.F./M.F. program.

Flagstaff is a welcoming city, but NAU is largely a residential university. Of the twenty-one residence halls, six have been set aside for freshmen. Two are twenty-four hour quiet dorms, another is a co-ed substance free dorm; other dorms have specific traditions of service or celebration.

The two obvious sources of recreation for NAU's students are the outdoors and Flagstaff, and both are attractive options during the week and on the weekend. Other activities flourish as well as NAU sponsors over two hundred clubs and activities including: Engineers Without Borders, the Forensic Science Club, Quidditch, Fencing, Kendo, and Flagstaff Hitmen.

The Lumberjacks compete in the Big Sky Conference of NCAA Division I. Like the rest of the crowd in the conference, NAU is in what is known as the Division I Football Championship Subdivision, formerly known as Division I AA. These schools are slightly less rabid in their pursuit of athletic competition – still producing excellent athletes but in slightly less concentrated masses. Rivals include Montana, Montana State, Northern Colorado, and Cal Poly.

Prescott College - Prescott, Arizona

Today, Prescott enrolls about 65 new students a year in what it calls its Resident Degree Program. The RDP is the program that most closely resembles college, in that it is intended to allow students four years in which to live and study in Prescott. Still "experimental," and highly experiential, Prescott asks each student to create his or her own program of study; this is a self-directed program. There are classes, and they are small (tiny?); teachers help provoke conversation and thought and mentor the journey that each Prescott student undertakes.

And the stats... 2015

Number of Applicants: 518 / 69% Accepted
Undergrad Enrollment: 848 59% female / 41% male
Avg. SAT Reading 460-630 and Math 430 -570 Avg. ACT: 20-28
Clearly, Prescott is for the rare student, often one who has tried a conventional college program and found it wanting. The admissions picture is hard to compare with other colleges, but here goes:

In addition to the usual paper submitted with an application, an interview is strongly recommended, in some case, required. My own feeling is that it would be foolish in the extreme to consider Prescott without making an extended visit.
Total Cost: $39,223.00
Received some form of financial assistance: 100%

Prescott College – "For the Liberal Arts, the Environment, and Social Justice."

Have no fear – Prescott is still one of the most genuinely experimental and experiential colleges in the nation; the city of Prescott may be charming in entirely conventional ways, but the college continues to challenge expectations.

Prescott began as an experiment encouraged by the Ford Foundation. Challenged to imagine the "college of the future" in 1965, educators imagined Prescott and placed it in a charming small city, once the capital of Arizona Territory, and a city rich with history and charm.

Called the "Most Midwestern City in the West," Prescott has more than eight hundred buildings on the National registry of Historic Places, many of which are Victorian. Notorious "Whiskey Row" was the city's "red light" district until it burned in the 1950's, and the legacy of pioneers, miners, and early settlers makes the city feel very much like a slice of Arizona's history. Festivals such as "Frontier Days," the Navajo Rug Auction, and the Gathering of Cowboy Poets keep the legacy alive.

Today there are four golf courses as well as the eight hundred registered buildings, and the city is rapidly expanding as planned communities spring up on the city's fringes.

The mix of cultures remains clear. The Yavapai-Prescott Indian Reservation is partially within the boundaries of the city, and five colleges and universities have programs located in Prescott.

They are in Prescott because the city is like Ojai or Mount Shasta – there's something … well… spiritual or otherworldly about the setting. Maybe it is the rarified air (Prescott is at an altitude of over five thousand feet); maybe it is in the spirit of the extraordinary landscape, or the presence of native peoples. How a city with golf courses feels spiritual I cannot say, but Prescott is one oddly wonderful place.

The experimental college dreamed up in the 1960's met the end that other experiments of the 60's found; it folded in 1974.

But, and here's where "The College that wouldn't die" come in, believers refused to let the dream slip away; the college was re-founded and re-invented in 1975, in makeshift classrooms (a former furniture store/ a converted dentist's office) until a proper set of buildings could be constructed.

Today, Prescott enrolls about 65 new students a year in what it calls its Resident Degree Program. The RDP is the program that most closely resembles college, in that it is intended to allow students four years in which to live and study in Prescott. Still "experimental;" and highly experiential, Prescott asks each student to create his or her own program of study; this is a self-directed program. There are classes, and they are small (tiny?); teachers help provoke conversation and thought and mentor the journey that each Prescott student undertakes.

The college does impose one clear set of expectations upon its students; they are to develop and embrace what the college class "environmental literacy." Much of the character of the college and of its academic program is attached to the environment in which the college is located. Key concepts at the heart of the Prescott experience are diversity, inclusion, and sustainability. In addition, Prescott is about initiative and resourcefulness.

For example, first year students are welcomed to the Prescott experience by backpacking fifty or sixty miles into the adjoining wilderness. Prescott believes in "learning by doing," and that active education begins right at the start. The college is surrounded by more than a million acres of national forest and almost eight hundred miles of hiking trails.

Courses are frequently taught in "the field." One might expect that the course in mountaineering or shamanism might be taught outdoors, but so are courses in history and creative writing. The college maintains several stations including the Kino Bay Center for Cultural and Ecological Studies in Sonora, Mexico and the Walnut Creek Station about forty five minutes from Prescott, It is at Walnut Creek that students encounter one of Prescott's unique courses - Ecopsychology, joining studies in Psychology, Human Development, and Environmental Studies.

No brief description can do justice to the remarkable initiatives undertaken at Prescott, so I'll just list a few of the courses or programs that seem unusual:

Adventure Based Environmental Education
Wilderness Leadership
Ecotherapy
Ethnobiology
Border Studies
Ecofeminism
Social Ecology

Other colleges operate with a semester system, or the 4-1-4 Plan, or, in some cases, a Block Plan. Prescott has its own elegant academic calendar: Three blocks of four weeks offer instruction in one course at a time, allowing intensive investigation of a subject. The blocks take place in September, January, and May, and set off the two -semester system.

As one might expect, in addition to a self-directed program, the college strongly encourages, field work, internships, and study off-campus. Many opportunities are created by the college in conjunction with local agencies and enterprises. Some of the available partnerships include the Arizona Wilderness Coalition, Centaur Leadership Services (an equine therapy program), the Kino Bay Center in Mexico (a field station), and an experimental agroecology farm.

All of which sounds like a remarkable undergraduate opportunity, and it is. There is one caveat, however, that I ought to mention at this point:

You won't see much in the way of a formal campus when you visit Prescott. There is a library and a performing arts building, and an admissions office, and a building for academic advising, but they are spread around town. You won't be enclosed on a campus. And, you won't see a residential complex; the college has built residential facilities housing, but many find housing in the city of Prescott. The college has a housing office that helps students find appropriate apartments and living arrangements, but there is residential life at Prescott despite its unusual campus design.

California

There are so many misconceptions about California that that it hard to know where to begin. I know people in other regions who think the entire state is filled with weirdness, and, although California has its share of oddities, California is huge and virtually a nation unto itself. And, after the description of Santa Fe and Prescott, California's colleges and universities are going to seem downright tame.

California is essentially made up of distinct regions – Northern or Upper California (from the Oregon line to Santa Rosa), The Sierra Nevada range (Yosemite, Sequoia, Mount Whitney, Lake Tahoe, King's Canyon) the Bay Area (from Marin County to San Jose), the Central Valley (Sacramento Valley and the San Joaquin Valleys – from Redding to Bakersfield), The Central Coast (Monterey Bay to Point Conception), The American Riviera (Santa Barbara), Los Angeles and the San Fernando Valley (from Thousand Oaks to Long Beach), San Diego, the Inland Empire (Riverside and San Bernardino), and the Imperial Valley (Coachella and the Salton Sea).

College visitors to California need to plan their trip with some care; the distances to be traveled can be daunting. For example, the distance from San Diego (University of California San Diego, San Diego State, University of San Diego) to Arcata (Humboldt State) is roughly the same distance as a drive from New York City to Charleston, South Carolina.

Most college searchers will start in San Francisco or Los Angeles, and those gateways offer very productive college exploration.

North of San Francisco, a visitor will find Sonoma State and Dominican University. Northeast of San Francisco, on the way to Lake Tahoe, a driver will find Sacramento State, U Cal Davis, and further north, Chico State. The newest campus of the University of California, at Merced, is about two hours southeast of San Francisco, due south of Modesto.

In what is called the East Bay, including Oakland and Berkeley, the traveler will find California Maritime Academy, Saint Mary's University, Mills College, U Cal Berkeley, and Cal State East Bay.

The University of San Francisco, San Francisco State, the Art Institute of California, and California College of the Arts are all in the City of San Francisco.

Driving south of the city toward the Pacific Coast Highway and the remarkable stretch of coastal views, a college searcher can visit Stanford, Notre Dame de Namur, (a university with the greatest heart and mission in the world – Oprah should be underwriting all that Notre Dame attempts to do) U Cal Santa Cruz, and California Polytechnic State University in San Luis Obispo.

San Jose is to the south of Oakland, and a drive slightly south and east opens up another gratifying trail. San Jose State is in San Jose; an adjacent community is Santa Clara, home to Santa Clara University and a Great America Amusement Park. Further east is Turlock, home to Cal State Stanislaus, and northeast is the port city of Stockton, site of the University of the Pacific. Merced, the newest of the University of California Campuses is south of Turlock, only a short drive from the west gateway to Yosemite National Park.

Debate rages as to where the Central Coast ends and Southern California begins, but the visiting driver can safely assume that once past Santa Barbara (U Cal Santa Barbara and Westmont College), all roads lead to So Cal.

The San Fernando Valley runs north of the City of Los Angeles and contains one of the Cal States (Northridge), California Institute of the Arts in Valencia, and California Lutheran University in Thousand Oaks. The Pacific Coast Highway picks up again south of Point Mugu and carries visitors from Malibu to Santa Monica, passing right by one of the most beautiful college settings at Pepperdine and winding on past Loyola Marymount to the colleges and universities south of Long Beach.

The City of Los Angeles is an easier city to drive in that many and will easily present its treasures. UCLA is the University of California in Los Angeles; Cal State Los Angeles and Cal State Dominguez Hills are both in the city, as are the Fashion Institute of Design and Merchandising (FIDM), the American Film Institute, Loyola Marymount University, Mount Saint Mary's College, and the Otis College of Art and Design.

USC is in the West Adams district of Los Angeles, about two miles from the heart of the city. Occidental College is in Eagle Rock in northeastern Los Angeles. Whittier College is in Whittier, southeast of Los Angeles.

Pasadena is the home of the Rose Parade and the Rose Bowl, and a city worth visiting in its own right. Cal Tech is located in the southern central section of Pasadena; the Art Center College of Design is in the Hills overlooking the Rose Bowl.

Claremont is east of Pasadena and home to the five undergraduate Claremont colleges: Pomona, Claremont McKenna, Scripps, Harvey Mudd, and Pitzer. Further east, heading into the Inland Empire, are UC Riverside and University of Redlands.

The last highly celebrated section of the state to be explored is Orange County. The OC is home to Disneyland, Knotts Berry Farm, and the beach communities that have given the county some notoriety. Much of Orange County is inland, former orange grove territory. Orange, for example, home of Chapman University and its extraordinary program in film and film studies, is a charming town that seems of another age. Cal State Fullerton, perennial baseball power, is in a small city outside of Anaheim, and the University of California, Irvine's "Anteaters" who have recently appeared in the College Baseball World Series is only moments from the coast.

It's a shame that the U Cal system is so very hard to crack. Each of the campuses has much to offer; applicants from outside the state have the best chance at Merced, Riverside, Irvine, and to some degree, Santa Cruz.

The California colleges profiled in this book include four in the California State University System: Cal State Stanislaus, San Francisco State, Sonoma State, and the California Maritime Academy.

Six of the profiled California colleges have associations with the Catholic Church: University of San Francisco, Santa Clara University, Dominican University, Saint Mary's University, Thomas Aquinas, and the University of San Diego. The profiled independent colleges are Whittier, located just outside the city of Los Angeles, and the University of Redlands, located in Redlands, west of Palm Springs.

California State Universities

There are twenty-three separate state universities in California in addition to the nine undergraduate campuses of the University of California. The twenty-three state universities are dispersed throughout the state and serve particular needs in particular settings. The newest of the Cal States is Cal State Channel Islands in Camarillo, north of Los Angeles; the others, for the most part, serve the particular needs of California's major cities.

San Diego State, San Jose State, and Fresno State are universities of considerable size. Cal Poly in San Luis Obispo is a strong Tech school with highly regarded programs in Engineering, Architecture, and Education; Cal Poly also draws quite widely from all parts of the state.

The four best-kept secrets in the Cal State system are the California Maritime Academy, Cal State Stanislaus, Sonoma State, and Cal State San Francisco.

The California Maritime Academy - Vallejo, California

This is a closely-knit group of earnest students who have a clear sense of profession. They enjoy their college life, play sports, and dominate, for instance, in rugby, in which enterprise they regularly defeat larger schools. Sailing is also a highly competitive sport at CMA, and the college turns out some of the finest sailors on the West Coast.

And the stats... 2015

Number of Applicants: 1,102 / 67% Accepted
Undergrad Enrollment: 1,047 14% female / 86% male
Avg. SAT Reading 460-580 and Math 500 -600 Avg. ACT: 19-26
Total Cost: $22,023.00 (in-state) $33,118.00 (out-of-state)
Received some form of financial assistance: 62%

Cal Maritime is one of only seven maritime academies in the country offering a degree. Located in Vallejo, at the northern end of what is called the East Bay, the academy looks for all intents and purposes like a military academy.

Students wear uniforms, muster in company formation, and earn rank for leadership performance. There is no obligation of military service upon graduation, however, although a significant number of students will participate in scholarship programs offered by the Coast Guard or the Navy Merchant Marine Reserve.

All students belong to the Corps of Cadets, and all are expected to learn the skill of command and the habit of responsibility in the corps. On the other hand, this is a state university, so uniforms are not required at the end of the class day, and weekends are open unless a training cruise on the Academy's training ship, the Golden Bear, is underway.

The Academy offers a degree in Mechanical Engineering, Marine Engineering Technology, Marine Transportation, International Business and Logistics, Facilities Engineering Technology, and Global Studies and Maritime Affairs.

Virtually all graduates intend to become involved in a nautical profession, although that profession may involve working exclusively stateside. The operation of every port in the world, for example, is in the hands of people who have been trained as these students are trained.

480

I confess myself most impressed by the giant lab simulating the approach to every port. Standing at the wheel, looking out at the horizon, watching New York or Hamburg come into view is a striking experience.

This is a closely-knit group of earnest students who have a clear sense of profession. They enjoy their college life, play sports, and dominate, for instance, in rugby, in which enterprise they regularly defeat larger schools. Sailing is also a highly competitive sport at CMA, and the college turns out some of the finest sailors on the West Coast.

Although Cal Maritime is a state school, it has considerable liberty in selecting the first year class. The Academy's current policy is to accept all qualified students with the exception of those applying to the program in Marine Transportation. That program is "impacted" and much more competitive.

California State University - Stanislaus - Turlock, California

Here's the best thing about Stan State – it's a true state university with more than a hundred major and minor programs, including the only undergraduate degree in Cognitive Science in the state, and ... the total undergraduate population on campus is under eight thousand students!

And the stats... 2015

Number of Applicants: 6,269 / 73% Accepted
Undergrad Enrollment: 7,848 64% female / 36% male
Avg. SAT Reading 450-560 and Math 460 -570 Avg. ACT: 20-24
Total Cost: $19,961.00 (in-state) $31,121.00 (out-of-state)
Received some form of financial assistance: 83%

Stanislaus is actually located in Turlock, a small city of about seventy thousand just outside of Modesto, and here's the best thing about Stan State – it's a true state university with more than a hundred major and minor programs, including the only undergraduate degree in Cognitive Science in the state, and... the total undergraduate population on campus is under seven thousand students!

Stanislaus is on a leafy, well-manicured campus of about two hundred and fifty acres on the edge of Turlock. The setting is quite pretty, as the campus is built around several ponds (complete with ducks). The facilities are good, newly constructed, and attractive, and the residence halls are cleverly built as condo-complexes with patios, swimming pools, and barbeque areas. The central dining hall is a pretty place to meet and dine, and the food is pretty darned good for a public dining hall.

Cal State Stanislaus plays a true Division II athletic schedule, although the soccer teams take on Division I opponents. The Women's soccer team is particularly ambitious and successful. The men's golf team won a string of national championships before moving up to Division II and has remained highly competitive. Baseball is also a very popular spectator sport; the team is excellent and has sent a number of players into major league baseball.

Those outside the region might not expect this university to sponsor a society for Hmong students, Nearby Fresno, however, has a population of more than twenty thousand Hmong, almost five percent of the city's population. Stanislaus has been at the forefront of universities offering support to first generation Hmong college students.

Sonoma State University - Rohnert Park, California

Sonoma State is a jewel of a university, currently enrolling about eight thousand five hundred undergraduates on a sparkling campus with extraordinary residential opportunities.

And the stats... 2015

Number of Applicants: 14,438 / 80% Accepted
Undergrad Enrollment: 8,512 62% female / 38% male
Avg. SAT Reading 440-550 and Math 440 -550 Avg. ACT: 18-23
Total Cost: $23,655.00 (in-state) $34,815.00 (out-of-state)
Received some form of financial assistance: 63%

Rohnert Park is a planned community, adjacent to the Armstrong Redwood State Preserve, the Annandel State Park, and Sugarloaf Ridge State Park, about seven miles south of Santa Rosa in Sonoma County. Extensive outdoor recreation, including the Tomales Bay State Park, is easily accessible, as are all the pleasures of the nearby Napa Valley.

Sonoma State is a jewel of a university, currently enrolling about eight thousand five hundred undergraduates on a sparkling campus with extraordinary residential opportunities.

Instruction is offered in six separate divisions maintained by the university. The divisions include a School of Arts and Humanities, A School of Business and Economics, a School of Education, a School of Extended Education, a School of Science and Technology, and a School of Social Sciences. The most popular majors are Business, Biology, Kinesiology, Communications, Psychology, Pre-Nursing, English, Criminal Justice, and History.

Located only an hour north of San Francisco, Sonoma State feels like a country retreat with all the energy and activity of a true college campus. Roughly twenty percent of the undergrads are affiliated with fraternities or sororities; seven of each have a place on campus. An extensive program of on-campus activities is also available for the entire student body, and a number of special events enliven the school year.

Much of that activity is planned for and around the residential communities, and it is in the organization of residential life that Sonoma State is both unique and impressive.

Students may elect to live in very comfortable special interest housing or learning communities, but the majority choose to join one of Sonoma's "Villages" – each of which is essentially a condominium neighborhood. The names of the villages reveal the legacy of nearby "wine country" as they are Beaujolais, Cabernet, Sauvignon, Verdot, Zinfandel, and Tuscany.

A high spirited residential life team organizes activities throughout the year, often grabbing a group for a trip to the city, to a Giants game, to the Great American theme park. Residential life is uncommonly happy at Sonoma, no matter what choice of residence a student picks.

Three recent initiatives have expanded the university's resources considerably. The campus expanded to include a new residential quadrant known as Sauvignon Village, Charles Schulz (creator of Charlie Brown and Snoopy) endowed the new Information Center, an expansion of the library facilities, and a new music center with concert hall, now the home of the Santa Rosa Symphony.

The Sonoma State Seawolves play in Division II and have won national championships in men's and women's soccer and in golf. The basketball teams draw big crowds, and water polo is increasingly popular as a spectator sport. Seawolf pride is evident and part of the reason morale on the small state university's campus is so exceedingly high.

San Francisco State University - San Francisco, California

San Francisco State is the most diverse student body anywhere, and the university supports diversity of every kind! Campus organizations are in the hundreds and many of them are attached to issues of race, ethnicity, gender, sexual orientation, and political causes at every point along the spectrum. There is a palpable level of activism and engagement among students and a very clear commitment to student from this highly evolved city university. In addition, SF State hosts the largest number of international students of any institution in the United States.

And the stats... 2015

Number of Applicants: 31,963 / 66% Accepted
Undergrad Enrollment: 25,938 57% female / 43% male
Avg. SAT Reading 430-550 and Math 440 -560 Avg. ACT: 18-24
Total Cost: $24,206.00 (in-state) $35,366.00 (out-of-state)
Received some form of financial assistance: 70%

Cal State San Francisco was at the heart of the student movement in the 1960's and in the midst of most political and social movements in the years since. The university calls itself, " a public urban university with a conscience," and that identity allows the university to offer a particularly effective education to the populations it serves.

There are three compelling reasons to consider SF State:

In the first place - San Francisco!

SF State is located in one of the most fascinating, exciting, culturally rich cities in the country. Living in San Francisco is expensive, and student housing in apartments is reasonable. I can't imagine a more stimulating urban experience than living in San Francisco and going to SF State.

Second, San Francisco State is the most diverse student body anywhere, and the university supports diversity of every kind! Campus organizations are in the hundreds and many of them are attached to issues of race, ethnicity, gender, sexual orientation, and political causes at every point along the spectrum. There is a palpable level of activism and engagement among students and a very clear commitment to student from this highly evolved city university. In addition, SF State hosts the largest number of international students of any institution in the United States.

You will truly meet the world at SF State.

Finally, SF State offers programs that are first-rate and not always found elsewhere. The university's motto is *Experientia Docent*- experience teaches – and hands-on education is at the heart of some of the university's most celebrated programs.

Obviously, community based programs and internships abound, but the hands-on approach is also significant in the fields that have been recognized as uncommonly successful at the university.

Interested in Advertising? Graphic Design? Extraordinary programs are offered at SF State.

Bioscience, Film, Broadcast Journalism, Creative Writing, Teacher Education, Physical Therapy, Multimedia Studies, Human Sexuality, Jewish Studies – all are considered among the best in the nation.

Obviously, the program in International Relations remains excellent. SF State was one of the first universities in the country to offer a program in International relations, and theirs is still considered one of the best.

The two "sexiest" programs (No, not Human Sexuality – although that is a remarkable program) are Broadcast and Electronic Communication Arts and Film. Without hyperbole, these are two of the most influential programs of their kind, and an aspiring media student could not find a more powerful area of study with greater resources at hand.

SF State (the SF Gators – from the Golden Gate) plays a Division II athletic schedule and offers a ton of recreational sports and clubs to meet the needs of its incredibly diverse student population.

Dominican University of California - San Rafael, California

Residential life is active and happy, although the proximity to San Francisco (twelve miles) and to the beach, and to the mountains, and to Napa Valley, and to Yosemite makes on-campus life a bit less of an issue than it might be in some other small colleges. Dominican's kids get around, and transportation in every direction is easy to find. There are some significant on-campus activities, and the residential halls build considerable spirit and sense of community. The single greatest unifying experience, however, is in supporting the successful athletic program.

And the stats... 2015

Number of Applicants: 2,076 / 81% Accepted
Undergrad Enrollment: 1,485 74% female / 26% male
Avg. SAT Reading 470-570 and Math 470 -580 Avg. ACT: 20-25
Total Cost: $60,016.00
Received some form of financial assistance: 99%

San Rafael is the County Seat of Marin County, and Marin County - just across the Golden Gate Bridge from San Francisco - is one of the five counties with the highest per capita income in the United States. San Rafael is of particular interest to movie fans because the city has been the backdrop for films such as American Graffiti and because the film and game industries have built technological empires in San Rafael. The city is home to LucasArts, THX, Broderbund Software, and Mind Control Software, among other cutting edge enterprises.

So, the delightful campus of Dominican University, located virtually in the heart of downtown San Rafael is all the more delightful for the quaint charm of some of its original buildings. The university describes itself as "an independent university of Catholic heritage," and that description allows the long tradition of educational service by the Dominican Sisters to be honored even as the university takes on a wider mission in the contemporary world.

Dominican was founded in 1890 by the Dominican Sisters of San Rafael who quickly established a flourishing school and college on the site the university currently occupies. The college was the first in California to award a B.A. degree to women and remained active and progressive, becoming fully coeducational in 1970. The heritage of the Dominican Sisters is kept alive in the unaffiliated university's mascot – the Penguin. The title of the campus newspaper? The Habit.

The campus is a bit odd in that it is literally in a neighborhood, and in that the campus is divided into several sections. The front half of the campus is essentially the original school building and a multi-purpose mansion, once the summer home of the de Young family. Known as "Meadowlands," the stately manor house is a rambling center of social activity, a dormitory, a recreational space, and more. The university's early teaching spaces were built adjacent to "Meadowlands," and many classes are held on the "old" half of the campus. Crossing a quiet street, the visitor will find the newer buildings that have completed the university's academic and residential plan. Slightly removed from the neighborhood setting are the extensive playing fields, courts, and impressive athletic facilities.

Dominican is a small (1500) university with a wide selection of courses and major programs. The university's mission remains centered on educating ethical and responsible global citizens, so many of its programs are connected with preparation for a profession. For example, the university offers an undergraduate degree in Nursing and a degree in Occupational Therapy as part of its School of Health and Science.

The School of Business and Leadership offers degrees in Accounting, Finance, International Business, Marketing, and Management. The School also houses an Institute for Leadership Studies, a Center for Sustainability, and an office coordinating the university's extensive program of study abroad. Partnerships with universities in the Philippines, Spain, Indonesia, and Thailand make travel easy.

The School of Education and Counseling Psychology offers a degree in Liberal Studies/Teacher Education, combining a general education with preparation for certification. Field-work begins as early as the Freshman year.

Most of the liberal arts are offered in the School of Arts, Humanities, and Social Science, including an excellent set of programs in the creative and performing arts. A recent alliance with Alonzo King's LINES Ballet School allows Dominican students to earn a degree in dance while working with a professional company. Students from Dominican have been invited to dance with LINES Ballet in San Francisco and on tour in Europe.

A particular advantage for Dominican students currently is the speaker series sponsored by the Institute for Leadership. The ISL line-up recently has included author, Jodi Picoult, actor, Ted Danson, financial pundit, Suze Orman, and Caroline Kennedy.

Residential life is active and happy, although the proximity to San Francisco (twelve miles) and to the beach, and to the mountains, and to Napa Valley, and to Yosemite makes on-campus life a bit less of an issue than it might be in some other small colleges. Dominican's kids get around, and transportation in every direction is easy to find. There are some significant on-campus activities, and the residential halls build considerable spirit and sense of community. The single greatest unifying experience, however, is in supporting the successful athletic program.

The Penguins play in the Pacific West Conference of NCAA Division II, having recently left the NAIA. The shift is a statement, moving Dominican into the mainstream of California collegiate sports and identifying the athletic program as an important part of the university's life. The construction of the Conlon Athletic Center with an impressive training facility, weight room, and basketball court has pulled the program up a full level. The university offers twelve varsity sports, including a strong program in lacrosse.

Twelve miles from San Francisco, a beautiful location, a student/faculty ratio of 11:1, and sound academic preparation for profession or graduate school... how can a student go wrong?

University of San Francisco - San Francisco, California

Part of the university's success comes in its determination to prepare students to take their place in the world with an awareness of social justice and an appreciation of diversity of cultures. USF is extremely diverse; almost forty percent of enrolled undergraduates are Asian, African-American, Latino, or Native Hawaiian/Pacific Islander. The University's mission is to educate leaders who will, "fashion a more humane and just world."

And the stats... 2015

Number of Applicants: 17,488 / 60% Accepted
Undergrad Enrollment: 1,268 62% female / 38% male
Avg. SAT Reading 510-590 and Math 520 -640 Avg. ACT: 22-27
Total Cost: $60,170.00
Received some form of financial assistance: 72%

Put on your hiking shoes! San Francisco is a city of hills and the University of San Francisco is perched atop one of the tallest. The campus is lovely, fifty acres of prime San Francisco real estate including playing fields, an impressive gymnasium, and about one hundred and fifty steps straight up from the street to the front door of the Lone Mountain campus.

There are several issues to clarify from the start. Like Boston University, New York University, and the University of Chicago, the University of San Francisco is not a public institution. Founded as Saint Ignatius Academy on Market Street in San Francisco by Jesuit brothers, the university has moved and grown. Now located near Golden Gate Park, the university enrolls more than five thousand undergraduate students and another three thousand graduate students in six schools and colleges - A School of Law, the School of Arts and Sciences, A School of Nursing, the School of Business and Professional Studies, the School of Education, and a School of Continuing Education. Undergraduates are enrolled in Arts and Sciences, Business and Professional Studies, Nursing, and Continuing Education.

It is to the university's credit that an institution of this size is often referred to by undergraduates as a "small school." Graduates and current students rave about close relationships with professors, and many report that they have enjoyed classes of no more than ten or twelve students. There is a good sense of community and a real bond between students and

491

the university, all the more impressive in that San Francisco is a notable distraction to anyone of college age.

Part of the university's success comes in its determination to prepare students to take their place in the world with an awareness of social justice and an appreciation of diversity of cultures. USF is extremely diverse; almost forty percent of enrolled undergraduates are Asian, African-American, Latino, or Native Hawaiian/Pacific Islander. The University's mission is to educate leaders who will, "fashion a more humane and just world." That mission is tied to the university's Catholic colleges and legacy as a Jesuit university, and its roots in the Catholic Church remain important in the university's vision of itself; USF is one of the twenty-eight Jesuit colleges and universities in the United States, as are Georgetown and Boston College.

The undergraduate population does include Catholics, of course, (about forty percent of students) but the great draw is a sound professional and pre-professional education in one of the most exciting cities in the world. Against all odds, the sense of community among the five thousand students is fairly strong, although almost all admit that the pull of the city is great enough to make on-campus parties somewhat less interesting than options in SF. Because the mix of cultures is so rich, and because the mix in San Francisco is so rich, one of the university's great advantages is in allowing students to become immersed in a world greater than they had expected.

In San Francisco, a city known for restaurants and exquisite cuisine of every kind, the dining facilities at the University are excellent and numbers of fine food options are available on campus. How fair is that? Great location. Great views. Great people. And now, Great Food!

In a city in which real estate is a prized commodity, the university's dormitories are handsome, safe, and beautifully located on the flat, close to the gymnasium and every form of transportation.

At some point, I suppose I should pause long enough to describe the academic opportunities at USF, and, once again, there is an embarrassment of riches – almost a hundred majors or programs available to undergraduates.

Starting with the College of Arts and Sciences, the student finds, in addition to the usual liberal arts options, the following departments: Art and Architecture, Asian Studies, Exercise and Sport Science, and Performing Arts and Social Justice. These programs include uncommon majors as Advertising and Architecture and Community Design.

The School of Business and Professional Studies offers Accounting, Entrepreneurship and Innovation, Business Administration, Hospitality Industry Management, International Business, Marketing, Business Economics, Information Systems, Public Administration, and Organizational Behavior and Leadership.

The School of Nursing offers the Bachelor of Science in Nursing in a program combining coursework and clinical labs.

Most students will encounter the USF Core Curriculum, a two-year sequence of courses intended to provide a solid grounding in academic skills of reasoning and expression. The university maintains a requirement that all native English speakers study a foreign language.
It goes without saying that in addition to all the resources of the city, the university provides extensive recreational facilities, clubs, organizations, and social opportunities. A small proportion of the student body will enter into Greek life. At any given time, a number of fraternities and sororities will offer the opportunity to experience close community and shared social values.

Finally, athletics at the University of San Francisco has a storied and complicated history.

The first chapter has everything to do with the university's role as an agent of change and social justice.

USF was a football powerhouse in the early 1950's.

Ten member of the undefeated 1950 football team went on to play in the NFL; three were inducted into the Professional Football Hall of Fame. This exceptional team included two African-Americans - Ollie Matson, Rookie of the Year with the Chicago Cardinals and Hall of Fame running back with the Cardinals, Rams, Lions, and Eagles, and Burl Toler, who would go on to become the first African-American official in the NFL.

The Dons of USF, then, were one of America's most accomplished teams, and were invited to play in the Orange Bowl - without Matson and Toler. The university refused the invitation. The statement from the team was clear: "We're going to play with 'em, or we're not going to play." Without the infusion of cash from a bowl appearance, the University was forced to give up the football program in the following year.

From 1954 to 1956, however, the USF Dons basketball team won sixty games in a row and a national championship. The team was led by basketball greats Bill Russell and K.C. Jones, and was the first national championship team to start three African-Americans.

The prominence of soccer in college athletics today is a fairly recent phenomenon. At USF, however, soccer was a signature sport as early as the 1930's. In part, soccer emerged in cities with significant immigrant families. It was no accident that St. Louis and San Francisco were the first great centers of collegiate soccer in the United States. USF has won a number of national championships and is numbered among the great soccer traditions in collegiate athletics.

So, a fabulous location, extensive professional programs, a beautiful campus, and rich traditions – how can USF long remain a secret outside the region?

Saint Mary's College of California - Moraga, California

Saint Mary's has SPIRIT, and I mean the campus is alive with hearty, vocal, boisterous school spirit – the gymnasium literally rocks when Saint Mary's Gaels play the bulldogs of Gonzaga in some of the best basketball found in Division I. And, the college also holds an abiding and palpable sense of community spirit – for the college community and in service to the wider world.

And the stats... 2015

Number of Applicants: 4,865 / 76% Accepted
Undergrad Enrollment: 2,961 59% female / 41% male
Avg. SAT Reading 490-600 and Math 500 -610 Avg. ACT: 22-27
Total Cost: $59,327.00
Received some form of financial assistance: 95%

I am in danger of over-selling this gem, and I know my enthusiasm may be a bit off-putting, but on my first visit to the campus, I was stunned, surprised, entranced, enchanted, and so on...

What makes Saint Mary's so special?

In the first place, the setting is gorgeous. The campus feels secluded and safe; Moraga is a small town, adjacent to Lafayette and near Walnut Creek, both very spiffy East Bay suburbs about ten miles from Oakland and about twenty from San Francisco. One of the great advantages, I think, of the Saint Mary's campus is that the Bay Area Rapid Transit (BART) line is easily accessed from the campus, so a quick train ride puts a Saint Mary's student in the heart of San Francisco.

Best of both worlds from my point of view.

In the second place, Saint Mary's has SPIRIT, and I mean the campus is alive with hearty, vocal, boisterous school spirit – the gymnasium literally **rocks** when Saint Mary's Gaels play the bulldogs of Gonzaga in some of the best basketball found in Division I.

There is also an abiding and palpable sense of community spirit – for the college community and in service to the wider world.

The college puts it this way:

"At Saint Mary's it's ... about energy, idealism. Enthusiasm. It's the kind of thing where you know you're smart (and compassionate, and courageous) and you're done apologizing for it."

It is rare to find a college in which students are so active and so genuinely dedicated to their studies, their school, and their world. At the risk of making the Saint Mary's students sound like saints (they are, after all, perfectly normal college humans), there is something different about the kind of person who chooses to attend a college such as Saint Mary's.

One of the differences has to be in admiring the legacy of the De La Salle Christian Brothers, some of whom still live and work on campus. Saint Mary's is affiliated with the Roman Catholic Church, and as it has at Notre Dame, Georgetown, and Boston College, the rigor of Catholic education has helped to create a strong academic environment.

At Saint Mary's, that rigor is expressed in two significant programs – the Collegiate Seminar and the Integral Program.

As the college puts it, "The Marines have Boot Camp; we have Collegiate Seminar."

Actually, the Seminar is a kinder, gentler experience; a small group sits around a table and discusses one of the great works of Western Civilization. The works themselves are significant, but the magic of the process is in the seminar. Reading line–by–line, attacking the work individually and with the group's insight, the seminar challenges each student to read actively and to learn to shape a response with reasoned precision.

Students take two of the seminars in their first year and two more during the course of their time at Saint Mary's. In addition to the academic skills attained in the process, each participant has worked on equal footing with each student and with the professor. Students not only claim mastery of the work they have studied, they develop habits of mind that serve them well, no matter what major field they decide to pursue.

Some who are particularly attracted to the seminar experience may elect to enter into the Integral Program, a four–year seminar, in which the small group studies together intensively. The program allows some room for elective courses, but this is essentially a Great Books curriculum along the lines of that presented by the St. John's Colleges.

"It's a simple idea," the college suggests. " Read and discuss the world's greatest thinkers. Then go out and be one."

The life of the mind is heady stuff, but Saint Mary's is determined in connecting the experience in the classroom with a life of purpose and quality. Students are involved with community service to a degree unmatched in any liberal arts college; an office coordinating service projects is in the heart of the campus and always buzzing. The proof is in the outcome, however, and more than ten percent of a Saint Mary's graduating class will end up in a major service organization, such as the Peace Corps or Teach for America.

I know, this all sounds very noble and high-minded, but college is supposed to be fun.

The students at Saint Mary's do work hard, but they are among the happiest and most satisfied of any group of college kids. Social events abound and they are well supported. Dance, Theater, Music, goofy hi-jinx – all are much appreciated. The college is very diverse – almost forty percent are people of color – and the ways of enlivening an afternoon or evening are equally diverse. It has to be said, however, that one notable characteristic of Saint Mary's is a stunningly effective athletic program. The college is relatively small (2100 students) and yet it competes with major powers at the top level of Division I.

This, by the way, is nothing new. Saint Mary's football was a sensation in the 1920's, defeating teams such as USC and Texas Tech. Today, football is but a memory, and the nationally ranked basketball team has claimed the public spotlight.

The Gaels have a part to play in the annual basketball frenzy known as "March Madness." In 2010, they scrapped their way to the "Sweet Sixteen," eventually falling to a tough Butler team. Obviously, a team's successes vary from season to season, but there is no inconsistency in the throbbing intensity of crowd support in McKeon Pavilion when the Gaels play at home. One of the smallest venues in Division I, the home court is literally ringed with rabid spectators. 3500 frenzied Gaels fill the small arena with noise from opening tip-off to the last basket.

Saint Mary's offer a total of fourteen Division I varsity sports and ten athletic clubs of very high quality. The Saint Mary's rugby team, for example, has been among the country's top ten teams, competing with Berkeley and Ohio State.

Among the varsity teams, women's basketball, volleyball, softball, and tennis teams are perennially successful. Both men's and women's soccer teams are nationally ranked.

Over-sell? I hope not. Saint Mary's is one-of-a-kind, an active, happy, purposeful, beautiful college with a distinguished legacy of service. It is one secret that deserves to be much more appreciated.

University of the Pacific - Stockton, California

A major component of the curriculum at Pacific is the expectation that most students will engage in meaningful internship or research. Many students also find cooperative programs, earning a salary while learning on-the-job. Some cooperative placements have been at DreamWorks Studio, NASA, and the White House. Active and engaged students enjoy an education designed to prepare them to take their place in a meaningful career. The liberal arts are at the heart of the General Education Program, and the emphasis on effective expression remains consistent throughout.

And the stats... 2015

Number of Applicants: 15,183 / 55% Accepted
Undergrad Enrollment: 3,810 52% female / 48% male
Avg. SAT Reading 500-630 and Math 530 -680 Avg. ACT: 23-30
Admissions information at the University of the Pacific is slightly skewed by the extremely competitive programs in pre-Pharmacy and Pre- Dentistry.
Total Cost: $58,829.00
Received some form of financial assistance: 90%

The University of the Pacific is located on a gorgeous campus in the port city of Stockton. Stockton has had its difficulties, as have many of California's cities in an era of economic recession, but the university's campus is elegant, impressive, and safe.

Pacific College is the heart of the university and the oldest chartered university in the state. Many visitors will find the campus feels familiar; it has been the backdrop to many movies, frequently doubling for a picturesque Ivy League campus. For example, it was from a classroom at Pacific that Indiana Jones headed out with the *Raiders of the Lost Ark.* The shaded, well-organized campus is both handsome and sensible; it is easy to find one's way around, and all facilities are easily accessible.

UOP is a very interesting model of small university in that it enrolls about thirty-five hundred undergraduates in Pacific College and offers advanced degrees from nine professional schools and a graduate school. Pacific's Law School is in Sacramento and the Dental School is in San Francisco; the other programs are on the Stockton campus. The prominence of the professional programs adds considerable clout to the Pacific degree and assists Pacific's graduates in getting to professional programs in Music,

Dentistry, Law, Business, Pharmacy, Engineering, and International Studies.

Undergrads attending Pacific College will find a number of programs that are unique to the U of P. For example, undergraduate students can take cross-disciplinary courses while in the School of International Studies. Honors students can begin their course of study in the Law School, the Dental School, or the School of Pharmacy while finishing the B.A. The Music major in Pacific's Conservatory of Music includes Music Management and Music Therapy. The Business Administration Program includes specialization in Business Law and Real Estate. The Engineering program includes a course of study in Bioengineering.

A major component of the curriculum at Pacific is the expectation that most students will engage in meaningful internship or research. Many students also find cooperative programs, earning a salary while learning on-the-job. Some cooperative placements have been at DreamWorks Studio, NASA, and the White House.

Active and engaged students enjoy an education designed to prepare them to take their place in a meaningful career. The liberal arts are at the heart of the General Education Program, and the emphasis on effective expression remains consistent throughout.

The university houses three important centers, each of which is a resource for undergraduates in any program.

The first of these, The John Muir Center, is a repository for Muir's correspondence and for the history of the environmental movement in the United States.

The Jacoby Center for Public Service and Civic Leadership acts a forum for interdisciplinary examination of contemporary issues, bringing experts from various fields to the center and promoting open exchange. The Jacoby Center also coordinates the programs that carry students off campus and into significant engagement in civic affairs. UOP sends students to the Washington Semester and places others in Sacramento where they have the opportunity to get a hands-on introduction to state government.

The Humanities Center celebrates the humanities and the arts, sponsoring performances and events, ranging from coffee houses to an evening with Jane Austen. The center is the home of the college's literary magazine, Calliope, produced by students interested in English and the Visual Arts.

There is a rich residential life beyond the classroom at Pacific, and the quality of student residential life is impressive. Fraternities and sororities are very active and attract roughly 25% of students. Each residence takes on a character of its own and provides a sense of community and an active social life. Some of the residential options are called Residential Learning Communities, and they allow students of similar in interests to live and work together. Covell Hall is the largest of these, welcoming more than three hundred students who have chosen Social Justice as a point of interest. Other interests include Earth and Environmental Living, Pacific Inter-American Community, and a residence set aside for Freshmen in a Learning Community. The Quad Communities are ten small communities located on the south end of campus. There are also apartment communities for upper-class students.

Residential life is taken seriously, and the variety of programs offered through the Recreation Program is impressive. Pacific has claimed the tiger as its mascot, and Tiger Training presents eager students with a personal trainer to effect total fitness. Rec Sports include dodgeball, floor hockey, flag football, ping pong, badminton, and walleyball, and a comprehensive pool celebrating "March Madness." Club sports include soccer, lacrosse, flag football, rock climbing, mixed martial arts, swimming, rugby, tae kwan do, tennis, and water polo. The newest of Pacific's teams has introduced rowing, training athletes from September to May.

The Pacific Tigers play in the NCAA Division I Big West Conference, although the university has let the football program go. The flagship program at Pacific is basketball, which is extremely successful, having a spot in the NCAA post-season tournament four times.

Most Pacific students are involved in intercollegiate or recreational sports, and the modern athletic facilities allow every imaginable activity.

I'm about to provide the statistical breakdown of enrollment and admissions, but I want to pause just to make sure applicants are aware that the demographic makeup of Pacific's students is remarkable. Roughly 35% of the 3400 students enrolled at the college are white non-Hispanic. Approximately 34% are Asian/Pacific Islander. International students, Black students, Hispanic students are also well represented

Thomas Aquinas College - Santa Paula, California

Imagine driving south from the sun dappled Ojai Valley toward tiny Santa Paula, passing orange groves, avocado ranches, and what passes for a Mediterranean landscape, following a curvy mountain pass to the view of what can only be described as a jaw-droppingly stunning example of the mixture of Renaissance and Spanish Mission architecture in a fifteen thousand square foot chapel, Our Lady of the Most Holy Trinity Chapel, gleaming in a rosy California sunset.

And the stats... 2015

Number of Applicants: 185 / 83% Accepted
Undergrad Enrollment: 378 49% female / 51% male
Avg. SAT Reading 620-710 and Math 560 -640 Avg. ACT: 24-31
Total Cost: $35,706.00
Received some form of financial assistance: 83%

The great danger in writing about Thomas Aquinas is that I may make it sound precious or simply quirky when, in fact, it could not be a more serious-minded and purposeful institution. This is not a college for everyone, and the usual collegiate hi-jinx are relentlessly absent, but it is a community with a strong sense of purpose, a really clear mission, and an abiding commitment to the life of the mind and the care of the soul. Faith and reason in lively balance amid one of the most serene collegiate settings imaginable!

Imagine driving south from the sun dappled Ojai Valley toward tiny Santa Paula, passing orange groves, avocado ranches, and what passes for a Mediterranean landscape, following a curvy mountain pass to the view of what can only be described as a jaw-droppingly stunning example of the mixture of Renaissance and Spanish Mission architecture in a fifteen thousand square foot chapel, Our Lady of the Most Holy Trinity Chapel, gleaming in a rosy California sunset.

The Chapel is the heart of this campus and it is an exceptionally inspiring building. Remember, this campus is as close to the middle of nowhere as any campus in Ventura County could possibly be, and this chapel has the gravitas of the Wieskirche in Bavaria. Parking near the chapel the visitor will begin to see that there actually is a campus that has grown up beyond the chapel. The college is relatively new, founded in nineteen seventy-one in response to what was seen as a crisis within the Catholic Church. The general progression in the culture to extreme secularization and permissive social behavior, especially in colleges and universities, was at odds, some in the Church believed, with the principles of rigorous intellectual exercise and precepts of the faith itself. It may not be immediately obvious to the casual visitor, but the reestablishment of the Socratic response to the Great Books was revolutionary within the framework of contemporary Catholic education. Saint Thomas Aquinas, the thirteenth century Dominican scholastic, held two opinions that have clearly been central to the mission of Thomas Aquinas College – truth is true wherever it is found (thus the Great Books) and the world can be known as it is (thus the sciences).

So, this extraordinary college of Liberal Arts and Sciences has taken its place among the few colleges determined to teach from the Great Books core curriculum. At Thomas Aquinas, that means following the classical definition of the liberal arts: The Trivium and the Quadrivium –Grammar, Logic, and Rhetoric followed by Geometry, Arithmetic, Astronomy, and Music. These are the disciplines necessary to the pursuit the highest forms of intellectual discourse. The college puts it succinctly – "The liberal arts are not the only or even the most important part of liberal education, but they are fundamental to it. Only thinking which is disciplined, vigorous, and animated by wonder produces knowledge and wisdom."

So, what exactly does one study in the freshman year? Well, one enters into a conversation with the Great Books, followed by thoughtful exchange in seminars taught in the Socratic method. The college has an excellent faculty in residence, but the premise is that the authors themselves are the primary teachers, especially Thomas Aquinas. The Great Books and authors include: *The Holy Bible,* representative translations of *Plato's Republic* and *Aristotle's Poetics and Rhetoric,* Fabre's *Souvenirs Entomologiques,* Galen *On the Natural Faculties,* Harvey *On the Motion of the Heart and Blood in Animals,* Linnaeus, Pascal, Archimedes, Mendel, Euclid's *Elements,* Homer'*s Iliad and Odyssey,* Aeschylus '*Agamemnon, The Libation Bearers, and Eumenides, Sophocles' Oedipus Rex, Oedipus at Colonus, and Antigone,* Herodotus ' *Histories,* Plutarch'*s Lives (Lycurgus, Pericles, Aristides, Alcibiades, Alexander)* , Euripides' *Hippolytus,*Thucydides ' *History of the Peloponnesian War,* Aristophanes ' *The Birds and The Clouds.*

Whew! And the following three years are every bit as rich, adding Dante, Chaucer, Shakespeare, Aquinas, Descartes, Galileo, Newton, Mozart, Cervantes, Machiavelli, Hobbes, Milton, Racine, Locke, Hume, Swift, Leibniz, Rousseau, Kant, Einstein, Tolstoy, Adam Smith, Tocqueville, Twain, Austin, Marx, Ibsen, Dostoevsky, Darwin, Melville, Elliot, Freud, Jung, Cather, and O'Connor.

And now, for the rest of the story. Socratic discussions begin in the classroom, but they don't end in the classroom. Not only do the discussions have an organic agency of their own, time and space is provided in each of the residences for those discussions to continue, often as an upper class student enters into conversation from a point of view not yet experienced by a younger student.

At Thomas Aquinas, the life of the mind is accompanied by the life of the spirit. While a statement of faith is not required of students, it is expected that each student will read, think, and converse within a greater framework provided by his or her Catholic faith and expected that faith is strengthened by regular attendance at the daily Chapel services.

It is that expectation and the requirement that each member of the faculty take an Oath of Fidelity and a Profession of Faith that puts Thomas Aquinas outside of the parameters established for this volume.

Thomas Aquinas is an exceptional and fascinating college. It is a lovely place with an active and responsive student body. The sense of community is powerful and empowering. Graduates are grateful for the qualities of mind they have developed in their years at Thomas Aquinas; they go on to careers in law, medicine, the sciences, business, education, and public service with an uncommonly grounded liberal education. About eleven percent take up a religious vocation; the majority of graduates take the legacy of Thomas Aquinas into the greater world.

Whittier College - Whittier, California

Whittier College is a small college with big ambitions. The curriculum is enormous for a school of its size, and its facilities extensive. One of the notable distinctions of the college is that it is designated a Hispanic Serving Institution – at least twenty-five percent of enrolled students are Hispanic. In fact, Whittier is a remarkably diverse student community; sixty-one percent of Whittier's students are American minorities. The faculty is equally diverse; unlike most college faculties, Whittier's includes a significant number of minority professors, and, unlike most, the teaching faculty is almost fifty percent female.

And the stats... 2015

Number of Applicants: 4,850 / 62% Accepted
Undergrad Enrollment: 1,626 55% female / 45% male
Avg. SAT Reading 470-580 and Math 590 -590 Avg. ACT: 20-25
Total Cost: $56,125.00
Received some form of financial assistance: 94%

The Fighting Poets of Whittier College take their name from a celebrated Quaker poet, John Greenleaf Whittier, and thereby hangs the tale of how a completely modern and impressively effective college came to be associated with a Nineteenth Century poet.

The town of Whittier, now a large suburb of Los Angeles, was an agricultural wonderland, settled in the early Nineteenth Century by members of the Religious Order of Friends – Quakers. The town prospered, and "Quaker Brand" citrus became known as the measure of quality. It was at the height of the town's agricultural prosperity that Whittier College was founded on seventy-five of the most attractive acres in town. Los Angeles has grown to meet the town, but the town – now a city of ninety thousand – retains its central square and old world charm.

Whittier College is a small college with big ambitions. The curriculum is enormous for a school of its size, and its facilities extensive. One of the notable distinctions of the college is that it is designated a Hispanic Serving Institution – at least twenty-five percent of enrolled students are Hispanic. In fact, Whittier is a remarkably diverse student community; sixty-one percent of Whittier's students are American minorities. The faculty is equally diverse; unlike most college faculties, Whittier's includes a significant number of minority professors, and, unlike most, the teaching faculty is almost fifty percent female.

This small college with big ideas presents a liberal education in two notable fashions.

Most students at Whittier will be engaged in the Liberal Education Program – a series of courses designed to develop problem solving skills and effective expression of thought. The program also emphasizes the connections between disciplines and cultural perspectives. Whittier's student will go on to declare a major field of study, but in their first years, they are exposed to a breadth of curriculum and encouraged to learn to think and write effectively.

About a quarter of Whittier's students enter into the Whittier Scholars program. The Scholars plan and carry out a self-designed course of study with the assistance of a faculty mentor. This is a program for the student who is highly motivated and self-directed.

There is a clear sense that Whittier intends to meet the needs of its students, and as a result, its breadth of curriculum provides far greater options than schools of comparable size. I was impressed (and slightly disturbed) for example, to find that advanced students of anatomy had access to cadavers on campus. The full description of major fields includes all of the usual courses in the arts and sciences as well as Business Administration, Education and Child Development, Environmental Studies, Film Studies, Gender and Women's Studies, Kinesiology and Leisure Science, an accelerated entry into Whittier's School of Law, and a pre-professional program in Physical Therapy and Recreational Therapy.

One of the conversations sponsored by the admissions office is an on-going set of nominations by current students of best professors. The number of nominations is impressive, but the range is also notable. A professor in Urban Studies is the most energetic; a professor sponsoring research on snake venom provided the most interesting research project. Isabel Allende clearly emerges as the most inspiring guest speaker in the past year.

Whittier is equally active outside the classroom. A web magazine called Quaker Campus keeps an up-to-date eye on events of interest to students. What becomes clear quickly is that, although Whittier is in a neighborhood of a suburban city adjacent to L.A., this college is all about a residential collegiate experience.

The residence halls are modern and comfortable and nicely set on the seventy-five-acre campus; the residential life staff is active and eager to provide both recreation and support. It is through the residences that many special events emerge, such as Haunted Houses, Sportsfest competitions, and Helping Hands Day.

One of the practices that set Whittier apart, however, is that while there are no national fraternities or sororities on campus, a tradition of literary and service "societies" has grown up with considerable social clout. There are five societies open to women, (Athenians, Ionians, Metaphonians, Palmers, and Thalians,) and four societies open to men (Franklins, Lancers, Orthogonians, and William Penns). One society, the Sachsens, is coed. The societies pride themselves on maintaining academic excellence and providing leadership and service.

They also have a very good time.

I want to mention two traditions at Whittier that struck me as very impressive – the Holiday Concert and the Pacific Islander Luau.

I think the celebration of spring as carried out in a campus-wide luau is a wonderful way to engage in some appropriate collegiate hi-jinx while recognizing a cultural tradition important to the region.

The Holiday Concert has evolved from a very traditional performance of Christmas Revels to the recent "Season of Love," a concert/dinner featuring the Whittier College Choir and the voices of the Broadoaks Children's Choir. The event is for the benefit of Broadoaks School,

Broadoaks is an academic program at Whittier, a demonstration school offering excellent education for children from two to fourteen. The school serves the community and is a model of early childhood education; the program serves Whittier's students seeking training and certification in education.

Whittier's students are happy and active and eagerly engaged in numbers of academic and service organizations. They also join clubs and club sports in droves. One club unique to Whittier is the Artorian Order of the Knights of Pendragon – a Medieval and renaissance based role playing club that includes LARPing (Live Action Role Playing).

More traditional activities include, a Dance Team, a Cheer Squad, an Equestrian Club, a Martial Arts Club, a Rugby club team, and an Ultimate Frisbee Club.

Varsity athletes at Whittier compete in NCAA Division III against comparable programs in Southern California. Sports at Whittier have been in place for more than a hundred years, but the addition of lacrosse, first as a club sport, and then as a varsity team sport, brought Whittier some attention on the West Coast as one of the first varsity lacrosse programs in the region. The Fighting Poets play football, soccer water polo, softball, volleyball, cross country, track, tennis, golf, and baseball. The athletic facilities are at a slight distance from the center of campus, but are well appointed and well used.

University of Redlands - Redlands, California

Redlands is known at both the undergraduate and graduate levels for an excellent School of Music, and a graduate program in the College of Arts and Sciences offering course work in Communicative Disorders and Geographic Information Systems. That program brings specialists from around the globe, including many sent by the Department of Defense. Also offered through graduate programs are advanced degrees in Business, Education, and a doctoral program in Leadership for Educational Justice. Redlands also has some exceptional athletic teams, including a powerful soccer team that won twenty victories last season on its way to the NCAA championship tournament.

And the stats... 2015

Number of Applicants: 4,533 / 73% Accepted
Undergrad Enrollment: 3,779 57% female / 43% male
Avg. SAT Reading 500-600 and Math 500 -600 Avg. ACT: 22-27
Total Cost: $60,874.00
Received some form of financial assistance: 95%

The cheer is known as "Och Tamale," and it is chanted when the Redlands Bulldogs score, at homecoming, and when alumni meet on the path of life.

Och Tamale gazolly gazump
Dayump dayadee yahoo
Ink damink dayadee gazink
Dayump, deray, yahoo
Wing wang trickey trackey poo foo
Joozy woozy skizzle wazzle
Wang tang orkey porkey dominorky
Redlands! — Rah, Rah, Redlands!

Ok, maybe not so much on the path of life, but it is a cherished tradition and one of the many memories happy graduates of Redlands take with them when they bid farewell to this fine small university. Redlands is a small (2400) liberal arts college with several significant graduate divisions and what is essentially an experimental college within a traditional college setting. It is also one of those jaw-dropping, "can this be real?" absolutely beautiful campus neatly set under the San Bernardino Mountains in a very pretty city about ninety minutes from Los Angeles.

Redlands is known at both the undergraduate and graduate levels for an excellent School of Music, and a graduate program in the College of Arts and Sciences offering course work in Communicative Disorders and Geographic Information Systems. That program brings specialists from around the globe, including many sent by the Department of Defense. Also offered through graduate programs are advanced degrees in Business, Education, and a doctoral program in Leadership for Educational Justice. Redlands also has some exceptional athletic teams, including a powerful soccer team that won twenty victories last season on its way to the NCAA championship tournament.

The University of Redlands was established in the town of Redlands when the area was a booming center of citrus cultivation and shipping. Located about ten miles east of San Bernardino and about sixty miles from Los Angeles, Redlands is on the way to Palm Springs, and like that desert oasis, perches amidst mountains and flatland. The city of Redlands still reflects the prosperity of those bygone citrus days, and is still known as "The Jewel of the Inland Empire."

The university was born of boom times and optimism, a characteristic obvious in the college's original statement of mission:

> "The University of Redlands aims to mould the mind and the heart so that in the conflict of life, keenness and conscience shall go forth together. It seeks to impress its pupils with the idea that making men is more important than making money; that it is better to live a life than make a living."

Today the phrase the university uses to describe its hopes for itself is, "life changing." One description of Redlands' students is that they are "entrepreneurial," by which the university means they set out to make things happen. Both academic and residential initiatives have been conceived in order to allow students to develop habits of mind and personal skills that allow them to live and work as independent thinkers and citizens of purpose.

That's a tall order, and Redlands is but a human enterprise; strong feelings on the part of students and graduates, however, seem to indicate that much the university's missions is working out nicely.

The establishment of five Centers of Distinction, for example, helps to give the undergraduate program focus and particular energy. The five centers are: The Johnston Center for Integrative Studies, The Banta Center for Business, Ethics, and Society, The School of Music, The Truesdail Center for Communicative Disorders, and the Center for Educational Justice.

Each of the five demonstrates the directions Redlands has chosen to pursue in the last half century.

The Music School is a conservatory, allowing Redlands' students to find the highest level of instruction and performance. Music has long been central to Redlands' mission and has occupied an important place in the curriculum from the start. The establishment of a formal program at the undergraduate and graduate levels has allowed performers and music educators to find professional training in the context of a liberal arts education.

The Truesdail Center for Communicative Disorders allows graduate students in the field to work in clinical practice in Southern California. Undergraduates studying Speech and Language Pathology have the advantage of a clinical training program in place on campus, and investigate issues involving speech pathology, auditory pathology, stuttering, cleft palate, and autism. A program in Communicative Disorders has been in place at Redlands for more than a half century.

The Center for Educational Justice offers the only Ph.D. program in the country in the area of Educational Justice, and is active in sponsoring symposia and lectures on equity and social advocacy.

The Banta Center for Business, Ethics, and Society is a forum for the examination of issues of ethics as they relate to business and management.

The Johnston Center for Integrative Studies is a fascinating on-going experiment, devised by the university in the 1960's in response to the call for "relevance" in education.

Students seeking an independent, self-directed, highly personalized academic experience can enter into a contract with a student-faculty Graduation Contract Committee. The contract will be individualized, but there are certain goals, including a cross-cultural experience, which are part of the contract's expectation.

To further promote the distinctively collaborative ethos of the Johnston Center, students who enter into Integrative Studies integrate those studies with the challenges of living in a self-governing learning community.

In a community meeting resembling the process at Marlboro or at the Quaker colleges, the entire community – faculty and students – seek consensus. Academic policies are initiated in this process, as are the events that sustain and refresh the community.

There is no greater experiment than that of working out the competing interests of a group living at close quarters. The skills of political compromise and adaptation learned in the seeking of consensus may be as valuable as the integrative studies themselves.

That is a lot of information about the life academic at Redlands, and it would be a mistake to picture student life as an academic grind.

The wonderful mix that is the Redlands student body includes the experiential residential life of Johnston and eleven fraternities and sororities. More than eighty clubs and organizations flourish, including Sweet Charity, A caBellas and Eight Hole Punch (devoted to a cappella singing), African Drumming circles, an Improv Company, a dance Company, a student run radio station, active student government, and a remarkable number of diversity and cultural organizations. The Latina Network, African-American Association, and the Middle Eastern Cross-Cultural Association are but a few of the associations devoted to issues surrounding diversity and cultural identity.

In addition to the fraternities and sororities, two associations have emerged with the goal of providing service and promoting awareness of current issues. Rangi Ya Giza, a brotherhood, dedicates itself to community service and action against injustice, and to offering encouragement and appreciation of LGBT members of the Redlands community; Waddada Wa Rangi Wengi is a sisterhood dedicated to raising awareness of issues of social injustice, diversity, and gender.

So, fraternities, consensus, a cappella, and sisterhood… not bad for a small university!

Finally, Redlands competes in NCAA Division III, probably most successfully over the years in tennis and golf. The women's tennis team has recently won a national championship, and both men's and women's teams are traditionally strong. The facilities at Redlands are excellent; the Division III tennis championships were held at Redlands in 2003, and the NCAA Division III golf championship was held at an adjoining golf course.

Och Tamale!

Intramural and club sports are also popular and include the usual array of outdoor activities possible in a region with great wilderness opportunities. In addition, Redlands offers a Dance Team, a Surf Club, Lacrosse, Quidditch.

University of San Diego - San Diego, California

Students love the campus and the city of San Diego. To a degree rarely found among the cynical college-aged crowd, these students express gratitude for the privilege of going to school on a campus they find exceptionally beautiful, with food service that is exceptionally healthy and responsive, and among people they genuinely like. The academic life at USD is very good, and students speak warmly about the quality of instruction and the responsiveness of their instructors. The hardest part about going to USD from all accounts is leaving after graduation.

And the stats... 2015

Number of Applicants: 14,247 / 50% Accepted
Undergrad Enrollment: 5,741 55% female / 45% male
Avg. SAT Reading 550-650 and Math 570 -670 Avg. ACT: 26-30
Total Cost: $59,729.00
Received some form of financial assistance: 81%

Some things you should know about USD before reading any farther:

1. Whether you know it or not, you want to be in San Diego. No, I mean, you REALLY want to be in San Diego. Most people from outside the region hear a lot about California's beaches, surfers, Yosemite National Park, fragrant orange groves, the fog in San Francisco, and, while there are many great places to visit, for long-term comfort and peace of mind, you want to be in San Diego. Tired of frigid January? Average high for San Diego, a comfy 65 degrees. Growing weary of pulse-stopping heat in July? Average high for San Diego, ocean breezes and 75 degrees.

2. San Diego is a very pleasant city. One of the most pleasant areas is Mission Bay; the University of San Diego sits on a plateau overlooking Mission Bay, literally ten minutes from one of the great beaches in the universe.

3. Most colleges have to make do with the remnants of buildings thrown up in the nineteenth century. USD was built virtually all in one piece in the nineteen fifties (except for the athletic facilities and adjoining residences), looks uniformly fabulous in a cohesive style I call "Old California Mission" and San Diegans call "Spanish Renaissance", and kept the style intact when it expanded after receiving a very generous bequest from the estate of McDonald's Joan B. Kroc (School of Peace Studies). The next large gift

was also relatively "foodie" arriving from weight-loss tycoon, Jennie Craig (Jennie Craig Pavilion).

4. San Diego is a great city, lots of fun, and easy to negotiate. Two other universities add to the mix of college-aged students (San Diego State University and the University of California San Diego) creating a lively social scene.

The University of San Diego is a Catholic university (Sacred Heart), and like most of the Catholic universities profiled in this book, has a confirmed sense of social mission deriving from the founding of the university. And, like the others in this book (except Thomas Aquinas) being Catholic doesn't really matter very much in the student's experience of the university. I generally overlook mission statements, but the President of USD, Mary E. Lyons, stated the university's position with some grace:

> "USD is founded and sustained by a belief in the essential goodness of creation, the worthiness of a lifelong commitment to understanding and working on behalf of the human condition."

The university enrolls about fifty-five hundred undergraduates, approximately fifteen hundred grad students in the various graduate schools, and another fifteen hundred in the School of Law. The emphasis is clearly on undergraduate education, and most residential life is attached to the undergraduate experience. All freshmen live on campus and about half of upper class students choose to stay on campus.

The description of academic offerings is fairly straightforward, although the establishment of the Kroc School of Peace Studies has added a conspicuous new set of courses. The undergraduate world is divided into a College of Arts and Sciences, the Hahn School of Nursing and Health Sciences, the School of Business Administration, and the Joan B. Kroc School of Peace Studies. Graduate programs in Health Sciences, Leadership and Education Sciences and the Institute for Nonprofit Education and Research allow some students the chance to take graduate programs as well.

This is a happy school.

Students love the campus and the city of San Diego. To a degree rarely found among the cynical college-aged crowd, these students express gratitude for the privilege of going to school on a campus they find exceptionally beautiful, with food service that is exceptionally healthy and responsive, and among people they genuinely like. The academic life at USD is very good, and students speak warmly about the quality of instruction and the responsiveness of their instructors. The hardest part about going to USD from all accounts is leaving after graduation.

514

Lots of praise for many departments, but I have heard the most ringing endorsement of all the natural and physical sciences and the very strong programs in Business Administration. The Kroc School is fairly new, but its emphasis on spiritual matters has been of great importance to those who have found their way there.

Having used the word "spiritual" it is probably time to address the misconceptions that are bound to pop up in a setting as profoundly advantaged as this.

USD has been called the University of Spoiled Daughters, and it cannot be denied that blonde girls from the O.C. do often enroll; there are wealthy kids here, but the university is made of up a wide diversity of peoples and enrollment is made up of almost 40% underrepresented minorities. One of the "pretty girls" responded to the observation that the campus appeared to be made up of models by asserting that the lifestyle at the university is healthy; from her point of view, the uncommonly effective dining service provides healthy food options, including excellent vegetarian and vegan options and the incredible opportunities for healthy recreation, including the use of two gorgeous gymnasiums, make a healthy lifestyle very compelling. "We do take care of ourselves," she said, "how is that a problem?"

Another concern for some applicants looking only at the viewbook is what seems to be a relatively underemphasized extra-curricular life. Actually, there are a slew of very active organizations on campus, offering points of connection for virtually any student; similarly, sports are actually very well supported and enjoyed. What visitors from other regions can hardly appreciate is the wealth of opportunities available in a climate that allows a student to be outdoors virtually all-year long. The beach is a huge draw, and if sun and surf aren't enough, the university sponsors an incredible variety of outdoor adventures, including: A Pre-Orientation Adventure, a trip during Thanksgiving Break to Havasu Falls, an Easter Break Trip to Utah, the Costa Rica Spring Break trip, and throughout the year – Backpacking, Canoeing, Canyoneering, Hiking, Horseback Riding, Kayaking, Biking, Mud Caving, Rock Climbing, Snorkeling, Surfing, Snowboarding and Skiing.

Residential life is well organized and efficient; an interesting variety of student residences are available, including some very handsome townhouse apartments adjacent to the athletic facilities. It is true that a good number of students will live off campus at some point, finding housing in Mission Beach, between the Pacific Ocean and Mission Bay.

The University of San Diego Toreros play in the West Coast Conference of Division I. Torero football plays in the Pacific Football league of the Football Championship Subdivision, but the rest of the sports are entirely in the West Coast Conference, allowing some fierce rivalries to emerge. It happens that by virtue of size, athletic ambition, and founding date, small Catholic universities – USD, Gonzaga, Saint Mary's, Loyola Marymount, Santa Clara, and the University of San Francisco – are tucked into the West Coast Conference along with outliers, Brigham Young University and Pepperdine. Brigham Young is also in the Mountain West Conference and is a much larger school (over thirty-four thousand whereas most of the rest are under nine thousand). There is enthusiasm for all of the Torero's varsity teams, but basketball is king, and the Craig Pavilion rocks when the Toreros are at home. USD also offers excellent men's soccer, golf, and rowing, and strong women's programs in basketball and volleyball.

The Pacific Northwest - Oregon and Washington

The Pacific Northwest has become very attractive to a college-aged and post-college population. Both Portland and Seattle have their own mystique, and each has its own peculiar subculture. Bellingham is also emerging as a small city with a big reputation for beauty, comfort, and a lively cultural scene.

There is far more to the region that prominent cities, however, and the visitor to the region can enjoy a remarkable variety of climates, topography, and adventure. After all, the largest boundary of the region runs from the Rockies to the Pacific coast and from the California line all the way to the Yukon.

For the purposes of this guide, however, we'll include the states of Oregon and Washington, and leave the exploration of Idaho and British Columbia to another day.

The region is actually defined by several kinds of geographic realities, exactly the sort of conditions that Lewis and Clark had to contend with on their journey westward.

There are five major mountain chains in the region - the Rockies, the Coast Mountains, the Cascades, the Olympic Mountains, and the Columbia Mountains. Two rivers play a significant part in creating boundaries - the Snake River runs from Wyoming to the Columbia Watershed the eastern boundary of Oregon and Washington and the western boundary of Idaho and the Columbia that separates Washington from Oregon. Finally, there are volcanoes, and I mean active volcanoes, in the region - Mount Rainier, Mount Hood, Mount St. Helens, and Mount Baker.

Portland, Seattle, Tacoma, and Bellingham are all port cities, and all are defined to some degree by their setting as ocean or river cities. The Columbia River carries more water than any river in the U.S. except the Mississippi and allows heavy freight to plow all the way from Portland to Lewiston, Idaho, the region's easternmost port city.

Some of the region is temperate rain forest, some of the most concentrated rain forest on the continent; some of the region is part of the Great Basin Desert. Eastern Washington is wheat rich in the southeastern portion of the state and pine rich in the northeastern sector.

For the purposes of college visiting, the best advice is to start in Portland or Seattle and head south or north. There are four colleges of interest in the eastern part of the region – Whitman, Gonzaga, Washington State, and Whitworth, but all are more easily accessed from Portland or Seattle than from any other jumping off point.

All four of the colleges lie along the eastern border of Washington.

Whitman College is an exceptional liberal arts college, handsome, happy, and increasingly competitive. Recently, the Forbes College review placed Whitman as the sixteenth best college in the nation, ahead of all but the most celebrated Ivies and Stanford. Whitman is located in Walla Walla (the town so nice they named it twice!), an agricultural oasis and wine-producing phenomenon on the edge of the Palouse, grassland converted to agriculture. I would put Whitman in the company of Bates, Bowdoin, Colby, Hamilton, Kenyon; it is an exceptional college and uncommon in that it attracts some of the nicest kids on the West Coast.

North of Walla Walla, just across the border from Moscow, home of the university of Idaho, is Pullman and Washington State University. Known to locals as "Wazzu," WSU offers all the opportunities of a major research university with extraordinary facilities in areas having to do with agriculture. Washington State's Cougars play in the Pac 10 (now Pac 12).

North of Pullman is the city of Spokane, directly west of Coeur d'Alene, Idaho. Spokane was known for rich natural resources – mining and lumber – but is now diversified by a number of industries, including booming high-tech and biotech corporations. Gonzaga is located about a half mile from downtown Spokane in a residential neighborhood. Whitworth, profiled in this book, is on a suburban campus of about two hundred acres.

From Portland, a visitor can drive a few miles outside the city limits, to the northeast, into some of the most astoundingly beautiful farmland anywhere. The small town of Forest Grove, one of Oregon's oldest towns, is the location of Pacific University, one of the colleges profiled in this book. Another easy drive from Portland takes the visitor south to McMinnville, where Linfield College is located. Linfield is a strong liberal arts college, enrolling about two thousand students on an impressive campus in a town approximately thirty-five miles south of Portland and the capital of Oregon's wine industry. For the wine lover, antique shopper, and boutique browser, McMinnville is a treasure.

George Fox University, an interesting small university, enrolling about three thousand students is located in Newburgh, a small city within the Portland metropolitan-area. George Fox began as a Quaker College, but is now a Christian university. George Fox is found in the center of Newburgh.

Salem, home of Willamette University, is the state capital and the center of the Willamette Valley. The University is literally across the street from the state buildings. You'll find more about Willamette as it is profiled in this book.

Continuing on the drive south from Portland, the visitor will land at Oregon State University in Corvallis and the University of Oregon in Eugene. Both of these public options are highly reputed and each has its own distinctive campus culture and areas of academic strength.

OSU is the land-grant university in Oregon and has more majors, minors, and programs than any institution in the state, many of which are nationally known. The forestry program is considered the best in the nation, but all studies having to do with agriculture, engineering, mineral science, and environmental science are outstanding. OSU is also the home of several distinctive graduate programs, including the school of Veterinary Science. Go, Beavers!

The University of Oregon is the state's flagship university and currently one of the very "hot" public universities, in part due to the strength of programs in the university, and in equal measure due to the generally groovy nature of the city of Eugene. It also helps that the Oregon Ducks are national football champions and one of the most exciting teams in college football. Go, Ducks!

Within the city limits of Portland are four distinctive institutions, one of which is Portland State University, a public university, with the largest enrollment of any institution in the state. PSU is a major research university in the heart of downtown Portland. The University of Portland is a large Catholic university (Order of the Holy Cross) with an outstanding program in preparation for professional schools; it is also a soccer powerhouse – its women's teams have twice won national Division I championships!

Reed College and Lewis & Clark College are located in neighborhoods in Portland.

Reed is located in the Eastmoreland neighborhood and is one of the nation's most celebrated small colleges, highly regarded for the percentage of graduates who go on to pursue the Ph.D. Reed is an exceptionally interesting campus, featuring handsome Tudor/Gothic buildings, the "Honor Principle," which covers all aspects of student life, and an unofficial motto – "Communism, Atheism, and Free Love" –which slyly acknowledges the college's radical reputation. Reed is an intellectual hotbed and one of the most challenging of colleges in the country.

Lewis and Clark College is located in a beautiful rural neighborhood in southeast Portland. Lewis & Clark is one of the colleges I feel most strongly about and one that I hope will find an even wider audience as a result of appearing in this book. The southernmost university in Oregon is Southern Oregon University, yet another public gem, profiled in this guide

The state capital of Washington, Olympia, is the home of the remarkable Evergreen State College. The drive to Evergreen from central Olympia takes the visitor into a forested wonderland. Seattle is the northernmost major city in the United States and home to the University of Washington, Seattle University and Seattle Pacific University, as well as the Cornish School of the Arts and the Art Institute of Seattle.

The University of Washington, known locally as "U Dub", is located in the University District of Seattle and is one of the great universities, one of the universities considered a Public Ivy and deservedly among the most competitive of public universities.

Seattle University is a Jesuit Catholic University with the largest enrollment of any private institution in the Pacific Northwest, currently enrolling more than eight thousand undergraduates in a variety of programs. Seattle University is known for its service learning programs and for its commitment to social justice. Each year students at Seattle University contribute hundreds of hours of community service in the community and in the city. Seattle University is located in the First Hill neighborhood of Seattle, also known as "Pill Hill" for the concentration of medical and health care facilities in the neighborhood.

Seattle Pacific University is a Christian University founded by Free Methodists. The University enrolls more than three thousand students and is located in the Queen Anne Hill neighborhood, northwest of central Seattle.

South of Seattle, on Puget Sound, Tacoma is home to several institutions of interest to the college visitor.

Both University of Puget Sound and Pacific Lutheran University are profiled in this book. UPS is located in the north end of Tacoma in a quiet neighborhood, and Pacific Lutheran is in Parkland, a suburb of Tacoma.

The last two of the universities and colleges profiled in this book are Whitworth University in Spokane on the eastern edge of Washington and Western Washington University in Bellingham, on Bellingham Bay about ninety miles north of Seattle. Even if you think WWU is not for you, take a trip to Bellingham! It's a beautiful city, surrounded by pine forest, with views of Bellingham Bay and the San Juan Islands.

Southern Oregon University - Ashland, Oregon

Student life at SOU can be described as simultaneously active and laid back. Lots of social events spring up, lots of clubs and organizations meet, lots of teams play sports, and lots of kids head out to climb, or kayak, or run the rapids, or ski, or hike. The pace of life is consistent with the vibe of Ashland itself; people tend to appreciate the beauty around them and stop to look around.

And the stats... 2015

Number of Applicants: 2,731 / 71% Accepted
Undergrad Enrollment: 5,406 57% female / 43% male
Avg. SAT Reading 460-580 and Math 450 -550 Avg. ACT: 20-25
Total Cost: $23,028.00 (in-state) $36,606.00 (out-of-state)
Received some form of financial assistance: 82%

Once again, I am in danger of gushing too enthusiastically about the opportunity in one of the loveliest regions in the country; I'm always in danger of losing credibility, but I'm certain some applicants will love Southern Oregon.

There are really three significant reasons to consider Southern Oregon (SOU) very seriously.

1. SOU is located in Ashland, Oregon.

2. SOU is one of two Public Liberal Arts Universities in the West.

3. SOU is the only place I know that has a department of Shakespeare Studies with the opportunity to intern with a professional theater.

Ashland is one of the most scenic, charming, welcoming, enchanting small cities in the Pacific Northwest.

Many people know Ashland as the home of the Oregon Shakespeare Festival, perhaps the most successful repertory theater in the United States. The Festival runs from March through November, attracting audiences from across the country and around the world. An elegant Shakespearean theater presents under the sky/stars, a modern large-scale theater offers elaborate sets and special effects, and a nifty black box theater allows the presentation of theater in the round. No longer strictly a

Shakespearean company, the OSF produces contemporary dramas, rollicking musicals, adaptations of novels and films, plays in translation, and classic works as well.

Hordes of playgoers need restaurants, coffee shops, shops, boutiques, and hotels, and Ashland provides them all. The city's amenities are not seasonal, however, because Ashland enjoys a spectacular autumn show of colors and excellent vineyards, attracting an entirely different population as it does in the winter and spring.

As the first snows fall, skiers arrive to enjoy the well -groomed runs on Mount Ashland, operating at almost eight thousand feet. Outdoor adventures also include some of the best river rafting and fishing in the region as the Rogue River courses south from Grant's Pass. Hikers climb down from the Pacific Crest Trail that runs right through Mount Ashland's Alpine meadows. Outdoor Magazine names Ashland one of the premiere locations for variety of outdoor opportunities.

And ... Ashland has a lively small university that enjoys all the benefits the city has to offer. SOU is located on a wooded campus at the southern end of the city, within walking distance of all things necessary to a rich college life. The community happily supports the university, which is also the home of the region's public radio station. Concerts and lectures, football and basketball, bring students and townsfolk together frequently.

I've profiled Saint Mary's College in Maryland, University of Montevallo, University of North Carolina at Asheville, Sonoma State, and The Evergreen State College, all of which are public liberal arts colleges, supported by their state and determined to offer a quality liberal arts education with small classes, instruction by professors rather than teaching assistants, and opportunities for discussion and exchange of ideas. SOU had a distinguished past as the state's primary school of education, and education and business still get a good number of students. More than a third of SOU's students arrive with no guess at their eventual major, open to the array of subjects they'll meet in the first two years. Recently, SOU has developed a unique academic division known as the "Houses". At this point, the Houses are not residential, although they may become residential as the program matures. Students apply to one of the three Houses in order to combine study, discussion, mentorship, and project-based experiential learning directed toward positive change. The Houses are open to students pursuing any major. The collaboration is meant to build communities of learners working together toward a shared goal. SOU has developed three separate Houses, each with a distinctive flavor. Skeptic House uses an interdisciplinary approach to contemporary issues, such as global warming or vaccinations. Social Justice House brings students to work with local governmental agencies on issues such as homelessness, poverty, and human rights. The Green House takes students to Mount Ashland, local farms, and the Rogue River in collaborative projects directed toward sustainability.

In case the emphasis on the Houses and Shakespeare seem too unlikely, it's worth noting that this small university offers a ton of options with regards to majors and programs. In addition to the usual arts, sciences, language, literature, math, and humanities programs, SOU boasts strong programs in Business Administration, Innovation and Leadership, Financial Mathematics, Creative Writing, and Computer Science. I do want to mention two programs of note. SOU is affiliated with the Oregon Health Sciences University (OHSU) which is in Portland operates the best and most modern health facility in the Northwest. The SOU affiliation allows the university to offer an exemplary program in Nursing, pairing students with internships at the main campus. The second interesting program is the Outdoor Adventure Leadership program which teaches technical skills necessary to safety in the wilderness, group leadership and communication skills, risk management, and expedition planning.

Now for Shakespeare. SOU has a large and ambitious professional program in theater; majors are offered in Acting, Costuming, Directing, Dramaturgy, Film Techniques, Musical Theater, Sound, Stage Lighting, Stage Management, and Stage Scenery. Shakespeare Studies is not a major but a collaborative minor combining the resources of the university, the 10,000 volume Margery Bailey Renaissance Library, and the facilities and expertise of the Oregon Shakespeare Festival. SOU's Summer Shakespeare Intensive is based entirely on the productions staged in Ashland during the season. Each year students participate in the productions, as actors, stage designers, lighting interns, costume interns. SOU offers the BFA degree, indicating professional standards of instruction.

Student life at SOU can be described as simultaneously active and laid back. Lots of social events spring up, lots of clubs and organizations meet, lots of teams play sports, and lots of kids head out to climb, or kayak, or run the rapids, or ski, or hike. The pace of life is consistent with the vibe of Ashland itself; people tend to appreciate the beauty around them and stop to look around. Classes and exams bring some challenges, but SOU doesn't seem as frenzied as many similar institutions. One hallmark of life at SOU is an innovative dining program. Lots of colleges have a dining hall and lots have food courts. SOU's dining facility (known as The Hawk) provides eight stations offering distinctive cuisine. Students can try pan-Asian fusion, Vegetarian and Vegan options at the station called "Chopped", Mexican food, Burgers and fries, freshly baked pizzas straight from the stone oven. Dormitories offer large rooms and comfortable common space. In what I think is among the most important of amenities, SOU's dorm have laundry facilities that are sparkling, clean, operational, and effective. Anyone who has had to pack up a bag of wet laundry because the college's dryers only whisper a hint of warmth will know what it means to have facilities that work.

All the usual clubs and organizations flourish at SOU. The university hosts a Public Radio station (WJPR) with opportunities for student involvement. Raider sports gather considerable enthusiasm and several significant social events follow the calendar of important games. "Beak Week" (Raiders' mascot is a hawk) in November, just before Homecoming is an opportunity for the university to meet a wide range of interests. A recent Beak Week featured a lecture on Exploring the Racial Divide, a performance by a famous mentalist, an ice cream social, Karaoke, a workshop on diversity, and a visit from a naturalist presenting live birds of prey. Among the organizations available are the SOU Step, the Magic the Gathering Club, Medieval Arts Club, the Foodie Club, a Cosplay Club, the Criminology Club, Dulcet (an a cappella group), a Beekeeping Club, the Anthropology Club, the Native American Student Union, the Percussion Club, the Queer Resource Center, Smash Club (playing Super Smash Brothers), SOU Poetry Slam, SOU Sign Club (American Sign Language), SOU Paranormal Club (SOUP), the Tango Club, and The Next Best Thing, an Improvisational Comedy Club.

Club sports and recreational activities include an Outing Center and all activities that might be found in this outdoor wonderland. Other club sports are baseball, lacrosse, soccer, climbing, rugby (both for men and women), tennis, golf, skiing and snowboarding, disc golf, and caving.

The athletic program is affiliated with the NAIA rather than the NCAA, and, although comparisons are tricky, many sports fans consider the NAIA as an equivalent to the top of NCAA Division II. Playing in the Cascade Collegiate Conference, Raiders teams have been notably successful. The first NAIA championship football game televised by CBS Sports included the Southern Oregon Raiders; SOU once again played in the national championship in 2015. Sports offered include football, cross-country, men's and women's soccer, women's volleyball, men's and women's basketball, track and field, softball, and wrestling for both men and women. SOU's football program has had great success, as has cross-country, volleyball, and wrestling.

Willamette University - Salem, Oregon

No matter what they take, Willamette's students are vocal in appreciation of their teachers, many of whom have volunteered in supervising research. Accessible, professional, informed – the Willamette faculty gets high marks and have a great deal to do with the strong feelings students have about their academic preparation at the college.

And the stats... 2015

Number of Applicants: 5,729 / 81% Accepted
Undergrad Enrollment: 2,166 57% female / 43% male
Avg. SAT Reading 540-670 and Math 540 -650 Avg. ACT: 24-30
Total Cost: $57,046.00
Received some form of financial assistance: 99%

Willamette is the oldest university in the Western United States, and Salem is the capital of Oregon and a thriving small city of about one hundred and thirty thousand less than an hour's drive south of Portland. Both its history and its location serve to make Willamette a surpassingly interesting small university in the region.

Willamette is primarily an undergraduate college of liberal arts, enrolling roughly eighteen hundred students on a sixty-five acre campus literally across the street from the state capital. The university also operates a School of Law, a School of Education, and a School of Management, all of which enroll another eight hundred graduate students.

A visitor to Willamette will be struck by the pleasant design of the campus, the more effective for its tidy efficiency and handsome architecture. Unlike some colleges that have grown up in city settings, Willamette feels very much its own space; the campus offers well manicured lawns, shady paths, quiet vistas overlooking a winding stream in a plan that makes eminently good sense.

The buildings range from the original red brick Renaissance style of Waller Hall, the oldest building on campus, built in the shape of a Greek cross, and recently renovated, to the modern brick and glass of the Hatfield Library, named for Senator Mark Hatfield, alumnus of Willamette and former member of the faculty. The plaza adjacent to the library overlooks the Mill Race a lovely winding stream that forms the letter "W" when viewed from the University Center. Traditionally, the lovely stream is available for dunking a student on his or her birthday. Willamette has managed to design a campus that is cohesive and yet varied in its architecture. Elements such as the Jackson Plaza and a stand of redwood trees, the beaux-arts facade of Salem's former Post Office, and the sleek entrance to the Ford Art Museum bring this well-organized campus considerable visual delight.

There are a number of other reasons to find Willamette delightful, including a strong program in the liberal arts, a year-long residential program in Japan on the sister-campus of Tokyo International University of America, close mentoring relationships with an outstanding faculty, and the opportunity to pursue some programs only available in a small comprehensive university. The relationship with a Japanese university not only promotes an outstanding program in Japanese at Willamette and the opportunity to live and study in Japan, but also brings almost a hundred Japanese students to Willamette, enriching the life of the college and fortifying language instruction.

In addition, Willamette's students can earn a Bachelor's degree in Music Performance, Music Education, Music Composition, Music Improvisation in Contemporary Practice, and a double degree in Music and Liberal Arts. They can begin their work in the excellent Atkinson Graduate School of Management, earning the BA and MBA in five years. Also available is an accelerated B.A./J.D. program through the College of Law, and a B.A./M.A.T. program through the College of Education

It all begins in the first year with the College Colloquium, a seminar introducing Willamette's newest students to seasoned faculty and to an array of topics from which they can choose. Recent Colloquia have included: Arts and Identity in South Africa; Beer, Wine, and Whiskey – Society Under the Influence; Getting Down and Dirty with Classical Music; Public Vows – The Meaning of Marriage in the United States.

Not only is the Colloquium a powerful introduction to the skills of thought and expression expected of Willamette's students, the course also introduces the student to the professor who will be his or her advisor until a major is declared.

One point of appreciation/contention is with the required course of general education, known as Modes of Inquiry. In addition to a foreign language requirement, all Willamette students are expected to complete work in each of six of six broadly defined elements – Understanding the Natural World, Creating in the Arts, Analyzing Arguments, Thinking Historically, Understanding Society, and Interpreting Texts. Most graduates are pleased to have been exposed to a wide view of education, while some professionally minded students have ached to jump more quickly into study in a major field.

No matter what they take, Willamette's students are vocal in appreciation of their teachers, many of whom have volunteered in supervising research. Accessible, professional, informed – the Willamette faculty gets high marks and have a great deal to do with the strong feelings students have about their academic preparation at the college.

This is a work hard/ live sensibly group of earnest kids. The percentage of students involved in extracurricular activities, including a number of orchestral and vocal music groups, theater, and intramural sports is exceptionally high. An active and engaged group of students, some of whom are environmentally sensitive, vegan, and earth-friendly, mixes well with those who still wear high school letter jackets and enjoy video games. Quirky intellectuals, athletes, radioheads, political activists, and community servants get along happily. Some describe Willamette as a "hippie" school; others call it "preppy." Fraternities and sororities continue to attract wholesome and athletic men and women, although many of Willamette's athletes will remain unaffiliated. The mix of types at Willamette is impressive and the more impressive for the ease with which students move from group to group; warm good will appears to be the prevalent mode in every quarter of the campus, and a wide variety of personalities are comfortable in the mix.

Another notable aspect of life at Willamette is a commitment to engagement in the wider world. Willamette students study abroad, and many take on service-learning – internships that serve communities other than Willamette.

The Lilly Project for the Theological, Spiritual and Ethical Exploration of Vocation, for example, is a program designed to allow the explore the big questions – meaning of life, etc. – and to think about what vocation will best meet the student's life path. The program, sponsored by the university and assisted by funds from the Lilly Foundation, quotes poet, Mary Oliver – "*Tell me, what is it you plan to do with your one wild and precious life?*" A significant initiative taken by the university is the Native American Advisory Council, established in order to build connections between statewide native leaders, native alumni, and current native students in order to work in service of native communities. The Chemawa Indian School Partnership Program is an example of that initiative, as it challenges Willamette to assist native students in transitioning to a college-prep curriculum.

Residential life at Willamette is varied and sane. The Greeks have a place in residential life, but do not dominate. A number of "theme" or special interest residences are available, including Keneko Commons, a residential option that combines an emphasis on sustainability, Japanese heritage, and the opportunity for students to learn from each other. Keneko Commons welcomes more than three hundred students who enjoy self-government and a variety of activities planned by and for the Keneko community.

Another interesting historical legacy at Willamette is the prominence of intramural sports, established at the university before a program in interscholastic sports had been implemented. Almost seventy percent of students jump into the intramural leagues (soccer, indoor football, flag football, basketball, and volleyball) and into tournaments such as BCS Football bowl challenge, March Madness bracket challenge, dodgeball, mushball, and racquetball.

In addition, Willamette supports an extraordinary number of clubs and organizations, including Broadway Dancers, a Cheer Squad, a Climbing Club, a Cycling Club, Ice Hockey, Juggling, Martial Arts, Lacrosse, Fishing, and Rugby. A Fitness program offers Yoga, Pilates, Cardio Kick, Hip Hop, Aikido, African Dance, and Salsa Dance. Willamette's Bearcats play in NCAA Division III in the Northwest Conference against rivals Whitman, Lewis & Clark, Linfield, and Whitworth. Willamette is proud of having produced 51 NCAA All-Americans in the last decade. One not-commonly-found athletic option available at Willamette is rowing, a sport that is growing in popularity year by year.

Pacific University - Forest Grove, Oregon

I'll turn to the academic picture in a moment, and that picture is bright, but the single most important feature of Pacific is its extraordinary ability to attract a superior faculty and the most engaging and thoughtful student body possible. There are clubs, activities, service projects, and athletic triumphs galore, and they add to the quality of life at Pacific, but the every-day leadership, ambition, and kindness of students in this university is outstanding.

And the stats... 2015

Number of Applicants: 2,665 / 80% Accepted
Undergrad Enrollment: 1,840 59% female / 41% male
Avg. SAT Reading 480-600 and Math 500 -600 Avg. ACT: 21-26
Total Cost: $52,296.00
Received some form of financial assistance: 100%

Although the Metro line does travel from downtown Portland to Forest Grove, it would be a real mistake to think that this charming town is essentially a suburb of. It is in some of the most beautiful rolling farm country you will ever find, and it is a welcoming and entirely captivating small town with a bustling main street and happy shops and shoppers, but it is NOT Portland. The city is approximately thirty minutes east of Forest Grove and accessible by car, bus, and light rail. The good news is that this lovely campus is tucked into one of the most pleasant and peaceful environments a student might wish to find. And, although Forest Grove is not a city, Pacific is the real thing as a liberal arts college and one of the most engaging college opportunities available in the Pacific Northwest. The university began with a legacy of service, is affiliated with the United Church of Christ, and welcomes students from every quarter. International students found their way to Pacific early on, and the university has a long-established presence in Hawaii and Japan.

The college had its roots in the 1850s, when Portland was a community of about eight hundred, and the largest settlement was Oregon City. The oldest building, a beautiful white clapboard house, was the first school in Oregon. Survivors of the Applegate Trail started the school to educate and care for the orphaned children who came to Forest Grove by foot from Massachusetts. Marsh Hall, the university's main building is the oldest collegiate building west of the Mississippi. The visitor to Forest Grove will be torn between exploring the tree-shaded and thoughtfully designed campus of Pacific University and the attractive shops and buildings in the central district of town. Fortunately, for the visitor and the sixteen hundred students at Pacific, moving from one to the other is no problem, as the campus flows easily into town. There are college towns in which the residents appear to feel put upon by students, and towns such as Forest Grove in which the town and university have grown and prospered together. Ask around. Maggie's Buns, Pizza Schmizza are routinely clogged with Pacific's students, and parents enjoy staying at the McMenamin's Lodge on the edge of town. For students, "Fo Gro" is a comfortable home-away-from-home.

Oh, and the town and campus are stunning in the fall when the leaves turn.

A university is obviously more than its buildings, but it has to be said that Pacific has a remarkably interesting and cohesive campus, having managed to preserve the best in the original red brick buildings while welcoming innovation as well. The Carnegie Building, originally a library, now the home of the Psychology Department is a wonderfully exotic checkerboard of brick. The university publishes a map of the trees on campus, and the play of light and shade across the green lawns and pathways is delightful. It doesn't always translate into substance, but the immediate judgment a visitor is inclined to hold is that this small university is PROSPEROUS. The grounds are immaculately maintained, the buildings are in spectacularly good shape, and the quality of every facility is immediately obvious. Perhaps the obvious support the university has received is best reflected in the observation that ninety-nine percent of all undergraduates receive some form of financial assistance from the university.

I'll turn to the academic picture in a moment, and that picture is bright, but the single most important feature of Pacific is its extraordinary ability to attract a superior faculty and the most engaging and thoughtful student body possible. There are clubs, activities, service projects, and athletic triumphs galore, and they add to the quality of life at Pacific, but the every-day leadership, ambition, and kindness of students in this university is outstanding.

Although Pacific now offers programs at locations other than Forest Grove, the heart of the institution is with the sixteen hundred students enrolled in the undergraduate College of Arts and Sciences. In addition to the commonly expected majors in the Arts, Sciences, and Humanities, Pacific offers degree-granting programs in Accounting, Anthropology, Bioinformatics, Business Administration, Disability Studies, Exercise Science, Gender and Sexuality Studies, Integrated Media, Peace and Social Justice, and Social Work.

The impressive buildings I've mentioned serve particular functions in the hosting of Centers and Programs that set Pacific apart.

The first of these is the Berglund Center for Internet Studies. The center examines both theoretical issues and issues of implementation in looking at the impact of the Internet in contemporary society.

Pacific is a university committed to sustainability in all its endeavors. The B Street Permaculture Project centers the efforts of the Pacific community to organize information about and sensitivity to issues of sustainability.

The Center for Gender Equity promotes dialogue and programs to enhance gender equity at the university.
The English Language Institute offers tuition in English to International students, thus supporting the university's determination to serve the world and incidentally offering English proficient students the opportunity to be of service.

The Center for Civic Engagement organizes service projects and opportunities for students to donate time and talent to local causes.

The Malheur Field Station is located at the edge of the Malheur National Wildlife Refuge in Oregon's High Desert. The station is used for field study in the fall and spring.

The Tom McCall Center for Policy Innovation and works to connect Pacific's students with policy makers.

Other programs of interest include an active program of Study Abroad, the work done in the field of Peace and Social Justice, International Studies, and a Conducting Apprenticeship Program that allows budding conductors to work with the Oregon Symphony.

Academically sound, the university is also a bustling and busy place outside of the classroom. Among the social activities most enthusiastically commended are the annual luau – the largest luau celebrated outside of Hawaii – and the Mensch Festival.

The MENSCH Festival of Music and Art is a two-day music and arts festival designed to promote civic awareness of various issues through music, art, displays, booths, installations, and demonstrations. Why called "Mensch"? "Mensch" is the German word for a person who does the right thing, stands up for the right causes, walks the walk, and who cares about other human beings. The festival is fun and brings great performers to campus (Blue Scholars, Snubb Fam, The Chengs) but also addresses a specific issue each year. Recent themes have included sustainability, gender equality, and the support of young artists.

It should come as no surprise then, that the four fraternities and four sororities on campus are seen as pleasant enough, but not at the heart of the life of the college. Students have a great time on campus, in town, in the dorms, and are actively involved in a range of activities including: Anime, the Rainbow Coalition, KickBoxers, Jiu Jitsu, Animal Ethics, Dance and Choreography, Big Brothers/Big Sisters, Archery, ultimate frisbee, lacrosse, Circle K, Oregonians Against Trafficking Humans, Politics and Law Forum, and World Awareness.

Music and Theater are both highly regarded, and Pacific's students have access to all musical performances are exceptionally popular. Those who want to join in a production or ensemble can join regardless of major. Options include: A wide range of ensembles that include Chamber Singers, Concert Choir, Symphonic Band, Pacific Philharmonic, Jazz Choir, Jazz Band, Pep Band and various chamber ensembles.

Finally, for reasons that may seem obscure, Pacific's athletic teams are known as The Boxers. Apparently, a statue was given to the university by a missionary laboring in China. The object, which came to be called "Boxer" –something like a lion/dragon/griffin – was put on display in front of the Chapel. It was only a matter of time before Boxer was taken by one group and recaptured by another. The appearance of the captured Boxer by a fraternity, team, or club was called a "flash", and in time an organized combat between classes arrived, called The Boxer Toss. The longest recorded Boxer Toss took nine hours in nineteen twenty-nine.

Where is Boxer now? No one knows. Stolen one final time, Boxer has retreated into the shrouds of time and now exists only as a mascot name for Pacific's teams. The advantages to having such a mascot are many, none better than having the chance to call quick facts about the place "Boxer Briefs".

The Boxers compete in NCAA Division III, playing in the Northwest Conference against such traditional rivals as Lewis and Clark, Whitman, the University of Puget Sound, and Willamette. Men (Boxers) compete in football, baseball, basketball, cross-country, football, golf, soccer, swimming, tennis, track and field and wrestling. Women's programs (Boxers) are offered in basketball, cross country, golf, lacrosse, softball, soccer, swimming, tennis, track and field, volleyball and wrestling. Yes, women's wrestling. Club sports include cheerleading and handball. Intramurals include the usual tilts plus mushball and racquetball.

Lewis and Clark College - Portland, Oregon

Occasionally misrepresented as a "hippie" or "Crunchy Granola" school, Lewis and Clark is one of only four colleges in the United States to have been honored with a Truman Foundation Honor Institution Award recognizing the college's success in preparing its students for careers in public service. Lewis and Clark has produced Rhodes Scholars and is highly regarded for preparing its graduates well for careers in every profession and for eminent graduate programs. And, the cross-country team is among the strongest in the region while the women's soccer program continues to churn out All-Americans... and both have the highest grade point averages among all teams.

And the stats... 2015

Number of Applicants: 6,243 / 65% Accepted
Undergrad Enrollment: 2,179 59% female / 41% male
Avg. SAT Reading 520-620 and Math 540 -650 Avg. ACT: 24-27
Total Cost: $57,690.00
Received some form of financial assistance: 92%

The stereotypical Lewis & Clark student is smart, independent, slightly on the "quirky" side, eminently kind, and happy, happy, happy with this beautiful college on a spectacular estate on the outskirts of Portland. The phrase L&C kids like to use about themselves is "laid-back", and when the phrase implies open-minded, inclusive, generous earnestness, it fits. There is real diversity of types at Lewis & Clark, although flannel shirts and Birkenstocks continue to dominate, and real acceptance of every sort of student. Occasionally misrepresented as a "hippie" or "Crunchy Granola" school, Lewis and Clark is one of only four colleges in the United States to have been honored with a Truman Foundation Honor Institution Award recognizing the college's success in preparing its students for careers in public service. Lewis and Clark has produced Rhodes Scholars and is highly regarded for preparing its graduates well for careers in every profession and for eminent graduate programs. And, the cross-country team is among the strongest in the region while the women's soccer program continues to churn out All-Americans.

Genuinely nice people encouraging other genuinely nice people find themselves on one of the most impressive college campuses anywhere. How nice? Well, student volunteers give up their own study time to prepare relaxing diversions in the library during exam weeks. Snacks, Disney movies, and massages are made available through their kind efforts.

There simply is not another campus like this anywhere in the U.S.

Not only is the setting magnificent – a beautifully manicured estate with gardens, a reflecting pool, and a stunning view of Mount Hood – Lewis & Clark is actually within the city limits of Portland, only moments away from a wonderfully arts-active, boutique-filled neighborhood and a bus-ride away from the center of the city. The shuttle to Pioneer Square is known as the "Pio Express" or "The Raz". Portland is perhaps the most "happening" city for young people right now, with an incredible array of concert, arts, sports, and dining venues; Portland is at the heart of the "Food Cart" movement, and L&C is only minutes away from the world's best "Cart Cuisine."

So, Portland is fantastic, the campus is fantastic, the students are uncommonly decent, and the faculty?

Lewis & Clark's students cannot cheer heartily enough to show their appreciation of a teaching faculty that is fully engaged in the care and encouragement of undergraduates. One student put it this way, "My professors know my name. I've been to their homes. A professor I've never even had went out of his way to ask me how my semester in London had gone."

First year students begin their academic adventure at L&C with a program entitled Exploration and Discovery. This two-semester seminar is required of all students new to the college. The first semester introduces some of the great texts and provokes discussion and extensive writing in response to significant ideas. In the second semester, the seminars branch into a number of topics – war, the environment, vampires, etc. The particular character of a seminar has much to do with the professor assigned to teach; they arrive from every department. But no matter how the course is delivered, it invariably leads to animated conversation outside of the classroom, far into the night.

Lewis & Clark enrolls about nineteen hundred students in the liberal arts college and also operates a distinguished School of Law and a highly regarded Graduate School of Education. The Liberal Arts are uniformly excellent, and the college offers some programs that fall outside of the usual array of undergraduate courses, such as: Japanese Painting, African-American Literature, International Economics, Marine Biology, Computer Architecture, Buddhism, Theatrical Lighting.

The energy with which the humanities are pursued and the emphasis on the arts draws a lot of attention, but the college is equally well known for its strength in the natural and physical sciences. The opportunity for original research and collaboration with professors is widely appreciated.

And then, more than half of every graduating class has taken advantage of the opportunity to study in off-campus and overseas programs.

The college has long been known for the number of graduates who have served in the Peace Corps, and is among the most actively concerned with promoting sustainability. National Public Radio recognized the quality of the college's radio production of "Unfinished Journey: The Lewis and Clark Expedition," broadcasting the thirteen-part series on more than a hundred stations across the country. Recently, the college's introduction of a study-abroad program in Vietnam was profiled for its emphasis on Vietnamese culture, politics, and economy. And finally, recent graduates have won a number of post-graduate fellowships, including Fulbright and Truman Scholarships. It is a particular triumph for Lewis and Clark to have had a current senior awarded the Rhodes Scholarship.

Outside of the classroom, Lewis & Clark manages somehow to balance independence and community. Residential life is, well, laid-back; students report comfortable visiting room-to-room and the occasional campus-wide social event. Students are fond of theme parties such as an "Animal-Fantasy" party, Luau, and the traditional Welcome Back Picnic in which welcoming Pioneers do the dance known as the "hippie flail" to marimba music on the lawn in front of Templeton Student Center. (Music students at Lewis & Clark can study Japanese koto as well as the African marimba). The Outing Club is especially active and ambitious, sponsoring trips to the mountains (about an hour) or to the beach (about an hour). Longer trips can carry students to the Redwoods of Northern California or the Grand Canyon.

Music is huge at L & C. A cappella groups are enjoying real popularity. Coffee house performances of every kind are on stage most weekends. Campus radio station, KLC, calls itself the last bastion of rock and roll and Portland is a hotbed of indie music. Main stage concerts and performances are also available on most weekends.

The attraction of Portland cannot be over-stated. Saturday Market, major league athletic teams, and Powell's Books (the largest bookstore in the country) are all within an easy bus ride.

There are no fraternities or sororities, so social and community activities are generated by students for students. The Ultimate frisbee club attracts a lot of attention, but popular leagues sponsor competition in dodgeball and kickball. Club sports include lacrosse, rugby, sailing, and Tae Kwan Do.

Varsity sports compete in NCAA Division III in the Northwest Conference, and in tribute to the explorers who trekked to the Pacific Northwest, Meriwether Lewis and William Clark, teams are known as the Pioneers. My favorite mascot is "Pio" currently a gigantic Newfoundland dog, who in his civilian life is known as "Buddy". The college offers eighteen interscholastic sports, including baseball, basketball, football, tennis, golf, rowing, swimming, cross country, and track. Athletes often play more than one sport, and friends follow the fortunes of Pioneer teams.

The Evergreen State College - Olympia, Washington

There are no students along for the ride at Evergreen. The individual is responsible for the collaborative success of each seminar. No passive note taking in a large lecture hall. Students draw up and Education Plan with the help of academic advisors, and take one course at a time in order to allow ideas and perspectives to emerge from many sources. I'll identify some of the seminars shortly, but it is important to note that professors are very much involved in the creation of the courses, working collaboratively from the start. That collaboration of teachers from very different disciplines helps to create the vibrant exchange that is at the heart of an Evergreen seminar.

And the stats... 2015

Number of Applicants: 1,544 / 99% Accepted
Undergrad Enrollment: 3,878 504% female / 46% male
Avg. SAT Reading 460-630 and Math 420 -570 Avg. ACT: 19-26
Total Cost: $22,803.00 (in-state) $35,856.00 (out-of-state)
Received some form of financial assistance: 87%

Throw out every idea you have ever had about a state university. Evergreen State College is the State of Washington's public Liberal Arts College, established in the nineteen sixties in response to what seemed creeping emphasis on the pre-professional, semi-vocational, intellectually arid experience found by many students in their college years. The state set aside a thousand acres of stunningly beautiful forest along the coastline of Puget Sound, adjacent to Washington's capital city, Olympia. From the start, the Evergreen State College was intended to be entirely experimental and non-traditional, and that founding impulse remains at the heart of the distinctive and remarkable experience that is Evergreen.

The campus is characterized as suburban which is an absolute misrepresentation. Yes, the drive from central Olympia probably takes about fifteen minutes, but once the visitor has entered the college, time and space seem to dissolve. Douglas Fir, Western Hemlock, Cedar, Grand Fir, Big Leaf Maple, Red Alder, Black Cottonwood, Bitter Cherry, and Pacific Madrone stand close to every byway and building. The college has been committed to sustainability from the start and has worked hard to maintain this second-growth forest as a living resource of the community. The campus is an island of green serenity in a loud, fast-moving world.

Two elements of the design of the campus, aside from the lush greenery, are noteworthy and eminently reflective of the college's mission. The first is in the administration of residential life. All the usual amenities and services are provided; resident advisors help cushion the transition to college life, and social events happen with regularity. The differences are these: The dorms are named A. B, C, and D. There was a movement to call them Gryffindor, Hufflepuff, Ravenclaw, and Slytherin, but times have changed, and the sleek cement structures remain simply alphabetical in their identity. Assignment to a room as a freshman is somewhat more complex, however, in that Evergreen is sensitive to personal issues in ways that most private colleges are not. Allergen free and quiet options are available to freshmen, and even greater range is available in the subsequent years. For example, what had been called the gender-neutral apartment style residence is now known as Rainbow Fort. The description of the residence speaks to the enlightened policies of this state school:

> *Safe-space housing for students who identify as: lesbian, gay, bisexual, pansexual, queer, questioning, transgender/gender non-conforming/gender queer, and/or intersex, as well as committed allies. This housing is designed to promote personal growth and community-building within a safe and supportive environment. Gender is not used as a designation in making housing assignments here.*

The other manifestation of the responsible leadership taken by this college came with the building of the Longhouse and the design of the ethnobotanical garden. The Longhouse was designed as a Northwest Coast Longhouse and specifically intended to provide a space in which thoughtful exchange could bring sensitivity to issues of cultures in a pluralistic community. Then Longhouse is a meeting place, and a cultural center promoting indigenous arts and cultures, and also acting as space of welcome and hospitality. Evergreen offers a Masters of Public Administration Tribal Concentration degree – a program designed by the college with the assistance of the The Northwest Indian Applied Research Institute (NIARI)

Students who have completed the program include staff and faculty with tribal affiliations including, among others: Apache, Colville, Kootenai, Makah, Native Hawai'ian, Port Gamble S'kallam, Quinault, Rocky Boy Cree, Salish, Skokomish, Snoqualmie, Suquamish, Tulalip, and Turtle Mountain Band of Chippewa Indians.

Although the curriculum is not organized around departments and majors, one set of studies is carried out through Native American and World Indigenous Peoples' Studies.

The Longhouse stands as a warm and welcoming statement of respect for the indigenous people of the Northwest and as a resource for a community dedicated to responsible inquiry.

OK, now to the curriculum.

There isn't one. Not in the conventional sense.

There are no students along for the ride at Evergreen. The individual is responsible for the collaborative success of each seminar. No passive note taking in a large lecture hall. Students draw up and Education Plan with the help of academic advisors, and take one course at a time in order to allow ideas and perspectives to emerge from many sources. I'll identify some of the seminars shortly, but it is important to note that professors are very much involved in the creation of the courses, working collaboratively from the start. That collaboration of teachers from very different disciplines helps to create the vibrant exchange that is at the heart of an Evergreen seminar.

How does a student get a grade?

Actually, no grades are given. Upon the completion of a seminar, students carry out a self-assessment and met with faculty to discuss academic progress. The result of observation, the self-evaluation, and the discussion is a one-page evaluation that becomes the student's academic record.

Some of the most fascinating reading I have done has been in perusing the description of seminars at Evergreen. This volume is not large enough to offer a fair sample, so I will simply offer three that struck me as particularly interesting.

American Stories was a seminar that suggested that the participant examine history and culture by immersing themselves in stories. One of the required texts, Thomas King's *The Truth About Stories,* begins with the warning – "Stories are wondrous things. And they are dangerous." Other texts included: *Lydia's Open Door, White Noise, Enrique's Journey, The Things They Carried, Housekeeping, Sula, The Adventures of Huckleberry Finn, O Pioneers!, Semiotics, Democracy in America, The Age of Innocence, The Lone Ranger and Tonto Fistfight in Heaven*, and *This House of Sky.*

How about Order and Chaos?

"There must be chaos in one's heart to be able to give birth to a dancing star."

--F. Nietzsche

Great developments in science and the arts—in fact all creative work—often occur at a tense juncture between the poles of order and chaos. How have artists and scientists have creatively tried to make sense of their world?

Greeks and Romans to Shakespeare and Moliere, opera, non-western performance, and other great traditions in music, dance, and visual art culminating in the work of Anton Chekhov. Greek astronomy (the Venerable model) and pantometry through the innovations of Copernicus, Galileo, Newton and Darwin. Brecht, Beckett, the advent of moving image, and other developments in science and the arts. Credits may be awarded in History of Science, Classical Astronomy, Theatre History, Performance Studies.

The reading list, as you might expect was equally divergent:
Beckett, Samuel. Waiting for Godot
Frayn, Michael. Copenhagen
Harmon, Katharine. You Are Here
Kushner, Tony. Angels in America
Rosenthal, Jeffrey. Struck by Lightning
Sondheim, Stephen and James Lapine. Sunday in the Park with George
Stoppard, Tom. Rosencranz and Guildenstern Are Dead
Zukav, Gary. The Dancing Wu Li Masters

Finally, <u>Music, Math, and Motion.</u> As expected, the description pulls the student almost immediately into collaborative inquiry.

The composition of music and the analysis of sound, using scientific methodology, creative insight, and contemporary technology, will be the intertwined pathways of our program. We will address subjects such as music and sound, rhythms and pulses, harmonics and resonances, the physical, geometrical, and psycho-physical bases of sound, acoustics and vibration systems.

A composer/musician and a mathematical physicist will collaborate to offer a common sense, accessible and deeply engaging introduction to these subjects for interested non-specialists. Our math and physics will be at a pre-calculus level, though students may do research projects at a more advanced level if they choose. Interdisciplinary projects could include electronically creating music from physical formulae, analyzing the behavior of sound in different environments, or other ideas. This program is designed for those who find their art increasingly mediated by technology, for those who seek artistic outlets for their science, or for anyone who desires to understand the interweaving of art and science. Student work will be evaluated through assignments such as homework, workshops, exams, performances, compositions, general participation, written and oral reports, and seminar essays.

Obviously, Evergreen State College is not for everyone, and many who find their way here have tried to satisfy their intellectual curiosity at another institution before realizing that Evergreen would allow them to plan their own education, find like-minded and very interesting collaborators, and place them in one of the most extraordinary campus settings in the world. Fun? Sure, and the usual kind. Lots of activities and clubs, but much of the energy of the place is in the seminar. Students are connected with their own education and rave about the experience. One student described it as, "a learning buffet – almost too rich!" They also talk about the music scene in Olympia and the relative proximity of Seattle, Portland, and Mount Rainier. Should the description of a college in which inquiry is absorbing and an organic garden is a Mecca, and a Longhouse suggests inclusive respect cause you to think that Evergreen students are all cut from the same cloth...think again. There is no typical "Greener". Most are socially conscious and environmentally aware, but the diversity on this campus is real.

Pacific Lutheran University - Tacoma, Washington

PLU's students are friendly, kind, and active; they are inclusive and happy. The overwhelming sense is that they are entirely at home, entirely earnest, and entirely comfortable in the company of their classmates and teachers.

And the stats... 2015

Number of Applicants: 3,438 / 75% Accepted
Undergrad Enrollment: 2,926 63% female / 37% male
Avg. SAT Reading 490-610 and Math 490 -600 Avg. ACT: 22-29
Total Cost: $50,258.00
Received some form of financial assistance: 99%

You might expect that a university with a Lutheran heritage, founded by serious-minded Scandinavian Lutherans, mostly Norwegians, might be slightly on the grimly purposeful side.

In fact, Pacific Lutheran is lively, a little bit quirky, and - dare I say it? - fun.

The university is set in a quiet corner of suburban Tacoma, on a campus of about one hundred and fifty acres, divided into two sections - an Upper Campus and a Lower Campus. The Upper Campus was the original site of the university; in fact, Harstad Hall was once the entire university. Today, a charming collection of older buildings, mostly red brick, meets the visitor on the Upper Campus, and slightly more modern buildings - and a golf course! -are found on the Lower Campus.

Lest my description of a quirky, fun, university mislead you, let me quickly establish the basic facts:

 PLU is a small university, enrolling about thirty-five hundred students in the College of Arts and Sciences, the School of Arts and Communication, the School of Business, the School of Education and Movement Studies, and the School of Nursing. The bachelor's degree is offered in the usual liberal arts and sciences, Business, Nursing, Communications, Music, Music Education, Music Arts, Physical Education, Computer Science, and Fine Arts.

PLU's First Year Experience is a well-crafted and thoughtful transition to a challenging curriculum. The excursions, retreats, and workshops are helpful, and the First Year Writing Seminars have been designed to provide an engaging first encounter with PLU's curriculum. Some recent seminars have included Dreams, Vanished Peoples and Lost Civilizations, and Sustainability: Balancing Self, Community, Environment.

But there's no way around it – the Pacific Northwest has a Scandinavian heritage, and that means Lutheran, and that means hard-working, civic minded, and musical. I'll return to the many Scandinavian virtues exemplified in this excellent university, but for the moment, I'd like to concentrate on music.

The most recent and highly visible representation of the outstanding music program at PLU was the appearance of the Plutonics on America's Got Talent. The a cappella group was chosen from thousands who auditioned and appeared before twelve million people last summer. Talented as the Plutonics are, they are but a small part of a tradition of vocal and orchestral music at Pacific Lutheran that emerged with the university's founding in 1880.

The celebrated Choir of the West is made up of fifty undergraduates and is widely considered to be one of the most outstanding collegiate choirs in the world. The Choir travels extensively, and performs an ambitious schedule of concerts throughout the year. Freshmen and sophomores, for the most part, will work their way up to the Choir of the West, if they are uncommonly talented. In their first years, they are likely to sing with the University Chorale, a group of another forty to fifty voices. There are, in addition, the University Men's Chorus, the University Singers, and Opera Workshop, and the Chapel Choir. For those who live in the area, including graduates, the Choral Union is an excellent community chorus.

More than a hundred-and-forty performances are held in the Mary Baker Russell Music Center each year. Lagerquist Concert Hall is a stunning venue, and the facility, as well as the variety of orchestral opportunities (University Symphony, University Wind Ensemble, University Jazz Ensemble, and the University Concert Band) make clear that PLU advantage in offering all that a conservatory might while allowing study in a variety of academic disciplines.

Students at PLU call themselves the "Lutes" and the campus the "Lutedome," indicating that the total involvement of students in life on campus creates a Lute bubble. From what I have observed, the level of engagement is extraordinary, and extraordinarily healthy.

There are parties and late night adventures, but, for the most part, they are the exception rather than the rule, in part because these Lutes have a ton of significant interests, and in part because they uniformly value the quality of the education they find at PLU. Professors get very high marks and classes in every department win praise. Almost all entering students comment on the demands made in the first years; the workload is notable and expectations are high.

What also comes across is that support is easily available and that hard work is entirely worthwhile. Several programs have emerged as having had significant success in the past few years, none more than programs in Media Studies.

The university's Emmy-winning communication team is known as MediaLab, first initiated as an extracurricular activity in print journalism. Since 1997, however, the MediaLab projects have expanded to include videography, photography, and public relations. Two recent documentaries have garnered considerable attention. "Oil Literacy" and "Illicit Exchanges: Canada, the U.S. and Crime," have piled up awards in several broadcast competitions. A current project investigates a little-understood phenomenon – "Compassion Fatigue." The title of the documentary is "Overexposed," and it documents the stress experienced by firefighters and professional caregivers.

It is no accident that the projects under examination in MediaLab chronicle significant contemporary issues; for all the allure of the "LuteDome", students are actively engaged in lives of service. An annual Holocaust Conference brings survivors to the campus, and the University Diversity Center will take students to the South to look at history of the Civil Rights Movement in the context of contemporary city life.

PLU's students are friendly, kind, and active; they are inclusive and happy. The overwhelming sense is that they are entirely at home, entirely earnest, and entirely comfortable in the company of their classmates and teachers.

The campus coffee shop, Garfield Street, serves exquisite cuisine using locally grown products; a helpful sophomore created a bicycle cooperative so that travel around the large campus was made easier. Another determined that handles and brakes were unnecessary, so created a unicycling course and club. More than eighty clubs and activities thrive – from a film society and active theater company to a popular radio station.

Residential life is equally cheerful, drawing students from all classes in well-appointed, reasonably sized dormitories. There are no fraternities or sororities so much organized social activity takes place in and around the residence halls. The Cave, the campus informal performance space, like a coffee house, is open to any who would like to take the stage. "OR", the outdoor recreation organization carries students into the wilderness, making camping, hiking, biking, snowshoeing, and rock climbing gear available to those who would venture to the mountains or the beach. Of course, any and all other "Lute-Gear" is available at "LuteWorld," the campus store.

The life of the Lute may seem distant from the rough and tumble beer soaked world of many college students, and so, the question might be asked: Is Pacific Lutheran a good march for someone not Scandinavian, not musical, not Lutheran?

About twenty percent of enrolled students are Lutheran; more than twice as many belong to other denominations, and almost thirty percent have no religious affiliation at all. Almost forty percent are people of color. The experience of living and working in this handsome, happy university (with a golf course!) seems to work for all sorts of students from all sorts of backgrounds. The only caution I have heard from students at PLU is one that applies to the entire region – the weather can be an unexpected challenge for those from less watery climates.

Sports play a significant part in promoting spirit, and good support is found for almost all of the club and varsity sports. PLU has won the All-Sports trophy more than any other college in the Northwest Conference, and the football team was especially successful during the tenure of legendary coach, Frosty Westering, who rang up thirty-two consecutive winning seasons in leading PLU to four national titles.

The rowing team also has a rich tradition of competition, the more impressive in having held the dual regatta with UPS since 1964.

University of Puget Sound - Tacoma, Washington

I'll end up making quite a bit out of the university's distinctive size – bigger than most of its peers and smaller than most universities. UPS offers a variety of residential choices not available at most small colleges. In the same fashion, this small university also offers close relationships with teachers in a curriculum somewhat broader than that found at comparable schools.

And the stats... 2015

Number of Applicants: 5,583 / 79% Accepted
Undergrad Enrollment: 2,553 57% female / 43% male
Avg. SAT Reading 560-680 and Math 550 -650 Avg. ACT: 25-30
Total Cost: $57,908.00
Received some form of financial assistance: 100%

University of Puget Sound, informally known as UPS, is a small university (there are three graduate programs – School of Education/ School of Occupational Therapy/School of Physical Therapy) and a large (almost 2600) college of liberal arts. Loyal "Loggers" love their school because they feel it has many of the advantages of a larger community with all the advantages of a cozy liberal arts college.

The campus is tidy, well organized, well maintained, and nicely positioned in a thriving neighborhood the northern end of Tacoma. The city has experienced some growth in recent years and the center of the city has seen major renovation, and the introduction of a light rail line, making travel within the city and to Seattle increasingly easy. Tacoma is a perfectly fine city with every amenity a college student might need and an extraordinary Museum of Glass featuring the work of celebrated local glass artist, Dale Chihuly, whose massive glass sculptures are prominently displayed at UPS and Pacific Lutheran. , The great attraction for social and cultural events, however, is Seattle, about thirty miles to the north.

I'll end up making quite a bit out of the university's distinctive size – bigger than most of its peers and smaller than most universities – and one aspect of that distinction is a campus that is fairly large and circumscribed by neighborhood streets. The central campus is made up of three handsome quadrangles, all of which reflect the predominant red brick Tudor-Gothic architecture, a style that causes some to make reference to

Hogwarts when describing their school. The newer buildings are spacious and well appointed and fit in well with the more traditional style of earlier generations of academic building. All athletic facilities are located on one end of the campus, including extensive playing fields and a remarkable tennis pavilion. The center of the campus is largely academic and its borders are residential.

There is an aspect of life at UPS that will seem a bit different – the university is residential, but most students live out of the residence halls after the first year.

A thriving Greek system will welcome a good number; at last count there were four residential fraternities and four residential sororities, located in a row along Union Avenue, across the street from the main campus. A fifth fraternity will likely be housed near campus soon.

Other houses are also available for students who band together out of friendship or common interests. The university owns fifty-five houses along the perimeter of the campus and makes them available to students through a lottery. Theme houses include: Adventure Living, Broadway House, Art Abode, Delicious Warm Beverage House, Harry Potter House, Creativity Cottage, Love Your Body House, Foreign Language and Culture House, Live Green House, The Outhaus (Wilderness), Track and Cross Country House, Recreational Options Forgoing Liquor House, and the Nom Nom House.

Obviously, UPS offers a variety of residential choices not available at most small colleges. In the same fashion, this small university also offers close relationships with teachers in a curriculum somewhat broader than that found at comparable schools.

Of the twelve hundred courses offered annually, some in the Core Curriculum which will include Argument and Inquiry, Five Approaches to Knowing, and Interdisciplinary Studies. In addition to the commonly found departments, UPS offers Asian Languages and Cultures, Business and Leadership, Global Development Studies Physical Education, Gender Studies, Environmental Policy and Decision Making, Exercise Science, Latin American Studies, Communication Studies, and Classics.

Particular enthusiasm has emerged around the Theatrical Arts, Comparative Sociology, Political Science, and Journalism, although the sciences are highly respected and contribute to the heaviest workload.

The programs in Business and Leadership and the conservatory-style School of Music come closest to professional programs at UPS and both are very well regarded. In addition to the ordinary majors in performance and education, the Music School offers a program in Music Business.

The interest in music is evident outside of the classroom as several fine organizations make the campus hum. The Logger Pep band is, well…peppy. The a cappella group M-Pact and the Gospel Hummingbirds are both active and well received.

Curtain Call is the student group responsible for mounting musical productions at UPS, often producing a musical review each semester.

And, obviously, Music House calls those who want to wallow in music even in their residential life.

Fraternal Life is a significant aspect of the UPS experience for about thirty percent of students. "Recruitment" (rush) takes place in the spring for most first year students, although sophs and transfers can rush in the fall. Social life on campus is largely found in houses and cross-house entertaining, around the major athletic events in the school year, and in "road trips" to Seattle.

There are a number of vigorous activities on campus as well, including an Alpine Ski Club, a Fencing Club, a Nerf Squad, and a Writer's Guild. Recreational and Club Sports include Ultimate Frisbee, Water Polo, and Rugby.

There are a number of traditions or practices still observed at UPS, some of which are remarkable.

For example, it is believed that the doors of the Memorial Field House are huge because the building once welcomed circus elephants to the venue. In fact, that belief is entirely justified, as the Field House was the largest performance space in Tacoma for many years, welcoming shows, rodeos, and the circus. The elephant story is actually even more dramatic as an elephant in the Shrine Circus fell through the temporary floor.

Log Jam is the traditional back-to-school Barbeque made all the more exciting in that a helicopter flies over the assemblage and drops ping pong balls that can be redeemed for prizes.

The most puzzling tradition, however, has to do with "The Hatchet." The hatchet was discovered in 1908 and was immediately seen as a fitting symbol for a school with the nickname, "The Loggers." From that point on, the hatchet was fair game, appearing on display and routinely stolen until it reappeared at some public event.

After twelve years in which the hatchet was mysteriously absent, it reappeared in 1998 and was placed in a high-security case in the lobby of Wheelock Student Center. The most recent "heist" involved distracting the

Security team by pulling a fire alarm, breaking the heavy glass, and unbolting the hatchet from its mount. To my knowledge, the hatchet is still missing.

Western Washington University - Bellingham, Washington

The visitor to WWU is likely to be struck by the university's location – Two hundred-and-fifty beautifully manicured acres overlooking Bellingham Bay and Puget Sound. The grounds are spectacular; an arboretum adjoins the campus, and the university is celebrated for its outstanding sculpture garden, one of the finest in the country. Western is a relatively small university, enrolling about thirteen thousand undergraduates, and as a result, undergraduates get a superior education and a superior college experience at a public school price.

And the stats... 2015

Number of Applicants: 9,285 / 85% Accepted
Undergrad Enrollment: 14,152 55% female / 45% male
Avg. SAT Reading 500-610 and Math 500 -600 Avg. ACT: 22-27
Total Cost: $423,221.00 (in-state) $34,663.00 (out-of-state)
Received some form of financial assistance: 74%

Each region has one irrefutable, grotesquely overlooked, absolutely stunning public university – in the Pacific Northwest, that would be Western Washington University.

And, just as Texas has Austin and Michigan has Ann Arbor, Western Washington has Bellingham. The small city of Bellingham is on Bellingham Bay, about fifty miles north of Seattle, twenty miles south of Vancouver, British Columbia, and west of Mount Baker and Lake Whatcom. The town is pretty, sure, and beautifully set against sky, sea, and mountains, the climate is reasonably mild (Bellingham is in what is called the Banana Belt of the Northwest), but the real story about Bellingham is the vibrant arts scene and a music sub-culture to rival any city in the country.

It is entirely typical that Bellingham has taken as its nickname, "City of Subdued Excitement"; it's a happening city with a laid-back attitude. Among the contemporary musical groups spawned by the Bellingham music scene are: Death Cab for Cutie, The Posies, Crayon, Idiot Pilot, Mono Men, the Trucks, Black Eyes, Federation X, Neckties, No-Fi Soul Rebellion, and Shook Ones.

Music isn't the only attraction in Bellingham. Linux Fest Northwest draws a particular group of computer enthusiasts and rebels. The Bellingham Music Festival promotes orchestral music, and the Imperial Sovereign Court of the Evergreen Empire has been raising money for charity for decades in an event that crowns a drag queen. Bellingham Pride celebrates LGBT people and their friends, and Wig Out/Wig Walk is a spring bacchanal held on the day before the Ski to Sea Race which tumbles from Mount Baker to the sea.

Local Theater is strong as well, in part due to the collaboration of the city and the university's excellent performing arts department. Several distinguished theaters in the city offer a wide range of productions throughout the year. One Bellingham celebrity, Ryan Stiles, star of the popular television show, *Whose Line Is It Anyway,* has established an improvisational theater company performing nightly at his Upfront Theater.

So, Bellingham is a super nifty city, and the convergence of astounding outdoor opportunities will surely attract those who long for adventure in the Pacific Northwest – what does Western Washington University have to offer?

Well, Western is consistently named the best master's-granting university in the Pacific Northwest, is among the universities selected by Forbes and the US News and World Report as one of the best in the nation, and is always among the bargains touted by Kiplinger's Personal Finance magazine and the Princeton Review.

Automobile Magazine named Western Washington possibly the best school in the country for total car design, and the team from Western continues to top all U.S. universities in Automotive X Project competition. As I write, undergrads at WWU are working on delivering a car that gets one hundred miles to a gallon of gas.

Sound like a tech school? They do have an electron microscope on campus and a neutron generator (for when we get low on neutrons?), but Western Washington has also been recognized for the excellence of the philosophy department, of particular importance because the university has developed a unique program – Philosophy, Politics, and Economics, modeled after the interdisciplinary program at Oxford.

The liberal arts are strong; the sciences are strong. And, in case the university has not met your needs in any of its divisions (College of Business and Economics, College of Fine and Performing Arts, College of Humanities and Social Sciences, Huxley College of Environmental Studies, College of Science and Technology, and College of Education), the university presents Fairhaven College, a small interdisciplinary liberal arts college within the university.

Fairhaven began as an experiment in self-directed education in the 1960's, providing much of the groundwork necessary to the state's founding of the entirely self-directed public university, Evergreen State University in Tacoma.

Today, Fairhaven welcomes about 450 students to a seminar based interdisciplinary program dependent upon the student's initiative and interest. Although much of the direction of inquiry is provided by students, certain priorities are clear. Fairhaven expects its students to take strategies from various disciplines in order to sharpen their thinking and communicative skills. In addition, there is a commitment to cultural pluralism, reflected in the makeup of the student body and teaching faculty in Fairhaven College. About a third of Fairhaven's students come from out of state, and about thirty percent are people of color. About a third are the first generation to attend college. Similarly, the faculty is about thirty percent people of color.

Bottom line at Fairhaven? A narrative assessment of work replaces a conventional grading system. Graduates have no difficulty in pursuing graduate work from the college, meeting success in applying to law school, business school, and professional schools.

Whew! A Vehicle Research Institute, a Computer Science department with an edge at Microsoft, and a college within a college! Anything else worth mentioning at the curricular level?

Well, Western Washington is the first in the Pacific Northwest to offer a bachelor's program in Emergency Planning and Management, directed through the Huxley School of Environmental Studies. WWU is also active in building bridges with the Northwest Indian College, the tribal college on the Lummi Reservation adjacent to Bellingham. The American Cultural Studies Program in Fairhaven College offers one significant point of transfer, and Native American Studies, and Native American Literature in particular, are among the most celebrated of the university's programs.

The visitor to WWU is likely to be struck by the university's location - Two hundred-and-fifty beautifully manicured acres overlooking Bellingham Bay and Puget Sound. The grounds are spectacular; an arboretum adjoins the campus, and the university is celebrated for its outstanding sculpture garden, one of the finest in the country.

Western is a relatively small university, enrolling about fourteen thousand undergraduates, and as a result, undergraduates get a superior education and a superior college experience at a public school price.

552

Classes are taught by professors rather than Teaching Assistants, an important difference when comparing Western to the flagship university in Seattle. There are no fraternities or sororities, and the active, happy campus is an inclusive place. Western's students speak glowingly of their experience in the classroom, in the residence halls, and on the remarkably handsome campus. The students tend to be liberal, kind, and welcoming, and the mix of interests on campus keeps the place hopping.

The performing arts are well respected and highly visible; most weekends feature a performance of one kind or another, from a full production in the theater to a series of improv performances through the residence halls, to an a cappella concert in the student center. The university's improvisational "team" has won national championships in national competition. The city of Bellingham is attractive and easy to access, and the opportunity for outdoor adventure is limitless. One student came to WWU because the School of Education is so highly regarded, but found that she could hardly stand to stay indoors to study because the campus is so beautiful - not a bad distraction!

Fairhaven operates a program known as "Outback," which allows any students at WWU to get involved with sustainable agriculture; a short walk behind the Fairhaven Complex is the university's arboretum and an ambitious vegetable garden. The Wade King Recreation center offers a climbing wall, an aquatic center, intramural and recreational sports, and massage.

Three notable extracurricular activities distinguish WWU and reflect the mix of personalities attracted to the university. The Model UN team has emerged as a power in the region and demonstrated uncommon poise and preparation in winning top honors at the National Model UN in New York City. The automotive design team brought their entry in world competition to the highest level, engineering a car achieving one hundred and twelve miles per gallon. The Human Powered Submarine team has also won honors in the International Submarine Race in Maryland.

The intramural program looks similar to most others, with the exception of a league devoted to competition in XBox FIFA soccer, NFL football, and NBA basketball. Sports clubs are especially active at this Division II school, traveling across the region to compete. Among the most successful are the ice hockey and lacrosse clubs, although the climbing club takes on some fairly knotty challenges throughout the year. The Men's Rugby team is known as the Warthogs, the Women's Rugby team the Flames - both travel extensively. Cycling is active in every season, and the Sailing Club recently placed second in the Western Canada Cup.

The Western Washington Vikings compete in NCAA Division II against colleges of similar size in the Pacific Northwest, Western Canada, and

Alaska. Viking pride creates bonds in every season, but the passion is most clear at the basketball court.

Whitworth University - Spokane, Washington

Unlike the majority of Christian Colleges, Whitworth admits students without regard to race, religion, age, national origin, sex, marital status, or disability. The invitation to join in Whitworth's mission is clearly stated – if you want an outstanding education and a supportive Christian community, apply to Whitworth.

And the stats... 2015

Number of Applicants: 4,247 / 75% Accepted
Undergrad Enrollment: 2,370 59% female / 41% male
SAT Not Required Avg. = 1778
Total Cost: $50,329.00
Received some form of financial assistance: 98%

Whitworth and Thomas Aquinas are the only colleges with a Christian profession in this book. There are other colleges profiled that have denominational affiliations and the heritage of Christian faith, but Whitworth is the only institution represented here that challenges all students to integrate their learning with Christian faith.

I include Whitworth for three reasons:

1. Unlike the majority of Christian Colleges, Whitworth admits students without regard to race, religion, age, national origin, sex, marital status, or disability. The invitation to join in Whitworth's mission is clearly stated – if you want an outstanding education and a supportive Christian community, apply to Whitworth. There is no required statement of faith.

2. Unlike the majority of Christian Colleges, Whitworth does not compel its faculty to sign a statement of faith, although it does expect each prospective faculty member to describe his or her own personal faith. Those expectations are presented in a manner that demonstrates the university's commitment to open inquiry.

    "When we hire new faculty we expect that they be able to articulate a clear Christian commitment, but we do not ask faculty to sign a doctrinal statement. To do so would limit the rich mix of denominational and theological diversity that Whitworth has enjoyed since its founding. We see Whitworth as one of the relatively few remaining higher education institutions where

protestant mainliners, evangelicals, Anabaptists, Catholics, and Orthodox faculty can engage one another on the widest variety of important intellectual and social issues. Review of our faculty handbook will attest that Whitworth does not take an institutional stand on controversial social and political issues, leaving members of our faculty free to engage the issues from their varied intellectual and theological perspectives and to model constructive dialogue, even disagreement, for our students."

3. Because Whitworth does not take an institutional stand on controversial social and political issues, I can recommend the university to anyone seeking the experience of learning in a Christian community.

Finally, and of course, I include Whitworth because it is an exceptionally beautiful, thoughtful, and effective university with an uncommonly well balanced and happy student body.

Whitworth's well appointed campus is located on two hundred acres of pine forest in the north part of Spokane. Known as the "Lilac City," Spokane is just across the border from Idaho and shares metropolitan resources with Coeur d'Alene.

Seattle and Portland probably best represent the "Pacific" part of the Pacific Northwest, but Spokane, for me, is the epitome of the great Northwestern expanse. Gold, silver, and lumber first brought settlers to Spokane, and the establishment of the Northern Pacific linked the city with the rest of the region. Today, Spokane is the largest city between Seattle and Minneapolis, serving Washington, Idaho, British Columbia, and Alberta. This sparkling, pine forested city has every modern amenity and is only four hours from the western entrance to Glacier National Park. Yellowstone, Banff, and Jasper National Parks are within an eight-hour drive. The region offers spectacular wilderness, some of the finest golf courses in the country, ski resorts, and a number of well-established vineyards.

Although Whitworth was established in 1890, the architecture on campus is predominantly Northwestern-modern, well designed and entirely in keeping with the attractive setting in which the university has grown. I don't ordinarily provide a building-by-building description of the campus, but in the case of Whitworth, the extensive and handsome facilities are both remarkable and reflective of the university's character.

The building that originally housed all students, all classrooms, the dining room, and all offices, still stands. McMillan Hall is a gabled red brick dormitory, now housing seventy men. The largest dormitory, Warren Hall, houses about two hundred students. Several dormitories have been completed in the last decade; Duvall and East Hall are large, modern, and present varieties of living options, "pods" for six students and rooms for one, two, or three. This residential university of almost twenty-four hundred students provides comfortable living spaces for virtually all of its students, including a "village" that offers about eighty students the chance to live in an apartment on campus.

Weyerhaeuser Hall, completed in 2004, is an attractive modern building that accommodates the university's administrative offices, the Whitworth School of Global Commerce and Management, two computer labs, seven classrooms, the Regional Resource and Learning Center, and the Weyerhaeuser Center for Christian Faith and Learning.

Red brick Dixon Hall is a classroom building and the home of the School of Education, Westminster Hall, a comfortable wooden building provides the offices of the modern language, kinesiology, English, theology and athletic training departments.

An impressive center for the visual arts was built in 2008 – the Lied Center offers more than 20,000 square feet of studio space for ceramics, sculpture, drawing, painting, mixed media, printmaking, a computer laboratory, and two galleries.

The Johnston Science Center is home to instruction in biology, physics, and chemistry, and contains two greenhouses, an auditorium, and a lecture hall. The Lindamen Center contains the mathematics and computer science departments, philosophy, communication studies, and the International Education Center.

The monolithic red brick Music Center has seventeen practice rooms, classrooms, a music library, an orchestra room, and a recital hall.

The Theater department is located in the Cowles Auditorium, a main stage auditorium that can seat 1200 people for theatrical performances, concerts, lectures, and other public performances.

The Seeley Mudd Chapel is a lovely modern brick building nestled in a pine grove. Regular Chapel services are held here on Tuesday and Thursday mornings, and on Tuesday evening.

Athletic facilities include extensive playing fields, the Pine Bowl where football and track train and compete, the Scotford Tennis Center with three indoor courts, the Aquatics Center which features a six-lane, 25 yard competition pool, the Scotford Fitness Center, and the Fieldhouse, a large facility with basketball court, volleyball court, training room, ballet loft, batting cage, and indoor track.

This very attractive campus serves its students uncommonly well, and allows the community to engage in the academic enterprise the university has embraced.

The curriculum contains more than sixty academic programs, including distinctive work in theology and philosophy. Other popular majors include: Journalism, Kinesiology, Art, Medieval and Early Modern Studies, Music, Technical Theater, Economics, Biochemistry, and Peace Studies.

Not surprisingly, students very much appreciate the university's attempt to join the life of the mind and the life of the heart.

One student put it this way, "If you want to be challenged in every way, you'll find energy and excitement here. This is not a place where everyone takes the same point of view or the same kinds of beliefs. The work is hard and always worthwhile, but you have to be open-minded and caring."
The faculty is notably open-minded, interested in their students and actively promoting critical thinking. Original research and collaborative work is common, and the teachers win high praise from a very satisfied student body.

Finally, Whitworth is an athletic power in the Northwest Conference, until very recently undefeated in basketball over the course of several seasons. Over the past decade, more than one hundred Whitworth Pirates have been recognized as All-Americans, and almost as many have been named Academic All-Americans.

It goes without saying that Whitworth's athletic programs and Whitworth's athletes dedicate themselves to playing at the highest level of competition while honoring the university's mission. Sportsmanship is the hallmark of Pirate teams.

Whitworth is not for everyone, but for those who welcome the particular character of this generous and happy school, it may be an excellent option in this beautiful region.

Acknowledgements

I have had many mentors as a college counselor, most notably John Kushan, former Director of Admissions at Kenyon College and Bill Hiss, former Dean of Admissions and now Vice President for External affairs at Bates College. I am grateful to Jim Hendrix, former Dean of Admissions at Davidson College, Jim Rogers, former Director of Admissions at Brown University, Bill Shain, formerly Dean at Macalester College, and Bill Mason, formerly Dean at Bowdoin College – all of whom were kind enough (or brave enough) to allow me to sit in on the deliberations of admissions committees, often for more than a week at a time.

I owe a debt of gratitude to Dwight Hatcher, my colleague at Berkshire School and a widely admired Assistant Director of Admissions at Kenyon College. Dwight could easily have written the ultimate college guide all by himself, but he was generous in asking me to join him in editing the project sponsored by Houghton Mifflin, *The Guidance Information System Guide to American Colleges and Universities*.

I am grateful to my colleagues in boarding schools, independent day schools, public high schools, and parochial schools – all of whom work at one of the hardest jobs in secondary education. Much maligned in film and fable, college counselors are a rare breed, often working above and beyond the call of duty to provide students and parents with informed guidance at a time when they most have need of it. I cannot begin to recognize the hundreds of dedicated admissions officers working at colleges and universities across the country. I am proud to have worked with men and women such as Mary Lou Bates at Skidmore, David Borus now at Vassar, Gary Ripple at William and Mary, Jane Reynolds, former Dean at Amherst, Arnoldo Rodriguez at Pitzer, Dan Saracino at Santa Clara, Tom Parker, former Director at Williams and Dean at Amherst, and Ted O'Neil at the University of Chicago.

Nothing takes the place of actually stepping on a college campus, and my family has made it possible for me to step on entirely too many. My children, Padgett, Bailey, and Grayson have missed out on family vacations and family time, and have been dragged on college visits across the country. My endlessly patient wife, Mary, too often carried the family alone while I stopped in at one more college bookstore. I could not be more grateful for their love and support.

Going far above and beyond, Padgett. My favorite and toughest editor, read this manuscript more than once, and provided the technical assistance that permits whatever coherence it may possess. He is the master of all things conceptual and now expert in the field of college admissions.

Finally, I owe an enormous debt to the thousands of students who have taught me everything I know.

Peter Arango
Phoenix, Oregon

Index

Made in the USA
Lexington, KY
16 May 2017